**The European Canton Trade 1723**

# The European Canton Trade 1723

Competition and Cooperation

edited by
Marlene Kessler, Kristin Lee and Daniel Menning

DE GRUYTER
OLDENBOURG

Painting on the cover from the Cod. gall. 674 in the Bayerische Staatsbibliothek München.

ISBN 978-3-11-042623-6
e-ISBN [PDF] 978-3-11-042143-9
e-ISBN [EPUB] 978-3-11-042153-8

**Library of Congress Cataloging-in-Publication Data**
A CIP catalog record for this book has been applied for at the Library of Congress.

**Bibliografische Information der Deutschen Nationalbibliothek**
Die Deutsche Nationalbibliothek verzeichnet diese Publikation in der Deutschen Nationalbibliografie; detaillierte bibliografische Daten sind im Internet über http://dnb.dnb.de abrufbar.


Typesetting: fidus Publikations-Service GmbH, Nördlingen
Printing and binding: CPI books GmbH, Leck
♾ Printed on acid-free paper
Printed in Germany

MIX
Papier aus verantwortungsvollen Quellen
FSC® C083411
FSC www.fsc.org

www.degruyter.com

# Acknowledgment

This source edition brings together a selection of primary sources on eighteenth-century European commerce with Canton, China. Taking different angles, but all referring to the same sailing year, the documents provide an intimate look at western experiences and opinions of the maritime travel to as well as business strategies, commodities and political, social and cultural customs of the East Indies. They, in the process, provide new insights into early modern globalization.

The edition originates from an in-class project at the Eberhard-Karls University in Tübingen, Germany. The concept behind the project was to encourage students not only to read secondary and published texts on the Canton trade, but to also work with historical material in its original form – discovering the difficulties of transcribing manuscripts with now unfamiliar words, letters and abbreviations and having to locate for themselves information that might help to understand the text. Yet, the project aimed not to stop here but to turn students' work into something that would contribute to a larger scholarship on the early China trade.

Teams of students took responsibility for individual parts of this edition. Anna Weininger and Lukas Weyell worked on the "Instructions" and the "Supercargo's Diary". Julia Ehrmann and Sascha Fietze were in charge of the "Navigational Journal". Jan Ruhkopf, together with the assistance of Marlene Kessler, took care of the French "Relation du Voÿage". Afterwards, we as editors rechecked transcriptions and comments as well as added further footnotes where we thought they provided clarification, thereby taking responsibility for the edition as a whole.

The project received financial aid from the *Förderverein Geschichte an der Universität Tübingen e. V.*, which allowed us to procure photocopies of the original manuscripts. Ewald Frie, as head of the Department for Modern History, provided additional money from the budget of his chair for the printing subvention. We are grateful to both for the support.

St. Louis/Tübingen, November 2015

# Table of Contents

# List of Figures

# Introduction

There can be too much of a good thing, or so United English East India Company (EIC) captain Daniel Small reported to company merchants in October 1723. Small wrote from his ship the Duke of Cambridge at Whampoa, a deep-sea anchorage on the Pearl River located just downstream of Canton, China. He had just received news of an incoming supply of year-old tea, purchased by EIC supercargoes upriver at a discounted price. And the Englishman, who also served as the general commander of the company's ships for that season, was convinced his vessel could hold no more weight and *also* successfully navigate the narrow river channels and shallow island shoals he would have to so as to return to England intact in 1724. The merchants' response to his concerns from the Chinese city was ominous: "We must and doe, by these presents Acquaint You ... Yourself and Owners are Answerable for all losses that may Accrue to the said Company."[1]

Much, too, has been written about the development of European commerce with the East Indies – the general, contemporary name for the area east of the Cape of Good Hope – particularly from the western perspective. Certain recent turns in the scholarship, fortunately, have prevented the field from feeling, like the captain of the Duke of Cambridge, overly saturated. In particular, increased linguist education and dialogues among a global scholarly community have revealed primary sources previously unknown, untapped or inaccessible to western researchers.[2] These refreshed narratives reveal overlapping and competing webs of eastern and western personalities and highlight the diversity of interests that informed the China trade. While the four sources that follow offer limitedly European views of such eastern exchanges, we envision them within and expect them to read as part of this complex historiography. They contest visions of a unified and dominant western mercantile presence in the East Indies, highlighting instead the ways in which strivings for company as well as personal profits did not always coincide among European traders and mariners, even those travelling on the same ships. The narrative that results reveals westerners had as much to professionally negotiate among themselves on their way to and in eighteenth-century Canton, as they did with the Chinese.

1 See pages 210–3.

2 For example, see Paul A. Van Dyke, *The Canton Trade: Life and Enterprise on the China Coast, 1700–1845* (Hong Kong: Hong Kong UP, 2005); Paul A. Van Dyke, *Merchants of Canton and Macao: Politics and Strategies in Eighteenth-Century Chinese Trade* (Hong Kong: Hong Kong UP, 2011); Weng Eang Cheong, *Chinese Merchants in Sino-Western Trade, 1684–1798* (Surrey: Curzon, 1997). Also, John E. Wills, Jr., ed., *China and Maritime Europe, 1500–1800: Trade, Settlement, Diplomacy and Missions* (New York: Cambridge UP, 2011).

## Historical Context

The treaties of Utrecht (1713) and Rastatt (1714), which ended the War of the Spanish Succession, concluded a quarter century of almost uninterrupted large-scale warfare in continental Europe. Some fighting did continue along the periphery. Austria and the Republic of Venice, for example, pushed back the Ottoman Empire on the Balkan Peninsula and in the eastern Mediterranean Sea until 1718. Russia, meanwhile, successfully contested the Swedish hegemony in the Baltic Sea until 1721, in a conflict that occasionally drew in Poland, Prussia, Denmark, Hanover and Great Britain. Yet, the Spanish question had been one of pan-European – even global – dimensions, pitting not only Louis XIV's French armies against Austria, the Dutch Republic and Great Britain but inspiring conflict among French, British and Spanish settlers and their native allies in North America and encouraging privateering – or state-sponsored piracy – in the East and West Indies.[3]

Trade during wartime was risky at best. Commercial lines were rerouted due to hostility between ports, and non-military, even privately-owned, ships and their cargos were captured or destroyed for flying enemy flags, like the Spanish-American silver fleet in 1702.[4] Continued conflicts after the War of the Spanish Succession only highlighted for merchants the desirability of doing business in peaceful waters. In the Baltic Sea, for example, a traditional space of inter-European trade, Charles XII of Sweden issued passes to privateers during the later 1710s. This necessitated armed escorts for private merchant vessels – not exactly a convenience for traders whose profits relied on the quick and cheap transport of commodities. Ultimately, the communicative and military disruptions caused by this regional conflict resulted in the visible decline of ship passages through the Danish-Swedish Sound and of the Baltic trade as whole between 1714 and 1719.[5]

The peace that, nevertheless, ensued in western and central Europe after 1713 and 1714, with only a minor interruption between 1718 and 1719, was significant for several reasons, particularly in the context of the following sources. First, diplomati-

3 For an introduction to these conflicts, see Matthias Schnettger, *Der spanische Erbfolgekrieg* (München: C.H. Beck, 2014); M.A. Thompson, "Louis XIV and the Origins of the War of the Spanish Succession", in: *Transactions of the Royal Historical Society* 4 (1954), 111–34; Paul W. Mapp, *The Elusive West and the Contest for Empire, 1713–1763* (Chapel Hill: University of North Carolina Press for the Omohundro Institute of Early American History and Culture, 2011), 122–43; Robert I. Frost, *The Northern Wars. War, State and Society in Northeastern Europe, 1558–1721* (London: Routledge, 2000), 226–329; David Denis Aldridge, *Admiral Sir John Norris and the British Naval Expeditions to the Baltic Sea 1715–1727* (Lund: Nordic Academic Press, 2009).

4 Henry Kamen, "The Destruction of the Spanish Silver Fleet at Vigo in 1702", in: *Bulletin of the Institute of Historical Research* 39 (1966), 165–73.

5 These statistics are available at the Sound Toll Registers Online: http://dietrich.soundtoll.nl/public/stats.php? tat=py [23.10.2015].

cally, it secured a French Bourbon monarch on the Spanish throne, although with the promise that these two kingdoms never would unite under one ruler. Second, geographically, the two treaties transferred control of the Southern Netherlands – roughly modern-day Belgium and Luxemburg – from Spain to the Austrian Habsburgs. Third, militarily, the war cemented claims of British and Dutch naval supremacy as well as administrative associations of maritime activity and state power.[6] Finally, commercially, with the end of most state-sponsored privateering in 1713 and 1714, merchants in central and western Europe began to look for new, non-local economic opportunities. One such lucrative space that seemed fairly safe, immensely profitable and welcoming to foreigners was the East Indies.

Europeans had long had contact with Asian markets. Silks and spices travelled westward through the Mediterranean Sea regularly by the Middle Ages, and an acknowledgement of their demand inspired the Spanish to pursue their first Atlantic voyage westward – the miscalculated travels of Cristoforo Colombo in 1492.[7] It was the Portuguese, however, who mastered the sea route eastward to the Indian Ocean and South China Sea first in 1488 and the 1510s, respectively. By 1557, they attained the first European toehold in southern China, renting the island and port city of Macao from the Chia-ching Emperor.[8] The Portuguese quickly were followed by western competitors, who sought to benefit from new access to eastern commodities and inhabitants. The Spanish crown established an annual sailing of silver galleons westward from Acapulco, New Spain to Manila in 1565 – where mariners accessed a variety of spices as well as Chinese silks and porcelains. Dutch merchants, meanwhile, challenged Lisbon's and Hamburg's control of European spice distribution beginning in 1595, when their first exploratory commercial venture left Amsterdam for Bantam, in modern-day Java. Even the Jesuits, a Roman Catholic religious order, looked to the east to expand their pool of spiritual adherents, moving into Macao in 1577 and advancing into other imperial-controlled settlements during the 1590s.[9]

---

**6** See David Armitage, *The Ideological Origins of the British Empire* (New York: Cambridge UP, 2000), 100–24; Douglas Coombs, *The Conduct of the Dutch: British Opinion and the Dutch Alliance during the War of the Spanish Succession* (The Hague: Martinus Nijhoff, 1958); James Bender, *Dutch Warships in the Age of Sail, 1600–1714: Design, Construction, Careers and Fates* (Yorkshire: Seaforth Publishing, 2014).

**7** For a brief introduction to the early silk and spice trades, see Valerie Hansen, *The Silk Road: a New History* (New York: Oxford UP, 2012); Paul Freedman, *Out of the East: Spices and the Medieval Imagination* (New Haven, CT: Yale UP, 2008); Christine R. Johnson, *The German Discovery of the World: Renaissance Encounters with the Strange and Marvelous* (Charlottesville: University of Virginia Press, 2008).

**8** Chu Hou-ts'ung, or the Chia-ching Emperor (1507–1567) was the eleventh emperor in the Chinese Ming Dynasty. See James Geiss, "The Chia-ching reign, 1522–1566", in: Cambridge History of China, vol. 7, 440–510.

**9** For more on this early competition, see Holden Furber, *Rival Empires of Trade in the Orient, 1600–1800* (Minneapolis: University of Minnesota Press, 1976); Kenneth R. Andrews, *Trade, Plunder and Settlement: Maritime Enterprise and the Genesis of the British Empire, 1480–1630* (New York: Cam-

The potential of Asian commerce in the sixteenth century, however, especially beyond the trade in pepper and other spices, largely outpaced European demands. Much speculation in the 1600s, as a result, went to increasing domestic consumer interests in eastern products. To mitigate the risks of uncertain markets, individual merchants joined together to form nation-based (and often government-supported) joint-stock companies, which spread the profits and downfalls of such commercial ventures among a range of investors. An early example focused on the East Indies was the Dutch *Verenigde Oostindische Compagnie* (VOC), founded in 1602. English merchants, too, sent several ships east after 1591 and founded their first of several companies – a predecessor to the 1708 EIC – in 1600. The firm had 1,318 subscribers during its first thirty years.[10] Expanded non-essential consumerisms, contemporary politics, and a bit of luck encouraged merchants in these firms to introduce untested goods to Europe. The Dutch capture of several Portuguese merchant vessels – notably the São Tiago (1602) and Santa Catharina (1603) – during wartime and the profitable sale of their cargos, for example, spurred the demand for and thus the import of Chinese porcelains into the Dutch Republic. The marriage of Portuguese princess Catherine of Braganza to English monarch Charles II in 1662, meanwhile, brought with it control of Bombay, which was quickly rented to the EIC for the palsy annual sum of £10, as well as the courtly habit of drinking imported teas.[11] The EIC even ventured to import 250,000 ready-made cotton shirts and shifts to England from India in 1664, or roughly 1 for every 2 Londoners, in an attempt to inspire new demands, although domestic linens had filled this need hitherto. By 1684, British cotton imports increased to more than one million pieces per annum.[12]

---

bridge UP, 1985); Douglas A. Irwin, "Strategic Trade Policy and Mercantilist Trade Rivalries", in: *The American Economic Review* 82.2 (1992), 134–9. For more on early conversion efforts, see Willard Peterson, "Learning from Heaven: the introduction of Christianity and other Western ideas into late Ming China", in: Cambridge History of China, vol. 8, 789–839; Liam Matthew Brockey, *Journey to the East: The Jesuit Mission to China, 1579–1724* (Cambridge, MA: The Belknap Press of Harvard UP, 2007).

**10** Alison Games, *The Web of Empire: English Cosmopolitans in an Age of Expansion, 1560–1660* (New York: Oxford UP, 2008), 83.

**11** John Styles, "Product Innovation in Early Modern London", in: *Past & Present* 168 (2000), 140–8; Anne E.C. McCants, "Poor consumers as global consumers: the diffusion of tea and coffee drinking in the eighteenth century", in: *The Economic History Review* 61 (2008), 172–200; Annerose Menninger, *Genuss im kulturellen Wandel. Tabak, Kaffee, Tee und Schokolade in Europa (16.–19. Jahrhundert)* (Stuttgart: Franz Steiner, 2008); K.N. Chaudhuri, *The Trading World of Asia and the English East India Company 1660–1760* (Cambridge: Cambridge UP, 1978), 385–405.

**12** Beverly Lemire, "Transforming Consumer Custom: Linen, Cotton and the English Market, 1660–1800", in: *The European Linen Industry in Historical Perspective*, eds. Brend Collins and Philip Ollerenshaw (New York: Oxford UP, 2003), 191. Also, Giorgio Riello, *Cotton: The Fabric that Made the Modern World* (New York: Oxford UP, 2015); Amelia Peck (ed.), *Interwoven Globe: the Worldwide Textile Trade, 1500–1800* (New Haven: Yale UP, 2013).

Seventeenth-century investments paid off well for the EIC and VOC. The EIC, for example, not only expanded but created an English demand for cotton textiles by the early 1700s – which persisted despite protectionist legislation banning their import – as well as began to re-export the cloth to continental Europe, Africa and the Americas. Furthermore, by the time of the War of the Spanish Succession, the EIC and VOC almost completely monopolized trade to the East Indies. Indeed, they not only exercised monopoly rights for their own countries – which disallowed any private English or Dutch ventures into the Indian Ocean and subsequently the South China Sea. They additionally shut out France, their greatest continental competitor, which could not protect its commercial ships during the war. Only the Danish East India Company also sent vessels east fairly regularly until 1714, albeit in small numbers.[13] This control limited the number of eastern commodities available in Europe – increasing their lucrativeness and producing high rewards for merchants, mariners and shareholders. The EIC, in particular, made annual profits from 11.1 to 22.2 % between the summers of 1709 and 1716.[14]

Such returns were high enough to attract new interest after the war's end, beyond the VOC and EIC. Ships sailed east from the Southern Netherlands in the spring of 1715. They were supported by local and imported financing from England and the Netherlands, as well as a cosmopolitan array of personnel tempted into foreign service by better pay, larger cargo allowances and expanded opportunities for professional advancement outside of their monopolistic native companies. The first two ships leaving the port of Ostend for India ultimately earned their owners a 100 % return on their invested capital. Subsequent sailings also netted substantial profits, albeit smaller.[15] Another trading venture focused on Mocha in the Arabian Peninsula was discussed in Hamburg in 1715 – this one supposedly failing due to an inability to procure ship insurance locally and the unwillingness of insurers in Amsterdam and London to support potential competitors. City traders then discussed joining the

13 Erik Gøbel, "Danish Companies Shipping to Asia, 1616–1807", in: *Ships, sailors and spices. East India Companies and their shipping in the 16th, 17th and 18th centuries*, eds. Jaap R. Bruijn and Femme S. Gaastra (Amsterdam: NEHA, 1993) 113.

14 Chaudhuri, *Trading World*, 440.

15 Jan Parmentier, *Oostende & Co. Het verhaal van de Zuid-Nederlandse Oost-Indiëvaart 1715–1735* (Gent: Ludion Press, 2002), 137. Additional works on Ostend's East India trade include: Ibid., *Tea Time in Flanders. The Maritime Trade between the Southern Netherlands and China in the 18th Century* (Gent: Ludion Press, 1996); ibid., "The Private East India Ventures from Ostend: The Maritime and Commercial Aspects, 1715–1722", in: *International Journal of Maritime History* 5.2 (1993), 75–102; ibid. and Karel Degryse, "Maritime Aspects of the Ostend Trade to Mocha, India and China (1715–1732)", in: Ships, eds. Bruijn and Gaastra, 139–75; G. Hinchcliffe, "An Ostend East Indiaman, 1718–1720", in: *The Mariner's Mirror* 59.3 (1973), 291–7. A more extensive bibliography is available online: http://www.oostende.be/product.aspx?id=5974 [12.11.2015].

Ostenders in 1723 but to no avail.[16] The late 1710s and early 1720s, in fact, saw a veritable boom in joint-stock company promotion and speculation. Shares were purchased not only by merchants but more modest income-earners hoping for quick returns. French natives reinvested in their country's commerce to the east (and the west) by 1719, encouraged by economist John Law. Portugal, Spain, Naples, and Denmark thought about mirroring such activities in 1720. Sweden, too, looked into chartering a joint-stock company for the China trade in 1719 and 1720 – an investment that Russia, its primary enemy in the Northern War, was considering as well. Even King Fredrik William I of Prussia was approached in 1721, for permission that an Englishman residing in Rotterdam might sail under his flag into the Indian Ocean.[17] This large interest, the high-rate of investment and related commercial returns, of course, could only persist so long in a competitive environment. Eventually, many speculative bubbles burst – notably those surrounding the French Compagnie du Mississippi and English South Sea Company in 1720.[18]

In China, which opened several harbors to Europeans in 1685, rising demands by Europeans for commodities after 1714 increased initial sale prices. And, as costs went up for buyers in Asia, returns in the west diminished as well, as goods flooded once monopoly-controlled markets. This impacted both old and new businesses. The rate of EIC profits dropped to between 3.7 and 11.8 % annually during the years 1717 to 1722. In two of these six years, 1718 and 1722, the company actually lost money on its eastern trade.[19] Profits also decreased for the VOC and Ostenders, with the latter losing substantial money (between 1.75 and 75 % per voyage) on three of its ships in 1719. The next three years returned similarly disappointing results.[20] The EIC and VOC reacted

---

**16** For a view from 1720, see Bericht über die Hamburger Ereignisse Anno 1720. In: Staatsarchiv Hamburg – 111-1, Cl VII, Lit. Ka 165, vol. 4a, unfol., 7–9. For 1723, see Ernst Baasch, "Hamburg und die Compagnie von Ostende", in: *Zeitschrift für Social- und Wirthschaftsgeschichte* 5 (1897), 309–19.

**17** We are grateful to Stefano Condorelli (Berne) for sharing with us his unpublished working paper, "The 1719-1721 stock euphoria: a pan-European perspective", which provides information on the European-wide diffusion of schemes for East India trading companies. For the Prussian case, see Victor Ring, *Asiatische Handlungscompagnien Friedrich des Großen. Ein Beitrag zur Geschichte des preußischen Seehandels und Aktienwesens* (Berlin: Carl Heymanns Verlag, 1890), 5–6. For the Danish Company, see Stephan Diller, *Die Dänen in Indien, Südostasien und China (1620–1845)* (Wiesbaden: Harrassowitz, 1999), 65–6.

**18** See Richard Dale, *The First Crash: Lessons from the South Sea Bubble* (Princeton, NJ: Princeton UP, 2005); François R. Velde, "Was John Law's System a bubble? The Mississippi Bubble revisited", in: *The Origins and Development of Financial Markets and Institutions: from the Seventeenth Century to the Present*, eds. Jeremy Atack and Larry Neal (New York: Cambridge UP, 2009), 99–120; Helen Julia Paul, *The South Sea Bubble: an Economic History of its Origins and Consequences* (London: Routledge, 2010).

**19** Chaudhuri, *Trading World*, 440. The bursting of the South Sea Bubble contributed to the troubles in 1722.

**20** Parmentier, Oostend, 137–9.

to this new economic climate in a very focused way: they blamed their troubles on the Southern Netherlands, which they believed illegally robbed their own ventures of money and men. The companies' reactions were threefold. First, each reasserted monopoly rights domestically. The EIC petitioned King George I in 1716 to enforce punishments on the emigration of British merchants, mariners and investors sailing to the East Indies. In 1719, the king's ambassador extended this complaint to Holy Roman Emperor Charles VI's court in Vienna. The British Parliament, too, supported the company's effort to restrict competition from Britons not holding a royal patent to trade, by issuing several acts between 1719 and 1721 that prohibited the activity of English, Scottish, Welsh and Irish commercial agents "under foreign Commissions."[21] The Dutch Republic reacted similarly, also forbidding its sailors from joining ships that sailed east from abroad.[22]

The two companies, secondly, pursued an aggressive economic strategy against the Ostenders. Merchants sailing from the Southern Netherlands seemed most economically harmful to EIC directors in Mocha and Canton. Thus, they decided to mainly challenge them there. The strategy was simple: to get ahead of their competitors, they began to send more ships to the East Indies in 1719 and to send them earlier in the year. By arriving in the Indian Ocean and South China Sea before the Ostend vessels, it was hoped the EIC would benefit from lower commodity prices and, possibly, have the opportunity to buy out export supplies. This included the cheap black Bohea teas that made up a majority of Ostend cargos in China (and which previously was not a British commercial priority).[23] These vessels then were to rush back to Europe, where their fresh, cheap goods would flood western markets. If everything worked as planned, the Ostenders would face bad buying and selling conditions in China and Europe. This intention was summed up in a single sentence from 1720: "Cost what it will we must try to make these Interlopers sick of their voyages for tea."[24] The VOC again followed a similar strategy, asking their Batavian representatives in 1723 to buy

---

21 See page 34, ft. 68. Also, Gerald B. Hertz, "England and the Ostend Company", in: *English Historical Review* 22 (1907), 265; Philip J. Stern, *The Company-State: Corporate Sovereignty and the Early Modern Foundations of the British Empire in India* (New York: Oxford UP, 2011), 194–6.

22 Michel Huisman, *La Belgique commercial sous l'empereur Charles VI. La Compagnie d'Ostende.* Étude *historique de politique commerciale et colonial* (Bruxelles: Lamertin 1902), 104; Victor Enthoven, "Dan maar oorlog! De reactive van de Republiek op de Oostendse Compagnie", in: *Noord-Zuid in Oost-Indisch perspectief*, ed. Jan Parmentier (Zutphen: Walburg pers., 2005), 131–48; Femme S. Gaastra, "War, Competition and Collaboration: Relations between the English and Dutch East India Company in the Seventeenth and Eighteenth Centuries", in: *The Worlds of the East India Company*, eds. H.V. Bowen, Margarette Lincoln and Nigel Rigby (Woodbridge: Boydell Press, 2004), 55–7.

23 Chris Nierstraz, " The Popularization of Tea: East India Companies, Private Traders, Smugglers and the Consumption of Tea in Western Europe, 1700–1760", in: *Goods from the East, 1600–1800: Trading Eurasia*, ed. Maxine Berg (New York: Palgrave Macmillan, 2015), 266–268.

24 "Instruction to the supercargoes of the Canton ships in 1720." Cited after H.B. Morse, *The Chronicles of the East India Company trading to China, 1635–1834, vol. 1* (Oxford: Clarendon Press, 1926); R. N.

out those Chinese silks that were particularly demanded by ships from the Southern Netherlands.[25]

Finally, the EIC and VOC jointly worked to increase the navigational risks to their Ostend competitors on the open sea. Legislation, in both England and the Dutch Republic, promoted the arrest of any national mariners found traveling on non-national ships east of the Cape of Good Hope. The two companies additionally closed those ports they controlled along the eastern route limitedly to Ostend ships (and not, for example, to their French competitors). This meant that vessels from the Southern Netherlands could not anchor at Cape Town, Batavia, or Saint Helena for fresh water, provisions or aid following moments of sickness or damage.[26] Ultimately, the EIC and VOC hoped their combined obstructions would make Ostend merchants' eastern trade more trouble, and less profitable, than it was worth.

The Ostenders, however, also were proactive against failing returns and foreign opposition. Their response was to minimize internal competition and, in 1722, they sent ships east owned collectively. The impact was immediate. Profits rose for the ships that left Ostend in 1723, increasing to between 83 and 104.4 % on single voyages.[27] Additionally, after several failed attempts by different consortia to get a monopoly charter from Charles VI for the East India trade before 1720, lobbying proved successful. The Emperor finally was willing to charter a joint-stock company and to provide patronage and political protection by 1721. After long deliberations, the *Generale Keijserlijcke Compagnie* (GIC) formally was founded in December 1722. The company began with an initial investment capital of six million silver florins as well as a thirty-year monopoly for trade along the African coast and in the East Indies. It promised the emperor 3 % of its returns before December 1724 and 6 % thereafter for his diplomatic sponsorship. It also concentrated its overseas sailings on the ports of Ostend and Bruges, near the North Sea. The GIC sent its first official vessels to the East Indies in 1724.[28] Its success was based on its efficiency. It reserved smaller percentages of profits for managers at home (thus attracting talent willing to travel

---

Banerji, *Economic Progress of the East India Company on the Coromandel Coast (1702–1746)* (Nagpur: Nagpur University, 1974), 197–202.

**25** Kristof Glamann, *Dutch-Asiatic Trade 1620–1740* ('S-Gravenhage: Martinus Nijhoff, 1981), 149; Jan Parmentier, "Vriend en vijand: de Zuid-Nederlanders en de VOC tijdens de achttiende eeuw", in: Noord-Zuid, ed. ibid., 149–66.

**26** Parmentier, Tea Time, 51–7; Conrad Gill, *Merchants and Mariners of the 18th Century* (London: Edward Arnold, 1961), 16.

**27** For more on the role of competition in Ostend trade, see Parmentier, Private, 89–94. For the profits: ibid., Oostend, 139–40; R. Baetens, "Investering en rendement bij de Generale Indishe Compagnie: de handel op Bengalen vergeleken met de Chinahandel", in: *Album aangeboden aan Charles Verlinden ter gelegenheid van zijn dertig jaar professoraat* (Ghent: Universa, 1975), 17–42.

**28** Michal Wanner, "The Establishment of the General Company in Ostend in the Context of the Habsburg Maritime Plans, 1714–1723", in: *Prague Papers on the History of International Relations* (2007), 32–61; Huisman, Belgique, 197–266; Hertz, "England and the Ostend Company," 261–262.

abroad), bought and refurnished used EIC ships, made shorter overseas sailings and benefitted from latecomer access to cartographical knowledge.[29]

Yet, these developments in Europe accounted for only half of the trade. In eastern spaces like Canton, located along China's Pearl River, representatives of the EIC, GIC and many other European and Asian kingdoms encountered one another face-to-face during the 1720s.[30] There, the conflicts between these companies had less meaning, as the competitors jointly were classified as foreigners by the Chinese government. The Ch'ing emperors maintained strict restrictions on this trade – dictating which commodities were exportable from China, which *hong* (or Chinese) merchants could trade with non-Chinese ships, the ways these sales could be financed, and even where and for how long Europeans might reside in their settlements.[31] Company agents economically struggled in this setting not only against one another, but especially to identify a western commodity actually wanted by the Chinese, beyond exported bullion, and in their attempts to buy desirable eastern products at a good quality-to-price ratio from the *hong* merchants. It was an uncomfortable reminder that their control had only limited reach in the East Indies – which perhaps only increased its value in the west.

The initial success of the GIC, however, did not last. Though, the Habsburg connection initially seemed to procure the new firm some opportunities, notably unfettered access to Spanish American ports and their silver supplies following the Vienna treaties of 1725, the company's competition mostly soured.[32] A contemporary British law expressly prohibited crown subjects from buying stock in the GIC. The Dutch, meanwhile, joined the English, Prussian and French Herrenhauser Alliance in August 1726, which specifically aimed against the "upstart" Ostend Company.[33] War seemed possible. Great Britain made this threat visceral by expanding its armies from 18,000 to 26,383 men by 1727 and by staring discussions of a European naval blockade. Austria simply could not get its allies in central and eastern Europe interested in recommencing armed conflict, and Charles VI ultimately caved to demands to temporarily suspend the GIC in 1727. The decision was made permanent in 1731, with the guarantee that the English, Dutch and French monarchs recognize the succession

29 Parmentier, Private, 76–85; ibid. and Degryse, Maritime.

30 The VOC did not directly sail to Canton until 1729. This was because they could access Chinese commodities via the interregional, or country, trade from their other settlements. Yong Liu, *The Dutch East India Company's Tea Trade with China, 1757–1781* (Boston: Brill, 2007).

31 For an overview of the early Canton trade, with a sensitivity to Chinese activities, see page 1, ft. 2.

32 Hertz, Ostend, 263–4.

33 Michal Wanner, "The Ostend Company as phenomenon of international politics in 1722–1731", in: *Prague Papers on the History of International Relations* (2006), 29–63; Hertz, 268; G.C. Gibbs, "Britain and the Alliance of Hanover, April 1725–February 1726", in: *The English Historical Review* 73 (1958), 404–30; Basil Williams, "The Foreign Policy of England under Walpole", in: *The English Historical Review* 15 (1900), 665–98.

Charles VI's daughter Maria Theresa.[34] Some vessels continued to trade – or more correctly smuggle – through the Southern Netherlands during the 1730s and 1740s, but the eastern Ostend trade mostly ended.[35] Despite this success, the VOC and EIC never regained the completeness of their one-time monopolies. Expanded interest in the East Indies, rather, only increased over time. New companies were chartered during the eighteenth century, including the Danish Asiatic Company in 1730, Swedish East India Company in 1731 and Prussia Asiatic Company during the 1750s.[36] In addition, towards the end of the century free trade arguments gained more and more recognition, perhaps the most notable voice being Adam Smith, who launched his attacks at the East India Company in his *An Inquiry into the Nature and Causes of the Wealth of Nations* (1776).[37] Thus, while commodities changed, intense competition among and between European companies remained the norm until the VOC and EIC's respective dissolutions in 1800 and 1874.

## On the Sources

The edited texts in this volume delve into this complex, transoceanic commercial world – following the experiences of four EIC and two Ostend ships that traveled to and traded in Canton between 1722 and 1724. They particularly were selected to highlight two themes – competition and cooperation – which manifest themselves across the sources in a variety of ways. Competition, as already suggested, not only existed between EIC and Ostend ships. EIC directors, ship captains and supercargoes, too, had differing visions of how their sailings should proceed and how they might interact with potential competitors abroad. As an example, apparent in the following sources, EIC directors supported the British law to detain all British mariners in the East Indies not sailing on British ships. The EIC travelers themselves, however,

---

**34** Huisman, Belgique, 354, 411–412; Ernst Schütz, *Die Gesandtschaft Großbritanniens am immerwährenden Reichstag zu Regensburg und am Kur(Pfalz-)Bayerischen Hof zu München 1683–1806* (München: C.H. Beck, 2007), 64–72.

**35** Hertz, Ostend, 268–79; Jeremy Black, *Trade, Empire and British Foreign Policy, 1689–1815* (London: Routledge, 2007), 124–6; Heinz Duchhardt, *Das Zeitalter des Absolutismus* (München: R. Oldenbourg Verlag, 1998), 95–7; L. Michielsen, "Het einde van de Oostendsche Kompagnie", in: *Bijdragen tot de geschiedenis* 28 (1937), 128–43; Helma Houtman-de Smedt, "The ambitions of the Austrian Empire with reference to East India during the last quarter of the eighteenth century", in: *Merchants, Companies and Trade: Europe and Asia in the Early Modern Era*, ed. Sushil Chaudhury and Michel Morineau (New York: Cambridge UP, 1999), 227–39.

**36** Diller, Dänen; Martin Åberg, "The Swedish East India Company 1731–66. Business Strategy and Foreign Influence in a Perspective of Change", in: *Scandinavian Journal of History* 15 (1990), 97–108; Ring, Asiatische.

**37** Gary M. Andersonan Robert D. Tollinson, "Adam Smith's Analysis of Joint-Stock Companies", in: *Journal of Political Economy* 90.6 (1982), 1237–56.

made no effort to enforce this instruction and even gave a nine-gun salute to their two Ostend competitors when the latter arrived in China in 1723.[38] This suggests, for those at sea or entering unfamiliar markets, the desire for information shared among experienced merchants and mariners could sometimes – even often – supersede western politics.

More generally, the texts provide a general impression of the early Canton trade from a multi-angled European perspective. The expectations and narratives the manuscripts lay out are much informed by where the authors composed their texts – in Europe or in route – as well as by their intended audiences. The EIC directors and supercargoes reports, for example, reveal a sensitivity to current European cultural trends (i.e. what will sell at home) and potential demands in the Chinese market (i.e. what will sell abroad). Given that the professional advancement of these authors relied on profit-maximization, this focus would be expected. The Ostend diary, meanwhile, written as post-facto commentaries on prior commercial travels, makes the journey to the East Indies seem like a curiosity-filled adventure. Its amused, ethnographic descriptions differ most from an EIC navigational journal, which highlights the day-to-day, and sometimes hour-by-hour, drudgery of sailing a cargo-laden ship from London to Canton and back. The captain's attempts to combat weather, wind, currents and cartographical challenges highlight the reality that – despite these authors' sometimes cultural arrogance – Europeans in 1723 were still trying to figure out the long-distance trade with China.

## The English East India Company

The three English sources selected and edited for this volume form part of the well-studied India Office Records (IOR), housed today at the British Library in London. The collection contains a variety of private papers and printed manuscripts, but many of its early holdings on the Canton trade represent manuscripts officially commissioned and stored by the EIC, to be used as commercial receipts, proceeding transcripts and navigational aides by future company merchants and mariners.[39] The chosen EIC texts fall into this latter category.

The volume begins with a selection of commercial instructions, composed by the EIC Court of Directors and given to its representatives on the four vessels that sailed from London to Canton in 1722. They have been transcribed from sections of the outgoing "Letter Book 18, 1721-1723," catalogued IOR/E/3/101. These instructions were intended to serve as guides for company agents while abroad and away from official oversight. They include directives on a range of expected and imagined issues, such

---

**38** Gill, Merchants, 24.

**39** M.I. Moire, *A General Guide to the India Office Records* (London: The British Library, 1988).

as what route vessels should (or should not) take for their sailing, what goods supercargoes should buy and at what rates, and how company agents should deal with any decisions left unspecified while in the East Indies. The EIC directors themselves were a diverse group – representing a range of nativities, trade experiences and current investments – but they shared a common interest in the final European market for imported Chinese commodities.[40] Their text thus traces the company's suggested process of attaining highest profits, including eliminating Ostend competition, rather than the necessary compromises of actual acts of commercial negotiation abroad.

The 101-page "Diary and consultations of the Council in China for 1723" was recorded by William Fazakerley, chief supercargo for the four aforementioned EIC vessels and a passenger on the Duke of Cambridge. It today is catalogued IOR/G/12/24. The text records the *in-situ* deliberations of the company's merchants abroad, as well as their recommendations to their ships captains and their contact with other Europeans sailing along the African coast and in the Indian Ocean.[41] Fazakerley offers only a short narrative of the fleet's actual travel to the east, encompassing just sixteen pages of his original diary. The majority of his text focuses on the actual acts of buying and selling he and his fellow EIC merchants negotiated with their *hong* counterparts upon reaching the Pearl River, including detailed lists of teas, textiles, porcelains and other goods purchased, their costs and packaging. The diary nods to the EIC's tacit partnership in 1723 with several specific Chinese merchant firms, notably that of Tan Suqua. Yet, it was written for and deposited with the EIC directors upon Fazakerley's return to Europe, who used it to gauge his and their other agents' effectiveness. Its aim, as a result, was to emphasize the agency and activity of only western traders in Canton.

The navigational journal for the ship Hertford – "Hertford: Journal, 1 October 1722 to 2 November 1724" and catalogued IOR/L/MAR/B/656 – was compiled by Francis Nelly, captain of one of the four aforementioned EIC ships. Nelly was very familiar with the eastern passage, having sailed with and commanded English trading ventures to the region since at least 1700.[42] His original journal is 157 pages and divided into two parts, the outward and homeward journeys, only the former of which is included in this volume. The return can be accessed via this edition's corresponding online material.[43] The text is highly organized and, except when the Hertford was at anchor, tabulated to record variations in ship speed, water depth as well as current ship coordinates with sometimes hourly regularity. Ostensibly, Nelly also was to provide his

40 See the examples of Henry Lyell, William Gosselin, Simon Theunemans and John Drummond. See page 42, ft. 97; 44, ft. 112; 45, ft. 113, 115.

41 For later Dutch consultation books, see Paul A. Van Dyke and Cynthia Viallé (eds.), *The Canton-Macao Dagregisters, 3 vol., 1762–1764* (Macau: Instituto Cultural, 2006–2009).

42 See Anna: Journal, 5 February 1700 to 31 January 1702, in: British Library (BL) – IOR/L/MAR/A/CXLIV; Mary Doreen Wainwright and Noel Matthews, *A Guide to Western Manuscripts and Documents in the British Isles relating to South and South East Asia* (New York: Oxford UP, 1965), 324-5.

43 See http://www.degruyter.com/view/product/456197?format=B&rskey=5ZojLY&result=3.

notes to the EIC directors upon his return to England, to improve the navigational information available to future company mariners. He did so in 1724. The journal, however, also clearly captures the lived challenges of sailing an eighteenth-century vessel into the open sea and against unfavorable weather, winds and tides as well as the captain's chosen sailing tactics to combat such conditions and recover from inevitable breakages. It thus traces in detail not only the EIC passage to China but, like the supercargo's diary, one EIC agent's attempts to convey to his employers his efficient leadership, despite difficulties.

All of the English manuscripts edited for this volume are the direct result of conducting a single journey to the East Indies. They highlight the variety of ways in which persons involved in the Canton trade not only experienced but perceived and justified their overlapping commercial work.

## The Ostend Sailing

The provenance of the Ostend manuscript "Relation du voyage fait en 1723" is somewhat more complicated and remains only partially reconstructed.[44] The text consists of nine letters totaling 210 pages, which were bound into a single volume. It was written by the same hand throughout, yet the calligraphy is of varying qualities. Today the manuscript is in the possession of the Bayerische Staatsbibliothek in Munich, catalogued as Codex gallicus 674. The library acquired the text at auction in 1830, as part of a lot previously owned by Pierre Antoine Noel Bruno Comte Daru (1767–1829), a French poet, historian and financier. It is unknown how the manuscript came into the possession of the Comte Daru.[45] Also unrecorded in both the catalogue and manuscript itself are the name of its author and the year(s) it was written. Historians Conrad Gill and Jan Parmentier both ascribe the manuscript to Henri Carlos Ghyselinck, a native of the Southern Netherlands and supercargo of the Ostender St. Joseph in 1723. Although this is mostly speculation, it may explain the limited degree of French language proficiency sometimes suggested by the text. Gill additionally suspects that Ghyselinck used notes taken during his journey to compose these letters at

44 For a contemporary Ostend travelogue to India, see Floris Prims, *De oorlog van Mijnheer Cobbé; geschiedenis van de reis van Cobbé, van zijn onderhandelingen met den Nabab en van zijn Oorlog tegen de Mooren 1722–1724* (Antwerpen: Leeslust, 1927). For GIC travels to China, see J. Rotsaert, *De reis van het keyserlyck compagnieschip genaempt De Keyzerinne, gemonteerd met 30 stukken canon en 108 zielen. Equipatie gecommandeert per Capteyn Joan de Clerck, gedestineerd naar Canton in China, uyt gevaren van Oostende op den 20 January 1725* (Sint-Andries: Heemkundige Kring "Maurits Van Coppenolle", 1963).

45 For more on this auction sale, see *Catalogue des Livres imprimé et manuscrits composant la bibliothèque de Feu M. le Comte Daru* [...] (Paris: J.S. Merlin, 1830), 110.

a later date.[46] However, a closer inspection of the manuscript shows that the text is only partially original. Large sections were copied from contemporary manuscripts and publications, thus opening the possibility that the author may not be Ghyselinck and may not have sailed to China at all in 1723. The time of the text's composition can at least be estimated with some precision. Internal clues indicate it was written after 1735, or when the East India trade was being discussed in the Habsburg territories and Prussia.[47] The source, therefore, is not as straightforward in its origin and character as the EIC texts. Nevertheless, it consolidates interesting western perceptions of the East Indies, which would have informed the encounters of EIC and Ostend traders in 1723 and thereafter.

## Editorial Principles

The following transcriptions maintain their original spelling. A majority of the manuscripts' line breaks, however, have not been retained, due to the practicalities of publication. The one exception is the navigational journal, where all possible care has been taken to retain the source's original appearance. To shorten the documents, repetitive headers of pages and months have been deleted without indication. In all other places where repetitions were deleted, omissions were marked by "[...]". The page numbers of the original texts have been inserted in square brackets at the start of each new page, if no other easy way of identifying source locations was available (e.g. dates). Any additional comments made by the editors within the text also have been inserted in square brackets. Finally, it should be noted that western authors often struggled to record the Chinese names, places and words they heard in the East Indies. We have favored the Wades-Giles system of romanization in our notes and tried to use these terms in their 1723 context.

**46** Parmentier, *Oostende*, 64, 110; ibid., Tea Time, 139; Gill, Merchants, 19–28.
**47** For more on these plans, see ibid., 28; Ring, Asiatische, 5–29.

# Edited Documents

**Ship Hartford's Sea Journal from China to England**

Additional Online Content
see http://www.degruyter.com/view/product/456197?format=B&rskey=5ZojLY&result=3

# 1 Documents from the East India Company Directors

## Orders & Instructions given by the Court of Directors of the United Company of Merchants of England Trading to the East Indies.[1] To Mess.rs William Fazakerley[2], Richard Morton[3], Edmund Godfrey[4], Thomas Atkyns[5], Tho.as Carter[6], Thomas Dade[7], & Devereux Bacon.[8]

[164r] 1. We the said Court of Directors reposing Special Trust and Confidence in your Ability & Integrity, have elected you to be a standing Council for Mannaging Our Affairs in China, And to Act in the same manner as any other Chief and Council at Our Settlements abroad[9] to whom We Consign Our Outward bound Shipping, We have appointed and do hereby appoint M.r William Fazakerley to be first of the said Council, M.r Richard Morton to be second, M.r Edmund Godfrey to be third, M.r Thomas

---

**1** Queen Elizabeth I granted a Royal Charter to the joint-stock "Governor and Company of Merchants of London Trading into the East Indies" in December 1600, after several independent English excursions to the Indian Ocean in the 1590s. This company operated under a monopoly until 1694 and thus largely without competition, until the chartering of "The English Company Trading to the East Indies" in 1698. The two companies merged in 1708, officially forming "The United Company of Merchants of England Trading into the East Indies". Hereafter, no British merchants outside of the EIC were permitted to trade between Europe and Asia. The Court of Directors, composed of 24 members elected by stockholders, met regularly as the Company's overall governing body. See "United Company Court Minutes ('Court Books')", 1710–1833, in: BL – IOR/B/51–185. For general histories of the EIC, see Philip Lawson, *The East India Company: A History* (London: Longman, 1993); John Keay, *The Honourable Company. A History of the English East India Company* (London: HarperCollins, 1991).

**2** William Fazakerley (dates unknown) regularly served as chief supercargo for EIC ships to Canton in the 1720s and early 1730s. In 1730, he, fellow Englishman James Naish and Cantonese trader Tan Suqua were accused by a Chinese competitor of defrauding the company, by invoicing higher purchase prices than actually procured. These claims likely were concocted to reduce Suqua's favor with the EIC, but they continued to embroil Fazakerley in controversy and disrupt his business until 1735. Gill, Merchants, 22; Van Dyke, Merchants, 105–14.

**3** Person unknown.

**4** Edmund Godfrey (dates unknown) later became a senior shipping authority for the EIC, whom he worked for into the 1750s. See Barry Crosbie, *Irish Imperial Networks: Migration, Social Communication and Exchange in Nineteenth-Century India* (New York: Cambridge UP, 2011), 51.

**5** Person unknown.

**6** Person unknown.

**7** Person unknown.

**8** Person unknown.

**9** The "President and Council" at the EIC trading posts in Asia were responsible for representing the company vis-à-vis Asian rulers and their officials, for administrating overseas settlement, trade and defense and for selling European imports and buying Asian commodities. In contrast to the Canton case, however, the President and Council stayed in Asia all year. See, for EIC governance abroad, Stern, Company-State; H.V. Bowen, *The Business of Empire: the East India Company and Imperial Britain, 1756–1833* (Cambridge: Cambridge UP, 2006).

Atkyns to be fourth, M.r Thomas Carter to be fifth, M.r Thomas Dade to be Sixth, and M.r Devereux Bacon to be Seventh and last of the said Council, And do direct you the said Council to take the charge of all the Cargos of the said Companys Ships now outward bound which shall be consign'd unto You or in absence of any to such of You as shall be then present as hereinafter mention'd, To dispose of all the Goods, Merchandizes & Treasure in the said Cargos, To invest the Proceed thereof in such Goods & Merchandizes and according to such directions as We shall give you for that Purpose, and to do such further Acts and things as We shall hereunder or hereafter order to require for the most benefit and Advantage of the said United Company, We have also elected M.r Samuel Skinner[10] to be Secretary & Accountant to You, but not to be of Council or have any Vote therein unless in the case of any of yor deaths & then he is to be youngest of Council together with his aforesaid Station.

[164v] 2. The Ships We intend to Consign unto You are the Duke of Cambridge[11] 430. Tons, Cap.t Daniel Small[12], The Princess Anne[13] 380. Tons Captain Nicholas Luhorne[14], The Mountague[15] 380. Tons Cap.t John Gordon[16], and the Hartford[17] 440 Tons, Cap.t Fran.s Nelly[18], What Goods & Treasure will be laden on board each & to what Amount, You will be fully Apprized of by their respective Invoices and Bills

**10** Person unknown.

**11** The Duke of Cambridge housed between 80 and 86 crewmembers and 36 guns while active, from 1717 to 1725. This was her fourth, and final, voyage. She also stopped at Bombay on her homeward sailing.

**12** Daniel Small (dates unknown) was captain of the Duke of Cambridge during her second and third voyages to Madras and Bengal (1716–1717, 1719–1720) and during her fourth voyage, this sailing to Canton.

**13** The Princess Anne housed between 70 and 76 crewmembers and between 28 and 30 guns while active, from 1716 to 1729. This was her third voyage.

**14** Nicholas Luhorne (d. 1723) was captain of the Princess Ann during her second voyage to Mocha (1719–1720) and during her third voyage, this sailing to Canton.

**15** The Montagu housed between 76 and 80 crewmembers and 24 guns while active, from 1719–1731. This was her second voyage.

**16** John Gordon (dates unknown), a native of Scotland, was captain of the Montagu during her first voyage to China (1719–1720), her second voyage, being this sailing to Canton, and her third voyage to Madras and Bengal (1726–1727). See George McGilvary, *East India Patronage and the British State: the Scottish Elite and Politics in the Eighteenth Century* (New York: Tauris Academic Studies, 2008), 116.

**17** The Hertford housed between 84 and 92 crewmembers and 36 guns while active, from 1717 to 1735. This was her third voyage. See the edited "Ship Hartfords Sea Journall from England to China" in this volume.

**18** Francis Nelly (dates unknown) was captain of the Hertford from her third voyage, this sailing to Canton, to her fifth voyage, also to China (1730–1732). He possibly died during this last excursion.

of Lading[19] which with their Charterpartys[20] you will find enclosed in their several Packets, whereto refer You, We have appointed Mess.[rs] Fazakerley & Carter to take Passage on the Duke of Cambridge, Mess.[rs] Morton & Dade on the Mountague, Mess.[rs] Godfrey & Bacon on the Princess Anne, & Mess.[rs] Atkyns and Skinner on the Hartford. We shall order all the Ships to keep Company together, and the Captains to appoint a Rendevouz in case of unavoidable Seperation, Whereby We propose you will Arrive all together at your Consign'd Port of Canton.

3. We hereby direct, That all of you do by all Opportunitys during the Voyage out and home give an Account of your Proceedings to that time to the Court of Directors of the United Company of Merch.[ts] of England Trading to the East Indies in London, or in case of Seperation then so many of you as are present.[21] That all & every of you do duly and constantly observe perform and comply with your Covenants, & the Particular Directions, Cautions & Prohibitions in these Orders and Instructions or such others as shall hereafter be given you, and any others to which they may relate. However that We may be the better Assured you do so, We hereby direct & order That each of you do at your return to England give to the Court of Directors of the said United Company for the time being an Account in Writing how far you have comply'd with these Instructions, or any others to be given you Paragraph by Par.[a] It being a standing Order of the said Court, That no Mony shall be paid to any SupraCargo[22] (and you are in the Nature of SupraCargo's) on account of Commission or otherwise till such Account is given, We further direct That you do each of you except the Chief take a Copy of these and any any [sic] other subsequent Instructions, assoon as you can after you put to Sea

19 A bill of lading is a commercial document, agreed between a merchant or supercargo and the ship captain transporting their goods. It details the individual items loaded onto a vessel, their quantity and their ultimate destination, and it is signed by sender, transporter and final recipient, thus operating much like a receipt.

20 A charter party was the pre-departure agreement reached between the EIC, here the ship's charterer, and the ship's owners. In contrast to the VOC, the EIC usually did not own the ships it used for its East Indies trade but relied on shipping consortia. Charter parties covered several topics, including the amount of freight to be paid to the captain and crewmembers upon their successful return. They extended either for a set amount of time or covered travels between specific geographies. The EIC favored the former option in 1722, making them liable for demurrage, a fee for keeping a ship longer than stated in its original contract. K.N. Chaudhuri, "The English East India Company's Shipping (c. 1660–1760)", in: Ships, ed. Bruijn and Gaastra, 49–80.

21 See copied letters to the Directors in the edited "Diary & Consultation Book of the Council for China for the Year 1723" in this volume.

22 Supercargoes represented the Company, or more generally the owners of the cargo, on any sailing vessel. They were responsible for selling exported merchandize and for procuring and securing additional goods for the return voyage. Morse, Chronicles, 66–77.

Outward, and at your return deliver it in to the Secretary each mentioning therein the times when written.[23]

4. We exhort you all to a sober & orderly behaviour & to demean yo.rSelves in yo.r several aforemention'd Stations respectfully one towards another, avoiding all Occasions of dissention during yo.r Voyage out, in China & homeward bound by w.ch & your Fidelity & diligence you will further recommend Your Selves to Our good Opinion, We particularly forbid all manner of Gaming for Mony or Goods.

### [165r] First as to your Voyage Outwards

5. It is of great Importance to Us, That you arrive in China assoon as possible as well to have the more time there to do your business in, and to give the Earlyer dispatches to these Ships as hereinafter directed, as to be before hand at Canton in case any Ostenders or other Interlopers[24] should this year be design'd thither, We should be Glad if all the Ships Companys remain so well in health that there may be no necessity for any to touch at the Cape[25], and to this end have order'd each of the four Captains to take in sufficient Water & Provisions here to serve them to Batavia[26] because as some of you must know the Winds often make it difficult to get in & out of the Cape, by which the Voyages of several Ships have been detarded, but this We leave to your discretion in case of necessity by unforeseen Accidents. We likewise shall order all said Captains to keep in so high a Latitude as not to come in sight of the Cape or of any Pyrates that may lye off it in hopes of Prey.[27]

---

23 For company bookkeeping in eighteenth-century Canton, see Paul A. Van Dyke, "Bookkeeping as a Window into Efficiencies of Early Modern Trade: Europeans, Americans and Others in China Compared, 1700–1842", in: *Narratives of Free Trade: the Commercial Cultures of Early US-China Relations*, ed. Kendall Johnson (Hong Kong: Hong Kong UP, 2012), 17–32.

24 An "interloper" was an independent English trader, especially here merchants and crewmembers who sailed for non-British companies. See *Remarks on Trade in a Dialogue between a Committee-man and an Interloper* (London, 1683).

25 Members of the VOC founded Cape Town, in modern-day South Africa, in 1652, as a provisions entrepôt for ships engaged in the East Indies trade. See M. Boucher, "The Cape and Foreign Shipping, 1714–1723", in: *South African Historical Journal*, 6.1 (1974), 3–29; Kerry Ward, *Networks of Empire: Forced Migration in the Dutch East India Company* (New York: Cambridge UP, 2009), 127–78.

26 Batavia, now Jakarta, was a settlement on the northern coast of the Indonesian island of Java. It was the main VOC political and trading site in the region after 1619 and 1674, respectively, a regular market for the Chinese junk trade, and a frequent site of navigation and re-provisioning for European vessels sailing to Canton. See Liu, Dutch, 17–42; Jaap R. Bruijn, "Between Batavia and the Cape: Shipping Patterns of the Dutch East India Company", in: *Journal of Southeast Asian Studies* 11.2 (1980), 251–65.

27 For more on piracy near Cape Town and in the Indian Ocean, see Boucher, Cape; Arne Bialuschewski, "Pirates, Slavers, and the Indigenous Population in Madagascar, c. 1690–1715", in: *The International Journal of African Historical Studies* 38.3 (2005), 401–25; Robert J. Antony, *Elusive Pirates,*

6. If any of the Ships should by Casualty of Storms or otherwise loose a Mast or be disabled from a speedy Prosecution of her Voyage, We hereby empower & direct that if the Chief or any of the next three of the aforesaid Council are on board they do shift into such of the other Ships as on a Consultation to be held by so many of you as are then in Company shall be judg'd most for Our General benefit, and if it should happen that any Ship should be disabled, We hereby direct that her Treasure be taken out, and put on board the other Ship or Ships in Company to be the sooner at Canton invested, and that such disabled Ship follow after as well as she can.[28] If when you are at Sea it shall appear any one of the Ships prove a better Sailer than that on which M.[r] Fazakerley takes Passage, We direct That he if he thinks fitting may change Ships with those of the Council on board her, because We would him assoon at China as possible in case of inevitable Seperation especially when got beyond Batavia.

7. Besure advise the Captains of each of the aforesaid Ships to keep well to the Eastward Outward bound to prevent falling to the Leeward of Java head[29] in the Easterly Monsoon[30], because for want of that care some of Our Ships have lost their Passage and y.[e] Comp.[a] a Years time of the return'd Cargo's.[31]

8. We propose all the Ships shall call in at Batavia and therefore We direct You or such of You as shall be on board [165v] to hasten the respective Captains to get away from thence within five to ten days in which time they may if diligent be fully supply'd with Wood Water & Refreshments. If a longer time should be necessary for the Recovering the Mens healths, You will be able to judge and give Orders accordingly[32], If you find any Cap.[t] making Unnecessary delays Protest against him for it is to be fear'd some Pretence or other may be started for longer stay, when the true reason is

*Pervasive Smugglers: Violence and Clandestine Trade in the Greater China Seas* (Hong Kong: Hong Kong UP, 2010).

**28** This happened to the EIC in 1722, when her ship the Sir Robert Walpole broke her main and foremast fifteen days after leaving London. She harbored in Cádiz for repairs. Afterwards, the Walpole fell to the leeward of the Sunda Strait and again missed the trade winds to get to China in 1722. Morse, Chronicles, vol. 1, 171.

**29** Java Head, now Tanjung Layar, is a mountainous cape on the extreme west coast of Java, marking the entrance to the Sunda Strait.

**30** The Southwest Monsoon extended from April to August, when strong winds and heavy rainstorms pushed north across the Indian Ocean. The storm reversed regional currents, thus allowing European ships easier travel to eastern Asia. The summer monsoon, however, also was violent in June and July, interrupting much regional dhow sailing and even closing some ports. See Edward A. Alpers, *The Indian Ocean in World History* (Oxford: Oxford UP, 2014), 7.

**31** Again, the Walpole encountered this problem in 1722. See paragraph above.

**32** For more on the impact of long sea voyages on sailors' health, see Mark Harrison, *Medicine in an Age of Commerce and Empire: Britain and its Tropical Colonies, 1660–1830* (New York: Oxford UP, 2010); Kevin Brown, *Poxed and Scurvied: the Story of Sickness and Health at Sea* (Barnsley: Seaforth Publishing, 2011).

to take in Pepper or other Private Trade[33], Protest also against any Cap.$^{t}$ that you find endeavouring to loose the Company of the rest in the Outw.$^{d}$ Passage, However if it should happen that the Ship in which M.$^{r}$ Fazakerley is should not get to Batavia so soon as any other of them, In that case We require such first arriv'd Ships to stay for him till he comes, Provided it be within Ten Days, for We would have him get to China on or with the first Ship of ours if possible. If by unforeseen Accidents the Passage Outward should be so tedious that a long stay for him at Batavia would hazard the Ships Passage to Canton, then We require the Ships to make the best of their way from Batavia to Maccoa[34] & so up to Wampo[35], and there wait for M.$^{r}$ Fazakerley, It being Our desire that he should be present, and give his Advice therein as having had much longer experience in the Trade of China than any of you besides.

9. And for this reason We would not have any Contract for Goods made till M.$^{r}$ Fazakerley Arrives as hoping he will live & get early to Canton, but in case of his death or absence so long, that you have reason to fear he will loose his Passage, then if M.$^{r}$ Morton, M.$^{r}$ Godfrey, & M.$^{r}$ Atkyns or any two of them are there, We give them leave to proceed in such part of the Contracts as shall appear to require most haste till the rest of you arrive, We have told you before that you are all to be One Council & Act joyntly in the Mannagement of Our Affairs according to Our Instructions herein (or hereinafter to be) given you. You are to sit in Council in the Stations before directed from the times of your respective Arrivals[36]

10. By the Copy of each Capt.$^{ns}$ Instructions enclosed in y.$^{e}$ Packet of the Ship you will see he hath Orders at large to follow yours, Nevertheless you must give him no Orders contrary to these Instructions or the Covenants in his Charterparty.[37] In the

33 Seamen had an interest in private trade to increase their salary. The companies, however, only permitted a limited amount, so as not to infringe on the space and commodities available for owners'/charterers' perusal. See, for private or illicit trading, Om Prakash, *On the Economic Encounter Between Asia and Europe, 1500–1800* (Surrey: Ashgate Publishing, 2014); Earl H. Pritchard, "Private Trade between England and China in the Eighteenth Century", in: *Journal of the Economic and Social History of the Orient* 1.2 (1958), 221–56; Antony, Elusive; Van Dyke, Merchants, 28–9.

34 The Portuguese were the first, and only, Europeans to establish a permanent foothold in China. They did so via their settlement on the island of Macao, located in the Pearl River delta, in 1557. Given its oceanic access, and potential for easy smuggling, the Chinese government did not support direct trade to this port. The Portuguese, similarly, did not allow non-Catholics to reside therein, thus necessitating yearly fleets from Great Britain. See Rogério Miguel Puga, *The British Presence in Macau, 1635–1793* (Hong Kong: Hong Kong UP, 2013); Brockey, Journey; Van Dyke, Merchants.

35 Whampoa, in modern-day Guangdong Province, was the last deep-sea port servicing Canton, located about midway between Macao and the city. European merchants had to anchor their deep-draught transoceanic vessels here and travel by regional watercraft a further 20 kilometers up the Pearl River to the markets at Canton.

36 See such activities indicated in the edited "Diary & Consultation Book of the Council for China in the Year 1723" in this volume.

37 See the captains' instructions, pages 51–61.

Cap.n's Instructions is a Clause relating to the Mariners behaviour at Batavia when they touch there, Remind the Cap.tns of it & do your endeavour to have it Obey'd, do You also observe it as if particularly directed to your Selves.

## [166r] Secondly as to your Mannagement in China

11. The French Factory[38] being as We are fully inform'd very capacious and sufficient to receive you, We last year recommended it to M.r Naish[39] & his Council to hire it if possible[40], If they had it you are the likelier to get it, but if otherwise endeavour for it, & if not procurable than for any other as large and as properly Situated by the River side. We understand that Factory has sufficient room to receive the greatest part of the Goods you are like to have at any one time together, for We expect and hereby Order that as fast as your Goods come in, You hasten them away on Ship board, but if it will not hold all, then you must rent another, and it would be best if adjoining to that you first took, however whatsoever large Factory you get, We require all of you to reside there, by which means as you will keep but One Table, The ffactory Expenses, Presents to the Government[41] & other charges will be lessen'd, and so will the rent too. If you can make it serve without renting a Second, for if you should be a little strait'ned

**38** Various French companies had been trading at Canton since 1699. They joined in 1719 to form the *Compagnie perpétuelle des Indes*, also known as the *Compagnie des Indes Orientales*. A French vessel, the Toulouse, sojourned in Canton in 1722, but, no company ships arrived in 1723. See Pierre Boulle, "French Mercantilism, Commercial Companies and Colonial Profitability", in: *Companies and Trade: Essays on Overseas Trading Companies during the Ancien Régime*, eds. Leonard Blussé and Femme Gaastra (The Hague: Leiden UP, 1981), 97–117; Catherine Manning, *Fortunes à Faire: The French in Asian Trade, 1719–1748* (Surrey: Ashgate Publishing, 1996); Furber, Rival, 201–11.

**39** James Naish (dates unknown) was a merchant and supercargo who worked for the EIC and the Ostend Company in China from 1716 to the 1730s. He, along with fellow supercargo William Fazakerley, was accused of defrauding the company by several rivals in the 1730s. See "Diary of James Naish at Canton and Macao," 13.1.1731 to 24.6.1731, in: BL – IOR/G/12/32.

**40** Europeans, by imperial decree, were restricted from owning property in Canton and entering the city independently. Instead, they were rented factories – so called because they were where commercial factors lived – outside the city walls from Chinese merchants. These residences were situated next to one another. See Jonathan Farris, "Dwelling Factors: Western Merchants in Canton", in: *Investing in the Early Modern Built Environment: Europeans, Asians, Settlers and Indigenous Societies*, ed. Carole Shammas (Boston: Brill, 2012), 163–90.

**41** Gift-giving based many European and Chinese relations. Cantonese traders received armor, jewels and red wine from foreigners and gave in return small chests of fine tea, bundles of silk and porcelain. Local officials similarly provided fresh provisions to newly arrived ships, while expecting a fee for their administrative services. Morse, Chronicles, vol. 1, 81; Van Dyke, Merchants, 61–4. See also page 218, ft. 87.

you may make use of the Merchants Hongs[42] for the China Ware, but as to the Tea, Take constant care it be lodg'd in your Factory assoon as bought or even such of it as shall be brought to You for Sale if you are like to buy it.[43] If you should be necessitated to rent a Second House one or two of you (as you shall agree upon) must every Night lodge in it for the Security of the Goods there, and keeping the better decorum among the Seamen that are to watch & guard it from time to time.[44] Nevertheless mannage with that prudence that the Chineeses may esteem you all as but one house as well as one Concern for they will be glad of a handle to get double Presents.

12. If any of the Council dye before compleating the Investm.ts the Survivours (taking M.r Skynner to their Assistance to be youngest of Council) are to carry them on, which We hereby direct them to do, And the Court of Directors for the time being, Will at your return consider & order what part of the deceaseds reward or allowance shall remain for his or their Executors or Administrators, & what part thereof be shared among the Survivours.

13. You being to Act jointly in the whole Mannagement of these Ships Cargo's, as well for disposing of the Outward bound Stock to most Advantage, as Investing the Proceed according to Our Orders, and therewith Lading Our Ships at China, We expect and Order, That none of you conceal from the rest any [166v] part of said Mannagement, That you hold Consultations twice a Week or oftner when Necessary, That all of you when at Canton or so many as are be duly Summon'd thereto, That all the Results of your Debates, All proposals for making Contracts, and those Contracts when made, The particulars of all Presents, when, to whom, and why made, & every other Transaction relating to Our Affairs be settled in Council as the Majority then present shall agree, and that the whole be enter'd in the Consultation book[45], and Sign'd so soon as the Entrys can from time to time be made, but to besure within three days, That if in the Debates at any Consultat.n any of you should differ in Opinion from the rest (as sometimes may happen where both sides may mean very honestly[46], he or they shall

42 The *hong* were Chinese merchants, officially licensed by the Emperor to work as intermediaries between Chinese suppliers and European traders in Canton. This was a limited position, with only thirteen established houses by 1687. *Hong* traders not only worked commercially with foreigners; they also were responsible for visitors' professional and personal conduct, including serving as collateral for the latters' import-export fees and gifts. They also helped Europeans locate suitable supplies, warehouses, temporary residences, translators and river pilots. The official aim of this system was to provide Chinese oversight of foreign commerce, as well as to limit attempts to create and benefit from competition among Chinese merchants. The EIC primarily worked with one *hong* in 1723, Tan Suqua. Cheong, Hong Merchants; Van Dyke, Merchants, 79–102.

43 Directors in Europe constantly feared Chinese frauds when delivering tea, which did sometimes happen. For Ostend examples, see Parmentier, Tea Time, 101–5.

44 Supercargoes regularly had armed seamen guard company factories in Canton. Ibid., 99–100.

45 See the edited "Diary & Consultation Book of the Council for China for the Year 1723" in this volume. For more on consultation and packing books, Van Dyke, Bookkeeping; ibid., Merchants, 25–6.

46 The former bracket remains unclosed in the original document.

have liberty to enter their dissent at the end of said Consultation Entry with their reasons to be judg'd of here at yo.ʳ return, but those reasons must be given in & enter'd in two or three days at furthest. However We expect and require such difference in Opinion be not made a handle for heat or Animosity then or afterwards.

14. As all the China Cargo's are Consign'd to you by Name, or such of you as shall be then present, We direct that you keep one General set of Books (as well as one Consultation book) in a regular Method that therein be enter'd every days buying, selling, or other Mercantile affairs proper to be inserted. Keep also a regular Account of all Silver & Goods deliver'd out or receiv'd in for Our Account, and of all particular Disbursements & Expences, Be as frugal in your Presents as the nature of the case will admit, & enter in Consultation the reason, to be examin'd at your return.

15. Keep likewise a packing Book of the Contents of every Parcell laden on board each of the Ships inserting therein the true Tares[47] of all the Weighable Goods and entring said Account of Tares in the respective Invoices.

16. Thô We have appointed M.ʳ Skinner to be Secretary and Accountant, yet We are sensible he is not sufficiently Skill'd in framing a Pair of Books, Therefore We direct That the Chief Second and Third do take the Charge of the Journal and Ledger more immediately upon themselves, at least in framing the Journal Parcells, and revising the rest, for so far as M.ʳ Skynner can assist therein, & in Copying over your Draughts he is (if you appoint him) to do it. We do not particularly order which of you shall keep the Packing Book, and do other Writing work, but leave it to you the Council to settle the whole among your Selves so as that each [167r] of you may bare his proper Share therein, and in all other the business as it happens wherein We expect you allot every one a reasonable proportion to prevent Uneasiness among you.

17. Use all possible frugality in Housekeeping and the nec.ʳʸ Expences in China, and as we shall allow you Twenty five Pounds p. head for Fresh Provisions Outwards, and Wine during the Voyage, and shall send Four Pipes of Canary[48] in Chests on the four Ships for the use of the Factory to present the Mandarines[49] and treat the Merchants, and to dispose of the Surplus which We hope will be at least one half of it, for Our Account, and likewise allow each of you Fifteen Pounds for Fresh Provisions

47 A tare was a unit of weight used in the Canton trade. It calculated the gross weight of commodities, minus their containers and packaging, and it was used for taxation.

48 This might refer to sack, a sweet, fortified white wine from the Canary Isles. Canary wines were especially popular in England by the late 1600s, with King Charles II chartering the short-lived *Governor and Company of Merchants trading to the Canary Islands* in 1665 to improve their direct import.

49 A mandarin was a political official in imperial China. The title was obtained by passing an official examination or by purchasing a civic degree. See pages 308, 333, 352–3. It gave the earner the privilege of adding *qua* or *guan* to their name, of wearing certain insignia and of avoiding corporal punishment. It thus offered the potential of social improvement. Van Dyke, Merchants, 14.

Homeward, We therefore direct That nothing further be brought to the Companys Account for Wine either in China or in the Voyage out or home.[50]

18. We hope none of you will transgress or Omit to perform any part of these Instructions. If you do We hereby acquaint you, the Offenders will render themselves unworthy Our future Service, That the Company will put their Covenants in suit against them, & insist on the forfeiting the Allowance or Reward mention'd therein to be made them, It being so mention'd on supposition they faithfully and diligently do their duty in performing said Covenants. This We tell you by way of Remembrance, & for caution that none may incur the Penalty.

19. On your Arrival in China, You will know on Enquiry whether there is like to be during your stay any Change of the Hoppo[51], If there be endeavour to get the present Hoppos Grant for whatever is in his Power at a reasonable rate, because it will be so much clear profit to him, use your best discretion in Agreeing on the Best terms you can for Measurage of the Ships[52], and all other demands but take the necessary precaution to prevent being Embarrast between the Old and New Hoppo.

20. Take all fitting Opportunitys to represent to the Chineeses That if they desire the Continuance of Our Trade at Canton & that We should not desert that Port as We have Chusan and Amoy[53], We expect they show it by their using you well That you be

**50** For more on daily life in the Canton factories and on Chinese-European relations, see Cynthia Viallé, "Daily Life of the Dutch in Canton and Nagasaki: a Comparison Based on the VOC *Dagregisters* and Other Sources", in: *Itinerario* 37.3 (2013), 153–71; May-Bo Ching, 'Chopsticks or Cutlery? How Canton Hong Merchants Entertained Foreign Guests in the Eighteenth and Nineteenth Centuries", in: Narratives, ed. Johnson, 99–116.

**51** The Hoppo was the Chief Superintendent of Customs and the emperor's representative at Canton. All Europeans had to obtain his written permission to do business there, in the form of a chop. A chop was an official permit that allowed European vessels to travel up the Pearl River, to unload their cargoes in Canton, and to finally depart with trade goods. Cheong, Hong Merchants, 193–212.

**52** The Hoppo or his officials measured all ships before unloading, from foremast to mizzenmast and from side to side, in an elaborate ceremony. These evaluations indicated the duty due on each vessel, with longer ships owning more money. Gifts also were exchanged at this time, with the Hoppo often giving fresh provisions and Europeans contributing a standard 1,950 taels as the emperor's present. See, for an elaborate description, pages 191, 193, 374. Also Van Dyke, Canton, 24–30; 190, ft. 24.

**53** Chusan, now Zhoushan, is an island located off the coast of eastern China. Nearby ports, Ningpo and Amoy, now Xiamen, often were considered as alternative depots for European trade. English and French ships stopped at the settlements in the 1680s and 1690s. Yet, strained relations with local merchants as well as complaints over the quality of goods caused the companies to end this trade by 1705. Europeans–sometimes with the support of their *hong* associates–repeatedly threatened to remove their business back to these ports, especially when facing unfavorable Cantonese prospects. The EIC acted on these threats with several failed attempts in 1734, 1735 and 1736. Eventually, in 1757, the Emperor closed Ningpo and Amoy to foreigners. Both ports continued to serve as regional hubs of the junk trade, with Amoy dominating from 1717 to 1740. See Ng Chin-keong, *Trade and Society: the Amoy Network on the China Coast, 1683–1735* (Singapore: Singapore UP, 1983); Morse, Chronicles, vol. 1, 127–34; Cheong, Hong Merchants, 28–9.

receiv'd in all places with respect, Have no New Impositions laid on you, Have free liberty to trade with whom you please without Confinement, Insist also on free liberty To choose Linguists[54] & China Servants and dismiss them as you see fit, To repair and purchase all manner of Stores for your Ships, & that no demand be in future made on you for your Guns Sails Powder or Arms being brought ashore.[55]

[167v] 21. Two or three years since the Chineeses attempted a Combination among themselves, & settled a Draught to that purpose to joyn together, The meaning of which was to set their own prices on the Goods to be sold Europeans, and to have their proportions of the real profit on said Goods, whoever appeard to be the Seller, But the next Years SupraCargo's brought Us word they could not Agree among themselves & so it dropt, after said SupraCargo's had complain'd to the Governour of the Province of this Imposition.[56] We hope they will not make another attempt that way but if they have already or should do it while you are there, you must also strenuously oppose it in the best manner you can. Let the Merchants and if necessary the Hoppo & Mandarines know you are under our positive Orders not to be ty'd to buy of any particular people, By a proper Address remind them of the General Loss the Mandarines Hoppos Merchants & inferiour Tradesmen of all sorts suffer'd at Amoy by the like ill treatment, and if you cant have as fair Treatment as formerly, You will try your fortune at another report. If they should attempt to Insult you or hinder the Merchants from bringing you the Goods you have contracted for or offer other Injurys of the like kind, Tell them plainly you will neither offer or suffer such things, You know how to make your selves amends, if they will force you to it as was done some Years since at Amoy where a Junk was seiz'd for reparation of the Injurys done to the Madrass[57] Traders[58], of which when

---

**54** European supercargoes and their *hong* counterparts commonly communicated in a form of pidgin English or Portuguese. All official requests, however, had to be made in Chinese. Teaching the language to foreigners was forbidden, under penalty of death. As a result, Europeans had to hire state-sponsored linguists to intermediate between themselves and Chinese officials. These linguists, in turn, performed the difficult task of balancing European requests with Chinese rules of deportment and imperial law. Van Dyke, Canton Trade, 77–93.

**55** In the early years of the Canton trade, supercargoes had annual audiences with the Hoppo, in which they asked for a number of privileges. See pages 188, 372–4. Also, Van Dyke, Canton Trade, 20–1.

**56** Canton's merchants formed a guild in 1720 and 1721, to check abuses, balance foreign influence and prevent commercial monopolies. It was a precursor to the later *Co-Hong*. Morse, Chronicles, vol. 1, 163–7.

**57** Madras, now Chennai, is located off the Bay of Bengal, on the east coast of India. It boasted the first purposefully-built English fort and first Anglican church in India. It was a hub of the country trade and, with EIC support, a major center of exports to Europe, especially cotton textiles. See Radhika Seshan, *Trade and Politics on the Coromandel Coast: Seventeenth and Early Eighteenth Centuries* (Delhi: Primus Books, 2012).

**58** This refers to the 1716 seizing of a loaded Chinese junk by a private British vessel, the Anne. In contrast to the Europe-Asia trade, which the EIC monopolized, the company did allow private traders in the inter-Asian country trade. These country traders sometimes caused disputes. In the case of the Anne, after being detained in Amoy for fifteen months, it was forced to leave by local officials without

Complaint was made at Court to the Emperour he said the Merchants must take care not to abuse Strangers, and that the Law of Retalliation[59] was but just if they did. Try at least how far thus speaking big, & seeming Resolute to Act so, may influence them, Consider whether if you should have occasion it may not be proper to show your Resolution by leaving Canton & ordering the Ships to fall down from Wampo where they usually lye to Typa Cabrada[60] and so to Maccao. Probably this will make them believe you are in earnest and bring them at least to some tollerable Complyance.

22. We positively forbid your and do you from time to time before Witness acquaint the Capt.[ns] and all on board the Ships That We forbid their running ashore any Goods, whatever on pretence of saving the Customs, because such running Goods if discover'd will cause great Embarrasments and delays to the hazard of the Ships Voyage.[61]

23. Take care that whatever Marriners or other English come ashore behave themselves Civilly and Soberly, suffer none [168r] of them to be Guilty of any riotous disorder, lest thereby the Companys Estate or Concerns be prejudiced, and the Chineeses good Opinion of the English be lessen'd or lost.[62]

24. What Woollen Goods Lead and other Our Produce shall be laden on board these Ships the respective Invoices will inform you Do your utmost endeavour to sell all the Woollen Goods for Mony that We may know the true worth of each sort. What you cant sell for Mony, Barter for Goods without any Silver with them.[63] Enter a Particular Account thereof in your Books, and in the Consultation enter the Memorandum of it, adding thereto what such Goods receiv'd in barter, could have been bought

collecting all its outstanding debts. To settle these matters, the Anne's crew commandeered a Chinese ship, valued at 80,000 taels, and sold its cargo in Madras. News of the incident, and the insult to the Europeans, reached the Emperor, who punished his Amoy officials. This act won EIC favor. Morse, Chronicles, vol. 1, 146–53.

59 The law of retaliation, or *lex talionis*, is a moral principle, which allows for punishment in the form of the crime. It is most commonly expressed as "an eye for an eye."

60 Typa-quebrada, now Taipa, is the northernmost of Macao's two main geographic islands. It sustained the main Portuguese settlement in the 1700s, as well as allowed nearby anchorage on the Pearl River delta.

61 All crewmembers were entitled to some private trade in Canton, its extent depending on their ranking on the ship. If they tried to evade paying taxes in China, however, the Hoppo usually charged companies accounts. In general, Ostend allowances for private trade until 1723 were greater than those of EIC ships. Parmentier, Tea Time, 66–73.

62 The alcoholic intoxication of sailors was not uncommon in Canton, with some supposedly dying due to bad Chinese punch. For more on seamen's lives in Canton, ibid., 98–9.

63 According to its charter, at least ten percent of EIC exports to Asia had to consist of commodities other than bullion. Yet, most British manufactures did not find ready markets in the East or only sold in limited quantities. EIC directors, therefore, constantly sought goods that would retail well in Asia and fulfill or even better exceed the ten percent rule. One such item they repeatedly tried was English woolens. See Andre Gunder Frank, *ReOrient: Global Economy in the Asian Age* (Berkeley: University of California Press, 1998), 74; Caroline Frank, *Objectifying China, Imagining America: Chinese Commodities in Early America* (Chicago: University of Chicago Press, 2011).

for with Silver, wherein Act sincerely, That We may be at a certainty of the real worth of our Woollen Goods in the Chineeses Opinion as well of the sorts as Colours.

25. We are told the Chineese Warehouses are clear'd of the Old Remains of the English Manufacture, do you make a strict Enquiry whether this Account be true. If not what sorts, quantitys, and of what Colour do yet remain, and for what reason, however if there be none surely what now sent will go off the better, and that We may find Encouragement to encrease the quantity hereafter. This will be a National benefit as it will encrease the Consumption of Our own Manufacture (which We earnestly recommend to you to endeavour) and as it will lessen the sending out Bullion: which costs more than the same Number of Ounces paid here for Goods. Enquire also what other English or European Commoditys, and in what quantitys will Vend in China, and at what rates that We may send them rather than Bullion if only to be done without loss. Enter in your Consultations the Result of these Enquirys, & be very particular therein.[64]

26. It is agreed on all hands that Lead[65] hath been and yet is a Staple Commodity and will sell for good profit & ready Mony if you Mannage prudently and don't suffer the crafty Chineeses to impose upon you, for which reason We hint this Caution.

27. We have sent a Ton of Jamaica Pepper or Pimente[66] for a Tryal. We are told it will sell well, take care to make the most of it, and let Us know how it goes off, & whether We may increase the quantity & how far another Season.

28. The Invoices will show you what Scales Weights and Stationary Ware are put on board the respective Ships for your Use.

[168v] 29. We last Year gave M.r Naish and the rest of the Council directions how to Act in case they meet with any Competitors in Trade at Canton Ostenders or others, If they should have taken any Methods to disappoint them which have Answer'd, do You the same or such as may most effectually discourage their return thô We again suffer as We have done this two Years, for We must continue Our utmost endeavours to beat them out of that Trade, which We look upon to be a certain Interloping upon Us, carry'd on at first & still continued by Our own Country Men under the Cover of Foreign Commissions. But in regard Secrecy is absolutely necessary in all Transac-

64 Here, the directors state the classical mercantilist view of exporting manufacture and importing as little of it in exchange for specie as possible, thus hoarding as much bullion domestically as possible. For an introduction to this theory, see Jürgen G. Nagel, *Abenteuer Fernhandel. Die Ostindienkompagnien* (Darmstadt: WBG, 2007), 37–9.

65 *Hong* merchants required lead to line the wooden chests used by Europeans to transport tea. This kept out dampness, preserved the tea's aroma and taste, and allowed for the stacking of chests without crushing its leaves. The EIC also used lead, supplied in London, as ballast on their outward voyage and in the country trade. Van Dyke, Merchants, 37–8; Liu, Dutch, 47.

66 Europeans discovered allspice, or Pimento, during Christoforo Colombo's voyages to the Caribbean. Spanish explorers likened the plant's dried berries to black pepper kernels, thus also giving it the name Jamaica Pepper.

tions of this kind, and that the least taking of Air is enough to blow them up, therefore We leave the particular Mannagement hereof to M.r Fazakerley & M.r Atkyns who must know more of these Interlopers proceedings than any other of You, and thereby better Enabled to offer his Opinion to M.r Fazakerley of what he thinks the best method to bring about Our Intention.

30. In case of M.r Fazakerley's death We would have M.r Morton as then Chief to succeed him & act in said mannagem.t If M.r Atkyns dye then We direct M.r Fazakerley or the Chief for the time being to take to his Assistance any one of You he judges fittest.

31. If any Interlopers come to Canton and you cant bring about Our Intention in the preceeding Paragraphs you must then proceed as the Circumstances & Necessitys of Affairs at the time will permit, so as may most conduce to Our Interest in General, as well for Embarrassing & disappointing them, which will be Our Interest in the long run, As for Providing the Company such Cargos as may turn to their most Advantage by buying them good & as cheap of their kind as possible.

32. In the Packet[67] you will find two Printed Acts of Parliament forbidding his Majestys Subjects to Trade or go to the East Indies under Foreign Commissions or Colours or otherwise contrary to Law, One of them giving Us power to seize any such Subjects.[68] We hereby direct & Empower you to Seize and bring to England any of them which you shall find at China or elsewhere within the Limits of the Comp.as Charter to Answer for their Offence, if you can come at them.

33. We apprehend that by the late great demands at Canton for Tea to fill up the Tonnage that has been sent from Europe thither this last two or three Years[69], the Merchants will have great quantitys at their Hongs or within their reach up in the [169r] Country.[70] In this case with good mannagement you will have an Opportunity to pick out the best, and buy the cheaper for frequent Experience hath shown they will sell it at almost any rate rather than let it lye dead on their hands, and the same reason still continues, & with dexterity may be Implor'd to good Advantage.

---

**67** For the contents of the supercargoes' 1722 packets, see pages 50–1.

**68** "An Act for the better Securing of the lawful Trade of his Majesty's Subjects to and from the East Indies; and for the more effectual preventing all his Majesty's Subjects trading thither under foreign Commissions," *Statutes of the Realm*, 5 George I, c. 21, 1719; "An Act for the further preventing his Majesty's Subjects from trading to the East Indies under foreign Commissions," *Statutes of the Realm*, 7 George I, c. 21, 1721. This legislation was passed with the Ostend interlopers specifically in mind. Hertz, England.

**69** In the fall of 1720, for example, there were five EIC, two Ostend, one French and four country ships in Canton, loading cargos mostly composed of porcelain and tea. Morse, Chronicles, vol. 1, 161.

**70** Tea was not grown in or around Canton. Bohea, in particular, had to be carried by Chinese laborers for six days from east-central China over the Bohea Mountains to Poyang Lake. There, the leaves were loaded onto shallow river craft and sent (sometimes pulled) up the Jiang River. Laborers again carried the tea over the Danxia Mountains, via a pass between Guǎngdōng and Guangxi, before finally reaching the Beijiang River. The leaves then could be shipped on larger vessels to Canton. Van Dyke, Merchants, 14–6.

34. Herewith you will receive Our Orders for Investments which you must comply with as if herein Incerted Verbatim, As well with relation to the sorts and quantitys of Goods to be Provided, as the directions & cautions therein given.[71]

35. The Ships now sending being large & probably may take in more Goods than let for, therefore We say do you lade no more than the Charterparty Tonnage on any one of the four, lest you should want for the rest, but when that is Compleated If any part of your Investment remains, load it as the Tonnage then on your hands can take in proportionably to each Ship.

36. To encourage your Zeal for Our Service, Your hearty Applicat.$^{n}$ in the pursuing Our Interest Vigourously & faithfully, and your Obeying these, and any other Orders, We shall judge proper to give you, We have Resolved and do agree to allow to such of you as shall arrive in China, shall dispose of the said four Ships Outward bound Cargo's, shall make and consign the Investm.$^{ts}$ according to Our directions & duly comply with all Our Orders and Instructions the Summs following Viz.$^{t}$ To M.$^{r}$ Fazakerley Two thousand five hundred Pounds, To Mess.$^{rs}$ Morton Godfrey & Atkyns each Fifteen hundred Pounds To M.$^{r}$ Carter Twelve hundred Pounds To M.$^{r}$ Dade One Thousand Pounds To M.$^{r}$ Bacon Seven hundred Pounds, and to M.$^{r}$ Skinner Five hundred Pounds to be paid out of the Produce of the Sales of the four Ships Cargo's before mention'd here in England. But if any of you shall not fully observe & duly comply with all Our said Orders & Instructions then We hereby declare it to be part of Our Agreement with you, that it shall be in the power of the Court of Directors of this Company for the time being to make such Deductions, and Defalcations out of the said Allowances, as the said Court when assembled shall judge reasonable, We further add as part also of Our Agreement with you, That if it shall happen (which God forbid) That any one of the said four Ships should miscarry in the Voyage Out or home then one fourth part of the above mention'd allowances to be severally made you shall be abated. If any two of the said four Ships should so miscarry, [169v] then you are severally to be abated one half of the said Allowances If three of the said Four Ships should miscarry, You are severally to be abated three fourth parts of the said Allowances, and if all four Ships should miscarry, in their said Voyages out or home then you are not to have expect or demand any part of the said Allowances before mention'd.

37. We have also agreed and resolved as a further Encouragem.$^{t}$ to allow you to carry out in Forreign Silver[72] Viz.$^{t}$ M.$^{r}$ Fazakerley Fifteen hundred Pounds Value Mess.$^{rs}$ Morton Godfrey and Atkyns each Nine hundred Pounds Value, Mess.$^{rs}$ Carter & Dade each Six hundred Pounds Value & Mess.$^{rs}$ Bacon and Skynner each Five hundred Pounds Value on the Conditions following and not otherwise Viz.$^{t}$ That the said

---

**71** For the orders for investments, see pages 47–9.

**72** The export of bullion from Great Britain was prohibited by law, although the EIC often found exemptions. See K.N. Chaudhuri, *The English East India Company: the Study of an Early Joint-Stock Company* (London: Routledge, 1965), 124–35.

respective Sums be Invested in China in Gold[73], and if any Opportunity presents of sending the said Gold to Fort S.$^{t}$ George[74], That it be sent thither consign'd to the said Companys President & Council there for your respective Accounts to be Invested by such Person or Persons as you shall severally desire and return'd you on Our Shipping in Diamonds[75], Or that the Produce thereof be paid into the Companys Cash there, and the Amount so paid in remitted to England by Bills of Exchange for your said Accounts as you shall severally choose:[76] But if you have no Opportunity to send said Gold to Fort S.$^{t}$ George We allow you to bring it to England or if all or any of you shall choose to joyn the said fforeign Silver with the Companys Cargos to be return'd to England on the usual terms, We permit you so to do.

38. We have further agreed to allow you to carry out as a separate Adventure to be laid out in China, and the produce return'd to England on Our Shipping for your own Accounts on the Companys usual terms & Conditions Viz.$^{t}$ M.$^{r}$ Fazakerley to the Value of Two hundred Pounds, Mess.$^{rs}$ Morton Godfrey & Atkyns each One hundred and fifty Pounds Value, Mess.$^{rs}$ Carter and Dade each One hundred & thirty Pounds Value, & Mess.$^{rs}$ Bacon and Skinner each One hundred Pounds Value.[77]

39. Tea being the Principal and Bulky Article to be provided by Our aforesaid Orders for Investments We direct you to take special care in the purchase of the several

---

**73** Although the Chinese used a silver-based currency, the export of gold from China also was forbidden by imperial decree. This noted, the metal retained a value fifteen times greater than silver in Europe. It thus was highly profitable for European companies to export gold from Canton, which was smuggled via *hong* merchants also at high returns. Gill, Merchants, 36.

**74** Fort St. George was an EIC fort and administrative center, located in Madras, India.

**75** British traders and Jewish craftsmen living in England began to significantly invest in the diamond trade in the late 1600s, making London the chief market for uncut stones by 1700. The EIC tried to acquire a monopoly of this trade several times, especially those supplies coming from mines in Burma and India. By the late 1600s, however, it gave up on these claims and allowed the private trade in diamonds, for a fee. See Tijl Vanneste, *Global Trade and Commercial Networks: Eighteenth-Century Diamond Merchants* (London: Pickering & Chatto, 2011); Søren Mentz, *The English Gentleman Merchant at Work: Madras and the City of London, 1660–1740* (Copenhagen: University of Copenhagen Press, 2005), 110–25.

**76** A bill of exchange was a medium to transfer money across distance, without sending hard specie. Rather, a merchant wanting to send money from Madras to England could give it to the EIC. The company then would use this money to buy commodities and ship them to England, where the EIC would sell them. From the proceeds of this sale, the EIC would pay out the Madras sum to the merchant's intended recipient in London as stated in the written bill of exchange, sometimes at a preferred exchange rate. This protected finances and was a means for companies to finance their Asian trade without themselves having to ship bullion. The differing exchange rates between silver and gold in Asia and Europe finally made it a profitable venture for supercargoes. See Femme S. Gaastra, "Private Money for Company Trade. The Role of the Bills of Exchange in Financing the Return Cargoes of the VOC", in: *Itinerario* 18 (1994), 65–76.

**77** In contrast to the other European companies, the EIC did not fix the amount of private trade allowed ships' crews and supercargoes in terms of space but of value. Parmentier, Tea Time, 67–8.

sorts and quantitys therein enumerated, That it be sound, very good of the kind, and all carefully Pack'd in Tootenague[78], whether in Chests or Tubs. That the Wood be first Season'd and the Camphire[79] smell of it taken away as also the smell of the Soldering Oyl in the Tootenague, because either of them will prejudice the Tea, That none of the Tea be false Packt as [170r] sometimes hath been, and discover'd on Opening that the top hath been good, and the sides middle or bottom bad. That as far as you can do it you get the Chests of an equal Size as to Tare, and to hold an equal Weight of Tea, That the English Weight & not the China Weight of the Tares of the several Containers of Tea whether Chests or Tubs &c.[a] be cut thereon or burnt in by a Marking Iron to be Visible to the Buyers, This We have promised the Commissioners of the Customs shall be done to prevent disputes with the Buyers, because the Customhouse Officers have not allow'd sufficient Tares, and the Tea hath been forced to be Stript, & thereby damaged to Ascertain the real Tares, That the several Tares of the Tea be also enter'd in the Invoices wherein be exact because if We chance to allow a higher Tare, then the Buyers imagine it will be so much dead loss to Us, If they think it too little they will not bid with chearfulness, and will besides oblige Us if found so on stripping to make good the want, whereas they always expect a little Supertare, and give the more for the Lott as they think it is so.

40. Take great care no Camphire be laden with the Tea in any Ship, lest its Scent spoil it, and give Orders That no more Arrack[80] be put on board than only what necessary for Stores and stow'd so that its Scent maynt prejudice the Tea.

41. To prevent false Package We order you to open & View all the Bohea[81], Pecko[82], and Congou[83] Tea, because it generally comes down in Cannisters and Basketts, and

---

**78** A European ship rated 800 to 900 tons required 400 to 600 pounds of ballast to prevent its capsizing. Tutenag, or tutenague, was an alloy of copper, zinc and nickel, produced in China and used by many westward-bound Europeans for this purpose. In England and the Netherlands, retailers sold the metal as spelter, zinc and later paktong, and craftsmen used it as a surrogate for silver in manufacturing domestic objects.

**79** Camphor is a type of tree, similar to cinnamon and native to Borneo, Sumatra, China and Japan. Its wood and roots produce a fragrant gum when fired, which was sought as medicine but necessitated its stowage away from odor-absorbing teas. Camphor wood also was used to pack textiles, as its smell repelled insects.

**80** Arrack was an Asian liquor, typically distilled from sugarcane in the early 1700s. It formed the basis of certain punches popular among Europeans in the East and in England.

**81** Bohea, a black tea from the Bohea Mountains, was the most frequently exported Chinese tea, often accounting for sixty to eighty percent of tea cargos in Canton. Its best varieties sold at moderate prices, while its coarser and damaged versions sold quite cheaply.

**82** Congou, or Congo, was a black tea that was more costly than Bohea but especially popular in the British Isles. It was made from smaller, more delicate leaves harvested in May.

**83** Peco, or Pekoe, was among the most costly varieties of black tea. Its leaves were gathered in April, and the finished beverage often was flavored with added materials.

is less liable to damage by Opening than the Green Tea[84], Repack it all in Chests, Take care each chest be fill'd with Tea of the same sort & Goodness and well mixt before put in to prevent the Buyers Complaint if they find a Chest of two sorts of Goodness, for they affirm If in mingling Tea, Good & Ordinary be put together, the Ordinary spoild the Good, But if the Good was mixt with other of or near the same goodness, and the worse kept by it self, the Good would have sold the worser sort if put up in the same Lott, and they could have afforded to give the more for the whole than if it had been unskilfully blended and of this We had a plain proof in the Tea by the Carnarvon[85] and Hartfords former Voyage.[86]

42. Thô the Green Tea generally comes down in Tubs & hath been seldom found to be false pack'd & the Opening & Repacking it will make it more dusty and hazard the loss of its flavour yet you must open every now and then some of the Tubs promiscuously to discover and prevent any design'd Cheat, [170v] Repack what so open'd in Chests. If you could get its first Package in Chests, they would stow better than in Tubs.

43. We are the more particular in these directions because We expect the loss by such Impositions in the Tea or other Goods as hereafter mention'd shall be made good by you.

44. Mark and Number all the Chests and Tubs of Tea of each sort from one onward successively with the Letter **B** for Bohea, **S** for Singlo[87], and so for the other sorts of Tea to distinguish them before Opening.

45. The Chineeses are as dextrous in putting Cheats on those they deal with in other Goods as well as Tea, When We have order'd Tootenague to be provided they have put into the Slabs, refuse Iron, and other Rubbish & sometimes Lead as being cheaper than the Tootenague, thô the thicker Slabs seem more liable to be Adulterated, yet the thiner have been found equally bad, the only way to prevent the Cheat is to break the Slabs at least a good part of them. If they are pure they will sell the better for being so proved, When We have Order'd the providing Silks their Cheats have appear'd Viz.[t] The first four or five yards of the Peice very good the rest Stark naught.

84 All teas derived from the same plant, *Camellia sinensis*, with their differences stemming from where the plant grew, when its leaves were harvested, and how it was processed. Black teas were dried, fermented and roasted. Green teas, in contrast, were dried but not fermented, thus making them susceptible to quicker decay. Popular green tea varieties were Hyson, young Hyson, Tonkai, Singlo, Bing, Imperial, gunpowder and Ankai.

85 The Carnarvon, rated 370 tons, sailed to Canton in 1718 and 1720. On her 1720 voyage, William Fazakerley was her chief supercargo. Morse, Chronicles, vol. 1, 99–101, 107.

86 The Carnarvon and Hertford both sailed to Canton in 1718. This discovery of mixed teas must have occurred in England, as the ship's supercargoes, arriving early in the season, expressed pleasure at their choice of product. Ibid., 158–60.

87 Singlo was a variety of green tea especially liked in Great Britain and the German states. It typically offered a better-quality leaf, but lower demands resulted in lower pricing in Europe.

If the whole Piece hath been true made they have made them damp to weigh the more[88] When Raw Silk hath been Order'd it hath been wetted for the same reason and often false pack'd in the middle of the respective bundles, sometimes the Chests & Tubs of Goods have been chang'd in the Factory after made up, at other times between the Factory and being water born, but the most succesfull practice of their Cheats hath been in changing the Goods in their Passage down to the Ship.[89] To prevent the Evil of changing the Goods any where, We hereby direct, that you Employ Trusty Persons of the Ships Companys, which by Charterparty & the Capt.ns Instructions they are to supply you withall as well to watch them in the Factory as to see them water born, and to guard them to the Ship acquaint the Capt.ns from time to time what you want that they be furnisht with good fire arms & other offensive Weapons to defend themselves and the Goods if any should offer to change rob or plunder them and as a further Security advise the exact weight & mark of every Chest, and other Package to the Officer who is to receive them on board with Orders to him to see they answer that Account, and if not the Cheat will be discover'd and satisfaction like to be got. If any Tootenague be sent down advise the quantity of Slabs & weight for they have cut off pieces from the Slabs to lessen the weight thô not the Number. [171r] Enter in your Diarys the names of the Persons so daily employ'd and the sorts, quantitys, marks & weights of what they take the charge of, Caution them to avoid Drinking to excess or whatever may hinder their watch, & in an especial manner to take care to have a good bulk-head or safe partition in the boat or Vessel between the Goods and the Places where the Chineeses and their familys lye in or have frequent resort to and set a watch at every such Place, for generally it is from thence the Mischief of Thievery or change comes. We mention these things as so many Cautions to prevent your being Cheated.

46. Buy up for the use of Our Island S.t Helena[90] to be laden on all the Ships to touch there to the Amount in the whole of four to five or six Chests containing each One hund.rd Cattee Pots of Tea, part Singlo, part Bohea of the middling sorts, also a Chest or two of China Ware part Coffee & Tea cups with some Bowles in Sizes for Punch larger and smaller, send the Remainder of the Charterparty One p.Cent as far as

---

**88** Ostend traders, too, experienced this same fraud. Parmentier, Tea Time, 107.

**89** All import and export cargos had to be transported between Canton and Whampoa on so-called "chop boats," which were owned by Chinese merchants and manned by their countrymen. Transportation on European boats was prohibited, because it was believed to make customs evasion easy. Van Dyke, Canton Trade, 22–3.

**90** St. Helena is an island in the southern Atlantic Ocean, which the EIC controlled from 1659 to 1834. Given its location on the Southeast Trade Winds and Atlantic currents, which pushed returning European ships north, it became a refueling station for EIC and VOC vessels. See Stephen Royle, *The Company's Island: St. Helena, Company Colonies and the Colonial Endeavour* (New York: Palgrave, 2007); Philip Stern, "Politics and Ideology in the Early East India Company-State: the Case of St. Helena, 1673–1709", in: *The Journal of Imperial and Commonwealth History* 35.1 (2007), 1–23.

two or three Tons in the whole in Sugar including in the quantity a little China root[91], order the Captain to stow these Goods to be easily come at when the Ship reaches the Island, and take care he signs Bills of Lading for them. Give Our Governour & Council there an Invoice of the whole to be a charge upon them for the quantum & Value to Credit Our Account London, for the same, and bring Us another for Our Notice.

47. You must take care to provide on Consulting the Capt.$^{ns}$ a sufficient quantity of China Ware & Quick Silver[92] for Stiffening the Ships including their respective Iron Kintlage[93] to prevent the danger of their being Crank sided homeward bound, Do what you can to put the several sorts of China Ware each by it Self, and to pack it as well as possible to preserve it from breakage, & so close as to loose no room.

48. Consult the respective Captains as to the sorts and quantitys of Goods to be first and from time to time sent on board, giving them due Notice that their Ships be stow'd to most advantage for Tonnage and Sailing. That the Tea be Stow'd as much as possible in the after part of the Ship between Decks, and abast the Well in the Hold to the bulk head in the Breadroom, That a Bulk head be made at the after part of the Well, and batten'd to prevent the Steam moistning and damaging the Tea, That the Breadroom be fill'd with Tea, and the residue of it be Stow'd where it may be best preserv'd from dampness.

[171v] 49. You being Our Representatives We hereby direct That you well consider the Charterparty Covenants & Capt.$^{ns}$ Instructions and take care they be duly comply'd with by the Captains and Ships Companys for so far as concerns them, and by you for what concerns Us or your Selves, and among others that no more Tonnage be taken up than allow'd by Charterparty as in Fol. 8. That all Goods receiv'd into, or deliver'd out of the Ship be enter'd into Books as in Fol. 6. and do you see the Entrys duly made, and the Pages Number'd, and put the Letters of your Names to each Page, ent'ring the Number of Pages, when Compleated as a Mem.$^{o}$ in your Consultation book, and give Us the Account, give the Captains notice in Writing, That We direct they Register severally with you assoon as possible the Accounts of their own & Ships Companys Private Trade on the Penalty contain'd on Fol. 6. Enclosed We send you the Companys Tenth By Law[94] & Order of Encouragement for Preventing Clandestine Trade for your

91 China root was a Chinese herb, probably the fungus *fuling*, valued as a medicine since its introduction to Europe in the 1500s. It was believed to cure colds, headaches and gout as well as to improve burns.

92 Quicksilver, or mercury, was produced in China and demanded as a cure-all in European medicine. It also aided Europe-bound ships as a form of ballast, as noted here.

93 Kentledge refers to scraps or pigs of iron, used on European ships as a permanent form of ballast. Unlike tutenag, porcelain and quicksilver, it was viewed as a necessary naval store and not retailed separately.

94 This might refer to the EIC policy that "no orders shall be sent by the directors to, or obeyed by, any persons employed in the service of this Company, in India, or any other parts beyond the Cape of Good Hope, or at St. Helena, but such as shall be signed by thirteen or more of the directors." See

Notice, We also order each of you to deliver into the Chief a Register of his own Private Trade, & that the same Register together with what the Chief has in Private Trade be enter'd in the Consultation book for Our Notice.

50. Send Us a particular Account of what you can learn of all Ships which shall be at Maccao or Canton or any other Port in China during your Stay, and of the Ships Annually Trading thither as to their Burdens, Guns, Number of Men To what Nation belonging, After what manner built, and Enter these Informations in your Diary.

**Thirdly as to your return home.**

51. We would have Our ships dispatcht to us two of them at a time for their greater security against Pyrates who probably may lye off the Cape of Good Hope to intercept our homeward bound Shipping, for which reason do you give the Capt.$^{ns}$ Orders that they take special care to keep out of Sight of the Cape, or of any Ships that may be cruizing thereabouts and make the best of their way directly to S$^{t}$ Helena for Refreshments and thence to England.

52. You must consign each Ships cargo to be sent Us by Invoice and Bill of Lading to the United Company of Merchants of England Trading to the East Indies taking care the Invoices be settled with the Bills of Lading assoon as possible after the Goods are on board and severally sign'd at furthest in ten days [172r] send Duplicates of each Ships Invoice, Bill of Lading, Copy of all Register'd Goods & Account of all material Occurrences to that time by the other Ship then dispatcht, Prepare in the Voyage homeward Copy of the same to be sent Us from the first Port you touch at, but keep all Original books & other Papers to be deliver'd Us on your Arrival at London.

53. Observe the same directions on the dispatch of the two later ships.

54. We would have you take passage on the two last ships returning to England.

55. These are Our present Orders and determinations touching the mannagement of Our Affairs committed to your care as aforesaid, But if before your getting to Sea, We should see cause to make any Alterations therein, We have desired Josias

Peter Auber, *An Analysis of the Constitution of 'The East India Company'* (London: Kingsbury, Parbury, & Allen, 1826), 225.

Wordsworth[95], Joseph Herne[96] & Henry Lyell[97] Esq.$^{rs}$ and S.$^{r}$ Mathew Decker Bar.$^{t}$[98] to Communicate to You those Alterations. Therefore if they or any three of them shall send you any Orders or Instructions differing from these, you must observe them in the same manner as if Sign'd by the whole court any thing herein beforemention'd to the contrary notwithstanding.[99]

56. Since writing the above We have thought fitt to entertain M$^{r}$ Roger Wheatley[100] to be Writer to you Our Council and have agreed to give him a Gratuity or reward for his Service of One hundred Pound on the same conditions with the Gratuitys or Rewards granted to you besides Twenty Pounds for Fresh Provisions outward and Fifteen homeward he is to do whatever you shall appoint him to in Our service, and to comply with all the rules in these Our Instructions which you must acquaint him withall for so far as relates to him in his Station as Writer and in case of any of your decease before the compleating the Investments. We intend he shall come into the benefit of such part of the deceas'ds gratuity or reward in the same manner as before mention'd with relation to the rest of you as the Court of Directors for the time being shall think fitt and as if his Name had been before herein inserted. We have also agreed to allow him to carry out the Value of One hundred Pounds in foreign Bullion for Purchase of Gold and Fifty Pounds as a Private Adventure on the terms before granted to you.

**95** Josias Wordsworth (1660–1736) was chairman of the Court of EIC Directors in 1717, 1722–1723, 1728 and 1733–1735. See Charles C. Prinsep, *Record of Services of the Honourable East India Company's Civil Servants...as well as lists of the directors of the East India Company; Chairmen and Deputy Chairmen of the Direction* (London: Trübner & Company, 1885), xviii–xx.

**96** Joseph Herne (c. 1683–1723) was deputy chairman of the Court of EIC Directors in 1722. He came from two well-connected English merchant families and, as M.P. for Dartmouth from 1715 to 1722, argued in favor of EIC policies in Parliament. See Romney Sedgwick (ed.), *The House of Commons, 1715–1754: the History of Parliament* (New York: Oxford UP, 1970), 131.

**97** Henry Lyell (1665–1731) was a Swedish-born merchant and an EIC director in 1723. He additionally served as chairman of the Court of EIC Directors in 1718, 1721 and 1726. *The Gentleman's Magazine: or, Monthly Intelligencer* (London: F. Jefferies, 1731), 82; Prinsep, Records, xix.

**98** Matthew Decker (1679–1749) was an Amsterdam-born merchant who established himself in London in 1702. He served as chairman of the Court of EIC Directors in 1725 and 1730–1732 as well as published several tracts on taxation and long-distance commerce. King George I gave him the title of baronet in 1716. See David Patrick and Francis Hindes Groome (eds.), *Chambers Biographical Dictionary* (London: W&R Chambers, 1902), 286.

**99** Although not formally established until 1784, the EIC used small, secret committees to convey orders and recommendations relating to trade and colony policies in private. They especially concerned themselves with matters relating to shipping. See C.H. Philips, "The Secret Committee of the East India Company", in: *Bulletin of the School of Oriental and African Studies* 10.2 (1940), 299–315.

**100** Roger Wheatley (dates unknown) was a European trader, likely born in Macao, who worked at various times for the EIC and the private country trade. In 1726, he was arrested at Batavia for attempting to retail blue chintz illegally to Dutch settlers, and he was deported to Madras. Furber, Rival, 277–9.

57. We find in the Supra Cargo's Accounts of One of Our China Ships. One hundred forty three Tales[101] (a pretty large Sum) [172v] charged as Customs paid for the Sailors and other Persons small Parcells of Goods whose Owners they could not discover, and the reason given for their paying the Mony was they thought it conformable to the Comp.[as] Instructions (and you have the same now) but We cant see the Strength of the Inference they would draw from it, That because We bid them (as We now do you) to tell the Captains and all on board, That We forbid their running any Goods on pretence of saving the Customs, lest it cause Embarrasments or delays in Our Affairs. That therefore We may pay the Customs on the Mariners Goods. The SupraCargos tell Us it was impossible to prevent it, because the Linguist never bring in the Account till the Ship is just ready to Sail, and without it be paid, they cant have their Chopp[102] or Clearance from the Hoppo, and to send down to the Ship to know the particulars and whose Goods would take up more time, and prove more prejudicial than the Mony was worth. This doth not Satisfy Us, nor can We allow such Articles, and therefore to prevent the like charge in future, We order you to give the Linguist directions assoon as you can to place nothing to Our Account for Customs, but only on Our own Goods, for if he do you will not pay it, but if any of the mariners shall desire the Customs on their Goods to be paid at the Factory. Do you take an Account who they are, howmuch, & on what Goods that they may repay it You. Or if any of them should not have Mony left after buying their Goods, and pretend they did not know of any Dutys to be paid, then take their Note for the Amount to be paid out of their Wages, & direct the Captain to enter it into the Pursers books[103], as is done w.[n] they take up Goods in the Ship & make it Us good here, this liberty We would have to extend to only small Parcells as abovemention'd & to those Men you keep with You at the Factory, or Employ in looking after what is brought from or carry'd to the Ship, but not for any round Sums, nor to any of y.[e] Superior Officers belonging thereto or any others. We are

Your very Loving Friends
London 30th Nov.[r] 1722.

---

**101** The tael was a form of Chinese specie. It was worth 10 maces, 100 candareen and 1.000 catty. One tael equated to about six English shillings, eight pence. The denomination also was used to measure weight.

**102** This refers to the Grand Chop or *yang chuanpai* – a written document from the Hoppo certifying that customs had been paid and that a ship was allowed to leave Whampoa. Ships trying to sail without it were liable to cannon fire from Chinese forts along the Pearl River. As ships had to wait for tides at several bars on their descent towards the open sea, this made unapproved departures precarious. Van Dyke, Canton Trade, 32.

**103** The purser was the ship officer responsible for its money supplies. See, for extant examples, "Duke of Cambridge: Pay Book," 1722–1725, in: BL – IOR/L/MAR/B/700D(2); "Herford: Pay Book," 1722–1724, in: BL – IOR/L/MAR/B/656-I(2).

| | |
|---|---|
| Josias Wordsworth | Chairman |
| Joseph Herne | Deputy |
| John Bance[104] | Mat. Decker, |
| Henry Kelsey[105], | John Gould[106], |
| John Eccleston[107], | Rob.t Hudson[108], |
| Edward Owen[109], | Jo.s Wordsworth Jun.r[110], |
| Abra.m Addams[111], | Will.m Gosselin[112], |

---

**104** John Bance (d. 1755) was an EIC director from 1722 to 1730, a director of the Bank of England and M.P. for Westbury, England in 1732. He apprenticed as a merchant in Amsterdam and continued to trade with Hamburg throughout his political career. Sedgwick, House of Commons, 106, 195.

**105** Henry Kelsey (d. 1728) was an EIC director in 1723. See *The Present State of Europe: or, the Historical and Political Monthly Mercury* (May 1723), 99.

**106** John Gould (ca. 1695–1740) was chairman of the Court of EIC Directors in 1727 and deputy chairman in 1726 and 1733. He succeeded his uncle, Nathaniel Gould, as M.P. of New Shoreham, England in 1729. Sedgwick, House of Commons, 74.

**107** John Eccleston (b. 1678) was a London silk merchant, practicing Quaker and EIC director from 1721 to 1735. A twelve-fold screen that he purchased from China in ca. 1725 now survives in the Peabody Essex Museum. See Norman Penney, "The Quaker Family of Eccleston", in: *The East Anglian: or, Notes and queries on subjects connected with the counties of Suffolk, Cambridge, Essex and Norfolk* 13 (1910), 25–6.

**108** Robert Hudson (d. 1735) was an EIC director during the 1720s and 1730s. *The London Magazine: or, Gentleman's Monthly Intelligencer* (January 1735), 47.

**109** Edward Owen (d. 1729) was an EIC director in 1723, who possibly worked as a merchant in India during the 1690s. He had a son, nephew and niece living in Bombay in 1720. See Vahé Baladouni and Margaret Makepeace, *Armenian Merchants of the Seventeenth and Early Eighteenth Centuries: English East India Company Sources* (Philadelphia: American Philosophical Society, 1998), 8–11; George K. McGilvary, *Guardian of the East India Company: the Life of Laurence Sulivan* (New York: Tauris Academic Studies, 2006), 2.

**110** Josias Wordsworth, Jr. (1691–1749) was an EIC director from 1721 to 1736 and chairman of the Court of EIC Directors in 1736. He inherited from his uncle, Josias, Sr., another EIC director, his fortune as well as a very successful commercial firm specializing in Baltic trade. The Wordsworths were the primary suppliers of Swedish iron to the British Navy Board, who insisted on this product for their anchors. See Chris Evans, Owen Jackson and Göran Ryden, "Baltic Iron and the British Iron Industry in the Eighteenth Century", in: *Economic History Review* 55.4 (2002), 646.

**111** Abraham Addams (d. 1740) was deputy chairman of the Court of EIC Directors in 1724 and 1734. Prinsep, Records, ix, xix.

**112** William Gosselin (d. 1748) was an EIC director during the 1720s. He was from a prominent London family and, while his religious sentiments are unclear, formed intimate and business attachments with several prominent Huguenot families in England. James Parker, *The Directors of the East India Company* (PhD diss., University of Edinburgh, 1977), 159.

Henry Lyell, Sim.[o] Theunemans[113],
John Heathcote[114], Jn.[o] Drummond[115],

[173r] We whose Names are hereunder written have examin'd the Instructions deliver'd to Us with this Paper Writing importing it to be a Draught of those Instructions containing Fifty' seven Paragraphs, Dated the 30.[th] of November 1722. & Signed by sixteen of the Court of Directors whose Names are Copy'd on the other Side, And We find the said Instructions, and the said Draught thereof to agree, Witness our hands this fourth day of December 1722.

Will.[m] Fazakerley
Rich.[d] Morton
Edm.[d] Godfrey
Tho.[s] Atkyns
Tho.[s] Carter
Tho.[s] Dade
Devereux Bacon
Sam.[l] Skinner Jun.[r]
Roger Wheatley

**113** Simon Theunemans (dates unknown) was an EIC director from 1720 to 1732 and likely of Dutch descent. In 1694, he obtained letters patent for his method of printing decorative motifs on oilcloth. Prinsep, Records, xvii.

**114** John Heathcote (ca. 1689–1759) was an EIC director from 1716 to 1724 and 1728 to 1731, a director of the Bank of England and M.P. for Grantham, England in 1715. Sedgwick, House of Commons, 121–124.

**115** John Drummond (1676–1742), a Scotsman, established himself as a merchant and banker in the Amsterdam tin trade by the early 1700s. He eventually relocated to London and there served as an EIC director, member of the Royal African Company and M.P. for Perth, Scotland. Ibid., 402.

## Supplementall Orders to the Chief and Council appointed to Mannage the Affairs in China of the United Company of Merchants of England Trading to the East Indies, and to each of the said Council.

Gentlemen

We the Court of Directors of the said United Company have reason to believe some of the Country Ships[116] and People belonging to Our Settlements at Fort S.$^{t}$ George, Bombay[117], or other Places in the East Indies under Our Protection may be at Canton at the same time with you, and that it is probable some of the Ostenders or other Ships under Forreign Commissions or pretence of Foreign Authority may be also there with some of his Majestys Subjects on board who first set on foot this new upstart Trade so prejudicial to the General Trade of this Nation as well as of the Company and peradventure some of the Captains or SupraCargo's of said Country Ships may be induced to joyn with or Assist them on Account of former Acquintance, or for the sake of some private Advantage to themselves. And it being so Notorious & demonstrable. That what ever contributes to the encouragement [173v] or Support of such Foreigners Trade is detrimentall to the Commerce of these Kingdoms, Therefore that We may do what in us lyes to stop the further Progress thereof, We hereby direct and Order you, & every one of you To give publick Notice to the Supra Cargos, Captains, and all others belonging to such Country Ships Viz.$^{t}$

That We desire and positively Order and require them and every one of them, That they shall neither directly or indirectly by themselves or any others Assist, Countenance or have any manner of dealing with any of the People belonging to such

116 The country trade encompassed commerce between Asian ports. African, Asian and European merchants all joined in this exchange, although it favored smaller regional vessels (i.e. dhows, ketches, brigs and schooners) until the late 1700s. Chinese merchants' participation specifically was known as the junk trade, so named after their wooden sailing vessels. British natives were highly successful in the country trade since the 1720s, although regulated by covenant agreements. Nevertheless, the EIC directors here express fear of cooperation between the English and Ostenders, which would aid foreign competition and thus damage their trade. See Furber, Rival, 264–97; Sucheta Mazumdar, *Sugar and Society in China: Peasants, Technology, and the World Market* (Cambridge, MA: Harvard UP, 1998); Eric Tagliacozzo and Wen-Chin Chang (eds.), *Chinese Circulations: Capital, Commodities, and Networks in Southeast Asia* (Durham, NC: Duke UP, 2011); K.N. Chaudhuri, *Trade and Civilization in the Indian Ocean: an Economic History from the Rise of Islam to 1750* (New York: Cambridge UP, 1985), 94. One British country trader, who worked in Canton in the early 1720s, was John Scattergood. Several records relating to his professional activities are extant in: BL – Mss Eur C387.

117 In 1687, the EIC transferred its regional headquarters from Surat to Bombay, a settlement on the west coast of India. It remained a key center of European trade, particularly in pepper and cotton cloths. See Marguerite Eyer Wilbur, *The East India Company, and the British Empire in the Far East* (New York: Oxford UP, 1945), 156–68.

Foreign Ships or others on their behalf But on the contrary do what in them lyes to discourage their further Trade.[118]

If you shall find they dont sincerely comply with these Our Orders besure to put down in Writing the Names of the Persons with the Instances of such their non complyance and treachery to their Country, for Our Information at your return wherein be particular, And let them severally know, That We will not suffer them longer to enjoy the benefit of our Protect.$^{n}$ or remaining in India if within our reach. We are

Your Loving Friends
London 30$^{th}$ Nov.$^{r}$ 1722. [...][119]

## List of Goods to be Provided in China for the Ships going out in the Year 1722.

| | |
|---|---|
| *Raw Silk* One hundred and twenty Chests of the finest sort if to be had from One hundred and twenty to One hundred & forty Tale p. Pecull[120], but if the said One hundred and twenty Chests cant be bought at that Price then to bring y$^{e}$ less. | Ch.$^{ts}$ 120 |
| *Taffaties*[121] the best sort goods Blacks One Thousand | [P.$^{s}$] 1000 |
| *Ditto Colour'd.* Three Thousand, One half to be cloth or hair Colours | 3000 |
| [174r] *Gorgorons*[122] *Black* Five hundred | 500 |
| *Ditto Colour'd* Seven hundred, One half to be Cloth or hair Colours | 700 |
| *Poises*[123] *flower'd White* Four hundred | 400 |

118 For evidence of (illicit) commercial relationships between British country traders and Ostend ships, see John Scattergood's activities in 1721 and 1722: BL – Mss Eur C387/3.

119 These signatures exactly mirror those of the preceding directors' orders, pages 44–5. They will be similarly shortened and acknowledged in the remainder of this document.

120 A pecul is a Chinese measurement, equaling about 133.33 pounds or 60.48 kilograms.

121 A taffeta was a highly demanded, plain-weave silk, that was available in numerous colors, stripes and patterns. It was manufactured in Persia, India and China as well as in Europe since the Middle Ages. Chinese taffeta was known to be thicker than its competitors.

122 A gorgoroon, or grogram, is a stiff, ribbed silk and often woolen-mixed textile, originally from China.

123 A poisee is a Chinese satin, or silk, likely painted or printed with floral designs. See Leanna Lee-Whitman, "The Silk Trade: Chinese Silks and the British East India Company", in: *Winterthur Portfolio* 17.1 (1982), 31-3.

| | |
|---|---|
| *Ditto flower'd Colour'd* Four hundred | 400 |
| *Ditto of two Colours* Four hundred & fifty | 450 |
| *Bed Damasks*[124] great flowers and a New Pattern according to the Chineeses own Fancy Two hund.d directors' orders, pages 44-5. | 200 |
| *Ditto of two Colours* Three hundred | 300 |
| *Masquerades*[125] of the best sort grave Colours Two hund.d | 200 |
| *Lampases*[126] One hundred | 100 |
| N.B. If something New bring a quantity accord.g to its Value. | |
| *Tea* Seven thousand two hundred sixty five Pecul Viz.t | 7265 |
| *Bohea Tea* Four thousand Pecul | |
| *Congou*<br>*Pecho* } what quantity you can get good & reasonable | |
| *Singlo* the best Two thousand Pecul | |
| *Bing*[127]<br>*Hyson*[128] } What q.ty you can get good & reasonable | |
| For what quantity you fall short in Congou, Pecho, Bing and Hyson make up in Bohea & Singlo in proportion two thirds in the Bohea, and one third in Singlo. | |
| *Quick Silver* Fifteen Tons | Tons 15 |
| Besure to take care it be securely Packt. | |
| *All usefull China Ware* Eight Hundred Chests of which Bowles, Dishes, and Plates of all Sizes as many as you can get | Ch.ts 800 |
| *Scollop Shells* none. | |
| *Tea Cannisters* none. | |
| *Large Milk Pots* none. | |
| *Large Chocolate Cups* none. | |
| *Chocolate cups* with handles none. | |

124 Damasks are heavy silk textiles, composed of one color but featuring designs created by alternating weave patterns. The heavy cloth was regularly used by Europeans for bed covers, curtains and domestic upholstery.

125 Mascades or mascardoes – known to English buyers as masquerades – were silks, likely used as hair-cloths in early modern Europe. See Eric Kerridge, *Textile Manufactures in Early Modern England* (Manchester: Manchester UP, 1985), 56.

126 Lampas was a type of twill cloth produced in Asia with silk wefts and typically featuring figures or designs woven directly into the fabric. This might refer to the cloth also known as *persiannes*.

127 Bing, or Imperial, was a high-quality and costly green tea. It did not keep well in transport, however, and thus was only exported in small amounts.

128 Hyson was the mostly highly valued green tea in eighteenth-century England and favored by both the British Crown and upper nobility. As such, it eventually was taxed at a higher rate than other varieties.

Althô We Calculate the above to be the Quantity and sorts of Wrought Silks, yet We do not so exactly limit to those Particulars, but that if it shall appear more advantageous according to the late Prices here to abate in some, & encrease in others. We do allow thereof. And for better Guidance therein We send herew.$^{th}$ the last Prices the several sorts sold for Viz.$^{t}$

| | |
|---|---|
| *Taffaties Black* p. Essex in September 1721. at | 58.6 p. P.$^{s}$ |
| *Ditto Colour'd* p. Carnarvon Septem.$^{r}$ 1719 . | 50.6 |
| [174v] *Gorgorons Black* p. Essex Septem.$^{r}$ 1721. at | 74.6 p. P.$^{s}$ |
| *Ditto Colour'd* p. Sarum D.$^{o}$ | 80._ |
| *Poises flower'd white* p Essex D.$^{o}$ | 88._ |
| *Ditto flower'd Colour'd* p. Sarum D.$^{o}$ | 75._ |
| *Ditto two Colours* p. Essex D.$^{o}$ | 92._ |
| *Bed Damasks* p. Carnarvon D.$^{o}$ 1719 | 88._ |
| *Lampasses* p. Townshend D.$^{o}$ 1718 | £ 5. 15._ |
| *Bed Damasks* two Colours<br>*Masquerades* | } find none of late. |

The undermention'd sorts of Wrought Silks We have wrote for none of late because they sold so very low Viz.$^{t}$

| | |
|---|---|
| *Pelongs*[129] p. Essex | 14.6 |
| *Gelongs*[130] p. D.$^{o}$ | 10.9 |
| *Paunches*[131] *flower'd* sold for | 10.6 Ditto 10.10 ½ |

But if all or any of these Species can be met with extreamly cheap so as likely to turn to good Account here at the above Prices, buy up what you see fit as far as Three Thousand Pounds in the whole £3000

*Sago*[132] sufficient for Package in China Ware.

Sign'd by Order of the Court of Directors
Tho. Woolley[133] Secty.

---

129 A pelong was a variety of Chinese silk.

130 Gelongs were a type of silk crepe, particularly used by Europeans as neck-cloths.

131 A paunch was another variety of Chinese silk – available plain, colored, and patterned.

132 Sago is a flour-like foodstuff produced by palms in southeast Asia. It was used for packing porcelain by the EIC in the early 1700s – a tendency later slowed as sago was known to expand when wet. Given that crews often packed porcelain items in the lower, most water-prone parts of their ships, this often caused breakages.

133 Thomas Woolley (1664–1728) was secretary of the EIC in London for almost twenty-five years. See *The Historical Register, Containing An Impartial Relation of all Transactions, Foreign and Domestick* 13 (1728), 32.

## List of the Companys Packet by the Chief & Council for China on the Duke of Cambridge.[134]

N.$^{o}$ 1. Companys Instructions to Mess.$^{rs}$ Fazakerley, Morton, Godfrey, Atkyns, Carter, Dade & Bacon, dated 30.$^{th}$ Novem.$^{r}$ 1722.

2. Supplemental Orders to the Chief and Council for China, dated 30.$^{th}$ November 1722.

3. Packet from the Secret Committee dated the 30$^{th}$ November 1722. Superscrib'd Viz.$^{t}$ To Mess.$^{rs}$ Fazakerley, Morton, Godfrey, Atkyns, Carter, Dade & Bacon appointed of Council for mannaging the Companys Affairs in China. To be open'd when are arriv'd at Wampo in China, and not before.[135]

4. Invoice of the Duke of Cambridge amounting to £ 36133.10[136].

5. Bill of lading of D.$^{o}$ Ship.

6. Copy of the Duke of Cambridge's Charterparty.

N.$^{o}$ 7. [175r] List of Goods to be Provided in China for the Ships going out in the Year 1722. Sign'd by the Secretary.

8. Copy of Cap.$^{t}$ Daniel Smalls Instructions dated 30$^{th}$ Novem.$^{r}$ 1722.

9. Manifest of Bullion and Goods Lycenc'd to be Shipt aboard the Duke of Cambridge. Sign'd by M.$^{r}$ Thomas Lewes.

10. Companys Indulgence.[137]

11. Copy of the Companys Tenth By-Law & Order of Encouragement

12. An Act of Parliament Entituled. An Act for the better Securing the Lawfull Trade of his Majestys Subjects to and from the East Indies, and for the more effectual preventing all His Majestys Subjects Trading thither under Foreign Commissions.

13. An Act of Parliament Entituled. An Act for the further preventing His Majestys Subjects from Trading to the East Indies under Foreign Commissions & for encouraging and further Securing the Lawfull Trade thereto, and for the better Regulating the Pylots of Dover, Deale, & the Isle of Thanet.

---

**134** The packets for the remaining three EIC ships were all similar. Any differences are noted, where relevant, in the footnotes.

**135** This paragraph was not included in the Hertford's packet.

**136** The other ships' packets noted differing total invoices of £ 31706.10.10 (Montagu), £ 28911.0.10 (Princess Ann) and £ 33222.14.4 (Hertford). See additionally "Duke of Cambridge: Ledger," 1722–1725, in: BL – IOR/L/MAR/B/700D(1); "Hertford: Ledger," 1722–1724, in: BL – IOR/L/MAR/B/656-I(1).

**137** An indulgence was an official grant by the EIC for its representatives to participate in private trade. See pages 35–6, 57–8. Also, Jean Sutton, *The East India Company's Maritime Service, 1746–1834: Masters of the Eastern Seas* (Woodbridge: The Boydell Press, 2010), 277–80.

14. Patterns of 20 Bales of Broadcloth[138], and 32 Bales of Long Ells p. Duke of Cambridge deliver'd to M.r Fazakerley apart.[139] [...]

## Orders and Instructions Given by the Court of Directors of the United Company of Merchants of England Trading to the East Indies, To Cap.t Daniel Small Commander of the Ship Duke of Cambridge, and to the commander for the time being.[140]

[176r] 1. We the said Court of Directors having Freighted the Ship Duke of Cambridge whereof you are Commander to serve Us in Peace and Warfare, and to proceed to such Ports and Places in the East Indies or elsewhere whereunto you shall be directed, We do therefore Order you on Receipt hereof to set Sail and Proceed as Wind and Weather will permit to the Port of [176v] Canton in China whereto you are Consign'd, On your Arrival deliver to Mess.rs William Fazakerley, Richard Morton, Edmond Godfrey, Thomas Atkyns, Thomas Carter, Thomas Dade, & Devereux Bacon, Whom We have appointed to be One Council for Mannaging Our Affairs in China, or to such of them as shall be then present all the Treasure, Goods, and Effects on board your Ship Consign'd to them by Invoice and Bill of Lading, and you are to receive all such Goods in return of Our said Cargo, as they shall Order and Sign the Bills of Lading for the same, and to follow all other their Orders agreeable to your Charterparty, & when Dispatcht by them to make the best of your way in your return to England accord.g to the Instructions they give you, Where We pray God to bring you in safety.

2. Such of Our said Council as shall during this Voyage or any Part of it be on board you, are to have the preference and Chair at Sea and on Shore, and the use of all the Great Cabbin according to Charterparty Viz.t all the Room aft the Whip Staff except the necessary room for the Steersman.

3. If you shall receive any Orders from Josias Wordsworth, Joseph Herne and Henry Lyell Esq.rs & S.r Mathew Decker Bar.t or any three of them whom We have appointed to be a secret Committee to give Instructions to Our Outward and homeward bound Shipping, You must comply with & obey them as fully as if the same were Sign'd by the whole Court.

---

**138** Broadcloth was a densely-woven, sturdy woolen textile, produced in England since the sixteenth century. It was commonly used for outerwear, as its tight construction was warm and watertight.

**139** The Montagu's packet noted differently here: "Pattern of 19 Bales of Broad Cloth and 32 Bales of Long Ells p. Mountague deliver'd to Mr Morton apart." The remaining ships did not carry any English woolens and thus did not have patterns included in their packet.

**140** The orders for the remaining captains were similar, except for changes noted on page 58, ft. 160.

4. We direct that the Duke of Cambridge, Princess Anne, Mountague & Hertford, who are all bound for China do proceed and keep Company thither to prevent the Hazard of Pyrates and to stand by and assist each other if attackt by them all the Commanders have the like Orders, for We have reason to fear some Pyrates may yet be abroad in the East Indies or lying off the Cape, and the Greenwich's Cowardly & treacherous deserting the Cassandra[141] when attackt by the Pyrates is yet fresh in Our mind, We tell you this that you mayn't be Guilty of the like if you Value Our Service, or the Publick benefit, We have appointed & do hereby direct Captain Small to be Commodore as being the Senior Commander, and that you do all before your putting out to Sea meet and agree upon proper Signals and Places of Rendezvous for your speedier joining in case of separation.

5. We strictly require you to keep up the Worship of God on board your Ship and good Orders among your Men taking care of their healths during the whole Voyage.

6. You must carry along with you a Mediterranean Pass[142] there being many Algerine Rovers[143] abroad which you are likely to meet [177r] withall in your Outward or Homeward bound Voyage you must also carry with you the full Number of English Mariners according to the direction of the Act of Navigation[144] and your Covenant in Charterparty.

**141** In 1720, Madagascar pirates attacked two EIC ships, the Cassandra and Greenwich, and one Ostend ship anchored in Muskat, Oman. The latter two fled, leaving the Cassandra to engage the pirates alone. Ultimately, she ran aground on some nearby rocks, and her crew was forced to abandon the vessel to seek shelter ashore. See John Pinkerton, *A General Collection of the Best and Most Interesting Voyages and Travels in Various Parts of Asia*, vol. 2 (London: Longman, Hurst, Rees, Orme & Brown, 1819), 270.

**142** Beginning in 1662, these passes guaranteed free navigation of the Mediterranean for English ships by the Admiralty. They were secured with the support of, and financial contributions to, the Barbary states of North Africa and compulsory after 1682. By the 1730s, over 1,200 passes, printed on parchment and carried onboard vessels, were distributed each year. See Tristan Stein, "Passes and Protection in the Making of a British Mediterranean", in: *Journal of British Studies* 54.3 (2015), 602–31.

**143** Algerine Rovers were Moorish privateers from North Africa, particularly the Barbary Coast. They were active not only in the Mediterranean but also along the continent's eastern and western coasts. Europeans also referred to them as "salleemen." See C.R. Pennell, *Piracy and Diplomacy in Seventeenth Century North Africa: the Journals of Thomas Baker, English Consul in Tripoli, 1677–1685* (London: Associated UP, 1989); Adrian Tinniswood, *Pirates of Barbary: Corsairs, Conquests, and Captivity in the Seventeenth-Century Mediterranean* (New York: Riverhead Books, 2010).

**144** The first Navigation Act, passed by English Parliament in 1651, required that most imports to England be shipped on English-built ships with majority English crews. In 1660, the ordinance was strengthened to stipulate that all colonial trade must now be on English ships with crews composed of at least 75 % English sailors and an English captain. "An Act for Increase of Shipping and Encouragement of the Navigation of this Nation," *Acts and Ordinances of the Interregnum*, 1651. "An Act for the Encouraging and increasing of Shipping and Navigation," *Statutes of the Realm*, 12 Charles II, c. 18, 1660.

7. We positively require and order That you do not directly or indirectly either for your Self or any other Person carry out any Bullion Goods or Merchandizes or any Letters but what you shall be Lycenc'd by Us or some Committee appointed by Us for that purpose shall Lycence you to carry and that you use your utmost endeavours to prevent all your Officers and Seamen from carrying out any Bullion Goods Merchandizes or Letters without the like Lycence.

8. Take immediate care on receipt hereof to have and keep your arms fix'd, To station your Men at their several Quarters, To put your Ship in a good posture of defence, To have a sufficient Number of cartridges fill'd with Powder and a proportionable quantity of Shot to be always in readiness during this Voyage in case of a sudden Assault, Trust no Colours, be very Watchfull at all times against surprizes and cautious of speaking with any Ship; and if you can avoid it speak with none during every part of the Voyage[145], Be very industrious to find out the trim of your Ship for her better Sailing.

9. We have great reason to believe some of the Captains of the Ships in Our Service have while they were in India disposed of part of their Ships Ordnance, Fire Arms, Powder and Shot and thereby render'd themselves less defensible. in case of an Enemys Attacking them, We do hereby positively forbid you and the Captain for the time being to Sell or otherwise part with any except in case of absolute necessity to Our Presidents, Agents, or Chiefs & Councils, and that only for the Use of Our Settlements under Penalty of an utter incapacity in Our Service.

10. Use all possible endeavours to Expedite your outward bound Voyage, and when by Judgement you are within Forty or Fifty Leagues of the Western Islands[146], Shape the Course, Wind and Weather will permit so as to keep at least Thirty Leagues to the Westward of the Canary Islands[147], and thence Proceed towards China directly to Batavia, which We hope you will be enabled to do, having had Our previous Notice to take in here a sufficient quantity of Water & Fresh Provisions for that purpose, because the Pyrates have lain off the Cape to intercept the Outward and homeward bound East India Shipping and possibly may do so this next Spring, for which Reason [177v] We direct that you don't if possible put into the Cape or come so near it as to be

**145** It was common for seamen on their homeward journey to speak to other ship's crews to get updates on the latest political and military developments in Europe. This also was an opportunity for outgoing ships to transmit personal mail.

**146** This refers to the Azores, a group of nine volcanic islands located 1,360 kilometers west of Portugal.

**147** The Canary Islands are an archipelago of seven islands, located about 100 kilometers west of modern-day Morocco. Although discovered by Portuguese sailors in the 1300s, the Spanish began to colonize them in 1402, a process not completed until 1495. For more on these islands and early exploration, see Felipe Fernández-Armesto, *The Canary Islands after the Conquest: the Making of a Colonial Society in the Early Sixteenth Century* (New York: Oxford UP, 1982); John Thornton, *A Cultural History of the Atlantic World, 1250–1820*, (New York: Cambridge UP, 2012), 15–19, 187–188.

seen by any Ships lying off or Cruizing near it, but keep in a high Latitude however if many of your Men should fall down Sick and thereby you are forced to touch somewhere by the way, choose with the advice and Consent of so many of Our China Council aforesaid as you can Consult withall, and of your Officers in Writing any Port not Prohibited in Charterparty, which you judge least liable to the danger of Pyrates or other Enemys, Remember the Pyrates & Sallee Men used to Visit S.t Jago[148] and the Isle of May[149], therefore put into none of the Cape DeVerde Islands[150], for Pyrates have lately been there, and probably will again. Be sure keep at least twenty or thirty Leagues to the Westward of the said Islands, Wherever you touch carry it civilly to the Governour & Inhabit.ts to prevent complaints, while you are at an Anchor in any Place outward or homeward bound or in the East Indies, keep a good look out at Topmast head, and keep the same look out during the whole Voyage when at Sea.

11. We forbid your touching at the Brazills[151] Outward bound on Penalty of an utter incapacity of continuance in our Service unless you can give Us very satisfactory reasons of the absolute necessity you are under of proceeding thither.

12. We likewise forbid your making any deviation Outward or homeward or breaking Bulk, for if you do, We shall put in Suit the Bonds you have enter'd into on these Accounts.

13. We expect that you do advise Us by all opportunitys in your Outward and homeward bound Voyage and during your stay in the East Indies of all Occurrences worthy Our Notice directing your Letters to Us in London.

14. Take care to clean and tallow your Ship as often as you have Opportunity while you remain in any Port during your present Voyage.

---

**148** St. Jago, now Santiago, was the principal island in the Cape Verde archipelago in the early 1700s, housing a large port and the bishop's seat. Vessels to the East Indies often stopped here on their outward journeys to refresh their water and food supplies. Pirates, however, also favored these islands, because the nearby meeting of trade winds and currents allowed them access to ships traveling to and from Europe as well as along the African and American coasts. See Iídio Cabral Baleno, "Pressões externas. Reacções ao corso e à pirataria", in: *História geral de Cabo Verde, vol. 2*, ed. Maria Emília Madeira Santos (Lisboa: Instituto de Investigação Científica Tropical, 1995), 125–88.

**149** Maio is the easternmost of the leeward Cape Verde islands. It is located about 30 kilometers east of Santiago.

**150** The Cape Verde Islands are located in the central Atlantic Ocean, 560 kilometers west of Senegal. European explorers discovered the archipelago around 1456, which then were uninhabited. By the 1500s, they prospered as an important entrepôt for slave ships travelling to the Americas and returning East Indies vessels. In 1720, they were still popular as stops for ships going to Asia.

**151** Ships taking the Southeast Trade Winds could sail to the South American coast, if they did not catch eastern countercurrents early enough. Ostend ships specifically aimed for Brazil in the 1720s, especially the settlements of Rio de Janeiro, Bahia, and Pernambuco. They used these areas to re-provision, as they were banned from EIC and VOC harbors at St. Helena and Cape Town. Gill, Merchants, 26.

15. Two of Our Ships bound to China some years since thô dispatcht from hence in due Season lost their Passage for want of Judgment, because they did not keep far enough to the Eastward, but fell to the Leeward of Java head in the Easterley Monsoon, of which We give you this caution to prevent your doing the like.

16. When you arrive at Batavia you must not stay there longer than you can provide your Selves with Wood, Water & refreshments, which with diligence may be effected in five to ten days at furthest unless by reason of your Mens Sickness you find an absolute necessity to remain somewhat longer [178r] for recovering their health, and here We think it proper to acquaint you, that having had of late very great complaints of the unkind usage the Supra Cargos and officers met with there.[152] We enquired into the reasons and are inform'd it was at least in part occasiond by the English carrying on a Trade thither and selling great quantitys of European Commoditys contrary to the standing Rules of the Hon.ble the Netherlands East India Company, and their Government at Batavia and that some of Our People when on Shore have been complain'd of for their riotous and disorderley behaviour, both which are not at all to be excused, nor can We by any means allow of, wherefore to prevent all such occasions of misunderstanding between the Dutch East India Company and Us, We hereby positively forbid you to Use or Exercise any manner of Trade or Merchandize whatsoever at Batavia, other than such as shall be allow'd of by the Standing Orders and Rules of the Government there, and for which they shall give you free liberty, as We suppose they will for purchasing Refreshments for the Ships Companys, or for Necessarys for the Ships in case by the Accidents of the Voyage you shall be in Want of any, and we peremptorily require, That if you or any of your Ships Companys shall have occasion to go on Shore for procuring such Supplys or Refreshments, they behave themselves respectfully to the Government, and civilly and without Offence to all other Persons whatsoever, as they will answer it at their Peril if ever We shall know they in any degree break these Our Orders, But if M.r Fazakerley (who takes Passage on the Duke of Cambridge and has Our liberty to shift her, and go on board any other of the Outward bound China Ships) finds she sails better should not Arrive at Batavia by the time you are ready to depart, you must stay till he comes, provided such stay doth not exceed Ten days, because We would have him Arrive with the first of Our Ships at China if possible, But if by unforeseen accidents the Passage outward should be so tedious that such stay at Batavia should hazard your Passage to China, in that Case you must make the best of your Way from Batavia to Maccao, and so up to Wampo,

---

**152** The English and the Dutch fought three wars against each other in the seventeenth century (1652–1654, 1665–1667, 1672–1674). While at peace in 1723, and while the British could anchor at Batavia in contrast to prohibited Ostenders, tensions between the EIC and VOC lingered. See Alastair Hamilton, Alexander H. de Groot, and Maurits H. van den Boogert (eds.), *Friends and Rivals in the East: Studies in Anglo-Dutch Relations in the Levant from the Seventeenth to the Early Nineteenth Century* (Boston: Brill, 2000); Furber, Rival.

there to stay for M.r Fazakerley and follow the Orders of such of Our aforesaid Council as shall be or Arrive there for your further proceedings

17. On your Arrival at China and while you stay there be very carefull to keep all your Ships Company within y.e due bounds of Sobriety and Civil deportment, suffer none of them [178v] to be guilty of any Riotous disorder or excess, Lest thereby the Peoples healths and the English Reputation with the Chineeses be endanger'd or Our Estates and Concerns in China prejudiced. We positively forbid you or any others running any Goods on pretence of saving the Customs due to the Government, give them all timely and due notice of this to prevent all mischievous consequences on that Account.

18. We direct and order you particularly to Regard and strictly to Observe all the Covenants and Agreements contain'd in your Charterparty of which you have a Copy with Marginal Notes for your easier Perusal & Notice, and among other things To put up and continue the Order of Encouragement as directed in Fol. 3. To touch at no Places prohibited as in Fol. 4 & 5. To take care that the Journals and the Boatswains and others Books be kept and Entrys made therein of all Goods Bullion and Effects taken into or deliver'd out of the Ship, and for whose Account, and all those Books produced and deliver'd as Covenanted in Fol. 5 & 6. To take care no Goods or Bullion be Laden on board during this Voyage, except such as shall be Lycenc'd or Indulged, for if there be We shall exact the Penaltys mention'd in said Fol. 6. of which We give you this warning that you may not incur them, Remember in these last Clauses the Covenants are made stronger than in the late Charterpartys, to prevent the Exorbitant Excesses of private and unlicenced Trade out or home, and the Encroachment of Commanders on the Ships Tonnage from Port to Port abroad.[153]

19. We hereby direct that neither your Self nor the Commander for the time being do Lade for your own Private Account or suffer any others to Load on board your Ship in the East Indies or elsewhere within the Limits of the Companys Charter to be brought from thence unto or towards Europe any Goods or Merchandizes but what shall be duly Register'd with Our Council aforesaid them on the Place, or in case of their Total absence with the Captain, in which Registers the several sorts, Quantitys and Values of each Species of Goods shall be express'd, and all the Numbers in words at length as well as figures, and that Copys thereof be deliver'd to the Court of Directors for the time being within ten days after the Ships unlading in England, of this give due Notice to all your Officers, Mariners, and other Persons on board, and acquaint them that the Goods if Unregister'd will be forfeited when discover'd. We further direct that neither they or you do bring from the East Indies or elsewhere any

153 The exact reference here is unclear. It was common, however, for ships' captains to carry as much private cargo home as possible, as this constituted their main voyage income. Parmentier, Tea Time, 67–71.

Packet or Letter but what shall be sent up to the East India house in London[154] and deliver'd to the Court of Directors for the time being or their Order.[155]

[179r] 20. Take care no Camphire be brought in the Ship Duke of Cambridge by any Person or on any Account whatsoever, lest the Scent of it spoil the Tea, and for the same reason let no more Arrack be brought in the Ship than what shall be for necessary Stores, and besure it be stow'd in such Places as will best prevent its doing the Tea harm by its Steam or Scent.

21. Our Council aforesaid are directed to Consult you what Sorts and Quantitys of Goods are to be first sent on board for the Ships better Stowage, and most advantage for her Tonnage and Sailing, and as We have Order'd them to fill you up with Tea after your Kintlage Goods are on board you must follow their Orders about the Stowage thereof, which We have told them shall be Viz.[t] as much of it as possible in the afterpart of the Ship between Decks, and abast the Well in the Hold to the Bulk head of the Breadroom, That a Bulkhead be made at the After part of the Well, and batten'd to prevent the Steam moistning and damaging the Tea, that the Breadroom be fill'd with Tea; and that the residue of it be stow'd where it may be best preserved from dampness.

22. We hereby acquaint you, and do you acquaint your Officers, That We will permit your Self or the Commander of this Ship for the present Voyage, and the Officers to bring home one half of the Three p.Cent Tonnage allow'd you and them by Charterparty in Tea, and no more on Condition that there be paid the Company Fifteen p.Cent on the Gross Amount thereof as Sold at the Companys Candle[156], and also Five p.Cent charged thereon by Act of Parliament[157], and Two p.Cent more for General Charges and not otherwise, excepting hereout the Two hundred weight of Tea for every hundred Tons the Ship Duke of Cambridge is Lett for, which is allow'd by the

---

**154** The East India House was located on Leadenhall Street, in London. Before it was rebuilt in 1726, the company met in an Elizabethan mansion on this site known as Craven House. By 1661, the facade of the building was decorated with wooden ornaments and paintings of EIC ships. George Walter Thornbury, *Old and New London: a Narrative of its History, its People and its Places* (London: Petter & Galphin, 1878), 183–94.

**155** This measure was meant to allow EIC directors control of Asia-Europe mail lines. Scattergood, a country trader who often flouted company dictates, in contrast, regularly sent letters via Ostenders. See: BL – Mss Eur C387/3.

**156** Candle auctions were popular in early modern England. They allowed for the public auction of individual commodities only for the amount of time one inch of a candle remained lit, an effort to ensure fairer and more consistent bids. Here, the EIC used them at their London house to retail Canton imports. Items had to be quickly paid in full, ensuring their sale to those of financial means. Lawson, East India, 61–2.

**157** See, for an example of such excise taxes, "An Act for laying additional Duties on Hides and Skins, Vellum and Parchment, and new Duties on Starch, Coffee, Tea, Drugs, Gilt and Silver Wire, and Policies on Insurance, to secure a yearly Fund [...] of one million eight hundred thousand Pounds towards her Majesty's Supply," *Statutes of the Realm*, 10 Anne I, c. 26.

Comp.^as Printed Indulgence, and in case your Self or the Commander of this Ship for the time being, and the Officers do bring home more Tea than is herein mention'd, We hereby declare that We will Seize upon and proceed to the forfeiture of such Surplus Tea, and double the Value according to the Act of Parliament[158] for that purpose as being Traded in contrary to the Companys Lycence, and We give you this due Notice that you may not incur the Penalty.

23. Be very carefull that neither your Self nor any of your Mariners or other Persons do Sell or deliver out of the Ship untill her return to England any Goods Laden on board your said Ship, lest thereby you bring your Owners and Us into trouble by Causing the Bond given at the [179v] Customhouse to prevent Breaking Bulk which is in Ten Thousand Seven hundred and fifty Pounds[159] Penalty to be put in Suit and by bringing on your Self and the Ships Company divers other ill Consequences. We must likewise tell you that by an Act of Parliament[160] lately past, all such Goods so run from on board are forfeited, thô the Goods should escape yet the Value will be sued for and recover'd by Information afterwards even by any of your Seamen from the Persons who can be proved Guilty, and We require you to give publick Notice hereof to all the Ships Company, that none may pretend Ignorance of the Law, We understand some of our Captains have pretended this Clause as a Justification to them not to deliver out any Necessarys to Our Governour and Council at S.^t Helena, thô they were shown Our Orders to the Governour and Council to demand them of our returning Commanders out of Our Cargos, We mention this that you do supply them according to those Orders if you can come at the Goods tak'g receipts for what you deliver, which you must give into the Court at your return, And if Our said Council or such of them as shall be in China shall Lade any Goods on board for S.^t Helena, do you take care they be so stow'd so as to be readily come at on your Arrival there, and deliver'd accordingly.

24. We desire and direct that you be always respectfull aiding and assisting to Our said Council or such of them as shall be in China in whatever may promote our Interest, Favour the Investment and forward the speedy Lading of the Ship, and if they shall buy any part of their China Cargo on board Ship, that you clear the Ship, and make it fitt to receive and examine the Goods as they are brought on board by the Chineeses for Sale, and also to take care to Stow them away seasonably and properly in the Hold or other Places of the Ship as the Council aforesaid shall direct agreeable to your Charterparty and these Our Instructions, That you treat the Chineeses civilly, and take care none of the Ships Company offer them any affront, That the said Council have the use of your Boats at all times when they shall have occasion for them

**158** "An Act for preventing the Frauds and regulating Abuses in His Majesties Customes," *Statutes of the Realm*, 13 & 14 Charles II, c. 11.

**159** The bonds for the other ships were: Princess Ann and Montagu, £9,500, Hertford, £11,000.

**160** "An Act against clandestine Running of uncustomed Goods, and for the more effectual preventing of Frauds relating to the Customs," *Statutes of the Realm*, 5 George I, c. 11.

for Our Service, That while they keep a Factory on shore you furnish them with the Number of Mariners mention'd in your Charterparty to assist them there, and to carry from and bring to the Ship any Treasure, Goods, or Merchandizes, besure let all the Mariners be able trusty Persons, If there should be a necessity of their having more hands on some particular occasions [180r] and the Affairs of the Ship will allow of it, that you furnish them therewith, all which if you perform will effectually recommend you to the Companys favour at your return, and shall meet with our Encouragement.

25. When our Council aforesaid have compleated their Investments and Laden the same on board, you or your Purser must Sign Bills of Lading for the Goods by them Shipt and observe the dispatches you receive from them for leaving Canton from whence If you are dispatcht for England and are not otherwise particularly directed, you must make the best of yo.r way for Our Island S.t Helena using all possible diligence in getting early about the Cape of Good Hope, when you come near the Island be cautious how you make it keeping a strict watch, and a constant look out to prevent falling into any Pyrates or other Enemys hands who may lye thereabouts to surprize you, On your Entrance into S.t Helena road bring your Ship to an Anchor before you come open with Chapp'd Valley near to Mundens point[161], if you dont meet with good Anchor hold sooner, and then send your Boat ashore to give the Governour an Account who you are, because he hath Our Orders to fire upon any unknown Ship that shall attempt to pass that point and come into the Road for fear she should prove an Enemy and attempt to Surprize Our Ships there as the French did the Queen and Dover[162] while you are in the road keep a good look out and a strict guard stay no longer there if a Single Ship than to refresh your Men and to get in the necessary supplys Supplys, but hasten away to the River of Thames. But if any of Our returning Ships shall be at S.t Helena on your Arrival or during your stay, then you must keep them Company for mutual Security & consult together how you may best Associate in case you meet with an Enemy in order to which, in regard We know not what Commanders may be upon the Place, We cannot appoint your Stations, but require you, that laying aside all occasions of misunderstanding, you rank your Selves according to Seniority in Command, and be always on your Guard, and trust no Colours whatsoever.

26. You will see by the Covenants in Charterparty Fol. 5. you are not in your homeward Voyage to put into any of the Western Islands, or Plymouth[163], or any Port of England or Ireland or any other port of Europe, except in case of unavoidable danger

**161** Munden's Point is a small peninsula on the northern side of St. Helena, named for the English naval captain who re-seized the island from the Dutch in 1673.

**162** In June 1706, two large ships flying Dutch flags approached St. Helena and the two EIC vessels anchored there. The former overran the British ships, quickly hoisted the French flag, and brought the seized vessels out-of-range before land batteries could organize. Royle, Company's Island, 153–4.

**163** Plymouth is a coastal settlement located in southwest England. Its harbor was an important center for the fishing industry as well as coastal English and continental trade by the late fifteenth century.

or by particular directions, which We expect you comply with, and that you make the best of your way into [180v] the Downes[164] if wind permits, into whatever Place you put send Us by the double conveyances advice of your Arrival with Copy of your Bill of Lading, and a short Account of your Voyage. If you do not We shall reckon you unworthy Our future service. If you can reach the Downes or if by contrary Winds you shall be obliged to put into some other Port in England, you must from thence send up your purser with such Packets as contain Our Letters and Advices, and with all other Letters aboard your Ship together with Copy of your Bill of Lading, and the Account of all Private Trade, Parcells of Goods, and Tokens on board, & if We shall afterwards understand that your self or any of your Officers or Mariners do conceal any such Letters, Goods, or Tokens, We shall make them know our Resentments of which give them all notice that they may not plead Ignorance.

27. If you happen to be supply'd during this Voyage by any of His Majestys Officers with Provisions or Naval or Ordnance Stores send Us by the first opportunity an Exact Account thereof advising also when and where the same were deliver'd, and by whom and a Duplicate thereof by the next to prevent the disputes which may otherwise arise (as they formerly have) between the Commissioners of the Navy, Victualling & Ordnance and Us on the like Account.

28. We hereby direct when you send ashore the Treasure on board you Consign'd to Our Council as aforesaid (which must every chest be buoy'd) That your self or the Purser, or other Person you shall appoint do accompany it, and be present at the delivering, opening, and examining to see if it comes out according to the Invoice, if by any accident it can't be immediately Open'd it is to be lodged in a proper Place; and you or the Person so appointed is to have a Lock upon it till it can be so examin'd, Our Council have Copy of these Instructions & therefore will conform themselves thereunto.

29. We have before directed you to keep Company but thinks your so doing for mutual Security of our Effects on board the four China Ships of such Consequence, We add thereto as follows That if upon any pretence whatsoever (except a plain unavoidable necessity) you do seperate from any Ship, that shall be dispatcht with you, or that you shall fall in Company with untill you are got to the Westward of the Cape of Good Hope or if in case of an Assault by an Enemy Outward or homeward you don't stand by and to the utmost assist one another in defence of your Selves, and of the Companys Estate on board such Consorting Ships, We shall deem you Unworthy and Uncapable of serving [181r] the Company any longer. We put this Clause also into the Captains Luhorne Gordon, and Nellys Instructions.

164 The Downs are a portion of the southern North Sea, located just off the coast of Deal, England. They offered ocean-going ships a sheltered anchorage and were often a congregation point for London-based vessels.

30. We have directed Our Council for China That if by any Unhappy accident any one of the Four China Ships should be disabled so as that the keeping her Company should endanger the Passage of the rest, they do in the first place contribute all they can to the Assistance of the disabled Ship, and then take out the Companys Treasure on board & put it into the other Ship or Ships in Company to be the sooner carryed to and Invested in China leaving such disabled Ship to follow after, and that the first four of the said Council have liberty to Shift out of any of the said four Ships that shall meet with the like accident into one or more of the rest, This We mention for your Notice and Observance.

31. Our said Council have with them Printed Copys of the late Acts of Parliament empowering the Company to Seiz any of His Majestys Subjects they shall find within the Limits of the Companys Charter, belonging to or that came out of any Ships under Foreign Commissions or Authority. And Our directions to Seiz them accordingly, and to bring them to England if they can catch them. We do therefore direct, That you aid and assist them in the Execution of Our said Orders, and do receive on board and secure the Persons so Seized to England to answer for their said Offence.

32. We have by a smarting late experience found how hazardous it is for Our returning Shipping to go into the Cape especially if their Arrival there is late in the Season[165], & yet thô the Commanders are not insensible of it they will make one pretence or other for putting in w.$^{n}$ the true reason is for the benefit of Private Trade, wherefore We positively direct & order That you do not on any pretence w.$^{t}$soever except in case of being disabled by Storms or other such like real & inevitable necessity venture to put into y.$^{e}$ Cape homeward bound as you Value being continued in Our service, & would avoid putting in Suit your Charterparty Covenants for breach of Orders. We are

Your Loving Friends
London 30.$^{th}$ Nov.$^{r}$ 1722. [...]

**165** The Canton trading season lasted four months, from September or October to the following January. This related to the easterly currents of the Southwest Monsoon, ending in August, and the westerly currents of the Northeast Monsoon, commencing in January. Van Dyke, Merchants, 52. The incidence hinted at here was the blowing aground of three EIC ships in Cape Bay in 1721. See pages 179–180, ft. 5.

## To Cap.[t] Daniel Small and to the Commander for the time being of the Ship Duke of Cambridge.[166]

[181v] By the order of Encouragement in Charterparty mention'd in your Instructions which accompany this, you will see what care We have taken of your Men to excite their Courage in case of being Attackt by an Enemy. We have thought of something yet further while the Pyrates are so rife in India and may be where you are consign'd to, and it is this We now empower you in case you should find your self in danger of being Attackt by Europe Pyrates to promise your Ships Company a Gratuity of Three Chests of Our Treasure which may be hoisted up out of the Breadroom; and lye ready to be distributed as soon as the Engagement is over, and then We would have you divide the said Three Chests among the Officers and Ships Company in proportion to their several Wages as they are enter'd upon your Books, and as to your Self We will reward you at your return agreeable to your good Conduct & Courage. In case of any Persons kill'd their Shares are to be reserved by you for the benefit of their Familys here, which We will see distributed.

[182r] We leave the mannagement of this Order to your prudence We suppose you will not make the Promise till you apprehend the Pyrate is resolutely bent to Assault you. We are

Your Loving Friends
London 30.[th] Novem.[r] 1722. [...]

**166** Parallel orders were given to all three remaining captains.

# 2 Ship Hartford's Sea Journal from England to China

## Ship Hartfords Sea Journall from England tow.ds China Commencing October 1st Anno Dom: 1722

[...]

A Journal of our Intended Voyage by God's Permission in the Good Ship Hartford of London from England towards China commencing October 1:st 1722 kept by me Francis Nelly Commander

Att 4 PM Launched from the Dock:yard of M:r Abraham Wells[1] & Warpt Down to Deptford[2], and took in ye Bridle of the upper Moarings

From Wednesday the 2:d to Saturday. 12:th Variable Winds and Weather, have been Rigging the Ship

Sunday: the 13:th Rec:d on board 16½ Tunns of Iron Kentlidge from the Francis[3] Cap:t Newsham.[4] Winds Easterly fair Weather

Munday. 14:th to Tuesday 23:d Variable winds and Weather, Received on board 45 Tunns ½ of Iron Kentlidge from the Frances, Almost Compleated our Rigging

Wednesday. 24:th Foggy Weather. Received on board 25 Tuns of Ballast, and 578 Slåbbs of Lead and 67 Piggs[5] of D:o belonging to the Honourable United East India Company

Thursday. 25:th Received on board 25 Tunns of Ballast wch makes in all on board 100 Tunns, Likewise Rec:d Ten Tunns of Empty water butts[6], Wind SSW hazey Weather

Friday. 26:th to Sunday 28:th Dark Cloudy Weather with Intermitting Squalls, Wind in the SW Quarter, Rec.d on board 16 Tunns of Empty water Casks

---

1 Abraham Wells (ca. 1690–1752) was a shipwright and dock owner for the EIC.

2 Deptford is a town located just southeast of London on the Thames River. It served as the first Royal Navy dockyard from the sixteenth to nineteenth centuries. Many ships ultimately chartered by the EIC were built in this harbor and at nearby Blackwall. For help identifying the location of this and the next English locales, see J.W. Norie, *Sailing directions for the river Thames, from London, to the Nore and Sheerness* (London: J.W. Norie and Co., 1817).

3 The Frances, rated about 400 tons, housed between 78 to 84 crewmembers and 30 guns while active, from 1721 to 1733. In 1722, she had just completed her inaugural voyage to Canton and Bengal.

4 Thomas Newsham (dates unknown) was captain of the Frances during her first and second voyages, to Canton and Bengal (1720–1722, 1723–1725).

5 A pig, or ingot, is a piece of metal cast into a shape suitable for transport and trade. In the instance of iron, this usually was a rectangular bar, although the size and thus weight of each pig varied widely.

6 These were watertight wooden barrels. They could be refilled with freshwater supplies from several harbors on the way to Canton or filled with rainwater while at sea. Generally, eighteenth-century ships preferred to carry enough fresh water to provide between one-and-a-half and two pints for each crewmember and passenger daily.

## Ship Hartford at Depthford

October.

Munday 29:th Moderate Gales w:th fair Weather Rec.d on Board our Gun Carriages two Cables for best Bowers and one for Small Bower

Tuesday. 30:th Fair Weather, Moderate Gales in the SW Quarter Rec.d on board 15 Tunns Small beer for Sea Store, Mounted our upper deck Guns, pass'd by for Gravesend[7] the Ships Mountague and Duke of Cambridge

Wednesday: 31:st to Friday 2.d November. Small Gales in the SW Quarter, fair weather. Rec:d on board our Sails bent them, also our Anchors and bent our Cables, took in 11 Tuns of Water Casks

Saturday. 3:d Moderate in the NW Quarter. Came on board Willson[8] Pylott[9], cast of our bridles and rid by a hawser[10].

Sunday. 4:th Small breezes, thick hazey Weather, Att 2 PM Cast of from Depthford, and at 6 D:o anchored near Dagnam[11], Breach in 7 fa:

Munday: 5:th At 3 PM having a Small breeze at WNW Run downe to Greenhive[12], there Anchor'd in 10 fa: Att 6 AM Weighed, Att 9 Anchor'd at Gravesend and Moar'd Ship

Tuesday: 6:th Hard Gales of Wind with thick hazey Weather Struck yards and Topmasts, Bent our Small Bower Cable to our Sheat Anchor

Wedneday. 7:th Fair Weather wind in the SW Quarter Rec.d on board our provisions of Beef and Pork, and Spliced our best Bower Cables together

Thursday. 8:th to Sunday. 18:th Variable winds &Weather Rec:d on board Sundry Stores for the use of the Ship

Munday:19: to Munday. 26:th Dark Cloudy Weather with Rain, Nothing more Remarkable

Tuesday: 27:th to Friday. 30:th November. Variable Winds and Weather, Bent our Sails and gott up yards and Topmasts

7 Gravesend is located about 50 kilometers east of London, on the Thames River.

8 Person unknown.

9 Pilots were skilled seamen with intimate knowledge of local waters, who either themselves steered deep-riding vessels along difficult channels or navigated smaller vessels that directed or towed these ships. After the early 1600s, many pilots were appointed by local mayors or aldermen and needed an official certificate.

10 The Hartford, here, is being pulled to open water, rather than simply navigating a channel behind a pilot ship.

11 Dagenham is located about 15 kilometers east of London, on the Thames River.

12 Greenhithe is located about 30 kilometers east of London, on the Thames River.

## Ship Hartford at Gravesend 1722

December

Saturday. 1:st, Squally w:th Rain ye Wind W:terly

Sunday. 2:d Squally weather with Raine wind WSW Rec:d on board thirty Six Chests said to be treasure of w:ch Thirty two belongs to the Honourable United East India Company, the other private

Munday. 3:d to Thursday. 6.th Variable winds and Weather prepair for Sailing, the Duke of Cambridge Montague & Princess Ann Pass'd by for ye Hope[13], paid river pay

Friday. 7:th The most part Calm. Att 9 AM Weighed and at 11 D:o Anch.d in y:e Middle of Hope, Att 12 D:o weighed at the Same time Came on board Mess:rs Thomas Atkins Supracargoe & Sam:ll Skinner-Secretary for affairs the Honou. Company in China

Saturday. 8:th Fair Weather & Variable Winds, Att 1 PM Weighed and at 4 D:o Anc:d below y.e Hope, Att 8 D:o Weighed and at 10 Anch.d short of the Noar[14], Joyning Comp.y w:th y.e Duke of Cambridge Princess Anne and Montague. Att 9 AM, We all Weighed and at 5 P.M: Anch.d in 8 fa: the black beacon[15] bearing N½W and the Isle of Shippy[16] S:o Shearness[17] SW

Sunday: 9th Light Winds S:oerly fair Weather Still Continue at Anchor

Munday: 10:th The Wind SSW. Att 7 A:M: Weighed w:th the Ships of our Comp.y & run down to the Buoys, but our Pylote fearing there was not water enough. bore away for y:e Deeps and there Anchored in 7 fa: ye buoy of the Spaniard bea:rg SSW & Reculv:er[18] SSE

Tuesday the 11:th This Morning at 8: weighed in Compy w:th the Ships, Att 12 Anchored at Margett[19] in 11 fa: the N:o foreland SEBE Burginton[20] Church SW & Marg:tt Church SEBS.

Wedenesday: 12:th Fresh Gales of Wind, Att 4 AM: weighed and made the best of our way turning through the Gull Stream[21] for the Downes

---

**13** The Hope was a bend in the Thames River, located over 50 kilometers east of London. It now encompasses the portion of the river between Tilbury and Cliffe, or roughly from Gravesend to the Thames River estuary.

**14** The Nore is a sandbank in the Thames River estuary. The British Navy used it for anchorage.

**15** The "black beacon" and the "Spaniard" were buoys, marking out sandbars for ships travelling on the channel between the Nore and the Downs.

**16** The Isle of Sheppey is located 46 miles east of London, on the Thames River estuary.

**17** Shearness is a town located on the northwest coast of the Isle of Sheppey. It housed a commercial port and dockyards for the Royal Navy since the sixteenth century.

**18** Reculver is a coastal village, located east of the Isle of Sheppey.

**19** This refers to Margate, a seaside town located on the Isle of Thanet. It borders the Thames River estuary and the North Sea.

**20** This likely refers to Birchington-on-Sea, a coastal village located between Reculver and Margate.

**21** The Gull Stream is a current off the eastern coast of England and near Goodwin Sand, which allows passage from the North Sea to the English Channel.

Thursday: 13:th Fresh Gales of Wind at WSW. Att 1 PM Anch.d in the Downes in 7 fa: the S:o foreland SBW½W Walmer Castle[22] SW½S:o and Sand Down Castle[23] WNW, Moor'd Ship and Struck Yards and Topmasts

**In the Downs – 1722**

Friday: 14:th to Saturday: 15:th Mostly Close hazey Weather and fresh Gales W:terly, This day Came in the Duke of Cambridge Princess Ann and Mountague, Sent our Empty Casks for Beer and water, w:ch we received on board today

Sunday: 16:th to Wednesday: 19:th We have had fair Weather and Moderate Gales of Wind, till this night, then blowing very hard at W:t and SW: w.ch Occasion'd us to Veer away our best Bower to the Long Service we found in the Morning Severall Ships had Drove

Thursday: 20:th Att 2 this morn.g the Wind veered about to the WSW a Moderate Gale then hove in our best Bower Cable to ye Moaring Service

Friday. 21:st Moderate Weather Wind in the NW Quarter, Rec.d on board Water and Beer, as we do every day

Saturday. 22:d to Wednesday the 26:th Moderate gales between the NNW and W:t w:th fair Weather, Gott up Yards and Topmasts

Thursday: 27:th The former part the Wind at N:o and NNW, the latter Wind Easterly: Att 10 AM Unmoar'd Ship, Waiting for the Tyde to Weigh

22 Walmer Castle, built by Henry VIII between 1539 and 1540, is located on England's east coast near Deal.

23 Sandown Castle, built by Henry VIII in 1545, was located on the eastern side of the Isle of Wight. It was in ruins by 1723.

## Ship Hartford From England Tow:ds China 1722[/3]

| H | K | F[24] | Courses | Winds | Friday: 28:th December. |
|---|---|---|---|---|---|
| 1 | | | | ESE | Small Gales of Wind, the first and latter |
| 2 | | | | | Part, the other Moderate: at 2 P.M. |
| 3 | | | | | Weighed in. Company w:th the Duke |
| 4 | | | | | of Cambridge Daniel Small Princess |
| 5 | | | | | Ann Nich:s Luhorn Mountague John |
| 6 | | | | | Gordon Commanders, all bound for |
| 7 | | | | R.B.T.S.s | China Att 4 D:o the North foreland bore |
| 8 | | | | | NBE & Sandown Castle NW. Att 8 D:o |
| 9 | 6 | 3 | SWBW½W | SE | Dungeness[25] Light bore NBE distance |
| 10 | 6 | 4 | | | 3 Leagues. Course from d:o with the |
| 11 | 6 | 3 | | | bearings included make to be S:o50d West |
| 12 | 5 | 4 | | | Distance 70 miles Southing 45 miles |
| 1 | 5 | 2 | WSW½W | SSE | Westing 53 miles. |
| 2 | 5 | 3 | | | |
| 3 | 6 | 3 | | | |
| 4 | 5 | 3 | | | |
| 5 | 3 | 3 | | S:o | |
| 6 | 2 | 3 | WbS | SbW | |
| 7 | 2 | 3 | | | |
| 8 | 2 | 9 | | | |
| 9 | 2 | 9 | | | |
| 10 | 2 | 9 | | S:o O.R.B.T.S. | |
| 11 | 1 | 4 | | | |
| 12 | 2 | 2 | 64 Miles | | |
| 1 | 1 | 2 | WbS.o | SbE | Saturday: 29:th |
| 2 | 1 | 2 | | | Small Gales of wind the first part with |
| 3 | 1 | 5 | | SSE | fair Weather, the Latter fresh Gales and |
| 4 | 1 | 4 | | | Cloudy Weather Att Noon Saw Land |
| 5 | 3 | 4 | WNW | ESE | bearing NNE dis:t 8 Leagues |
| 6 | 4 | 4 | | | |
| 7 | 4 | 4 | | | |
| 8 | 3 | 4 | | | Course make to be (w:th regard to all |
| 9 | 3 | 4 | | | known Impediments) West Distances 110 |
| 10 | 2 | 4 | | | Miles |
| 11 | 3 | 4 | | | |
| 12 | 3 | 4 | WNW½W | SE | Southing from Dungeness 0d 45 Miles |
| 1 | 4 | 3 | | | Westing from d:o 3 43 d:o |
| 2 | 5 | 3 | | ESE | |
| 3 | 4 | 3 | | | |
| 4 | 5 | 3 | WBN | S:o | |
| 5 | 6 | 2 | W:t | | |
| 6 | 6 | 5 | | SSE | |
| 7 | 6 | 5 | | ESE | |
| 8 | 7 | 2 | | | |
| 9 | 7 | 2 | | S:o | |
| 10 | 6 | 3 | | | |
| 11 | 6 | 3 | | | |
| 12 | 6 | 1 | 103 Miles | | |

24 These columns commonly appear in eighteenth-century captain's logs. The "H" stood for each progressing hour, in a 24 hours day. The "K" recorded the ship's speed, evaluated in knots. The "F" indicated fathoms as fractions of knots when recording speed.

25 Dungeness is a coastal headland, located southeast of London and between Dover and Hastings.

| | | | | | |
|---|---|---|---|---|---|
| 1 | 6 | 4 | WBS.° | S:° | Sunday: 30: |
| 2 | 7 | 3 | | SBW | Fresh Gales of wind the first part, the |
| 3 | 7 | 3 | R.M.T.S. | SSE | latter Hard Gales with drizling rains |
| 4 | 4 | 2 | | | Handing and Reefing our Topsails as p$^{r}$ |
| 5 | 3 | 2 | R.F.T.S. | | Logg |
| 6 | 4 | 2 | | S:° | |
| 7 | 5 | 2 | | | Course make to be S:° 78$^{d}$ W:$^{t}$ Distance 97 |
| 8 | 5 | 3 | WSW | | Miles Southing 20 miles Westing 94 miles |
| 9 | 4 | 3 | | | |
| 10 | 3 | 3 | SWBW I:2:$^{d}$ | R.M.T.S:$^{e}$ SSW | Southing from Dungeness 1$^{d}$ 05$^{m}$ |
| 11 | 3 | 3 | WSW | S:° | Westing from D:° 4 17 |
| 12 | 3 | 3 | WBSo In: | 2.$^{d}$ R.F:T.S$^{l}$ SbW | |
| 1 | 5 | 3 | | | |
| 2 | 5 | 3 | | | |
| 3 | 4 | 3 | | Squalls | |
| 4 | 5 | 3 | | Rain | |
| 5 | 2 | 3 | | | |
| 6 | 2 | 3 | WSW | S° | |
| 7 | 2 | 6 | | H:$^{d}$ F.T.S:$^{l}$ | |
| 8 | 2 | 5 | | | |
| 9 | 3 | 5 | | | |
| 10 | 2 | 5 | SWBW | SBE | |
| 11 | 2 | 5 | | | |
| 12 | 3 | 4 | 98 Miles | | |
| H | K | F | Courses | Winds | Monday: 31: December 1722 |
| 1 | 3 | ” | WSW | S.° Sq$^{ly}$ Rain | Hard Gales the first part with Cloudy |
| 2 | 4 | ” | | | Weather and drizling Rains, The latter |
| 3 | 3 | ” | | H.M.T.S. Wore | moderate gales. |
| 4 | 3 | ” | ESE | Sqly Rain | |
| 5 | 3 | ” | | | |
| 6 | 3 | ” | | D.° | |
| 7 | 2 | 3 | | | |
| 8 | 2 | 5 | EBS.° | SBE | |
| 9 | 3 | ” | | | |
| 10 | 3 | ” | | | Course make to be N:° 66$^{d}$ E:$^{t}$ Distance 19 |
| 11 | 3 | ” | ESE | S.° | Miles Northing 7 miles Easting 17 miles |
| 12 | 2 | ” | | | |
| 1 | 2 | ” | | | |
| 2 | 2 | ” | | | Southing from Dungeness 0$^{d}$ 58$^{m}$ |
| 3 | 2 | ” | | | Westing from Do 4 00 |
| 4 | 2 | 3 | | | |
| 5 | 1 | 2 | | | |
| 6 | 1 | 2 | | | |
| 7 | 1 | ” | EBS.° | SBE Set MTS | |
| 8 | 1 | ” | | Set F.T.S. TK$^{t}$ | |
| 9 | 2 | ” | WSW½S.° | O:$^{t}$ 2.$^{d}$ R.B.T.S. | Sett up Topmasts Shrouds and Backstays |
| 10 | 2 | ” | | | |
| 11 | 3 | ” | | SSE O:$^{t}$1:$^{st}$ R D.° | |
| 12 | 3 | 6 | 59 Miles | | |

| | | | | | |
|---|---|---|---|---|---|
| 1 | 3 | 2 | WSW | SBE Squaly | Tuesday: 1: January |
| 2 | 2 | „ | | | Fresh Gales of wind with drizling rains in |
| 3 | 2 | 2 | | | the night |
| 4 | 5 | 4 | | | |
| 5 | 4 | 5 | | | Att 9 AM Carried away our Topmast, |
| 6 | 3 | 1 | | | Stript the Rigging and gott him upon deck |
| 7 | 7 | „ | SWBW | | |
| 8 | 6 | 4 | | | Course make to be S:° 58$^{d}$ West Distance |
| 9 | 4 | 2 | | | 111 Miles Southing 58 miles Westing 93 |
| 10 | 5 | 3 | | | miles |
| 11 | 9 | 2 | | | |
| 12 | 5 | „ | | | Southing from Dungeness 1$^{d}$ 56$^{m}$ |
| 1 | 3 | 4 | WSW½S.° | SSE | Westing from D.° 5 33 |
| 2 | 5 | „ | | | |
| 3 | 4 | „ | | | Stowed our Longboat |
| 4 | 5 | 4 | | | |
| 5 | 3 | „ | | | |
| 6 | 6 | 5 | | | By my Acc:$^{t}$ from Dungeness (this day |
| 7 | 9 | „ | | | noon) I take the Lizard[26] to bear N:° 50 E:$^{t}$ |
| 8 | 7 | „ | | | dis:$^{t}$ 96 miles |
| 9 | 5 | 1 | WBS:° | | |
| 10 | 3 | 4 | | | |
| 11 | 5 | 2 | | | |
| 12 | 6 | 4 | 111 Miles | | |
| 1 | 5 | 3 | WSW | SBE | Wednesday: 2:$^{d}$ |
| 2 | 5 | 3 | | | Fresh Gales of wind with fair weather |
| 3 | 3 | „ | W½S.° | | Gott up another, and at 8 A:M: broke our |
| 4 | 5 | 6 | W.$^{t}$ | | Cross=jack=yard. |
| 5 | 5 | 5 | WSW | | |
| 6 | 6 | 5 | | | Course w:$^{th}$ yesterdays bearings from the |
| 7 | 5 | 4 | WBS.°½S:° | | Liz.$^{d}$ make to be S:° 54 West Distance 244 |
| 8 | 5 | 5 | | | Miles Southing 144 miles Westing 196 |
| 9 | 5 | 5 | | | miles Difference of Longitude 296 Miles |
| 10 | 6 | 5 | WSW | | |
| 11 | 6 | 4 | | | |
| 12 | 6 | 1 | | | Lat:$^{d}$ Observed 47$^{d}$ 40$^{m}$ N:° |
| 1 | 5 | „ | | | Meridian Distance 9 16 W:$^{t}$ |
| 2 | 5 | 9 | | | Difference of Longitude 4 56 W:$^{t}$ |
| 3 | 5 | „ | | | Variation allowed 9 30 W:$^{t}$ |
| 4 | 5 | 9 | | 2:$^{d}$ R.M.T.S:$^{l}$ | |
| 5 | 7 | „ | | | |
| 6 | 7 | „ | | SSE | |
| 7 | 6 | 5 | | | |
| 8 | 8 | „ | | | |
| 9 | 7 | „ | SWBW | | |
| 10 | 7 | „ | WSW | | |
| 11 | 7 | 1 | | | |
| 12 | 7 | 1 | 147 Miles | | |

26 The Lizard is a peninsula, located off the coast of Cornwall in southwestern England. It was infamous for shipwrecks.

| H | K | F | Courses | Winds | Thursday: 3: January |
|---|---|---|---|---|---|
| 1 | 7 | 4 | SWBW | SSE | Fresh Gales of wind with fair weather |
| 2 | 7 | 4 | WSW | | |
| 3 | 7 | 6 | | | Course make to be S:° 50$^{d}$ W:$^{t}$ Dis:$^{t}$ 159 |
| 4 | 8 | „ | | SE | Miles Southing 98$^{m}$ Westing 122.$^{m}$ |
| 5 | 7 | 9 | | | Difference of Longitude 180 Miles |
| 6 | 8 | „ | SWBW | | |
| 7 | 8 | „ | | | Lat:$^{d}$ Observ'd 46$^{d}$ 02$^{m}$ N.° |
| 8 | 7 | 2 | | H:$^{d}$ M:T:S:$^{l}$ | Meridian Distance 5 18 W:$^{t}$ |
| 9 | 6 | „ | | | Difference Longitude 7 56 W:$^{t}$ |
| 10 | 7 | „ | | | Variation allowed 9 00 W:$^{t}$ |
| 11 | 7 | 3 | | Set D° | |
| 12 | 6 | „ | | | |
| 1 | 7 | 2 | | | |
| 2 | 7 | 2 | | | Setup Standing Rigging and Topmast |
| 3 | 6 | 6 | | | Shrouds and Backstags |
| 4 | 7 | „ | | | |
| 5 | 6 | 3 | | | |
| 6 | 6 | 4 | SW½W | | |
| 7 | 5 | 3 | | | |
| 8 | 5 | 3 | | | |
| 9 | 5 | „ | SW½S:° | | |
| 10 | 5 | „ | | | |
| 11 | 4 | 3 | | | |
| 12 | 4 | 1 | 159 Miles | | |
| 1 | 6 | „ | SW½S | SE | Friday: 4:$^{th}$ |
| 2 | 5 | 5 | | | Fresh gales of wind the first part, the |
| 3 | 5 | 2 | | | Latter Small gales with fair weather |
| 4 | 4 | 3 | | O:$^{t}$ 2:$^{d}$ R.B.T.S:$^{l}$ | |
| 5 | 5 | 2 | SWBS:° | | P:$^{r}$ Observation am to the S:° w:$^{d}$ of the |
| 6 | 5 | 1 | | | Log. the Error Impute to Course and |
| 7 | 5 | 2 | | | Distances |
| 8 | 5 | 1 | | | |
| 9 | 4 | „ | | | Course make to be S:° 22 West Distance |
| 10 | 5 | „ | | | 106:$^{m}$ Southing 98$^{m}$ Westing 40$^{m}$ |
| 11 | 4 | 5 | | SEBE | Difference of Longitude 57 Miles |
| 12 | 4 | 2 | | | |
| 1 | 5 | „ | | | Lat:$^{d}$ Observ'd 44$^{d}$ 24$^{m}$ N.° |
| 2 | 4 | 3 | | | Meridian Distance 5 58 W:$^{t}$ |
| 3 | 3 | „ | | | Difference Longitude 8 53 d:° |
| 4 | 2 | 4 | | | Variation allowed 8 30 d:° |
| 5 | 2 | 6 | | | |
| 6 | 2 | 9 | | O:$^{t}$ A: Reefes | |
| 7 | 2 | „ | | | |
| 8 | 1 | 4 | | | |
| 9 | 1 | 4 | | SBW | |
| 10 | 2 | 2 | | SSW | |
| 11 | 2 | „ | | | |
| 12 | 2 | „ | Dis:$^{t}$ 93Miles | | |

| | | | | | |
|---|---|---|---|---|---|
| 1 | 2 | 3 | SWBS.° | SEBE | Saturday: 5:$^{th}$ |
| 2 | 2 | 2 | | | Small gales of wind the first part, the |
| 3 | 1 | 5 | | | latter moderate w:$^{th}$ fair Weather. |
| 4 | 2 | ” | | EBS.° | |
| 5 | 2 | 3 | | | Course make to be S:° 27$^{d}$ West Distance |
| 6 | 2 | 3 | | | 110 Miles, Southing 98:$^{m}$ Westing 50 |
| 7 | 3 | 5 | | SEBE | miles difference of Longitude 68 miles |
| 8 | 4 | 3 | | | |
| 9 | 3 | ” | | | Lat:$^{d}$ Observ'd 42$^{d}$ 46$^{m}$ N:° |
| 10 | 4 | ” | | SE | Meridian Distance 6 48 W:$^{t}$ |
| 11 | 4 | ” | | | Difference of Longit$^{d}$ 10 01 d:° |
| 12 | 3 | 3 | | | Variation allowed 8 00 d:° |
| 1 | 3 | 3 | | | |
| 2 | 3 | 5 | | ESE | |
| 3 | 5 | 4 | | | |
| 4 | 6 | 2 | | | |
| 5 | 6 | 2 | | | |
| 6 | 6 | ” | | | |
| 7 | 6 | 6 | | | |
| 8 | 6 | 6 | | | |
| 9 | 6 | 1 | SSW | | |
| 10 | 6 | ” | | | |
| 11 | 6 | ” | | SEBE | |
| 12 | 6 | ” | 105 Miles | | |
| H | K | F | Courses | Winds | Sunday: 6: January |
| 1 | 4 | 6 | SSW | SE | Moderate gales of wind the first part, |
| 2 | 5 | ” | | | the latter Small, with Some Rain in the |
| 3 | 5 | 2 | | | morning |
| 4 | 5 | ” | | | |
| 5 | 6 | ” | | ESE | Course make to be South 23$^{d}$ West dis- |
| 6 | 5 | 4 | | SE | tance 76 Miles Westing 30 miles Southing |
| 7 | 7 | ” | | | 69 miles difference of Longitude 40 miles |
| 8 | 7 | ” | | | |
| 9 | 6 | 2 | SSW½W | 1:$^{st}$ R.B.T.S. | Lat:$^{d}$ Observ'd 41$^{d}$ 47$^{m}$ N:° |
| 10 | 5 | ” | | | Meridian Distance 7 08 W:$^{t}$ |
| 11 | 4 | 4 | SSW | | Difference Longitude 10 41 d:° |
| 12 | 5 | ” | | | Variation allowed 8 00 d:° |
| 1 | 5 | 3 | SWBS:° | SEBS.° | |
| 2 | 5 | 3 | | | |
| 3 | 4 | 3 | | | |
| 4 | 4 | ” | | Sq&R.$^{n}$ | |
| 5 | 4 | 3 | NW | WSW | |
| 6 | 2 | 2 | NNW | W$^{t}$ | |
| 7 | 1 | 3 | | TK.$^{t}$ | |
| 8 | 1 | 3 | SEBE | SBW | |
| 9 | 2 | 3 | | | |
| 10 | 2 | ” | | | |
| 11 | 2 | ” | EBS.° | SBE | |
| 12 | 2 | 1 | 104 Miles | | |

| | | | | | |
|---|---|---|---|---|---|
| 1 | 2 | 4 | SEBE | SBW | Monday 7:$^{th}$ |
| 2 | 2 | 4 | SEBE½E | | Small gales the first part, the latter fresh |
| 3 | 2 | 2 | SEBE | Wore | with Squalls and Rain |
| 4 | 1 | 5 | WSW | S.º | |
| 5 | " | 3 | | | Course make to be S:º 9$^{d}$ W:$^{t}$ Distance 69 |
| 6 | 1 | " | | | Miles Southing 67 miles Westing 10 miles |
| 7 | 1 | 3 | SSW½W | SEBE | difference of Longitude 12 miles |
| 8 | 2 | 3 | SSW | | |
| 9 | 2 | " | | | Lat:$^{d}$ Account 40$^{d}$ 30$^{m}$ N.º |
| 10 | 1 | " | | | Meridian Distance 7 08 W.$^{t}$ |
| 11 | 2 | 3 | | SE | Difference of Longit:$^{d}$ 10 53 d:º |
| 12 | 1 | " | | | Variation allowed 8 00 d:º |
| 1 | 1 | " | S:º | ESE | |
| 2 | 1 | " | | | |
| 3 | 1 | 3 | | | |
| 4 | 2 | " | SBW | NNE | Sett up Topmast Shrouds and backstays |
| 5 | 3 | 3 | SSW | WNW | |
| 6 | 6 | 3 | | N.º Rain | |
| 7 | 7 | 3 | | NNE D.º | |
| 8 | 8 | " | | D.º | |
| 9 | 8 | 3 | | NBW D.º | |
| 10 | 7 | " | In 2.$^{d}$ R.F. | T.S. NBWN.º | |
| 11 | 8 | " | | | |
| 12 | 8 | " | In 2.$^{d}$ R. | M:TS 83$^{Ms}$ | |
| 1 | 9 | " | SSW | NWBN | Tuesday: 8:$^{th}$: |
| 2 | 6 | 5 | | Sq.$^{ll}$ w:$^{th}$ R.$^{n}$ | Fresh gales of wind with Continuall Sq:$^{lls}$ |
| 3 | 9 | " | | | and Rain |
| 4 | 9 | " | | | |
| 5 | 9 | 2 | SSW½W | d.º d:º | Course make to be S:º 13:$^{d}$ West Dis:$^{t}$ 170 |
| 6 | 9 | 4 | | d.º d:º | miles Southing 165 miles Westing 38 |
| 7 | 7 | " | | | miles Difference of Longitude 49 miles |
| 8 | 8 | 3 | SSW | Squaly | |
| 9 | 8 | " | | WNW | Lat:$^{d}$ Account 37$^{d}$ 45$^{m}$ N:º |
| 10 | 8 | 4 | | | Meridian Distance 8 56 W.$^{t}$ |
| 11 | 8 | " | | | Difference of Longit$^{d}$ 11 42 d:º |
| 12 | 6 | 3 | | | Variation allowed 7 30 d:º |
| 1 | 7 | " | | | |
| 2 | 7 | 3 | | | |
| 3 | 7 | 3 | | | |
| 4 | 7 | 5 | | | |
| 5 | 7 | 2 | | | Setup Topmast Shrouds and Backstays |
| 6 | 7 | " | | | |
| 7 | 7 | " | | | |
| 8 | 6 | 4 | | | |
| 9 | 6 | 4 | | WBN.º | |
| 10 | 5 | " | SBW | WBS.º | |
| 11 | 4 | " | SBE | SWBW | |
| 12 | 4 | " | 178 Miles | | |

| H | K | F | Courses | Winds | Wednesday: 9.$^{th}$ January |
|---|---|---|---|---|---|
| 1 | 5 | 3 | ESE | S.$^{o}$ | Fresh Gales of Wind with fair |
| 2 | 4 | 2 | | Wore | Weather |
| 3 | 5 | " | SW | SSE | |
| 4 | 7 | 2 | SWBS:$^{o}$ | SE | p:$^{r}$ Observation the Ships has not gone So |
| 5 | 6 | " | Out all | Reefes NEBE | far to the S:$^{o}$ ward as the Log gives p$^{r}$ 44 |
| 6 | 6 | " | | | Miles the Error Impute to the Distance |
| 7 | 7 | 6 | SSW | | |
| 8 | 6 | 2 | SWBS.$^{o}$ | | Course with regard to Impediments |
| 9 | 7 | " | | | known is S:$^{o}$ 26$^{d}$ West Distance 93 Miles |
| 10 | 6 | 3 | | NEBN | Southing 83$^{m}$ Westing 41$^{m}$ Difference of |
| 11 | 7 | " | | | Long.$^{d}$ 51 Miles |
| 12 | 7 | " | | | |
| 1 | 7 | 1 | | | Lat:$^{d}$ Observ'd 36$^{d}$ 22$^{m}$ N.$^{o}$ |
| 2 | 6 | " | | NNE | Meridian Distance 9 37 W:$^{t}$ |
| 3 | 6 | 2 | | | Difference of Longit$^{d}$ 12 32 W.$^{t}$ |
| 4 | 6 | 1 | | Sm:$^{ll}$ raine | |
| 5 | 6 | 3 | | | |
| 6 | 6 | 4 | | | |
| 7 | 7 | " | | | |
| 8 | 7 | " | | | |
| 9 | 7 | 3 | | | |
| 10 | 6 | " | | | |
| 11 | 7 | 2 | | | |
| 12 | 7 | 1 | 156 Miles | | |
| 1 | 7 | 4 | SWBS.$^{o}$ | NNE | Thursday: 10:$^{th}$ |
| 2 | 7 | 4 | | | Fair weather w:$^{th}$ fresh Gales of wind |
| 3 | 7 | 3 | | | the first part: the latter Small |
| 4 | 7 | " | | | |
| 5 | 7 | 2 | | | A Difference between the Log & observa: |
| 6 | 7 | 2 | | | 15 miles; The Error Impute to y$^{e}$ Distance |
| 7 | 7 | 2 | | | |
| 8 | 6 | 4 | | | Course allowed to be S:$^{o}$ 26 W:$^{t}$ Distance |
| 9 | 5 | 5 | | | 116 Miles |
| 10 | 5 | 3 | | | |
| 11 | 5 | 4 | | | Lat:$^{d}$ Observ'd 34$^{d}$ 37$^{m}$ North |
| 12 | 6 | " | | | Meridian Distance 10 27 West |
| 1 | 4 | 3 | | | Difference of Longit$^{d}$ 13 34 W:$^{t}$ |
| 2 | 4 | 4 | | | |
| 3 | 5 | " | | | |
| 4 | 5 | " | | | |
| 5 | 5 | 2 | | | |
| 6 | 5 | " | | NBW | |
| 7 | 4 | 3 | | | |
| 8 | 4 | 4 | | | |
| 9 | 4 | 4 | | | |
| 10 | 4 | 3 | | | |
| 11 | 3 | " | | | |
| 12 | 3 | 1 | 134 Miles | | |

| | | | | | |
|---|---|---|---|---|---|
| 1 | 3 | 2 | SWbS | NBE | Friday: 11:$^{th}$ |
| 2 | 3 | ” | | | Small gales of wind, fair weather |
| 3 | 2 | 5 | | | and a Western Swell |
| 4 | 1 | ” | | | |
| 5 | 1 | ” | | | Att 8 this morning Saw Land bearing SSE |
| 6 | ” | 3 | | | 20 Leagues distant, which Land Judge to |
| 7 | 1 | ” | | | be the Island Madera[27] |
| 8 | 1 | 2 | SSW | | |
| 9 | ” | 4 | | | Course make to be South 27$^{d}$ West Dist |
| 10 | ” | 5 | | | 58 Miles, Southing 51 miles Westing 26 |
| 11 | 1 | ” | | | miles Difference of Long:$^{d}$ 32 miles |
| 12 | 1 | ” | | | |
| 1 | 1 | ” | | | Lat:$^{d}$ Observ'd 33$^{d}$ 46$^{m}$ N:$^{o}$ |
| 2 | ” | ” | | | Meridian Distance 10 53 W:$^{t}$ |
| 3 | ” | ” | | | Difference of Long:$^{d}$ 14 06 W.$^{t}$ |
| 4 | ” | ” | Calm | | |
| 5 | ” | ” | | | |
| 6 | ” | ” | | | |
| 7 | 2 | ” | SW½W | SSE | |
| 8 | 2 | ” | Land SSE 20 | Leagues | |
| 9 | 2 | ” | WSW | | |
| 10 | 3 | ” | WBN | SWBS$^{o}$ | |
| 11 | | | up WBS.$^{o}$ of | WNW SBW | |
| 12 | ” | ” | 27 Miles | | |
| H | K | F | Courses | Winds | Saturday: 12:$^{th}$ January |
| 1 | 5 | ” | WBN | SWBS.$^{o}$ | Fresh Gales of wind with abundance of |
| 2 | 6 | ” | | | Rain attended with Lightning |
| 3 | 4 | 3 | W:$^{t}$ In 1$^{st}$ | R.B.T.S. SSW | |
| 4 | 5 | ” | | | Hand reeft and Set Sails as p$^{r}$ Log: Saw a |
| 5 | 3 | ” | WBN | SWBS.$^{o}$ | Saile this morning bearing NWBW |
| 6 | 3 | ” | W½S.$^{o}$ | SBW | |
| 7 | 3 | ” | WBS:$^{o}$ | | Course I allow to be N:$^{o}$ 60$^{d}$ West Distance |
| 8 | 3 | 3 | In: 2:$^{d}$ | R.B.T.S. | 60 Miles |
| 9 | 4 | ” | | | |
| 10 | 3 | ” | WSW | S.$^{o}$ | Lat:$^{d}$ p:$^{r}$ Account 34$^{d}$ 16 N:$^{o}$ |
| 11 | 3 | 2 | | | Meridian Distance 11 45 W:$^{t}$ |
| 12 | 3 | 2 | SWBW | H:$^{d}$ F.T.S. | Difference of Long:$^{d}$ 15 09 W:$^{t}$ |
| 1 | 2 | ” | W½S.$^{o}$ | SbW H.$^{d}$ MT.S. | |
| 2 | 2 | ” | | | |
| 3 | 1 | 3 | WBN | SWBS:$^{o}$ Rain | |
| 4 | 1 | ” | Lightning at | SW | |
| 5 | 1 | 6 | West | SSW | |
| 6 | 2 | 5 | WNW | SW Light:$^{g}$ | |
| 7 | 2 | 4 | WBN.$^{o}$ Set | MT.S. SWBS.$^{o}$ | |
| 8 | 1 | ” | | | |
| 9 | 1 | ” | WNW | SW | |
| 10 | 1 | 3 | W.$^{t}$ | SSW | |
| 11 | 1 | 4 | WBS.$^{o}$ | SBW | |
| 12 | 2 | ” | 67 Miles | Small Rain | |

27 Madeira is an island located in the northern Atlantic Ocean, slightly southwest of Portugal. It was discovered by the Portuguese in 1418 and employed in largescale sugar, then wine, cultivation in the 1700s. EIC ships did not regularly stop at Madeira on outward voyages but sailed to its west. See David Hanock, *Oceans of Wine: Madeira and the Emergence of American Trade and Taste* (New Haven: Yale UP, 2009).

| | | | | | |
|---|---|---|---|---|---|
| 1 | 2 | ” | WBS.$^{o}$ | SBW Sq$^{l}$&R.$^{n}$ | Sunday: 13:$^{th}$ |
| 2 | 2 | ” | | | Fresh gales of wind with Intermitting |
| 3 | 1 | 5 | WBN | SWBS.$^{o}$ | Squalls. |
| 4 | 1 | 4 | a Sail | bearing NNW | |
| 5 | 1 | 3 | WBS.$^{o}$ | SBW | Att 8 this morning found our Maintop- |
| 6 | 1 | ” | West | SSW | mast Sprung[28] a little above y$^{e}$ Capp |
| 7 | 1 | 2 | | Sq:$^{l}$&R.$^{n}$ | unrigg'd it and gott it down |
| 8 | 1 | ” | | | |
| 9 | 2 | 3 | Set F.T.S. | Small D:$^{o}$ | Course make to be S:$^{o}$ 67$^{d}$ W:$^{t}$ Distance |
| 10 | 1 | 3 | | | 46 Miles |
| 11 | ” | 4 | WBN | SWBS$^{o}$ D:$^{o}$ | |
| 12 | 1 | ” | | | Lat:$^{d}$ p:$^{r}$ Account 34$^{d}$ 00$^{m}$ N.$^{o}$ |
| 1 | 1 | ” | WSW | S:$^{o}$ | Meridian Distance 12 27 W:$^{t}$ |
| 2 | 1 | 2 | | | Difference of Longitude 15 54 W:$^{t}$ |
| 3 | 1 | 4 | SWBW | SBE | |
| 4 | ” | 3 | SWBS.$^{o}$ | SEBS:$^{o}$ | |
| 5 | 2 | ” | | | |
| 6 | 3 | ” | SW:$^{t}$ | SSE | |
| 7 | 4 | ” | Out 2:$^{d}$ | R.B.T.S.$^{l}$ | |
| 8 | 3 | ” | | | |
| 9 | 4 | 3 | SW½S.$^{o}$ | | |
| 10 | 4 | 2 | | | |
| 11 | 4 | ” | SWBS.$^{o}$ | SEBE | |
| 12 | 3 | 4 | 50 Miles | | |
| 1 | 2 | 5 | SSW½W | SE Squaly | Monday: 14:$^{th}$ |
| 2 | 3 | ” | | Rain | Fresh Gales of wind with Squalls of Wind |
| 3 | 4 | ” | | Set M.T.S. | and Rain |
| 4 | 4 | 5 | | | |
| 5 | 5 | ” | SW½S:$^{o}$ | | Att 1 P.M: Gott up a New Maintopmast |
| 6 | 5 | 4 | | In 3:$^{d}$ R.M.T.S. | and at 3 D:$^{o}$ Set Maintopsaile |
| 7 | 5 | ” | SSW | SEBE | |
| 8 | 5 | ” | | | Course Judge S:$^{o}$ 33$^{d}$ W:$^{t}$ Dis:$^{t}$ 110 Miles |
| 9 | 5 | ” | | | |
| 10 | 5 | ” | | | Lat:$^{d}$ p:$^{r}$ Account 32$^{d}$ 26$^{m}$ N.$^{o}$ |
| 11 | 4 | 6 | SBW | | Meridian Distance 13 27 W:$^{t}$ |
| 12 | 5 | ” | | | Difference of Longitude 17 06 W:$^{t}$ |
| 1 | 4 | ” | | | |
| 2 | 5 | ” | | | |
| 3 | 5 | ” | | | |
| 4 | 5 | 2 | | | |
| 5 | 5 | ” | | | Bore away this Morning and Sett up |
| 6 | 5 | ” | | | Shrouds and backstays |
| 7 | 5 | 9 | S:$^{o}$ | ESE | |
| 8 | 5 | 4 | | | |
| 9 | 5 | ” | | EBS H:$^{d}$ F.T.S. | |
| 10 | 2 | ” | bore away | W.$^{t}$ | |
| 11 | 4 | 2 | Set F.T.S. | and out 3:$^{d}$ | R.MT.S. |
| 12 | 5 | 4 | 114 Miles | | |

**28** This means that the topmast cracked, typically due to problems with the rigging. This compromised the mast's integrity and increased the likelihood that it would fall in severe weather.

| H | K | F | Courses | Winds | Tuesday: 15:$^{th}$ Janunary 1723 |
|---|---|---|---|---|---|
| 1 | 6 | 4 | SBE | EBS:° | Fresh Gales with Cloudy Weather. |
| 2 | 7 | " | SBW | | |
| 3 | 7 | 4 | | ESE | Course made good is S:° 15$^{d}$ W:$^{t}$ Distance |
| 4 | 7 | 3 | | | 150 Miles Southing 144 miles Westing 38 |
| 5 | 7 | " | | | miles Difference of Longit.$^{d}$ 44 miles |
| 6 | 6 | 3 | SBW½W | | |
| 7 | 7 | " | | | |
| 8 | 6 | " | SBW | | Lat:$^{d}$ p:$^{r}$ Account 29$^{d}$ 56$^{m}$ North |
| 9 | 6 | 4 | S:° | | Meridian Distance 14 05 W:$^{t}$ |
| 10 | 5 | " | | | Difference of Longit.$^{d}$ 17 50 W:$^{t}$ |
| 11 | 5 | " | | | |
| 12 | 5 | 3 | SBW | SEBE | |
| 1 | 5 | 1 | SBW½W | | |
| 2 | 5 | " | SBW | | |
| 3 | 5 | 3 | | | |
| 4 | 6 | 3 | S:° | EBS:° | |
| 5 | 6 | " | | | |
| 6 | 6 | 3 | | East | |
| 7 | 7 | " | | | |
| 8 | 7 | 3 | | | |
| 9 | 7 | 5 | | | |
| 10 | 8 | " | | EBS:° | |
| 11 | 7 | 3 | | | |
| 12 | 7 | " | S½W | 156 Miles | |
| 1 | 6 | 4 | S.° | EBS.° | Wednesday: 16:$^{th}$ |
| 2 | 6 | 2 | | | Fresh gales of Wind Cloudy Weather and |
| 3 | 5 | " | | | Intermitting Squalls |
| 4 | 5 | " | | | |
| 5 | 6 | " | | | Course all known Impedim:$^{ts}$ Allowed |
| 6 | 6 | " | | | is South 13:$^{d}$ West Distance 146 Miles |
| 7 | 6 | 4 | | | S:°ing 142 miles Westing 32$^{m}$ diff Long:$^{d}$ |
| 8 | 7 | 3 | | | 37 miles |
| 9 | 7 | " | | | |
| 10 | 7 | " | | | Lat:$^{d}$ Observed 27$^{d}$ 34$^{m}$ N:° |
| 11 | 6 | 5 | | | Meridian Distance 14 37 W:$^{t}$ |
| 12 | 6 | 4 | SBW½W | ESE | Difference of Long:$^{d}$ 18 17 W:$^{t}$ |
| 1 | 4 | 4 | | | |
| 2 | 5 | 3 | | | |
| 3 | 6 | 3 | | | |
| 4 | 5 | " | | | |
| 5 | 5 | 5 | SBW | | |
| 6 | 7 | " | SWBS:° | SEBE | |
| 7 | 8 | " | | | |
| 8 | 6 | 5 | | | |
| 9 | 5 | " | | | |
| 10 | 4 | " | SSW | ESE | |
| 11 | 5 | " | | | |
| 12 | 5 | " | 144 Miles | | |

| | | | | | |
|---|---|---|---|---|---|
| 1 | 6 | 4 | SSW | EBS.° | Thursday: 17:$^{th}$ |
| 2 | 6 | 2 | | | Fresh Gales of wind with Squalls |
| 3 | 5 | ” | SWBS:° | | |
| 4 | 5 | ” | In 3:$^{d}$ R.F. | T.S. SE | Course make to be S:° 32$^{d}$ West Distance |
| 5 | 6 | ” | | | 100 Miles Southing 85 miles Westing 53 |
| 6 | 6 | ” | SSW In 3.$^{d}$ | R.M.T.S. | miles Difference of Longit.$^{d}$ 59 miles |
| 7 | 6 | 4 | | | |
| 8 | 7 | 3 | | H.$^{d}$ F.T.S. | Lat:$^{d}$ Observe'd 26$^{d}$ 09$^{m}$ N:° |
| 9 | 7 | ” | | | Meridian Distance 15 30 W:$^{t}$ |
| 10 | 7 | ” | | Set D.° | Difference of Long:$^{d}$ 19 26 W:$^{t}$ |
| 11 | 6 | 5 | | | |
| 12 | 6 | 4 | | | |
| 1 | 4 | 4 | | | |
| 2 | 5 | 3 | | | |
| 3 | 6 | 3 | | | |
| 4 | 5 | ” | | | |
| 5 | 5 | 5 | | | |
| 6 | 7 | ” | | | |
| 7 | 8 | ” | | H.$^{d}$ F.T.S. | |
| 8 | 6 | 5 | | | |
| 9 | 5 | ” | SWBS.° | | |
| 10 | 4 | ” | | | |
| 11 | 5 | ” | | Set D:° | |
| 12 | 5 | ” | 100 Miles | | |
| H | K | F | Courses | Winds | Friday: 18:$^{th}$ January |
| 1 | 3 | ” | SWBS:° | SEBS:° | Small Gales of wind with Thunder Light- |
| 2 | 3 | ” | | Out 3.$^{d}$ R.F.T.S. | ning and Rain in the Night |
| 3 | 3 | 4 | | | |
| 4 | 5 | ” | | | Course Judge to be S:° 43$^{d}$ W:$^{t}$ Distance 66 |
| 5 | 2 | ” | WBS:° | SBW Th:$^{d}$& Lig:$^{t}$ | Miles Southing 48 miles Westing 45 miles |
| 6 | 3 | 3 | | | Difference of Long:$^{d}$ 51 miles |
| 7 | 2 | 5 | SW | SSE D.° D.° | |
| 8 | 2 | 5 | | | Lat:$^{d}$ Observ'd 25$^{d}$ 21$^{m}$ N:° |
| 9 | 3 | ” | SWBS.° | SEBS:° | Meridian Distance 15 15 W:$^{t}$ |
| 10 | 2 | ” | | D:° D.° | Difference of Long:$^{d}$ 20 17 W:$^{t}$ |
| 11 | 2 | ” | | | |
| 12 | 1 | 3 | SW | SSE | |
| 1 | 2 | ” | SWBS:° | SEBS:° | |
| 2 | 1 | 3 | | | |
| 3 | 1 | ” | Lightning to | the N:°ward | |
| 4 | 2 | 3 | | | |
| 5 | 3 | ” | SSW | SE | |
| 6 | 2 | 3 | | | |
| 7 | 2 | 2 | | Out all Reefs | |
| 8 | 2 | 5 | SWBS:° | SEBS:° | |
| 9 | 2 | ” | | | |
| 10 | 1 | 4 | | | |
| 11 | 1 | ” | SWBW | SBE | |
| 12 | 1 | ” | 57 Miles | | |

| | | | | | |
|---|---|---|---|---|---|
| 1 | 1 | 3 | SW | SSE | Saturday: 19.th |
| 2 | 1 | " | SWBW | SBE | Small Airs with Calms |
| 3 | 1 | 2 | bore away | | |
| 4 | 1 | 4 | WBN | SBW | Course make to be S:o 50d W:t Distance 10 Miles Southing 6 miles Westing 8 miles Difference of Long.d 9 miles |
| 5 | " | " | Calm | | |
| 6 | " | " | | | |
| 7 | " | " | | | |
| 8 | " | " | | | |
| 9 | " | 4 | EBS:o | SBE | Lat:d Observ'd 25d 15m N.o |
| 10 | " | 3 | | | Meridian Distance 16 23 W:t |
| 11 | " | " | | | Difference of Long:d 20 26 W:t |
| 12 | " | " | Calm | | |
| 1 | " | " | | | |
| 2 | " | " | | | |
| 3 | " | " | | | |
| 4 | " | " | | | |
| 5 | " | " | | | |
| 6 | " | " | | | |
| 7 | " | " | | | |
| 8 | " | " | | | |
| 9 | " | " | | | |
| 10 | " | " | | | |
| 11 | " | " | | | |
| 12 | " | 5 | SWBS:o | 7 Miles SEBS:o | |
| 1 | " | " | Calm | | Sunday: 20:th |
| 2 | " | " | | | Small Airs with Calms |
| 3 | " | " | | | |
| 4 | " | 3 | SE | WNW | Course made good is S:o 30d E:t Distance 10 Miles Southing 8 miles Easting 5 miles Difference of Long:d 6 miles |
| 5 | 1 | " | S.o | | |
| 6 | 1 | 3 | SBE | | |
| 7 | " | " | Calm | | |
| 8 | " | " | | | Lat:d p:r Account 25d 06m N:o |
| 9 | " | 3 | S½E | NBW | Meridian Distance 16 18 W:t |
| 10 | " | 5 | | | Difference of Long:d 20 20 W.t |
| 11 | " | 5 | | | |
| 12 | " | 5 | | | |
| 1 | " | 5 | | | |
| 2 | " | 4 | | | |
| 3 | " | " | Calm | | |
| 4 | " | " | | | |
| 5 | " | " | | | |
| 6 | " | " | | | |
| 7 | " | " | | | |
| 8 | " | " | | | |
| 9 | " | " | | | |
| 10 | " | " | | | |
| 11 | " | 4 | SEBE | N:o | |
| 12 | " | 5 | 8 Miles | | |

| H | K | F | Courses | Winds | Monday: 21.$^{st}$ January |
|---|---|---|---|---|---|
| 1 | ” | ” | | | Small breezes the first part, the latter fine |
| 2 | ” | ” | Calm | | pleasant Gales. |
| 3 | ” | ” | | | |
| 4 | 1 | ” | ESE | NBE | Course Allowed to be S:° 25:$^{d}$ E:$^{t}$ Distance |
| 5 | 1 | ” | SEBS:° | | 79 miles, Southing 72 miles Easting 33 |
| 6 | 2 | ” | SSE | | miles Difference of Long.$^{d}$ 36 miles |
| 7 | 2 | ” | | ENE | |
| 8 | 3 | ” | SEBS:° | | Lat:$^{d}$ p:$^{r}$ Account 23$^{d}$ 56$^{m}$ N:° |
| 9 | 2 | ” | | | Meridian Distance 15 45 W:$^{t}$ |
| 10 | 2 | 3 | | | Difference of Long:$^{d}$ 19 34 W:$^{t}$ |
| 11 | 2 | ” | SSE | | |
| 12 | 3 | 3 | | | |
| 1 | 2 | 5 | | EBN | |
| 2 | 2 | 2 | | | |
| 3 | 3 | 3 | | NEBE | |
| 4 | 5 | ” | | | |
| 5 | 5 | ” | | | |
| 6 | 5 | 3 | | EBN | |
| 7 | 6 | ” | | | |
| 8 | 6 | ” | | | |
| 9 | 6 | 5 | | | |
| 10 | 6 | 2 | | ENE | |
| 11 | 6 | ” | | | |
| 12 | 5 | ” | 79 Miles | | |
| 1 | 4 | ” | SSE | EBN | Tuesday: 22. |
| 2 | 5 | ” | | | Fresh Gales fair weather and smooth |
| 3 | 5 | 3 | | | Water |
| 4 | 5 | 4 | | | |
| 5 | 6 | ” | | | Course make to be S:° 14:$^{d}$ E:$^{t}$ Distance |
| 6 | 3 | ” | | | 140 Miles Southing 136 miles Easting 33 |
| 7 | 7 | ” | | | miles Difference of Long:$^{d}$ 36 miles |
| 8 | 7 | ” | | | |
| 9 | 6 | 4 | | | Lat:$^{d}$ Observ'd 21$^{d}$ 38$^{m}$ N.° |
| 10 | 6 | 4 | | | Meridian Distance 15 12 W:$^{t}$ |
| 11 | 6 | 4 | S½E | EBS.° | Difference of Longit.$^{d}$ 19 08 W.$^{t}$ |
| 12 | 6 | ” | S:° | Lightning ESE | |
| 1 | 6 | ” | | | |
| 2 | 5 | 9 | | | |
| 3 | 4 | ” | SBE | EBS.° | |
| 4 | 5 | ” | | | |
| 5 | 6 | ” | SSE | E:$^{t}$ | |
| 6 | 6 | ” | SBE | EBS:° | |
| 7 | 5 | 4 | | | |
| 8 | 5 | 4 | | | |
| 9 | 5 | ” | S½E | ESE | |
| 10 | 5 | ” | | | |
| 11 | 6 | 3 | | | |
| 12 | 6 | 2 | 135 Miles | | |

| | | | | | |
|---|---|---|---|---|---|
| 1 | 7 | ” | SSE | EBN | Wednesday: 23.$^{d}$ |
| 2 | 6 | 2 | | | Fine fresh Gales with hazey weather |
| 3 | 7 | ” | | | |
| 4 | 7 | ” | | | Course make to be S:$^{o}$ 20$^{d}$ E:$^{t}$ Distance |
| 5 | 7 | ” | | | 170 Miles Southing 150 miles Easting 57 |
| 6 | 7 | ” | | | miles Difference of Long.$^{d}$ 61 miles |
| 7 | 7 | ” | | | |
| 8 | 7 | 4 | | | Lat:$^{d}$ p:$^{r}$ Acc.$^{t}$ 18$^{d}$ 58$^{m}$ N.$^{o}$ |
| 9 | 7 | 3 | | ENE | Meridian Distance 14 15 W:$^{t}$ |
| 10 | 5 | 4 | | In 1:$^{st}$ R.B.T.S. | Difference of Long:$^{d}$ 18 07 W.$^{t}$ |
| 11 | 6 | 3 | | | |
| 12 | 6 | 3 | | | |
| 1 | 7 | ” | | | |
| 2 | 7 | 2 | | | |
| 3 | 7 | 3 | | | |
| 4 | 8 | ” | | | |
| 5 | 7 | 4 | | | |
| 6 | 7 | ” | | | |
| 7 | 7 | 4 | | E:$^{t}$ | |
| 8 | 7 | 3 | | | |
| 9 | 6 | 3 | | | |
| 10 | 7 | 4 | | ENE | |
| 11 | 8 | ” | | | |
| 12 | 7 | ” | 70 Miles | | |
| H | K | F | Courses | Winds | Thursday: 24: January. |
| 1 | 7 | ” | SSE | ENE | Fresh gales of Wind & hazey wea: |
| 2 | 7 | ” | | | |
| 3 | 7 | ” | | | Course make to be S:$^{o}$ 14$^{d}$ E:$^{t}$ Distance |
| 4 | 7 | ” | | | 157 Miles Southing 150 miles Easting 37 |
| 5 | 7 | ” | | | miles Difference of Longit.$^{d}$ 39 miles |
| 6 | 7 | ” | | In 2.$^{d}$ R.M.T.S. | |
| 7 | 7 | ” | | | Lat:$^{d}$ p:$^{r}$ Account 16$^{d}$ 23$^{m}$ N:$^{o}$ |
| 8 | 6 | ” | | In 2.$^{d}$ R.F.T.S. | Meridian Distance 13 38 W:$^{t}$ |
| 9 | 6 | ” | | | Difference of Long:$^{d}$ 17 28 W:$^{t}$ |
| 10 | 6 | 5 | | | |
| 11 | 7 | ” | | | |
| 12 | 7 | ” | | | |
| 1 | 7 | ” | | | |
| 2 | 5 | 4 | | | |
| 3 | 5 | 3 | | | |
| 4 | 6 | ” | | | |
| 5 | 5 | 3 | SBW | Out 2.$^{d}$ R.B.T.S. | |
| 6 | 6 | ” | | | |
| 7 | 7 | ” | | | |
| 8 | 7 | 2 | | Out 1:$^{st}$ R.B.T.S. | |
| 9 | 7 | 3 | | | |
| 10 | 7 | 3 | | | |
| 11 | 7 | 4 | | | |
| 12 | 7 | 1 | 161 Miles | | |

| | | | | | |
|---|---|---|---|---|---|
| 1 | 6 | „ | SBW | NEBE | Friday: 25: |
| 2 | 5 | 4 | | | Moderate Gales of wind and hazey |
| 3 | 5 | 4 | | | Weather |
| 4 | 6 | 2 | | | |
| 5 | 6 | 4 | | | |
| 6 | | | Bro:$^{ht}$ too | Up SEBE off | SSE D.R.B.T.S. |
| 7 | „ | „ | | of SEBS:$^{o}$ | |
| 8 | „ | „ | up ESE off | SE Sound:$^{d}$ no | gr.$^{d}$ |
| 9 | „ | „ | | | |
| 10 | „ | „ | | | Course make to be S:$^{o}$ 15$^{d}$ W:$^{t}$ Distance |
| 11 | „ | „ | | | 75 Miles |
| 12 | „ | „ | | | |
| 1 | „ | „ | up SEBE off | SE no ground | Lat:$^{d}$ Observ'd 15$^{d}$ 11$^{m}$ N.$^{o}$ |
| 2 | „ | „ | | NEBN | Meridian Distance 13 57 W.$^{t}$ |
| 3 | „ | „ | up ESE | off SE | Difference of Longitude 17 48 W.$^{t}$ |
| 4 | „ | „ | lost sight of | y$^{e}$ Princess Ann | |
| 5 | „ | „ | | | Lost Company with the Princess Ann, and |
| 6 | „ | „ | | | this morning Saw Three Saile bearing |
| 7 | 3 | „ | Made Saile | Out all Reefs | down for us, upon which the Commo- |
| 8 | 5 | „ | SWBW | NEBE | dore[29] made the Signall for the Line[30], Att |
| 9 | 5 | „ | SW | NE | 10 D:$^{o}$ they Came up w:$^{th}$ us, being the |
| 10 | 2 | „ | SWBW | NEBE | Barrington[31] |
| 11 | 6 | „ | | ENE | Prince Augustus[32] and Craggs[33], for Mocho |
| 12 | 5 | „ | WSW 56 M.$^{s}$ | | |

29 The title of commodore was given to the senior captain of a sailing fleet, charged with decisions impacting all ships. Here, it refers to John Gordon, captain of the Montagu. Gill, Merchants, 20.

30 This was a defensive strategy, which required fleet ships to sail in close proximity to one another and to pay particular attention to the commodore's vessel for possible further commands.

31 The Barrington, rated 450 tons, housed 88 to 90 crewmembers and 30 guns. It sailed from the Downs to Mocha, Goa, Karwar, Thalassery and Kochi in 1722 and 1723, before returning to England in 1724. This ship and its fleet companions, the Prince Augustus and Craggs, were later rumored to be lost.

32 The Prince Augustus, rated 495 tons, housed 99 to 111 crewmembers and 32 to 36 guns. It was sailing to Mocha in 1723.

33 The Craggs, a frigate of 380 tons, housed 76 crewmembers and 26 to 28 guns. It travelled from Falmouth, England to Mocha on its second voyage, from 1722 to 1723.

| | | | | | |
|---|---|---|---|---|---|
| 1 | 7 | ” | W½N | NE | Saturday: 26.th |
| 2 | 7 | 3 | | | Fresh Gales of wind. Lay too in the night |
| 3 | 8 | ” | | | and in the Morning made Sail again |
| 4 | 8 | ” | | | |
| 5 | 8 | 2 | WBN | | Att 9 this morning Saw the Island S.t Jago |
| 6 | 5 | ” | | | West 3 Leagues, Att Noon anchor'd in |
| 7 | | | Lay too up | NNE | Port Braya[34] road in 10 fa: the high peak |
| 8 | ” | ” | NBW off | NW. NEBE | bearing NW the W:termost land WSW and |
| 9 | ” | ” | | | E:termost NEBE Dis:t from Shore 2 Miles |
| 10 | ” | ” | | | |
| 11 | ” | ” | | | |
| 12 | ” | ” | | | |
| 1 | ” | ” | | | |
| 2 | ” | ” | | | |
| 3 | ” | ” | up NNW | off NWBW | |
| 4 | ” | 6 | | | |
| 5 | ” | ” | up NBW | off NWBW | |
| 6 | 4 | ” | Made Saile | NNE | |
| 7 | 7 | ” | | | |
| 8 | 7 | ” | 63 Miles | | |
| 9 | ” | ” | Saw Land | W:t 3 Leagues | |
| 10 | ” | ” | | | |
| 11 | ” | ” | | | |
| 12 | ” | ” | Anch.d in | 10 fa: water | |

## Ship Hartford att S:t Jagoe

Sunday: 27: January. Fresh Gales of Wind and fair Weather, This Morning Sent our Long boat ashoar with Empty water Casks, and in the Evening She Returned with Water

Monday. 28: Fair Weather and a Moderate Gale at NE:t Received on Board Water

Tuesday. 29:th Fair Weather with Moderate Sea and Land Breezes of Wind This Morning Stayed our Masts and Sett up Our Rigging fore and Aft, Also Sent our Long Boat to S:t Jagoe Town[35], but Could get No Provisions, for which She went

Wednesday. 30:th Att 6 this Morning Unmoar'd Ship and att 8 D:o Weighed in Company with the Duke of Cambridge Mountague and an Ostend Ship[36] bound for Bengall Att 10 D:o Brought too and hoisted in our Boats, Unbent our Cables and Stowed our Anchors This Noon the Island S:t Jago bore NNW about 10 Leagues

---

**34** Praia de Santa Maria was a major town on the southern coast of Santiago, in the Cape Verde Islands. By 1723, it began to eclipse its nearby rival, Ribeira Grande, as the island's administrative and commercial capital.

**35** This refers to another major town on the southern coast of Santiago. The Portuguese named it Ribeira Grande when founded in 1462, and it was the isle's main settlement until too frequent pirate attacks caused the majority of its inhabitants to flee to the nearby – and better protected – town of Praia.

**36** The Carolus Sextus, rated 450 tons, housed 87 crewmembers and 36 guns. She was sailing to the Coromandel coast and Bengal in 1723, returning in 1724 with a profit of 104.4 percent. Parmentier, Oostende, 139.

## Ship Hartford From S:t Jago tow:ds China 1723

| H | K | F | Courses | Winds | Thursday: 31: January |
|---|---|---|---|---|---|
| 1 | 6 | 5 | S½E | NE | |
| 2 | 7 | 2 | | | Moderate gales of wind & fair weather |
| 3 | 7 | 5 | | | Yesterday Noon the body of S.t Jagoe |
| 4 | 8 | „ | | | NNW 10 Leagues from whence I take my |
| 5 | 8 | „ | | | Departure |
| 6 | 8 | „ | | | |
| 7 | 7 | 2 | | | Course to this Noon is S:o 10d E:t Distance |
| 8 | 7 | 4 | | | 217 Miles |
| 9 | 7 | 3 | SBE | | |
| 10 | 7 | 3 | | | Lat:d Observ'd 11 d 39 m N. o |
| 11 | 7 | 3 | | | Meridian Distance 0 36 E: t |
| 12 | 7 | 3 | | | Difference of Long:c 0 37 E: t |
| 1 | 7 | 4 | | | |
| 2 | 7 | 5 | | | |
| 3 | 6 | 3 | | | |
| 4 | 6 | „ | | | |
| 5 | 7 | „ | | | |
| 6 | 7 | „ | | | |
| 7 | 8 | „ | | | |
| 8 | 8 | „ | | | |
| 9 | 7 | 4 | | | |
| 10 | 7 | 3 | | | |
| 11 | 7 | 5 | | | |
| 12 | 8 | „ | 179 Miles | | |
| 1 | 7 | 3 | SBE | NE | Friday: 1:st February 1723 |
| 2 | 7 | 4 | | | Moderate Gales of Wind with fair Weather |
| 3 | 8 | „ | | | |
| 4 | 6 | 5 | | | Course make to be S:o 11d E:t Distance |
| 5 | 7 | „ | | | 163 Miles Southing 159 miles Easting 30 |
| 6 | 8 | „ | | | miles Difference of Long.d 31 miles |
| 7 | 8 | 3 | | | |
| 8 | 8 | „ | | | Lat:d Observ'd 9 d 00 m N. o |
| 9 | 8 | „ | | | Meridian Distance 1 06 E. t |
| 10 | 7 | 5 | | | Difference of Longitd 1 08 E. t |
| 11 | 7 | 2 | | | |
| 12 | 7 | „ | | | |
| 1 | 6 | „ | S½E | | |
| 2 | 6 | „ | | | |
| 3 | 6 | „ | | | |
| 4 | 5 | „ | | | |
| 5 | 5 | 5 | | | |
| 6 | 6 | „ | SBE | | |
| 7 | 5 | 5 | | | |
| 8 | 6 | 4 | | | |
| 9 | 6 | 3 | | | |
| 10 | 6 | 3 | | | |
| 11 | 6 | „ | | | |
| 12 | 6 | „ | 163 Miles | | |

| | | | | | |
|---|---|---|---|---|---|
| 1 | 5 | ” | S½E | NEBN | Saturday: 2: |
| 2 | 5 | ” | | | |
| 3 | 4 | 3 | SBE | | Moderate Gales of wind and fair weather |
| 4 | 4 | 3 | | | |
| 5 | 4 | 2 | | | Course make to be S:$^{o}$ 12$^{d}$ E:$^{t}$ distance |
| 6 | 4 | ” | | NBW | 118 miles Southing 115 miles Easting 24 |
| 7 | 4 | ” | | | miles Difference of Long.$^{d}$ 25 miles |
| 8 | 3 | 3 | | | |
| 9 | 4 | ” | | | Lat:$^{d}$ Observ'd 7$^{d}$ 05$^{m}$ N.$^{o}$ |
| 10 | 4 | 4 | | | Meridian Distance 1 30 E.$^{t}$ |
| 11 | 4 | 3 | | | Difference of Long.$^{d}$ 1 33 E.$^{t}$ |
| 12 | 4 | 3 | | | |
| 1 | 4 | 2 | | | |
| 2 | 4 | 3 | | | |
| 3 | 4 | 3 | | | |
| 4 | 4 | 2 | | NNE | |
| 5 | 4 | ” | | | |
| 6 | 4 | ” | | | |
| 7 | 4 | 4 | | | |
| 8 | 5 | ” | | | |
| 9 | 5 | 1 | | | |
| 10 | 5 | 3 | | | |
| 11 | 5 | ” | | | |
| 12 | 5 | 3 | 108 Miles | | |
| H | K | F | Courses | Winds | Sunday: 3: February. 1723 |
| 1 | 4 | ” | SBE | NNE | Moderate Gales of wind with fair wea: |
| 2 | 4 | 3 | | | Lightning in the Night |
| 3 | 4 | 3 | | | |
| 4 | 5 | ” | | | Course allowed, S:$^{o}$ 13$^{d}$ E:$^{t}$ Distance 122 |
| 5 | 5 | 3 | | | miles Southing 120 miles Easting 27 |
| 6 | 4 | ” | | | miles diff:$^{e}$ of Long:$^{d}$ 27 miles |
| 7 | 4 | ” | | | |
| 8 | 4 | 4 | | | Lat:$^{d}$ Observ'd 5$^{d}$ 05$^{m}$ N:$^{o}$ |
| 9 | 5 | 4 | | NBE | Meridian Distance 1 57 E:$^{t}$ |
| 10 | 6 | ” | | | Difference of Long:$^{d}$ 2 00 E:$^{t}$ |
| 11 | 5 | ” | | NNE | |
| 12 | 5 | 2 | | | |
| 1 | 4 | 4 | | | |
| 2 | 4 | 3 | | | |
| 3 | 4 | 3 | Light:$^{g}$ out | of the SE board | |
| 4 | 5 | ” | | | |
| 5 | 5 | ” | D.$^{o}$ | D.$^{o}$ | |
| 6 | 5 | ” | | | |
| 7 | 5 | 3 | | | |
| 8 | 4 | 3 | | | |
| 9 | 5 | ” | | | |
| 10 | 4 | ” | | | |
| 11 | 4 | 4 | | | |
| 12 | 4 | ” | 114 Miles | | |

| | | | | | |
|---|---|---|---|---|---|
| 1 | 3 | „ | SBE | NBE | Monday: 4:$^{th}$ |
| 2 | 2 | „ | | | Small Gales of wind with showers of Rain |
| 3 | 1 | 5 | | | in the Night |
| 4 | 2 | „ | | | |
| 5 | 1 | 4 | | | Course judge to be S:$^{o}$ 13$^{d}$ E:$^{t}$ Distance 52 |
| 6 | 1 | „ | | | miles Southing 50 miles Easting 12 miles |
| 7 | 1 | 2 | | | Difference of Long:$^{d}$ 12 miles |
| 8 | 1 | „ | | | |
| 9 | 1 | „ | | | Lat:$^{d}$ Observ'd 4$^{d}$ 15$^{m}$ N.$^{o}$ |
| 10 | 1 | „ | | | Meridian Distance 2 09 E.$^{t}$ |
| 11 | 1 | 3 | | | Difference of Long.$^{d}$ 2 12 E.$^{t}$ |
| 12 | „ | 3 | | | |
| 1 | „ | 3 | | | |
| 2 | „ | 3 | | | |
| 3 | „ | 3 | | Rain | |
| 4 | „ | 5 | | D:$^{o}$ | |
| 5 | 1 | „ | | | |
| 6 | 1 | „ | | | |
| 7 | 1 | „ | | | |
| 8 | 2 | „ | | | |
| 9 | 2 | „ | | | |
| 10 | 1 | 4 | | | |
| 11 | 1 | 3 | | | |
| 12 | 1 | 4 | 31 Miles | | |
| 1 | 1 | 4 | SBE | NBW | Tuesday: 5:$^{th}$ |
| 2 | 1 | 3 | | | |
| 3 | 2 | 3 | | | Small Gales of wind the first part the |
| 4 | 2 | 4 | | | latter fresh Gales with abundance of |
| 5 | 2 | 4 | | | Lightning and Rain |
| 6 | 3 | „ | | | |
| 7 | 3 | 3 | | | Course with regard to all known Impedim.$^{ts}$ |
| 8 | 4 | 3 | | | make to be S:$^{o}$ 12:$^{d}$ E:$^{t}$ Distance 93 miles |
| 9 | 5 | „ | | | Southing 91 miles Easting 19 miles |
| 10 | 4 | 2 | | | |
| 11 | 5 | „ | | | Lat:$^{d}$ Account 2$^{d}$ 44$^{m}$ N:$^{o}$ |
| 12 | 5 | „ | | | Meridian Distance 2 28 E:$^{t}$ |
| 1 | 1 | 3 | | NNW hard R.$^{n}$ | Difference of Longit.$^{d}$ 2 31 E:$^{t}$ |
| 2 | 2 | 3 | | Light:$^{g}$ & D.$^{o}$ | |
| 3 | 3 | 3 | | | |
| 4 | 3 | 4 | | | |
| 5 | 3 | 6 | | | |
| 6 | 4 | 3 | | | |
| 7 | 5 | „ | | | |
| 8 | 5 | 2 | | D.$^{o}$ D.$^{o}$ | |
| 9 | 5 | „ | | | |
| 10 | 6 | „ | | | |
| 11 | 6 | „ | | | |
| 12 | 5 | 6 | 93 Miles | | |

| H | K | F | Courses | Winds | Wednesday: 6: February. |
|---|---|---|---|---|---|
| 1 | 5 | 3 | SBE½E | NBW | |
| 2 | 5 | „ | | | Moderate Gales of wind with Rain |
| 3 | 4 | 3 | | | |
| 4 | 4 | 3 | | | p:$^{r}$ Observation am 34 miles to the |
| 5 | 2 | 3 | SSE | NNW | S:$^{o}$ward of the Log: the Error Impute to |
| 6 | 2 | „ | | NE | the Distance |
| 7 | 1 | „ | SBE | E.$^{t}$ Rain | |
| 8 | „ | 5 | | | Course make to be South Distance 111 |
| 9 | „ | 4 | | | Miles |
| 10 | „ | 3 | | | |
| 11 | 2 | „ | | | Lat:$^{d}$ Observ'd 0$^{d}$ 53$^{m}$ N:$^{o}$ |
| 12 | 3 | „ | SBW | SEBE | Meridian Distance 2 28 E.$^{t}$ |
| 1 | 4 | „ | | | Difference of Long.$^{d}$ 2 34 E.$^{t}$ |
| 2 | 3 | 4 | | | |
| 3 | 5 | „ | | | |
| 4 | 5 | „ | S.$^{o}$ | ESE | |
| 5 | 5 | „ | SBW | SEBE | |
| 6 | 4 | „ | SSW | SE | |
| 7 | 2 | 3 | | | |
| 8 | 3 | 2 | S.$^{o}$ | ESE | |
| 9 | 2 | „ | | | |
| 10 | 2 | 3 | | | |
| 11 | 3 | 3 | | | |
| 12 | 5 | 3 | 77 Miles | | |
| 1 | 4 | „ | SBW | SEBE | Thursday: 7:$^{th}$ |
| 2 | 4 | „ | | | |
| 3 | 1 | 3 | | | Small Gales of wind and fair weather |
| 4 | 1 | 4 | | | |
| 5 | 2 | 3 | | | p:$^{r}$ my Observation the Ship is 15 miles |
| 6 | 2 | 3 | SWBW | SBE | more to the S:$^{o}$ward then the Log: gives |
| 7 | 1 | „ | | | the Error Impute to the Distance |
| 8 | 2 | „ | | | |
| 9 | 1 | 3 | | | Lat:$^{d}$ Observ'd 0$^{d}$ 13$^{m}$ N.$^{o}$ |
| 10 | 1 | „ | | | Meridian Distance 1 19 E:$^{t}$ |
| 11 | | | Calm | | Difference of Long.$^{d}$ 1 22 E:$^{t}$ |
| 12 | „ | 4 | WBN | SWBS.$^{o}$ | |
| 1 | 1 | „ | | | Course allow to be S:$^{o}$ 50$^{d}$ W:$^{t}$ Distance |
| 2 | 1 | „ | | | 63 Miles |
| 3 | 1 | „ | W½S.$^{o}$ | SBW | |
| 4 | 1 | 3 | | | |
| 5 | 2 | „ | WSW | S:$^{o}$ | |
| 6 | 2 | 3 | SWBW | SBE | |
| 7 | 1 | „ | | | |
| 8 | 1 | „ | | | |
| 9 | 1 | 3 | SW | SSE | |
| 10 | 2 | „ | | | |
| 11 | 1 | 3 | | | |
| 12 | 1 | 3 | SWBW | 39 Miles | |

| | | | | | |
|---|---|---|---|---|---|
| 1 | 1 | ” | WSW | S:° | Friday: 8:$^{th}$ |
| 2 | 1 | ” | | | |
| 3 | 1 | ” | | | Small breezes with Squalls and Rain in |
| 4 | ” | 5 | | | the Night |
| 5 | ” | 4 | | | |
| 6 | ” | 3 | | | Course I allow to be S:° 68$^{d}$ W:$^{t}$ Distance |
| 7 | ” | 5 | SWBW | SBE | 23 miles Southing 9 miles W:$^{t}$ing 21 miles |
| 8 | ” | 3 | WBS.° | SBW | |
| 9 | ” | 3 | West | SSW | Lat:$^{d}$ Account 0$^{d}$ 4$^{m}$ N:° |
| 10 | ” | 4 | | Small Rain | Meridian Distance 1 19 E:$^{t}$ |
| 11 | 1 | 2 | | | Difference of Long:$^{d}$ 1 22 E:$^{t}$ |
| 12 | ” | 3 | WBN | SWBS.° | |
| 1 | ” | 6 | WBS.° | SBW | |
| 2 | 2 | 4 | SWBS.° | SEBS.° | |
| 3 | 4 | 2 | | Sq$^{ly}$ R.$^{n}$ | |
| 4 | 3 | ” | | | |
| 5 | 2 | 4 | SSW | SE D.° | |
| 6 | ” | ” | } | | |
| 7 | ” | ” | } Calm | | |
| 8 | ” | ” | } | | |
| 9 | ” | 3 | | | |
| 10 | ” | 5 | | | |
| 11 | ” | ” | } | | |
| 12 | ” | ” | } Calm | | |
| | | | Distance | 23 Miles | |
| H | K | F | Courses | Winds | Saturday: 9: February. |
| 1 | ” | ” | } | | The first part Calm with Rain, the other |
| 2 | ” | ” | } | | Small gales and fair Weather |
| 3 | ” | ” | } | | |
| 4 | ” | ” | } Calm | & Raine | Course Allow to be S:° 45$^{d}$ W:$^{t}$ Distance 31 |
| 5 | ” | ” | } | | miles Southing 22 miles Westing 22 miles |
| 6 | ” | ” | } | | |
| 7 | ” | ” | } | | Lat:$^{d}$ Observ'd 0$^{d}$ 18$^{m}$ South |
| 8 | ” | ” | } | | Meridian Distance 0 58 East |
| 9 | 1 | 3 | NEBE | SEBE Wore | Difference of Long:$^{d}$ 1 00 East |
| 10 | 1 | ” | SSW½W | SE | |
| 11 | 2 | ” | SW | SSE | |
| 12 | 2 | ” | | | |
| 1 | 3 | ” | | | |
| 2 | 3 | ” | | | |
| 3 | 2 | ” | | | |
| 4 | 1 | 3 | | | |
| 5 | 2 | 4 | SWBS:° | SEBS:° | |
| 6 | 2 | 4 | SSW | SE | |
| 7 | 2 | ” | SBW½W | SEBE | |
| 8 | 2 | ” | | | |
| 9 | 3 | 3 | | | |
| 10 | 3 | 4 | | | |
| 11 | 3 | ” | | | |
| 12 | 1 | 6 | 37 Miles | | |

| | | | | | |
|---|---|---|---|---|---|
| 1 | 1 | 3 | SBW | SEBE | Sunday: 10:$^{th}$ |
| 2 | 2 | „ | | | |
| 3 | 1 | 4 | SEBS:° | SEBS:° | Small Gales of Wind with Rain in the |
| 4 | 1 | 3 | | | night |
| 5 | 1 | 4 | | | |
| 6 | 1 | 3 | | | Course make to be S:° 38:$^{d}$ W:$^{t}$ Distance |
| 7 | 2 | „ | SW | SSE | 51 miles Southing 40 miles Westing 31 |
| 8 | 2 | 3 | SWBS:° | SEBS: ° | miles |
| 9 | 1 | „ | | | |
| 10 | 1 | 3 | | | Lat:$^{d}$ Observ'd 0$^{d}$ 58$^{m}$ S: ° |
| 11 | 1 | „ | SW | SSE Rain | Meridian Distance 0 27 E:$^{t}$ |
| 12 | 1 | 3 | | | Difference of Long:$^{d}$ 0 29 E:$^{t}$ |
| 1 | 3 | „ | SWBS:° | SEBS:° | |
| 2 | 2 | 3 | | | |
| 3 | 2 | „ | | | |
| 4 | 1 | 5 | SSW | SE | |
| 5 | 2 | 3 | | | |
| 6 | 2 | 3 | | | |
| 7 | 3 | 3 | | | |
| 8 | 3 | 4 | | | |
| 9 | 3 | 5 | SW | SSE | |
| 10 | 3 | 5 | | | |
| 11 | 3 | 3 | SWBS:° | SEBS:° | |
| 12 | 4 | 3 | SW½S:° | 55 Miles | |
| 1 | 4 | „ | SWBS:° | SEBS:° | Monday. 11: |
| 2 | 4 | „ | | | Moderte Gales of wind and Smooth Water, |
| 3 | 4 | 3 | | | with Rain in the night |
| 4 | 5 | „ | | | |
| 5 | 4 | „ | | | Course make to be S:° 33$^{d}$ W:$^{t}$ Distance |
| 6 | 4 | „ | | | 120 Miles Southing 100 miles Westing |
| 7 | 5 | „ | SSW½W | SE | 65 miles |
| 8 | 5 | „ | | | |
| 9 | 4 | „ | SBW½W | SEBE | Lat:$^{d}$ Observ'd 2$^{d}$ 38 S: ° |
| 10 | 4 | 3 | SSW | SE | Meridian Distance 0 38 W.$^{t}$ |
| 11 | 5 | 2 | | | Difference of Long.$^{d}$ 0 37 W.$^{t}$ |
| 12 | 4 | 3 | SWBS:° | SEBS.° | |
| 1 | 5 | „ | | Rain | |
| 2 | 5 | „ | | | |
| 3 | 5 | 5 | | | |
| 4 | 5 | „ | | Sq$^{l}$ & R.$^{n}$ | |
| 5 | 5 | 3 | SSW | SE D.° | |
| 6 | 5 | 5 | | | |
| 7 | 4 | 2 | | | |
| 8 | 4 | 2 | | | |
| 9 | 3 | 3 | | | |
| 10 | 3 | 4 | | | |
| 11 | 4 | „ | | | |
| 12 | 4 | „ | 109 Miles | | |

| H | K | F | Courses | Winds | Tuesday: 12. February |
|---|---|---|---|---|---|
| 1 | 5 | 2 | SWBS:$^{o}$ | SEBS:$^{o}$ | |
| 2 | 5 | 3 | | | Fresh gales of wind w:$^{th}$ smooth water |
| 3 | 5 | 1 | | | |
| 4 | 4 | 2 | | | Course make to be S:$^{o}$ 36$^{d}$ W:$^{t}$ Distance |
| 5 | 4 | 1 | | | 131 mile Southing 106 miles Westing 76 |
| 6 | 4 | 3 | | | miles difference of Long.$^{d}$ 77 miles |
| 7 | 5 | „ | | | |
| 8 | 4 | 3 | | | Lat:$^{d}$ Observ'd 4$^{d}$ 24$^{m}$ S:$^{o}$ |
| 9 | 4 | „ | SSW | SE | Meridian Distance 1 54 W:$^{t}$ |
| 10 | 4 | „ | | | Difference of Long.$^{d}$ 1 54 W:$^{t}$ |
| 11 | 5 | „ | | | |
| 12 | 5 | „ | | | |
| 1 | 5 | „ | | | |
| 2 | 6 | „ | | | |
| 3 | 6 | 2 | | | |
| 4 | 6 | 2 | | SEBE | |
| 5 | 5 | „ | | | |
| 6 | 5 | „ | | | |
| 7 | 7 | 3 | | | |
| 8 | 6 | 5 | | | |
| 9 | 7 | 2 | | | |
| 10 | 7 | „ | SBW½W | | |
| 11 | 6 | 4 | | | |
| 12 | 6 | 2 | 131 Miles | | |
| 1 | 5 | „ | SBW½W | SEBE | Wednesday: 13: |
| 2 | 5 | „ | | | |
| 3 | 5 | „ | | | Fresh Gales, Cloudy Weather with Squalls |
| 4 | 6 | „ | | Cloudy | and Raine |
| 5 | 6 | 2 | | | |
| 6 | 6 | „ | | | Course S:$^{o}$ 21:$^{d}$ W:$^{t}$ Distance 134 miles |
| 7 | 4 | 3 | SBW | | Southing 127 Westing 49 Diff Long:$^{d}$50$^{m}$ |
| 8 | 6 | „ | | | |
| 9 | 6 | „ | | | Lat:$^{d}$ Observ'd 6$^{d}$ 27 S:$^{o}$ |
| 10 | 6 | „ | | Sq.$^{ll}$ and R.$^{n}$ | Meridian Distance 2 43 W:$^{t}$ |
| 11 | 6 | 6 | | | Difference of Long:$^{d}$ 2 44 W:$^{t}$ |
| 12 | 6 | 2 | | | |
| 1 | 5 | 5 | | | |
| 2 | 5 | 2 | | | |
| 3 | 6 | 1 | SBW½W | SE | |
| 4 | 5 | 3 | | | |
| 5 | 6 | 2 | | | |
| 6 | 6 | 3 | | | |
| 7 | 6 | 1 | | | |
| 8 | 6 | 3 | | | |
| 9 | 6 | „ | SBW | SEBE | |
| 10 | 6 | „ | | | |
| 11 | 7 | 3 | SSW | SE | |
| 12 | 7 | 4 | 134 Miles | | |

| | | | | | |
|---|---|---|---|---|---|
| 1 | 6 | 3 | SSW | SE:$^{t}$ | Thursday: 14:$^{th}$ |
| 2 | 6 | 1 | | | |
| 3 | 6 | 4 | | | Fresh gales of Wind with Squalls and |
| 4 | 7 | „ | SBW | SEBE | Raine |
| 5 | 6 | „ | SBW½W | SE | |
| 6 | 6 | „ | | | Course make to be S:$^{o}$ 23$^{d}$ W:$^{t}$ Distance |
| 7 | 6 | „ | | | 132 Miles, Southing 121 Westing 51 |
| 8 | 5 | 3 | SBW | SEBE | Difference of Longitude 52 miles. |
| 9 | 5 | 3 | | Sq:$^{l}$ & R.$^{n}$ | |
| 10 | 4 | „ | | | Lat:$^{d}$ By Account 8$^{d}$ 28$^{m}$ S:$^{o}$ |
| 11 | 4 | 3 | | fair | Meridian Distance 3 34 W.$^{t}$ |
| 12 | 5 | 3 | SSW | SE | Difference of Long.$^{d}$ 3 36 W.$^{t}$ |
| 1 | 5 | 4 | | | |
| 2 | 5 | 3 | SBW | SEBE | |
| 3 | 6 | „ | | | |
| 4 | 5 | 3 | | | |
| 5 | 6 | 3 | | | Could not Observe the Sun being near our |
| 6 | 5 | „ | SBW½W | SE Sq.$^{l}$ & R.$^{n}$ | Zenith |
| 7 | 6 | „ | SBW | SEBE D.$^{o}$ | |
| 8 | 4 | „ | | Cloudy | |
| 9 | 5 | „ | | | |
| 10 | 5 | „ | | | |
| 11 | 4 | 2 | SBW½W | SE | |
| 12 | 4 | 5 | 132 Miles | | |
| H | K | F | Courses | Winds | Friday: 15. February |
| 1 | 5 | „ | SBW | SEBE | |
| 2 | 5 | „ | | | Moderate Gales of wind with Cloudy |
| 3 | 5 | „ | | | Weather. |
| 4 | 5 | „ | | | |
| 5 | 5 | 3 | | | Course make to be S:$^{o}$ 24$^{d}$ W:$^{t}$ Distance |
| 6 | 5 | „ | | | 116 Miles Southing 106$^{m}$ Westing 46 |
| 7 | 4 | 2 | SBW½W | SE | miles Difference of Long:$^{d}$ 47 miles |
| 8 | 5 | „ | SBW | SEBE | |
| 9 | 5 | 4 | S½W | ESE | Lat:$^{d}$ p:$^{r}$ Account 10$^{d}$ 14$^{m}$ S:$^{o}$ |
| 10 | 5 | 2 | | | Meridian Distance 4 20 W:$^{t}$ |
| 11 | 5 | 3 | | | Difference of Longit.$^{d}$ 4 23 W:$^{t}$ |
| 12 | 4 | 4 | SBW | | |
| 1 | 4 | 3 | S½W | | |
| 2 | 4 | 4 | | | |
| 3 | 3 | 3 | SW | SSE | |
| 4 | 4 | „ | SSW | SE | |
| 5 | 5 | „ | SBW½W | SEBE | |
| 6 | 5 | 3 | | | |
| 7 | 5 | „ | SSW | SE | |
| 8 | 4 | 3 | | | |
| 9 | 5 | „ | SBW | SEBE | |
| 10 | 6 | „ | | | |
| 11 | 6 | „ | S.$^{o}$ | ESE | |
| 12 | 3 | 1 | 117 Miles | | |

| | | | | | |
|---|---|---|---|---|---|
| 1 | 2 | 3 | SW | SSE | Saturday: 16. |
| 2 | 1 | 3 | | Sm:$^{ll}$ Rain | Small Gales the first part w:$^{th}$ rain |
| 3 | 1 | 2 | WSW | S:$^{o}$ | the latter fresh Gales |
| 4 | 1 | ” | S½W | ESE | |
| 5 | 1 | ” | | | Course make to be S:$^{o}$ 20$^{d}$ W:$^{t}$ Distance |
| 6 | 2 | 3 | SBW | | 100 Miles Southing 94 Westing 34 Differ- |
| 7 | 3 | 6 | | | ence of Long:$^{d}$ 36 Miles |
| 8 | 4 | ” | S½W | | |
| 9 | 4 | 3 | | | Lat:$^{d}$ Observ'd 11$^{d}$ 48$^{m}$ S.$^{o}$ |
| 10 | 4 | 5 | | | Meridian Distance 4 54 W:$^{t}$ |
| 11 | 5 | ” | | | Difference of Long:$^{d}$ 4 59 W:$^{t}$ |
| 12 | 5 | 3 | | | |
| 1 | 6 | 3 | SBW½W | SEBE | |
| 2 | 7 | ” | | | |
| 3 | 5 | 3 | SBW | | |
| 4 | 5 | ” | | | |
| 5 | 5 | ” | | | |
| 6 | 5 | 3 | M: Amp:$^{d}$ 4° | 30' E:$^{t}$ S:$^{o}$erly | |
| 7 | 6 | ” | | | |
| 8 | 5 | 4 | | | |
| 9 | 5 | 4 | | | |
| 10 | 5 | 4 | S½W | ESE | |
| 11 | 5 | ” | | | |
| 12 | 4 | 1 | 103 Miles | | |
| 1 | 3 | ” | S½W | SEBE | Sunday: 17.$^{th}$ |
| 2 | 4 | ” | | | |
| 3 | 4 | 3 | SBW | | Moderate gales of wind with fair Weather |
| 4 | 5 | ” | | | |
| 5 | 5 | ” | | | Course allow'd to be S:$^{o}$ 14$^{d}$ W:$^{t}$ Distance |
| 6 | 4 | 6 | | | 107 Miles Southing 97 Westing 24 Dif- |
| 7 | 4 | 3 | | | fernce of Long:$^{d}$ 25 |
| 8 | 4 | 4 | | | |
| 9 | 5 | ” | | | Lat:$^{d}$ Observ'd 13$^{d}$ 25$^{m}$ S:$^{o}$ |
| 10 | 5 | 1 | | | Meridian Distance 5 18 W:$^{t}$ |
| 11 | 5 | 3 | | | Difference of Long.$^{d}$ 5 24 W:$^{t}$ |
| 12 | 5 | 3 | S:$^{o}$ | ESE | |
| 1 | 5 | ” | | | |
| 2 | 5 | ” | | | p:$^{r}$ Observation the Ship is not so farr to |
| 3 | 4 | 6 | | | the S:$^{o}$ward as the Log. allows p$^{r}$ 17 miles |
| 4 | 5 | ” | | | the Error Attribute to the Distance |
| 5 | 4 | 3 | | | |
| 6 | 4 | 6 | | | |
| 7 | 5 | 1 | | | |
| 8 | 5 | ” | | | |
| 9 | 6 | ” | | | |
| 10 | 5 | 4 | | | |
| 11 | 5 | 4 | | | |
| 12 | 5 | ” | 117 Miles | | |

| H | K | F | Courses | Winds | Monday: 18: February |
|---|---|---|---|---|---|
| 1 | 4 | „ | S:$^{o}$ | ESE | |
| 2 | 3 | 5 | | | Moderate Gales of Wind & fair Weather |
| 3 | 2 | „ | SBW | SEBE | |
| 4 | 2 | 1 | SBE | EBS.$^{o}$ | Course make to be South Distance 80 |
| 5 | 3 | 4 | S.$^{o}$ | ESE | Miles. |
| 6 | 3 | 3 | | | |
| 7 | 2 | „ | | | Lat:$^{d}$ Observ'd 14$^{d}$ 45$^{m}$ S:$^{o}$ |
| 8 | 3 | 4 | | | Meridian Distance 5 18 W:$^{t}$ |
| 9 | 3 | 3 | | | Difference of Long:$^{d}$ 5 24 W:$^{t}$ |
| 10 | 4 | „ | | | |
| 11 | 4 | 3 | | | |
| 12 | 4 | „ | | | |
| 1 | 5 | „ | | | |
| 2 | 5 | „ | SBE | EBS.$^{o}$ | |
| 3 | 5 | 2 | | | |
| 4 | 5 | 3 | | | |
| 5 | 3 | 5 | S.$^{o}$ | ESE | |
| 6 | 3 | 3 | | | |
| 7 | 3 | 4 | S½E:$^{t}$ | EBS:$^{o}$ | |
| 8 | 2 | 3 | | | |
| 9 | 3 | 2 | SBE | Small R.$^{n}$ | |
| 10 | 3 | 5 | | | |
| 11 | 3 | 4 | SBE½E | East | |
| 12 | 3 | 2 | 88 Miles | | |
| 1 | 3 | 4 | SBE | EBS:$^{o}$ | Tuesday: 19: |
| 2 | 3 | „ | | | |
| 3 | 2 | „ | S½E | ESE | Small Gales the first part, the latter Mod- |
| 4 | 3 | „ | | | erate. Cloudy Weather |
| 5 | 4 | „ | | Sm:$^{ll}$ Rain | |
| 6 | 4 | 3 | | | Course make to be S:$^{o}$outh Distance 102 |
| 7 | 4 | 4 | | Sq:$^{ll}$ and D:$^{o}$ | Miles |
| 8 | 3 | 5 | | | |
| 9 | 4 | 3 | SBE | EBS:$^{o}$ | Lat:$^{d}$ Observ'd 16$^{d}$ 27$^{m}$ S:$^{o}$ |
| 10 | 5 | „ | SBE½E | E:$^{t}$ | Meridian Distance 5 18 W:$^{t}$ |
| 11 | 5 | 3 | SBE | EBS:$^{o}$ | Difference of Long:$^{d}$ 5 24 W:$^{t}$ |
| 12 | 5 | 1 | | | |
| 1 | 5 | „ | | | |
| 2 | 5 | 3 | | | |
| 3 | 5 | „ | | | |
| 4 | 5 | „ | | | |
| 5 | 5 | „ | | Sq:$^{ll}$ & Rain | |
| 6 | 5 | „ | | | |
| 7 | 4 | 2 | | | |
| 8 | 3 | 3 | | | |
| 9 | 2 | 2 | | | |
| 10 | 4 | „ | | | |
| 11 | 5 | 4 | | | |
| 12 | 4 | 5 | 103 Miles | | |

| | | | | | |
|---|---|---|---|---|---|
| 1 | 5 | ” | SBE | EBS:$^{o}$ | Wednesday: 20: |
| 2 | 4 | 4 | | | |
| 3 | 5 | 3 | | | Moderate Gales of wind with Sq$^{ls}$ in the |
| 4 | 3 | ” | SSE | E.$^{t}$ | Night. |
| 5 | 1 | 2 | | | |
| 6 | 2 | ” | | | Course make to be S:$^{o}$ 5:$^{d}$ E:$^{t}$ Distance |
| 7 | 4 | ” | | | 112 Miles Southing 112 Easting 9 miles |
| 8 | 4 | 4 | | | Difference of Long:$^{d}$ 10 miles |
| 9 | 5 | 3 | SBE½E | EBS:$^{o}$ | |
| 10 | 5 | 4 | | | Lat:$^{d}$ Observed 18$^{d}$ 19$^{m}$ S:$^{o}$ |
| 11 | 5 | ” | | | Meridian Distance 5 09 W:$^{t}$ |
| 12 | 5 | ” | | | Difference of Long:$^{d}$ 5 14 W:$^{t}$ |
| 1 | 4 | ” | | | |
| 2 | 5 | 3 | | | |
| 3 | 5 | ” | | | |
| 4 | 5 | ” | | | |
| 5 | 5 | ” | SBE | E:$^{t}$ | |
| 6 | 5 | ” | | | |
| 7 | 6 | ” | | | |
| 8 | 7 | ” | | | |
| 9 | 7 | ” | | | |
| 10 | 6 | ” | SBE½E | | |
| 11 | 4 | ” | SSE | | |
| 12 | 1 | 5 | 112 Miles | | |

| H | K | F | Courses | Winds | Thursday: 21: February |
|---|---|---|---|---|---|
| 1 | 2 | ” | SSE | E:$^{t}$ | Small Gales of wind with fair wea: |
| 2 | 3 | ” | | | |
| 3 | 2 | 3 | | | Course make to be S:$^{o}$ 5:$^{d}$ E:$^{t}$ Distance |
| 4 | 2 | 3 | SBE | EBS:$^{o}$ | 69 miles Southing 68 Easting 6 miles |
| 5 | 2 | 4 | | | Difference of Longit.$^{d}$ 7 miles |
| 6 | 2 | ” | | | |
| 7 | 2 | ” | | | Lat:$^{d}$ Observ'd 19$^{c}$ 27$^{m}$ S:$^{o}$ |
| 8 | 3 | ” | | | Meridian Distance 5 03 W:$^{t}$ |
| 9 | 3 | 6 | | | Difference of Long:$^{d}$ 5 07 W: |
| 10 | 3 | 3 | | | |
| 11 | 3 | 5 | | | |
| 12 | 3 | 3 | SBE½E | EBS:$^{o}$ | |
| 1 | 4 | ” | | | |
| 2 | 3 | ” | | | |
| 3 | 3 | 4 | | | |
| 4 | 3 | 3 | | | |
| 5 | 3 | ” | | | |
| 6 | 3 | ” | | | |
| 7 | 3 | 3 | | | |
| 8 | 3 | 3 | | | |
| 9 | 2 | ” | SBE | | |
| 10 | 2 | ” | | | |
| 11 | 1 | 3 | | | |
| 12 | 1 | ” | 68 Miles | | |

| | | | | | |
|---|---|---|---|---|---|
| 1 | 2 | „ | SBE | EBS:$^{o}$ | Friday: 22: |
| 2 | 1 | 4 | S:$^{o}$ | ESE | |
| 3 | 2 | 3 | SBE | EBS | Small Gales of wind with Rain in the |
| 4 | 2 | „ | | | night |
| 5 | 1 | „ | | | |
| 6 | 1 | „ | | | Course South Distance 77 miles |
| 7 | 1 | „ | | | |
| 8 | 1 | „ | | | p:$^{r}$ my Observation am 25 Miles to y:$^{e}$ |
| 9 | „ | 4 | | | S:$^{o}$ward of Acc.$^{t}$ the Error Impute to the |
| 10 | „ | 3 | | | Distance |
| 11 | 1 | „ | S:$^{o}$ | ESE | |
| 12 | 1 | 3 | SSE | E:$^{t}$ | Lat:$^{d}$ Observ'd 20$^{d}$ 37$^{m}$ S.$^{o}$ |
| 1 | 2 | „ | | | Meridian Distance 5 03 W:$^{t}$ |
| 2 | 1 | „ | Rain and | Lightning | Difference of Long.$^{d}$ 5 07 W:$^{t}$ |
| 3 | 1 | „ | | | |
| 4 | 1 | „ | SBE | EBS.$^{o}$ | |
| 5 | „ | 4 | | | |
| 6 | 1 | 3 | | | |
| 7 | 3 | „ | | | |
| 8 | 4 | „ | | | |
| 9 | 4 | 4 | SSE | E:$^{t}$ | |
| 10 | 4 | „ | SBE | EBS.$^{o}$ | |
| 11 | 2 | 3 | SBW | SEBE | |
| 12 | 2 | „ | 42 Miles | | |
| 1 | 2 | 3 | SSE | EBN | Saturday: 23: |
| 2 | 1 | 4 | | | |
| 3 | 1 | 5 | | NEBN | Small Gales of wind with Squalls and |
| 4 | 1 | „ | | | Rain in the night |
| 5 | 1 | „ | | | |
| 6 | 1 | „ | var: p$^{r}$ Amp.$^{d}$ | 5° 54' E:$^{t}$ | Course allowed to be S:$^{o}$ 10$^{d}$ E:$^{t}$ Distance |
| 7 | „ | 3 | | | 48 miles Southing 47 Easting 8 miles |
| 8 | „ | 5 | | | Difference of Long.$^{d}$ 9 miles |
| 9 | 1 | „ | | Sq:$^{ll}$ & R.$^{n}$ | |
| 10 | 1 | „ | | | Lat:$^{d}$ Observ'd 21$^{d}$ 24$^{m}$ S:$^{o}$ |
| 11 | 1 | „ | | | Meridian Distance 4 55 W:$^{t}$ |
| 12 | 1 | 3 | | | Difference of Long:$^{d}$ 4 58 W:$^{t}$ |
| 1 | 1 | 3 | | | |
| 2 | 1 | 3 | | | |
| 3 | 2 | 3 | SBE½E | ENE | |
| 4 | 3 | „ | | | |
| 5 | 2 | 1 | | | |
| 6 | 2 | 1 | | | |
| 7 | 2 | 4 | SSE | | |
| 8 | 3 | „ | | | |
| 9 | 3 | „ | | | |
| 10 | 3 | 6 | | | |
| 11 | 3 | 3 | | | |
| 12 | 3 | 2 | 46 Miles | | |

| H | K | F | Courses | Winds | Sunday: 24: February |
|---|---|---|---|---|---|
| 1 | 1 | 4 | SEBS.° | NE | |
| 2 | 1 | 4 | | | Small Gales of Wind and Cloudy Weather |
| 3 | 1 | 3 | | | |
| 4 | 1 | " | | | Course make to be S:° 20$^{d}$ E:$^{t}$ Distance 76 |
| 5 | 1 | " | | | Miles, Southing 71 miles Easting 26 miles |
| 6 | | | Calm var: 6$^{d}$ | 00$^{m}$ E:$^{t}$erly | Difference of Long:$^{d}$ 28 miles |
| 7 | 1 | " | S½E | EBN | |
| 8 | 1 | " | SBE | EBS.° | Lat:$^{d}$ Observ'd 22$^{d}$ 35$^{m}$ S:° |
| 9 | 2 | 3 | SSE | East | Meridian Distance 4 29 W.$^{t}$ |
| 10 | 3 | 3 | | | Difference of Long:$^{d}$ 4 30 W.$^{t}$ |
| 11 | 3 | " | | | |
| 12 | 3 | " | | | |
| 1 | 3 | 2 | | | |
| 2 | 3 | 2 | | | Att 9 This morning M:$^{r}$ Tho:$^{s}$ Atkins (supra |
| 3 | 4 | " | | NNE | Cargo) departed this Life |
| 4 | 4 | " | | NEBE | |
| 5 | 3 | " | | | |
| 6 | 4 | " | | | |
| 7 | 4 | 3 | SEBS:° | ENE | |
| 8 | 4 | 5 | | | |
| 9 | 4 | 5 | | | |
| 10 | 3 | " | | | |
| 11 | 3 | 3 | | | |
| 12 | 2 | 4 | 64 Miles | | |
| 1 | 1 | 3 | SSE | N:° | Monday: 25: |
| 2 | 2 | " | | NNW | |
| 3 | 2 | " | | | The first part Small gales the latter |
| 4 | 1 | " | | | Moderate |
| 5 | 1 | " | | | |
| 6 | 1 | " | | | Course make to be S:° 26:$^{d}$ E:$^{t}$ Distance |
| 7 | " | " | Calm | | 46 miles Southing 42$^{m}$ Easting 19 miles |
| 8 | " | " | | | Difference of Long:$^{d}$ 21 miles |
| 9 | 1 | " | SEBE | | |
| 10 | 1 | " | | Lighting | Lat:$^{d}$ Obs:$^{d}$ 33$^{d}$ 17$^{m}$ S:° |
| 11 | 3 | " | | | Meridian Distance 4 10 W.$^{t}$ |
| 12 | 1 | " | SEBS:° | EBN | Difference of Long:$^{d}$ 4 9 W.$^{t}$ |
| 1 | 3 | " | | | |
| 2 | 3 | 3 | SSE | | Committed the body of M:$^{r}$ Tho$^{s}$ Attkins |
| 3 | 4 | 5 | SEBS:° | | to the Deep and fired 26 Guns[37] |
| 4 | 4 | " | | | |
| 5 | 3 | 3 | SE | | |
| 6 | 3 | 3 | | | |
| 7 | 3 | 3 | SEBS:° | | |
| 8 | 3 | 3 | | | |
| 9 | 3 | 3 | | | |
| 10 | 3 | " | | | |
| 11 | 5 | " | | | |
| 12 | 5 | 2 | 58 Miles | | |

**37** For more on maritime funerals, see Marcus Rediker, *Between the Devil and the Deep Blue Sea: Merchant Seamen, Pirates, and the Anglo-American Maritime World, 1700–1750* (New York: Cambridge UP, 1987); David James Stewart, *The Sea Their Graves: an Archaeology of Death and Remembrance in Maritime Culture* (Gainesville: UP of Florida, 2011).

| | | | | | |
|---|---|---|---|---|---|
| 1 | 3 | ” | SE | NE | Tuesday: 26: |
| 2 | 3 | 4 | | | |
| 3 | 2 | 5 | | NNE | Moderate Gales of wind and fair Weather |
| 4 | 3 | ” | | | |
| 5 | 3 | 3 | | | Course make to be S:° 40$^{d}$ E:$^{t}$ Distance |
| 6 | 4 | ” | var: 5°30' E:$^{t}$ | | 98 miles Southing 75 miles Easting 68 |
| 7 | 2 | 4 | | | Difference of Long:$^{d}$ 69 miles |
| 8 | 2 | 4 | | | |
| 9 | 3 | ” | | | Lat:$^{d}$ Observ'd 24$^{d}$ 31$^{m}$ S.° |
| 10 | 4 | ” | | | Meridian Distance 3 07 W:$^{t}$ |
| 11 | 4 | ” | | | Difference of Long:$^{d}$ 3 00 W:$^{t}$ |
| 12 | 4 | ” | | | |
| 1 | 4 | 3 | | | |
| 2 | 4 | 2 | | | |
| 3 | 4 | 2 | | | |
| 4 | 4 | ” | | | |
| 5 | 4 | ” | | NNW | |
| 6 | 4 | ” | | | |
| 7 | 3 | 3 | | | |
| 8 | 4 | ” | | | |
| 9 | 4 | 5 | | | |
| 10 | 5 | 5 | | | |
| 11 | 6 | ” | | | |
| 12 | 6 | 2 | 95 Miles | | |
| H | K | F | Courses | Winds | Wednesday: 27: February |
| 1 | 5 | ” | SE½S:° | NWBN | |
| 2 | 5 | 3 | | | Moderate gales of wind with fair Weather |
| 3 | 5 | 4 | | | |
| 4 | 4 | ” | SE | NW | Course make to be S:° 40$^{d}$ E:$^{t}$ Distance |
| 5 | 4 | ” | | | 116 miles Southing 89 miles Easting 75$^{m}$ |
| 6 | 4 | ” | | | Difference of Long:$^{d}$ 83 miles. |
| 7 | 3 | ” | | | |
| 8 | 2 | 5 | | | Lat:$^{d}$ p:$^{r}$ Account 26$^{d}$ 01$^{m}$ S:° |
| 9 | 2 | 5 | | NWBN | Meridian Distance 1 52 W.$^{t}$ |
| 10 | 4 | ” | | | Difference of Long:$^{d}$ 1 37 W.$^{t}$ |
| 11 | 4 | 2 | | | |
| 12 | 5 | 5 | | | Variation 5 00 E.$^{t}$ |
| 1 | 6 | ” | | NNW | |
| 2 | 6 | 3 | | | |
| 3 | 4 | 3 | | | |
| 4 | 4 | ” | | Sq:$^{ll}$ & R:$^{n}$ | |
| 5 | 4 | 4 | | NBW D:° | |
| 6 | 4 | 4 | ESE | | |
| 7 | 5 | 5 | | | |
| 8 | 5 | 4 | | | |
| 9 | 5 | 3 | | | |
| 10 | 5 | 3 | | | |
| 11 | 6 | 3 | | | |
| 12 | 6 | ” | 172 Miles | | |

| | | | | | |
|---|---|---|---|---|---|
| 1 | 6 | 2 | SE½S:$^{o}$ | NWBN | Thursday: 28: |
| 2 | 6 | 3 | | | |
| 3 | 6 | 3 | | | Fresh Gales of wind & fair Weather |
| 4 | 6 | " | SE | NW | |
| 5 | 6 | " | | | Course allowed to be S:$^{o}$ 50$^{d}$ E:$^{t}$ Distance |
| 6 | 6 | " | | | 166 miles Southing 106$^{m}$ Easting 127 m:$^{s}$ |
| 7 | 7 | " | | | Difference of Long:$^{d}$ 142 miles |
| 8 | 7 | " | | | |
| 9 | 7 | 3 | | NWBW | Lat:$^{d}$ Observ'd 27$^{d}$ 47 S:$^{o}$ |
| 10 | 7 | 3 | | | Meridian Distance 00 15 E:$^{t}$ |
| 11 | 7 | " | | | Difference of Long.$^{d}$ 00 45 W:$^{t}$ |
| 12 | 7 | " | | | |
| 1 | 6 | 5 | | NNW | |
| 2 | 6 | 3 | | | |
| 3 | 6 | 4 | | | |
| 4 | 6 | 3 | | Sq.$^{l}$ & Rain | |
| 5 | 7 | 5 | | NBW D.$^{o}$ | |
| 6 | 8 | " | ESE | | |
| 7 | 8 | 3 | | | |
| 8 | 8 | 3 | | | |
| 9 | 8 | 4 | | | |
| 10 | 8 | 2 | | | |
| 11 | 8 | 4 | | | |
| 12 | 8 | " | 172 Miles | | |
| 1 | 8 | " | ESE | NNW | Friday: 1: March |
| 2 | 7 | 3 | | | |
| 3 | 6 | " | ESE½S:$^{o}$ | | Fresh gales the first part, the latter Small |
| 4 | 6 | 3 | | | with fair weather |
| 5 | 6 | " | | | |
| 6 | 6 | 1 | SEBE | | Course allow to be S:$^{o}$ 61$^{d}$ E:$^{t}$ Distance |
| 7 | 7 | " | ESE | | 138 miles Southing 67 Easting 121 m:$^{s}$ |
| 8 | 7 | 3 | | | Difference of Long:$^{d}$ 136 miles |
| 9 | 6 | 5 | | | |
| 10 | 6 | " | | | Lat:$^{d}$ Observ'd 28$^{d}$ 54$^{m}$ S:$^{o}$ |
| 11 | 5 | 4 | | | Meridian Distance 2 16 E:$^{t}$ |
| 12 | 6 | " | | | Difference of Long.$^{d}$ 3 01 E:$^{t}$ |
| 1 | 6 | " | | | |
| 2 | 6 | 3 | | | |
| 3 | 7 | 3 | | | |
| 4 | 7 | " | | | |
| 5 | 5 | 5 | | | |
| 6 | 5 | 2 | Var: p. Am:$^{d}$ | 3$^{d}$ 22$^{m}$ E:$^{t}$ | |
| 7 | 5 | 2 | | | |
| 8 | 4 | 5 | ESE½S:$^{o}$ | | |
| 9 | 4 | " | | | |
| 10 | 3 | " | | | |
| 11 | 2 | " | | | |
| 12 | 2 | 3 | 138 Miles | | |

| H | K | F | Courses | Winds | Saturday: 2: March |
|---|---|---|---|---|---|
| 1 | 2 | " | ESE½S:° | NNW | |
| 2 | 2 | " | | | Small Gales of wind w:$^{th}$ fair Weather |
| 3 | 2 | 4 | | | |
| 4 | 2 | " | | | Course allowed to be S:° 58$^{d}$ E:$^{t}$ Dis:$^{t}$ 40 |
| 5 | 1 | 5 | | | miles Southing 21 miles Easting 34 miles |
| 6 | 1 | 3 | | | Diference of Long.$^{d}$ 39 miles |
| 7 | 1 | 4 | | | |
| 8 | 1 | " | | | Lat.$^{d}$ Observ'd 29$^{d}$ 15$^{m}$ S.° |
| 9 | 1 | " | | NBE | Meridian Distance 2 50 E.$^{t}$ |
| 10 | 1 | 3 | | | Difference of Long$^{d}$ 3 40 E.$^{t}$ |
| 11 | 2 | " | | | |
| 12 | 2 | 3 | | NNE | |
| 1 | 2 | " | | | |
| 2 | 2 | 2 | | | |
| 3 | 2 | 3 | | | |
| 4 | 2 | " | | | |
| 5 | 1 | " | | | |
| 6 | 1 | 3 | var p$^{r}$ Amp.$^{d}$ | 3° 30' E.$^{t}$ | |
| 7 | 1 | 4 | | | |
| 8 | 1 | " | | | |
| 9 | 1 | " | | | |
| 10 | 1 | " | SSE | E.$^{t}$ | |
| 11 | 1 | 3 | | | |
| 12 | 2 | " | SEBE | NEBE | |
| 1 | 1 | " | SE | ENE | Sunday: 3: |
| 2 | 1 | " | | | |
| 3 | " | 3 | | | Small gales the first part with abundance |
| 4 | " | 4 | | | of Lightning in the Night |
| 5 | 1 | " | | | |
| 6 | 2 | " | SEBS.° | EBN | Course w:$^{th}$ regard to all known Impedim.$^{ts}$ |
| 7 | 2 | 3 | Lightning in | the SW | make to be S:° 22$^{d}$ E:$^{t}$ Distance 58 Miles |
| 8 | 3 | 3 | SE | ENE Light:$^{g}$ | Southing 53 Easting 22 Diff. of Long.$^{d}$ |
| 9 | 2 | " | | | 25 m.$^{s}$ |
| 10 | 1 | " | | | |
| 11 | 3 | " | | | Lat:$^{d}$ p:$^{r}$ Account 30$^{d}$ 13$^{m}$ S:° |
| 12 | 3 | " | | } D.° | Meridian Distance 3 12 E.$^{t}$ |
| 1 | 2 | " | | | Difference of Long:$^{d}$ 4 05 D:° |
| 2 | 1 | 2 | SEBS:° | EBN | Variation p:$^{r}$ Amplitude 3 00 D:° |
| 3 | 1 | " | | | |
| 4 | 1 | " | SBE | EBS:° | |
| 5 | 1 | 2 | | | |
| 6 | 1 | 2 | | | |
| 7 | 3 | 3 | S.° | ESE | |
| 8 | 3 | 3 | SBE | EBS.° | |
| 9 | 4 | 3 | | | |
| 10 | 4 | 3 | | | |
| 11 | 5 | " | | | |
| 12 | 3 | 4 | 58 Miles | R.B.T.S:$^{l}$ | |

| | | | | | |
|---|---|---|---|---|---|
| 1 | 3 | 3 | SSE | E.$^{t}$ | Monday: 4: |
| 2 | 3 | 5 | SBE | EBS:$^{o}$ | |
| 3 | 3 | 3 | S:$^{o}$ | ESE | Moderate gales of wind with fair Weather: |
| 4 | 3 | 3 | SSE | East | |
| 5 | 2 | 6 | | | Course make to be S:$^{o}$ 9$^{d}$ E:$^{t}$ Distance 87 |
| 6 | 2 | 3 | SBE | EBS.$^{o}$ | miles Southing 85 Easting 14 Dif Long:$^{d}$ |
| 7 | 4 | ” | SSE | E.$^{t}$ | 16 |
| 8 | 4 | ” | | | |
| 9 | 3 | 3 | SEBS:$^{o}$ | EBN | Lat.$^{d}$ Observ'd 31$^{d}$ 38$^{m}$ S:$^{o}$ |
| 10 | 3 | ” | | | Meridian Distance 3 26 E.$^{t}$ |
| 11 | 4 | ” | | | Difference of Long:$^{d}$ 4 21 E.$^{t}$ |
| 12 | 4 | 3 | SSE | E.$^{t}$ | |
| 1 | 5 | ” | | | |
| 2 | 5 | 2 | SBE½E | | |
| 3 | 5 | ” | | | |
| 4 | 4 | 4 | SSE | | |
| 5 | 4 | 4 | | | |
| 6 | 4 | 3 | | | |
| 7 | 4 | 5 | | | |
| 8 | 5 | ” | | | |
| 9 | 4 | 3 | | | |
| 10 | 4 | 5 | | | |
| 11 | 4 | ” | SEB S:$^{o}$ | EBN | |
| 12 | 4 | 1 | 98 Miles | | |
| H | K | F | Courses | Winds | Tuesday: 5: March |
| 1 | 3 | 3 | SE | ENE | |
| 2 | 3 | 4 | | | Moderate gales of wind with fair Weather |
| 3 | 3 | ” | | | |
| 4 | 3 | ” | | | Course make to be S:$^{o}$ 43$^{d}$ E:$^{t}$ Distance |
| 5 | 3 | ” | | | 101 Miles Southing 74 miles Easting 68 |
| 6 | 4 | ” | | | miles difference of Long.$^{d}$ 80 miles |
| 7 | 4 | ” | | | |
| 8 | 4 | 2 | | | Lat:$^{d}$ Observ'd 32$^{d}$ 52$^{m}$ S:$^{o}$ |
| 9 | 4 | 3 | | | Meridian Distance 4 34 E.$^{t}$ |
| 10 | 4 | 2 | | | Difference of Long:$^{d}$ 5 41 E.$^{t}$ |
| 11 | 5 | 3 | | | |
| 12 | 5 | 3 | | | |
| 1 | 4 | ” | | | |
| 2 | 5 | ” | | | |
| 3 | 3 | 6 | | | |
| 4 | 4 | ” | | | |
| 5 | 4 | 5 | | | |
| 6 | 4 | ” | | | |
| 7 | 4 | ” | | | |
| 8 | 4 | 5 | SEBE | NE | |
| 9 | 4 | ” | | | |
| 10 | 5 | ” | | | |
| 11 | 5 | 3 | | | |
| 12 | 4 | 3 | 101 Miles | | |

| | | | | | |
|---|---|---|---|---|---|
| 1 | 3 | 5 | ESE | NE | Wednesday: 6: |
| 2 | 3 | 2 | | | |
| 3 | 4 | 4 | SEBE½E | | Moderate gales of wind and fair Weather |
| 4 | 4 | 3 | variation | 2° 20' E:$^t$ | |
| 5 | 5 | „ | | | Course allow to be S:$^o$ 58$^d$ E:$^t$ Distance |
| 6 | 5 | „ | | | 110 miles Southing 58 miles Easting 95 |
| 7 | 5 | 2 | | | miles difference of Long.$^d$ 114 miles |
| 8 | 5 | 3 | | | |
| 9 | 5 | 3 | | | Lat:$^d$ Observ'd 33$^d$ 50$^m$ S:$^o$ |
| 10 | 6 | „ | ESE | | Meridian Distance 6 09 E:$^t$ |
| 11 | 5 | 3 | | | Difference of Long.$^d$ 7 35 E:$^t$ |
| 12 | 5 | 3 | | | |
| 1 | 5 | 5 | ESE½E | NBE | |
| 2 | 5 | „ | EBS:$^o$ | | |
| 3 | 3 | 3 | | | |
| 4 | 4 | „ | | | |
| 5 | 3 | 4 | | | |
| 6 | 2 | 3 | | | |
| 7 | 3 | „ | | | |
| 8 | 3 | „ | SEBE | | |
| 9 | 3 | „ | | | |
| 10 | 3 | 5 | EBS:$^o$ | NBW | |
| 11 | 4 | 3 | | | |
| 12 | 4 | 6 | 103 Miles | | |
| 1 | 4 | „ | E½S:$^o$ | NNW | Thursday: 7:$^{th}$ |
| 2 | 2 | 3 | | | |
| 3 | 2 | „ | | | Fresh Gales of wind, fair Weather |
| 4 | 3 | 3 | | | |
| 5 | 4 | „ | | | Course make to be S:$^o$ 85$^d$ E:$^t$ Distance |
| 6 | 4 | 3 | E.$^t$ | NBW | 123 Miles Southing 10 miles Easting 123 |
| 7 | 4 | „ | | | miles difference of Long.$^d$ 148 miles |
| 8 | 4 | 1 | | | |
| 9 | 4 | 2 | | | Lat:$^d$ Observ'd 34$^d$ 00$^m$ S:$^o$ |
| 10 | 4 | 2 | | | Meridian Distance 8 12 E:$^t$ |
| 11 | 5 | „ | | | Difference of Long:$^d$ 10 03 E:$^t$ |
| 12 | 5 | „ | | | |
| 1 | 6 | „ | | | |
| 2 | 6 | „ | | | |
| 3 | 7 | „ | | | |
| 4 | 7 | 3 | | | |
| 5 | 7 | „ | | | |
| 6 | 7 | 1 | | | |
| 7 | 7 | „ | | | |
| 8 | 7 | 5 | | | |
| 9 | 5 | „ | | | |
| 10 | 5 | 3 | E½S:$^o$ | NBE | |
| 11 | 5 | 3 | | | |
| 12 | 5 | „ | 123 Miles | | |

| H | K | F | Courses | Winds | Friday: 8: March |
|---|---|---|---|---|---|
| 1 | 5 | „ | E$^{t}$ | NNW | |
| 2 | 4 | 4 | E½S:$^{o}$ | | Fresh gales of wind fair Weather |
| 3 | 4 | 2 | | | |
| 4 | 4 | 3 | | | Course Judge to be East Dis:$^{t}$ 177 Miles |
| 5 | 5 | 3 | | | Difference of Long:$^{d}$ 216 miles |
| 6 | 6 | 4 | Var: p:$^{r}$ | Amp.$^{d}$ 1$^{d}$ 39$^{m}$ | |
| 7 | 6 | 2 | | E:$^{t}$ | Lat:$^{d}$ Observ'd 34$^{d}$ 00$^{m}$ S:$^{o}$ |
| 8 | 7 | „ | | | Meridian Distance 11 11 E:$^{t}$ |
| 9 | 8 | „ | | | Difference of Long$^{d}$ 13 39 E:$^{t}$ |
| 10 | 7 | 3 | | | |
| 11 | 8 | „ | | | |
| 12 | 8 | „ | | | |
| 1 | 8 | „ | | | |
| 2 | 8 | „ | | | |
| 3 | 8 | 4 | | | |
| 4 | 8 | 4 | E:$^{t}$ | | |
| 5 | 9 | „ | | | |
| 6 | 9 | „ | | | |
| 7 | 9 | „ | | | |
| 8 | 9 | „ | | | |
| 9 | 9 | „ | | | |
| 10 | 9 | „ | | | |
| 11 | 8 | 3 | | | |
| 12 | 8 | 3 | 177 Miles | | |
| 1 | 8 | „ | East | NNW | Saturday: 9: |
| 2 | 8 | 3 | | | |
| 3 | 8 | 3 | | | Fresh Gales w:$^{th}$ great rains in the Night – |
| 4 | 7 | „ | Saw a Saile | bearing SSE | Came up with a Sloop from England |
| 5 | 8 | „ | EBS:$^{o}$ | | |
| 6 | 8 | „ | E.$^{t}$ | | Course make to be S:$^{o}$ 85 E:$^{t}$ Distance |
| 7 | 8 | 3 | | | 160 Miles Southing 14 miles Easting 160 |
| 8 | 8 | 3 | | Rain | miles difference of Long:$^{d}$ 190 miles |
| 9 | 7 | 3 | | D:$^{o}$ | |
| 10 | 7 | 2 | | | Lat:$^{d}$ Observ'd 34$^{d}$ 14$^{m}$ S.$^{o}$ |
| 11 | 7 | „ | | | Meridian Distance 13 51 E:$^{t}$ |
| 12 | 6 | „ | | West | Difference of Long.$^{d}$ 16 49 E:$^{t}$ |
| 1 | 6 | „ | | In 1:$^{st}$ R.B.T.S. | |
| 2 | 6 | 3 | | WBN | |
| 3 | 6 | 2 | | | |
| 4 | 5 | 4 | | | |
| 5 | 5 | 5 | | | |
| 6 | 5 | „ | | W:$^{t}$ | |
| 7 | 5 | „ | | | |
| 8 | 5 | „ | | | |
| 9 | 4 | „ | | WNW | |
| 10 | 5 | 5 | | O:$^{t}$ R.B.T. S:$^{o}$ | |
| 11 | 6 | 3 | | WBN | |
| 12 | 7 | 3 | 161 Miles | | |

| | | | | | |
|---|---|---|---|---|---|
| 1 | 8 | „ | East | NW | Sunday: 10: |
| 2 | 8 | 3 | | Rain | |
| 3 | 8 | 4 | | | Fresh gales, Variable winds with Rain |
| 4 | 9 | „ | | | |
| 5 | 9 | „ | | | Course S:° 81:$^{d}$ E.$^{t}$ Distance 104 Miles |
| 6 | 8 | 3 | | | Southing 17 miles Easting 108 miles diff.$^{s}$ |
| 7 | 9 | „ | | | of Long:$^{d}$ 124 miles |
| 8 | 9 | „ | | | |
| 9 | 9 | „ | EBS:° Taken | a back at SSW | Lat:$^{d}$ p:$^{r}$ Account 34$^{d}$ 31$^{m}$ S:° |
| 10 | 3 | „ | | | Meridian Distance 15 33 E:$^{t}$ |
| 11 | 1 | 3 | EBN | SWBS:° | Difference of Long.$^{d}$ 18 53 E:$^{t}$ |
| 12 | 1 | „ | | | |
| 1 | 3 | „ | E.$^{t}$ | SSW | |
| 2 | 2 | 1 | | | |
| 3 | 3 | 3 | | | |
| 4 | 1 | 2 | | | |
| 5 | „ | 3 | | | |
| 6 | „ | 4 | | | |
| 7 | | | } Calm | | |
| 8 | | | | | |
| 9 | 2 | 2 | SSE | E:$^{t}$ 1:$^{st}$ R.B.T.S. | |
| 10 | 4 | „ | SEBS.° | NEBE | |
| 11 | 5 | „ | SE | ENE | |
| 12 | 6 | „ | ESE 112$^{ms}$ | NE | |
| H | K | F | Courses | Winds | Monday: 11: March |
| 1 | 9 | 3 | East | NNW | |
| 2 | 9 | 3 | | | Fresh Gales Variable as p.$^{r}$ Logg |
| 3 | 9 | 5 | | NW | |
| 4 | 9 | 5 | | | Course make to be N:° 72$^{d}$ E:$^{t}$ Distance |
| 5 | 7 | 4 | | Rain | 162 miles Dif Long.$^{d}$ 188 miles Easting |
| 6 | 8 | „ | | | 156 miles Dif Long.$^{d}$ 188 miles. |
| 7 | 7 | 3 | | WNW | |
| 8 | 8 | 2 | | | Lat:$^{d}$ p:$^{r}$ Account 34$^{d}$ 12$^{m}$ S:° |
| 9 | 8 | 4 | | | Meridian Distance 18 09 E:$^{t}$ |
| 10 | 9 | „ | | | Difference of Long:$^{d}$ 22 01 E:$^{t}$ |
| 11 | 9 | „ | | | |
| 12 | 9 | „ | | | |
| 1 | 3 | 4 | | SSE | |
| 2 | 3 | „ | EBN | SEBS:° | |
| 3 | 4 | „ | | | |
| 4 | 5 | „ | | | |
| 5 | 5 | „ | E.$^{t}$ | SSE | |
| 6 | 6 | „ | EBN | SEBS.° | |
| 7 | 5 | „ | | In 2.$^{d}$ R.M.T.S. | |
| 8 | 6 | „ | ENE | | |
| 9 | 5 | 4 | | In 2.$^{d}$ R.F.T.S. | |
| 10 | 6 | 6 | | SE | |
| 11 | 5 | 5 | | | |
| 12 | 6 | 1 | 167 Miles | | |

| | | | | | |
|---|---|---|---|---|---|
| 1 | 7 | „ | ENE | SE Rain | Tuesday: 12: |
| 2 | 6 | 3 | | | |
| 3 | 5 | 6 | | | Fresh Gales, Some Rain the former part |
| 4 | 6 | „ | | | |
| 5 | 6 | 3 | | | Course allow'd N:$^{o}$ 55$^{d}$ E:$^{t}$ Distance 130 |
| 6 | 6 | „ | | O:$^{t}$ 2$^{d}$ R.M.T.S. | Miles, Northing 74 miles Easting 106 |
| 7 | 6 | 3 | EBN | SEBS.$^{o}$ | miles difference of Long.$^{d}$ 128 miles |
| 8 | 5 | 2 | | | |
| 9 | 5 | 2 | | | |
| 10 | 5 | „ | | | |
| 11 | 5 | 4 | | | |
| 12 | 6 | „ | | | |
| 1 | 5 | „ | | Rain | Lat:$^{d}$ p:$^{r}$ Account 32$^{d}$ 58$^{m}$ S:$^{o}$ |
| 2 | 5 | 1 | | | Meridian Distance 19 54 E.$^{t}$ |
| 3 | 5 | 5 | | | Difference of Long.$^{d}$ 24 09 E.$^{t}$ |
| 4 | 6 | 2 | | | |
| 5 | 6 | 4 | | | |
| 6 | 6 | „ | | In 2.$^{d}$ R.M.T.S. | |
| 7 | 6 | „ | | | |
| 8 | 5 | 4 | | | |
| 9 | 5 | 4 | | | |
| 10 | 5 | 4 | | | |
| 11 | 6 | 3 | ENE | | |
| 12 | 7 | „ | 134 Miles | | |
| 1 | 7 | „ | ENE | SE | Wednesday: 13. |
| 2 | 6 | „ | | | |
| 3 | 5 | 4 | NEBE | SEBE | Fresh gales the Major part and fair |
| 4 | 5 | 4 | | | Weather |
| 5 | 4 | 3 | | | |
| 6 | 4 | „ | NE | ESE | Course allow'd S:$^{o}$ 75:$^{d}$ E:$^{t}$ Distance 30 |
| 7 | 4 | 2 | NEBE | SEBE | miles Southing 7 miles Easting 29 miles |
| 8 | 3 | „ | ENE | SE TK.$^{t}$ | Difference of Long.$^{d}$ 35 miles |
| 9 | 2 | „ | S$^{o}$ | ESE | |
| 10 | 1 | 3 | | | Lat:$^{d}$ p$^{r}$ account 33$^{d}$ 05$^{m}$ S:$^{o}$ |
| 11 | 2 | 4 | SBW | SEBE | Meridian Distance 20 23 E.$^{t}$ |
| 12 | 2 | „ | | | Difference of Long:$^{d}$ 24 44 E.$^{t}$ |
| 1 | 3 | „ | SBE | EBS$^{o}$ | Variation p$^{r}$ Azim:$^{th}$ 3 40 West |
| 2 | 3 | „ | | | |
| 3 | 3 | „ | | | |
| 4 | 3 | „ | | | |
| 5 | 2 | 3 | | | |
| 6 | 3 | „ | | | |
| 7 | 3 | 2 | | | |
| 8 | 2 | „ | | O:$^{t}$ 2 R.B.T.S.[1] | |
| 9 | 2 | „ | | | |
| 10 | 3 | „ | SSE | E.$^{t}$ | |
| 11 | 3 | „ | SEBE | NEBE | |
| 12 | 2 | 6 | 85 Miles | | |

| H | K | F | Courses | Winds | Thursday: 14 March. 1723 |
|---|---|---|---|---|---|
| 1 | 2 | " | SBE | EBS:$^{o}$ | |
| 2 | 1 | " | SE | ENE | Small Gales of Wind, fair Weather |
| 3 | 1 | " | | | |
| 4 | 1 | " | SEBE | NEBE | Att 6. P.M: Saw a Sail bearing NBE which I |
| 5 | " | " | | } | take to be the Sloop we Saw the 9:$^{th}$ |
| 6 | " | " | | } Calm | |
| 7 | 1 | " | SE½E | | Course allow to be S:$^{o}$ 33$^{d}$ East Distance |
| 8 | 1 | " | | | 37 Miles |
| 9 | " | 4 | SE | ENE | |
| 10 | " | 3 | | | Lat:$^{d}$ p:$^{r}$ Account 33$^{d}$ 36$^{m}$ S:$^{o}$ |
| 11 | " | " | | } | Meridian Distance 20 43 E.$^{t}$ |
| 12 | " | " | | } Calm | Difference of Long.$^{d}$ 25 08 E.$^{t}$ |
| 1 | 1 | " | | | Variation p$^{r}$ Even:$^{gs}$ Azim:$^{th}$ 4 13 W:$^{t}$ |
| 2 | 1 | 2 | SEBE | NEBE | |
| 3 | 1 | 3 | | | |
| 4 | 1 | " | ESE | NE | |
| 5 | 1 | 1 | | | |
| 6 | 1 | 4 | SEBE | NEBE | |
| 7 | 1 | 6 | | | |
| 8 | 2 | 4 | SE | ENE | |
| 9 | 2 | 1 | | | |
| 10 | 2 | 3 | | | |
| 11 | 3 | " | SE½E | | |
| 12 | 3 | 4 | | | |
| 1 | 4 | " | SEBE | NEBE | Friday: 15: |
| 2 | 5 | " | | | |
| 3 | 5 | 2 | | | Fresh gales with abundance of Rain |
| 4 | 5 | 3 | | | |
| 5 | 2 | 4 | | In 1:$^{st}$ R.B.T.S. | Course I judge to be S:$^{o}$ 20$^{d}$ E:$^{t}$ Distance |
| 6 | 3 | " | SBE | EBS:$^{o}$ Rain | 90 Miles, Southing 85 miles Easting 31 |
| 7 | 4 | 3 | | | miles difference of Long.$^{d}$ 37 miles |
| 8 | 5 | 2 | | | |
| 9 | 3 | 3 | | | Lat:$^{d}$ p:$^{r}$ Account 35$^{d}$ 01$^{m}$ S:$^{o}$ |
| 10 | 2 | 4 | SEBS:$^{o}$ | EBN 2:$^{d}$ R.B.T.S. | Meridian Distance 21 14 E:$^{t}$ |
| 11 | 2 | 5 | SE | ENE Rain | Difference of Long.$^{d}$ 25 45 E:$^{t}$ |
| 12 | 3 | 2 | SEBS$^{o}$ | EBN D.$^{o}$ | |
| 1 | 5 | " | SBE½E | EBS.$^{o}$ | |
| 2 | 5 | 3 | SSE | East | |
| 3 | 3 | 4 | | | |
| 4 | 3 | 4 | | | |
| 5 | 3 | 4 | S$^{o}$ | ESE | |
| 6 | 4 | 2 | | | |
| 7 | 4 | 5 | | | |
| 8 | 4 | 3 | SBE | EBS.$^{o}$ | |
| 9 | 2 | 5 | | | |
| 10 | 2 | 4 | | | |
| 11 | 3 | 2 | | | |
| 12 | 2 | 5 | 93 Miles | H.$^{d}$ F.T.S. | |

| | | | | | |
|---|---|---|---|---|---|
| 1 | 2 | „ | SBE | EBS:o | Saturday: 16: |
| 2 | 2 | „ | So | ESE | |
| 3 | 1 | 4 | SBE | EBS.o 3.d R.MT. | S. & H.d D.o |
| 4 | 2 | „ | SSE | E:t Rain | |
| 5 | 1 | 4 | SBE½E | | Fresh gales of wind w:th continuall |
| 6 | 1 | 2 | SSE | | Squalls and Rain, a Sea from y:e E:tward |
| 7 | 1 | 2 | | | |
| 8 | 1 | 3 | | | Course Allow'd South Distance 24 m:s |
| 9 | 1 | 2 | | | |
| 10 | 1 | 3 | | | Lat:d p:r Account 35 d 25 m S:o |
| 11 | 1 | 2 | | | Meridian Distance 21 14 E:t |
| 12 | 1 | 4 | | | Difference of Long.d 25 45 E:t |
| 1 | 1 | 4 | | | |
| 2 | 1 | 2 | | | |
| 3 | 1 | „ | So | ESE | |
| 4 | 1 | „ | SBW | SEbE | |
| 5 | „ | „ | Calm | Set M.T.S. | |
| 6 | „ | „ | Calm | | |
| 7 | „ | „ | | Set F.T.S. | |
| 8 | „ | „ | | | |
| 9 | 1 | „ | SBE | EBS.o | |
| 10 | 1 | 4 | SEBE | NEbN | |
| 11 | 3 | „ | East | NNE O:t AR.s | |
| 12 | 5 | „ | 34 Miles | | |
| H | K | F | Courses | Winds | Sunday: 17: March |
| 1 | 5 | 3 | EBN½N | N:o In 2.dR. | |
| 2 | 3 | „ | | BT:S:s | Fresh Gales of Wind with abundance of |
| 3 | 4 | 3 | EBN.o | | Rain, an Eastern Sea: |
| 4 | 5 | „ | | | |
| 5 | 4 | 2 | ENE | | Course make to be N:o 83d E:t Distance |
| 6 | 4 | „ | | | 136 Miles, Northing 16 m:s Easting 135 |
| 7 | 4 | 6 | | | m:s difference of Long.d 164 m:s |
| 8 | 5 | 4 | | | |
| 9 | 5 | 2 | | | Lat:d p:r Account 35 d 09 m S:o |
| 10 | 6 | „ | | | Meridian Distance 23 29 E:t |
| 11 | 6 | 3 | | | Difference of Longd 28 29 E:t |
| 12 | 6 | „ | EBN½N | | |
| 1 | 6 | 2 | EBN.o | | |
| 2 | 6 | 3 | | | |
| 3 | 6 | „ | | | |
| 4 | 5 | 2 | | | |
| 5 | 6 | „ | EBN½N.o | | |
| 6 | 6 | 3 | EBN.o | | |
| 7 | 6 | 3 | | | |
| 8 | 6 | 5 | | | |
| 9 | 7 | „ | | | |
| 10 | 7 | 2 | | | |
| 11 | 6 | 5 | | | |
| 12 | 6 | 1 | 137 Miles | | |

| | | | | | |
|---|---|---|---|---|---|
| 1 | 6 | 4 | EBN | N:$^{o}$ Rain | Monday: 18: |
| 2 | 7 | ” | | | |
| 3 | 6 | 3 | | | Fresh Gales of Wind with Sq:$^{lls}$ |
| 4 | 7 | ” | | | and Raine |
| 5 | 6 | 2 | | In 3:$^{d}$ R.M.T.S. | |
| 6 | 7 | ” | | | Course make to be N:$^{o}$ 81:$^{d}$ E:$^{t}$ Distance |
| 7 | 7 | ” | E:$^{t}$ | | 124 miles, Northing 19 m:$^{s}$ Easting 122$^{ms}$ |
| 8 | 7 | ” | | | difference of Long:$^{d}$ 148 m:$^{s}$ |
| 9 | 6 | 3 | EBN.$^{o}$ | Rain | |
| 10 | 6 | ” | | | Lat:$^{d}$ p:$^{r}$ Account 34$^{d}$ 50$^{m}$ S:$^{o}$ |
| 11 | 6 | ” | | | Meridian Distance 25 31 E:$^{t}$ |
| 12 | 4 | 5 | | NNW | Difference of Long:$^{d}$ 30 57 E:$^{t}$ |
| 1 | 3 | 5 | | | |
| 2 | 3 | ” | | WNW | |
| 3 | 4 | ” | | | |
| 4 | 3 | ” | | W:$^{t}$ | |
| 5 | 3 | 6 | | Out R.B.T.S. | |
| 6 | 3 | 5 | | | |
| 7 | 4 | ” | | | |
| 8 | 4 | ” | | | |
| 9 | 5 | ” | | | |
| 10 | 5 | 3 | | | |
| 11 | 5 | 1 | | | |
| 12 | 3 | 5 | 126 Miles | | |
| 1 | 3 | 3 | EBN | WBS:$^{o}$ | Tuesday: 19: |
| 2 | 3 | 4 | | Rain | |
| 3 | 3 | ” | | | Fresh Gales, Cloudy Weather w:$^{th}$ |
| 4 | 3 | 3 | | | Squalls |
| 5 | 4 | 2 | | | |
| 6 | 5 | 3 | East | | Course make to be N:$^{o}$ 84 E.$^{t}$ Distance 145 |
| 7 | 5 | ” | | | miles, Northing 16 m:$^{s}$ Easting 144 m:$^{s}$ |
| 8 | 6 | ” | | | difference of Long.$^{d}$ 176 m:$^{s}$ |
| 9 | 5 | ” | | | |
| 10 | 4 | ” | | | Lat:$^{d}$ Observ'd 34$^{d}$ 34$^{m}$ S.$^{o}$ |
| 11 | 4 | ” | | | Meridian Distance 27 55 E:$^{t}$ |
| 12 | 3 | 3 | | | Difference of Long.$^{d}$ 33 53 E:$^{t}$ |
| 1 | 6 | ” | | | |
| 2 | 6 | 3 | | SWBW | |
| 3 | 7 | 3 | | Squaly | |
| 4 | 8 | ” | | | |
| 5 | 7 | 4 | | | |
| 6 | 8 | ” | | | |
| 7 | 8 | ” | | | |
| 8 | 8 | 4 | | SW | |
| 9 | 8 | ” | | | |
| 10 | 8 | 3 | | | |
| 11 | 9 | 3 | EBS$^{o}$ | | |
| 12 | 9 | ” | 145 Miles | | |

| H | K | F | Courses | Winds | Wednesday: 20: March |
|---|---|---|---|---|---|
| 1 | 8 | „ | EBS.$^{o}$ | SW | |
| 2 | 8 | „ | | | Fresh Gales the first part, the latter |
| 3 | 7 | „ | | | Small |
| 4 | 6 | 3 | | | |
| 5 | 4 | 3 | | | Course with regard to all known Imped- |
| 6 | 4 | 4 | | | im$^{ts}$ make to be N:$^{o}$ 82 E:$^{t}$ Distance 100 m:$^{s}$ |
| 7 | 4 | „ | E½S.$^{o}$ | | Northing 14 m:$^{s}$ Easting 99 m:$^{s}$ difference |
| 8 | 5 | „ | | | of Long.$^{d}$ 120 m$^{s}$: |
| 9 | 4 | 4 | | | |
| 10 | 4 | 4 | | | Lat:$^{d}$ Observ'd 34$^{d}$ 20$^{m}$ S.$^{o}$ |
| 11 | 5 | „ | | | Meridian Distance 29 34 E:$^{t}$ |
| 12 | 5 | „ | | | Difference of Long.$^{d}$ 35 53 E:$^{t}$ |
| 1 | 4 | „ | | WSW | |
| 2 | 3 | 4 | | | |
| 3 | 3 | 4 | E:$^{t}$ | | |
| 4 | 4 | „ | | | |
| 5 | 3 | 3 | | WBS:$^{o}$ | |
| 6 | 2 | 5 | | | |
| 7 | 3 | „ | | | |
| 8 | 2 | „ | | | |
| 9 | 2 | 5 | | | |
| 10 | 1 | 3 | | W:$^{t}$ | |
| 11 | 1 | „ | | | |
| 12 | 2 | „ | 100 Miles | | |
| 1 | 2 | 2 | E½S.$^{o}$ | WBN:$^{o}$ | Thursday: 21: |
| 2 | 2 | 2 | | | |
| 3 | 2 | 2 | | | Small Gales of Wind, fair Weather |
| 4 | 2 | 2 | | | |
| 5 | 2 | 2 | | | Course allow to be East Distance 88 Miles |
| 6 | 3 | 3 | Var:p$^{r}$ med:$^{m}$ 2 | Az:$^{th}$ 11$^{d}$06$^{m}$ W.$^{t}$ | difference of Long.$^{d}$ 106 m:$^{s}$ |
| 7 | 3 | 3 | EBS.$^{o}$ | | |
| 8 | 3 | 3 | | | Lat:$^{d}$ p:$^{r}$ Account 34$^{d}$ 20$^{m}$ S:$^{o}$ |
| 9 | 3 | 3 | | SWBW | Meridian Distance 30 12 E:$^{t}$ |
| 10 | 3 | 3 | | | Difference of Long.$^{d}$ 37 29 E:$^{t}$ |
| 11 | 3 | 3 | | | |
| 12 | 4 | 4 | | | |
| 1 | 3 | 3 | | | |
| 2 | 2 | 2 | | SSW | |
| 3 | 4 | 4 | | | |
| 4 | 4 | 4 | | | |
| 5 | 3 | 3 | | | |
| 6 | 4 | 4 | | | |
| 7 | 4 | 4 | | | |
| 8 | 4 | 4 | | | |
| 9 | 5 | 5 | | | |
| 10 | 6 | 6 | | | |
| 11 | 5 | 5 | | | |
| 12 | 5 | 5 | 88 Miles | | |

| | | | | | |
|---|---|---|---|---|---|
| 1 | 6 | ” | EBS½S.$^{o}$ | SSW | Friday: 22: |
| 2 | 6 | 3 | | SW | |
| 3 | 6 | 5 | EBS$^{o}$ | SSW | |
| 4 | 7 | ” | | | Fresh gales of Wind with Cloudy |
| 5 | 5 | ” | | SBW | Weather |
| 6 | 5 | ” | Var:p$^{r}$ med:$^{m}$ 2 | Az: 11° 55' W:$^{t}$ | |
| 7 | 4 | 3 | | | Course make to be N:$^{o}$ 70$^{d}$ E:$^{t}$ Distance |
| 8 | 4 | ” | | | 122 Miles, Northing 41 m:$^{s}$ Easting 115 |
| 9 | 3 | 3 | E:$^{t}$ | SSE | m:$^{s}$ difference of Long.$^{d}$ 138 m:$^{s}$ |
| 10 | 5 | 3 | EBN | SEBS.$^{o}$ | |
| 11 | 5 | ” | ENE | SE | Lat:$^{d}$ p$^{r}$ Account 33$^{d}$ 39$^{m}$ S:$^{o}$ |
| 12 | 5 | ” | | | Meridian Distance 32 07 E:$^{t}$ |
| 1 | 5 | 5 | East | SSE | Difference of Long.$^{d}$ 39 57 E:$^{t}$ |
| 2 | 6 | ” | EBN$^{o}$ | SEBS.$^{o}$ | |
| 3 | 5 | ” | | | |
| 4 | 5 | 2 | | | |
| 5 | 6 | ” | | | |
| 6 | 5 | 3 | | | |
| 7 | 4 | 3 | | | |
| 8 | 4 | 3 | East | SSE | |
| 9 | 5 | ” | EBN | SEBS.$^{o}$ | |
| 10 | 5 | 3 | East | SSE | |
| 11 | 5 | 3 | | | |
| 12 | 5 | 3 | 127 Miles | | |
| H | K | F | Courses | Winds | Saturday: 23: March |
| 1 | 5 | 3 | E½S.$^{o}$ | SBE | |
| 2 | 5 | 4 | E:$^{t}$ | | Fresh Gales of Wind. Cloudy Weather |
| 3 | 6 | ” | | SSE | |
| 4 | 4 | 3 | | In 2.$^{d}$ R.B.T.S. | Course make to be N:$^{o}$ 85$^{d}$ E:$^{t}$ Distance |
| 5 | 4 | 3 | EBS.$^{o}$ | SBE | 106 miles, Northing 98 m:$^{s}$ Easting 106 |
| 6 | 4 | 3 | | | m:$^{s}$ difference of Long.$^{d}$ 126 m:$^{s}$ |
| 7 | 5 | ” | | | |
| 8 | 5 | 2 | EBS½S.$^{o}$ | S:$^{o}$ | Lat:$^{d}$ p:$^{r}$ Account 33$^{d}$ 31$^{m}$ S:$^{o}$ |
| 9 | 5 | 3 | | | Meridian Distance 33 53 E:$^{t}$ |
| 10 | 6 | 3 | | | Difference of Long.$^{d}$ 42 03 E:$^{t}$ |
| 11 | 4 | ” | ESE | H:$^{d}$ F.T.S. | |
| 12 | 4 | 3 | | | |
| 1 | 3 | 3 | | | |
| 2 | 4 | ” | | | |
| 3 | 3 | 2 | SEBE | SBW | |
| 4 | 3 | ” | | | |
| 5 | 3 | 6 | | | |
| 6 | 3 | 3 | | Set F.T.S. | |
| 7 | 4 | 3 | | | |
| 8 | 4 | ” | | | |
| 9 | 4 | 3 | | | |
| 10 | 4 | ” | | | |
| 11 | 5 | 2 | | | |
| 12 | 6 | ” | 100 Miles | | |

| | | | | | |
|---|---|---|---|---|---|
| 1 | 5 | 4 | SEBS.° | SBW | Sunday: 24: |
| 2 | 6 | „ | | | |
| 3 | 6 | 2 | | | Fresh Gales of Wind with Some Rain in |
| 4 | 6 | 2 | | | the Night |
| 5 | 6 | 3 | | | |
| 6 | 6 | 3 | | | Course make to be N:° 84$^{d}$ East Dis:$^{t}$ 115 |
| 7 | 4 | 3 | | | miles, Northing 12 m:$^{s}$ Easting 113 m:$^{s}$ |
| 8 | 3 | „ | SSE | SW | difference of Long:$^{d}$ 136 m:$^{s}$ |
| 9 | 4 | 3 | SEBS.° | SWBW | |
| 10 | 4 | 3 | | | Lat:$^{d}$ Observ'd 33$^{d}$ 18$^{m}$ S:° |
| 11 | 5 | „ | | | Meridian Distance 35 46 E:$^{t}$ |
| 12 | 4 | „ | | | Difference of Long:$^{d}$ 44 19 E:$^{t}$ |
| 1 | 5 | „ | SE | SSW | |
| 2 | 2 | „ | | SWBS:° | |
| 3 | 3 | 5 | SEBS.° | Rain | |
| 4 | 3 | 3 | | | |
| 5 | 4 | 3 | | | |
| 6 | 3 | 3 | | | |
| 7 | 4 | „ | | | |
| 8 | 4 | 3 | | | |
| 9 | 5 | 5 | | | |
| 10 | 5 | „ | | | |
| 11 | 6 | 4 | | | |
| 12 | 5 | „ | 115 Miles | | |
| 1 | 5 | „ | SE | SSW | Monday: 25: |
| 2 | 5 | „ | | | |
| 3 | 4 | 3 | | | Moderate gales of wind and fair Weather |
| 4 | 5 | „ | | | |
| 5 | 5 | „ | ½ past Saw | Land | Att 4 P.M: Saw Land and att 8 D:° Tackt |
| 6 | 4 | „ | SEBS° | SWBS°Va:14°W$^{t}$ | and Stood off till 5 A:M: then Stood in & |
| 7 | 2 | 3 | SE½E | SBW | this Noon the Table Land[38] bore SEBS:° |
| 8 | 2 | „ | | TK:$^{t}$ | Distance 14 Leagues |
| 9 | 2 | „ | WSW | S:° | |
| 10 | 3 | „ | | | Course make to be S:° 78 E:$^{t}$ Distance |
| 11 | 1 | 5 | SWBW | SBE | 36 Miles |
| 12 | 2 | „ | WSW | S.° | |
| 1 | 3 | 3 | | | Lat:$^{d}$ Observ'd 33$^{d}$ 25$^{m}$ S.° |
| 2 | 4 | „ | WBS.° | SBW | Meridian Distance 36 21 E:$^{t}$ |
| 3 | 3 | 3 | W$^{t}$ | SSW | Difference of Long$^{d}$ 45 01 E:$^{t}$ |
| 4 | 3 | 2 | | | |
| 5 | 3 | „ | W½S.° | SBW TK:$^{t}$ | Note. I make the Table Land to lie in Lat:$^{d}$ |
| 6 | 2 | „ | SE | SSW O.$^{t}$R.BT:S. | 33° 45 S.° M: Dis:$^{t}$ from the Island S:$^{t}$ Jago |
| 7 | 3 | „ | Saw 3 Saile | | 36 57 E:$^{t}$ & Diff Long:$^{d}$ 45° 46 $^{E}$t |
| 8 | 3 | 3 | | | |
| 9 | 3 | 3 | | | |
| 10 | 3 | 3 | | | |
| 11 | 3 | 4 | | | |
| 12 | 3 | 3 | Table Land | SEBS:° 14 lea: | |

38 This likely refers to the area around Table Bay, located to the north of and overlooked by Cape Town. Although known for its shipwrecks, the bay offered ships some shelter and crucial access to fresh water.

| H | K | F | Courses | Winds | Tuesday: 26: March |
|---|---|---|---|---|---|
| 1 | 4 | " | SEBS° | SWBS.° | |
| 2 | 4 | 3 | | | Moderate Gales of Wind with fair Weather |
| 3 | 5 | " | | | – Stood off and on in the Night as p:$^{r}$ Logg |
| 4 | 6 | " | SSE | SW | |
| 5 | 5 | " | | | Att 6 P.M. Cape Bona Esperance[39] bore |
| 6 | 4 | " | | | S½E Penguin Island[40] SE½E and the |
| 7 | 2 | " | Cape S½E | 16 Leag$^{s}$: Tackt | N:°ermost Land NNE |
| 8 | 2 | 2 | W½S.° | SBW | |
| 9 | 2 | " | | | Att 8 AM: the Table Land SEBS:° the Pitch |
| 10 | 2 | " | | | of Cape bona Esperance (being a round |
| 11 | 3 | 3 | | | Hummock[41]) S½E |
| 12 | 4 | " | WBS.° | | |
| 1 | 4 | 3 | | | Att Noon the Cape S:° the N:°ermost |
| 2 | 4 | 5 | | Tackt | land in Sight NEBN:° and the Table Land |
| 3 | 5 | " | SEBE | SBW | SBE½E |
| 4 | 4 | 3 | ESE | S.° | |
| 5 | 2 | 3 | SEBE | SBW | |
| 6 | 2 | 4 | Table Land | SEbS 12 Leag:$^{s}$ | |
| 7 | 2 | " | SEBS.° | SWBS.° | |
| 8 | 2 | " | | | |
| 9 | 2 | " | SSE | SW | |
| 10 | 1 | 2 | | | |
| 11 | 1 | " | | | |
| 12 | 1 | " | 77 Miles. | Cape SBE 16 | Lea.s |

39 The Portuguese explorer Bartolomeu Dias was the first European to round the Cape of Good Hope, located near the southern tip of Africa and which allowed access between the Atlantic and Indian oceans, in 1488. Cape Town was the Dutch settlement located near this headland.
40 Penguin Island is one in a collection of small islands off the southwest coast of Africa, near Cape Town. Merchants began to visit the area in the 1600s to collect guano, which was sold as fertilizer in Europe and the Americas. See Gregory Cushman, *Guano and the Opening of the Pacific World: a Global Ecological History* (New York: Cambridge UP, 2013).
41 A hummock is a small hill, typically less than 15 meters high. Sailors frequently used descriptions of land markers to identify their location and communicate it to others, especially in written sources.

## Ship Hartford in Table Bay

March

Wednes:[d] 27[th] Fresh gales of wind and fair Weather, att 4 PM Anchored in Table Bay in Company with the Duke of Cambridge and Mountague Cap:[t]: Daniel Small and John Gordon

found here the Princess Ann Cap:[t] Luhorn and the Ships Sarum[42] and Carnavan Cap:[ts] Geo: Newton[43] and Josias T[h]waits[44],

Att 8 PM Moor'd Ship with our 2 Bowers the bearings of the Land as followeth (viz) Lyons Rump[45] SWBS:[o] Charles Mount[46] South and Penguin Island N½E Depth of water 5 fa: Saluted the Fort with Eleven Guns[47]

Thursday 28 The first part light breezers intermixt w:[th] Calms the latter fresh gale at SE. Struck yards and Topmasts

Our Long boat Attempted to go ashore in the Even:[g] for water but was forced to return again. Sent her ashore in the Morning, at which time New Moor'd Ship a Dutch Ship having Tript our anchor

This Morning Came in the Ships Barrenton Prince Augustus, and Craggs, Cap:[ts] Hunter[48] Reeves[49], and Grantham[50] for Moco

Friday 29[th] Moderate Gales of Wind with fair weather Our Longboat made 2 Trips with water

---

**42** The Sarum, a frigate of 400 tons, housed 80 crewmembers and 36 guns while active, from 1715 to 1728. Its third voyage, extending from 1723 to 1724, primarily focused on Bengal.

**43** George Newton (dates unknown) was captain of the Sarum during her first through fourth voyages, to Bombay, Canton, Bengal and Bengal respectively (1715–1718, 1719–1721, 1722–1724, 1725–1728).

**44** Josiah Thwaites (1691–ca. 1729) was captain of the Carnarvon from 1720 to at least 1724. In 1725, the Receiver of Customs indicted him for the "running of goods", or smuggling, and fined him £2,800. See petition of Judith, widow of Josiah Thwaites," 3 December 1729, in: *Calendar of Treasury Books and Papers, 1729–1730*, vol. 1, ed. William A. Shaw (London: Her Majesty's Stationery Office, 1897).

**45** Lion's Rump, now Signal Hill, is a flat-topped hill located in western Cape Town. It served as an early lookout and signal point for the Dutch settlement.

**46** King Charles Mount, now Devil's Peak, is a promontory located in southern Cape Town.

**47** A thirteen-gun salute typically indicated the presence of a superior naval officer. It was common practice by European and American sailors, however, to also salute a newly unfurled flag with thirteen guns. Sutton, East India, 86.

**48** John Hunter (dates unknown), a Scotsman, was captain of the Barrington during her three voyages to Mocha and India (1722–1724, 1725–1727, 1729). McGilvary, East India, 116.

**49** Thomas Ryves (ca. 1690–1723) was captain of the Prince Augustus during her inaugural voyage to Mocha and India (1722–1725). He died near Bombay during this sailing.

**50** Caleb Grantham (d. 1762) was captain of the Craggs during her second voyage, being this sailing, to Mocha (1722–1724) and during her third and fourth voyages to Madras and Bengal (1725–1727, 1729–1730). He worked as captain and ship-owner for the EIC into the 1740s. Ultimately, Grantham joined the Elder Brethren of Trinity House and was appointed Governor of the London Hospital. He then bought a manor for his family in West Thurrock. See Derek Morris, "Stepney and Trinity House", in: *East London Record* 13 (1990), 36–37.

Saturday. 30th Sea and Land wind, Continue watering Ship
Sunday 31st Fresh Gales in the SE Quarter, Continue Watering the Ship
April
Monday: 1:st Light Variable winds in the Day, in the Night fresh gales. Rec.d on board water
Tuesday 2 Fresh gales in the SE Quarter, Scrubb'd Ship and paid her Sides with Tarr[51]
Wednesday 3.d Light Sea and Land Winds, received on board water
Thursday 4 Gott up Yards and Topmasts, Winds in ye SE Quarter, Sailed hence the Disbovery[52] for Engl.d
Friday 5th Made the Signall for Sailing, the winds in the SE Quarter
Saturday 6 Variable Winds, and Calms, Made the Signall to Unmoare but being little wind and Calm Continue our Anchors as they were
Sunday 7th Variable winds allround, Att 6 AM Unmoard and hove Short and Att 9 D:o weigh'd the Wind then WBS:o Saluted the Fort w:th 11 Guns
Monday 8th Att 4 P.M Looking very Cloudy and likely to blow, so that there was no likelyhood of Turning out of the Bay, the Commadore made the Signall to bear away and Anchor, which we did in fathoms 5. Lyons rump WBS:o Charles Mount SBW and Penguin Island NBE – Att 6 PM Moar'd Ship and Att 6 this morning Unmoard again and Att 10 D:o Weighed with ye Wind at North. Penguin Island bearing at Noon N½W:t

51 This refers to the act of caulking a ship.
52 The Bouverie, or Desbouverie, rated 420 tons, housed 84 men and 30 guns while active, from 1709 to 1723. This was her fourth, and final, voyage. Captained by James Chambré, she was returning from Madras, Balasore and Calcutta.

## Ship Hartford from the the Cape tow:$^{ds}$ China

| H | K | F | Courses | Winds | Tuesday: 9:$^{th}$ April |
|---|---|---|---|---|---|
| 1 | | | | | |
| 2 | | | Table Land | SSE & Penguin | SE 2 Leag:$^{s}$ |
| 3 | | | | | |
| 4 | | | D:$^{o}$ D:$^{o}$ | SSE 7 Leagues | Variable Winds, Att 4 PM the Table Land |
| 5 | 4 | 4 | WBN | SWBS:$^{o}$ | bore SSE 7 Leagues from whence I take |
| 6 | 5 | ” | | In 2.$^{d}$ R.B.T.S. | my Departure |
| 7 | 5 | ” | W$^{t}$ | SSW | |
| 8 | 5 | ” | | | Course from thence to this day Noon is S:$^{o}$ |
| 9 | 5 | 3 | | | 77$^{d}$ W:$^{t}$ Distance 80 Miles, S:$^{o}$ing 15 m:$^{s}$ |
| 10 | 7 | ” | | | |
| 11 | 6 | ” | | | Lat:$^{d}$ Observ'd 34$^{d}$ 04$^{m}$ S.$^{o}$ |
| 12 | 4 | 3 | WBS:$^{o}$ | SBW In F.T.S. | Meridian Distance 1 15 W. |
| 1 | 3 | 3 | | | Difference of Long$^{d}$ 1 29 W. |
| 2 | 3 | 3 | | | Variation allowed 14 30 W. |
| 3 | 3 | 5 | | | |
| 4 | 4 | ” | W:$^{t}$ | SSW Set F.T.S. | |
| 5 | 3 | ” | WBS:$^{o}$ | SBW | |
| 6 | 5 | 3 | | | |
| 7 | 4 | ” | | | |
| 8 | 5 | ” | WSW | S:$^{o}$ | |
| 9 | 4 | ” | | | |
| 10 | 3 | 2 | | | |
| 11 | 3 | ” | | | |
| 12 | 3 | 2 | 92 Miles | | |
| 1 | 4 | ” | WSW | S:$^{o}$ | Wednesday: 10: |
| 2 | 3 | 3 | | | |
| 3 | 4 | 3 | | | Moderate gales of wind with fair |
| 4 | 3 | 6 | | | Weather |
| 5 | 4 | 3 | | | |
| 6 | 4 | 3 | SWBW | SBE | Course make to be S:$^{o}$ 60$^{d}$ W:$^{t}$ Distance |
| 7 | 4 | 3 | | | 100 Miles Southing 50 m:$^{s}$ Westing 88 m:$^{s}$ |
| 8 | 4 | 4 | | | difference of Long.$^{d}$ 108 m:$^{s}$ |
| 9 | 4 | 3 | | | |
| 10 | 4 | 5 | | | Lat:$^{d}$ Observ'd 34$^{d}$ 53$^{m}$ S.$^{o}$ |
| 11 | 5 | ” | | | Meridian Distance 2 43 W.$^{t}$ |
| 12 | 5 | 2 | | | Difference of Long.$^{d}$ 3 17 W.$^{t}$ |
| 1 | 5 | ” | | | Variation allowed 14 00 W.$^{t}$ |
| 2 | 5 | ” | SE | SSE | |
| 3 | 5 | ” | | | |
| 4 | 5 | ” | | | |
| 5 | 4 | 5 | SWBS:$^{o}$ | SEBS:$^{o}$ | |
| 6 | 5 | ” | | | |
| 7 | 5 | ” | | | |
| 8 | 5 | ” | | | |
| 9 | 6 | ” | SSW | SE | |
| 10 | 5 | ” | | | |
| 11 | 5 | ” | S$^{o}$ | ESE | |
| 12 | 4 | 2 | 113 Miles | | |

| | | | | | |
|---|---|---|---|---|---|
| 1 | 4 | ” | SBE | EBS.$^{o}$ | Thursday: 11 |
| 2 | 4 | ” | | | |
| 3 | 4 | ” | S½E | | Moderate Gales of Wind, fair |
| 4 | 3 | 5 | S$^{o}$ | ESE | Weather |
| 5 | 4 | ” | SBW | SEBE O:$^{t}$ AR.$^{s}$ | |
| 6 | 4 | ” | | | Course make to be S:$^{o}$ 4$^{d}$ E:$^{t}$ Distance |
| 7 | 4 | 3 | | | 88 Miles Southing 87 m:$^{s}$ Easting 6 m:$^{s}$ |
| 8 | 4 | ” | | | difference of Long.$^{d}$ 7 m:$^{s}$ |
| 9 | 4 | 3 | | | |
| 10 | 5 | ” | | | Lat:$^{d}$ Account 36$^{d}$ 30$^{m}$ S:$^{o}$ |
| 11 | 4 | ” | S$^{o}$ | ESE | Meridian Distance 2 37 W:$^{t}$ |
| 12 | 5 | ” | | | Difference of Long.$^{d}$ 3 10 W:$^{t}$ |
| 1 | 4 | ” | S½W | | Variation Allowed 14 00 W:$^{t}$ |
| 2 | 4 | 2 | | | |
| 3 | 3 | 5 | SBE | EBS:$^{o}$ | |
| 4 | 5 | ” | | | |
| 5 | 4 | ” | | | |
| 6 | 4 | ” | | | |
| 7 | 4 | ” | | | |
| 8 | 3 | 5 | | | |
| 9 | 2 | 5 | SE | ENE | |
| 10 | 2 | 1 | | | |
| 11 | 1 | ” | SEBE | NEBE | |
| 12 | 1 | 2 | 91 Miles | | |
| H | K | F | Courses | Winds | Friday: 12: Aprill 1723 |
| 1 | ” | ” | } Calm | | |
| 2 | ” | ” | | | Small Airs till 6 PM then fresh Gales and |
| 3 | ” | 3 | SEBE | N:$^{o}$ | fair Weather |
| 4 | 1 | ” | | NBW | |
| 5 | 3 | ” | ESE | | Course Judge to be S:$^{o}$ 85$^{d}$ E:$^{t}$ Distance |
| 6 | 5 | ” | | | 108 Miles Southing 9 m:$^{s}$ Easting 107 m.$^{s}$ |
| 7 | 7 | ” | | | difference of Long.$^{d}$ 134 m:$^{s}$ |
| 8 | 6 | 5 | | | |
| 9 | 6 | ” | | | Lat:$^{d}$ p:$^{r}$ Account 36$^{d}$ 39$^{m}$ S:$^{o}$ |
| 10 | 7 | ” | | | Meridian Distanc 0 50 West |
| 11 | 6 | ” | | WSW | Difference of Long.$^{d}$ 1 24 West |
| 12 | 6 | 3 | | | Variation Allowed 14 30 West |
| 1 | 6 | ” | | | |
| 2 | 4 | 4 | | WNW | |
| 3 | 5 | ” | | | |
| 4 | 5 | ” | | O:$^{t}$ 2.$^{d}$ R.B.T.S. | |
| 5 | 5 | ” | | Rain | |
| 6 | 4 | 2 | | | |
| 7 | 5 | ” | | SBW | |
| 8 | 6 | ” | | | |
| 9 | 4 | ” | | In 1:$^{st}$ R.B.T.S. | |
| 10 | 6 | ” | | S$^{o}$ | |
| 11 | 6 | ” | EBS$^{o}$ | SBE In2$^{d}$. R. | BT.S. |
| 12 | 6 | 4 | 112 Miles | | |

| | | | | | |
|---|---|---|---|---|---|
| 1 | 6 | 4 | EBS.° | S:° Sq$^{l}$ & R.$^{n}$ | Saturday: 13: |
| 2 | 5 | 3 | | H.$^{d}$ F.T.S. | |
| 3 | 4 | 3 | ESE | | Fresh Gales of Wind with Squalls and |
| 4 | 5 | " | EBS.° | SBE | Rain |
| 5 | 4 | " | | Wore | |
| 6 | 2 | 3 | SWBW | In 3.$^{d}$ R.M.T.S. | Course make to be S:° 31$^{d}$ W:$^{t}$ Distance |
| 7 | 2 | " | SWBS° | SEBS° | 32 Miles Southing 27 m:$^{s}$ Westing 16 m:$^{s}$ |
| 8 | 2 | " | | | difference of Long.$^{d}$ 20 m:$^{s}$ |
| 9 | 3 | " | SW | SSE | |
| 10 | 3 | 5 | SWBS° | SEBS° | Lat:$^{d}$ p:$^{r}$ Account 37$^{d}$ 06$^{m}$ S:° |
| 11 | 3 | " | | Set F.T.S. | Meridian Distance 1 06 W:$^{t}$ |
| 12 | 3 | 4 | SSW | SE | Difference of Long:$^{d}$ 1 44 W:$^{t}$ |
| 1 | 3 | 3 | SBW | SEBE H.$^{d}$ F.TS | |
| 2 | 3 | 4 | SSW | SE | |
| 3 | 3 | " | SBW | SEbE | |
| 4 | 2 | " | SSW | SE | |
| 5 | 2 | 3 | SBW | SEBE | |
| 6 | 2 | 3 | | | |
| 7 | 3 | " | | | |
| 8 | 3 | " | | | |
| 9 | 3 | 2 | SSW | SE | |
| 10 | 2 | " | | | |
| 11 | 2 | " | SWBS.° | SEBS.° | |
| 12 | 1 | 5 | 77 Miles | | |
| 1 | 1 | " | SBW | SSE | Sunday: 14: |
| 2 | " | " | } | | |
| 3 | " | " | } Calm | | Small Airs till 4 PM then fresh Gales with |
| 4 | 4 | " | SSE | SW Squaly | Intermitting Squalls & Rain |
| 5 | 5 | " | ESE | H.$^{d}$ M.T.S. | |
| 6 | 4 | " | East | In3$^{d}$ R & H$^{d}$ F.T.S | Course make to be N:° 56$^{d}$ W:$^{t}$ Dis:$^{t}$ 80 |
| 7 | 3 | 3 | E½N | SSE Rain | miles Northing 45 m:$^{s}$ Easting 66 m:$^{s}$ |
| 8 | 4 | " | | Set M.T.S. | difference of Long.$^{d}$ 82 m:$^{s}$ |
| 9 | 5 | " | East | | |
| 10 | 6 | 3 | EBS.° | SBE | Lat:$^{d}$ p:$^{r}$ Account 36$^{d}$ 21$^{m}$ S:° |
| 11 | 4 | 3 | | H.$^{d}$ M.T.S. | Meridian Distance 00 00 ---- |
| 12 | 3 | 3 | | | Difference of Long$^{d}$ 00 22 West |
| 1 | 3 | " | | | Variation allowed 14 30 West |
| 2 | 3 | " | | Set M.T.S. | |
| 3 | 3 | 3 | | Set F.T.S. | |
| 4 | 4 | " | East | SSE H$^{d}$ F.T.S. | |
| 5 | 5 | 3 | EBS.° | S:° | |
| 6 | 5 | " | | | |
| 7 | 4 | 5 | | | |
| 8 | 4 | 3 | | | |
| 9 | 3 | 3 | | SBE | |
| 10 | 3 | 4 | | | |
| 11 | 3 | 4 | | Set F.T.S. | |
| 12 | 3 | 5 | 88 Miles | | |

| H | K | F | Courses | Winds | Monday: 15: Aprill |
|---|---|---|---|---|---|
| 1 | 3 | 4 | EBS.$^{o}$ | SBE | |
| 2 | 3 | ” | | | Fresh Gales of Wind with Cloudy Weather |
| 3 | 3 | 3 | EBN | SEBS.$^{o}$ | |
| 4 | 3 | 3 | | Tackt | Course make to be West Distance 33 Miles |
| 5 | 1 | ” | SW | | difference of Long.$^{d}$ 40 m:$^{s}$ |
| 6 | 1 | ” | | H.$^{d}$ F.T.S. | |
| 7 | 2 | ” | SWBS.$^{o}$ | SEBS.$^{o}$ | Lat:$^{d}$ p:$^{r}$ Account 36$^{d}$ 21$^{m}$ S:$^{o}$ |
| 8 | 2 | ” | | Set F.T.S. | Meridian Distance 0 33 West |
| 9 | 4 | ” | SW | SBE Light:$^{s}$ | Difference of Long.$^{d}$ 1 02 West |
| 10 | 3 | ” | | | Variation allowed 14 30 West |
| 11 | 3 | 3 | | | |
| 12 | 3 | ” | | H.$^{d}$ F.T.S. | |
| 1 | 3 | 2 | | | |
| 2 | 3 | 2 | SWBW | SBE | |
| 3 | 4 | ” | | Set F.T.S. | |
| 4 | 3 | 3 | | | |
| 5 | 4 | ” | WSW | SSE | |
| 6 | 3 | 3 | | | |
| 7 | 3 | ” | | | |
| 8 | 4 | ” | | Tackt | |
| 9 | 3 | 3 | ESE | S:$^{o}$ O:$^{t}$3$^{d}$ R.BT. | S:$^{s}$ |
| 10 | 4 | ” | | | |
| 11 | 3 | ” | SEBE | SBW | |
| 12 | 2 | 2 | ESE 72$^{m}$ S:$^{o}$ | O:$^{t}$ 2.$^{d}$ R.BT:S. | |
| 1 | 3 | 2 | SEBE | SWBS:$^{o}$ | Tuesday: 16: |
| 2 | 4 | ” | | | |
| 3 | 6 | 2 | | SW | Fresh Gales of Wind w:$^{th}$ Intermitting |
| 4 | 6 | ” | | | Squalls and Raine |
| 5 | 5 | 3 | ESE | | |
| 6 | 5 | ” | | | Course with regard to all known |
| 7 | 6 | ” | SEBE | WBN | Impedim:$^{ts}$ make to be S:$^{o}$ 79$^{d}$ E:$^{t}$ Distance |
| 8 | 4 | ” | | | 155 Miles Southing 29 m:$^{s}$ Easting 152 |
| 9 | 4 | ” | ESE | | m:$^{s}$ diff Long:$^{d}$ 190 m:$^{s}$ |
| 10 | 5 | ” | | WNW Rain | |
| 11 | 5 | 3 | | | Lat:$^{d}$ p:$^{r}$ Account 36$^{d}$ 50$^{m}$ S:$^{o}$ |
| 12 | 6 | 6 | Light.$^{g}$ in the | SW board | Meridian Distance 1 59 East |
| 1 | 8 | ” | | | Difference of Long:$^{d}$ 2 08 East |
| 2 | 7 | ” | D:$^{o}$ and Rain | In 3.$^{d}$ R.F.T.S. | Variation Allowed 15 30 West |
| 3 | 8 | ” | | In 3.$^{d}$ R.M.T.S. | |
| 4 | 8 | 3 | hard Sq.$^{ll}$ & | R:$^{n}$ H.$^{d}$ F.T.S. | |
| 5 | 7 | 3 | | | |
| 6 | 7 | ” | | | |
| 7 | 7 | 4 | | | |
| 8 | 7 | ” | | | |
| 9 | 6 | 3 | | Set F.T.S:$^{l}$ | |
| 10 | 8 | ” | Squaly | SW | |
| 11 | 7 | 3 | | Out 3$^{d}$ R.BT.S. | |
| 12 | 8 | 1 | 155 Miles | Out 2.$^{d}$ R. D.$^{o}$ | |

| | | | | | |
|---|---|---|---|---|---|
| 1 | 7 | „ | ESE½S.° | SW | Wednesday: 17: |
| 2 | 6 | 5 | | | |
| 3 | 7 | „ | | | Fresh Gales the most part, fair |
| 4 | 7 | 4 | | | Weather |
| 5 | 6 | „ | | | |
| 6 | 5 | „ | | | Course S:° 68:$^{d}$ E:$^{t}$ Distance 115 Miles |
| 7 | 5 | 3 | | | Southing 42 m:$^{s}$ Easting 105 m:$^{s}$ differ- |
| 8 | 5 | 4 | | SSW | ence of Long.$^{d}$ 130 m:$^{s}$ |
| 9 | 6 | „ | ESE | | |
| 10 | 5 | „ | | | Lat:$^{d}$ Observ'd 37$^{d}$ 55$^{m}$ S:° |
| 11 | 4 | „ | | | Meridian Distance 3 44 E:$^{t}$ |
| 12 | 4 | „ | | | Difference of Long$^{d}$ 4 18 E:$^{t}$ |
| 1 | 3 | „ | | | |
| 2 | 2 | 4 | | | Variation allowed 16 30 W:$^{t}$ |
| 3 | 1 | 5 | | WNW | |
| 4 | 1 | „ | | | |
| 5 | „ | „ | | | |
| 6 | „ | „ | } Calm | | |
| 7 | 3 | „ | | NBE | |
| 8 | 3 | „ | | NEBN | |
| 9 | 3 | „ | | NE | |
| 10 | 4 | „ | | | |
| 11 | 5 | „ | SEBE | | |
| 12 | 5 | 3 | | 107 Miles | |
| | | | ESE | | |

| H | K | F | Courses | Winds | Thursday: 18: Aprill |
|---|---|---|---|---|---|
| 1 | 5 | 3 | ESE | NEBN | |
| 2 | 5 | 4 | | | Fresh Gales, fair Weather, a Swell from |
| 3 | 6 | 3 | | | the NEward |
| 4 | 6 | „ | ESE½S.° | | |
| 5 | 4 | 2 | ESE | | Course make to be S:° 83$^{d}$ E:$^{t}$ Distance |
| 6 | 4 | 3 | | NE | 145 Miles Southing 16 m:$^{s}$ Easting 143 |
| 7 | 5 | 3 | | | m:$^{s}$ difference of Long.$^{d}$ 180 m:$^{s}$ |
| 8 | 5 | 4 | | In 1:$^{st}$ R.B.T.S. | |
| 9 | 6 | 4 | | | Lat:$^{d}$ Observ'd 37$^{d}$ 51$^{m}$ S:° |
| 10 | 6 | „ | | | Meridian Distance 5 57 E.$^{t}$ |
| 11 | 7 | „ | | Sq$^{ll}$ & Cloudy | Difference of Long.$^{d}$ 7 18 E.$^{t}$ |
| 12 | 7 | „ | | | Variation ~~pm~~ Amp.$^{d}$ 16 54 W:$^{t}$ |
| 1 | 6 | 3 | | | |
| 2 | 5 | 3 | | In 2.$^{d}$ R.B.T.S. | |
| 3 | 6 | „ | | NEBN | |
| 4 | 5 | 3 | | | |
| 5 | 7 | „ | EBS.° | NNE | |
| 6 | 7 | „ | | | |
| 7 | 7 | „ | | NEBN | |
| 8 | 6 | „ | ESE | Out AReefs | |
| 9 | 6 | „ | | | |
| 10 | 6 | 3 | | | |
| 11 | 6 | 3 | | NBE | |
| 12 | 6 | 1 | 145 Miles | | |

| | | | | | |
|---|---|---|---|---|---|
| 1 | 7 | ” | ESE | NEBE | Friday: 19: |
| 2 | 7 | 3 | | | |
| 3 | 7 | 3 | | | Fresh Gales the first part, the Latter Calm |
| 4 | 8 | ” | | | |
| 5 | 6 | ” | | | Course make to be S:$^{o}$ 85$^{d}$ E:$^{t}$ Distance |
| 6 | 5 | ” | ESE½E | | 88 Miles Southing 8 m:$^{s}$ Easting 87 m:$^{s}$ |
| 7 | 4 | ” | ESE | | difference of Long.$^{d}$ 110 m:$^{s}$ |
| 8 | 4 | ” | | | |
| 9 | 6 | 3 | | | Lat:$^{d}$ p:$^{r}$ Account 37$^{d}$ 59$^{m}$ S:$^{o}$ |
| 10 | 6 | ” | | | Meridian Distance 7 24 E.$^{t}$ |
| 11 | 4 | 3 | | | Difference of Long$^{d}$ 9 08 E.$^{t}$ |
| 12 | 4 | 5 | | | |
| 1 | 4 | 3 | | | Variation allowed 17 30 W:$^{t}$ |
| 2 | 3 | 2 | | | |
| 3 | 2 | 3 | | | |
| 4 | 3 | 2 | | | |
| 5 | 2 | 3 | Thick and | foggy | |
| 6 | 2 | ” | | | |
| 7 | ” | ” | | | |
| 8 | ” | ” | | | |
| 9 | ” | ” | Calm | | |
| 10 | ” | ” | | | |
| 11 | ” | ” | | | |
| 12 | ” | ” | 88 Miles | | |
| 1 | ” | ” | | | Saturday: 20: |
| 2 | ” | ” | Calm | | |
| 3 | ” | ” | | | Calm and foggy the first part, the Latter |
| 4 | ” | ” | | | fresh Gales and fair Weather |
| 5 | 1 | ” | ESE | NNE | |
| 6 | 1 | 2 | | | Course make to be S:$^{o}$ 85$^{d}$ E:$^{t}$ Distance |
| 7 | 3 | 3 | | | 100 Miles, Southing 10 m:$^{s}$ Easting 99 |
| 8 | 4 | ” | | | m:$^{s}$ difference of Long.$^{d}$ 126 m:$^{s}$ |
| 9 | 5 | ” | | | |
| 10 | 5 | 2 | | | Lat:$^{d}$ Observ'd 38$^{d}$ 09$^{m}$ S.$^{o}$ |
| 11 | 7 | ” | | | Meridian Distance 9 04 E:$^{t}$ |
| 12 | 6 | ” | Light:$^{g}$ in | the N:$^{o}$ board | Difference of Long.$^{d}$ 11 14 E:$^{t}$ |
| 1 | 6 | 5 | | | Variation allowed 18 30 W:$^{t}$ |
| 2 | 7 | 3 | | | |
| 3 | 6 | 3 | D:$^{o}$ in y$^{e}$ W:$^{t}$ | board: NWBW | |
| 4 | 6 | ” | | In 2:$^{d}$ R.B.T.S. | |
| 5 | 5 | 3 | D:$^{o}$ in y$^{e}$ E.$^{t}$ | board | |
| 6 | 3 | 3 | | | |
| 7 | 3 | ” | | Out AR:$^{s}$ | |
| 8 | 5 | ” | | | |
| 9 | 5 | ” | | | |
| 10 | 7 | 3 | | | |
| 11 | 7 | 3 | | | |
| 12 | 7 | 4 | 104 Miles | | |

| H | K | F | Courses | Winds | Sunday: 21: Aprill |
|---|---|---|---|---|---|
| 1 | 7 | 3 | EBS.$^{o}$ | WBN | |
| 2 | 7 | 5 | | In 3.$^{d}$ R.F.T.S. | Fresh Gales attended with Squalls and |
| 3 | 7 | 3 | EBS½S.$^{o}$ | | Rain |
| 4 | 7 | 3 | | H.$^{d}$ F.T.S. | |
| 5 | 6 | 4 | | In 3.$^{d}$ R.M.T.S. | Course make to be N:$^{o}$ 76$^{d}$ E:$^{t}$ Distance |
| 6 | 7 | „ | | | 176 Miles Northing 42 m:$^{s}$ Easting 170 |
| 7 | 7 | 4 | EBS$^{o}$ | | m:$^{s}$ difference of Long.$^{d}$ 213 m:$^{s}$ |
| 8 | 7 | 3 | | | |
| 9 | 8 | „ | | | Lat:$^{d}$ Observ'd 37$^{d}$ 26 S.$^{o}$ |
| 10 | 8 | 4 | | | Meridian Distance 11 54 E:$^{t}$ |
| 11 | 7 | 3 | | | Difference of Long.$^{d}$ 14 47 E:$^{t}$ |
| 12 | 7 | 4 | | | |
| 1 | 7 | 6 | | | Variation Allow'd 20 00 W:$^{t}$ |
| 2 | 7 | „ | | Squalls & Rain | |
| 3 | 6 | 3 | | | |
| 4 | 7 | „ | | WBS$^{o}$ | |
| 5 | 7 | „ | | WSW | |
| 6 | 6 | „ | | Set F.T.S. | |
| 7 | 7 | 4 | | | |
| 8 | 7 | „ | | | |
| 9 | 8 | „ | | | |
| 10 | 8 | „ | | | |
| 11 | 8 | „ | ESE | SWBW | |
| 12 | 8 | „ | 178 Miles | | |
| 1 | 8 | 4 | ESE | SWBW | Monday: 22: |
| 2 | 9 | „ | | Sq$^{lly}$ & Rain | |
| 3 | 8 | 4 | | | Fresh Gales of wind with Squalls |
| 4 | 8 | 3 | | | and Rain |
| 5 | 7 | „ | | | |
| 6 | 8 | 3 | | | Course make to be S:$^{o}$ 87$^{d}$ E:$^{t}$ Distance |
| 7 | 7 | 3 | SEBE | D.$^{o}$ D.$^{o}$ | 157 Miles Southing 7 m:$^{s}$ Easting 156 m:$^{s}$ |
| 8 | 7 | 4 | | | difference of Long.$^{d}$ 196 m:$^{s}$ |
| 9 | 7 | 4 | ESE½S$^{o}$ | | |
| 10 | 5 | „ | | | Lat:$^{d}$ Observ'd 37$^{d}$ 44$^{m}$ S:$^{o}$ |
| 11 | 5 | „ | | | Meridian Distance 14 30 E:$^{t}$ |
| 12 | 7 | „ | | | Difference of Long.$^{d}$ 18 03 E:$^{t}$ |
| 1 | 7 | 3 | | | |
| 2 | 7 | „ | | | Att 8 PM broke Maintopsailyard & Split |
| 3 | 7 | „ | ESE | SW D.$^{o}$ D.$^{o}$ | the Saile This Morn:$^{g}$ gott up another |
| 4 | 6 | 4 | | | |
| 5 | 6 | „ | | | |
| 6 | 6 | „ | | | |
| 7 | 5 | „ | | | |
| 8 | 5 | 4 | | | |
| 9 | 4 | 4 | | | |
| 10 | 4 | 3 | ESE½S$^{o}$ | | |
| 11 | 3 | 4 | ESE | SWBW | |
| 12 | 4 | 2 | 157 Miles | Set M.T.S. | |

| | | | | | |
|---|---|---|---|---|---|
| 1 | 1 | 3 | SEBE | SE | Tuesday: 23: |
| 2 | 1 | 3 | | | |
| 3 | 3 | „ | ESE | WNW | Small Gales with some Raine in the Night |
| 4 | 4 | 3 | | | |
| 5 | 4 | 4 | | In 2$^{d}$ R.F.T.S. | Course make to be N:$^{o}$ 85 E:$^{t}$ Distance |
| 6 | 4 | „ | | In D.$^{o}$ M.T.S. | 89 Miles, Northing 8 m:$^{s}$ Easting 89 m:$^{s}$ |
| 7 | 4 | 3 | | | difference of Long.$^{d}$ 112 m:$^{s}$ |
| 8 | 3 | 2 | | | |
| 9 | 3 | 3 | ESE½S.$^{o}$ | Sq$^{ll}$ & Rain | Lat:$^{d}$ Observ'd 37$^{d}$ 36$^{m}$ S:$^{o}$ |
| 10 | 3 | 2 | | | Meridian Distance 15 59 E:$^{t}$ |
| 11 | 3 | „ | | | Difference of Long.$^{d}$ 19 45 E:$^{t}$ |
| 12 | 4 | „ | | | Variation allow'd 22 30 W:$^{t}$ |
| 1 | 4 | 2 | ESE | | |
| 2 | 4 | 2 | | | |
| 3 | 4 | 3 | | | |
| 4 | 4 | 4 | | | |
| 5 | 3 | 4 | | | |
| 6 | 5 | „ | | NW O:$^{t}$ AR:$^{s}$ | |
| 7 | 4 | 3 | | | |
| 8 | 4 | „ | | | |
| 9 | 4 | 3 | ESE½S.$^{o}$ | | |
| 10 | 4 | „ | | | |
| 11 | 2 | 3 | | | |
| 12 | 3 | 2 | 89 Miles | | |
| H | K | F | Courses | Winds | Wednesday: 24: Aprill |
| 1 | 5 | 3 | SEBE | NNW Sq:$^{ll}$ | |
| 2 | 5 | 4 | | | Fresh gales of wind with fair Weather |
| 3 | 6 | 3 | | | |
| 4 | 6 | 4 | | | Course make to be S:$^{o}$ 80$^{d}$ E:$^{t}$ Distance |
| 5 | 4 | „ | | In 1$^{st}$ R.B.T.S. | 176 Miles |
| 6 | 2 | „ | | | |
| 7 | 5 | 3 | ESE | N:$^{o}$ | Lat:$^{d}$ Observ'd 37$^{d}$ 54$^{m}$ S:$^{o}$ |
| 8 | 6 | 3 | | | Meridian Distance 18 47 E.$^{t}$ |
| 9 | 5 | 3 | | | Difference of Long.$^{d}$ 23 11 E.$^{t}$ |
| 10 | 7 | „ | SEBE | | |
| 11 | 7 | 4 | SEBE½E | | Variation allow'd 23 30 W.$^{t}$ |
| 12 | 8 | „ | | | |
| 1 | 8 | 4 | SEbE | | |
| 2 | 8 | 3 | | | |
| 3 | 9 | „ | | | |
| 4 | 9 | „ | SSE | NBE | |
| 5 | 8 | 3 | | | |
| 6 | 8 | „ | | | |
| 7 | 8 | „ | SEBE½E | | |
| 8 | 7 | 5 | | | |
| 9 | 9 | 3 | | Squaly | |
| 10 | 9 | „ | | | |
| 11 | 7 | 1 | | In 2.$^{d}$ R.B.T.S. | |
| 12 | 8 | „ | 171 Miles | In 3.$^{d}$ R.B.T.S | |

| | | | | | |
|---|---|---|---|---|---|
| 1 | 9 | „ | ESE | NBE | Thursday. 25: |
| 2 | 9 | „ | | | |
| 3 | 9 | „ | | | Hard gales of Wind w:$^{th}$ Intermitt:$^{g}$ Squalls |
| 4 | 9 | „ | | | |
| 5 | 9 | „ | | | Course make to be N:$^{o}$ 85$^{d}$ E:$^{t}$ Distance |
| 6 | 9 | „ | | | 170 Miles, Northing 15 m:$^{s}$ Easting 169 |
| 7 | 9 | 3 | | | m:$^{s}$ difference of Long.$^{d}$ 224 m.$^{s}$ |
| 8 | 9 | 3 | | | |
| 9 | 8 | 5 | EBS½S.$^{o}$ | | |
| 10 | 9 | „ | | | |
| 11 | 9 | „ | | Squall & R.$^{n}$ | |
| 12 | 7 | „ | ESE | H:$^{d}$ MT:S. taken | a back at SW |
| 1 | 6 | „ | ENE | | |
| 2 | 5 | „ | ESE | | Lat:$^{d}$ p:$^{r}$ Account 37$^{d}$ 39 S:$^{o}$ |
| 3 | 4 | 3 | | | Meridian Distance 21 36 E.$^{t}$ |
| 4 | 3 | „ | | | Difference of Long$^{d}$ 26 55 E.$^{t}$ |
| 5 | 3 | „ | hard Rain | W:$^{t}$ | Variation Allow'd 25 00 W:$^{t}$ |
| 6 | 3 | 3 | | | |
| 7 | 7 | 4 | Set M.T.S | WBN$^{o}$ | |
| 8 | 7 | 3 | ESE | fair | |
| 9 | 7 | 3 | | | |
| 10 | 7 | 5 | | | |
| 11 | 8 | „ | | | |
| 12 | 7 | 2 | 177 Miles | | |
| 1 | 7 | 4 | ESE | WBN | Friday: 26: |
| 2 | 7 | 3 | | | |
| 3 | 6 | „ | | | Fresh Gales of Wind, and the |
| 4 | 6 | „ | | | Major part fair Weather |
| 5 | 7 | „ | | | |
| 6 | 7 | „ | | | Course allow to be East, Distance 184 |
| 7 | 7 | 3 | | NW | Miles, difference of Long:$^{d}$ 232 m:$^{s}$ |
| 8 | 7 | 5 | | Small Rain | |
| 9 | 7 | 3 | | | Lat:$^{d}$ Observ'd 37$^{d}$ 35$^{m}$ S:$^{o}$ |
| 10 | 7 | 3 | | | Meridian Distance 24 40 E:$^{t}$ |
| 11 | 8 | „ | | | Difference of Long$^{d}$ 30 47 E:$^{t}$ |
| 12 | 8 | „ | | | Variation Allow'd 26 30 W:$^{t}$ |
| 1 | 6 | 4 | | NWBW | |
| 2 | 7 | 3 | | | |
| 3 | 8 | „ | | | |
| 4 | 8 | 4 | | | |
| 5 | 8 | 3 | | | |
| 6 | 8 | 3 | | | |
| 7 | 8 | „ | | | |
| 8 | 8 | 4 | | | |
| 9 | 9 | 3 | | | |
| 10 | 8 | „ | | | |
| 11 | 9 | 4 | | | |
| 12 | 1 | 0 | 188 Miles | | |

| H | K | F | Courses | Winds | Saturday: 27: Aprill |
|---|---|---|---|---|---|
| 1 | 9 | ” | ESE | NW | |
| 2 | 8 | 3 | | | Fresh gales the first part, the latter Small |
| 3 | 9 | ” | | In 3.$^{d}$ R.F.T.S. | and Cloudy |
| 4 | 8 | ” | | | |
| 5 | 7 | ” | ESE½S:$^{o}$ | WNW | Course make to be N:$^{o}$ 85$^{d}$ E:$^{t}$ Distance |
| 6 | 6 | 3 | | Rain | 130 Miles, Northing 10 m:$^{s}$ Easting 129 |
| 7 | 6 | ” | ESE | | m:$^{s}$ diff. of Long.$^{d}$ 162 m:$^{s}$ |
| 8 | 6 | ” | | | |
| 9 | 6 | 3 | | | Lat:$^{d}$ p:$^{r}$ Acc$^{t}$ 37$^{d}$ 25$^{m}$ S:$^{o}$ |
| 10 | 6 | ” | | | Meridian Distance 26 49 E.$^{t}$ |
| 11 | 4 | ” | | WBS.$^{o}$ | Difference of Long.$^{d}$ 33 29 E.$^{t}$ |
| 12 | 4 | 3 | | WBN | |
| 1 | 5 | 3 | | | Variation Allow'd 27 30 W:$^{t}$ |
| 2 | 5 | ” | | | |
| 3 | 5 | 5 | | | |
| 4 | 5 | ” | | | |
| 5 | 4 | 3 | | | |
| 6 | 4 | 4 | | | |
| 7 | 3 | 5 | | | |
| 8 | 5 | ” | | | |
| 9 | 4 | ” | | Out AR.$^{s}$ | |
| 10 | 2 | 2 | | | |
| 11 | 3 | 3 | | | |
| 12 | 4 | 5 | 134 Miles | | |
| 1 | 4 | 3 | ESE½S.$^{o}$ | WBN | Sunday: 28: |
| 2 | 4 | 4 | | WSW | |
| 3 | 5 | 3 | | | Moderate gales of Wind with |
| 4 | 5 | 4 | | SWBW | Cloudy Weather |
| 5 | 5 | 2 | | | |
| 6 | 3 | 5 | ESE In 1:$^{st}$ | R.MTS. & 2.$^{d}$ R. | FT.S. |
| 7 | 4 | 3 | | | |
| 8 | 5 | 3 | | SW | Course Allow'd to be N:$^{o}$ 86$^{d}$ E:$^{t}$ Dista 112 |
| 9 | 6 | ” | | | Miles, Northing 8 m:$^{s}$ Easting 111 m:$^{s}$ |
| 10 | 6 | ” | | WSW | diff$^{e}$ of Long.$^{d}$ 140 m.$^{s}$ |
| 11 | 5 | ” | | | |
| 12 | 6 | ” | | | Lat:$^{d}$ p:$^{r}$ Judgement 37$^{d}$ 17 S:$^{o}$ |
| 1 | 3 | 3 | | WBS.$^{o}$ | Meridian Distance 28 40 E.$^{t}$ |
| 2 | 3 | 3 | | | Difference of Long:$^{d}$ 35 49 E.$^{t}$ |
| 3 | 3 | 4 | | WBN | |
| 4 | 5 | ” | | | Variation Allow:$^{d}$ 27 30 W:$^{t}$ |
| 5 | 3 | 3 | | | |
| 6 | 3 | ” | | WNW | |
| 7 | 3 | ” | | | |
| 8 | 3 | ” | | Out 1$^{st}$ R.MT.S | |
| 9 | 4 | 3 | | Out 2.$^{d}$ R.FT.S. | |
| 10 | 5 | ” | | | |
| 11 | 6 | 4 | | | |
| 12 | 6 | 2 | 112 Miles | | |

| | | | | | |
|---|---|---|---|---|---|
| 1 | 6 | 3 | ESE | WNW | Monday: 29: |
| 2 | 7 | „ | | | |
| 3 | 7 | „ | | | Hard Gales of Wind attended with Squalls |
| 4 | 7 | „ | | | and Raine |
| 5 | 8 | „ | | | |
| 6 | 8 | „ | In 1:$^{st}$ R.MT. | S. Rain | Course make to be N:$^{o}$ 84$^{d}$ E:$^{t}$ Distance |
| 7 | 7 | 3 | | D.$^{o}$ | 200 Miles |
| 8 | 8 | „ | | | |
| 9 | 8 | „ | | | Lat.$^{d}$ Observ'd 36$^{d}$ 56$^{m}$ S:$^{o}$ |
| 10 | 7 | 4 | | | Meridian Distance 31 58 E:$^{t}$ |
| 11 | 8 | 3 | Lightning | WBS:$^{o}$ | Difference of Long$^{d}$ 39 59 E.$^{t}$ |
| 12 | 7 | 4 | | | |
| 1 | 7 | 5 | | | |
| 2 | 8 | „ | | WSW | |
| 3 | 7 | 4 | | | |
| 4 | 8 | „ | | | |
| 5 | 8 | „ | | | |
| 6 | 8 | „ | | WNW | |
| 7 | 8 | 3 | | W.$^{t}$ | |
| 8 | 8 | 4 | | | |
| 9 | 9 | „ | | | |
| 10 | 9 | 5 | | | |
| 11 | 9 | 3 | | | |
| 12 | 9 | 1 | 192 Miles | | |
| H | K | F | Courses | Winds | Tuesday: 30: Aprill |
| 1 | 9 | „ | ESE | W.$^{t}$ | |
| 2 | 9 | „ | | Squalls | Hard Gales of wind with hard |
| 3 | 9 | „ | SEBE | D.$^{o}$ | Squalls |
| 4 | 8 | „ | | | |
| 5 | 7 | „ | In 2.$^{d}$ R.F.T. | S. WNW | Course allowed to be N.$^{o}$ 81$^{d}$ E:$^{t}$ Dist 198 |
| 6 | 6 | 3 | SSE | | Miles, Northing 31 m:$^{s}$ Easting 190 m:$^{s}$ |
| 7 | 7 | „ | SEBE | W:$^{t}$ Sq$^{ll}$ & R.$^{n}$ | difference of Long.$^{d}$ 243 m:$^{s}$ |
| 8 | 7 | „ | | WNW | |
| 9 | 6 | 2 | ESE | | Lat:$^{d}$ p:$^{r}$ Account 36$^{d}$ 25$^{m}$ S:$^{o}$ |
| 10 | 7 | „ | | | Meridian Distance 35 16 E.$^{t}$ |
| 11 | 7 | „ | | | Difference of Long.$^{d}$ 44 02 E.$^{t}$ |
| 12 | 7 | „ | | | |
| 1 | 7 | 2 | | H.$^{d}$ F.T.S. | Variation allow'd 25 00 W:$^{t}$ |
| 2 | 8 | „ | ESE½S:$^{o}$ | | |
| 3 | 9 | 2 | Lightning in | the SW board | |
| 4 | 9 | 3 | D$^{o}$ | H.$^{d}$ M.T.S. | |
| 5 | 9 | „ | | | |
| 6 | 8 | „ | | | |
| 7 | 8 | „ | In 2.$^{d}$ R. and | Sett M.T.S. | |
| 8 | 9 | „ | EBS.$^{o}$ | | |
| 9 | 9 | „ | | | |
| 10 | 8 | „ | hard Sq.$^{lls}$ | hail and Rain | |
| 11 | 8 | 2 | | | |
| 12 | 9 | „ | 192 Miles | | |

| | | | | | |
|---|---|---|---|---|---|
| 1 | 9 | „ | EBS$^{o}$ | WBN | Wednesday: 1: May: |
| 2 | 9 | „ | hard Squalls | and Rain | |
| 3 | 8 | 4 | E.$^{t}$ | WNW | Hard gales of Wind and Rain, In y:$^{e}$ |
| 4 | 7 | 3 | | D.$^{o}$ | Morning having Light but of one Ship – |
| 5 | 8 | 3 | | In 3.$^{d}$ R.MT.S. | Steered to the N:$^{o}$ward as p$^{r}$ Logg, and fell |
| 6 | 9 | „ | | W.$^{t}$ | in with our Company |
| 7 | 9 | „ | hard Sq$^{lls}$ | with Lightning | |
| 8 | 9 | „ | | | Course N:$^{o}$ 63$^{d}$ E:$^{t}$ Distance 189 Miles |
| 9 | 9 | 3 | D.$^{o}$ | and Rain | Northing 85 miles Easting 168 miles Diff. |
| 10 | 9 | 3 | Lightning to | the S:$^{o}$w.$^{d}$ | of Long.$^{d}$ 207 miles |
| 11 | 7 | 4 | D$^{o}$ | WBS.$^{o}$ | |
| 12 | 8 | 3 | D.$^{o}$ in the | SE board | Lat:$^{d}$ p:$^{r}$ Account 35$^{d}$ 00$^{m}$ S:$^{o}$ |
| 1 | 8 | „ | D.$^{o}$ | D.$^{o}$ | Meridian Distance 38 04 E.$^{t}$ |
| 2 | 9 | „ | | | Difference of Long$^{d}$ 47 29 E.$^{t}$ |
| 3 | 8 | 3 | | | |
| 4 | 9 | „ | hard Squalls | | |
| 5 | 8 | „ | D$^{o}$ D$^{o}$ | SW | |
| 6 | 9 | „ | | H.$^{d}$ M.T.S. | |
| 7 | 8 | „ | | hard Sq.$^{lls}$ | |
| 8 | 7 | 3 | | | |
| 9 | 6 | „ | | | |
| 10 | 6 | „ | EBN$^{o}$ | | |
| 11 | 4 | 3 | NNE | | |
| 12 | 6 | 3 | 194 Miles | | |
| 1 | 7 | 3 | East | SWBW | Thursday: 2. |
| 2 | 7 | „ | ESE | O:$^{t}$ 3.$^{d}$ R.M.T.S. | |
| 3 | 8 | „ | SEBE | SW | Fresh gales of wind with Smooth Water, |
| 4 | 9 | „ | | | Cloudy Weather |
| 5 | 8 | „ | | | |
| 6 | 8 | „ | | | Course make to be East Distance 149 |
| 7 | 7 | 3 | | | Miles, difference of Long.$^{d}$ 180 m:$^{s}$ |
| 8 | 8 | „ | | | |
| 9 | 7 | 3 | ESE½S$^{o}$ | Squally | Lat:$^{d}$ p:$^{r}$ Account 35$^{d}$ 00$^{m}$ S:$^{o}$ |
| 10 | 7 | 3 | | | Meridian Distance 40 33 E.$^{t}$ |
| 11 | 5 | „ | ESE | | Difference of Long$^{d}$ 50 29 E.$^{t}$ |
| 12 | 6 | 3 | | Out 2.$^{d}$ R.F.T.S. | |
| 1 | 3 | 4 | | | |
| 2 | 3 | „ | SEBE | Small Rain | |
| 3 | 3 | 5 | | W.$^{t}$ | |
| 4 | 3 | 3 | ESE | | |
| 5 | 7 | 3 | | | |
| 6 | 5 | „ | | Out B.R.M.T.S. | |
| 7 | 4 | 3 | | WNW | |
| 8 | 5 | 2 | | | |
| 9 | 4 | 4 | SEBE | | |
| 10 | 6 | „ | | | |
| 11 | 6 | 5 | ESE | W:$^{t}$ | |
| 12 | 6 | 5 | 149 Miles | O:$^{t}$1:$^{st}$ R.F.T.S | |

| H | K | F | Courses | Winds | Friday: 3: May |
|---|---|---|---|---|---|
| 1 | 8 | „ | ESE | WNW | |
| 2 | 7 | „ | | | Moderate Gales of Wind w:$^{th}$ Cloudy |
| 3 | 7 | „ | | In 2.$^{d}$ R.F.T.S | Weather and Intermitting faint Squalls |
| 4 | 8 | „ | | | |
| 5 | 6 | 3 | | In 1:$^{st}$ R.M.T.S. | Course make to be S:$^{o}$ 80$^{d}$ E:$^{t}$ Distance |
| 6 | 6 | 4 | | | 155 Miles, Southing 6 m:$^{s}$ Easting 154 m.$^{s}$ |
| 7 | 7 | „ | | | diff. of Long.$^{d}$ 178 m:$^{s}$ |
| 8 | 7 | „ | | | |
| 9 | 7 | „ | ESE½S.$^{o}$ | | Lat:$^{d}$ Observ'd 35$^{d}$ 06$^{m}$ S:$^{o}$ |
| 10 | 7 | 3 | | | Meridian Distance 43 08 E.$^{t}$ |
| 11 | 7 | „ | | | Difference of Long.$^{d}$ 52 47 E.$^{t}$ |
| 12 | 7 | 4 | | | Variation Allow'd 23 00 W.$^{t}$ |
| 1 | 7 | 4 | | | |
| 2 | 7 | „ | SEBE | NWBW | |
| 3 | 5 | 5 | | | |
| 4 | 7 | 3 | | | |
| 5 | 6 | 4 | | | |
| 6 | 6 | 2 | | | |
| 7 | 6 | 3 | ESE½S.$^{o}$ | Squally | |
| 8 | 5 | 4 | Out 2.$^{d}$ | R.F.T.S. WSW | |
| 9 | 4 | 1 | ESE out 1:$^{st}$ | R.MT.S. WNW | |
| 10 | 4 | 3 | ESE½S.$^{o}$ | | |
| 11 | 4 | „ | | | |
| 12 | 4 | 3 | 159 Miles | | |
| 1 | 6 | 3 | SEBE | WSW | Saturday: 4: |
| 2 | 6 | „ | | Out 1:$^{st}$ R.F.T.S. | |
| 3 | 5 | 3 | | | Moderate Gales of Wind with Intermitting |
| 4 | 5 | 4 | | | faint Squalls, Attended with Rain |
| 5 | 6 | „ | | | |
| 6 | 6 | „ | | | Course make to be S:$^{o}$ 78$^{d}$ E:$^{t}$ Distance 170 |
| 7 | 5 | „ | SE | WNW | Miles Southing 49 m:$^{s}$ Easting 164$^{ms}$ diff. |
| 8 | 6 | 3 | | | of Long.$^{d}$ 202 m:$^{s}$ |
| 9 | 7 | 3 | | | |
| 10 | 7 | 5 | | | Lat:$^{d}$ Observ'd 33$^{d}$ 51$^{m}$ S:$^{o}$ |
| 11 | 8 | „ | | | Meridian Distance 45 52 E.$^{t}$ |
| 12 | 8 | „ | | | Difference of Long.$^{d}$ 56 09 E.$^{t}$ |
| 1 | 7 | 3 | SEBE | | Variation allow'd 22 00 W:$^{t}$ |
| 2 | 7 | 4 | | | |
| 3 | 8 | „ | SE | West | |
| 4 | 8 | 4 | | | |
| 5 | 7 | 5 | | | |
| 6 | 7 | 5 | | | |
| 7 | 8 | 3 | | | |
| 8 | 8 | 3 | | | |
| 9 | 7 | 3 | SE½E | Sq.$^{lls}$ & R.$^{n}$ | |
| 10 | 7 | 5 | | | |
| 11 | 8 | „ | SEBE | | |
| 12 | 8 | „ | 173 miles | In 2.$^{d}$ R.FT.S. | |

| | | | | | |
|---|---|---|---|---|---|
| 1 | 8 | 3 | ESE | WNW | Sunday: 5: |
| 2 | 7 | „ | | In 3.$^{d}$ R.F.T.S. | |
| 3 | 7 | „ | | | Fresh gales of Wind with Intermitting |
| 4 | 8 | „ | | | Squalls |
| 5 | 7 | 3 | SEBE | In 2.$^{d}$ R.M.T.S. | |
| 6 | 7 | 4 | | | Course make to be S:$^{o}$ 87$^{d}$ E:$^{t}$ Distance |
| 7 | 7 | „ | ESE | W:$^{t}$ | 185 Miles, Southing 10 m:$^{s}$ Easting 184 |
| 8 | 7 | „ | | | m$^{s}$ diff of Long.$^{d}$ 232 m:$^{s}$ |
| 9 | 8 | „ | ESE½S.$^{o}$ | | |
| 10 | 8 | 4 | | | Lat:$^{d}$ Observ'd 36$^{d}$ 01 S:$^{o}$ |
| 11 | 8 | 3 | | | Meridian Distance 48 56 E:$^{t}$ |
| 12 | 8 | „ | | | Difference of Long.$^{d}$ 60 00 E:$^{t}$ |
| 1 | 8 | „ | ESE | | Variation allow'd 20 30 W:$^{t}$ |
| 2 | 7 | 3 | | | |
| 3 | 8 | „ | | | |
| 4 | 7 | 4 | | | |
| 5 | 8 | 5 | ESE½S:$^{o}$ | | |
| 6 | 8 | 2 | | | |
| 7 | 7 | 4 | | Out 2.$^{d}$ R.F.T.S. | |
| 8 | 8 | „ | | | |
| 9 | 7 | „ | | | |
| 10 | 7 | „ | | | |
| 11 | 7 | „ | | | |
| 12 | 7 | „ | 185 Miles | | |
| H | K | F | Courses | Winds | Monday: 6: May. |
| 1 | 7 | 3 | ESE½S.$^{o}$ | WNW O$^{t}$ 1 R.M. | T.S. |
| 2 | 9 | „ | | | Fresh Gales of Wind attended with |
| 3 | 8 | 3 | | | Squalls |
| 4 | 8 | 4 | In 1:$^{st}$ R.MT. | S & 3.$^{d}$ R.F.T.S. | |
| 5 | 8 | 3 | | | Course Allow'd S:$^{o}$ 86 E:$^{t}$ Distance 203 |
| 6 | 8 | „ | | | miles, Southing 12 m:$^{s}$ Easting 202 m:$^{s}$ |
| 7 | 9 | „ | | | diff of Long.$^{d}$ 252 m:$^{s}$ |
| 8 | 9 | „ | | Squally | |
| 9 | 8 | „ | | | Lat:$^{d}$ Observ'd 36$^{d}$ 13$^{m}$ S:$^{o}$ |
| 10 | 8 | 3 | | | Meridian Distance 52 18 E.$^{t}$ |
| 11 | 8 | „ | ESE | | Difference of Long:$^{d}$ 64 12 E.$^{t}$ |
| 12 | 8 | „ | | | Variation Allow'd 19 00 W:$^{t}$ |
| 1 | 8 | 4 | | | |
| 2 | 8 | „ | | Sq$^{lls}$ & Rain | |
| 3 | 8 | „ | ESE½S.$^{o}$ | WNW D.$^{o}$ | |
| 4 | 8 | 4 | | In 2$^{d}$R.MT.S. D.$^{o}$ | |
| 5 | 7 | „ | ESE | W.$^{t}$ D.$^{o}$ | |
| 6 | 7 | 4 | | | |
| 7 | 7 | 6 | ESE½S.$^{o}$ | WSW O:$^{t}$ 2.$^{d}$ R. | M.T.S |
| 8 | 8 | „ | | | |
| 9 | 9 | „ | ESE | | |
| 10 | 9 | 5 | | Out R.B.T.S. | |
| 11 | 10 | „ | | | |
| 12 | 10 | 3 | 203 Miles | | |

| | | | | | |
|---|---|---|---|---|---|
| 1 | 10 | 4 | ESE | WSW | Tuesday: 7: |
| 2 | 10 | 2 | | | |
| 3 | 10 | " | EBS.$^{o}$ | | Fresh Gales of Wind, attended with |
| 4 | 10 | " | | | Squalls |
| 5 | 10 | " | EBS½S.$^{o}$ | Squalls | |
| 6 | 8 | " | | In 1 R.B.T.S. | Course make to be S:$^{o}$ 87$^{d}$ E:$^{t}$ Distance |
| 7 | 7 | 3 | | WSW Squaly | 191 Miles, Southing 6 m:$^{s}$ Easting 190$^{m}$ |
| 8 | 8 | " | | | diff of Long.$^{d}$ 234 m:$^{s}$ |
| 9 | 9 | " | ESE | | |
| 10 | 9 | 3 | ESE½S.$^{o}$ | SW | Lat:$^{d}$ p$^{r}$ Account 36$^{d}$ 19$^{m}$ S:$^{o}$ |
| 11 | 8 | 4 | | | Meridian Distance 55 28 E:$^{t}$ |
| 12 | 9 | 4 | | | Difference of Long$^{d}$ 68 06 E:$^{t}$ |
| 1 | 8 | " | | | |
| 2 | 7 | 3 | | | Variation p$^{r}$ Med:$^{m}$ 17 58 W:$^{t}$ |
| 3 | 7 | 5 | | | of Severall Azimuths |
| 4 | 8 | " | | WBN | |
| 5 | 8 | " | EBS$^{o}$ | WSW | |
| 6 | 6 | " | | | |
| 7 | 6 | " | | | |
| 8 | 6 | " | | | |
| 9 | 6 | " | | | |
| 10 | 5 | 3 | EBS½S.$^{o}$ | WNW | |
| 11 | 5 | " | ESE | | |
| 12 | 6 | 4 | 191 Miles | | |

| | | | | | |
|---|---|---|---|---|---|
| 1 | 7 | 3 | EBS.$^{o}$ | WBN | Wednesday: 8: |
| 2 | 8 | " | | | |
| 3 | 7 | " | | | Fresh Gales of Wind w:$^{th}$ Cloudy Weather |
| 4 | 6 | " | | Sm$^{ll}$ Rain | |
| 5 | 5 | " | EBN$^{o}$ | NW | West |
| 6 | 6 | 3 | Var:p$^{r}$ | Azim:$^{th}$ 17° 10' | |
| 7 | 8 | " | In 1 R.M.T. | S. & 2.$^{d}$ R.F.T.S. | Course make to be N:$^{o}$ 64$^{d}$ E:$^{t}$ Dis:$^{t}$ 190 |
| 8 | 8 | " | | | Miles, Northing 69 m:$^{s}$ Easting 176 m:$^{s}$ |
| 9 | 8 | 3 | | | Diff of Long.$^{d}$ 216 m:$^{s}$ |
| 10 | 8 | 4 | | | |
| 11 | 9 | " | | | Lat:$^{d}$ p:$^{r}$ Account 36$^{d}$ 00$^{m}$ S:$^{o}$ |
| 12 | 10 | " | | | Meridian Distance 58 24 E.$^{t}$ |
| 1 | 9 | 3 | E½N.$^{o}$ | | Difference of Long$^{d}$ 71 42 E.$^{t}$ |
| 2 | 8 | 4 | | Sq$^{lls}$ & R.$^{n}$ | |
| 3 | 9 | 6 | In 2.$^{d}$ R.M.T. | S D$^{o}$ D$^{o}$ | |
| 4 | 9 | 4 | | WNW D$^{o}$ | |
| 5 | 8 | " | | | |
| 6 | 7 | 3 | E½S.$^{o}$ | Small D.$^{o}$ | |
| 7 | 8 | " | | | |
| 8 | 8 | 2 | EBN | out 2.$^{d}$ R.B.T.S. | |
| 9 | 8 | 3 | EBN½N.$^{o}$ | | |
| 10 | 8 | 2 | ENE | out 1:$^{th}$ R.B.T.S. | |
| 11 | 9 | 2 | | | |
| 12 | 9 | " | 196 Miles | | |

| H | K | F | Courses | Winds | Thursday: 9: May. |
|---|---|---|---|---|---|
| 1 | 9 | " | NEBE | NW | |
| 2 | 9 | 4 | | | Fresh Gales of Wind with fair |
| 3 | 9 | 5 | | | Weather |
| 4 | 9 | " | | | |
| 5 | 7 | " | | In 2.$^{d}$ R.F.T.S. | Course make to be N:$^{o}$ 45$^{d}$ E:$^{t}$ Distance |
| 6 | 9 | " | | In 2.$^{d}$ R.M.T.S. | 182 Miles |
| 7 | 9 | " | ENE | | |
| 8 | 8 | 4 | NEBE | | Lat:$^{d}$ Observ'd 32$^{d}$ 42$^{m}$ S.$^{o}$ |
| 9 | 9 | 4 | | | Meridian Distance 60 32 E.$^{t}$ |
| 10 | 9 | 4 | | | Difference of Long$^{d}$ 75 14 E.$^{t}$ |
| 11 | 9 | " | | WBS$^{o}$ | Variation allow'd 16 00 W:$^{t}$ |
| 12 | 8 | " | | | |
| 1 | 7 | 5 | | | |
| 2 | 8 | " | | | |
| 3 | 8 | " | | | |
| 4 | 6 | 4 | | | |
| 5 | 7 | 4 | | | |
| 6 | 6 | " | | | |
| 7 | 5 | 3 | | Out AR.$^{s}$ | |
| 8 | 6 | " | | SWBW | |
| 9 | 5 | " | | | |
| 10 | 5 | 3 | | | |
| 11 | 5 | " | | | |
| 12 | 5 | 2 | 183 Miles | | |
| 1 | 5 | " | NEBE | SWBW | Friday: 10: |
| 2 | 4 | " | | | |
| 3 | 4 | 4 | | | Small gales of Wind with Calms |
| 4 | 4 | 3 | | | |
| 5 | 4 | " | | | Course make to be N:$^{o}$ 42$^{d}$ E:$^{t}$ Distance 50 |
| 6 | 4 | " | | S:$^{o}$ | Miles, Northing 38 m:$^{s}$ Easting 34 m:$^{s}$ diff |
| 7 | 3 | 4 | | | of Long.$^{d}$ 41 m:$^{s}$ |
| 8 | 3 | 3 | | SWBW | |
| 9 | 2 | 3 | | | Lat:$^{d}$ p:$^{r}$ Account 32$^{d}$ 01$^{m}$ S:$^{o}$ |
| 10 | 2 | " | | | Meridian Distance 61 06 E:$^{t}$ |
| 11 | 2 | " | | | Difference of Long$^{d}$ 75 55 E:$^{t}$ |
| 12 | 2 | " | | | |
| 1 | 1 | 6 | | SSW | Variation Allow'd 15 30 W:$^{t}$ |
| 2 | 1 | 2 | | | |
| 3 | 1 | 3 | | | |
| 4 | 1 | " | | | |
| 5 | 1 | " | | | |
| 6 | 1 | " | | | |
| 7 | 1 | " | | SWBW | |
| 8 | 1 | " | | | |
| 9 | " | " | } | | |
| 10 | " | " | } Calms | | |
| 11 | " | " | } | | |
| 12 | " | " | } 51 Miles | | |

| | | | | | |
|---|---|---|---|---|---|
| 1 | „ | „ | | | Saturday: 11: |
| 2 | „ | „ | | | |
| 3 | „ | „ | | | Small gales of wind and Calm |
| 4 | „ | „ | | | |
| 5 | „ | „ | Calm | | Course make to be N:° 18$^{d}$ E:$^{t}$ Distance 15 |
| 6 | „ | „ | | | Miles |
| 7 | „ | „ | | | |
| 8 | „ | „ | | | Lat:$^{d}$ p:$^{r}$ Account 32$^{d}$ 09$^{m}$ S:° |
| 9 | „ | „ | | | Meridian Distance 61 20 E.$^{t}$ |
| 10 | „ | „ | | | Difference of Long.$^{d}$ 76 12 E.$^{t}$ |
| 11 | 1 | „ | NBW | NEBE | |
| 12 | 1 | 3 | | | Variation allow'd 15 00 W:$^{t}$ |
| 1 | 2 | 3 | | | |
| 2 | 2 | „ | NW | NNE | |
| 3 | 2 | „ | | | |
| 4 | 2 | 3 | NWBW | NBE Tackt | |
| 5 | 2 | 4 | SEBE | NEBE | |
| 6 | 3 | „ | ESE | NE | |
| 7 | 4 | „ | | | |
| 8 | 4 | 3 | | | |
| 9 | 3 | 3 | | | |
| 10 | 2 | 5 | | | |
| 11 | 2 | „ | | In 1:$^{st}$ R.B.T.S | |
| 12 | 1 | 4 | EBN.° 34 m:$^{s}$ | NBE | |
| H | K | F | Courses | Winds | Sunday: 12: May. 1723 |
| 1 | 1 | „ | ESE | N:° | |
| 2 | 1 | 4 | | In 1 R.B.T.S. | Moderate gales of Wind, Cloudy Wea: |
| 3 | 2 | 4 | SE | ENE | |
| 4 | 2 | „ | | Tackt | Course make to be E:$^{t}$ Distance 6 Miles |
| 5 | 1 | 2 | NNW | NE | |
| 6 | 2 | „ | | | Lat:$^{d}$ p:$^{r}$ Account 32$^{d}$ 09$^{m}$ S:° |
| 7 | 2 | 3 | | | Meridian Distance 61 26 E:$^{t}$ |
| 8 | 2 | 3 | NBW | NEBE | Difference of Long.$^{d}$ 76 19 E:$^{t}$ |
| 9 | 3 | „ | | | Variation p$^{r}$ Med$^{m}$ |
| 10 | 1 | „ | NW | NNE | of Azim:$^{th}$ and Amplit:$^{d}$ 12 35 W:$^{t}$ |
| 11 | 2 | „ | | | |
| 12 | 4 | „ | NWBN | NEBN | |
| 1 | 5 | „ | NW | NNE | |
| 2 | 5 | 4 | | | |
| 3 | 5 | „ | NWBN | NEBN | |
| 4 | 4 | 2 | NW | NNE Tackt | |
| 5 | 3 | „ | SEBE | NEBE | |
| 6 | 3 | „ | | | |
| 7 | 2 | 5 | ESE Var: p$^{r}$ | Amp.$^{d}$ 12:30: | |
| 8 | 3 | 3 | | NE | |
| 9 | 6 | 3 | | | |
| 10 | 6 | „ | | | |
| 11 | 5 | „ | | | |
| 12 | 4 | 5 | 79 Miles | | |

| | | | | | |
|---|---|---|---|---|---|
| 1 | 2 | ” | ESE | NE | Monday: 13: |
| 2 | 1 | ” | | | |
| 3 | 1 | ” | | Squally | Small gales of Wind Cloudy Wea: |
| 4 | 3 | 3 | EBS.$^{o}$ | NEBN | |
| 5 | 3 | 3 | | In 2.$^{d}$R.BT.S.D:$^{o}$ | Course make to be E:$^{t}$ Distance 56 Miles |
| 6 | 3 | 4 | | H.$^{d}$ F.T.S. | |
| 7 | 3 | ” | | | Lat:$^{d}$ p:$^{r}$ Account 32$^{d}$ 09$^{m}$ S:$^{o}$ |
| 8 | 3 | ” | E½S.$^{o}$ | NNE | Meridian Distance 62 20 E:$^{t}$ |
| 9 | 3 | ” | E½N | Set F.T.S. | Difference of Long$^{d}$ 77 25 E:$^{t}$ |
| 10 | 3 | ” | | | Variation Allow'd 12 00 W:$^{t}$ |
| 11 | 2 | ” | EBN | NBE | |
| 12 | 2 | 2 | | | |
| 1 | 2 | ” | | | |
| 2 | 2 | 3 | | | |
| 3 | 2 | ” | | | |
| 4 | 2 | ” | ENE | N:$^{o}$ | |
| 5 | 2 | ” | EBN | NBE | |
| 6 | 2 | ” | | | |
| 7 | 2 | 2 | | Out 2:$^{d}$ R.BT.S. | |
| 8 | 3 | ” | | | |
| 9 | 1 | ” | EBS.$^{o}$ | NEBN | |
| 10 | 2 | 5 | E.$^{t}$ | NNE | |
| 11 | 2 | 3 | | | |
| 12 | 2 | 3 | EBN 57 M:$^{s}$ | NBE | |
| 1 | 1 | 5 | ENE | N.$^{o}$ | Tuesday: 14: |
| 2 | 2 | ” | | | |
| 3 | 2 | ” | NEBE | NBW | Small Gales of Wind, fair Weather |
| 4 | 2 | 3 | | | |
| 5 | 1 | 3 | EBN | NBE | Course make to be N.$^{o}$ 79$^{d}$ E:$^{t}$ Distance |
| 6 | 1 | ” | | In 2.$^{d}$ R.BT.S. | 28 miles, Northing 5 m:$^{s}$ Easting 27 m:$^{s}$ |
| 7 | 1 | ” | E$^{t}$ | NNE | difference of Long.$^{d}$ 32 m:$^{s}$ |
| 8 | ” | 3 | | | |
| 9 | 1 | ” | | | Lat:$^{d}$ Observ'd 32$^{d}$ 14$^{m}$ S:$^{o}$ |
| 10 | 1 | ” | | | Meridian Distance 62 47 East |
| 11 | 1 | ” | | | Difference of Long$^{d}$ 77 55 East |
| 12 | 1 | ” | | | Variation p$^{r}$ Azim:$^{th}$ 11 20 West |
| 1 | 1 | ” | EBS.$^{o}$ | NEBN | |
| 2 | 1 | ” | | | |
| 3 | 1 | ” | | | |
| 4 | 1 | ” | | Out 2.$^{d}$ R.BT.S. | |
| 5 | 1 | 3 | | | |
| 6 | 1 | 3 | | | |
| 7 | 1 | ” | E$^{t}$ | NNE out AR$^{s}$ | |
| 8 | 1 | 4 | EBS$^{o}$ | NEBN | |
| 9 | 1 | ” | ESE | NE | |
| 10 | 1 | ” | | | |
| 11 | ” | 4 | | | |
| 12 | ” | ” | 28 M:$^{s}$ | Calm | |

| H | K | F | Courses | Winds | Wednesday: 15: May. |
|---|---|---|---|---|---|
| 1 | 2 | „ | NW | NE | |
| 2 | 2 | „ | | | Small Gales of Wind, fair Weather |
| 3 | 2 | 2 | | | |
| 4 | 2 | „ | NWBN | NEBN | Course make to be N:$^{o}$ 57$^{d}$ E:$^{t}$ Distance 27 |
| 5 | 1 | „ | WNW | NNE | Miles, Northing 14 m:$^{s}$ Westing 22 m:$^{s}$ diff |
| 6 | 4 | 4 | | | of Long.$^{d}$ 27 m:$^{s}$ |
| 7 | 2 | „ | NW½W | | |
| 8 | 3 | 3 | | | Lat:$^{d}$ p:$^{r}$ Account 32$^{d}$ 00$^{m}$ S:$^{o}$ |
| 9 | 3 | „ | NWBN | NEBN | Meridian Distance 62 25 E.$^{t}$ |
| 10 | 3 | „ | | | Difference of Long$^{d}$ 77 28 E.$^{t}$ |
| 11 | 3 | 4 | NW | NNE | |
| 12 | 3 | „ | | | |
| 1 | 3 | 3 | | | |
| 2 | 3 | 4 | | | |
| 3 | 3 | „ | | | |
| 4 | 3 | „ | | | |
| 5 | 4 | „ | NWBW | NBE | |
| 6 | 3 | „ | | | |
| 7 | 2 | „ | | Tackt | |
| 8 | 2 | 6 | EBN | | |
| 9 | 4 | „ | | | |
| 10 | 4 | 2 | East | NNE | |
| 11 | 4 | „ | | | |
| 12 | 4 | „ | 73 Miles | | |
| 1 | 3 | 5 | EBN | NBE | Thursday: 16: |
| 2 | 4 | „ | | | |
| 3 | 4 | 2 | ENE | N.$^{o}$ | Moderate Gales of Wind with fair Weather |
| 4 | 4 | „ | | | |
| 5 | 3 | 3 | | | Course make to be N:$^{o}$ 75$^{d}$ E:$^{t}$ Distance 79 |
| 6 | 3 | „ | NEBE | NBW | Miles, Northing 20 m:$^{s}$ Easting 76 m.$^{s}$ diff |
| 7 | 3 | „ | | In 1:$^{st}$ R.BT.S. | Long.$^{d}$ 90 m:$^{s}$ |
| 8 | 2 | 5 | | | |
| 9 | 2 | 3 | | | Lat:$^{d}$ Observ'd 31$^{d}$ 40$^{m}$ S.$^{o}$ |
| 10 | 2 | 3 | | | Meridian Distance 63 41 E:$^{t}$ |
| 11 | 3 | „ | | Small Rain | Difference of Long$^{d}$ 78 58 E:$^{t}$ |
| 12 | 3 | „ | | Squalls | |
| 1 | 2 | 3 | | | |
| 2 | 2 | 2 | | | |
| 3 | 3 | 4 | | | |
| 4 | 3 | 2 | | | |
| 5 | 2 | 1 | | | |
| 6 | 2 | „ | EBN | NBE | |
| 7 | 4 | „ | E½N$^{o}$ | | |
| 8 | 4 | „ | | | |
| 9 | 4 | „ | | | |
| 10 | 4 | „ | | | |
| 11 | 4 | 2 | | In 2$^{d}$ R.BT.S | |
| 12 | 4 | „ | 79 Miles | | |

| | | | | | |
|---|---|---|---|---|---|
| 1 | 3 | 3 | ENE | N:$^{o}$ H:$^{d}$ F.T.S. | Friday: 17: |
| 2 | 3 | „ | NEBE | NBW Set D.$^{o}$ | |
| 3 | 3 | 5 | ENE | N.$^{o}$ | Cloudy Weather and Small gales |
| 4 | 2 | 3 | | | of Wind |
| 5 | 2 | 4 | | H:$^{d}$ F.T.S. | |
| 6 | 2 | 3 | | | Course make to be N:$^{o}$ 80$^{d}$ E:$^{t}$ Distance 48 |
| 7 | 2 | 2 | EBN | NBE | Miles |
| 8 | 3 | „ | | | |
| 9 | 2 | „ | In 3:$^{d}$ R & | H:$^{d}$ M.T.S. | Lat:$^{d}$ p:$^{r}$ Account 31$^{d}$ 32$^{m}$ S:$^{o}$ |
| 10 | 2 | „ | | | Meridian Distance 64 24 E:$^{t}$ |
| 11 | 2 | „ | East | NNE | Difference of Long$^{d}$ 79 53 E:$^{t}$ |
| 12 | 2 | „ | | Sq.$^{lls}$ & Rain | Variation Allow'd 11 30 W:$^{t}$ |
| 1 | 2 | 2 | | | |
| 2 | 2 | 3 | | hard Sq:$^{lls}$ & R.$^{n}$ | |
| 3 | 2 | „ | | | |
| 4 | 2 | 1 | | | |
| 5 | 2 | „ | E½N | NBE D.$^{o}$ | |
| 6 | 2 | „ | | | |
| 7 | 1 | 3 | | Set M.T.S. | |
| 8 | 1 | „ | ENE | N.$^{o}$ O:$^{t}$ 3:$^{d}$ R. D.$^{o}$ | |
| 9 | 1 | 4 | | | |
| 10 | 1 | 4 | EBN | NBE | |
| 11 | 2 | 1 | | | |
| 12 | 1 | 4 | 53 m:$^{s}$ | Wore Ship | |
| H | K | F | Courses | Winds | Saturday: 18: May 1723 |
| 1 | 2 | 2 | NW | NNE Rain | |
| 2 | 2 | 4 | | | Fresh gales and Cloudy Weather |
| 3 | 2 | „ | NWBW | NBE | |
| 4 | 3 | „ | | | Course make to be N:$^{o}$ 72$^{d}$ W:$^{t}$ Distance 11 |
| 5 | 2 | 3 | WNW | N:$^{o}$ | miles, Northing 3 m:$^{s}$ Westing 10 m:$^{s}$ |
| 6 | 1 | 3 | W$^{t}$ | NNW | |
| 7 | 1 | „ | Lightning in | y$^{e}$ SW board | Lat:$^{d}$ Obs:$^{d}$ 31$^{d}$ 29$^{m}$ S:$^{o}$ |
| 8 | | | Bro:$^{ht}$ too up, | NW off WNW | Meridian Distance 64 14 East |
| 9 | „ | „ | up WBN off | WSW | Difference of Long$^{d}$ 79 41 East |
| 10 | „ | „ | up W.$^{t}$ off | SWBW | |
| 11 | „ | „ | | | |
| 12 | „ | „ | | | |
| 1 | „ | „ | | | |
| 2 | „ | „ | | | |
| 3 | „ | „ | up W:$^{t}$ off | WSW | |
| 4 | „ | „ | | | |
| 5 | „ | „ | up W.$^{t}$ off | SW | |
| 6 | | | Wore Ship & | made Sail Var: | p$^{r}$ Am:$^{d}$ 11:$^{d}$ 42'W |
| 7 | 1 | 4 | NNE | NWBW Set F.S. | |
| 8 | 2 | „ | | Out AReefs | |
| 9 | 3 | „ | | | |
| 10 | 4 | 1 | NEBN | NWBN | |
| 11 | 3 | 6 | | | |
| 12 | 3 | 4 | 34 Miles | | |

| | | | | | |
|---|---|---|---|---|---|
| 1 | 4 | „ | NEBN | NW | Sunday: 19: |
| 2 | 4 | 3 | | In 1:st R.BTS. | |
| 3 | 3 | 3 | NNE | Squalls | Small gales of Wind, the first part. The latter moderate and fair Weather |
| 4 | 2 | „ | NEBN | NWBN | |
| 5 | 2 | 3 | | Sq:lls & R.n | |
| 6 | 3 | 3 | | | Course make to be N:o 22d E:t Distance 95 Miles, Northing 88 m:s Easting 37 m:s diff of Long.d 43 m:s |
| 7 | 3 | „ | | | |
| 8 | 3 | „ | NNE | NW | |
| 9 | 3 | 3 | NBE | NWBW | |
| 10 | 3 | „ | | | Lat:d p:r Account 30d 01m S:o |
| 11 | 3 | „ | | | Meridian Distance 64 51 East |
| 12 | 3 | „ | | | Difference of Longd 80 24 East |
| 1 | 3 | 3 | | | Variation pr PM Azim:th 10 18 West |
| 2 | 2 | 5 | NBE½E | In 2.d R.B.T.S. | |
| 3 | 2 | „ | NEBN | NWBN | |
| 4 | 2 | 4 | | | |
| 5 | 2 | 3 | | | |
| 6 | 2 | 3 | | | |
| 7 | 5 | „ | | | |
| 8 | 6 | „ | | WNW Out 2d R. | BT.S. |
| 9 | 6 | 3 | NNE | | |
| 10 | 6 | 3 | | | |
| 11 | 7 | „ | | | |
| 12 | 6 | 3 | 91 Miles | | |
| 1 | 6 | 3 | NBE | WNW | Monday: 20: |
| 2 | 7 | 1 | | Squalls & R.n | |
| 3 | 5 | „ | | | Moderate gales of Wind, fair Weather |
| 4 | 6 | 3 | | W:t | |
| 5 | 6 | „ | | | |
| 6 | 5 | 6 | | | Course make to be N:o 6d E:t Distance 130 Miles, Northing 139 m:s Easting 14 m:s diff of Long.d 16 m:s |
| 7 | 6 | 5 | | | |
| 8 | 6 | 3 | | WBNo | |
| 9 | 6 | „ | | | |
| 10 | 6 | 2 | | | Lat:d Obs:d 27d 51m S:o |
| 11 | 5 | 5 | | | Meridian Distance 65 05 E:t |
| 12 | 5 | 4 | | | Difference of Longd 80 40 E:t |
| 1 | 5 | 5 | | | Variation p:r AM Amp.d 10 33 W:t |
| 2 | 5 | 5 | | | |
| 3 | 5 | „ | | Sq:lls & Rain | |
| 4 | 3 | 2 | NBE½E | | |
| 5 | 5 | „ | NBE | W.t | |
| 6 | 4 | 5 | | | |
| 7 | 5 | 4 | NNE | | |
| 8 | 4 | „ | NE | | |
| 9 | 4 | „ | | Out 1:st R.B.T.S. | |
| 10 | 3 | 3 | | | |
| 11 | 4 | „ | | | |
| 12 | 4 | „ | 128 Miles | | |

| H | K | F | Courses | Winds | Tuesday: 21:$^{st}$ May |
|---|---|---|---|---|---|
| 1 | 3 | „ | NE | SW | |
| 2 | 4 | „ | | | Small Gales of Wind with Calms |
| 3 | 3 | 2 | | Squalls | |
| 4 | 3 | „ | | | Course make to be N:$^{o}$ 23$^{d}$ E:$^{t}$ Distance 59 |
| 5 | 1 | „ | Var: p$^{r}$ | Azim:$^{th}$ 10$^{d}$ W:$^{t}$ | Miles, Northing 54 m:$^{s}$ Easting 23 m:$^{s}$ diff |
| 6 | 1 | „ | | In 1:$^{st}$ R.B.T.S | of Long.$^{d}$ 26 m:$^{s}$ |
| 7 | 2 | „ | | | |
| 8 | 3 | „ | NEBN | | Lat:$^{d}$ Obs:$^{d}$ 26$^{d}$ 57$^{m}$ S:$^{o}$ |
| 9 | 3 | „ | NBE | SSW | Meridian Distance 65 28 E.$^{t}$ |
| 10 | 2 | 2 | | | Difference of Long$^{d}$ 81 06 E.$^{t}$ |
| 11 | 2 | „ | NNE | | |
| 12 | 2 | „ | | | p$^{r}$ Obs:$^{s}$ the Ship is not so far to y$^{e}$ N:$^{o}$w:$^{d}$ |
| 1 | 2 | „ | | | p:$^{r}$ 12 m:$^{s}$ as the Log: gives, y:$^{e}$ Error in |
| 2 | 1 | „ | Taken a back | | y$^{e}$ Dis:$^{t}$ |
| 3 | „ | „ | } Calm | | |
| 4 | „ | „ | | | |
| 5 | 2 | 3 | NEBN | EBS.$^{o}$ | |
| 6 | 2 | „ | | | |
| 7 | 2 | „ | Var:p$^{r}$ med:$^{m}$ | of Azim:$^{th}$ 10:° | 40'N |
| 8 | 2 | 5 | NE | SE | |
| 9 | 1 | 3 | | | |
| 10 | 1 | „ | | | |
| 11 | 1 | „ | WNW | SW | |
| 12 | „ | 6 | NBW | 46 Miles | |
| 1 | 1 | 5 | NEBE | SE | Wednesday: 22. |
| 2 | 1 | 2 | | | |
| 3 | 1 | 4 | | | Small airs of wind, & fair weather |
| 4 | 1 | „ | | | |
| 5 | 1 | 3 | NNE | | Course make to be N:$^{o}$ 45$^{d}$ E:$^{t}$ Distance 61 |
| 6 | 1 | „ | NE | ESE | Miles, Northing 43 m:$^{s}$ Easting 43 m:$^{s}$ dif |
| 7 | 2 | „ | ENE | SSE | Long:$^{d}$ 48 m:$^{s}$ |
| 8 | 2 | „ | | | |
| 9 | 1 | 4 | | | Lat:$^{d}$ Obs:$^{d}$ 26$^{d}$ 14$^{m}$ S:$^{o}$ |
| 10 | 1 | 5 | NE | SW | Meridian Distance 66 11 E:$^{t}$ |
| 11 | 1 | 1 | | | Difference of Long$^{d}$ 81 54 E:$^{t}$ |
| 12 | 1 | 5 | | | Variation p:$^{r}$ Amp$^{d}$ 9 55 W:$^{t}$ |
| 1 | 1 | „ | | | |
| 2 | 1 | 3 | | SSW | |
| 3 | 1 | 4 | | | |
| 4 | 2 | 3 | | | |
| 5 | 2 | 4 | | | |
| 6 | 2 | 3 | | | |
| 7 | 2 | 2 | | | |
| 8 | 3 | „ | NEBE | SW | |
| 9 | 3 | 3 | | | |
| 10 | 4 | „ | | | |
| 11 | 3 | 4 | ENE | SSW | |
| 12 | 3 | „ | 49 Miles | | |

| | | | | | |
|---|---|---|---|---|---|
| 1 | 3 | 3 | ENE | SSE | Thursday: 23: |
| 2 | 3 | „ | | | |
| 3 | 3 | 3 | | | Small Gales of Wind w:$^{th}$ Cloudy Weather |
| 4 | 4 | „ | NEBE | SEBE | |
| 5 | 4 | „ | | | Course make to be N:$^{o}$ 38$^{d}$ E:$^{t}$ Distance 74 |
| 6 | 2 | 3 | | | Miles |
| 7 | 3 | „ | ENE | SE | |
| 8 | 2 | „ | NEBN | EBS.$^{o}$ Rain | Lat:$^{d}$ Obs:$^{d}$ 25$^{d}$ 16$^{m}$ S:$^{o}$ |
| 9 | 1 | 3 | NNE | E:$^{t}$ | Meridian Distance 66 57 E:$^{t}$ |
| 10 | 1 | „ | NBW | NEBE | Difference of Long$^{d}$ 82 45 E:$^{t}$ |
| 11 | 1 | „ | NNW | NE | |
| 12 | 1 | „ | NEBN | EBS.$^{o}$ | Variation Allow'd 9 00 W:$^{t}$ |
| 1 | 1 | „ | | | |
| 2 | 1 | „ | | | |
| 3 | 1 | 3 | NEBE | SSE Sq$^{l}$ & R.$^{n}$ | |
| 4 | 3 | „ | ENE | | |
| 5 | 4 | 5 | NEBE | | |
| 6 | 2 | „ | | | |
| 7 | 2 | 3 | NE | ESE | |
| 8 | 4 | „ | | Sq:$^{lls}$ & R.$^{n}$ | |
| 9 | 4 | „ | NEBN | EBS.$^{o}$ | |
| 10 | 3 | 3 | | | |
| 11 | 4 | 3 | | | |
| 12 | 3 | 6 | 67 Miles | | |
| H | K | F | Courses | Winds | Friday: 24: May: 1723 |
| 1 | 4 | „ | ENE | SE Squaly | |
| 2 | 2 | „ | | SSE D.$^{o}$ | Small Gales of wind with Cloudy |
| 3 | 4 | 5 | | SE | Weather and Some Raine |
| 4 | 4 | 5 | | | |
| 5 | 4 | „ | | | Course made good N:$^{o}$ 48$^{d}$ E:$^{t}$ Distance 80 |
| 6 | 3 | „ | NEBE | SEBE | miles, Northing 53 m:$^{s}$ Easting 59 m:$^{s}$ diff |
| 7 | 3 | 2 | | | of Long.$^{d}$ 65 m:$^{s}$ |
| 8 | 3 | „ | | | |
| 9 | 3 | 3 | | | Lat:$^{d}$ p:$^{r}$ Account 24$^{d}$ 23$^{m}$ S:$^{o}$ |
| 10 | 3 | 3 | | | Meridian Distance 67 56 E:$^{t}$ |
| 11 | 3 | 4 | | | Difference of Long$^{d}$ 83 50 E:$^{t}$ |
| 12 | 2 | 3 | | | Variation Allow'd 8 00 W:$^{t}$ |
| 1 | 4 | 3 | | | |
| 2 | 3 | „ | | | |
| 3 | 3 | 2 | | | |
| 4 | 2 | 3 | | | |
| 5 | 2 | 4 | | | |
| 6 | 4 | „ | | | |
| 7 | 4 | „ | NE | ESE | |
| 8 | 4 | „ | | | |
| 9 | 2 | 3 | | | |
| 10 | 3 | „ | ENE | SE | |
| 11 | 3 | 6 | | | |
| 12 | 4 | 3 | 83 Miles | | |

| | | | | | |
|---|---|---|---|---|---|
| 1 | 2 | „ | ENE | SE | Saturday: 25: |
| 2 | 4 | 4 | | | |
| 3 | 4 | 3 | NEBE | SEBE | Small Gales of wind and Cloudy Weather |
| 4 | 5 | „ | | | |
| 5 | 3 | „ | | | Course make to be N:$^{o}$ 20:$^{d}$ E:$^{t}$ Distance 80 |
| 6 | 2 | „ | | | Miles, Northing 75 m:$^{s}$ Easting 27 m:$^{s}$ diff |
| 7 | 2 | 2 | | | of Long$^{d}$: 30 m:$^{s}$ |
| 8 | 1 | „ | | | |
| 9 | 3 | „ | | | Lat:$^{d}$ p:$^{r}$ Acc:$^{t}$ 23$^{d}$ 08$^{m}$ S.$^{o}$ |
| 10 | 4 | „ | | | Meridian Distance 68 23 E:$^{t}$ |
| 11 | 3 | 4 | | | Difference of long$^{d}$ 84 20 E:$^{t}$ |
| 12 | 3 | 3 | | | Variation p:$^{r}$ AM Amp.$^{d}$ 8 00 W:$^{t}$ |
| 1 | 3 | „ | | | |
| 2 | 2 | „ | NEBN | EBS:$^{o}$ | |
| 3 | 3 | „ | | | |
| 4 | 2 | 4 | NNE | East | |
| 5 | 4 | 5 | | | |
| 6 | 4 | 4 | | | |
| 7 | 4 | 4 | | | |
| 8 | 4 | „ | | | |
| 9 | 4 | „ | NBE | EBN | |
| 10 | 4 | „ | N.$^{o}$ | ENE | |
| 11 | 3 | 3 | | | |
| 12 | 2 | 6 | NBE 81 M:$^{s}$ | EBN | |
| 1 | 3 | 4 | NBE | EBN | Sunday: 26: |
| 2 | 3 | 3 | | | |
| 3 | 3 | 3 | N½E | | Small Gales of wind w:$^{th}$ Cloudy |
| 4 | 4 | „ | | | Weather |
| 5 | 3 | „ | N.$^{o}$ | ENE | |
| 6 | 2 | 3 | | Tackt | Course make to be N:$^{o}$ 82$^{d}$ E:$^{t}$ Distance 55 |
| 7 | 1 | „ | SE | | Miles, Northing 7 m:$^{s}$ Easting 54 m:$^{s}$ diff |
| 8 | 3 | „ | SEBS$^{o}$ | EBN | of Long.$^{d}$ 59 m:$^{s}$ |
| 9 | 3 | „ | | | |
| 10 | 3 | „ | EBS$^{o}$ | NEBN | Lat:$^{d}$ Observ'd 23$^{d}$ 01$^{m}$ S.$^{o}$ |
| 11 | 2 | „ | | | Meridian Distance 69 17 E:$^{t}$ |
| 12 | 3 | „ | | | Difference of Long$^{d}$ 85 19 E:$^{t}$ |
| 1 | 3 | „ | | | Variation p:$^{r}$ Very |
| 2 | 2 | 4 | | | good P.M Amplit$^{d}$ 7 00 W.$^{t}$ |
| 3 | 2 | 3 | | | |
| 4 | 2 | 4 | | | |
| 5 | 2 | 4 | E½S.$^{o}$ | NNE | |
| 6 | 2 | 2 | | | |
| 7 | 3 | 3 | | | |
| 8 | 3 | 5 | | Out 1.$^{st}$ R.MT.S. | |
| 9 | 4 | „ | | | |
| 10 | 4 | 3 | | | |
| 11 | 4 | „ | E$^{t}$ | | |
| 12 | 5 | 1 | 75 Miles | | |

| H | K | F | Courses | Winds | Monday: 27: May |
|---|---|---|---|---|---|
| 1 | 4 | „ | N½E | NBE | |
| 2 | 4 | 3 | | | Small Gales of Wind Variable as p$^{r}$ Logg, |
| 3 | 4 | „ | | | Cloudy Weather |
| 4 | 4 | 3 | | | |
| 5 | 3 | „ | ENE | N:$^{o}$ In1:$^{st}$ R.BT.S | Course make to be N:$^{o}$ 54$^{d}$ E:$^{t}$ Distance 73 |
| 6 | 4 | „ | | | miles, Northing 42 m:$^{s}$ Easting 59 m:$^{s}$ diff |
| 7 | 2 | „ | EBN | NBE | of Long.$^{d}$ 64 m:$^{s}$ |
| 8 | 3 | „ | ENE | N:$^{o}$ | |
| 9 | 2 | 3 | NEBE | NBW | Lat:$^{d}$ p$^{r}$ Account 22$^{d}$ 19$^{m}$ S:$^{o}$ |
| 10 | 2 | 3 | | | Meridian Distance 70 16 E:$^{t}$ |
| 11 | 3 | 2 | ENE½N | | Difference of Long$^{d}$ 86 23 E:$^{t}$ |
| 12 | 2 | 5 | NEBE | | Variation Allow'd 6 30 W:$^{t}$ |
| 1 | 2 | „ | | | |
| 2 | 2 | 5 | | | |
| 3 | 3 | „ | ENE | N:$^{o}$ | |
| 4 | 2 | 3 | | | |
| 5 | 3 | „ | NEBE | NBW | |
| 6 | 3 | 3 | | Out 1:$^{st}$ R.BT.S. | |
| 7 | 4 | 3 | | | |
| 8 | 4 | 3 | ENE | NNW | |
| 9 | 5 | „ | | | |
| 10 | 4 | „ | | | |
| 11 | 2 | „ | EBN | WBS:$^{o}$ Rain | |
| 12 | 1 | 6 | 78 Miles | | |
| 1 | 3 | „ | EBN | W:$^{t}$ Rain | Tuesday. 28: |
| 2 | 4 | „ | | | |
| 3 | 5 | „ | EBN½N | | Moderate Gales of Wind with Cloudy |
| 4 | 5 | „ | | | Weather |
| 5 | 5 | „ | | | |
| 6 | 3 | „ | EBN | In 1:$^{st}$ R.B.T.S. | Att 7 last night brought too for an Isl:$^{d}$ |
| 7 | 2 | „ | Tackt and | brought too | Sett down in Lat:$^{d}$ 22 S:$^{o}$ and at day light |
| 8 | „ | „ | up SSW off | WSW R$^{n}$ | Made Saile |
| 9 | „ | „ | | | |
| 10 | „ | „ | | | Lat.$^{d}$ p:$^{r}$ Account 22$^{d}$ 00$^{m}$ S:$^{o}$ |
| 11 | „ | „ | up SW off | WBS.$^{o}$ | Meridian Distance 70 51 E:$^{t}$ |
| 12 | „ | „ | | | Difference of Long$^{d}$ 87 01 E:$^{t}$ |
| 1 | „ | „ | up SWBS:$^{o}$ | off SWBW | |
| 2 | „ | „ | | | |
| 3 | „ | „ | | | |
| 4 | „ | „ | | | |
| 5 | „ | „ | up SWBW | off W:$^{t}$ | |
| 6 | „ | „ | Wore Ship | and Made Sail | |
| 7 | 4 | „ | NEBE | SSE O:$^{t}$ AR:$^{s}$ | |
| 8 | 4 | „ | NE½E | | |
| 9 | 5 | „ | NEBE | | |
| 10 | 4 | 5 | | | |
| 11 | 5 | „ | | | |
| 12 | 4 | 2 | 54 Miles | | |

| | | | | | |
|---|---|---|---|---|---|
| 1 | 3 | „ | NE | SSE | Wednesday: 29: |
| 2 | 5 | „ | | | |
| 3 | 6 | „ | | SEBS:$^{o}$ | Moderate gales of Wind and |
| 4 | 6 | „ | NE½E | SE | fair Weather |
| 5 | 5 | 3 | NEBN | | |
| 6 | 3 | 3 | | | Course make to be N:$^{o}$ 44$^{d}$ E:$^{t}$ Dist 90 |
| 7 | 2 | 2 | NE | SEBS.$^{o}$ | Miles, Northing 62 m:$^{s}$ Easting 62 m$^{s}$ diff |
| 8 | 4 | 3 | | | of Long.$^{d}$ 65 m:$^{s}$ |
| 9 | 3 | 3 | NE½E | | |
| 10 | 2 | 5 | | | Lat:$^{d}$ Observ'd 20$^{d}$ 58$^{m}$ S:$^{o}$ |
| 11 | 4 | 3 | | | Meridian Distance 71 57 E:$^{t}$ |
| 12 | 5 | „ | NE | | Difference of Long$^{d}$ 88 06 E:$^{t}$ |
| 1 | 3 | 5 | | S:$^{o}$ | |
| 2 | 4 | 3 | | | |
| 3 | 4 | „ | | | |
| 4 | 5 | „ | NEBE | SSW | |
| 5 | 4 | 2 | | | |
| 6 | 6 | „ | | | |
| 7 | 6 | 4 | | S:$^{o}$ | |
| 8 | 6 | „ | NE | SSE | |
| 9 | 5 | 5 | | | |
| 10 | 5 | 5 | | | |
| 11 | 6 | „ | | | |
| 12 | 5 | 3 | 114 Miles | | |
| H | K | F | Courses | Winds | Thursday: 30: May. |
| 1 | 2 | 6 | NE | SSE | |
| 2 | 3 | 3 | | | Moderate gales of Wind, fair Wea: |
| 3 | 4 | „ | | | |
| 4 | 4 | „ | | | Course make to be N.$^{o}$ 30$^{d}$ E:$^{t}$ Distance 74 |
| 5 | 2 | 5 | | In 1:$^{st}$ R.B.T.S. | Miles, Northing 64 m:$^{s}$ Easting 37 m:$^{s}$ diff |
| 6 | 5 | „ | NE½N | S$^{o}$ | of Long.$^{d}$ 40 m:$^{s}$ |
| 7 | 5 | „ | NE½E | | |
| 8 | 3 | 4 | | | Lat.$^{d}$ Observ'd 19$^{d}$ 54$^{m}$ S:$^{o}$ |
| 9 | 4 | „ | | | Meridian Distance 72 37 E |
| 10 | 3 | 4 | Brought too | | Difference of Long$^{d}$ 88 46 E |
| 11 | „ | „ | up SE off | E:$^{t}$ | Variation p:$^{r}$ P.M. Amp:$^{d}$ 5 45 W:$^{t}$ |
| 12 | „ | „ | | | |
| 1 | „ | „ | | | |
| 2 | „ | „ | up SE off | ENE | |
| 3 | „ | „ | up SE off | E.$^{t}$ | |
| 4 | „ | „ | Wore Ship & | made Saile | |
| 5 | 3 | „ | NNE | SW | |
| 6 | 4 | 6 | | Out 1:$^{st}$ R.B.T.S. | |
| 7 | 5 | „ | | S.$^{o}$ | |
| 8 | 4 | 3 | | | |
| 9 | 4 | 3 | NBE | | |
| 10 | 4 | „ | | | |
| 11 | 4 | 3 | NNE | | |
| 12 | 5 | 3 | 73 Miles | | |

| | | | | | |
|---|---|---|---|---|---|
| 1 | 5 | „ | NE | SSW | Friday: 31. |
| 2 | 6 | „ | | | |
| 3 | 5 | „ | | SBE | Moderate Gales of Wind with Cloudy |
| 4 | 5 | „ | | | Weather |
| 5 | 6 | „ | | | |
| 6 | 6 | „ | | | Course make to be N:$^{o}$ 40$^{d}$ E:$^{t}$ Distance160 |
| 7 | 6 | 2 | | | miles, Northing 120 m:$^{s}$ Easting 81 m:$^{s}$ |
| 8 | 6 | „ | | | diff of Long.$^{d}$ 86 m:$^{s}$ |
| 9 | 5 | „ | NEBN | SEBS:$^{o}$ | |
| 10 | 6 | „ | | Squally | Lat:$^{d}$ p:$^{r}$ Account 17$^{d}$ 54$^{m}$ S:$^{o}$ |
| 11 | 7 | „ | NE | In 1:$^{st}$ R.BT.S. | Meridian Distance 73 55 E:$^{t}$ |
| 12 | 7 | „ | | | Difference of Long$^{d}$ 90 12 d.$^{o}$ |
| 1 | 6 | 4 | | SE | Variation p:$^{r}$ P.M: Amp:$^{d}$ 5 40 W:$^{t}$ |
| 2 | 7 | „ | | | |
| 3 | 7 | „ | | | |
| 4 | 7 | 3 | | | |
| 5 | 8 | 5 | | | |
| 6 | 8 | 5 | | | |
| 7 | 8 | 5 | | | |
| 8 | 8 | 4 | | | |
| 9 | 7 | „ | | | |
| 10 | 7 | „ | | | |
| 11 | 8 | „ | | | |
| 12 | 8 | „ | 163 Miles | | |
| 1 | 7 | 5 | NE | SEBE | Saturday: 1: June 1723 |
| 2 | 7 | 4 | | | |
| 3 | 7 | 3 | | | Fresh Gales of Wind w:$^{th}$ Cloudy Weather |
| 4 | 7 | „ | | In 2:$^{d}$ R.B.T.S. | |
| 5 | 6 | 3 | | | Course make to be N:$^{o}$ 34$^{d}$ E:$^{t}$ Dist 150 |
| 6 | 6 | „ | | | Miles Northing 124 m:$^{s}$ Easting 83 m:$^{s}$ |
| 7 | 6 | „ | | | difference of Long:$^{d}$ 86 m:$^{s}$ |
| 8 | 7 | „ | NE½E | | |
| 9 | 6 | 3 | NE | | Lat:$^{d}$ p:$^{r}$ Acc:$^{t}$ 15$^{d}$ 50$^{m}$ S:$^{o}$ |
| 10 | 7 | „ | | | Meridian Distance 75 13 E:$^{t}$ |
| 11 | 6 | 5 | | | Difference of Long$^{d}$ 91 33 E:$^{t}$ |
| 12 | 6 | 2 | | Sq:$^{lls}$ & Rain | |
| 1 | 7 | „ | | | |
| 2 | 5 | 3 | | ESE | |
| 3 | 7 | 2 | | | |
| 4 | 6 | „ | | | |
| 5 | 6 | 5 | | | |
| 6 | 5 | 3 | | | |
| 7 | 5 | 3 | | | |
| 8 | 6 | „ | NEBN:$^{o}$ | | |
| 9 | 7 | „ | | | |
| 10 | 7 | 2 | | | |
| 11 | 7 | „ | | | |
| 12 | 5 | 6 | 158 Miles | | |

| H | K | F | Courses | Winds | Sunday: 2: June 1723 |
|---|---|---|---|---|---|
| 1 | 5 | 3 | NE | SEBS:° | |
| 2 | 6 | „ | | | Fresh gales of Wind with faint |
| 3 | 6 | „ | NE½N:° | | Squalls |
| 4 | 6 | „ | | | |
| 5 | 6 | „ | | | p$^{r}$ Obs: the Ship is not so farr to the |
| 6 | 6 | „ | | | N:°ward as the Log: gives p:$^{r}$ 22 miles, the |
| 7 | 6 | „ | | | Error Attribute to the Distance |
| 8 | 6 | „ | | | |
| 9 | 5 | 3 | NE | | Course make to be N.° 30$^{d}$ E:$^{t}$ Distance |
| 10 | 5 | 4 | | | 108 Miles, |
| 11 | 6 | 3 | | Out 2:$^{d}$ R.BT.S. | |
| 12 | 6 | „ | | | Lat:$^{d}$ Observ'd 14$^{d}$ 16$^{m}$ N:° |
| 1 | 5 | 3 | NE½N | ESE | Meridian Distance 76 10 E.$^{t}$ |
| 2 | 5 | „ | | | Difference of Long$^{d}$ 92 22 E.$^{t}$ |
| 3 | 5 | 2 | NE | | |
| 4 | 6 | „ | | | |
| 5 | 6 | „ | | | |
| 6 | 6 | „ | | | |
| 7 | 5 | 4 | NE½N° | | |
| 8 | 4 | 4 | | | |
| 9 | 6 | 3 | | | |
| 10 | 5 | 3 | | | |
| 11 | 5 | 3 | NEBN | EBN | |
| 12 | 5 | „ | 137 Miles | | |
| 1 | 5 | „ | NE | ESE | Monday: 3:$^{d}$ |
| 2 | 5 | 3 | | | |
| 3 | 5 | „ | | | Moderate Gales of Wind with |
| 4 | 5 | „ | | | fair Weather |
| 5 | 5 | „ | NE½N Var: | p$^{r}$ Az:$^{th}$ 4:° 14' | |
| 6 | 5 | 3 | NEBN | | Course make to be N:° 22 E:$^{t}$ Distance 102 |
| 7 | 5 | „ | | | miles Northing 93 m:$^{s}$ Easting 38 m:$^{s}$ diff |
| 8 | 5 | „ | | | of Long.$^{d}$ 39 m:$^{s}$ |
| 9 | 5 | „ | | | |
| 10 | 4 | 5 | | | Lat:$^{d}$ Observ'd 12$^{d}$ 43$^{m}$ S:° |
| 11 | 4 | „ | NE½N | | Meridian Distance 76 48 E:$^{t}$ |
| 12 | 4 | 2 | NEBN | | Difference of Long$^{d}$ 93 01 E:$^{t}$ |
| 1 | 4 | „ | | | |
| 2 | 4 | „ | | | |
| 3 | 4 | „ | | | |
| 4 | 3 | „ | | | |
| 5 | 4 | „ | | | |
| 6 | 4 | 4 | | | |
| 7 | 4 | 2 | NNE | | |
| 8 | 5 | „ | | | |
| 9 | 5 | 2 | | | |
| 10 | 4 | 4 | | Out 1:$^{st}$ R.FT.S. | |
| 11 | 5 | 3 | NNE½E | | |
| 12 | 5 | „ | 112 Miles | | |

| | | | | | |
|---|---|---|---|---|---|
| 1 | 5 | „ | NE½N | ESE | Tuesday: 4: |
| 2 | 4 | 4 | | | |
| 3 | 5 | „ | NEBN | | Fresh gales of Wind with fair Weather |
| 4 | 3 | „ | NBE | SE O:$^{t}$ 1 R.MT. | S. |
| 5 | 5 | 3 | Var.$^{s}$ p$^{r}$ | Azim:$^{th}$4°30'W.$^{t}$ | p$^{r}$ Obs: the Ship is 26 miles to the S:$^{o}$w:$^{d}$ |
| 6 | 5 | „ | In 1 R.BT.S | Sq$^{ll}$ & R$^{n}$ | of what the Log: allows, the Error I Attrib- |
| 7 | 5 | „ | | | ute to a S:$^{o}$erly Streame[53] |
| 8 | 6 | 3 | | | |
| 9 | 6 | 3 | | | Course make to be N:$^{o}$ 10$^{d}$ E:$^{t}$ Distance |
| 10 | 6 | 3 | | | 126 Miles |
| 11 | 7 | „ | | Out 1:$^{st}$ R.MT.S. | |
| 12 | 7 | „ | | | Lat:$^{d}$ Observ'd 10$^{c}$ 39$^{m}$ S:$^{o}$ |
| 1 | 6 | 4 | | | Meridian Distance 77 09 East |
| 2 | 6 | 3 | | | Difference of Long$^{c}$ 93 23 East |
| 3 | 7 | „ | | | |
| 4 | 7 | „ | | | |
| 5 | 8 | 2 | | | |
| 6 | 7 | 6 | O:$^{t}$ 1 R.FT.S. | SEBE | |
| 7 | 8 | 3 | | | |
| 8 | 8 | „ | | | |
| 9 | 8 | „ | | | |
| 10 | 7 | 3 | | ESE | |
| 11 | 7 | 2 | | | |
| 12 | 7 | „ | 155 Miles | | |
| H | K | F | Courses | Winds | Wednesday: 5: June |
| 1 | 7 | 2 | NBE | ESE | |
| 2 | 6 | „ | | | Fresh Gales of Wind, fair Wea: |
| 3 | 6 | 3 | | | |
| 4 | 2 | „ | | | Course make to be N:$^{o}$ 6$^{d}$ E:$^{t}$ Distance |
| 5 | 5 | 3 | | | 107 Miles |
| 6 | 6 | „ | | | |
| 7 | 2 | 3 | | | p:$^{r}$ my Observation the Ship is not so |
| 8 | 4 | „ | | | farr to the N:$^{o}$w:$^{d}$ as the Log: gives p:$^{r}$ 11 |
| 9 | 5 | 3 | | | miles, the Error impute to a S:$^{o}$erly Stream |
| 10 | 5 | „ | | SEBE | |
| 11 | 6 | „ | | | Lat:$^{d}$ Observ'd 8$^{d}$ 52$^{m}$ S:$^{o}$ |
| 12 | 6 | „ | | | Meridian Distance 77 49 East |
| 1 | 6 | 3 | NBE½E | | Difference of Long$^{d}$ 99 33 East |
| 2 | 6 | „ | | | Variation p:$^{r}$ Morn:$^{g}$ Amp:$^{d}$ 4 13 West |
| 3 | 3 | 2 | NBE | | |
| 4 | 4 | 3 | | | |
| 5 | 5 | „ | | | |
| 6 | 5 | 2 | | | |
| 7 | 4 | 3 | | SBE | |
| 8 | 5 | „ | | | |
| 9 | 5 | 3 | | | |
| 10 | 5 | 3 | | | |
| 11 | 5 | 4 | | | |
| 12 | 5 | „ | 123 Miles | | |

**53** Ocean streams were always difficult for seamen. They could significantly offset the ship from its estimated and intended, especially longitudinal, positioning, given that mariners only limitedly knew such streams' direction and intensity. For a map of Atlantic currents, see Andrew S. Cook, "Establishing the Sea Routes to India and China. Stages in the Development of Hydrographical Knowledge", in: Worlds, eds. Bowen, Lincoln and Rigby, 124.

| | | | | | |
|---|---|---|---|---|---|
| 1 | 5 | „ | NBE | ESE | Thursday: 6: |
| 2 | 5 | 5 | | | |
| 3 | 5 | „ | NBE½E | | Fresh gales till Morning then variable and |
| 4 | 4 | 5 | NNE Saw | Land NNE½E | Rain |
| 5 | 4 | 3 | N° | | |
| 6 | 3 | „ | NWBN | | Att 4 P.M Saw the Land of Java bearing N:° |
| 7 | 2 | „ | WNW | East | 15 Leag:$^{s}$ distance, |
| 8 | 3 | 2 | | | |
| 9 | 4 | „ | | ESE | Att 6 D:° Land from the NE½N:° to the |
| 10 | 4 | „ | | | NWBW distance 13 Leag:$^{s}$ being very high |
| 11 | 5 | „ | NWBW | | Land. |
| 12 | 4 | „ | | | Att 7 this morning Land from NEBN to |
| 1 | 3 | 3 | WNW | | NWBN high Land and this Noon y$^{e}$ Land |
| 2 | 3 | 3 | | | from NEBN to the NW:$^{t}$ being high Land |
| 3 | 3 | 2 | | | in Triple foulds |
| 4 | 2 | 5 | | | |
| 5 | 3 | „ | | | Course make to be N:° 41$^{d}$ W:$^{t}$ Distance |
| 6 | 4 | „ | | | 76 Miles |
| 7 | 3 | „ | NWBW | East | |
| 8 | 3 | „ | NW½N | NEBN | Lat:$^{d}$ p:$^{r}$ Account 7$^{d}$ 55$^{m}$ S:° |
| 9 | 1 | 3 | WNW | | Meridian Distance 76 29 E:$^{t}$ |
| 10 | 4 | „ | NWBW | East | Difference of Long$^{d}$ 93 43 E:$^{t}$ |
| 11 | 2 | 1 | NWBW½W | | |
| 12 | „ | 3 | 84 Miles | | |
| 1 | 3 | 3 | NWBW | SEBS:° | Friday: 7: |
| 2 | 2 | 4 | | | Moderate gales Variable & fair Weather – |
| 3 | 3 | 3 | | | a great Swell heaving in up on the Shoar, |
| 4 | 4 | 4 | | | the Land Still Continues Mountainous in |
| 5 | 4 | 6 | NW | ESE | foulds one over another |
| 6 | 4 | „ | NWBW | | |
| 7 | 4 | „ | | | Att 5 PM Land from EBN to NW½W |
| 8 | 4 | „ | WNW | | Att 8 AM: Land from NW½N to y$^{e}$ ENE |
| 9 | 3 | 4 | NWBW½W | SEBS:° | And att Noon the Extreams of the Land |
| 10 | 2 | „ | Sounded no | Gr.$^{d}$ at 110 fa: | from EBN to NWBW Dis:$^{t}$ about 3 Leag:$^{s}$ |
| 11 | 3 | 4 | WNW | | |
| 12 | 4 | 1 | WBN° | East | Course N:° 69$^{d}$ E:$^{t}$ Distance 60 miles |
| 1 | 3 | „ | | | |
| 2 | 3 | „ | WNW | | Lat:$^{d}$ Observ'd 7$^{d}$ 84$^{m}$ S.° |
| 3 | 3 | 3 | | | Meridian Distance 75 33 E:$^{t}$ |
| 4 | 3 | „ | | | Difference of Long$^{d}$ 92 46 E:$^{t}$ |
| 5 | 3 | 3 | WBN | | |
| 6 | 4 | 1 | WNW | | |
| 7 | 4 | „ | | | |
| 8 | 4 | 6 | NW | | |
| 9 | 2 | 2 | | | |
| 10 | 2 | 3 | | NNE | |
| 11 | 3 | 2 | | E:$^{t}$ | |
| 12 | 3 | „ | 84 Miles | | |

| H | K | F | Courses | Winds | Saturday: 8: June. 1723 |
|---|---|---|---|---|---|
| 1 | 3 | 3 | WNW | SE.$^{t}$ | Moderate Gales of wind and fair Weather |
| 2 | 4 | 4 | | SSE | Att 6 P.M. The Extreams of the Land from |
| 3 | 5 | „ | | | WNW to EBN Distance 4 miles from Shore |
| 4 | 6 | „ | Land from | WNW to EBN.$^{o}$ | |
| 5 | 6 | „ | dist from shore | 4 or 5 Lea:$^{s}$ | |
| 6 | 6 | „ | Extreams of | y$^{e}$ Land from | |
| 7 | 4 | „ | E½N to | NWBW dis.$^{t}$ of | Sho:$^{r}$ 4m:$^{s}$ |
| 8 | 5 | „ | | | |
| 9 | 5 | 4 | W½N | | Att 8 AM. Java head NW and Claps |
| 10 | 6 | 2 | West | SE | Island[54] W:$^{t}$ end NNW:$^{t}$ distance from the |
| 11 | 6 | 3 | | | head 7 Leagues |
| 12 | 5 | „ | WBN | | This Noon Java head bore NNW 2 Leag:$^{s}$ |
| 1 | 6 | „ | West | | Course from yesterday Noon to Java head |
| 2 | 5 | 2 | WBN | | is N:$^{o}$ 73$^{d}$ West Distance 128 Miles, So |
| 3 | 5 | „ | WNW | ESE | that I make the Said head Land to lie in |
| 4 | 4 | „ | | | Lat.$^{d}$ of 6$^{d}$ 58$^{m}$ South |
| 5 | 5 | „ | NNE | | And Meridian Distance from Cape bon |
| 6 | 4 | 3 | | | Esperance 73 39 East Difference of Longi- |
| 7 | 4 | „ | N$^{o}$ | | tude from D$^{o}$ 90 50 East |
| 8 | 5 | „ | NW½W | | The Land Since yesterday, Appears much |
| 9 | 6 | „ | NWBW | SEBE | lower then what we've before Seen of Java |
| 10 | 6 | 4 | NWBW½W | | head Appears like a Sm:$^{ll}$ Island till come |
| 11 | 6 | 3 | NW½W | | pretty near it |
| 12 | 6 | „ | 128 Miles | | |

## Ship Hartford at an Anchor in Mew[55] Bay

June

Sun:$^{d}$ 9$^{th}$ Att 4 PM the first point of Java bore SWBW and the Peak on Princess Island[56] NBW depth of water 20 fathom

Att 6 D:$^{o}$ Anchor'd in Mew Bay (for what reason I know not) with Small bower in 15 fa: water Sand and Oaze[57], the W:$^{t}$ermost point of Mew Island WBN, the Second point of Java NE Crocotore hill[58] NBE½E and the Peak on Princess Island NNW distance from Java Shore One League, Hoisted out Lon=boat and Moor'd Ship

---

**54** Clap's Island, now Pulau Deli, is located about 34 kilometers southeast of Java Head. The names of islands in the Java and South China seas have not remained consistent since 1723. Later sailing directions, however, can be useful in untangling this and the following early eighteenth-century locations. See *Sailing Directions for the Oriental, or East-India Pilot* (London: Robert Sayer and John Bennett, 1778); John Purdy, *The Oriental Navigatory: or, Directions for Sailing to, from, and upon the coasts of, the East-Indies, China, Australia, &c.* (London: James Whittle and Richard Holmes Laurie, 1816); James Horsburgh, *India Directory, or Directions for Sailing* (London: W.H. Allen & Co., 1836).

**55** Mew Bay is located between the unhabituated Mew Island and Java, about ten miles northeast of Java Head. It was a popular spot for European ships to rewater and secure provisions.

**56** Prince's Island, now Panaitan, is located at the western entrance of the Sunda Strait and just north of Java Head. Ships used the channel to its east to access the strait during the Southeast Monsoon.

**57** Oaze is a soft mud.

**58** Krakatoa was an active volcanic island, located in the middle of the Sunda Strait.

Mon:[d] 10 The Weather hott and Sultry have Employ'd our Boats in fetching wood and water, This Morning rec.[d] a Letter from William Fazackerly Esq:[r] &[a], Councill, the Substance of w:[ch] was that they thought proper we should proceed directly for China w:[th] out Touching at Batavia w:[ch] makes me Now to Understand the reason of our Anchoring in this Bay, but had I known it before I should not have Lost any time in Anchoring here, being Sensible of the Necessity I was in to proceed for Batavia, the Aforementiond Letter have Communicated to all my Officers who Jointly with me in Opinion thought the most Speediest way for our Arrivall in China was first to proceed for Batea there to Supply our Selves w:[th] Topmasts having but one on board but what broke and Sprung, Likewise two of my foreshrouds being broke in the hipp which will oblidge me to lift my Standing rigging and do think it highly Necessary to lift it all fore and Aft which will take up Some time in doing which time do think to Spend at the Aforementioned place Where can Supply our Selves with all Necessarys wanting

## Ship Hartford Working through the Streights of Sundy[59], to Batavia

June

Tuesd:[y] 11[th] Small breezes with Calms, finding it to no Purpose to weigh, Sent our Longboat for Wood and Water, And made Search for a Topmast but Could find none

Wednes:[d] 12 Unmoar'd Ship and at 11 at Night had a Small breeze at SE at which time Weighed in Company w:[th] y:[e] Princess Ann for Batavia

Att 6 this morning the Peak on Princess Island West and Crocotore hill NBE

Att Noon Crocotore N:[o] and the 3:[d] point of Java EBN Sultry Weather wind allround

Thurs:[d] 13 Variable Winds and fair Weather, Att 4 PM Princess Island WBS:[o] Crocotore Isle NBW and the 3:[d] point of Java ENE Depth of water 35 fa:

This Noon Twarth[60] the way bore NNE the Cap NE & Crocotore WbN depth of water 32 fa: Owsey ground

Friday 14 Small Winds and Calms, Att 3 P.M. being Calm Anchor'd with Stream Anchor in 28 fa: Soft owsey gro:[d] Crocotore hill bearing W:[t] the Cap NE and the body of y:[e] Island Twarth the Way N½E distance from Shore 1 league The tides Ever Since past the 2:[d] point of Java we find very Iregular the W:[t]ern Setting Near 14 or 16 hours and E:[t]ern 8 hours

59 This refers to the Sunda Strait, a body of water located between the modern-day Indonesian islands of Java and Sumatra. It also links the Indian Ocean and the Java Sea. Dutch sailors used the strait to first access the Spice Islands in the 1600s, thus evading their Portuguese competitors near Malacca to the north.

60 This refers to modern-day Sangiang, which VOC traders referred to as Dwars-in-den-weg and the EIC as Thwart-the-Way. It is located in the Sunda Strait, northeast of Krakatoa.

Att 5 P.M. Weighed a Small breeze in the SE Quarter and at 8 D:° the tide running Strong against us Anchor'd in 35 fa:

Att 6 AM. Weighed with a breeze at SE and at D:° found we Could not Stem the tides Anchor'd, Att 11 the W:tern tide being done weighed wind WBN, Att noon Cap NEBN and Button[61] NNE, the Island Twarth the Way N½W depth of water 33 fa:

Satur:d 15th Winds Variable with Sulltry hott Weather

Att 6 P.M. the Cap bore SWBS:° the Button SWBW and Bantam point[62] SEBE depth of water from 24 to 50 fa:

Att 7 D:° Sent the Yawl to to try the Stream and found it to the W:tward so strong we Could not Stemn it, then had depth of water 47 fa: Endeavour'd to gett in Shoar but Could not so was Oblidg'd to Anchor in that Depth This Morning found the Land to bear as follows, Bantam point SE½E Cap SWBS:° and Button WSW Distance from Shoar 3 Miles

Sunday 16 Att 2 P.M. Weighed with a fine Sea breeze at NE and Att 6 D:° the flood being done Anchor'd in 15 fa: wa Soft Owse Pullo Baby[63] NEBE Great Moody[64] SE and the SE End of pulo Panjang[65] S:° Since we weigh'd have had depth of water from 30 to 15 fa: Soft ground

Att 6 AM. Weighed wind SBE and are turning between Pulo Baby and Pulo Panjang Att 8 D:° Great Moody SW and Pulo Baby NBE depth of water 12 fa:

Att 11 D.° the tide being made to the W:tw:d and the Wind an End Anchor'd in 22 fa. wate:r E:t end of P:°Baby NNW the body of Wappen Island[66] EBN and Great Pulo Moody SW. Much Lightning in the Night

Mond:y 17 Att 2 P.M. Weighed with a Light Sea breeze at NEbE and at 4 D:° had Sight of the great Camboise[67] bearing ESE Mansettees Island[68] SE and the W:tend of Wappen Island NEbN depth of water 25 fa: to 15 d:°

---

**61** Button Island was a small isle, located northeast of Twart-the-Way and in the Sunda Strait. It possibly is modern-day Pulau Temperung.

**62** Bantam Point, also known as St. Nicholas Point, is a steep headland, located on the western coast of Java. It marks the meeting of the Sunda Strait and Bantam Bay – the latter located on its eastern shore.

**63** This refers to modern-day Pulau Tunda, located in the Java Sea about 13 miles northeast of Bantam Point.

**64** The Great Moody was an island located in eastern Bantam Bay. It likely is modern-day Pulau Pamujan Besar.

**65** Pulau Panjang is an island located in western Bantam Bay, just off the east coast of Bantam Point.

**66** Wapen's Island, now Pulau Tidung Besar, is located about 25 kilometers off the Java coast, midway between Bantam Point and Batavia.

**67** The Great Cambuys, likely modern-day Pulau Lancang Besar, is located off the northern Java coast. It, along with the Little Cambuys, marked the northern boundary of the channel used by ships approaching Batavia.

**68** Maneater Island, now Pulau Laki, is located about 8 kilometers southwest of the Cambuys islands. European ships traveled to its north, because of a shoal extending from Java to its southern coast. It marked the southern edge of the channel used by ships approaching Batavia.

Att 6 D:$^{o}$ the Camboise ESE Mansetters Isle SE and Wappen Isles W:$^{t}$End NEBE
Att 7 D:$^{o}$ Anchor'd in 20 fa: Soft owse the Great Camboise ESE Mansettees Isle SEbS:$^{o}$ and Pulo Parre[69] EBN
Att 6 AM Weighed a Small breeze in the SE Quarter Plying to Windward between Pulo Parre and the Great Camboise Soundings from 22 to 30 fa:
Att 11 D:$^{o}$ Anchor'd with Stream anchor in 22 fa: Soft ground Little Camboise SE½S:$^{o}$ E:$^{t}$end of Pulo Parre NEBE and Mansetters Isle SW

Tuesd:$^{y}$ 18 Att 2 P.M. Weighed with a faint Sea breeze in the NE Quarter but finding we could not Weather the Little Camboise[70] (att 5) Anchored in 12 fa: water the Great Camboise bearing NW and little Camboise NE the Island Onroost[71] SEbE Graduall Soundings between the Camboise and Pulo Parre from 22 to 12 fa:

Att 6 AM. Weighed the Wind at SW and run out to the NW of the little Camboise Making the best of our way to the E:$^{t}$ward Depth of water from 11 to 15 fa: soft ground. Course Chiefy EBS:$^{o}$

Att 10 D:$^{o}$ being Calm Anchor'd in 14 fa: Duffins Island[72] ENE Edam[73] E½S:$^{o}$ Amsterdam[74] SSE & Batavia road SE½S.$^{o}$

## Ship Hartford at an Anchor in Batavia Road

June

Wednes:$^{d}$ 19 Att 1 P.M. Weighed with a moderate Sea breeze at NNE and made the best of our way in for Batavia between the Islands Harlem[75] and Rotterdam.[76] Soundings graduall from 14 to 7 in which Depth at 7 P.M. Anch.$^{d}$ Soft ground the Westermost Beacon NW½N:$^{o}$ and Onroost Island NWBW, Edam NEbE and Eastermost Beacon NE½N:$^{o}$

---

69 Pulau Pari is an island located about 18 kilometers off the northern Java coast and 8 kilometers northeast of the Cambuys islands.

70 The Little Cambuys, likely modern-day Pulau Lancang Kecil, is located north of the Java coast.

71 Onroost Island, now Pulau Onrust, is located four miles northwest of Batavia. The VOC established a shipyard here in 1615 and a fort in 1656, but it mostly served as a temporary anchorage for colonial ships.

72 Duffen's Island, now Pulau Dapur, is a small island located in the north of modern-day Jakarta Bay. It also marked the northern boundary of the outer channel, allowing transoceanic vessels access to Batavia.

73 Edam Island, now Pulau Damar Besar, is located just north of Batavia, in modern-day Jakarta Bay.

74 Amsterdam Island, now Pulau Untung Jawa, is located about 5 miles off the Java coast and near the entrance to modern-day Jakarta Bay.

75 Haarlem Island, now Pulau Air Kecil, is located on the eastern side of the channel leading into modern-day Jakarta Bay.

76 Rotterdam Island, now Pulau Ubi Besar, is located on the western side of the channel leading into modern-day Jakarta Bay.

Att Sunrise this morning Saluted the fflagg with 13 guns Att 10 D:$^{o}$ Weighed and run in till we brought Onroost NW the Westermost Beacon NNW Edam and Eastermost Beacon in One, bearing NBE½E, there Anchor'd in 5 fa: Soft owse distance from Shoar 2 Miles

Thurs:$^{d}$ 20 Heel'd and Scrubb'd Ship on both Sides and paid out Bends with Pitch, Struck Yards and Topmasts

Friday 21 Our People are Employed in Unrigging our Foretopmast

Satur:$^{d}$ 22 Our People are Employed in fixing the rigging of our Foretopmast, Unbent our Sails and blackt our Yards

Sund:$^{y}$ 23 Winds Variable, Sultry hott Weather

Mond:$^{y}$ 24 This day Stript our Fore~~top~~mast and found 3 pair of the Shrouds broke in the Hip: which is what I all along fear'd. Are repairing them

Tuesd:$^{y}$ 25 Fair Weather, Are repairing our rigging, gott it over head

Wednes:$^{d}$ 26 Fair Weather, Staid our fore~~top~~mast and Sett up Fore Shrouds, reeft Foretopmast being Sprung, finding we Cannot be Supply'd here with Topmasts

Thurs:$^{d}$ 27 This Morning gott up Foretopmast rigg'd it & Top=gallent Mast and Gott the Yards a Cross, Sett up Topmastshrouds and Backstays

Friday 28 Fair Weather and little winds, Clear'd Water Casks to Send on Shoar. Thunder Lightning & Rain

Saturd:$^{y}$ 29 Employed our people in the rigging belonging to our Maintopmast

Sunday 30 Lifted our Main Shrouds, but find them in a better Condition then was Expected, the Weather in the Day fair, but in the night Thunder Lightning and Rain

July

Mond:$^{y}$ 1 Compleated the rigging of our Main Mast and Sett Main Shrouds up

Tuesd:$^{y}$ 2 Compleated the rigging of our Maintopmast & Sett up the Shrouds and backstays. Rec.$^{d}$ on board water

Wednes:$^{d}$ 3 I find the water on board to be bad, Started it and Sent our Long:boat on Shore for more which returned Loaded – The Day fair, the night attended with Thunder Lightning and Rain

Made the Signall for Sailing

## Ship Hartford from Batavia tow:$^{ds}$ China

July

Thurs:$^{d}$ 4 Fair Weather faint Land and Sea breezes, Att 7 This Morning Weighed in Company with the Princess Ann Saluted the flagg with 13 Guns, return'd 11 – Att 11 D:$^{o}$ the Sea breeze Came in which oblidged us to Anchor in 10 fa: water Soft ground. the Island Edam NNE Horn Isl.$^{d}$[77] NWBN and Onroost WBN:$^{o}$

Friday 5 Calm till 4 AM. then the Land wind Came of but being Cloudy did not Weigh till 7 D:$^{o}$ had a Gale at ESE. Steering N.$^{o}$ between Edam and Hoorn having graduall Soundings from 10 to 16 fa: then being Noon had the South Watcher[78] in sight bearing NBW

Satur.$^{d}$ 6 Att 2 P.M. the Sea Wind being faint and far N:$^{o}$erly So that Could not Weather the Thousand Island.[79] Came too with Stream Anchor in 26 fa: but found the Ship drive dropt the Small Bower which brought her up the S:$^{o}$ Watcher NNE and the Thousand Islands WBN:$^{o}$

Att 7 this morning Weighed with a light SE breaze but Could make no Advantage of it anchor'd w:$^{th}$ best bower in 26 fa: y$^{e}$ S:$^{o}$ Watcher E:$^{t}$ the Nights Clouds & Rain

| H | K | F | Courses | Winds | fa | Sunday: 7: July |
|---|---|---|---|---|---|---|
| 1 | | | | | | |
| 2 | | | | | | Hazey Weather and Moderate Gales |
| 3 | | | | | | |
| 4 | | | | | | Att 7 this Morning weighed and 8 d:$^{o}$ the |
| 5 | | | | | | South Watcher bore SE distance 1 League |
| 6 | | | | | | |
| 7 | | | | | | Latitude Observed 5$^{d}$ 20$^{m}$ South |
| 8 | | | | | | |
| 9 | | | | | | Courses Steer'd as p$^{r}$ Logg: and Depth of |
| 10 | | | | | | Water |
| 11 | | | | | | |
| 12 | | | | | | This Noon the Southermost of the Thou- |
| 1 | | | | | | sand Islands in Sight bearing NW½W:$^{t}$ |
| 2 | | | | | | |
| 3 | | | | | | |
| 4 | | | | | | |
| 5 | | | | | | |
| 6 | | | | | | |
| 7 | " | " | Weighed | ESE | | |
| 8 | " | " | S:$^{o}$ Watcher | SE 1 Leag:$^{e}$ | | |
| 9 | 4 | " | NBE | SE | 19 | |
| 10 | 4 | 3 | N½W | | 20 | |
| 11 | 4 | 5 | N$^{o}$ | | 18 | |
| 12 | 4 | 6 | | | 15 | |

77 Hoorn Island, now Pulau Anyer, is located southeast of Haarlem Island, in modern-day Jakarta Bay.

78 The South Watcher, now Pulau Peniki, is a small island, located about 19 miles northwest of Edam and east of the southernmost chain of the Thousand Islands.

79 The Thousand Islands are a chain of 110 islands, stretching from modern-day Java Bay to Banten Province. The VOC initially used them to defend and supervise the commerce of nearby Batavia.

| | | | | | | |
|---|---|---|---|---|---|---|
| 1 | 4 | 6 | N½E | SE | 14 | Monday: 8: |
| 2 | 5 | „ | | | 13 | Fair Weather with moderate gales of |
| 3 | 5 | „ | | | | Wind. Courses and Depth of water as p$^{r}$ |
| 4 | 5 | 1 | | | | Collums |
| 5 | 5 | 2 | | ESE | | |
| 6 | 4 | 5 | N$^{o}$ | | 14 | Att 8 This Morning Saw Tree Islands[80] |
| 7 | 5 | „ | N½W | | | WBS:$^{o}$ which place would Advise all that |
| 8 | 5 | 3 | | | | Comes this way to be Cautious how they |
| 9 | 6 | „ | NBW | | | Come under 7 fa: for you're imediatly in |
| 10 | 6 | 3 | | | 13 | 5:4: &: 3: fa: water hard Sand which Sand |
| 11 | 6 | „ | | | 15 | runs a great way to the Eastw:$^{d}$ So that if |
| 12 | 5 | 4 | | | 14 | you can from Masthead discern the Land |
| 1 | 5 | „ | | | 13 | you are in a fair way upon a NNE Course |
| 2 | 4 | 5 | | | 14 | for Luceparra[81] |
| 3 | 5 | 2 | | | 12 | |
| 4 | 6 | „ | | | | This Noon Luceparra bore NE distance 5 |
| 5 | 5 | 4 | NNW | | 15 | or 6 Leagues |
| 6 | 4 | 3 | | SEBE | 12 | |
| 7 | 5 | 2 | | | 12:7 | |
| 8 | 5 | 1 | Tree Isl.$^{d}$ W BS | 4 or 5 Leag.$^{s}$ | 7:9 | |
| 9 | 4 | 6 | | | 7 | |
| 10 | 4 | 3 | N$^{o}$ | | 5 | |
| 11 | 3 | 3 | NBE | | 5:3 | |
| 12 | 3 | 3 | NEBN Luce-pare | NE 5 or 6leag$^{s}$ | 4:5 | |
| 1 | 4 | „ | NEBN | SEBE | 5 | Tuesday: 9: |
| 2 | 3 | 5 | | | 4½ | Moderate Gales of Wind, & fair Weather |
| 3 | 3 | „ | NBE | | 4½ | Steering for Luceparra as p$^{r}$ Logg: |
| 4 | 2 | „ | N:$^{o}$ | | 5 | Att 4 P.M. had the first point of Sumatra[82] |
| 5 | 2 | „ | Oazey | ground | 5 | NBW and Lucepara E½N depth of water |
| 6 | 2 | „ | | | 4 | 5 fa: |
| 7 | „ | „ | run a gr.$^{d}$ | soft ouze | 2½ | Att 7 D:$^{o}$ having good Soundings & |
| 8 | „ | „ | | | | Endeavo:$^{r}$ to gett round the first point, |
| 9 | „ | „ | hove y$^{e}$ | Ship a floatin | 5 | had from 7 to 5 & 4 fa Soft ground. |
| 10 | „ | „ | | | | imediatly put the Helm a Port to bear |
| 11 | „ | „ | Anch.$^{d}$ w:$^{th}$ | best bower in | 5 | of into deeper water, but a Strong tide |
| 12 | „ | „ | Soft ground | | | under foot w:$^{ch}$ took us upon the Larboard |
| 1 | „ | „ | | | | Quarter which made the ship fall round |
| 2 | „ | „ | | | | off against her Helm and Occasion'd us |
| 3 | „ | „ | | | | to ground in ¼ less 3 fa: Soft mud, the |
| 4 | „ | „ | | | | first point then West, Handed our Sails, |
| 5 | „ | „ | | | | Shott our Stream Anchor out in 5 fa: and |
| 6 | „ | „ | | | | imediatly hove her off again and dropt |
| 7 | „ | „ | | | | our best bower Anchor – A very Strong |
| 8 | „ | „ | | | | Tide |
| 9 | „ | „ | | | | |
| 10 | „ | „ | | | | |
| 11 | „ | „ | | | | |
| 12 | „ | „ | | | | |

**80** Tree Island is a large bank on the east coast of Sumatra, surrounded by tall trees and appearing like an island. It forms a dangerous and sandy shoal near the mouth of the Tulangbawang River.

**81** Lucepara, now Pulau Maspari, is a small island located at the southern entrance of the Banka Strait and bordered, on its other side, by Sumatra. Deep-riding vessels travelled through the channel to its west.

**82** Sumatra is a large island located northwest of Java and in western Indonesia. It borders the Indian Ocean to the west, the Sunda Strait to the south, and the Banka Strait to the east.

Tues:$^{d}$ 9 Continued[:] This Morning day light being low water run a Warp out into 8 fa: Soft ground, Hove up our Best Bower in 8 fa: where must be Oblidg'd to Lye, till the Tides done to take up our Stream anchor, being Oblidg'd to Slip the Cable leaving a buoy upon the End there of

I would Advise every body that comes this way after you have Luceparra SE, not to come under 6 or 7 fathom but then besure it's Soft ground, Otherways you may be deceived and run upon the Sands that lie to y$^{e}$ N:$^{o}$w:$^{d}$ which is a hard Sand, the Sumatra Shoar mudd

Wednes.$^{d}$ 10 Att 10 This Evening being Slack Water, Sent the Long:boat to Weigh the Stream Anchor, but the Buoy rope broke which oblidg'd her to Weigh it with the Cable, She return'd with it at One in the Morning and Att 7 D:$^{o}$ Weighed with a fresh Gale at ESE, Graduall Sound:$^{gs}$ between the first and Second point of Sumatra from 8 to 16 fathom Soft ground

Att 8 D:$^{o}$ the first point of Sumatra bore SbE½E besure to keep the Sumatra Shoar on board for you'll find the Tides to heave you much upon the Banca[83] Shoar where you may meet Some difficulty to get Over to the Sumatra Shoar. We Were hove Over into 20 fa: hard Ground but having a fresh leading Gales hauld up West till we gott the Soundings of the Sumatra Shoar 15 fa:

This Noon Pulo Nanca[84] N½W & 2:$^{d}$ point of Sumatra NWBN distance 3 Leag:$^{s}$ depth of water 16 fa: Softgr.$^{d}$

Thurs:$^{d}$ 11 Pleasent Gales at SE, at 2 P.M Pulo Nanca NBE 3 leag:$^{s}$ depth of water 10 fa: Att 4 D:$^{o}$ P:$^{o}$ Nanca EBN½N and 3:$^{d}$ point NW 12 fa: the Ground being Somewhat hard Occasion'd us to believe the Soundings to be of the Banca Shoar, but when hauled up for the Sumatra Shoar found it shoal fa: 9:8:7 & a half 6 fa: bore away again to 10:11 and 12 fa: Soft gr.$^{d}$ being then pretty near Advanc'd to the 3:$^{d}$ p:$^{t}$

Att ½ past 6 D.$^{o}$ being dark Anch.$^{d}$ in 12 fa: found the Land to bear in the Morning as foll:$^{s}$ P:$^{o}$ Nanca EBS.$^{o}$ and 3:$^{d}$ p:$^{t}$ S:$^{o}$ dis:$^{t}$ 4 Miles

Att 7 AM weighed y$^{e}$ Wind at SEBE and at 9 D:$^{o}$ being Calm Anch.$^{d}$ in 13: fa: 4:$^{th}$ p.$^{t}$ W:$^{t}$ 3:$^{d}$ p:$^{t}$ SE½E & y$^{e}$ E:$^{t}$most Land of Banca E.$^{t}$ Distance from Sumatra Shoar 2 Leagues

Friday 12 Att 3 P.M Weighed with the Wind at NE the Weather dark and hazey

Att 4 D:$^{o}$ the fourth point of Sumatra bore WBS:$^{o}$ 3 Leagues depth of water 15 fa: hard Ground

Att 6 D:$^{o}$ the fourth point WSW½W and Monopin hill[85] NWBW Depth of Water 12 fa: hard ground

---

**83** The Banka Strait is located between the modern-day Indonesian islands of Bangka and Sumatra.

**84** The Nanka Islands were a group of three islands, located near the western coast of Banka Island and in the Bangka Strait. They served as convenient stopping points for ships in need of fresh water and wood.

**85** Monopin Hill is a prominent summit, visible from a long distance, on the northwest coast of Banca. Together with Batacarang Point, it marked the northern entrance to the Banca Strait.

Att 7 D:o being dark Anchor'd in 13 fa: – and at 6 this Morning Weighed, the Wind at South a Sm:ll gale Att 8 D:o the fourth point bore SWBS:o Monopin hill NW½N:o depth of water 10 fa: hard ground

We find our Soundings here very Irregular when under 10, or 11 fa: Imediately at a Cast of the Lead into 4 fa: which Surprized us. bore into 12 and 13 fa: in Three Casts of Lead have Since Sent our pinnace Ahead of the Ship to Sound Att 11 D:o being Calm Anchord in 14 fa: Monopin NWbN and 4:th point SbW

Satur.d 13 The former part Squally with some hard Showers of Rain, The latter part fair with a light breeze at S:o

Att 7 this Morning Weighed, and at 9 D:o being Calm Anchor'd in 13 fa: Clay ground, Monopin NBW½W 10. or 12 Miles

Sund:y 14 Att 5 P.M. having a breeze of Wind at East weigh'd

Att 6 D.o being Calm Anchord in 12 fa: hard Clay: the East Entrance of Pullambam[86] SoW½W, Monopin NBW.

Att 6 AM. Weigh'd a Moderate breeze at SEBE Steering WSW till 8 D:c then the East Entrance of Pullambam SBW½W depth of water 10 fa: Soft ground Then bore off NW and NWBN:o Soundings from 10 to 12: and 13 fa: Soft ground

This Noon Monopin NEBE Batacarang[87] Point NW and the Westermost Entrance of Pullambam SSW depth of water 13 fa: Soft ground

You'll find a Strong out Sett from the Rivers of Pullambam

**86** Palembang was a large town and trade-center located in interior Sumatra. This likely refers to the Musi River delta, which deposited just south of Batacarang Point and allowed sea travel to the settlement.

**87** Batacarang Point is a headway, located on the eastern shore of Sumatra. Together with Monopin Hill, it marked the northern entrance to the Banca Strait.

## Ship Hartford from Pulo Tamoon towards China

| H | K | F | Courses | Winds | Dep$^{t}$ | Monday: 15: July 1723 |
|---|---|---|---|---|---|---|
| 1 | " | " | NNW | SE from 12: | to 11 | Small Gales of wind with fair Weather |
| 2 | " | " | NBW½W | | 11:13 | Lightning in the night |
| 3 | " | " | NBW | | 13:15 | |
| 4 | " | " | Anchored | Soft Ground | 15:10 | Att 2 P.M. Monopin hill bore E½N and |
| 5 | | | | | | Batacarang p.$^{t}$ WBN½N depth of water 13 |
| 6 | | | | | | fa: Soft ground |
| 7 | | | | | | Att 4 D:$^{o}$ being Calm Anchor'd in 10 fa: |
| 8 | | | | | | Soft ground Monopin E½S.$^{o}$ and Bataca- |
| 9 | | | | | | rang W½N.$^{o}$ |
| 10 | | | | | | Att 5 AM. had a breeze at SEBE weigh'd |
| 11 | | | | | | and Steer'd as p$^{r}$ Log: |
| 12 | | | | | | Att 8 D:$^{o}$ Batacarang SW & Monopin |
| 1 | | | | | | SE½E graduall Soundings from 10 to 7 |
| 2 | | | | | | fathom |
| 3 | | | | | | Att 10 d:$^{o}$ Monopin SEBS:$^{o}$ 9 or 10 Leag.$^{s}$ |
| 4 | | | | | | |
| 5 | " | " | Weigh$^{d}$ NNE | SEBE | 10 | This Noon had Sight of the Seven |
| 6 | " | " | | | 9:8 | Islands[88] from |
| 7 | " | " | | | 8:7 | Mast head bearing NEBN and Monopin |
| 8 | " | " | | SSE | 7 | SSE |
| 9 | " | " | | | 7:10 | Distance 12 Leagues |
| 10 | " | " | | Oasy Ground | 10:13 | |
| 11 | " | " | | hard D$^{o}$ | 10 | |
| 12 | " | " | | D$^{o}$ D$^{o}$ | 13:14 | |
| 1 | " | " | NBE½E | SWBS$^{o}$ | 15.14 | Tuesday: 16: |
| 2 | " | " | | | 14.15 | |
| 3 | " | " | NNE | | 15 | Moderate gales till 7 P.M then Calm and |
| 4 | " | " | | | 14.15 | the Tide Setting to the Westward Oblidg'd |
| 5 | " | " | NBE | EBN | 15.13 | us to Anchor in 11 fa: Soft ground, |
| 6 | " | " | N$^{o}$ | ENE | 13 | |
| 7 | " | " | Anchored | Calm | 11 | Att ½ past 9 D:$^{o}$ having a moderate breeze |
| 8 | | | | | | Weighe'd as p$^{r}$ Log |
| 9 | " | " | Weighed | SE | | Att 4 P.M. Monopin S½E and the S:$^{o}$er- |
| 10 | 2 | 3 | NNE | | 11:13 | most of the Seven Islands ENE then depth |
| 11 | 4 | 3 | | | 13 | of Water 15 fa: Oazey ground |
| 12 | 3 | 3 | | SSE | | Att 6 D:$^{o}$ the body of the Seven Islands |
| 1 | 3 | 2 | | | | NEBE 3 Leagues |
| 2 | 3 | 2 | | | 13:15 | Att 6 AM. the Seven Islands SBE½E and |
| 3 | 2 | 5 | | | 15 | Pullo Taya[89] WBS:$^{o}$ 6 Leagues |
| 4 | 4 | " | | | 15:14 | This noon the Island Egelogotisa[90] NWBW |
| 5 | 5 | " | NBE | | 14:15 | 8 Leagues |
| 6 | 5 | " | | | 15 | |
| 7 | 4 | 2 | NNE | | 14 | |
| 8 | 4 | 4 | | | | |
| 9 | 5 | " | NNE½E | | 15 | |
| 10 | 5 | " | NNE | | | |
| 11 | 5 | 1 | NE | | | |
| 12 | 5 | 3 | 63 Miles | | 15:14 | |

**88** The Seven Islands were a chain of 260 islands, located east of Sumatra and extending from the Bangka Strait in the south to the Anambas in the north.
**89** This refers to modern-day Pulau Singkep, a small island located off the east coast of Sumatra and north of the Banca Strait.
**90** This refers to an island off the southeastern tip of Malaysia, possibly modern-day Pulau Bintam.

| | | | | | | |
|---|---|---|---|---|---|---|
| 1 | 4 | 4 | NE | SSE | 15 | Wednesday: 17: |
| 2 | 4 | 4 | | | 15:17 | |
| 3 | 4 | 6 | | | 17 | Moderate Gales of wind, fair |
| 4 | 5 | „ | NE½N | | | Weather |
| 5 | 5 | 5 | NEBN | | 17:19 | |
| 6 | 5 | 2 | | | 19 | True Course from Egelogotia to this Noon |
| 7 | 6 | „ | NE½N | | 20 | Make to be N:° 35$^{d}$ E:$^{t}$ Distance 88 Miles |
| 8 | 6 | 2 | | | | |
| 9 | 6 | 3 | | | 19:20 | Lat:$^{d}$ Observ'd 1$^{d}$ 4$^{m}$ N:° |
| 10 | 5 | 4 | NEBN | | 20 | |
| 11 | 5 | 3 | | | 20:22 | |
| 12 | 5 | 3 | NBE½E | | 22 | |
| 1 | 4 | „ | NBE | | 24 | |
| 2 | 4 | „ | | | 26 | |
| 3 | 3 | „ | NBW | | 25 | |
| 4 | 4 | „ | | | 26 | |
| 5 | 3 | 3 | | | 27 | |
| 6 | 2 | 3 | | | 27:26 | |
| 7 | 2 | 4 | NNW | | 26:30 | |
| 8 | 2 | „ | NWBN | | 32:29 | |
| 9 | 3 | 3 | | | 32 | |
| 10 | 3 | 4 | NNW no | ground at | 32 | |
| 11 | 4 | „ | NBW | D.° | | |
| 12 | 3 | 3 | 105 Miles | | 25 | |
| H | K | F | Courses | Winds | Dep:$^{h}$ | Thursday: 18: July. 1723 |
| 1 | 3 | 2 | N° | SBE | 25 | |
| 2 | 4 | „ | hard Sq:$^{ll}$ of | Wind & R:$^{n}$ | w:$^{th}$ Hail | Winds Variable with Squalls and Rain |
| 3 | 4 | „ | In 1:$^{st}$ R.B | T.S.&H.$^{d}$D.°D.° | D.° | |
| 4 | 1 | „ | NBE | WBN | 26 | Att 8 this morning Saw the Island Pulo |
| 5 | 1 | „ | NBW | SetB.T.S. | 27 | Auroe[91] distant 12 or 14 Leagues |
| 6 | 1 | „ | Out 1:$^{st}$ | R.F.T.S.SW | 28 | |
| 7 | 1 | 2 | | | 26 | This Noon Saw the Anamba Islands[92] |
| 8 | 1 | 5 | NNW | | 25 | NEBN and Pulo Auroe WBN 11 or 12 |
| 9 | 1 | „ | NNW½W | Out1R.MT.S. | 26 | Leagues |
| 10 | 1 | „ | | SSW | 28 | |
| 11 | 3 | 3 | NNW | | 30 | Lat:$^{d}$ Observed 2$^{d}$ 22$^{m}$ N:° |
| 12 | 2 | 2 | | | 35 | |
| 1 | 1 | „ | | | | |
| 2 | 1 | 3 | | WSW | | |
| 3 | „ | 3 | | | | |
| 4 | 1 | 3 | | | | |
| 5 | 1 | „ | | | | |
| 6 | 2 | „ | | | | |
| 7 | 2 | „ | | SW | | |
| 8 | 2 | 2 | NWBN | | | |
| 9 | 3 | „ | | SWBW | | |
| 10 | 3 | 2 | | | | |
| 11 | 3 | 2 | | | | |
| 12 | 2 | 5 | NWBW | 49:$^{ms}$SWBS° | | |

**91** Pulau Aur is located about 75 kilometers east of the Sumatran coast.

**92** The Anambas are a cluster in the Seven Islands archipelago, specifically those located nearest Sumatra. In the early 1700s, the Anambas retained political significance as an asylum for refuge princes from Indonesia. They also were key navigational and rendezvous points for country and European traders.

| | | | | | | |
|---|---|---|---|---|---|---|
| 1 | 2 | ,, | NWBN | SW | 35 | Friday: 19: |
| 2 | 3 | ,, | | | | |
| 3 | 4 | 3 | | | | The first part fair Weather, the night |
| 4 | 3 | ,, | | | | attend:$^{d}$ with Thunder Lightning and |
| 5 | 3 | 3 | NW | | | Rain, The latter part Cloudy |
| 6 | 3 | 3 | | | 36 | |
| 7 | 3 | 2 | NBE½E | S:$^{o}$Light:$^{g}$ | | Att 4 P.M. Pulo Auroe bore WBS½S 9 or |
| 8 | 4 | ,, | NNE | Softground | | 10 Leagues |
| 9 | 3 | 3 | | SSW | 35 | Att 6 D:$^{o}$ Pulo Auroe bore SWBW and Pulo |
| 10 | 3 | 2 | | Light$^{g}$ | 37 | Timoan[93] (from whence I take my Depar- |
| 11 | 2 | 3 | | D.$^{o}$SW | 40 | ture) West distance 10 Leagues |
| 12 | 3 | ,, | | D$^{o}$ | | |
| 1 | 4 | ,, | all round | D.$^{o}$SSW | | Course from thence to this Noon Allow to |
| 2 | 4 | 2 | D.$^{o}$ | D.$^{o}$ | | be N:$^{o}$ 43$^{d}$ E:$^{t}$ Distance 77 Miles |
| 3 | 4 | 3 | NEBN.$^{o}$Th$^{d}$ | Lig:$^{h}$Sq$^{ll}$&Rn | SSE 36 | |
| 4 | 3 | ,, | D$^{o}$ | D$^{o}$D$^{o}$SWBS$^{o}$ | | Lat:$^{d}$ p:$^{r}$ Account 3$^{d}$ 47$^{m}$ N:$^{o}$ |
| 5 | 1 | ,, | NBE½E | | | Meridian Distance 0 53 E:$^{t}$ |
| 6 | 1 | ,, | | Rain | 40 | |
| 7 | 2 | 3 | | SBWD$^{o}$ | | |
| 8 | 2 | 4 | | D$^{o}$ | 42 | |
| 9 | 3 | ,, | NNE | E$^{t}$D.$^{o}$ | | |
| 10 | 5 | 3 | NNE½E In | 1R.BT.S.SSE | D.$^{o}$ | |
| 11 | 5 | 3 | NNE | No ground at | 40 | |
| 12 | 4 | 5 | 80 M:$^{s}$ | Out 1:$^{st}$R.TB.S. | | |
| 1 | 4 | 3 | NNE | SSW | Fa | Saturday: 20: |
| 2 | 4 | 2 | NNE½E | No gr:$^{d}$ at | 50 | |
| 3 | 5 | ,, | | | | Moderate Gales and fair Weather |
| 4 | 5 | 5 | | | | |
| 5 | 5 | ,, | | | | True Course Judge to be N:$^{o}$ 23$^{d}$ E:$^{t}$ Dis- |
| 6 | 5 | 5 | | | | tance 104 Miles |
| 7 | 5 | ,, | NNE | | | |
| 8 | 5 | 5 | | | | Lat:$^{d}$ Observ'd 5$^{d}$ 22$^{m}$ N:$^{o}$ |
| 9 | 5 | 4 | NNE½E | | | Meridian Distance 1 33 E:$^{t}$ |
| 10 | 5 | 4 | | | | |
| 11 | 5 | 4 | NNE | | | |
| 12 | 4 | 5 | | | | |
| 1 | 4 | 5 | | | | |
| 2 | 5 | ,, | | No Ground at | 55 | |
| 3 | 4 | 6 | | Lightning | | |
| 4 | 4 | 2 | | | | |
| 5 | 4 | ,, | | | | |
| 6 | 3 | 5 | | | | |
| 7 | 4 | 2 | | | | |
| 8 | 4 | ,, | NNE½E | | | |
| 9 | 4 | ,, | | | | |
| 10 | 4 | ,, | | | | |
| 11 | 4 | 3 | | | | |
| 12 | 4 | 3 | 114 Miles | | | |

93 Pulau Tioman is an island located about 32 kilometers off the eastern Sumatra coast and northwest of Pulau Aur.

| H | K | F | Courses | Winds | Sunday: 21. July. 1723 |
|---|---|---|---|---|---|
| 1 | 3 | „ | NNE | SSW | |
| 2 | 2 | „ | Sq[ll] & Rain | NW | Small Gales of Wind with Cloudy Weather |
| 3 | 3 | 2 | | SSW | |
| 4 | 3 | „ | | | True Course Allow N:° 23[d] E:[t] Distance 71 M:[s] |
| 5 | 2 | 3 | | | |
| 6 | 2 | 3 | | | p:[r] Observation Am 10 miles to the N:°ward of the |
| 7 | 1 | 4 | | | Log: the Error Attribute to Distance |
| 8 | 1 | 3 | | | |
| 9 | 3 | „ | NEBN | | Lat:[d] Obs:[d] 6[d] 27[m] N:° |
| 10 | 2 | 2 | | | Meridian Distance 2 01 E:[t] |
| 11 | 2 | 1 | NNE | | |
| 12 | 2 | „ | | | |
| 1 | 2 | „ | | SWBW | |
| 2 | 2 | „ | | Lightning | |
| 3 | 3 | „ | | D° | |
| 4 | 2 | 3 | Sq[ll] & Rain | SWBS.° D.° | |
| 5 | 2 | 3 | D° D° | D° | |
| 6 | 2 | 3 | | | |
| 7 | 2 | 4 | | | |
| 8 | 3 | „ | NNE½E | | |
| 9 | 2 | 3 | NNE | | |
| 10 | 2 | 5 | | | |
| 11 | 3 | 3 | | | |
| 12 | 3 | „ | 60 Miles | | |
| 1 | 3 | „ | NNE | SWBS:° | Monday: 22: |
| 2 | 1 | 3 | | | |
| 3 | 3 | 2 | NNE½E | SBW | Small Gales of Wind with Lightning in |
| 4 | 3 | 2 | | | the Night |
| 5 | 3 | 3 | | | |
| 6 | 3 | 4 | Var p[r] | Amp:[d] 2° 12' | Course make to be N:° 25[d] E:[t] Distance 72 M:[s] |
| 7 | 2 | „ | | | |
| 8 | 3 | „ | | | Lat:[d] Observ'd 7[d] 32[m] N.° |
| 9 | 3 | 4 | | | Meridian Distance 2 31 E:[t] |
| 10 | 3 | „ | | | |
| 11 | 2 | 5 | | | |
| 12 | 2 | 5 | | | |
| 1 | 2 | 3 | | Light:[g] | |
| 2 | 2 | 3 | | D.° | |
| 3 | 3 | 2 | | D.° | |
| 4 | 3 | 2 | NNE | | |
| 5 | 3 | 2 | | | |
| 6 | 3 | 2 | | | |
| 7 | 3 | „ | | | |
| 8 | 3 | „ | | | |
| 9 | 3 | 3 | | SWBS.° | |
| 10 | 3 | „ | | | |
| 11 | 4 | „ | | | |
| 12 | 4 | 3 | 74 Miles | | |

| | | | | | | |
|---|---|---|---|---|---|---|
| 1 | 3 | 2 | NNE | SW | Dep | Tuesday: 23: |
| 2 | 4 | 3 | | | fa | |
| 3 | 3 | 2 | | | | Moderate Gales of wind with fair Weather |
| 4 | 3 | 2 | | | | |
| 5 | 3 | 3 | | | | Course make to be N:$^{o}$ 39$^{d}$ E:$^{t}$ Dis:$^{t}$ 104 M:$^{s}$ |
| 6 | 3 | 4 | Sounded | ground at | 25 | |
| 7 | 2 | 4 | Sandy | D$^{o}$ | 26 | Lat:$^{d}$ Observ'd 8$^{d}$ 52$^{m}$ N.$^{o}$ |
| 8 | 3 | 3 | | | 28 | Meridian Distance 3 35 E:$^{t}$ |
| 9 | 3 | 4 | | | 30 | |
| 10 | 3 | „ | | | | |
| 11 | 2 | 5 | | | | |
| 12 | 3 | 3 | | | | |
| 1 | 5 | „ | | | | |
| 2 | 5 | 4 | NEBE | | | |
| 3 | 5 | 5 | | WBS.$^{o}$ | | |
| 4 | 5 | 5 | Sq$^{ll}$ & Rain | WNW | 32 | |
| 5 | 6 | „ | Lightning | West | | |
| 6 | 5 | 4 | | | | |
| 7 | 5 | 3 | | | | |
| 8 | 5 | „ | No Ground | at | 40 | |
| 9 | 4 | 3 | NE | | | |
| 10 | 4 | 4 | | | | |
| 11 | 3 | 1 | | | | |
| 12 | 2 | 6 | 99 Miles | | | |

## Ship Hartford from the Junck Cattwicks Islands[94] tow:$^{ds}$ China

| H | K | F | Courses | Winds | Dep | Wednesday: 24: July: 1723 |
|---|---|---|---|---|---|---|
| 1 | 5 | 4 | NE | WBN | | |
| 2 | 5 | 2 | | | | Fresh Gales of Wind with dark |
| 3 | 5 | „ | | | | Cloudy Weather |
| 4 | 5 | „ | | | | |
| 5 | 4 | 5 | | | | Att 6 P.M: brought too for the |
| 6 | 4 | 5 | | In 1$^{st}$ R.B.T.S. | | Junck Cattwick Islands and at 9 |
| 7 | | | Bro:$^{ht}$ too up | WNW off NWBN | | this Morning Saw the Eastermost |
| 8 | | | | | | bearing NNE½E, then made Saile |
| 9 | | | Sound:$^{d}$ | Sandy gr:$^{d}$ w:$^{th}$ | 64 | |
| 10 | | | | grey Sand | 60 | By my Account I make this Island |
| 11 | | | up NWBW | off WNW, no gr.$^{d}$ | at 60 | to Lie in Latitude of 9$^{d}$ 4$^{m}$ N:$^{o}$ And |
| 12 | | | | | | East of Pulo Tamoon[95] 4 21 |
| 1 | | | up | WNW off NWBN | | |
| 2 | | | | No gro:$^{d}$ at | 70 | |
| 3 | | | | Light:$^{g}$ | | |
| 4 | | | | D.$^{o}$ | | |
| 5 | | | | D.$^{o}$ | | |
| 6 | | | Hard Sq$^{ll}$ | & R:$^{n}$ H.$^{d}$ M.T.S. | | |
| 7 | | | up NNW | off NBE hard R.$^{n}$ | | |
| 8 | | | | WSW no gr.$^{d}$ at | 75 | |
| 9 | | | Bore away | and Set M.T.S. | | |
| 10 | 6 | „ | NE | Rain | | |
| 11 | 5 | 3 | | | | |
| 12 | 5 | 2 | 47 Miles | | | |
| 1 | 5 | 3 | NE | WSW | Thursday: 25: | |
| 2 | 5 | 4 | | | | |
| 3 | 5 | „ | | | | Fresh Gales of Wind with Cloudy Sqly |
| 4 | 4 | „ | | SWBW | | Weather |
| 5 | 3 | 3 | | | | |
| 6 | 4 | „ | | | | Course from the Junck Cattwicks East Isle |
| 7 | 4 | 6 | | Lightning | | Make to be N:$^{o}$ 45 E: Distance 130 Miles |
| 8 | 5 | 3 | | hard Sq.$^{ll}$ | | |
| 9 | 5 | „ | | Light:$^{g}$ | | Lat:$^{d}$ p:$^{r}$ Account 11$^{d}$ 19$^{m}$ N.$^{o}$ |
| 10 | 5 | „ | | | | Meridian Distance 1 32 E.$^{t}$ |
| 11 | 5 | „ | | | | |
| 12 | 5 | „ | | | | |
| 1 | 6 | 3 | | Squaly & R.$^{n}$ | | |
| 2 | 7 | 3 | | D.$^{o}$ D.$^{o}$ | | |
| 3 | 6 | „ | | D.$^{o}$ D.$^{o}$ | | |
| 4 | 4 | 4 | | D$^{o}$ D.$^{o}$ | | |
| 5 | 5 | 3 | | WNW | | |
| 6 | 6 | „ | | | | |
| 7 | 6 | „ | | | | |
| 8 | 5 | 5 | | | | |
| 9 | 6 | 2 | | Drizling R.$^{n}$ | | |
| 10 | 2 | „ | NEBE | | | |
| 11 | 1 | 2 | | | | |
| 12 | 1 | 3 | 117 Miles | | | |

94 The Catwicks are a group of islands off the southeast coast of modern-day Vietnam. They include the Great Catwick, also known as Hon Da Ty or Round Island, the Little Catwick, also known as the Pyramid, and Pulau Sapata, also known as Hon Hai or Shoe Island. Ships to Canton travelled to the east of Pulau Sapata.

95 This refers to Pulau Tioman.

| | | | | | |
|---|---|---|---|---|---|
| 1 | 6 | „ | NE | NW | Friday: 26: |
| 2 | 7 | 2 | | | |
| 3 | 6 | 6 | | | Fresh Gales of Wind with Cloudy Weather |
| 4 | 5 | 5 | | | |
| 5 | 5 | „ | | | True Course allow to be N:$^{o}$ 39$^{d}$ E:$^{t}$ Dis- |
| 6 | 4 | „ | | | tance 130 Miles |
| 7 | 4 | „ | | | |
| 8 | 4 | 5 | | | p:$^{r}$ Observation am 15 miles, to the N:$^{o}$w:$^{d}$ |
| 9 | 5 | „ | | | of Acc.$^{t}$ The Error in the Distance |
| 10 | 4 | 4 | | | |
| 11 | 4 | 2 | | | Lat:$^{d}$ Observ 12$^{d}$ 57$^{m}$ N:$^{o}$ |
| 12 | 4 | 3 | | | Meridian Distance 3 04 E:$^{t}$ |
| 1 | 4 | 2 | | W:$^{t}$ | |
| 2 | 4 | 3 | | | |
| 3 | 4 | 2 | | Squally | |
| 4 | 5 | „ | | | |
| 5 | 4 | 4 | | | |
| 6 | 4 | 3 | | Sqly Rain | |
| 7 | 5 | „ | | | |
| 8 | 5 | „ | | WNW D.$^{o}$ | |
| 9 | 4 | „ | | W:$^{t}$ | |
| 10 | 4 | 3 | | | |
| 11 | 5 | 4 | | WNW Sq.$^{lls}$ | |
| 12 | 6 | 1 | 119 Miles | | |
| H | K | F | Courses | Winds | Saturday: 27: July: 1723. |
| 1 | 6 | „ | NE | WBN | |
| 2 | 5 | 6 | | | Variable Winds and Weather |
| 3 | 4 | 4 | | | |
| 4 | 3 | „ | | NW | True Course Allow N:$^{o}$ 46$^{d}$ E:$^{t}$ Distance 58 |
| 5 | 2 | 5 | NE½E | NNW | M:$^{s}$ find the same difference between the |
| 6 | 2 | „ | NEBE | NWBN | Logg and Observation |
| 7 | 2 | 3 | | | |
| 8 | 2 | 3 | | | Lat:$^{d}$ Observ'd 13$^{d}$ 37$^{m}$ N.$^{o}$ |
| 9 | 1 | „ | ENE | N$^{o}$ | Meridian Distance 3 44 E:$^{t}$ |
| 10 | „ | „ | | | |
| 11 | „ | „ | | | |
| 12 | „ | „ | | | |
| 1 | „ | „ | | | |
| 2 | „ | „ | Calm | | |
| 3 | „ | „ | | | |
| 4 | „ | „ | | | |
| 5 | „ | „ | | | |
| 6 | „ | „ | | | |
| 7 | „ | „ | | | |
| 8 | 1 | „ | NE | West | |
| 9 | 1 | 4 | | | |
| 10 | 1 | 3 | | | |
| 11 | 1 | 4 | | | |
| 12 | 1 | 3 | 37 Miles | | |

| | | | | | |
|---|---|---|---|---|---|
| 1 | 2 | „ | NE | NW | Sunday: 28: |
| 2 | 2 | „ | | | |
| 3 | 2 | 5 | | NWBW | Small Winds Variable with abundance |
| 4 | 2 | 5 | | | of Raine |
| 5 | 2 | „ | | | |
| 6 | 2 | „ | | | Course allow to be N:° 38$^{d}$ E:$^{t}$ Distance 64 |
| 7 | 2 | „ | | | Miles |
| 8 | 2 | „ | | | |
| 9 | 1 | „ | | Lightning | Lat:$^{d}$ p:$^{r}$ Acc:$^{t}$ 14$^{d}$ 27$^{m}$ N.° |
| 10 | 2 | „ | | D.° | Meridian Distance 4 24 E:$^{t}$ |
| 11 | 2 | 3 | | SBW | |
| 12 | 2 | „ | | Rain | |
| 1 | 3 | 2 | | WNW D.° | |
| 2 | 2 | 3 | | SW D.° | |
| 3 | 2 | „ | | D.° | |
| 4 | 3 | „ | | Light.$^{g}$ & D.° | |
| 5 | 3 | 3 | | WSW D.° | |
| 6 | 3 | 3 | | | |
| 7 | 4 | „ | | | |
| 8 | 5 | „ | NNE | WBN | |
| 9 | 4 | 4 | | | |
| 10 | 4 | 5 | | | |
| 11 | 5 | 3 | | | |
| 12 | 6 | 4 | 72 Miles | | |
| 1 | 6 | „ | NNE | WNW | Monday: 29: |
| 2 | 5 | 3 | | | |
| 3 | 3 | „ | NBE½E | NWBW | Hard Squalls, Winds Variable with |
| 4 | 2 | „ | NEBE | NBW Rain | Abundance of Rain as p$^{r}$ Logg |
| 5 | 3 | „ | NBE½E | NWBW D.° | |
| 6 | 3 | 3 | | SW D.° | Course make to be N:° 13$^{d}$ E:$^{t}$ Distance 108 |
| 7 | 5 | „ | NBE | WNW D.° | Miles |
| 8 | 4 | „ | | W:$^{t}$ D° | |
| 9 | 4 | „ | | D.° | Lat:$^{d}$ p:$^{r}$ Account 16$^{d}$ 12$^{m}$ N.° |
| 10 | 2 | „ | NEBN | NWBN D.° | Meridian Distance 4 48 E:$^{t}$ |
| 11 | 3 | „ | NBE | NWBW D.° | |
| 12 | 2 | 3 | | SW D.° | |
| 1 | 5 | „ | | SSW | |
| 2 | 6 | 3 | hard Sq$^{ll}$ | & R.$^{n}$ SW | |
| 3 | 3 | „ | NEBN | NWBN Rain | |
| 4 | 5 | „ | NBE | WBS° D.° | |
| 5 | 6 | „ | | WBN D.° | |
| 6 | 5 | 3 | | D.° | |
| 7 | 7 | „ | | D.° | |
| 8 | 7 | 3 | | WBS.° D.° | |
| 9 | 5 | 3 | | SW Sq$^{ll}$ & D.° | |
| 10 | 6 | 3 | | W$^{t}$ D.° D.° | |
| 11 | 5 | „ | N° | D.° D.° | |
| 12 | 6 | 4 | NNW | 112$^{Ms}$ DRBTS.D° | |

| H | K | F | Courses | Winds | Tuesday: 30: July: 1723 |
|---|---|---|---|---|---|
| 1 | 5 | 4 | NNW | WBS hard Sq.$^{l}$ | |
| 2 | 6 | " | | D.° D.° | Variable Winds with Continuall Sq:$^{lls}$ and |
| 3 | 6 | " | | | abundance of Raine |
| 4 | 5 | " | | W:$^{t}$ | |
| 5 | 5 | " | | | Course make to be N.° 26$^{d}$ W:$^{t}$ Distance |
| 6 | 5 | 2 | | D.° D.° | 108 M$^{s}$ |
| 7 | 4 | " | NBW½W | | |
| 8 | 3 | " | NNW | | Lat.$^{d}$ p:$^{r}$ Account 17$^{d}$ 48$^{m}$ N.° |
| 9 | 1 | 3 | | WSW Rain | Meridian Distance 4 01 E.$^{t}$ |
| 10 | 1 | " | | SSE | |
| 11 | 4 | " | | | |
| 12 | 5 | 4 | | S.° D.° | |
| 1 | 5 | 4 | | SSW | |
| 2 | 6 | " | | | |
| 3 | 5 | 2 | | | |
| 4 | 6 | 3 | | SW | |
| 5 | 5 | 2 | NW | | |
| 6 | 5 | " | O:$^{t}$ | 2$^{d}$ R.MT.S. | |
| 7 | 6 | " | | SEBS.°R.$^{n}$ | |
| 8 | 5 | " | | | |
| 9 | 5 | 2 | Out 2.$^{d}$ R. | FT.S.SW | |
| 10 | 3 | 4 | | D.° | |
| 11 | 2 | 3 | | | |
| 12 | 2 | 2 | 110 Miles | | |
| 1 | 2 | 2 | NW | SSE | Wednesday: 31. |
| 2 | 4 | " | | Rain | |
| 3 | 3 | 5 | | D.° | Fresh Gales the major part with |
| 4 | 4 | " | | D.° | Some Raine |
| 5 | 6 | " | | SW D.° | |
| 6 | 6 | " | | S.° | Course make to be N:° 40$^{d}$ W:$^{t}$ Distance |
| 7 | 4 | " | | | 104 M:$^{s}$ |
| 8 | 1 | 2 | | SE | |
| 9 | 2 | " | | | Lat:$^{d}$ Observ'd 19$^{d}$ 08$^{m}$ N:° |
| 10 | 2 | 3 | | | Meridian Distance 2 55 E:$^{t}$ |
| 11 | 3 | " | | | |
| 12 | 3 | 2 | | | |
| 1 | 5 | " | | | |
| 2 | 5 | 3 | | ESE | |
| 3 | 5 | 4 | | | |
| 4 | 5 | 4 | | | |
| 5 | 4 | 3 | | SE | |
| 6 | 5 | 3 | | Rain | |
| 7 | 4 | 4 | NNW | O.$^{t}$ 1 R.B.T.S. | |
| 8 | 4 | " | | | |
| 9 | 6 | 2 | | | |
| 10 | 7 | " | | | |
| 11 | 7 | " | | | |
| 12 | 6 | 5 | 109 Miles | | |

| | | | | | | |
|---|---|---|---|---|---|---|
| 1 | 6 | 6 | N.$^{o}$ | ESE | Dep$^{th}$ | Thursday: 1: August |
| 2 | 5 | 6 | | E:$^{t}$ Sq$^{l}$ & R.$^{n}$ | | |
| 3 | 5 | 4 | | | | Fresh gales of wind with Squalls |
| 4 | 4 | 6 | | | | & Rain |
| 5 | 6 | 6 | | | | |
| 6 | 6 | 3 | | | | Att 12 P.M: Brought too and |
| 7 | 6 | " | | EBN | | Sounded had depth of Water 50 |
| 8 | 6 | " | | | | fathom, Kept a good look out all |
| 9 | 6 | " | | E:$^{t}$ | | night |
| 10 | 7 | " | | | | Att 11 This Morning Saw Land |
| 11 | 7 | " | | Sq$^{ly}$ R.$^{n}$ & | | bearing NNW which Land do take |
| 12 | 4 | 4 | Bro:$^{ht}$ too | Sound:$^{d}$ ground | 50 | Island S:$^{t}$ John[96] to be. |
| 1 | 4 | 3 | | | | |
| 2 | 4 | 2 | | brown Sand | 55 | Note, this Land to the E:$^{t}$w:$^{d}$ |
| 3 | 4 | 3 | | fine D.$^{o}$ | 50 | Shews high but to the W:$^{t}$w:$^{d}$ like |
| 4 | 3 | 3 | | rocky gro:$^{d}$ | 45 | a p[ar]cell of Sm:$^{ll}$ Islands |
| 5 | 4 | " | | EBS$^{o}$ | | |
| 6 | 4 | 2 | | | | Lat:$^{d}$ Observ'd 21$^{d}$ 06$^{m}$ N:$^{o}$ |
| 7 | 3 | 4 | | | 40 | Meridian Distance 2 50 E:$^{t}$ |
| 8 | 4 | " | | | | |
| 9 | 3 | 5 | | | | |
| 10 | 3 | 4 | blew mud | mixt w:$^{th}$ Sand | 30 | |
| 11 | 3 | 2 | Saw Land | bearing NNW | | |
| 12 | 3 | " | 118 Miles | | 27 | |

96 St. John's Island, now Shangchuan Island, is located in the South China Sea, about 80 kilometers southwest of Macao. The Portuguese used it as a stopping point on their voyages to Japan in the early 1500s. It was the initial site of of Portuguese-Chinese trade from 1549 to 1553 and a place of Catholic pilgrimage, as the site of Saint Francis Xavier's death in 1552. The passage into eighteenth-century Macao was filled with a large number of islands and rocks, many of which are now joined together via natural or man-made land expansions. For a visual aid in identifying these islands, dated to the late 1700s, see *A chart of the China Sea from the island of Sanciam to Pedra Branca with the course of the river Tigris from Canton to Macao, corrected from the surveys made by Captn. Jph. Huddart and Captn. J.P. Larkins* (London: Laurie and Whittle, 1794). Also, refer to the map on page 259. Deep-riding vessels generally sailed to the city along its western islands. This was because of the shallow and rocky Macclesfield Bank located east of this passage and near the Great Ladrone.

| H | K | F | Courses | Winds | Dep. | Friday: 2: August. 1723 |
|---|---|---|---|---|---|---|
| 1 | 4 | „ | N° | EBS.° grey Sand | 23 | The first part moderate gales, |
| 2 | 4 | „ | NBE Deers | Isl.[d] 7 leag.[s] | 21 | hazey wea:[r] |
| 3 | 3 | 5 | NNE | | 19 | Att 4 P.M: the body of S:[t] Johns |
| 4 | 3 | „ | Saw y[e] great | Ladrone NEBN | 23 | bore NW 8 leag:[s] |
| 5 | 2 | „ | NE½N | NWBN | 18 | I allow this Island to lie in Lat:[d] |
| 6 | 1 | „ | In 1.[st] R.B.T.S. | Course Sand | 20 | 21[d] 22[m] N:° And East of y:[e] Junck |
| 7 | 1 | 4 | NE | ESE | 18 | Cattwicks 2 34 |
| 8 | 1 | 3 | NE½N | SEBE Rain | | Att the Same time the Eastermost |
| 9 | 3 | „ | | Tackt D.° | 19½ | of the Deer Isl:[ds97] NNW½W and |
| 10 | 1 | 3 | S½E Course | Sand and Shells | 20 | the Great Ladrone[98] appear- |
| 11 | 2 | 1 | Sq[ll] & R.[n] | D.° D.° D.° | 18 | ing like a hay Cock NEBN:° 10 |
| 12 | 2 | „ | | | 17 | Leagues |
| 1 | 1 | 5 | Wore to | y[e] E:[t]ward | | Att 8 this Morning the Great |
| 2 | 1 | „ | NE | ESE bro:[ht] too | 18 | Ladron ENE and Lantoa[99] NE½E |
| 3 | | | up NEBE | off NBE | 19 | Att Noon Great Ladroon NEBE 1 |
| 4 | | | up ENE off | NNE Made Sail | | League |
| 5 | 5 | „ | NE | | | D:° time blowing very hard |
| 6 | 5 | „ | | | | Oblidg'd us to Hand Both Top |
| 7 | 5 | 1 | Great Ladrone | ENE Tackt | | Sails and Try under Mizon |
| 8 | 2 | „ | | | | Made Sail at 5 AM as p[r] Logg |
| 9 | 1 | 6 | S° | | | |
| 10 | 2 | „ | SSE | E[t] | | |
| 11 | 1 | 4 | hard Squalls | and Rain | | |
| 12 | 1 | 3 | 56 M:[s] SE | ENE HB.T.S.[s] | | |

97 The Deer Islands are located just east of St. John's Island and on the southwest edge of the Pearl River delta.

98 The Great Ladroon Island, now part of the Wanshan Archipelago, is located southeast of Macao, where the Pearl River meets the South China Sea.

99 Lantau is a large island, with a prominent mountain range, located near the eastern edge of the Pearl River delta and directly across from Macao. It now constitutes the largest island of Hong Kong.

| | | | | | | |
|---|---|---|---|---|---|---|
| 1 | „ | „ | S:° DR. & | Set BT.S.ESE Sq$^{l}$ | & R.$^{n}$ | Saturday: 3: |
| 2 | „ | „ | SEBS° | EBN | 17 | |
| 3 | „ | „ | SE | ENE | | Very hard Squalls of wind and |
| 4 | „ | „ | | | 19 | Rain and a great Sea: Handing, |
| 5 | „ | „ | ESE | NE | 20 | Reefing, and Laying by as p$^{r}$ Logg |
| 6 | „ | „ | | | 21 | |
| 7 | 2 | „ | SEBE | NEBE | 22 | Att 4 P.M: Great Ladroon NE½N:° |
| 8 | 1 | 6 | | Tackt | | and the Westermost Land in sight |
| 9 | 1 | 3 | NBE | EBN | 23 | W½N:° |
| 10 | 1 | 5 | NBW | NEBE Tackt | | Att 5 A.M: Great Ladroon NEBN 7 |
| 11 | 1 | „ | East | NNE | 21 | Leagues |
| 12 | 2 | „ | EBN | NBE Light.$^{g}$ | 20 | Att 8 D:° d° d:° NNE½E 6 Lea: |
| 1 | 2 | „ | NEBE | NBW | 19 | |
| 2 | 2 | 3 | NE½N | NWBN D.° | | |
| 3 | 3 | „ | NEBN | | | |
| 4 | | | up NWBN | off WBN TK:$^{t}$ | Sq$^{ll}$ | & Rain |
| 5 | | | up NW off | WNW Wore & | Made | Sail |
| 6 | 1 | 3 | NEBE O:$^{t}$ 2.$^{d}$ | R.B.T.S. NBW | | |
| 7 | 3 | „ | Hard Sq$^{ll}$ | & R.$^{n}$ HB.T.S. | 22 | |
| 8 | 1 | 1 | Sqly EBS.° | NEBN | | A Tumbling Sea from the |
| 9 | | | Bro:$^{ht}$ too up | EBN.° off EBS° | | NE:$^{t}$ward |
| 10 | „ | „ | up EN off | E:$^{t}$ hard Sq$^{ll}$ & | R.$^{n}$ | |
| 11 | „ | „ | up E:$^{t}$ off | ESE D.° D.° D.° | | |
| 12 | | | 23 Miles, | up ESE off SE | | |
| 1 | | | up ESE off | SE NE hard Sq$^{l}$ | & R.$^{n}$ | Sunday: 4: |
| 2 | | | | D° d° | D.° | Lowred M: Yard & R.M.S. |
| 3 | | | up SEBE off | SEBS.° R: Mizen | D.° | |
| 4 | | | up SEBS.° | off SBE NEBE R. | & Set | F.S.$^{l}$: |
| 5 | 2 | „ | SSE | E:$^{t}$ Sq$^{l}$ & Rain | | |
| 6 | 2 | 4 | | D.° D.° | 20 | Hard Gales with very hard |
| 7 | 2 | „ | S½E | EBS° D.° | 23 | Squalls of Wind and Rain, which |
| 8 | 2 | „ | SBW | SEBE TK:$^{t}$ D.° | | Oblidged us to Reefe Courses, and |
| 9 | 1 | „ | NE | ESE | 28 | at 4 PM tho blowing very hard |
| 10 | 2 | 2 | NEBE | SEBE D.° | | Sett Courses being fearfull should |
| 11 | 2 | 2 | | D.° | | not with Lying a Try drive Clear of |
| 12 | 2 | 4 | ENE | SE D.° | 26 | the Deer Islands |
| 1 | 2 | 3 | | | 25 | Att 9 PM Wore Ship to the |
| 2 | 3 | „ | NEBE | SEBE Wore | | N:°ward and |
| 3 | 1 | 3 | SBW DR | & Set BT.S. Land | NNE$^{t}$ | att 3 AM Saw Land bearing NNE |
| 4 | 2 | „ | S:° Out Reef | Courses ESE | | then Wore Ship to the S:°ward |
| 5 | 2 | „ | | | | and Sett both Topsails Double |
| 6 | 2 | „ | SBE | EBS° Land from | | reeft lay Clear of the Land |
| 7 | 2 | 3 | | NNE to NW | | |
| 8 | 2 | 4 | S° | ESE Wore | | T.S. |
| 9 | 2 | „ | East | SSE HB.T.S | HB. | This Noon Land from NE to |
| 10 | 1 | 3 | Set BT:S. | Sq$^{ll}$ & R:$^{n}$ | Wore | NW:$^{t}$ the water very thick by the |
| 11 | „ | 4 | ESE | S.° Set MT.S. | | Violence of y:$^{e}$ Storm Raising so |
| 12 | 1 | 3 | EBS° | SBE Sq$^{ly}$ Rain | | great a Sea |
| | | | 40 Miles | | | |

| H | K | F | Courses | Winds | Dep | Monday: 5: August: 1723 |
|---|---|---|---|---|---|---|
| 1 | 1 | | SBW blew | Clay SEBS$^{o}$ | 23 | |
| 2 | 2 | „ | S$^{o}$ | ESE O:$^{t}$ 2 R.BT.S | | Moderate Gales with Some Rain |
| 3 | 2 | „ | SBE | EBS:$^{o}$ | | |
| 4 | 2 | „ | SEBS.$^{o}$ | EBN | | Att 2 PM the W:$^{t}$ermost Land |
| 5 | 1 | 4 | SSE | East | 22 | WNW and Eastermost NEBE 9 or |
| 6 | 1 | 3 | | | | 10 Leagues |
| 7 | 2 | 2 | Sandy and | Muddy ground | 25 | Att 5 D:$^{o}$ the E:$^{t}$ermost NEBE |
| 8 | 2 | 4 | SE½S$^{o}$ | ENE | | and W:$^{t}$ermost (being an Island |
| 9 | 3 | „ | SEBS$^{o}$ | EBN.$^{o}$ | | between S:$^{t}$ Johns and Deers |
| 10 | 2 | 3 | SSE | East | | Islands) WNW |
| 11 | 2 | 3 | | | | |
| 12 | 2 | 3 | SSE½E | EBN | | Course Make to be Dist:$^{t}$ |
| 1 | 2 | „ | | | | Miles |
| 2 | 2 | „ | SSE | E$^{t}$ | | |
| 3 | 1 | 4 | S$^{o}$ | ESE Sqly TK$^{t}$ | 30 | |
| 4 | 1 | „ | East | SSE Wore | | |
| 5 | „ | 3 | SSE | E:$^{t}$ DRBTS | Sq$^{l}$ & | R.$^{n}$ |
| 6 | „ | 4 | SEBE | NEBE | | D$^{o}$ |
| 7 | „ | 3 | SE Land | N.$^{o}$ & NBW, ENE | | |
| 8 | „ | 3 | S$^{o}$ | | 32 | |
| 9 | 1 | „ | O:$^{t}$ 2.$^{d}$ R. | BT.S. ESE Wore | | |
| 10 | 1 | „ | NE | | | |
| 11 | „ | 2 | O.$^{t}$ 1:$^{st}$ | R.BT.S. | 30 | |
| 12 | | | Calm | 34 Miles | | |
| 1 | „ | „ | | | 30 | Tuesday: 6: |
| 2 | „ | „ | Calm | | | Small Gales till 5 this morning |
| 3 | 1 | 3 | SEBS$^{o}$ | EBN.$^{o}$ | | then Moderate |
| 4 | „ | „ | Calm TK:$^{t}$ y$^{e}$ | Isl.$^{d}$ S.$^{t}$ Johns N | W½N | 12$^{Lgs}$ |
| 5 | 1 | 2 | ENE | SE | | |
| 6 | 1 | 4 | | | | Att 5 PM the Eastermost Land |
| 7 | 1 | 2 | EBN | SSE | | NEBE and the Island S:$^{t}$ Johns |
| 8 | 1 | 6 | | | | NWBN 12 Leag$^{s}$: |
| 9 | 3 | „ | | SBE mudd | 25 | |
| 10 | 2 | 2 | | | | Course from S:$^{t}$ Johns is N:$^{o}$ 75$^{d}$ E:$^{t}$ |
| 11 | 3 | „ | | | | Distance 60 Miles |
| 12 | 4 | 1 | | | | |
| 1 | 3 | 4 | | | | Att 11 AM Anchor'd in 15 fa: Soft |
| 2 | 3 | 2 | ENE | SW | | ground among the Deer Islands, |
| 3 | 2 | „ | NEBE | NWBW | | but beleiv'd one of them to be the |
| 4 | 2 | „ | | | 24 | Great Ladrone w:$^{ch}$ Occasion'd our |
| 5 | 4 | „ | NE½E | SBW | | Anchoring |
| 6 | 5 | „ | NNE | SW | | |
| 7 | 6 | „ | NBE | WBS$^{o}$ | 23 | Meridian Distance from S:$^{t}$ |
| 8 | 5 | „ | | | 22 | Johns is 0$^{d}$ 58$^{m}$ E:$^{t}$ |
| 9 | 5 | „ | NNE | SW | 21 | |
| 10 | 4 | „ | | | 19 | |
| 11 | 4 | „ | NW | Anchored | 15 | |
| 12 | „ | „ | 64 Miles | | | |

| | | | | | | |
|---|---|---|---|---|---|---|
| 1 | ” | ” | | WSW | | Wednesday: 7: |
| 2 | | | | | | Moderate Gales in the SW Quarter |
| 3 | | | | | | Att 8 P.M: two Saile Came in here |
| 4 | | | | | | (being mistaken as we were). |
| 5 | | | | | | being the Princess Ann (whom we |
| 6 | | | | | | lost Company w:th in the Storm |
| 7 | | | | | | and the King George[100] from Fort |
| 8 | | | | | | S:t George |
| 9 | | | | | | |
| 10 | | | | | | Att day Light this morning |
| 11 | | | | | | Weighed Steering to the Eastward |
| 12 | | | | | | and at 10 D:o had Light of the |
| 1 | | | | | | Great Ladroon, Att 1 D:o the |
| 2 | | | | | | Remarkable White Spott on the |
| 3 | | | | | | Island Colan[101] |
| 4 | | | | | | NWBN.o Mountania[102] NNE and |
| 5 | | | | | | Great Ladroon EBN½N° |
| 6 | ” | ” | Weighed | W:t | 15 | |
| 7 | 4 | ” | ENE | | | Att Noon the Spott on Colan W:t |
| 8 | 4 | 3 | | | | Mountain NBE and Great Ladroon |
| 9 | 5 | ” | NE½E | SW Oazy gr.d | 14 | E½N 3 Leagues |
| 10 | 5 | 4 | NEBE | | 13 | |
| 11 | 5 | 3 | | | 12 | |
| 12 | 5 | 4 | NE 30 M:s | | 10 | |

100 The King George, rated about 450 tons, housed 90 to 92 crewmembers and 30 guns while active, from 1715 to 1727. She travelled to Calicut, Goa, Combay, Madras, Bombay, Malacca, Surat and Canton on her third voyage, extending from 1720 to 1723. See page 199, for the cause of her delay.

101 Coloane is the southern of Macao's two main geographic islands. It was not heavily populated in the 1700s and rather used for salt farming and illicit trade.

102 Montanha, now Da Hengqin, is one of three large islands, located just west of Coloane.

## S:t John towards Wampo

| H | K | F | Courses | Winds | | Thursday: 8: August 1723 |
|---|---|---|---|---|---|---|
| 1 | " | " | | WSW | 9 | |
| 2 | " | " | | | 7 | The first part Moderate gales of |
| 3 | " | " | Anch:d mud | dy ground | 5½ | Wind and fair Weather |
| 4 | " | " | | | | |
| 5 | " | " | | | | Att 3 PM Anchor'd in 5 fa: Muddy |
| 6 | " | " | | | | Ground, the Great Ladroon SSE |
| 7 | " | " | | | | Linting[103] NEBN and the Castle at |
| 8 | " | " | | | | Macoa NW Dis:t from Shore 2 Miles |
| 9 | | | | | | |
| 10 | | | | | | Sent our Boat A Shoar for a Pylote[104] |
| 11 | | | | | | |
| 12 | | | | | | Att 6 in the Morning Weighed, the |
| 1 | | | | | | Wind as pr Logg |
| 2 | | | | | | |
| 3 | | | | | | |
| 4 | | | | | | |
| 5 | | | | | | |
| 6 | | | Weighed | SW | | |
| 7 | | | NBE | | 5 | |
| 8 | | | | | | |
| 9 | | | Almost | Calm | | |
| 10 | | | NNE | fine breeze | | |
| 11 | | | NEBN | | 6 | |
| 12 | | | NE | | 7:10 | |

Friday 9 Hazey Weather with Abundance of Rain Steer:g Sundry Courses

Att ½ past 4 PM Anchor'd in a half 5 fathom Water Oasey Ground the Peak on Linting SSE the Bogue of Tigris[105] NNW½W Distance 3 Leagues

Being Squaly thick and Cloudy, Could not Weigh

Satur:d 10 Hazey Weather, Att 4 PM Weighed Steering away Severall Courses till 5 D:o then was in ¼ 3 fa: being Dark and Hazey run back and Anchor'd in a ¼ less 5 fa:

Att 8 AM: Weighed with a fine Gale of Wind and at 9 D:o Cross'd the 4:th Barr[106], the least depth on it ¼ 3 afterwards Encreasing our water to 7 and 8 fathoms

Att 11 D:o Anchor'd within the Bogue in 7 fa: hard ground

---

**103** Lintin Island, now Nei Lingding, is located about 29 kilometers northeast of Macao and in the Pearl River delta.

**104** A number of pilots aided EIC ships approaching Canton. The first, fishermen, guided arriving vessels along the channel to Macao. A second group, those who aided Europeans up the Pearl River, often came from Macao and thus could communicate at least partially in Portuguese or pidgin English.

**105** Bocca Tigris, or the Bogue, marked the entrance to the Pearl River proper. It was a regular site of European anchorage. It was located just south of the area where the Dongjiang, a regional river, joins the Pearl River and near modern-day Humen.

**106** The fourth bar anchorage was located in the Pearl River delta, about 2 kilometers northwest of Lintin Island. It probably was part of a natural mud bank that extended from this island, known as the Lintin Sands.

Sunday 11 Small Airs of Wind with fair Weather Yesterday M:r John Hooper[107] Purser Departed this Life and this Morning buried him Ashoar[108]

### From the Bogue of Tigris tow:ds Wampo

August 1723

Mon:d 12 The first Moderate breezes of Wind and fair Weather

Att 1 PM Weighed with the Wind at SSW a Strong Tide under foot with us.

Att 3 D:o rece'd an Order from William Fazackerly Esq: President &c Councill, Not to proceed farther up the River till had their Orders, upon which Anchor'd in ½ 5 fa: the Piramid[109] bearing NWBW

Tues:d 13 Att 3 PM Rec.d an Order to proceed with all Conven:t Speed for Wampo and at 5 d:o weighed with a Small breeze at SWBS:o and in half an hour Cross'd the 2:d barr[110] in a half 2 fa. the Piramid then bearing WNW

Att 6 D:o Anchor'd in 4 fa: Soft ground Piramid W½N. Att 5 AM Weighed being Calm was Oblidg'd to Tow, but found Could not gain Anchor'd again in the Sam Depth of Water

Wednes:d 14 The first part hard Squalls with Cloudy Weather Att 6 AM: Weigh'd with a moderate Gale of Wind at ENE and at 8 D:o Cross'd the first barr the least water a foot 3

Att 10 D:o Anchor'd at Wampo in 5 fathom water, find Riding here the Duke of Cambridge Daniel Small and Mountague John Gordon Commanders, also 2 Ostend Ships Here we have Advice of our two former Consorts Meeting with a very hard Turfoon or Storm of Wind in so much that the Cambridge Sprung her Boultsprite and had like to losst her head, So that it was very fortunate for us that we proceeded to Batavia. Otherwise in that Weather we had, we must Infalliably have lost our Foremast and by that loss very probably a Greater we must Sustain

Thurs:d 15 Light Airs of Wind and fair Weather, Moar'd Ship with Swivle and Small bower, Unbent Sailes & Unrigg'd Top gallant Masts and Yards, gott them down

Friday 16 Intermitting Squalls and Rain, We have Employed our People in Unrigging Ship

---

107 Person unknown.

108 Englishmen who died in Canton or at Whampoa usually were buried on French or Danish-controlled islands, in common gravesites. For more on EIC burials in Southeast Asia, see Lindsay Ride and May Ride, *An East India Company Cemetery: Protestant Burials in Macao* (Hong Kong: Hong Kong UP, 1996); Nicolas Standaert, *The Interweaving of Rituals: Funerals in the Cultural Exchange between China and Europe* (Seattle: University of Washington Press, 2008).

109 The Pyramid was a navigational marker, likely one of the prominent hills or mountains located near the Whampoa Anchorage.

110 The second bar anchorage was located about fourteen to sixteen kilometers up the Pearl River from Bocca Tigris, before Whampoa.

## Ship Hartford Att Anchor att Wampo: 1723

August 1723

Saturday 17 Hard Gales of Wind, Cloudy weather

Sunday 18 Light Gales and Sultry hott Weather

Munday 19 Light breezes, Sultry hott Weather, Yesterday Came on board the Hoppo to Measure the Ship

Tuesday 20 Small breezers of Wind and fair Weather – Stript our Topmasts and gott them down and Standing rigging Set the Caulkers to work on the Lower Gundeck

Wednesday 21 Sent by Order of the Councill five Chests of the Honourable Companys Treasure for Canton, Winds and Weather Variable

Thursday 22 Friday 23 Saturday 24 Sunday 25Variable Winds and Weather, have Employed Some Hands at Banksall[111] about the rigging, Others in Clearing Hould & other Necessary uses, not any thing material otherwise

Munday 26 Tuesday 27 Wednesday28 Thursday 29 Friday 30 Saturday 31 Variable Winds and Weather, Continue Sending Our Stores ashore to Bankshall, Our Carpenters and Caulkers Employed upon the Gun Deck

September

Sunday 1 Munday 2 Tuesday 3 Wednesday 4 Variable Winds, Sultry hott Weather. Clear'd our Aufter Hould and the Limbers there, have also Quoiled our Cables down abaft, Continue Caulking & fix:[g] riging

Thursay 5 Friday 6 Saturday 7 Sunday 8 Variable Winds, hott Weather with Some Intermitting Showers of Raine, Rec.[d] on board Ballast from the Duke of Cambridge, fixt the Standing rigging of our Foremast Gott it over head, Also Compleated the Caulking of the Gun:deck, George Condell[112] Steward Deceas'd

Monday 9 Tuesday 10 Wednes:[d] 11 Thursday 12 Variable Winds and Weather Rec.[d] from the Duke of Cambridge Guns for Kentlidge, Gave the Ship a good heel and Scrubb'd her Bottom and Gave her a pair of Boot Tops. Clear'd limbers fore and Aft and put the Hold in a Condition to receive Goods, Our People fall down very fast of feavers and fluxes

Friday 13 Saturday 14 Sunday 15 Munday 16 Chiefly fair Weather, very Sultry Winds are variable Ommitted on the 12 Instant the Death of William Baxter[113] Quarteer, Continue fixing Riggin & Caulking Steereage

Tuesday 17 Wednesday 18 Thursday 19 Friday 20 The Weather moderate and fair, by which do Hope the Recovery of Our People who Still Continue Sick, Have Assisted

---

**111** Chinese officials established bankshalls, or small shacks, on the islands of the Pearl River near Canton. These acted as refueling stations for European vessels. There, crews could repair their riggings, keep livestock, purchase additional provisions, tend to sick sailors and socialize, oftentimes with the accompaniment of alcohol.

**112** Person unknown.

**113** Person unknown.

the Cambridge with Long:boat and Men, to bring down the Honourable Companys Tutanague

Saturday 21 Sunday 22 Munday 23 Tuesday 24 The Weather fair, Winds Variable. On the 21 In:$^{s}$ Lyon[114] Cook departed this Life of a feaver, People Still Continue Sick and Weak, Employed at Bankshall about riggin Gott the Main Shrouds overhead

Wednes:$^{d}$ 25 Thursday 26 Friday 27 The Weather fair, Omitted the Death of In:$^{o}$ Morris[115] Taylor on the 24:$^{th}$ Gott our Tops over head, Water'd the Gundeck and received on board Ballast

Saturday 28 Sunday 29 Munday30 The Weather Chiefly fair, Sent up the Honourable Comp:$^{ys}$ Lead, Our People Still Continue Sick, Sail'd from hence the Ship Walpole[116] for Madrass, Phinis Hazlewood[117] Coopers Mate Departed this Life

October

Tuesday 1 Wednesday 2 Thursday 3 Friday 4 Cheifly fair Weather, Gott the Topmast rigging over head and Gammon'd our Boltspritt. Our People Employ'd in the Rigging, those that are well of 'em

Saturday 5 Sunday 6 Monday 7 Tuesday 8 Cheifly fair Weather, Sent the Honourable Comp:$^{ys}$ Lead to Canton, Gott out Fore and Main Yards a Cross

Wednes:$^{d}$ 9 Thursday 10 Friday 11 Saturday 12 Sunday 13 Small Gales Variable, Cheifly fair Weather, Swaid up our Topmasts & Sett the Rigging up fore & Aft. Also Gott our Top: Sailyards a Cross, Our People upon Recovery y$^{e}$ Major Part

Monday 14 Tuesday 15 Wednes:$^{d}$ 16 Thursday 17 Variable Winds and Weather, Gott up our Cables between Decks, Stowing our Salt provisions[118] in y$^{e}$ Lazaretta

Friday 18 Saturday 19 Sunday 20 Monday 21 Small Gales of Wind with fair Weather, our People upon Recovery, Rece'd on board 50 Chests said to be Chinaware Belonging to the Honourable United East India Company

Tuesday 22 Wednes.$^{d}$ 23 Thursday 24 Friday 25 Small Gales of Wind with Intermitting Showers of Rain – Saild from hence the Boon[119] for Bombay

Saturday 26 Sunday 27 Monday 28 Small Variable winds, Reeving our Running Riging and fixing our Small blocks – Rec:$^{d}$ on Board China Ware of the Honourable Company's

---

**114** Person unknown.

**115** Person unknown.

**116** The Sir Robert Walpole, rated 495 tons, housed 134 crewmembers and 32 guns while active, from 1722 to 1737. For more on her problematic 1722 sailing, see page 25, ft. 28 and 31.

**117** Person unknown

**118** Salted provisions included beef, pork and fish. These often were preserved for months or even years, and they were eaten only after fresh food stores depleted. Salted meats needed to boiled several times before ingested, and they were widely associated with crew malnutrition and disease, especially scurvy.

**119** The Boone Frigat was a country ship, which sailed between Persia, Bombay, Madras and China. John Standard (dates unknown) was her captain in 1723. See *Records of Fort St. George. Diary and Consultation Book 1723* (Madras: Government Press, 1930), 54, 64.

Tuesday 29 Wednesday 30 Thursday 31 Variable Small Winds, Saild from hence the Duke of Cambridge for Bombay, Employ'd our People in bring:$^{g}$ on board Our Luggage from Bankshall

Novem:

Friday 1 Saturday 2 Sunday 3 Monday 4 Small Breezes of Wind, fair Weather, Employ'd Our People in fixing Rigging and Blacking our Yards. Sent up above Canton Water Casks to be filled w:$^{th}$ Water

Tuesday 5 Wednesday 6 Thursday 7 Friday 8 Fresh Gales with Intermitting Squalls, on the 5:$^{th}$ Ant:$^{oy}$ Crisdy[120] Midshipman Departed this Life, Rec:$^{d}$ on board Water, Our Longboat Assisting the Duke of Cambridge in bringing down the Company's Quicksilver

Saturday 9 Sunday 10 Monday 11 Tuesday 12 Fair Weather with Some Lightning and Rain in y:$^{e}$ Nights y$^{e}$ Wind in the NE Quarter, Rec.$^{d}$on board Water which we Stowd Under y$^{e}$ Cables

Wednesday 13 Thursday 14 Friday 15 Saturday 16 Sunday 17 Moderate gales Variable, On the 15:$^{th}$ W:$^{m}$ Newheok[121] Caulker departed this Life, fetching Lumber from Bankshall and Received on board Water

Munday 18 Tuesday 19 Wednes:$^{d}$ 20 Thurs:$^{d}$ 21 Fresh Gales the Major part, fair Weather, On the 18:$^{th}$ Tho:$^{s}$ Peach[122] Departed this Life, Scraped Our Quarters, Masts and Topmasts and rigg'd Topgallant Masts

Friday 22 Saturday 23 Sunday 24 Monday 25 Some rain with Small Gales. Compleated the mending Our Sails – Rec.$^{d}$ on board 50 Small Chests Quicksilver

Tuesday 26 Wednes:$^{d}$ 27 Thursday 28 Moderate Gales of Wind, Cloudy Weather, Rec:$^{d}$ on Board 20 Chests Raw Silk 45 D:$^{o}$ Quicksilver & 18 halfe ones D:$^{o}$

Friday 29 Saturday 30 Sun.$^{d}$ Decem: 1 Rec.$^{d}$ on board 20 Chests of Raw Silk 115 half Chests of Quick=Silver also 3 whole Chests of D:$^{o}$ the Wea: moderate w:$^{th}$ Rain

Munday 2 Tuesday 3 Wednes:$^{d}$ 4 Thursday 5 Fine fresh Gales and pleasant Weather, Rec.$^{d}$ on Board 200 Whole Chests of Bohea Tea and 50 half Chests D:$^{o}$ of the Honourable United East India Companys

Friday 6 Saturday 7 Sunday 8 Monday 9 Moderate Winds and Weather, Rec.$^{d}$ on Board 200 Whole Chests of Bohea Tea & fifty half Chests, also 18 Chests of Silk

Tuesday 10 Wednes.$^{d}$ 11 Thursday 12 Friday 13 Saturday 14 Moderate Gales of Wind, Received on Board our Stores, as Rice Beef &c. and also our Booms, We are Stowing Water and Wood

Decem:

Sunday 15 Monday 16 Tuesday 17 Wednes$^{d}$ 18 Fresh gales of Wind with Some Rain. Rec.$^{d}$ on board 20 Chests of Raw Silk. One hundred Chests of Green Tea: 338

---

**120** Person unknown.

**121** Person unknown.

**122** Person unknown.

Whole Chests of Bohea Tea: and 35 chestes of Peco: Tea of the Honourable United Company's

Thursday 19 Friday 20 Saturday 21 Sunday 22 Moderate gales of Wind. Our people Employed in Stow:[g] the Tea and getting the Ship in a Sailing Posture, Bent our Sails, and Rec.[d] on board 200 Chests of Congoa = tea and 200 of Green Belonging to y[e] Hono'ble united Company

Monday 23 Tuesday 24 Wednesday 25 Thursday 26 Friday 27 Moderate Gales in the NE Quarter, Rec.[d] on board Three hundred Chests Green tea and two hundred Chests Bohea Teas belonging to the Hono'ble United Company

## From Wampo tow:[ds] y:[e] 1:[st] Barr[123]

Decem: 1723

Saturd:[y] 28 Moderate Gales in the NE Quarter Att 8 AM Unmoar'd and at 10 D[o] Weighed with a Small Gale at NNE:[t] and gott down to the Edge of the first Barr there Anchord in 6 fa: & moar'd Ship

Sunday 29 Cloudy Weather and Small Rain the first part the latter fair

Att 8 am Unmoar'd and at 10 Weighed with a Small Gale at NE, but when was uppon the middle of the Barr, fell Stark Calm and the Ebb Coming on, grounded in a foot less 3 fathom, Imediately Shored the Ship and Carried out our Stream Anchor to the Eastward in 5 fa:wa.

Att 11 PM being near half flood the Ship Swung of the Ground hove in up on the Cable till were a peak then Waited the Tide of Ebb Designing this for our Upper or Western Anchor, Att 2 the Ebb Coming Wore away upon our Stream Cable and Carried out our Small Bower to the Eastward and Dropt it in 8 fa: Water

Monday 30 Tuesday 31 Cloudy Weather Unmoar'd Ship and new Birthed her in 8 fa: Our Hould being full have Caulked Down y[e] Hatches

## Att Anchor att the first Barr

Janu[ry]

Wednes[d] 1 Thursday 2 Friday 3 Saturday 4 Cloudy Weather with Fresh Gales of Wind. Clearing Our Bankshall of Lumber, Our Ship Now Draws Eighteen foot and one Inch

Sunday 5 Munday 6 Tuesday 7 Wednesd[y] 8 Small Gales and fair Weather. Received a Letter from Will[m] Fazackerly Esq. in which he desires, If can possibly to take on board forty or fifty Chests more of Peco Tea Advising me it would be of Great

123 The first bar anchorage was located about twenty-five kilometers up the Pearl River from Bocca Tigris, almost at Whampoa.

Service to the Comp:y Altho in my Opinion I think her Draught of Water is full enough to be a Jocant Ship at Sea: however have agreed thereto, and now having on Board 43 Chests more of Peco and Congo and 8 of Bohea, all our Stores &c on board Our Draught of Water now is Eighteen feet 5 Inches

Thursday 9 Friday 10 Saturday 11 Sunday 12 Cloudy Weather, gott all our things from ye Bankshall and everything in a readiness for Sailing, Cap:t Gordon wth my Self Wrote to the President and Councill Advising them of the Spring, and that we desired leave to proceed Over the 2:d barr, there to Lye to receive them but the Answer was they Could not procure a Chopp. So that must be Oblegdd to Wait the other Spring, before Can proceed having upon the height of the Spring in the best Channell no more than a Quarter 3 fathom

Monday 13 Tuesday 14 Wednesd 15 Thursdy 16 Cloudy Weather Waiting for Orders to Saile

[The journal of the return voyage can be found online:
http://www.degruyter.com/view/product/456197?format=B&rskey=5ZojLY&result=3]

# 3 Diary & Consultation Book of the Council for China for the Year 1723

# Diary & Consultation Book of William Fazakerley Esq. Chief, Richard Morton, Edmond Godfrey, Thomas Attkyns, Thomas Carter, Thomas Dade, & Deverux Bacon; Appointed a Councill for Mannageing the Affairs of The Hon.ble United Company of Merchants of England Trading to the East Indies in China for the Year 1723. Commencing 7th Decem.r 1722

**Decem.r**

7.th [1] This day We Repar'd on Board our Respective Ships in the Hope.

8th Mess.rs Fazakerley & Carter, Wrote to Tho.s Woolley Esq. Secretary To The Hon.ble Company from on Board the Cambridge, at the Nore, desiring him to Acquaint Our Hon.ble Mast.s that the SupraCargos gott yesterday on Board their Respective Ships, in order to proceed directly to Sea if the Wind permitts.

12. All our four Ships Anchor'd in Margarett Road.

13. The Hartford Arriv'd in the Downes.

15. The Cambridge, Mountague & Princess Ann arriv'd in the Downes.

16. We wrote to Tho.s Woolley Esq., adviceing him of the arrivall of the East India Ships / which were in Margarett Roads / in the Downes; that they were Supplying themselves, with Water & provissions in the Room of those Spent by their long passage thither, and would be ready to Sail by the first Oppertunity. [2]

27.th We Embarqu'd on our Respective Ships, and Sail'd out of the Downes.

**January 1722/23**

24th This Morning Miss'd the Princess Ann, being Extream hazey; and Saw three Ships, Steering directly for Us: At 8 A:M:d Spoke with them; they prov'd to be the 3 Mocha Ships, Barrington, Prince Augustus, and Craggs; but soon parted with them they, Steering to the S°ward, We to the Westw.d for the Island S.t Jago.

25. This Morning about 8 AM.d Saw the Island S.t Jago; & about Noon came to an Anchor in porto Prayja Bay; w[h]ere We found ~~in the Bay~~ ~~an Ostend~~ a Ship belonging to Ostend. Command.d by Cap.tn Harrisson[1], bound for Bengall, with

1 John Harrison (dates unknown) started his commercial career with the EIC but transitioned to the Ostend Company as second captain by 1720. The seaman refused an offer of £200 to return to EIC service in 1725, but he ultimately did so in 1728 once the GIC dissolved, paying a £1,500 fine. Gill, Merchants, 15, 45.

an Engineer on Board to Build a Fort ~~The Captain~~ and __ [Huoms][2] yre Supra-Cargo were both Subjects of the King of Great Britain.[3]

At a Consultation Holden ye 27th Jan.ry in Porto Praya Bay on Board the Hartford
Present William Fazakerley Esq. Chief &c.a Councill
Came to a Resolution to Write Our Hon.ble Mast.s the following Letter

S.t Jago 27th January 1723
Hon.ble S.rs

We have the Hon. of Acquainting You of Our touching at this place with the Cambridge, [3] Mountague and Hartford, the Captains having appointed this port as a Rendezvous in Case of Separation; We lost the Princess Ann, in hazey Weather two days agoe, but not finding her here, suppose She proceeded on her Voyage being a single Ship. we propos'd to take in some Water here, having been a good while from England; but the dryness of the Springs for want of Rain, has hinder'd Us of that benefitt; so We shall Sail to Morrow.

We found here at an Anchor the Ostend Ship, bound for Bengall in order to Attempt a Settlement there; and three days agoe, we fell in Company with the three Mocha Ships, who made the best of their way for that place; for fear of the lateness of the Season.

This being all we can Acquaint Yo.r Hon.rs of at present, with the tender of Our hum.ble Dutys; We remain
Y.r Hon.rs most Obedient Hum.ble Serv.ts

| | | |
|---|---|---|
| W. Fazakerley | | |
| Rich.d Morton | (Sign'd[4]) | William Fazakerley |
| Edm.d Godfrey | | Rich.d Morton |
| Thomas Carter | | ~~Edm.d Godfrey~~ |
| Tho.s Dade | | Tho.s Atkyns |
| Dev.x Bacon | | Tho.s Carter |

2 Private merchants from the Austrian Netherlands had been accessing trade in Bengal since 1715. After the chartering of the GIC in 1722, its members obtained formal permission from the local Muslim ruler to trade and quickly built a factory. See Michal Wanner, "Bankibazar – Ostend and Imperial Factory in Bengal, 1722–1744", in: *Prague Papers on the History of International Relations* (2009), 107–18; Jan Parmentier, *De holle compagnie. Smokkel en legale handel onder Zuidnederlandse vlag in Bengalen, ca. 1720–1744* (Hilversum: Verloren, 1992).

3 These supercargos were Peter Hambly (dates unknown) and Patrick Trehee (d. 1737). Both men, who were English natives and eventually retired in London, invested in commercial adventures to the East and West Indies from England and the continent throughout their lives. See Gill, Merchants, 61; Ric Berman, *Schism: the Battle that Forged Freemasonry* (Brighton: Sussex Academic Press, 2013), 250.

4 Hereafter, Council signatures will be abbreviated using the first initials of first and last names.

Sam.[l] Skinner Tho.[s] Dade
~~Dev.[x] Bacon~~

Saild from S.[t] Jago

[4] At a Consultation Held on Board the Hartford February 22.[d] 1722/23
present William Fazakerley Esq.[r] Chief &c.[a] Councill
Receiv'd the following paper from the Command.[rs] of the Cambridge, Mountague and Hartford.

**February 1722/23.**

22.[d]

We whose Names are hereunto Subscrib'd, at a Consultation held on board y.[e] Hartford do agree to touch at the Cape of Good Hope, either in Company, or in Case of Separation, as a Rendezvous; there being great probability of finding the Princess Ann there; besides, We think it very much for the benefitt of Our people, considering; the goodness of Our passage hitherto, is likely to afford Us sufficient time for so doing.
(Sign'd) Daniel Small
John Gordon
Francis Nelly

We do agree to the forgoing Resolution; besides, We think it very probable We may meet the homeward bound China Ships; [5] which may afford Us Advices, very advantagious, in Relation to the present Constitution of Affairs, in China.
[signed WF, RM, EG, TC, TD, DB, SS]

24.[th] M.[r] Thomas Attkyns 4[th] of Councill Died.

**March**

26 We arriv'd at the Cape, with the Cambridge, Mountague and Hartford; We found our Consort The Princess Ann, at an Anchor in the Bay; She arriv'd the 21[st] Ins.[t] The Sarum and Carnarvon arriv'd the same day with Us, and the 28[th] Arriv'd the three Outward bound Mocha Ship, and the Desboverie from Bengall.

28[th] Agreed to take on board Our Ships, all the Lead of the Hon.[ble] Companys, Sav'd out of the Nightingale Wreck[5] [6]

5 The Nightingale, rated 480 tons, housed 96 crewmembers and 30 guns. She was bound for Madras on her maiden voyage when she and two EIC vessels on the way back to England, the Addison and

## April

3$^{d}$ Gave Mess.$^{rs}$ Macktt[6], Gilbert[7] and Higginson[8] Receipts, for the Hon.$^{ble}$ Companys Lead, they putt on Board the Duke of Cambridge, Princess Ann and Mountague; being in all, One hundred forty Six piggs, and three Rolls.

At a Consultation Held at the Cape of Good Hope Aprill 4$^{th}$ 1723
We came to a Resolution to Write Our Hon.$^{ble}$ Mast.$^{rs}$ the following Letter.

Cape Good Hope 4$^{th}$ April 1723
Hon.$^{ble}$ S.$^{rs}$

We have the Oppertunity of tendering You Our Dutys from this place, where We arriv'd the 26$^{th}$ Ultimo, with the Cambridge, Mountague & Hardf.$^{d}$ here, We have rejoyn'd the Princess Ann, who was waiting for Us, having lost Us off of S.$^{t}$ Jago. the Sarum and Canarvon, Anchor'd the Same day we did, and y.$^{e}$ 27$^{th}$ came in the three Outward bound Mocha Ships, and the Desboverie from Bengall.

We are taking in all the Lead sav'd out of the Wrecks, being One hundred forty Six piggs, and three Rolls, which we shall carry to Your Hon.$^{rs}$ Account. The Mocha Ships, are taking in the Iron, and those for Madrass the Cloth so when the Addisson's Bales [7] /which We hear are about Sixty / are Sent home, there will be little of Your Concern left here that can be Recover'd.

M.$^{r}$ Thomas Attkyns our 4.$^{th}$ in Councill Died the 24$^{th}$ February; and M.$^{r}$ Skinner is brought in according to your Hon.$^{rs}$ Directions in Our Instructions.

We hear from Batavia, that the Wallpole was there, having lost her passage to China, by falling to Leeward of Java Head.

part of the Batavia Fleet, being 24 Ships Sail'd from this place for Holland, the 26.$^{th}$ Ultimo. there are about 4 more now here; they have added to their misfortunes

---

Chandos, blew aground at the Cape of Good Hope on 5 June 1721. *Records of Fort St. George: Diary and Consultation Book of 1722* (Madras: Superintendent, Government Press, 1930), 99.

**6** William Mackett (dates unknown) was captain of the Nightingale during her initial voyage, this shipwrecked sailing to Madras. He continued to work for the EIC during the 1730s and seems to have settled in Bengal by the early 1750s, where he had several children and served in colonial politics. See Samuel Charles Hill, *List of Europeans and others in the English Factories of Bengal at the time of the Siege of Calcutta in the year 1756* (Calcutta: Office of the Superintendent of Government Printing, 1902), 61–2.

**7** Thomas Gilbert (dates unknown) was captain of the Chandos during her initial voyage, this shipwrecked return sailing from Bombay to London.

**8** Richard Higginson (ca. 1689–1726) was a junior merchant, who sailed on the Nightingale in 1722. His father, Nathaniel Higginson, was the first mayor of Madras and established a mercantile firm in London, to where he relocated in 1700. Richard eventually, himself, was selected first mayor of the Madraspatham in 1726, but he died before the founding charter arrived there in 1727. See Henry Davidson Love, *Vestiges of Old Madras, vol. 2* (London: J. Murray, 1913), 223, 240.

last Year, the Loss of 2 other Ships one near Japon, and the other off of this place[9]: Eleven of their Outward bound Ships arriv'd here two days agoe.

We propose to Sail to Morrow, if the Cap.[tns] have taken on Board all their Lead.

This being all We can Collect worth y.[e] Hon.[rs] Cognizance; We Respectfully Conclude Our Selves,

Your[s] Hon.[rs] most Obed. & Hum.[ble] Serv.[ts]
Sign'd [...] [WF, RM, EG, TC, TD, DB, SS] [8]

8.[th] We Sail'd from the Cape with the Cambridge, Princess Ann, Mountague, and Hartford. Saw the two Madrass Ships, Sarum & Carnarvon und.[er] Sail, coming after Us.

10. Lost Sight of the Madrass Ships.

## June

7[th] Made the Land of Java
Came to Anchor at Muo Bay, in the Streights of Sindy, with Our four Ships.

At a Consultation Holden on Board the Hartford being at Anchor off of Muo Island June 10.[th] 1723.
Present William Fazakerley Esq. Chief &c.[a] Councill
Having some Conference, with the Comm. of the four Ships, in Relation to touching at Batavia; as upon our Declaration to Them that We thought it the Companys Interest, that they should all proceed directly for China; Understanding, that Cap.[tn] Nicholas Luhorne, and Cap.[tn] Francis Nelly, were of contrary opinions: [9] We Came to a Resolution to Send the following Letter to each of them. Vizt

On Board the Hartford Riding in the Streights of Sindy June 10.[th] 1723
Sr.

We think our Selves oblig'd to acquaint You, that it is our opinion you should proceed to China, with all Convinient Speed, without touching at Batavia; But if You have any Reasons to the contrary, we desire You will give Us them in writing that they may be a Justifycation for Us to Our Hon.[ble] Mast.[rs], as well as a Government to any of Us who shall Arrive in China before You, in Relation to compleating the Companys Investm.[ts]

---

**9** These likely refer to the VOC shipwrecks of the frigate *Valkenbos*, off Japan in August 1722, and the *Schonenberg*, just east of Capetown in November 1722. See Jacob Swart, *Verhandelingen en Berigten betrekkelijk het Zeewezen, de Zeevaartkunde en de Daarmede in Verband Staande Wetenschappen* (Amsterdam: G. Hulst Van Keulen, 1857), 226.

We are your Hum:$^{ble}$ Serv.t$^{s}$
(Sign'd) [...] [WF, RM, EG, TC, TD, DB, SS]

[10] At a Consultation Holden on Board the Duke of Cambridge being at Anchor off of Muo Island June 11.$^{th}$ 1723
Present William Fazakerley Esq. Chief &c.$^{a}$ Councill
We have Receiv'd two Letters, one Sign'd by Cap.$^{tn}$ Nicholas Luhorne ~~and~~ the other by Cap.$^{tn}$ Francis Nelly, both Dated this day, from on Board their Respective Ships. Vizt

Gentlemen

I have receiv'd your Letter; I should be very willing to have gone with you to China, but that my Ships Company Wants Refreshments, having had none for this Six Months past; likewise, want to unrigg my Foremast, my Cap Trus being broke; also, having lost Two of my Topmast, and all my Topsail Yards, which obliges me to go to Batavia, for Recruit, I shall make [11] all possible dispatch after you for China:
I am Gentlemen your Oblig'd Hum.$^{ble}$ Serv.$^{t}$
(Sign'd) Nicolas Luhorne
Princess Ann June 11.$^{th}$ 1723.

To William Fazakerley Esq. Presid.$^{t}$ &c.$^{a}$ Councill
June 11.$^{th}$ 1723.
Worshipfull S.$^{rs}$

Yesterday, I receiv'd yours, in which you Acquaint me, that it is your Opinions I should directly proceed for China, without touching at Batavia. You are sensible, that the putting into S.$^{t}$ Jago, and the Cape, was no Refreshments to my People, who have now been near Six months oblig'd to Live on Salt Provissions; however, should run the Risque of proceeding directly, was I not necessitated otherwise, having never a Topmast on board, / except my main topmast which is now up / but what is Sprung; also, two of my Fore-Shrouds are broke in the Hip, which obliges me to lift them all, and do think it highly necessary to lift all others of my standing Rigging; had I known before, that there was an occasion, for my so [12] Speedy arrivall in China, should not have Anchor'd here, but proceeded directly for Batavia; for which Port, design to Sett Sail to Morrow Morning Early, and shall make all possible dispatch after the other Ships, for China. I am Worshipfull S.$^{rs}$ your most Obed.$^{t}$ & Hum.$^{ble}$ Serv.$^{t}$
(Sign'd) Francis Nelly
Ship Hartford in the Streights of Sunday

Finding that against our opinions, they do persist in going to Batavia, we think it necessary, to Come to the following Resolution;

That Mess.[rs] Thomas Dade, Devereux Bacon and Samuel Skinner, should go upon the Princess Ann and Hartford, in Case of any Accident that may happen, in relation to the Companys Affairs, and We do think fitt to Order them, / in case the aforemention'd Commanders, should Stay there, longer than the Space of Ten days./To protest against the said Captains, for Account of The Hon.[ble] Court of Directors of The United East India Company and that they Buy for the Companys Account, Twenty [13] Leagures[10] of Arrack, giving the Captains an Order to Receive them on Board;

Orders Given To Mess.[rs] Dade, Bacon & Skinner. viz.[t]

To Mess.[rs] Thomas Dade, Devereux Bacon, and Samuel Skinner.
Gentlemen.

Since Capt.[tn] Nicholas Luhorne and Cap.[tn] Francis Nelly, have declar'd to Us in Writing, that they will touch at Batavia, Contrary to Our Opinions, given to Each of them in writing; We think it Consonant to Our Instructions, to Order you, to go upon their Ships, in Case of any Accident that might happen to the Companys affairs.

We would have You perswade them to Stay as little time as possible there, but in Case they should Exceed Ten days, then, You are to protest against them, for the Account of The Hon.[ble] Court of Directors, of The United East India Company [14] and to give them Notice of it, beforehand in Writing, because their Delays there, may very much Impeed the Companys Affairs in China.

We would likewise have You Buy Twenty Leagures of Arrack, for the Companys Account; and, give the Captains Orders, to Receive them on Board.

As, We do by this Order, give You as full a power to Act, as if We were all present, We don't doubt, / in Case of any necessity / of Your Acting every thing that may be for the Company Interest.

We are Gentlemen your Hum.[ble] Serv.[ts]
(Sign'd) [WF, RM, EG, TC]

Upon Captain Small's mentioning to Us, that the Companys Instructions to him as Commodore, do Imply, that he should not purposely leave any of the other Ships; We Come to a Resolution of Sending him, the following Order to proceed directly for China, for his Indimnification.

---

**10** A leagure, or leaguer, was a large cask of variable size, used to measure liquids. At one point, it equated to 159 imperial gallons.

[15] To Cap.[tn] Daniel Small Command.[r] of the Duke of Cambridge
Sir,

It is our Opinion, that all the Ships should proceed directly for China, without touching at Batavia; but, since Cap.[tn] Nicholas Luhorne, and Captain Francis Nelly have Acquainted Us they are of Contrary Sentiments, and You declare that the Companys Instructions to You as Commod.[r] Express Your not parting with any of the Ships, We send You this, to Desire and Order You to proceed directly for China; and We will Indemnifie You, for so doing
We are your Hum.[ble] Serv.[ts]
(Sign'd) [...] [WF, RM, EG, TC, TD, DB, SS] [16]
On Board the Duke of Cambridge Riding at Anchor off of Mew Island 11.[th] June 1723

12.[th] Last Night the Princess Ann & Hartford Saild for Batavia.
This Morning The Cambridge & Mountague Weigh'd & Saild from Mew Bay for Canton.

**July**

15.[th] Our Ships Arriv'd near Boca Tygris where We are Inform'd that the Wallpolee had been arriv'd at Wampoo about two Months and that there was a Manila Ship there likewise w.[ch] had been detain'd a whole Year by y.[e] Mandareens on Acco.[t] of mak.[ng] fire Arms in China against which there is a Strict prohibiton by y.[e] Laws of the Country[11]. We came to a Resolution Immediately to Send one of y.[e] Pinnaces up to Canton to Acquaint the SupraCargos of y[e] Wallpole of Our Arrivale hoping that they would as soon as possible Send Us an Acco.[t] of the pres.[t] posture of Affairs at Canton.

16. This morning We took our Leaves of the Ships in Our Pinnace thinking it proper to make all y[e] convenient Speed we possibly could up to Canton because upon our making the Coast of China we descry'd two Ships which by the Acco.[t] We Rec'd of a Countrey Ship in the Streights of Banca must undoubtedly be the two Ostenders[12] under y[e] Direction of Cap.[tn] Hall[13], and we did believe the Antici-

11 It is unclear which incident the authors refer to here.
12 These were the Marquis de Prié and St. Joseph. See the edited "Report of the Voyage of the Marquis de Prié and St. Joseph from Ostend to Canton in 1723" in this volume.
13 Thomas Hall (1692–1748) was an English merchant, who began his career as a captain in the EIC and joined the Ostend Company as a supercargo in 1718. He eventually established a successful tea import firm in London, while regularly exporting to the Dutch Republic, in the 1730s. To do so, he first had to pay a £2,100 indemnity for damages to the EIC caused by his Ostend adventures. Gill, Merchants.

pating of them a little time might be of Consequence to Our Affairs and if the Chineess should know of their being so near at our Heels it would infallably raise the price of Goods, in our passage up We mett M.r Pratt[14] who came to Congratulate Us on Our Arrivale He inform'd us that M.r Savage[15] & himself had directed a Letter to the SupraCargos of the Outward bound Comp.as Ships in Case [17] They should ~~touch~~ Send a shore at Maccao with Advice to them to detain their Ships there some time because the affairs in China were in a very unsettled Condition since the death of the late Emperor[16], that the Creditt of the Merch.ts who us'd to deal with the English was almost Ruin'd by the Overbearing power & Covetuousness of the Mandareens who would only lett those trade with the Europeans who would lett them be large Sharers in their Contracts We told M.r Pratt the Ships were too farr advanc'd to Order them back to Maccao but in Considiration of what he Acquainted Us with Send y.e Underwritten Order to Cap.tns Small & Gordon.

On Board the Wallpole at Wampoo 16th July 1723
Gentlemen

We are inform'd by M.r Pratt one of the SupraCargos of the Walpole that the Commerce at Canton is very precarious by the reason of the Impositions of the Mandareens therefore think it necessary to order you not to pass Over the uppermost Barr w.th Your Ships till You Receive farthur Directions from Us, Upon Our Arrivall at Canton You may Expect to hear from Us again when We have Inquir'd more particularly into this affair.

We are your hum.ble Serv.ts
(Sign'd) [...] [WF, RM, EG, TC]
To Cap.tn Daniel Small Command.r of the Duke of Cambridge & Cap.tn John Gordon Comman.r of the Mountague

[18] At a Consultation Holden at Canton July 17.th 1723.
Present William Fazakerley, Esq.r Richard Morton Edmund Godfrey Thomas Carter
We open'd and read our packetts from the Secrett Committee & took into consideration each paragraph whereby we find it pretty much intended that two of the Ships should be dispatcht with proper loadings for Bombay & Fort S.t George neither can We Considering the present circumstances of affairs at Canton be of a contrary opinion

---

**14** Edward Pratt (dates unknown) was a supercargo on the Sir Robert Walpole in 1723.
**15** John Savage (dates unknown) was a supercargo on the Sir Robert Walpole in 1723.
**16** The K'ang-hsi Emperor (1654–1722) was the second ruler in the Manchu Ch'ing Dynasty. It was under his reign that the Jingdezhen porcelain industry was reorganized for export trade and the Canton Hang, the precursor of the Thirteen *Co-Hong*, was established. See Jonathan Spence, "The K'ang-hsi Reign", in: Cambridge History of China, vol. 9.1, 120–82.

We shall endeavour to purchase as early as possible an advantagious Cargo for the Ship bound to Bombay and as We have a liberty to Load Tea & other Valuable Goods on the Ship bound to Fort S.[t] George we can Dispatch her from hence to arrive so early there that she may be sent home this Season & then it will be the same if she went directly from thence to Europe because this Deviation will Lay the Comp.[a] under no obligation to pay Demorage[17] & since M.[r] Fazakerley does assure Us that in the private packett from the secrett Committee directed to himself that the Ships Cambridge & Mountague are therein recommended to go the Round about Voyage, we have resolv'd that the Cambridge Captain Small shall go Consign'd to the President & Councill at Bombay & the Mountague [19] Captain Gordon to the Presid.[t] & Councill of Fort S.[t] George besides by the estimate we have made of our Cargoes we find that with the Tea we shall put aboard the Mountague the Hartford & Princess Ann will be able to Carry the whole quantity order'd in Our Instructions.
[signed WF, RM, EG, TC]

Since the above we have had several discourses with M.[r] Savage & M.[r] Pratt in relation to the Creditt of the Merch.[ts] & Prices of Goods they Acquainted Us that by the Wall-pooles early arrivall hire & being a single Ship they had an oppertunity of transacting their affairs at very reasonable prices that the arrivale of our two Ships & the notice of two more Coming would make considerable alterations[18] that they had made their Contract with Cumshaw[19] as being now the only person that could be dealt with, w.[th] any safety they added that the rest of the Merch.[ts] were by the Oppression of the Mandareens & owed them great summs of Mony, & that they believ'd he would hardly Contract for all our Ships they mention'd to Us Sending one or two of our Ships to Amoy where they said our buisness might be easily transacted and the doing of it [20] would frighten the Mandareens & the Merch.[ts] & oblige them to treat Us better for the future but we are of opinion that consonant to Charterparty we have no power to order any of the Ships from this Port without the Captains Consent to any other in China besides as Amoy is a port that has been so long unfrequented by any Europe

17 For more on EIC charter parties, see page 23, ft. 20.

18 Prices frequently increased as news of additional incoming European ships spread in Canton. The ship(s) that arrived before this knowledge usually had a considerable advantage in making contracts. Parmentier, Tea Time, 100.

19 Tan Suqua (d. 1761), or Cumshaw, was a *hong* merchant, with whom the EIC primarily traded in the 1720s. Suqua began his career in Amoy in the 1700s, moving to Canton in 1703. There, he began to be engaged by Europeans in 1716 and gained a near monopoly of the trade by 1730. In 1731, his success was temporarily set back, when two competitors accused him and his EIC contacts of inflating their books. He was imprisoned several times for this and other dealings with foreigners. Van Dyke, Merchants, 79–102; Weng Eang Cheong, "The Age of Suqua, 1720–1759: the Early Hong Merchants", in: *Asian Trade Routes: Continental and Maritime*, ed. Karl Reinhold Haellquist (London: Curzon Press, 1991), 217–30.

Shipping & consequently no Merch.[ts] Accustom'd to trade with them are there it would be almost Impracticable for the first Ship that went to make her Investm.[t] so as to save her passage home that Season & being inform'd here that goods that Goods for this Year & the last are much more reasonable than has been for many Years before We resolv'd to propose to Cumshaw the doing our buisness as being the most Credillable & to speak truly the only Merch.[t] that could go through so large a Contract hopeing that we might be able to effect it with him before the Arrivall of the Ostenders whom We suspected to be at our heels but did not know but by falling to the Eastw.[d] or some accident or other might be some distance of time after Us.

Receiv'd the following Letter from our Cap.[tn] Viz.[t]
Sirs,

Conformable to your Order this day Rec.[d] we have Moor'd our Ships Just without the Barr, shall now wait your further directions being oblig'd by Charterparty & Acquaint you of our Arrivall make use of this oppertunity the two Ostenders are Just without the boak this Evening we have nothing further to advice but remaine with all Respect
S.[rs] your hum.[ble] Serv.[ts]
Dan.[l] Small John Gordon
near y.[e] barr July 16. 1723
To William Fazakerley Esq. & Presid.[t] &c.[a] Councill

[21] To which we Sent y.[e] following Answer
Canton 17.[th] July 1723
Cap.[tn] Small Cap.[tn] Gordon
Gentlemen

We Receiv'd Yours & according to the Import there of Yo.[r] Demorage shall Commence the same as if at Wampoo, We not having been to wait on the Hoppoo Can't tell how long may be oblig'd to keep your Ships where they now are but should be glad of your Company here as soon as you think Convenient we are your
hum.[ble] Serv.[ts]
(Sign'd) [WF, RM, EG, TC]
To Cap.[tn] Daniel Small Cap.[tn] John Gordon On board their Ships in the River of Canton

This Evening the Ostinders pinnice Came up w.th Cap.tn Hall Command.r of the Marq.s D'prie[20] Cap.tn Pyke[21] Comman.r of the S.t Joseph[22] & M.r Robert Hewer[23]
They are all three English Men SupraCargoes of the two Ships the addition of these two Ships to ours has made a great uproar amongst the Merchants at Canton whom We had keept entirely ignorant of their Coming till the minuett of their Arrivall. Their Capitall is near a hundred Thousand pounds & their Investm.t we hear will be in Tea & wrought Silks. [22]

19th This day went to the Hoppo & Insisted on the following priviledges & all others usually granted to the English viz.t[24]

| | |
|---|---|
| First | That we might speak with him at all times without waiting. |
| Secondly | That we may have a Chop of Free Trade & his protection against Insults |
| Thirdly | that we may Chuse our own Lingust Compradore[25] & Serv.ts |
| Fourthly | That the SupraCargoes & Command.rs of the Ships pass the Hoppo boats with the Flagg flying in the boat without being searcht |
| Fifthly | That we have Liberty to provide all Naval Stores without Duty or Imposition |
| Sixthly | That we have our Chop for departure without delay or Embarrasment. |

Having receiv'd satisfactory promisses to all our demands, we gave an Order to Our Ships to Come to their Moorings at Wampoo

20.th Ever since the 16.th we have had frequent Conferences w.th Cumshaw in relation to Compleating Contract with him. he promiss'd us to under take our Buis-

**20** The Marquis de Prié, rated 300 to 360 tons, was captained by Englishman Thomas Hall. She housed 28 guns during her 1723 sailing to Canton. Her chief supercargo was Englishman Robert Hewer. Gill, Merchants, 19–28.

**21** Isaac Pyke (d. 1738) was an Ostend and EIC captain in the 1720s, as well as prior governor of St. Helena from 1714 to 1719. He again held the latter role from 1731 until his 1738 death. See *Isaac Pyke: Twice Governor of St. Helena* (London: Taylor and Francis, 1937).

**22** The St. Joseph rated slightly less than the Marquis de Prié. Her chief supercargo was Henri Carlos Ghyselinck. Gill, Merchants, 19–28; Parmentier, Private, 93.

**23** Robert Hewer (dates unknown) was an English merchant who served as supercargo and later chief supercargo on several GIC vessels in the 1720s. After experiencing severe financial troubles during the South Sea Bubble in 1720, Hewer wrote his acquaintance Thomas Hall, who procured for him work with the Ostend company. The Englishman regained his fortune through the East Indies trade by 1728 and returned to England – settling in Plymouth – in 1731, after an indemnity payment to the EIC of £750. Gill, Merchants, 47–50.

**24** For another sampling of such requests, see pages 372–4. Also, Van Dyke, Canton Trade, 20–1.

**25** A comprador was a Chinese supplier, who obtained routine goods and services either for European supercargoes or their associated ships. He also served as an intermediary between EIC traders and the Hoppo. Van Dyke, Canton Trade, 51–75; Morse, Chronicles, vol. 1, 179.

ness so reasonably as he could but that y.e Arrivall of the two Ostenders would hinder Us buying our goods at so reasonable a rate as We expected. We Consider'd we lay [23] Under a necessity of Coming to a speedy Conclusion because the Quantity of wrought Silks we had to buy would take up a great deal of time in making[26], & if we did not purchase our Bombay & Madrass Cargoes early the Arrivall of any Ships from those parts would vastly Inhanse the price of Goods proper for those Marketts, besides we Consider'd that the price he ask'd for the goods we should carry for Europe was not at all unreasonable considering the price of former Years & much cheaper than we could Expect before our Arrivall. We knew if we delay'd Our Coming to an agreement ~~with him~~ ever so long He must be the Merchant at last that we should be Oblig'd to Contract with for the running about to the Merchants with so large a Sum to lay out would have only rais'd the price of Goods upon Us & Confounded Us at last upon w.ch consideration came to an agreement with him to furnish Us with the following Goods This will Reduce our buisness under our thumbs & leave us a sufficient quantity of mony to lay out should we find at the latter end the price of goods to lower upon Us.

Acco.t of the Contract made with Cumshaw in Canton this 20.th July 1723.
Bohea Tea five thousand five hundred peculls at Tal.s 27 p. Pec.l
Tea Singlo 1000 peculls at Tales 16. p. Pecull
Nainkeen[27] Raw Silk Head S.t 100 pec.l at 145 p. D.o
Taffaties 25 to 26 Ta.s w.th 3000 pieces 6 Hand Long 38 Cov.ds[28] broad 2.Co2.Pts[29] at Ta. 4.3.M [24]
Gorgoroons 800 pieces 33 to 34 Tales Weight long 38 Covids broad 2 Cov.ds at Ta.s 5.1.M
Poysees 1000 p.s 38 Cov.ds long, broad 2 Cov.ds w.th 33 ta.s at Ta.s 5.9.
Bed Damasks 200 p.s 45 Ta.s W.th Long 38 Cov.ds broad 2 Cov.ds at Ta.s 7.5.M
Masquerades 200 p.s
Sampasses 100 p.s Long 38 Cov.ds broad 1.Cov5.Punt. a Ta.s
Quicksilver 300 peculls certain if to be gott 400 at 42 tales p. pecull

26 For more on contemporary silk production, see Shelagh Vainker, *Chinese Silk: a Cultural History* (London: The British Museum Press, 2004), 172–98; Gang Deong, *Maritime Sector, Institutions, and Sea Power of Premodern China* (Westport, CT: Greenwood Press, 1999), 66–70.

27 Nankeen was a durable cotton cloth, noted for its yellow coloring and used for men's trousers in eighteenth-century Europe.

28 A covid, or cubit, was a unit of linear measurement employed in China. One covid ranged from 14.1 to 14.6 English inches. Van Dyke, Canton Trade, 190, ft. 24.

29 A punto was a unit of linear measurement employed in China, equalling roughly 1.3 English inches or 1/10 covids. See Francis J. Grund, *The Merchant's Assistant* (Boston: Hilliard, Gray & Company, 1834), 91.

Virmillion[30] 100 pec.$^{l}$ at Ta.$^{s}$ 42 p. pecull
Sugar[31] 4000 pec.$^{l}$ at Ta.$^{s}$ 2.9.$^{M}$_ p.D.$^{o}$
Sugar Candy 1800 pec.$^{l}$ at Ta.$^{s}$. 5.9._ p.D.$^{o}$
China Root 400 pec.$^{l}$ at Ta.$^{s}$ 1.8_ p. D.$^{o}$
Allum[32] 1500 pec.$^{l}$ at Ta.$^{s}$ 1.6_ p. D.$^{o}$
Tutenague 2000 pec.$^{l}$ at Ta.$^{s}$ 6._ p. D.$^{o}$
Tea Peckho 100 pec.$^{l}$ at Ta.$^{s}$ 45._ p.D.$^{o}$ if very fine else none
Tea Congho 200 pec.$^{l}$ at Ta.$^{s}$ 45._ p. D.$^{o}$
Tea Bing 100 pec.$^{l}$ to agree y$^{e}$ price when See the Tea

He is to take our Cloth Lead & perpetuanos[33] all at prime Cost w.$^{ch}$ considering the Quality & little demand for those goods we take to be reasonable the SupraCargoes / as we are Inform'd / selling them last year at a great Loss

We have further agreed that he shall buy [25] for Us for the Companys Acco.$^{t}$ One or two hundred pieces of Gold at a reasonable rate in case we should want them [signed WF, RM, EG, TC]

25. This day an Armenian[34] ship came up to the River She was here last Year & went to Batavia & is return'd from batavia She is about 300 Tonns & has brought

---

**30** Vermilion is a bright red or scarlet coloring, made from powdered cinnabar. It was used in Chinese lacquerware but additionally served as a paint, textile dye and cosmetic in Europe.

**31** China had been active in the intra-Asian sugar trade since the mid-1500s, when its traders began directly exporting the foodstuff to Japan. By the 1720s, country ships regularly shipped sugar to India in exchange for silver and textiles, and transoceanic vessels transported limited supplies back to Europe. Mazumdar, Sugar, 60–119.

**32** Alum is a mineral, used by textile dyers in Asia and Europe since the medieval period to maintain fabric dyes. It was mined and used in China by the sixth century. Europeans also employed alum as ballast and as commodity for the country trade, especially to regional textile producers. See George Bryan Souza, "Country Trade and Chinese Alum: Raw Material Supply in Asia's Textile Production in the Seventeenth and Eighteenth Centuries", in: *Revista da Cultura* 11 (2004), 136–53.

**33** Perpetuanos, also known as purpetts, were hard-wearing, English-made woolens, retailed by overseas traders in Africa and Asia.

**34** Armenian traders, united by a shared ancestral homeland, were based out of New Julfa, a suburb of Isfahan, Persia. They traded throughout Europe, Africa and Asia during the medieval and early modern eras. For more on their extensive networks, see Baladouni and Makepeace, Armenian Merchants; Sebouh Aslanian, *From the Indian Ocean to the Mediterranean: the Global Trade Networks of Armenian Merchants from New Julfa* (Berkeley: University of California Press, 2011); Michel Aghassian and Kéram Kévonian, "The Armenian Merchant Network: Overall Autonomy and Local Integration", in: Merchants, eds. Chaudhury and Morineau, 74–94.

here about 1000 Peculls Pepper[35] a little Spice & some Tinn[36] the Master of her Acquaints Us that upon sailing out of batavia he Saw our two Ships, the Princess Ann & Hartford standing in so we have reason to Expect them here dayly

26. We waited on the Hoppo to Wampoo to take the Measuarage of our Ships w.ch was as follows

| | |
|---|---|
| Duke of Cambridge | 71 Covids 2 puntos Long |
| | 20 Covds ... 7 pts ... broad |
| Mountague | 67 Covds ... 6 pts ... Long |
| | 21 Covds ... 5 pts ... broad |

27. Finding the Hoppo notwithstanding the fair promises he had given Us / to be very insisting & very troublesome to Us in our buisness we thought it proper to send the following Letter to Boca Tygris to detain our two Ships from Batavia there till [26] further Orders. In order to bring him to more Reasonable Complyances

Canton July 27.th 1723
Gentlemen

Since our Arrival here we have meet with unexpected troubles from the Hoppo who has refus'd to grant Us the Priviledges due to all English Ships at this Port, we therefore think fitt to Order You not to come up with your Ships to Wampoo, but bring them to an Anchor at Boca Tygris or there about & not to Weigh from thence till you receive further Directions from
your hum.ble Serv.ts
(Sign'd) [WF, RM, EG, TC]
To Cap.tn Rich.d Luhorne & Cap.tn Francis Nelly Command.rs of the Princess Ann & Hartford.

Gave directions to Cap.tn Small & Cap.tn Gordon that each of them should send up ten Chests of the Comp.es Treasure in their Longboats Ordering it to be well Buoy'd & guarded

28. This day receiv'd into our Factory 20 Chests of Treasure as before Order'd

---

35 European demands for eastern spices only increased after initial contact in the Middle Ages. Since the late 1500s, imports focused on cloves, nutmeg, mace, cinnamon and especially pepper. Chaudhuri, English East India Company, 140–72; Freedman, Out of the East; Johnson, German Discovery.

36 Tin, originating in Indonesia, was another popular commodity in the country trade and used as ballast by European ships. Indian craftsmen employed the metal in coating household utensils and ceramics. Chinese tea producers, meanwhile, used tin to make canisters for transporting dried leaves. Chaudhuri, Trading World, 206, 221, 249; Van Dyke, Merchants, 22.

## August

4.th Wrote Captain Small the following Order for ten Chests of the Companys Treasure

Canton 4.th Aug.st 1723
Sir,
We hereby Order you to send up by your Longboat ten Chests of the Companys treasure taking care that [27] it be well buoy'd & that there be a sufficient number of hands to Secure it we are
Your most hum.ble Serv.ts
(Sign'd) [WF, RM, EG, TC]
To Cap.tn Daniel Small on board His Ship at Wampoo

5th Receiv'd the ten Chests of treasure agreeable to the above order & Weigh'd them off to Cumshaw & likewise the 20 Chests before receiv'd he desereing Us to advance it him on Acco.t of our Contract.

10.th This day our two Ships the Hartford & Princess Ann arriv'd from Batavia & came to an Anchor in the River below the first Barr, in the Evening M.r Wheatty came up & gave Us an Acco.t that Cap.tn Luhorne died y.e 24 July at the same time arriv'd the King George a Countrey Ship from Madrass the SupraCargoes on board her are Mess.rs Naish Colebrooke[37] & Barnes[38] her Lading is Chiefly pepper & a little Sandall Wood[39] & the Amo.t of their Stock is about forty odd thousand Pagodas

11.th Receiv'd a Letter from Mess.rs Dade & Skinner dated yesterday on Board the Hartford near Boca Tygris wherein they Acquaint Us of their arrival there that Morning that three days before they fell in Comp.a with a Countrey Ship call'd y.e King George Mess.rs Naish Colebrooke & Barnes SupraCargoes Cap.tn Wybourg[40] Comm.r [28] who inform'd them of the Boone Friggotts being at Madrass from whence She is to proceed to this place that the day before a small Moors Ship from the Coast of Mallabar[41] passt by them towards Wampoo & that the 24.th Ultimo Cap.tn Nicholas Luhorne Died of a violent Feavor. [...]

---

**37** Person unknown.

**38** Person unknown.

**39** Sandalwood is a fine-grained wood, native to India and eastern Indonesia. It was much demanded in the country trade for its use as incense in religious ceremonies and for its believed medicinal values.

**40** Person unknown.

**41** The Malabar Coast is located in southwestern India. The region not only attracted the commercial interest of the Portuguese, Dutch and English in the early 1700s, notably to supply pepper, spices (cardamom and cinnamon) and cotton cloths. It also formed a key entrepôt in the trading networks of

12.[th] Mess.[rs] Dade, Bacon & Skinner Arriv'd at our Factory & deliver'd in an Acco.[t] of their transactions since their departure from Mew Bay Sent the Cap.[tns] of the Hartford & Princess Ann the following Order to bring their Ships up to Wampoo Viz.[t]

Canton Aug.[t] 12.[th] 1723.
Gentlemen
By Order of the Chief & Councill You are hereby directed to proceed with your Respective Ships to their Moorings at Wampoo w.[th] all Convenient Speed I am Gentlemen your hum.[ble] Serv.[t]
(Sign'd) Sam.[l] Skinner
To Cap.[tn] Francis Nelly & Cap.[tn] Charles Hudson[42] On board their respective Ships near y[e] First Barr

[29] At a Consultation Holden at Canton Aug.[t] 16.[th] 1723.
Present William Fazakerley Esq. Rich.[d] Morton Edmund Godfrey Thomas Carter Thomas Dade Devereux Bacon Samuel Skinner
Read over all the preceeding Transactions in this Diary of Mess.[rs] William Fazakerley Richard Morton Edmund Godfrey & Thomas Carter and are of opinion they have Acted to their Utmost for the Interest of Our Hon.[ble] Masters
[signed TD, DB, SS] [30]

18.[th] This day the Hoppo went to Wampoo and measur'd our two Ships Hartford & Princess Ann which were as follows

| | | | | |
|---|---|---|---|---|
| Hartford a 2.[d] Rate | Long | 71 Cov.[ds] | 20 | puntos |
| | Broad | 22 Cov.[ds] | 3 | puntos |
| Princess Ann a 3.[d] Rate | Long | 66 Covids | 4 ½ | puntos |
| | Broad | 20 | 6 | |

the Islamic world. See Ashin Das Gupta, *Malabar in Asian Trade: 1740–1800* (New York: Cambridge UP, 1967).

**42** Charles Hudson (d. 1773) took over command of the Princess Ann, after the death of Nicholas Luhorne in 1723. He was born into a wealthy and titled family from Leicestershire, England and eventually became a long-term captain for the EIC. Chaudhuri, Trade, 144.

20.th Came up to Wampoo the small Moors[43] Ship before mention'd from Siam[44] Sent Cap.tn Francis Nelly & Cap.tn Charles Hudson each of them an Order for five Chests of the Hon.ble Companys Treasure Viz.t

Canton 20th Aug.t 1723
Cap.tn Francis Nelly
Sir,

We hereby Order you to Send up by your Longboat five Chests of the Hon.ble Companys Treasure taking Care that it be well Buoy'd & that there be sufficient number of men to Secure it We are
Sr. your hum.ble Serv.ts
(Sign'd) [TC, TD, DB, SS]
To Cap.tn Francis Nelly on board his Ship at Wampoo

[31] Canton August 20.th 1723
Cap.tn Charles Hudson
Sir,

We hereby Order you to Send up by your Long boat five Chests of the Hon.ble Companys Treasure taking Care that it be well Buoy'd and that there be a sufficient number of Men to Secure it We are
your hum.ble Serv.ts
(Sign'd) [TC, TD, DB, SS]
To Cap.tn Charles Hudson on Board his Ship at Wampoo

21. Receiv'd the treasure mention'd on the above Orders & deliver'd Eight of them to Cumshaw the other two took into Cash.
Cumshaw desiring that we would Send him all the Coarse Cloth & all the Purpetts Except Scarlett as soon as possible he having present occasion for them Sent Cap.tns Small & Gordon the following Orders

43 Islamic trading states were established in Sumatra, Java, Malacca and the Moluccas as well as around the Indian Ocean by the thirteenth century. They were crucial consumers of Chinese porcelain by the sixteenth century, and EIC merchants regularly noted their presence in Canton in the 1720s. See Carl T. Smith and Paul A. Van Dyke, "Muslims in the Pearl River Delta, 1700 to 1930", in: *Review of Culture* 10 (2004), 6–15; Chaudhuri, Trading World, 191–213; M.N. Pearson, *Merchants and Rulers in Gujarat: the Response to the Portuguese in the Sixteenth Century* (Berkeley: University of California Press, 1976).

44 Siam, or the Ayutthaya Kingdom, was located on the modern-day Gulf of Thailand from 1351 to 1767. It began to attract Portuguese and Dutch traders in the sixteenth century. See Marc Frey, "Eurasian Interactions: Siam and the Dutch East India Company during the Seventeenth Century", in: *Southeast Asian Historiography: Unravelling the Myths*, ed. Volker Grabowsky (Bangkok: River Books, 2011), 162–75.

Canton Aug.[t] 22. 1723.
Cap.[tn] John Gordon
S.[r],

You are hereby Order'd to Send up by this Boat the following Bales of the Companys Cloth [32] and Purpetts with a sufficient Number of Men to secure them We are Sir your hum.[ble] Sev.[ts]
(Sign'd) [RM, ~~EG~~, TC, TD, DB, SS]

Broad Cloth. Viz.[t]
N.[o] 977@980. 1003@1005. 1007@1012. being ~~13 Bl.~~[s]
Purpetts viz.[t]
N.[o] 9@15. 21@30. 127@136 & 142. being 28 Bales

Canton August 22[d] 1723
Cap.[tn] Daniel Small
Sir

You are hereby Order'd to Send up by this Boat the following Bl.[s] of the Companys Cloth & purpetts with a sufficient number of Men to Secure them We are
Sir your hum.[ble] Serv.[ts]
(Sign'd) [RM, TC, TD, DB, SS]

Broad Cloth viz.[t]
N.[o] 966@976. & 1002 being 12 Bales
Purpetts viz.[t]
N.[o] 1@8. 16@20. 117@126. 137@141. 82.103 & 104 being 31 Bales

[33] At a Consultation Holden at Canton August 24. 1723.
Present William Fazakerley Esq. Chief Richard Morton Edmund Godfrey Thomas Carter Thomas Dade Devereux Bacon Samuel Skinner
Read over the minutes of the transactions of Mess.[rs] Dade, Bacon & Skinner from Their leaving Us at Mew Island to Their Arrivall in China which we approv'd of and Confirm'd & Order'd to be Enter'd Underneath

Diary of Thomas Dade Devereux Bacon and Samuel Skinner Commencing 11.[th] June 1723.

This day We Receiv'd an Order from William Fazakerley Esq. Chief &c.[a] Councill for Mannaging the Affairs of the Hon.[ble] United Company of Merchants of England Trading to the East Indies in China Importing That as Captain Nicholas Luhorne Command.[r] of the Princess Ann and Captain Francis Nelly Command.[r] of the Hartford were determin'd to go to Batavia [34] They thought it proper to Order Us to go upon their Ships in Case of any Accident that might happen to the Companys Affairs

June

12.th Late last night we Sail'd from Muo Bay with the Princess Ann & Hartford for Batavia

18.th Arriv'd in the Road of Batavia, went ashore and waited on the Shabandarr[45] who gave Us liberty to Lodge on Shore. Receiv'd a Letter Sign'd by Mess.rs Savage and Pratt SupraCargoes on board the Wallpoole dated y.e 1.st April last w.ch day they Sail'd hence for Canton after a stay here of 4 months were they were inform'd of the Death of old Emperour of China.

20.th It being mention'd in Our Orders from William Fazakerley Esq.r Chief &c.a Councill to purchase twenty Leagures of Arrack for the Companys Acco.t / after having spoke to the Shabandarr / We drew up a petition to the Generall & Councill of this place[46] w.ch we deliver'd to the Shabandarr who promiss'd to tender it the first Consultation w.ch he said would be tomorrow night.

22.d Waited on the shabandarr to know what Answer was given to our Petition he then told Us the Councill would not sitt till the 25.th at night We then Acquainted him our time was very short & desir'd he would lett Us know the Generall & Councill Resolution as soon as possible & that when y.e Cap.tns were ready to sail we should not not stay an hour on any Acco.t [35]

24th Agreeable to the directions Receiv'd from Will.m Fazakerley Esq. Chief &c.a Councill Sent Captain Nichol.as Luhorne & Captain Francis Nelly the follow.g Letter

Batavia June 24.th 1723.
Sir,

By the directions given to Us by William Fazakerley Esq. Chief &c.a Councill for Mannaging the Affairs of the Hon.ble United East India Company in China We are to give You notice / as we hereby do / That if you continue at this Port longer than y.e space of ten days to be Reckon'd from Your first arrivall We shall be oblig'd to protest against you in the name & for y.e Acco.t of the Hon.ble The Court of Directors of the

45 *Shahbandar* was a term used throughout the Indian Ocean and South China Sea, to designate the office of harbormaster. At Batavia, the *shahbandar* met with newly arriving vessels, collected import-export duties, and monitored waterfront trade. See Leonard Blussé, "John Chinaman Abroad: Chinese Sailors in the Service of the VOC", in: *Promises and Predicaments: Trade and Entrepreneurship in Colonial and Independent Indonesia in the 19th and 20th Centuries*, eds. Alicia Schrikker and Jeroen Touwen (Singapore: National University of Singapore, 2015), 105.

46 The VOC managed its empire in the Indian Ocean and South China Sea via extensive bureaucratic networks, based in Batavia. There, a governor-general, council of merchants, supreme court and bookkeeper made commercial and political decisions for the company, which they reported back to Europe annually. Ward, Networks, 64–70. For a persepctive from ca. 1705, see Pieter van Dam, *Beschryvinge van de Oostindische Compagnie*, eds. F.W. Stapel and C.W. Th. van Boetzelaer (The Hague: Nijhoff, 1977).

United Company of Merchants of England Trading to the East Indies But as any delays here may very much Impeed Their Affairs in China We don't doubt of Your making all possible Dispatch We are
Sir, your hum.[ble] Serv.[ts]
(Sign'd) [TD, DB, SS]
to Cap.[tn] Nicholas Luhorne Command.[r] of the Ship Princess Ann

The same w.[th] y[e] foregoing Mutatis Mutandis was Sent to Cap.[tn] Francis Nelly Command.[r] of Ship Hartford [36]

26.[th] This morning We waited on the Shabandarr again when he told Us he had deliver'd our Petition to the Generall & Councill in Consequence of which We had Liberty to purchase Six Leag.[rs] Arrack and not more in Answer to which we told him we were not a little surpriz'd we should be allow'd but so small a quantity in proportion to the Necessity we had for it which was Sett forth in our petition since it was for Our Hon.[ble] Mast.[rs] Acco.[t] & further told him we should be Oblig'd to Acquaint Our Employers of it. he said he was very sorry but that it was not in his power to help it.
Finding we could not have liberty to purchase more than Six Leag.[rs] We Resolv'd to argee with a Chinaman who y.[e] Shabandarr Recommended to Us / no one else being able to Serve Us / for y.[e] Remain.[g] fourteen Leag.[rs] but he could help Us to no more than twelve which he agreed to put on board at forty Rix Doll.[rs] p. Leag.[rs] to be paid when y.[e] Arrack was all on board & not before.

July
1.[st] Sent Captain Nelly y.[e] following Order to Receive the Arrack on board his Ship

To Cap.[tn] Francis Nelly Command.[r] of the Hartford. [37]
Sir,
Please to Receive on board Eighteen Leagures Arrack in Six Large & thirty two small Casks Mark'd as & Marg.[t] for Acco.[t] of The Hon.[ble] United East India Company
We are your hum.[ble] Serv.[ts]
(Sign'd) [TD, DB, SS]
Batavia July 1[st] 1723

2.[d] Being inform'd by Captain Nelly that all the Arrack was safe on board his Ship we paid the Chinaman for it and have made William Fazakerley Esq. Chief &c.[a] Councill D.[rs] for the same
3.[d] Being Inform'd that some Dutch Ships would hence for Europe in Octob.[r] next we wrote Our Hon.[ble] Mast.[rs] the following Letter.

Batavia 3.$^{d}$ July 1723
Hon.$^{ble}$ S.$^{rs}$

We take this Oppertunity to Acquaint You of Our Arrivall in the Streights of Sindy the 7.$^{th}$ June with your four China Ships were we were inform'd by people who came on Board in prows that two Ships from Europe pass'd by to the Eastw.$^{d}$ 3 days before and Supposing them to be Ostenders a Consultation was call'd at which it was agreed to Acquaint the Cap.$^{tns}$ [38] in writing it would be for Your Hon.$^{rs}$ Interest all the Ships should proceed directly for China without Touching at Batavia but Captain Nicholas Luhorne & Captain Francis Nelly Acquainting Us they must of necessity go there. agreeable to y.$^{e}$ Hon.$^{rs}$ Instructions it was Resolv'd that Mess.$^{rs}$ William Fazakerley Eq. Chief and the three next of Council should go upon the Cambridge and Mountague which will make y.$^{e}$ best of their way for China to hasten y.$^{r}$ Hon.$^{rs}$ Investm.$^{t}$

Upon our arrivall here y.$^{e}$ 18.$^{th}$ Ultimo We Receiv'd a Letter sign'd by Mess.$^{rs}$ Savage & Pratt Supra Cargoes on board the Wallpole dated y.$^{e}$ 1$^{st}$ Aprill last / which day they Sail'd hence for Canton in which they Acquaint Us of their Stay here up wards of 4 months and that they were credibly inform'd / as we since have been / that y.$^{e}$ Old Emperour of China was Dead and is succeeded by his fourth Son.

One Armenian Ship sail'd out of this Road for Canton the day we arriv'd and we hear there will be two Ships there this Season from Madrass.

Having nothing more to Say worthy y.$^{r}$ Hon.$^{rs}$ Cognizance but that the Captains Intend to Sail to morrow We Beg leave to Subscribe Our selves
your Hon.$^{rs}$ most Obed.$^{t}$ Hum.$^{ble}$ Serv.$^{ts}$
(Sign'd) [TD, DB, SS] [39]

3.$^{d}$ The Captains acquainting Us they intended to Sail the next morning this Evening we went on Board having first waited on the Shabandarr to Return him thanks for his favours

4.$^{th}$ This morning Early Sail'd out of Batavia Road

24.$^{th}$ We Saw the Islands Junchattwicks and this Afternoon Captain Nicholas Luhorne Died of a violent Feavor which siez'd him y.$^{e}$ 22.$^{d}$

August

1 Saw the Great Ladroon Island in y.$^{e}$ Evening

3 This Morning we haed a very hard gale of Wind at NE.$^{t}$ which continu'd all Day

4 This Morning y.$^{e}$ Tuffoon is very much abated could not See the Princess Ann

6 We came to an Anchor among y.$^{e}$ Deer Islands & in y.$^{e}$ Evening y.$^{e}$ Princess Ann & King George a Countrey Ship belonging to Madrass came to an Anchor near Us. The countrey Ship is bound to Canton her SupraCargoes are Mess.$^{rs}$ Naish Colebrooke & Barnes Cap.$^{tn}$ Wybourg Command.$^{r}$ they inform'd Us of the Boon Friggotts being Arriv'd at Madrass from whence She is design'd for this port.

7 Sail'd from the Deer Islands this Morn.$^{g}$ w.$^{th}$ the Princess Ann Hartford & King George & in y.$^{e}$ Afternoon came to an Anchor off of Maccao.

8.$^{th}$ Having gott a pilott on board we Weigh'd from Maccao. The pinnace brought Us off a Letter Sign'd [40] by Mess.$^{rs}$ Savage and Pratt SupraCargoes of y.$^{e}$ Wallpole adviceing that a Manilla Ship had meet w.$^{th}$ a great deal of trouble y.$^{e}$ last year at Canton on Acco.$^{t}$ of their Making fire Arms there & that She was detain'd by the Mandareens the whole Year & is there now & that the King George y$^{e}$ last Year was threaten'd when ready to Sail to be unladen under pretence of searching for Yellow Silks[47], & that upon these Acco.$^{ts}$ they had at their first Arrivall magnified the force of their Ship to the Officers who came on board to take that acco.$^{t}$ & were in hopes it had good Effect.

10.$^{th}$ Came to an Anchor at Boca Tygris a Mandareen Boat Came on Board as usuale to be inform'd of the Ships Name Burthen & force and as Mess.$^{rs}$ Savage & Pratt in their Letter before mention'd seem to hint that ~~it would~~ magnificing the strength of their Ships had prov'd advantagious gave them the follow.$^{g}$ Acco.$^{t}$ of the Hartford.

That She burthen'd 500 Tonns, had 36 Gunns 120 Men. 30 Barrells powder, 60 small arms & 50 Swords.

This Morning dispatch'd a Boat for Canton with the following Letter for Mess.$^{rs}$ William Fazakerley Esq. Chief &c$^{a}$ Councill

To William Fazakerley Esq. Chief &c.$^{a}$ Councill
Gentlemen

We think it necessary to Acquaint you of the Ships Hartford & Princess Anns Arrivall at Bocha Tygris this Morning after a long passage[48] [41] of thirty Eight days from Batavia

The 7.$^{th}$ this Inst.$^{t}$ being the day before We Arriv'd at Maccao we fell in Company with the King George from Madrass Captain Wybourg Command.$^{r}$ Mess.$^{rs}$ Naish Colebrooke & Barnes SupraCargoes who Inform'd Us of the Boone Friggotts being arriv'd at Maddrass from whence She is design'd for this Port

Yesterday a Moors Ship pass'd Us while at Anchor 3 or 4 Leag.$^{s}$ without the Bocha it being so thick and hazey that our Pilott Grounded the Ship twice which oblig'd us to come too

The 24.$^{th}$ Ultimo near the Junchattwicks Captain Luhorne Died of a violent Feavour w.$^{th}$ w.$^{ch}$ he was siez'd y.$^{e}$ 22.

Having nothing more materiall to Acquaint you off We Subscribe ourSelves Gentlemen your hum.$^{ble}$ Serv.$^{ts}$

---

**47** It was forbidden to export "crimson or jonquil stuffs" (red or light yellow silks) from China by order of the emperor. These colors were limited to his wardrobe and restrictions against their sale were tightened again in the 1760s. C.J.A. Jörg, Porcelain and the Dutch China Trade (The Hague: M. Nijhoff, 1982), 84.

**48** It took VOC ships an average of 30 days to travel between Batavia and Macao. Ibid.

(Sign'd) [TD, SS]
Ship Hartford 10.th Aug.t 1723

12.th We arriv'd this Morning at Our Factory at Canton and Deliver'd in this Diary Commencing y.e 11.th June 1723 & Ending this Day
(Sign'd) [...] [WF, RM, EG, TC, TD, DB, SS] [42]

25.th Receiv'd from the Duke of Cambridge The Bales of Cloth & Purpetts mention'd in y.e Order Sent Cap.tn Daniel Small the 22.d Inst.

26. Receiv'd from the Mountague In consequence of the order Sent Cap.tn John Gordon on y.e 22.d Ins.t The Hon.ble Companys Bl.s of Cloth & Purpetts mention'd therein

27.th Deliver'd Suqua forty Bl.s Purpetts and one hundred thirty Eight pieces

28.th This morning M.r Cambell[49] came up to this Citty he is SupraCargoe of the Hanover[50] a ship about Six hundred Tonns burthen Cap.tn Timothy Tully[51] Command.r last from Madrass her Cargo is Pepper and Redwood[52] to the Value of about thirty Thousand pagodas[53]

He brings an Acco.t of the Arrivale of the Honble Companys Ships Sarum & Carnarvon at Madrass & that three days since a Moors Ship from the Coast of Mallabar arriv'd at Bocha Tygris having lost all her Masts.

This night had a Conference with the SupraCargoes of the Wallpole Ostend.rs & Countrey Ships about Signing a paper which Suqua brought to Us for that purpose and is to be deliver'd to the Tsontuek[54] and Foouen[55] after being translated & Examin'd it was [43] Sign'd by all present except Mess.rs Savage and Pratt the Contents are as follows

---

**49** Person unknown.

**50** The Hanover, rated about 470 tons, housed between 92 and 96 crewmembers and 30 and 32 guns while active, from 1712 to 1724. On this sailing, her fourth and captained by John Bond, the EIC ship travelled to Madras, Calicut, Bombay, Karwar, Mocha, Surat and Cochinchina.

**51** Timothy Tully (dates unknown) was an EIC captain during the 1720s and 1730s. See *A New Nautical Directory of the East-India and China Navigation* (London: S. Couchman, 1804), 489.

**52** Redwoods are coniferous trees, including brazilwood, barwood and camwood, whose ground and powdered timbers were used to make reddish to dark brown clothing dyes during the 1700s.

**53** The pagoda was an Indian gold coin. It was worth 3.5 rupees. The pagoda equated to about eight English shillings.

**54** The *zongdu*, *tsongtu* or *tsongtock* was the provincial Viceroy and the region's highest civil official. The function of the office was primarily military, but the zongdu frequently aided the *fuyuan* in routine civic affairs, especially problems with foreigners. Morse, Chronicles, vol. 1, xx.

**55** The *fuyuan*, or *foo-yuen*, was the provincial governor and subordinate colleague of the *zongdu* stationed at Canton. He was charged with civic affairs. Ibid.

Canton 28 August 1723

Whereas all y.[e] European Ships Trading to Canton this Year have meet with several Impositions and Grievances unpractic'd before the Underwritten Persons under whose Direction the Ships are have thought fitt to meet together in Consultation and advice with Suqua the principall Merch.[t] in this place about drawing up a petition to the Tsontuek & Foouen in Order to being Redresst.

The Substance of the petition is as follows

That the Europeans Trading here for many Years have found the present Tsontuek to be a very great friend to Them that he has always Represented to the Emperour that we were a Civill People and come a great way That we have Always brought Money & Goods to a great Value and after finishing our Buisness have left this place with a very good Character That we are Oblig'd to bring Gunnpowder & fire Arms to defend our Ships against the Enimies of our Countrey & Pyrates and for no other Reason and before this Year We never meet with any trouble on that Acco.[t] But now [44] Upon Arrivall at Bocha Tygris We are plagu'd by some Mandareens who have a mind to take out our Arms & powder and when we have pass'd Bocha Tygris they still insist to do the same at Wampoo this is not only against Custom but may indanger the Loss of some of our Ships by going down into the Hold

That we always us'd to have a free Import.[g] and Exporting our Goods having no Reinspection after being once pass'd by the Hoppoos Officers that now some Mandareens in hopes of getting money from Us threaten to Examine all our Goods when Shipt at their pleasure by going into the Hold after they are stow'd away this trouble will be so great that it will endanger lossing our passage as well as breaking our bulk and damaging our Goods and is an Imposition never laid upon us before

That the Soldier Mandareens Stop Sampans[56] to gett money out of them so that if we have any buisness of Consquence we can't persuade them to Go.

We desire that he will Redress these Grievances as well as confirm to Us all the Privileges We have had here to fore [45]

The same with the foregoing with little Alterat.[n] was deliver'd to the Foouen
The day Sent Suqua all the Broad Cloth we had in the factory

56 Sampans here were hired by Europeans to transport goods and passengers between ocean-going vessels and their associated factories on the shallower parts of the Pearl River. For contemporary images of these and other Chinese ships, see Jeremy Franks, "Eighteenth-Century Chinese Vessels at Canton. The Paintings at Skärva, Sweden", in: *The Mariner's Mirror* 83.1 (1997), 21–40.

**Septem.$^{r}$**

1 Deliver'd Suqua Twelve Bl.$^{s}$ Purpetts

At a Consultation Holden at Canton Septem.$^{r}$ 3.$^{d}$ 1723.
Present William Fazakerley Esq. Chief Richard Morton Edm.$^{d}$ Godfrey Thomas Carter Thomas Dade Devereux Bacon Sam.$^{l}$ Skinner
After Examining the Hongs of the Merch.$^{ts}$ for proper assortments of ChinaWare agreeable to our Instructions we could only find Suqua to be capable of furnishing Us with our desir'd quantity We had Chaffer'd with him Severall times about the prices of Each Assortment and now agreed to give him the following for the undermention'd Goods which he Comply'd with

[46] Acco.$^{t}$ of the Quantity Sorts and prices of China Ware bought of Suqua Septem.$^{r}$ 3.$^{d}$ 1723. Viz.$^{t}$
Musters[57]
N.$^{o}$ 1 300 Nests[58] Dishes blue & white 5 in a Nest at Tales 1.2.$^{M}$ -.-. p. Nest
5000. plates to Ditto at 3 Cand.[59] 5 Cash e@
2. 500. Nests Dishes pale blue & White 5 in a Nest at Tales 1.2.$^{M}$ -.-. p. Nest
10000 plates to D.$^{o}$ at 3 Cand. 5 Cash e@
3. 500. Nests Dishes paler blue & white 5 in a Nest at Ta.$^{s}$ 1.2.$^{M}$ -.-. p. Nest
10000 plates to D.$^{o}$ at 3 Cand. 5 Cash e@
4. 500. Nests Dishes pale blue & white 5 in a Nest diff.$^{t}$ figure at Tales 1.2.$^{M}$ -.-. p. Nest
10000. Plates to D.$^{o}$ at 3 Cand. 5 Cash e@
5. 500. Nests soop dishes pale blue & white 5 in a Nest at Ta.$^{s}$ 1.2.$^{M}$ -.-. p. Nest
10000 soop plates to D.$^{o}$ at 3 Cand. 5 Cash
6. 500. Nests soop Dishes pale blue & White diff.$^{t}$ pattern 5 in a Nest at ta.$^{s}$ 1.2.$^{M}$ -.-.
10000. Plates to D.$^{o}$ @ 3 Cand. 5 Cash e@
7. 300 Nests Dishes soop pale blue & white diff.$^{t}$ pattern 5 in a Nest @ ta.$^{s}$ 1.2.-.-.
6000. Plates D.$^{o}$ at 3 Cand. 5 Cash e@
8. 200 Nests Dishes dark blue & White 5 in a Nest at Ta.$^{s}$ 1.2.-.-. p. Nest
2500. plates to D.$^{o}$ @ 3 Cand. 5 Cash e@ [47]
9. 300. Nests Colour'd & frosted Soop Dishes 5 in a Nest Rim at Tal. 2.2.$^{M}$ -.-.
7000 plates to D.$^{o}$ at ta.$^{s}$ -.-.$^{M}$ 9$^{Ca}$ -.$^{C}$ e@

57 A muster was a sample of a commodity or cargo. It was used to check and ensure quality.
58 The EIC packaged their porcelain exports in nests, or small bundles, in the early 1700s.
59 A candareen was a conjoined unit of weight and Chinese monetary value in silver.

10. 150 Nests Soop Dishes Gold & Colours fluted & Gold Rim at Ta.s 3.1.-.-. p. Nest 5 in a Nest
2000 plates to D.o @ 1 Mace[60] 6 Cand.
11. 200 Nests Dishes Gold & Colo.rs baskett flower & go.d Rim 5 in a Nest @ Ta.s 2.2.-.-. p. Nest
4000 plates to D.o @ 9 Cand. e@
12. 330 Nests Dishes Gold & Col.rs Bamboo Tree & gold Rim 5 in a Nest @ Ta.s 2.2.-.-.
2000 plates to D.o @ 9 Cand. e@
13. 240 Nests Dishes Gold & Colours Spriggs & gold Rim 5 in a Nest @ ta.s 2.2.-.-.
3000 plates to D.o @ 9 Cand. e@
14. 300 Nests Dishes diff.t Col.rs Paddy Birds[61] & Den Gold Rim 5 in a Nest @ Ta.s 2.2.-.-.
6000 plates to D.o @ 9 Cand. e@
15. 120 Nests Dishes Gold & Col.rs flower pott & go Rim 5 in a Nest @ Ta.s 2.2.-.-. p. Nest
2000 plates to D.o @ 9 Cand. e@
16. 76 Nests Japan Dishes[62] Gold & Col.rs go Rim 3 in a Nest at Ta.s 1.3.-.-. p. Nest
17. 60 Nests Japon Dishes go & Col.rs go Rim lesser Seize diff.t figure 3 in a Nest at Ta.s 1.3.-.-. p. Nest [48]
18. 352 Nests Bowls white frosted blue & Whe Bord.r brown Rim 4 in a Nest at Ta.s 2.1.M
19. 150 Nests Dishes Gold & Col.rs blue Bord.r & gl Rim 5 in a Nest @ Ta.s 2.2.-.-. p. Nest
1800 plates to D.o @ 9 Candareens e@
20. 16 Nests Dishes green & Gold flower at bottom gold Rim 5 in a Nest at Ta.s 2.2.-.-.
174 plates to D.o @ 9 Cand. e@
21. 380 Nests Bowles green & Colours D.o Bord.r & gold Rim 4 in a Nest at Ta.s 3.3.-.-.
22. 750 Nests Bowles white frosted lesser Size w.h flower pott gold & Colour'd Bord.r & gd Rim 4 in a Nest at Ta.s 2.2.-.-. p. Nest
23. 170 Nests Bowles frosted inside Gold & Col.rs the same & g.o Rim 4 in a Nest @ Ta.s 2.-.-.
24. 500 Nests Bowles White w.th blue & white Bord.r & brown Rim lesser size 3 in a Nest @ Ta.s. [illegible]

---

**60** A mace was a conjoined unit of weight and Chinese monetary value in silver. It equated to ten candareens and 1/10 tael. Seven mace and two candareens commonly were worth one silver dollar, or yuan.

**61** Oversized birds were popular motifs on Chinese porcelains. The "paddy birds" noted here likely refer to depictions of regional cranes, egrets or pond herons.

**62** This likely refers to porcelain wares decorated with a lacquering technique known as japanning. It involved firing dishes with a thick black varnish, decorating them with Asian-inspired scenes, and polishing the completed pieces to a shine.

25. 500 Nests Bowles blue & White D.$^{o}$ Bord.$^{r}$ brown & diff.$^{t}$ figure 3 in a Nest @ Ta.$^{s}$ .-.5$^{M}$
26. 2000 Single Bowles blue & white D.$^{o}$ Bord.$^{rs}$ and brown Rim at Ta.$^{s}$ -.2$^{M}$.-.-. e@
27. 2000 Sneakers[63] blue & White D.$^{o}$ Bord.$^{rs}$ & brown Rim @ 1 mace e@
28. 10000 pair Cups & Saucers blue & W.$^{t}$ w.$^{th}$ Birds and brown Rim at 3 Candareens p. pair
29. 20000 pair Cups & Saucers blue & White diff.$^{t}$ figure brown Rim at 3 cand. p. Pair [49]
30. 10000 p.$^{r}$ Cups & Saucers blue & White Bord.$^{d}$ Top and bottom brown Rim at 3 Cand. p. Pair
31. 10000 pair Cups & Saucers blue & White diff.$^{t}$ figure @ 3 Cand. p. Pair
32. 1800 p.$^{r}$ Cups & Saucers blue & White D.$^{o}$ Bord.$^{r}$ and brown Rim at 3 Candareens p. pair
33. 8500 p.$^{r}$ Cups & Saucers blue & White Chequer'd & brown Rim at 2. Cand. p. pair
34. 10000 pair Cups & Saucers blue & White w.$^{th}$ Spriggs brown Rim @ 3 Cand. p. pair
35. 300 Single Bowles Gold & Colours D.$^{o}$ Bord.$^{r}$ and go Rim at 3 mace 5 Cand. e@
36. 500 Single Bowles gold & Col.$^{rs}$ gold Rim at 1 mace 6 Cand. e@
37. 39 Nests Dishes gold & Colours w.$^{th}$ blue & White Bord.$^{r}$ & Gold Rim 5 in a Nest @ Ta.$^{s}$ 2.2.$^{M}$
    500 plates to D.$^{o}$ @ 9 Can. Each

To take a few more or less of Each Muster as it shall happen
[signed WF, RM, EG, TC, TD, DB, SS] [50]

4.$^{th}$ Sent Cap.$^{tn}$ Daniel Small Command.$^{r}$ of the Duke of Cambridge & Cap.$^{tn}$ John Gordon Command.$^{r}$ of Ship Mountague Each of them the following Order to Send up all The Hon.$^{ble}$ Companys Bl.$^{s}$ of Cloth and purpetts from on Board their Ships vizt.

Canton 4.$^{th}$ Septem.$^{r}$ 1723
Cap.$^{tn}$ Daniel Small
Sir,

By Order of the Chief & Council you are hereby Directed to Send up by this Boat all the Bl.$^{s}$ of Cloth & purpetts on Board Your Ship belonging to the Hon.$^{ble}$ Company with a sufficient Number of your men to secure the same I am
your humble Serv$^{t}$
Sam.$^{l}$ Skinner

---

**63** Sneakers were small porcelain bowls – larger than tea bowls – used for punch. They were popular in Europe between 1710 and 1740.

The Same w.[th] the above Mutatis Mutandis was sent to Captain John Gordon

7.[th] Agreeable to an Order Sent Captain John Gordon the 4.[th] this Ins.[t] Receiv'd all the Bales of Cloth & purpetts from on Board the Mountague
Yesterday We began to Pack the China Ware bought of Suqua the 3.[d] this Ins.[t] [51]

9.[th] Agreeable to an Order Sent Captain Daniel Small Receiv'd from on Board the Cambridge all the Hon.[ble] Companys Bl.[s] of Cloth & purpetts.

11. This day arriv'd at Wampoo the Boone Friggotte belonging to Bombay but last from Madrass burthen about Six hundred Tonns Cap.[tn] – Standard[64] Comm.[r] M.[r] William Wake[65] SupraCargo We hear her Stock is about one hundred & twenty thousand Rupees[66] chiefly in pepper

At a Consultation Holden at Canton the 12.[th] Septem.[r] 1723.
Present William Fazakerley Eq. Chief Richard Morton Edmund Godfrey Thomas Carter Thomas Dade Devereux Bacon Sam[l] Skinner
The Consideration of so many large Ships Arriving this year from Madrass and Bombay brought us to consider what we had done in relation to Appointing the Mountague to go to Madrass [52]
We had Reason to believe the SupraCargoes of those Ships in the Acco.[ts] they gave of the wretches prices of all China goods at the aforesaid Ports by reason of the Marketts being overstockt and a great Quantity of those goods remaining unsold; they added to Us that the reason of Their Coming was to prevent the Rotting of their Ships in their Ports and that they could have no prospect of making an advantagious Voyage but knowing how much it is the Inclination of every person to Act the most Cunningly he Can for his own Interest We should not have given Creditt entirely to their Reports had they not been Confirm'd to severall of Us by private Letters from the Gentlemen of Fort S.[t] George with enclos'd Price Currants for having an Acco.[t] of four of the Companys Ships being bound to China they concluded that probably one of them might be order'd to their port and this indeed was the occasion of their writing to Us; they mention that without any of Ours they should have Seven Ships to be dispatch'd home this Year and that if we did consign them any one she would run the Risque of being

64 John Standard (dates unknown) was captain of a country ship, the Boone, in 1723. He initially relocated to Madras in 1716, before settling in Bombay by the early 1730s. There, he worked as a free trader. Love, Vestiges, 407.

65 William Wake (d. 1751) was a successful free trader, country merchant and supercargo based in India during the 1720s. He eventually joined the EIC, secured a role on its Bombay Council and served as colonial governor from 1742–1750. Holden Furber, "Asia and the West as Partners before 'Empire' and After", in: *The Journal of Asian Studies* 28.4 (1969), 714.

66 The rupee was an Indian silver coin. It was worth about ⅓ pagodas. The rupee equated to two English shillings, six pence in the early 1700s.

detain'd a whole Year in the Country without a prospect [53] of being Employ'd any way towards bearing the burthen of her Demorage
We likewise think that if Our Hon.ble Mast.rs had suspected the Wallpoles lossing her Passage that she only without the knowledge of any other Accid.ts would have alter'd their Designs of Ordering any of our Ships to Madrass she being a Ship of Six hundred Tonns & alone capable of Carrying a sufficient Quantity of Gruff Goods[67] to supply that Markett
We further consider'd that we are order'd in Case Tea was cheap / which we have found so / to put aboard of any Ship which should be bound to Madrass five or six hundred Chests of Bohea Tea which is almost half the Charterparty Tonnage & we think it much more for the Companys Interest / as affairs stand at present / to fill up the Ship with the Remainder of a Europe Cargoe that at the present price of goods must in all probability turn to better Acco.t than those do with a gruff Madrass Cargo which is dear, and by which the Company will infallibly be Loossers and the Ships passage to Europe endanger'd.
[54] We therefore after the maturest Consideration and nice Weighing of every Circumstance Resolv'd that it is greatly for the Interest of the Company that the Mountague instead of being Sent to Madrass should be Consign'd directly home provided We could prevail with our Merch.t to take back the Goods provided to go upon her to Madrass without any Loss to the Company
[signed WF, RM, TC, SS]

13.th We Confer'd with Suqua upon taking back the gruff Goods we had contracted ~~for~~ with him for, for the Mountague then design'd for Madrass he at first made great difficultys Urging that all the SupraCargoes of the Country Ships had already made their Investments and [55] these Goods would be turn'd upon his hands to a great Loss we told him that Loss would be made up to him for we must Buy other goods in their room and he would be Our Merch.t if he afforded them as Cheap as others to which at last he Consented

14.th Captain Gordon upon the Alternation of his Voyage acquainted Us, that he had bought fivety pecuIls of Quicksilver with design to Carry it to Madrass and desir'd Us if We had occasion for any more for the Companys Acco.t to take it off his hands so we agreed to buy it at the price it Cost him which was forty two Tales p. pecull.
Deliver'd Suqua all the Hon.ble Companys Cloth & purpetts.
Order'd the Captains to Send up all the Lead belonging to the Company and the four Casks of pimento

67 Gruff goods were coarse, bulk commodities imported by the EIC, including indigo, cotton yarns, saltpeter, gum resins, red- and sandalwood, sugar and wool. Chaudhuri, Trading World, 329–41.

16.[th] Agreeable to the above Order this day Rec.[d] from on Board the 4 Ships all the Hon.[ble] Companys Lead being Two Thousand Six hundred Sixty two p.[ces] & four Casks pimento
Deliver'd Suqua the four Casks pimento

[56] At a Consultation Holden at Canton Septem.[r] 17.[th] 1723.
Present William Fazakerley Esq. Chief &c.[a] Councill
Upon a Computation of the Bohea and Green Teas already contracted for, We find / the Mountague Voyage being alter'd / the Ships capable of Receiving a great deal more Tea and having the offer of a parcell of about Seven hundred pecULLS at a very low price because it was Tea of the last Year[68] We thought it proper to agree for it with the Merch.[t] provided the whole came up to the Muster he tender'd Us which we take to be sound & good especially it being no uncommon thing in the great quanities of Teas that we purchase to Receive part in it thô we agree for new and this inconvenience we can never avoid because [57] Our Merchant will so blend the old & New together that we can hardly discover it and if we do can seldom avoid taking it and we have generally observ'd that it has made little difference in the Price at home so we agreed with Chinqua[69] for about seven hundred peculls at nine tales the pecull he to pay the Custom.[70] We had further reasons for doing of this which were that the first sort of Bohea grew very scarse and the Ostenders were oblig'd to Pick up their Quantity were they could find it lett the quality be what it ~~will~~ would and we thought it would put a distress upon them. another Reason We had was by our being credibly inform'd that Suqua our Merchant with whom we made our first Contract had not secur'd his Quantity and was buying up all he could which made us fear if he was very much press'd he would light upon this Tea we have purchas'd so cheap and putt it upon Us at the price in Our first Contract the difference of Which Amounts to a great Summ of Money Having been sullicited severall times by Suqua to buy of him a greater Quantity of Singlo [58] Tea and finding by our discourse with the Cap.[tns] that they could receive it we promis'd to take a further quantity of Singlo Tea of him amot.[es] to about one thousand peculls at sixteen tales the pecull but Conditionally that if the Ships could not

68 At various times, Chinese merchants tried to sell prior year's teas for the same price as new teas to Europeans. It was therefore important for supercargos to assess the freshness of the product to determine the appropriate price and to adjust accordingly for teas that were not fresh. Parmentier, Tea Time, 101.
69 Chinqua (d. 1733) was bookkeeper of the Chinese merchant house of Tan Suqua. He eventually formed his own commercial firm in the 1730s. Van Dyke, Merchants, 79–102.
70 *Hong* merchants regularly agreed to stand as fiador, or security, for the foreign merchant vessels with whom they traded. This meant, even if not agreed to in contacts, they were liable to the Hoppo for any fees not paid. Jörg, Porcelain, 66–7; Van Dyke, Merchants, 23–4.

take the whole in or by any Accident We thought our selves oblig'd to remitt any part of it that then he should not Isist upon our taking it which he agreed to
[signed WF, RM, EG, TC, TD, DB, SS]

20.th Deliver'd Suqua all the Hon.ble Companys Lead any have made his Acco.t D.o to the same in our Books
This day we went down to Wampoo to Receive the Tsontuek Taujun[71] Foouen & Hoppoo who Came to See the European Ships [59]

23.th Between this day and the twentieth have been Employ'd in Weighing off and Shipping a great part of the Cambridges Cargo the particulars of w.ch will appear by the Packing Book

29.th The Linguist telling Us the Hoppoo intended all the Europeans should pay him Custom for the Wine and Arrack which they brought up from their Ships it was thought proper to go to the Hoppoo[72] and make Complaint that we believ'd the Linguist impos'd Us in telling Us that he thought of demanding Custom for our Wine & other Liquors he say'd the Linguist was not in fault for he had order'd him we then told him that at our first Arrivale he promiss'd we should Enjoy all the priviledges hitherto granted the English and should have no new Customs impos'd on Us that we hop'd he would keep to his word and not Insist we should pay Custom for Liquors it being an unpresidented thing He then say'd he only design'd we should for a little as three or four Chests We told him we desir'd he would not think of it, it never being pay'd by the English to any hoppoo he then Ask'd if we had any [60] thing to Say against paying for Dammer[73] and Oyl We told him we Expected to have all ~~the~~ Ships Stores Custom free but that if any quantity was bought we thought it Reasonable he then say'd all Eatables and drinkables should be Custom free that Dammer & Oyl for the Ships use should be likewise free but that he Expected Custom for any large Quantity with which answer taking our Leave we return'd to our Factory.

71 The *Tsiang Kün*, *taujun* or Tartar-General, was the commandant of the Manchu garrison located at Canton and in charge of provincial protection. He generally was not involved in civic administration, although officially he ranked higher than the *zongdu*. Morse, Chronicles, vol. 1, xx.

72 EIC supercargoes met with the Hoppo at his private residence to receive official commercial permits until the 1750s. After this first audience, however, they typically had to send Chinese sentries with any further communications and wait at the city's external gate for the Hoppo's response. Van Dyke, Canton Trade, 20–1.

73 Dammer was a natural resin, derived from trees native to southeast Asia and used as a substitute for pitch in naval upkeep.

## October

At a Consultation Holden at Canton October 3.[d] 1723.
Present Will.[m] Fazakerley Esq. Chief &c.[a] Councill
Having Packt all our ChinaWare bought of Suqua and finding the whole to Amount to little more than four hundred Chests We thought it not a sufficient quantity for y[e] three Ships being Order'd in our Instructions to Ship more proportionably on Each of them
[61] We therefore came to a Resolution to purchase more provided we could procure the Sortments that were directed of which this Citty is very barren this Year the Chineess thinking we should buy the old Customary Sorts such as Setts of Tea Equipages Scollop shells pattepans[74] and other dear useless Stuff
[signed WF, RM, EG, TC, TD, DB, SS]

At a Consultation Holden at Canton Octob.[r] 4.[th] 1723
Present William Fazakerley Esq.[r] Chief &c.[a] Councill
Agreed with Quiqua[75] for the undermention'd China Ware he to pay the Custom and to Deduct 1 p. Ct for Breakage[76]

[62] Acco.[t] of Sundry parcells ChinaWare bought of Quiqua viz.[t]
Must.[r]
N.[o] 38. 150 Nests Dishes Gold & Colours & Gold Rim 11 Dishes & 11 Plates to a Nest at Ta.[s] 5.8[M] -.-.
39. 150 Nests Bowles gold & Colours & gold Rim 4 in a nest @ Ta.[s] 1.3.[M] -.-. p. Nest
40. 160 Nests dishes posted blue & White 11 Dishes & 20 plates to a Nest at 3 ta.[s] 2 Mace p. Nest
41. 185 Nests Dishes Gold & Colours w.[th] a blue Bord[er] & gold Rim 4 Dishes & 18 plates to a Nest at Ta.[s] 2.8.2 p. Nest.
42. 300 Nests Bowles brown w.[th] blue & White pattern 3 in a Nest at Ta.[s] -.4.[M] -.-. p. Nest

74 Pattypans, also known as "spoon trays," were porcelain dishes with raised and scalloped sides common in eighteenth-century tea services. They could be used to bake small cakes but more commonly served as decorative tableware, featuring simple blue-and-white or floral designs.
75 This again refers to Chinqua, the bookkeeper of Tan Suqua's firm.
76 European merchants expected to lose between two and six percent of their porcelain exports, due to breakage. Some of these loses were assumed by Chinese merchants in their initial contracts, which largely fell under "free-on-board" agreements. These assigned *hong* traders responsibility (and financial liability) for any damages to supplied goods until they were loaded onto foreigners' ships at Whampoa. Jörg, Porcelain, 129; Van Dyke, Merchants, 35–6.

43. 200 Nests Soop Dishes Gold & Col[rs] blue bord. 11 Dishes & 20 plates to a Nest @ Ta.[s] -.5. p. Nest

To take a few more or less of Each Must.[r] as it shall happen

Order'd the Remainder of the Hon.[ble] Companys Treasure on Board the Cambridge to be sent up with particular Directions to the Command.[r] to have it well Buoy'd & Guard'd

began to pack the China Ware bought of Quiqua

[63] [signed WF, RM, EG, TC, TD, DB, SS]

At a Consultation Holden at Canton October 6.[th] 1723

Present William Fazakerley Esq. Chief &c.[a] Councill

Agree'd with Suqua for the undermention'd ChinaWare he to pay the Custom and to Deduct 1 p. C.[t] for Breakage Viz.[t]

Must.[r]

N.[o] 44. 300 Nests Bowles Gold & Colours D.[o] Bord.[r] and gold Rim 4 in a Nest at Ta.[s] 3.8.-.-. p. Nest

[64] Agreeable to the Order Sent Captain Small the 4.[th] this Inst. Receiv'd this day twelve Chests of Treasure w.[ch] with those Rec.[d] before makes Chests 32 the whole Summ p. the Duke of Cambridge.

[signed WF, TD, RM, DB, EG, SS, TC]

10.[th] Made an End of packing ChinaWare

13.[th] For these severall Days have been Employ'd in Weighing off and shipping part of the Duke of Cambridges Cargo the Particulars are as p. Packing Book

At a Consultation Holden at Canton Octob.[r] 17.[th] 1723

Present William Fazakerley Esq. Chief &c.[a] Councill

Read the following Letter from Mess.[rs] Savage and Pratt Supra Cargos of the Wallpoll

[65] Canton 17.[th] Ocotber 1723

Gentlemen

Captain Boddain[77] Acquaints Us that there is not room in the Ship Wallpoole for all the Tea we have provided and pack'd, unless some of the Coarse Goods which We

77 Charles Boddam (1680–1752), a native of Scotland, was captain of the Sir Robert Walpole for all four of her voyages, including this first travel to China (1721–1724). Boddam joined the EIC in 1710, settled in Madras in 1712, and earned his first captaincy in 1716. He sailed for the EIC until the Sir Robert Walpole's final voyage in 1739. McGilvary, East India, 115.

have Ship'd on Board are taken out: We therefore desire to know if you can take any of our SugarCandy upon the Duke of Cambridge bound to Bombay, or any part of the Tea upon either of your three Ships bound to England, provided the Wallpoole can't take it all in We are
Gentlemen: Yo.[r] most hum.[ble] Serv.[ts]
(Sign'd) J. Savage Edm.[d] Pratt

To which we Return'd the following Answer
Canton 17.[th] Octob.[r] 1723
Gentlemen

We have receiv'd Yours and observe the Contents of it and heartily wish so great a mistake had not happen'd had we been Appriz'd of it sooner, we [66] might have afforded you some Remedy but at present our Case is thus.

We have Contracted for as much Tea as the three homeward bound Ships can Carry with the China Ware, Silks &c.[a] that must be putt above of 'em

As to the Cambridge the Command.[r] Acquaints Us she draws so much Water that he can't take in near what we have provided for her, though its no more than the Companys Tonnage

We heartily ~~wish~~ desire for the Companys sake and your own, you may easily gett over this misfortune being
yo.[r] hum.[ble] Serv.[ts]
(Sign'd) [...] [WF, RM, EG, TC, TD, DB, SS]
To Mess.[rs] John Savage & Edm.[d] Pratt SupraCargoes of the Wallpoole [67]

20.[th] Yesterday and to Day have been Employ'd in sending aboard the homeward bound Ships all the ChinaWare being four hundred fivety Eight Chests viz.[t]

| | |
|---|---|
| On the Mountague | 155 Chests |
| On the Hartford | 154 D.[o] |
| On the Princess Anne | 149 D.[o] |
| | 458 |

This Evening some of our people from the Ships brought up word that one of our Boats with fivety Six Chests of ChinaWare going on Board the Hartford Struck upon piles under Water in the River and remains Sunck they told Us that M.[r] Nicholas Jackson[78] Chief Mate of the Hartford had been to her Assistance with the Long Boat and taken out several Chests that knowing them all to be wett and fearing a great deal of breakage he was procuring Boats to order them up to Canton to be Repack'd We immediately Sent for Our Linguist [68] Who did

78 Nicholas Jackson (dates unknown) served on EIC ships as a first and second mate from the 1720s until the 1770s. See *A Register of Ships, Employed in the Service of the Hon. The United East India Company* (London: Charles Hardy, 1800), 23, 46.

not think fitt to come to Us it being late and out of his power to Assist Us till the Morning.

21.st Our sunken China Ware came to our Stairs in three Sampans which we Landed as far as we had procur'd permission from the Hoppoo and shall go to Repacking of it as fast as we Can We are afraid of some Damage seeing severall of the Chests turn'd upside down which happen'd by the hurry they were in to gett the ChinaWare out there were severall Englishmen in the Boat to take care of her and we can find no other remedy in this misfortune but to gett the Boatmen punish'd as an Example to all others for the future

25.th having finish'd the Repacking of the sunken ChinaWare this day sent it on Board the Hartford

27.th Sent Cap.tn Small an Order to moor his Shipp over y.e first Barr

29.th Began to pack our Bohea Tea which we shall continue to do as the Weather permitts till the Ships are dispatch'd.

**Novem.r**

2.d For these 4 days have been Employ'd in shipping on the Duke of Cambridge & Princess Ann

[69] At a Consultation Holden at Canton November 4.th 1723
Present Will.m Fazakerley Esq. Chief &c.a Councill
Receiv'd the following Letter from Captain Daniel Small Commander of the Duke of Cambridge

Canton Nov.r 3.d 1723
Gentlemen

Understanding you design to Ship more goods on Board the Duke of Cambridge besides the Vermillion on Acco.t of the Hon.ble English East India Company this is to Acquaint you the Goods Receiv'd from here, being twenty hundred to the tunn, besides a good Quantity of Stores & Provissions [70] on Board for Europe, has already brought the Ship to Draw 17 foot 10 Inches water therefore with the Opinion of my Officers cannot receive more goods on board without running the Risque of the whole
I am Y.r most hum.ble Serv.t
(Sign'd) Dan.l Small

Came to a Resolution to Send Cap.tn Small the following Letter
Canton 4.th Novem.r 1723
S.r

We have receiv'd and consider'd y.$^{rs}$ of the 3. Ins.$^{t}$ and shall load no more Goods aboard of you; thô, according to Our Computation you want near fivety Tonns of y.$^{e}$ Charterparty Tonnage.

We must and doe, by these presents Acquaint You in the Name and for the Account of The Hon.$^{ble}$ United East India Company that [71] Yourself and Owners are Answerable for all losses that may Accrue to the said Company by your breach of this Article in your Charterparty We are
S$^{r}$ your hum.$^{ble}$ Serv.$^{ts}$
(Sign'd) [WF, EG, TC, SS]
Cap.$^{tn}$ Daniel Small Command.$^{r}$ of the Duke of Cambridge

The Duke of Cambridge not being able to take in any more goods We order'd our Linguist to gett the grand Chopp from the Hoppo for her dispatch and order'd the Invoice of her Cargo to be drawn out
[signed WF, RM, EG, TC, TD, DB, SS]

5.$^{th}$ This day the Cap.$^{tns}$ and SupraCargos of the Wallpoole Boone & King George left this Citty in Order to proceed to Madrass where they are all bound

[72] At a Consultation Holden at Canton Novem.$^{r}$ 6.$^{th}$ 1723.
Present William Fazakerley Esq. Chief Richard Morton Edmund Godfrey Thomas Carter Thomas Dade Devereux Bacon Samuel Skinner
The Invoice of the Duke of Cambridges Cargo being drawn out & Bills of Lading for the same being Sign'd Came to a Resolution to Write the Presid.$^{t}$ & Councill of Bombay[79] the following Letter

Gentlemen

This goes by the Duke of Cambridge Captain Daniel Small which We have Consign'd to you, with a Cargo for Account of The Hon.$^{ble}$ United East India Company enclos'd is an Invoice and Bill of Lading for the Goods Shipt aboard of her

[73] ~~the~~ The Arrivall of two such large Ships as the Boone & Hanover, from Madrass, bound to Yo.$^{r}$ Port and Surratt[80] was a great disappointment to Us however we hope the Cargo will come to a favourable Markett.

79 The EIC appointed its own governor of Bombay, beginning in 1668 when King Charles II began to lease them the colony. They moved their regional headquarters to the settlement from Surat the same year and continued to govern via a council from here until disbanded in 1862. See Emily Erikson, *Between Monopoly and Free Trade: the English East India Company* (Princeton: Princeton UP, 2014), ix–x.
80 Surat, now Suryapur, was a port located in western India. Although a popular country and early European trading entrepôt – the EIC built a factory there in 1612 – it was declining in favor by 1723. Chaudhuri, English East India Company, 16–73.

Canton has been crowded with Ships this Year, five of the Companys and two from Ostend, and five Countrey Ships including a small one from the Coast of Mallabarr

The Hartford, Mountague & Princess Anne are bound directly home with valuable Cargoes, by our having the good Fortune to Purchase all our Europe Goods at very reasonable prices.

Having nothing more, worth your Cognizance, to Acquaint you of. We Remaine
Gentlemen
your most hum.$^{ble}$ Serv.$^{ts}$
(Sign'd) [WF, RM, EG, TC, TD, DB, SS]
To The Hon.$^{ble}$ The Presid.$^{t}$ & Councill for the Direction of the Hon.$^{ble}$ United East India Companys Affairs at Bombay

[74] Order'd the following Sailing Orders to be Copy'd out & deliver'd to Morrow To Cap.$^{tn}$ Daniel Small with the Packett for the Hon.$^{ble}$ Presid.$^{t}$ & Councill at Bombay.

Canton 7.$^{th}$ Novem.$^{r}$ 1723
Sir

We Order you to proceed with all convenient Speed for the Port at Bombay wither You Go Consign'd To the Hon.$^{ble}$ The Presid.$^{t}$ and Councill for the Mannagement of The Hon.$^{ble}$ United East India Companys affairs heartily wishing You a safe arrival thither
We Remaine
S$^{r}$ Your hum.$^{ble}$ Serv.$^{ts}$
(Sign'd) [...] [WF, RM, EG, TC, TD, DB, SS]
To Cap.$^{tn}$ Daniel Small Command.$^{r}$ of the Duke of Cambridge [75]

7.$^{th}$ Dated & Sign'd the Sailing Orders to Captain Daniel Small and Deliver'd them & the Packett for the Hon.$^{ble}$ Presid.$^{t}$ & Councill of Bombay to him
Deliver'd the Duplicate of the Packett p. Duke of Cambridge to M.$^{r}$ Cambell SupraCargo of the Hanover bound directly to Bombay.

16.$^{th}$ The intervall of time between this day and the Date of the above Par.$^{a}$ has been wholy Employ'd in Packing & shipping our Tea so that nothing of Importance has happen'd worth committing to paper
This day Cap.$^{tn}$ Gordon sent us a Lettter notifying the Commencement of his Ships Demorage According to Charterparty ~~to~~ which we told him We would minute down

25.$^{th}$ Between this and the foregoing Date have been packing and sending on Board great quantitys of our Tea and likewise this Day sent on Board the Hartford the Quicksilver having taken such sufficient Care in its package that We think it impossible there should be any waste [76] this alteration in its package occasion'd some Arguments between Us and our Merch.$^{t}$ he Alleged that he was only bound to Answer for its Custom in its usuall Package and our alteration for its security would make the Gross weight be a great deal more than it could be if it was sent in its customary package and that he thought himself not oblig'd to answer for any more we thought what he urg'd to be very Just and so agreed to allow him the difference he should pay upon that Acco.[t]

26.[th] Upon our Packing the Raw silk we had Contracted for with Suqua we found to be so extraordionary good & of y.[e] right assortment for England that we told him if he had any more of the same goodness we would purchase it of him he said he had one hundred pecuлls which he would afford us at the same price to which we agreed

[signed WF, TD, RM, DB, EG, SS, TC] [77]

28 Adjusted with our Merch.[t] the tares of our Chests of Green Tea having tare'd & open'd about ten in each hundred

**Dec.[r]**

2.[d] Sent and Order to Cap.[tn] Nelly for Six Chests of Treasure

3.[d] Having finish'd the Packing of about five hundred Pecuлls of the Bohea Tea we had contracted for with Chinqua we told him we thought it not to be so good as the muster he first produc'd to Us he alledg'd the hardness of his bargain which we said was now nothing to Us but however knowing it to be so and to encourage him to lett Us have better for the future we agreed to allow him one tale p. pecuлl more for the Remaind.[r]

5.[th] Sent Cap.[tn] Gordon an Order for five Chests of Treasure and to Cap.[n] Nelly & Cap. Hudson Each of them to send five.

7.[th] Sent an Order to the Captains to bring up conceal'd in their Boat / as oppertunity permitted / the Remaind.[r] of the Treasure they had aboard their Respective Ships the Hoppo being very inquisitive & troublesome and upon the least suggestions [78] giving us a great deal of trouble and making a great many delays in the Shipping our goods

At a Consultation Holden at Canton Decem.[r] 8.[th] 1723
Present William Fazakerley Esq. Chief &c.[a] Councill
We took into Examination the state of Our Cash and found that we had a considerable ballance yett to lay out. We believ'd the quantity of Teas we had and should Receive would be sufficient to fill the Ships and so consequently we could do nothing with the remainder of our money but to invest in Raw or Wrought Silks if we bought the wrought they would in all probability be what the Weavers had turn'd upon their hands for not being good as we thought it more adviceable to Buy more Raw Silk there being a good deal in the place and some of it the Head sort we look'd at some that

Tinqua[81] had promissing to take it provided it was the [79] head sort but upon looking it over finding it to be very bad we refus'd it at least Chinqua with whom We had contracted for our Cheap Bohea Tea said he would engage to deliver us the head sort at one hundred forty five tales y.[e] Pecull in consideration that he gott nothing by his Tea and to encourage the man for the future We agreed to take one hundred peculls of him at the foregoing price
[signed WF, RM, EG, TC, TD, DB, SS] [80]

14.[th] Ever since the date of the foregoing parg[a] our time has been chiefly taken up in packing and sending on Board our Teas and wrought Silks

16.[th] We have been often pressing our Merch.[t] Suqua to make what possible haste he could in the delivery of the Remaind.[r] of the Teas we had contracted with him for Urgeing that it now began to grow late and that it was high time to bring every thing to a Conclusion We Agreed with him the Nett Weights of the Tea he had deliver'd and found he was still in debt to Us about fiveteen hundred peculls of the Bohea he then told Us that he had about one thousand more by him and that was all of our Contract that he had procur'd that if We press'd him he must find the Rest but he believ'd it would be difficult to find any that was good and that if he did we must waite [81] some considerable time for it he aded that the proportion of Congho Tea we had agree w.[th] him for was very small in referrence to the whole that he had a considerable quantity of that by him which was very good and could be deliver'd Us presently we took this into consideration and concluded that if We press'd him to deliver the Bohea it would in all probability take up too much of our time and that when we had waited for it we might very likely find fault with the Quality there being none good / as we very well knew / left in the place besides upon every little dispute w.[th] the Hoppoo he Stop'd the shipping of our goods by knowing that we must go away by a certain time lett the terms be what they would; that were insisted upon ~~besides~~ & further by our Instruct.[ns] we are order'd to buy any quantity of the Congho and ~~Bohea~~ Peckho Teas if we found them good and two hundred peculls of Congho has hardly any proportion to the quantitys we have Bought [82] so we came to the following Resolution that we would compleat the remaind.[r] of our Investm. as to the Tea in Congho Sort and agreed with Suqua for what we should Receive of him to pay the same price we had done for the first two hundred peculls we had contracted for which will be about a just proportion for the Cargo of Each Ship
[signed WF, RM, EG, TC, TD, DB, SS]

81 Tinqua (d. ca. 1775) was either Tan Suqua's business partner or one of his sons, employed in his merchant house. Van Dyke, Merchants, 79–102.

27.[th] Between this and y.[e] preceeding date we have been bussy'd in compleating the Shipping the greatest part of of y.[e] Remaind.[r] of our Cargoes and settling our affairs with our Merch.[ts] in order for our Dispatch We agreed to allow Suqua sixty nine tales 4 Mace 4 Candareens being the Difference he paid the Hoppo for our Extraordionary Gross Weight of the Quicksilver by the reason of our Altering its package for its [83] better security to Europe.
[signed WF, EG, TC, TD, DB, SS]

## January 1723/4

1.[st] Before this day we were never able to settle the price of our Bing Tea with Suqua having by Contract only agreed the Quantity and the price to be according to Its goodness upon our Examination of It We found it to be pretty good and after a great many squabbles we agreed to pay him 33 ta.[s] the pecull he Urging that he had keept it purposely for Us & that he could have had as much or more if he had Sold it to the Ostenders the whole is 203 Chests Cont.[a] Nett 122 peculls & 26 Cottys[82] and was all that was in y[e] Town Except a parcell of Cudgins[83]
[signed WF, TD, DB, EG, SS, TC] [84]

2.[d] The twelve.[th] of Last month the Two Ostend.[rs] Weigh'd out of the River of Canton to proceed for Europe they carry'd away about five thousand one hundred peculls of Tea chiefly the Bohea Sort between 4 & 500 pec.[l] QuickSilver and about 34000 peices of Wrought Silks and a small quantity of Raw amot.[g] to about 30 odd peculls besides ChinaWare for their Kintledge the direction of both the Ships was Chiefly under Cap.[tn] Thomas Hall M.[r] Robert Hewers was in the Commission w.[th] him there was one – Coombs[84] an Englishman and Butler[85] an Irishman Officers on Board the Ships besides these there were no other of the King of Englands Subjects that were of any consideration or Boor any Office on Board them.

3.[d] We thought we should have paid away our french Crowns[86] at 95 touch as Usual there being no distinktion in the Invoice but upon Examination of 'em we found

82 A catty is a unit of Chinese weight, equaling 16 taels or roughly 1 ⅓ pounds.
83 Cudgin (dates unknown), or Cawsanqua, was a *hong* merchant and Tan Suqua's chief Canton rival. The two shared the EIC cargo in 1721, 1722 and 1723, but Cudgin dominated the Ostend trade during the 1720s. He earned enough wealth to retire from active business in 1728, and he returned to his family estate at Ch'üanchow in 1731. Cheong, Hong Merchants, 144–7; Paul A. Van Dyke, "The Ye Merchants of Canton, 1720–1804", in: *Review of Culture* 13 (2005), 6–47.
84 Person unknown.
85 Person unknown.
86 This refers to a recent minting of French silver écus, ordered by King Louis XIV after 1709. Such coins featured the monarch's profile on the front and three crowns on the back. Because EIC mer-

these Ch.$^{ts}$ to be the wrong Sort and which never pass'd for more than 94 so we could have nothing to gainsay the allowing of it supposing [85] the Companys Cashier to be mistaken or misinform'd for there are none but thoose w.$^{th}$ the three Crowns stampt on them that Pass Current for 95.

8.$^{th}$ Upon Running over our Ballance w.$^{th}$ Suqua he insisted upon an allowance for taking back ~~hat~~ three hundred peculls of SugarCandy that we had bought of him for the Duke of Cambridge we did all we could to avoid it but he Urg'd that it was a perishable commodity and must lye upon his hands the whole Year since we did not take it and ~~now~~ at that time, every body had sercur'd their quantity so there was no getting Rid of it at any price we were forc'd to allow him one tale four mace p. pecull for the Loss and we hope this can be no detriment to the Company by the Ships not being able to take in her Charterparty Tonnage so, as we think the Owners are liable to this Loss We shall charge it to their Acco.$^{t}$ in the Books Accordingly ~~Read over our Instr~~

Read over our Instructions in relation to providing particular Stores to be putt on board [86] Each Ship for the use of the Island S.$^{t}$ Helena and order'd a sufficient Quantity to be bought Consonant thereto

[signed by WF, RM, EG, TC, TD, DB, SS]

10.$^{th}$ Having now Compleated our Invoices and ship'd all our Goods we had nothing left but to settle our Acco.$^{ts}$ w.$^{th}$ our Merchants and adjust with our Linguist the many little Demands we had from the Hoppoo about the Import and Export of private Merchandize and other small things for which with all the care that we were able to take we never [87] could find Owners this is a trouble has been Annually mett with in China and we have been always oblig'd at last to putt the expence to the Companys Acco.$^{t}$ this being but one hundred twenty six Tales is a small one for four Ships however for the Companys satisfaction we have a List of the particulars by Us

We were forc'd to be at another Expence which by the obstinency of y.$^{e}$ Hoppoo in giving Us great delays we could not avoid this was in relation to a Clock brought out in our Ships the owner of it could have Sold it for as much as we were oblig'd to pay him if not more but when the Hoppoo heard of it he order'd that no Merchant should dare to Buy it declaring he design'd it for the Emperour[87] the owner believing that the Hoppoo when he gott it in his possess.$^{n}$ would have it at his own price refus'd to Deliver it which we could not think

chants legally could not export silver coins from England, they relied on foreign currency to exchange in China. An ecu featuring three crowns was worth 95 touch, a measurement relating to tael weight, in contemporary Canton. Otherwise, it was worth 92 or 93 touch. Morse, Chronicles, vol. 1, 68.

**87** The Hoppo often requested to see European curiosities during a ship's measuring ceremony. This especially referred to mechanical instruments and luxuries. He aimed to pass along such goods to his superiors, all the while paying as little as necessary for them. *Hong* merchants typically incurred any financial loss resulting from this process. Van Dyke, Canton Trade, 25.

unreasonable it ~~then~~ being a private Concern and [88] then no way related to the Company the Hoppoo Urg'd that he look'd upon the Supra Cargos to have the entire direction of all the Ships and so consequently in our power to Act as we pleas'd in such an Affair possitively insisting that he would grant us no Chop nor lett us Ship any Goods till he he had the Clock deliver'd to him he was as good as his word so that after a considerable delay in our Affairs and our Factory was so full of goods that we were afraid of fire[88] or any other Accident we were forc'd to prevail with the owner of the Clock to deliver it to Us that we might Send it to y.[e] Hoppoo w.[th] our promise that we would be answerable for the price at which he could have Sold it to any other person which he said was 14 hundred Tales at this time the Hoppoo sent [89] Us back the Clock knowing that now we had neither time nor oppertunity to dispose of it but to a great Loss so the end of this base Useage was in paying fourteen hundred tales for the Clock as the Owner could have Sold it and Selling it for nine hundred & sixty.

We were forc'd to be at another Expence occasion'd by the troubles we meet with this Year for upon our first Arrivall the Hoppoo insisted upon the taking away our Flagg[89] as well as deny.[g] Us almost all the other priviledges that we had Insisted upon at our first Coming and he had pretended to grant we were threaten'd likewise that the Mandaryns did disign upon any Jealousy of Sending Silks on Board of the prohibited Colours that our Ships must be Search'd and Rummag'd at their pleasure ~~or~~ else we could not have our Dispatches this was the occasion of our Conference with the Gentlemen of all the other Ships and upon w.[ch] [90] We drew up and presented a Petition to the Jontusek and Foouen and had the Effect we desir'd the mannagment of this Affair could not be left to any but the principall Merchant Suqua and thereupon We promiss'd to Reimburse him the Charges he should be at which he said in Presents and ready mony Amounted to Seven hundred & twenty five Tales the Applications to the Officers of great men in this Country being very Expensive

The corruptions here are so Evident that we were oblig'd According to our words to allow him this great Charge which is something the Easyer because it is very near the whole Amo.[t] of the Acco.[t] of Presents for the 4 Ships which was always pretty considerable at this Port

[signed WF, RM, EG, TC, TD, DB, SS] [91]

**88** To minimize the risk of fire damage, foreign traders sometimes stored their goods in several different warehouses. The financial impact of fires, however, tended to hit *hong* merchants hardest, as it fell under their "free-on-board" agreements. Van Dyke, *Merchants*, 35–6; 150; 222.

**89** The Hoppo regularly granted foreign officers the privilege of moving quickly on the Pearl River by traveling on service boats that flew their flag. This was intended to aid business efficiency by allowing them to avoid time-consuming vessel searches at river checkpoints. It regularly was used—even promoted—by EIC merchants as a way to smuggle prohibited or taxable goods. Van Dyke, Canton Trade, 117–20.

12.$^{th}$ We this Day Receiv'd the following Letter from Cap.$^{tn}$ Gordon and Cap.$^{tn}$ Nelly viz.$^{t}$

S$^{rs}$

We think it Convenient to Acquaint You that our Ships draw Eighteen foot Water Desire Your Order and a Chop to go over the Second Barr this Spring to Morrow Its new Moon 'tis our Opinion that 'tis not safe for Us to goe over should we Stay till the Tides fall off, Desire your Answer which will Oblige
S$^{rs}$ Your Hum.$^{ble}$ Serv.$^{ts}$
(Sign'd) J. Gordon Fran.$^{s}$ Nelly
Near the 1.$^{st}$ Barr Jan.$^{ry}$ 12.$^{th}$ 1723/4

to which we Sent the following Answer
Canton 14.$^{th}$ Jan.$^{ry}$ 1723/4
Gentlemen

We Receiv'd yours and have Order'd the Linguist to procure the Chop which when We [92] have rece'd we shall send you the Order you desire When your People have done assisting the Princess Ann we desire You will send up the pinnaces designing to leave this place as soon as they Come. We are
yours &c$^{a}$
WF RM EG TC TD DB SS
To Cap.$^{tn}$ John Gordon & Cap.$^{tn}$ Fran.$^{s}$ Nelly

15.$^{th}$ We had now Ballanc'd our Acco.$^{t}$ with every body and after a great many disputes with our Merchant Suqua settled the difference with him for the Goods we oblig'd him to take back upon the alteration of the Mountague Voyage
When we first Acquainted him of this design he then told Us how great a sufferer he must be by the [93] Affairs that the Mountague should go directly home and we have no reason to doubt but the advantages that will accrue thereby will make this Loss appear but as a trifle.
The Loss upon the Sale of the Clock, the Acco.$^{t}$ of Presents to the Mandaryns pe D'Casas[90] &c.$^{a}$ and other little disbursements has brought Us in Debt more than we are able to pay under this necessity M.$^{r}$ Fazakerley Consented to advance the difficiency and paid Us 1339.$^{Tas}$ 8.$^{M}$2.$^{C}$5.$^{C}$ for w.$^{ch}$ he desir'd to have Creditt in the Companys Books ~~fo~~ as an Adventurer in the whole Stock this we have Liberty to grant by a Paragraph in our Instructions and we have Rec.$^{d}$ it on those Conditions
[signed WF, RM, EG, TC, TD, DB, SS]

**90** *Pay de casas* was the pidgin term for a steward in any administrative or commercial house in Canton. Morse, Chronicles, vol. 1, 166.

[94] We are sorry that we must take Notice that the Jamaica Pepper Sent out by the Company for an Experiment will not answer their Expectations we gave out several Musters to be seen by the Merchants and endeavour'd to dispose of it separately but they refus'd to buy it at all not knowing what to make of it and we had a sad Dispute with the Hoppoo by his disegning to make Us pay the Duty as Spice[91] which however we gott off so we were oblig'd to force it upon our Chief Merch.t at last at prime Cost who say'd he would Send it into the Countrey and Acquaint the Companys Serv.ts hereafter if it would be of any Consumption there

16. This Day we left Canton in order to Proceed to Sea directly

17.th Being this Morning gott on Board We Sent the Command.r of Each Ship the following Ordr

On Board ye Hartford 17 Jan.ry 1723/4
S.r

We hereby Order and desire you to proceed [95] with your Ship over the Second Barr with all Convenient speed We are
your hum.ble Serv.ts
(Sign'd) WF &c.a Councill

24.th The Bills of Lading of each Ship being Sign'd by the Command.rs we Sent to Each the following sailing Orders

S.r

We desire and Order You to Proceed with all Convenient Speed for the Port of London where You go Consign'd To The Hon.ble The Court of Directors of the United Company of Merchants of England Trading to the East Indies ~~after~~ heartily wishing you a safe Arrivall hither We Remain
yours &c.a
WF &c.a Councill [96]

91 Import and export duties varied based on products, and different fees had to be paid for each variety of tea. The categorization of (unknown) products therefore was important with regard to the overall profit. At times, Europeans tried to fool custom official by wrongly labeling their packaging. Van Dyke, *Canton Trade*, 31.

**Febr.$^{ry}$ 1723/4**

10.$^{th}$ At Sea Feb.$^{ry}$ 10.$^{th}$ 1723/4
Having Compleated our ~~Bills of Lading~~ Invoices ~~and~~ with their Duplicates & our Books the SupraCargoes upon the Ships Rec.$^{d}$ the Papers belonging to them respectively to be transmitted to the Hon.$^{ble}$ Court upon their Arrivale in England we likewise wrote the two following Letters

At Sea Febuary 10.$^{th}$ 1723
Hon.$^{ble}$ S.$^{rs}$

With this are enclos'd the Hartfords Bill of Lading Invoice and Register of private Trade for England with Invoice and Bill of Lad.$^{ng}$ for her S.$^{t}$ Helena Cargo and Duplicates of those of the Mountague & Princess Ann & Duke of Cambridge

We desire your Hon.$^{rs}$ reference to Our Invoices for the Quantity of our Goods and hope the Assortments will be very proper for the Markett our Bohea Tea Cost Us between 24 and 25 Tales the pecull and our Singlo 16 the Congho & Peckho [97] Teas were not in proportion so Cheap this Year as the others for we were oblig'd to give 45 Tales but they are very good and really what we bought 'em for the Imperial[92] cost 33 Ta.$^{s}$ the pecull.

The quantity of our Raw & Wrought Silks is very large by reason of the Cheapness of our other Goods and we believe our Assortm.$^{ts}$ of ChinaWare will be very well lik'd for Its all of the Usefull Sort and a new Must.$^{r}$ we have no more than 100 peculls of QuickSilver for Europe the price at 42 Ta.$^{s}$ the pecull is not dear considering what Its generally at at Canton but the reason we purchas'd no more was because to our great surprize the Ostenders carr'd home between 4 & 500 peculls.

We dispatch'd the Duke of Cambridge for Bombay the 7.$^{th}$ Novem.$^{r}$ with a Cargo Amounting to 36000 Tales we design'd to have dispatch'd [98] the Mountague for Madrass till the Arrivall of so many Countrey Ships from thence whose Cargoes added to the Wallpooles must infallibly overstock that Markett and We believe if Your Hon.$^{rs}$ had had the least Suspicion / before our coming out / of the Wallpooles lossing her passage That consideration alone alone without any other Accident wou'd have deswaded you from Ordering any other the same Year especially She being a Ship of Six hundred Tonns & alone capable of Carrying a sufficient Quantity of Gruff Goods for the Coast what we have done in this Affair we think must be entirely for your Hon.$^{rs}$ Interest and hope you'l approve of it.

We met with so many Impositions and Delays at our Coming away that it was the 15.$^{th}$ Ins.$^{t}$ before we could leave Canton and then thought we must have been oblig'd to have done it by force. Our Captains According to [99] Your Hon.$^{rs}$ Commands propose to keep Company but in Case of Separation and the Arrivall of any single Ship we

---

92 Imperial was another name for high-quality Bing tea. See page 48, ft. 127.

shall putt aboard each proper Duplicates of our Papers that you may be sufficiently appriz'd of our whole Transactions

Hopeing soon after these to pay Our personall Dutys to Your Hon.$^{rs}$ we Remaine your Hon.$^{rs}$ most Obed.$^{tt}$ Hum.$^{ble}$ Serv.$^{ts}$
(Sign'd) W. Fazakerley &c.$^{a}$ Councill
To the Hon.$^{ble}$ The Court of Directors of the United English East India Company [100]

At Sea February 10.$^{th}$ 1723/4
Hon.$^{ble}$ S.$^{rs}$

We think it our Duty to Acquaint you of the reasons we had for Entering the Bohea Tea in the Invoices at an Averidge w.$^{ch}$ we hope You'l approve of

After our first Contract for the Bohea Tea finding the Ships had room for more and that the head Sort grew Scarce as likewise that the Ostenders were buying up all they could lay their hands on for fear of missing their quantity We thought it proper towards disappointing of them / as well as to Secure our Selves against our Merchant with whom we had made our first Contract who wanted his Quantity and was buying up all he could / to purchase 7 or 800 pecults of Bohea from 9 to 10 tales the pecull It's a great part of it the growth of the preceed.[g] [101] Year but Sound and of a good Quality and we believe worse has been carry'd to England at a farr greater price

The publick knowledge of the Cheap Cost of any Commodity has been very often the cause of the depretiating It's Sale and we are of opinion the Buyers may blow upon it purely for that Reason / should they come to know it, and so by their Jealousy the whole Cargoe of Each Ship may suffer Your Hon.$^{rs}$ by perusing this will be sufficiently Appriz'd of our Intentions in this Matter and if what we have done Succeeds / which we don't at all doubt of / it may be of Consequence to Your Affairs in future Voyages to China; We are with great Respect
Your Hon.$^{rs}$ Most Obed.$^{tt}$ Hum.$^{ble}$ Serv.$^{ts}$
(Sign'd) W. Fazakerley &c.$^{a}$ Councill
to The Hon.$^{ble}$ The Committee of Secrecy in the Hon.$^{ble}$ Court of Directors of the United East India Company

# 4 Report of the Voyage of the Marquis de Prié and St. Joseph from Ostend to Canton in 1723

# Relation du voyage fait en 1723

## Lettre 1. Relation du Voÿage depuis le départ d'ostende Jusqu'a l'arriveé dans la Riviere de Canton dans La Chine[1]

[1] J'entrepens Monsieur de satisfaire vostre Curieusité sur le voyage que J'aÿ fait dans la Chine en qualité de marchand d'une Compagnie de negocians de Gand[2] et Anvers[3], qui les premiers d'entre tous les flamans (hors l'opinion de tous les Europeens) se sont avisez de faire endroiture, et sans l'entremisse des autres Nations un Commerce en ce païs la, et singulierement le Commerce de theé porcelaine soiries &.[a] que les flamans avoient toujours acheté des Anglois et des Hollandois; Je souhaite que ma relation avec la grace dela nouveauté, puisse encorre vous plaire par son exatitude, et par la verité des faits, et de son negoce qui ÿ sont rapportez.[4]

**Le Marquis de prié et le S$^{t}$. Joseph deux** Vaisseaux pour le Commerce le premier de 36. pieces de Canon, et Cent hommes d'equipage, et le deuxieme de 30. pieces avec quatre Vingt quatre hommes tout deux equipez pour un Voÿage de dix huit mois, sur le dernier des quels J'êtois embarqué, sortirent d'Ostende[5] sur la rade le 26 Janvier 1723. ou nous restames â l'ancre â cause du Vent Contraire Jus qu'a le 6 de febr. quand nous eumes le vent du [2] Nord est faisant route pour le canal lequel nous traversames avec le même vent et beau tems, mais nous fumes pas ausitôt venus sur les fonds, ou nous eumes le vent au sud ouest, nostre Commandant eut le maleur de rompre sa grande vergue, nous avons en même tems viré de bord en Courant sud, sud, est aÿant

1 As a general introduction to European travelogues about Asia in the 18th century, see Jürgen Osterhammel, *Die Entzauberung Asiens. Europa und die asiatischen Reiche im 18. Jahrhundert* (München: C.H. Beck, ²2010).

2 Ghent, or Gand, was a city in the Southern Netherlands, located on the Scheldt and Leie rivers. It is in the modern-day region of Flanders. For more on trading here and in nearby Antwerp, see Jan Parmentier, "In the Eye of the Storm: the Influence of Maritime and Trade Networks on the Development of Ostend and Vice Versa during the Eighteenth Century", in: *Trade, Migration and Urban Networks in Port Cities, c. 1640–1940*, eds. Robert Lee and Adrian Jarvis (Liverpool: Liverpool UP, 2008), 67–80; Mary Lindemann, *The Merchant Republics: Amsterdam, Antwerp and Hamburg, 1648–1790* (New York: Cambridge UP, 2014); Jeroen Puttevils, *Merchants and Trading in the Sixteenth Century: the Golden Age of Antwerp* (London: Pickering & Chatto, 2015).

3 Antwerp, or Anvers, was a city in the Southern Netherlands, located on the Scheldt River and along an estuary linked to the North Sea. It was a key regional mercantile center, until the closing of the Scheldt in 1648.

4 The preceding paragraph was adjusted and copied from: Jean de La Roque, *Voyage de l'Arabie Heureuse* (Paris: André Cailleau, 1716), 1–2.

5 Ostend was city in the Southern Netherlands, located on the North Sea. It was granted a commercial monopoly with Africa and the East Indies by Emperor Charles VI in 1723, thus founding the GIC or Ostend Company. See Michael W. Serruys, "The Port and City of Ostend and the Process of State Consolidation in the Southern Netherlands in the Seventeenth and Eighteenth Centuries: a Geopolitical Approach", in: *International Journal of Maritime History* 19.2 (2007), 319–47.

seré les huniers et reste a la cape sur la misene, pour attendre le dit nostre Commandant et avons reste de même Jusqu'a minuit que nous avons fait servir, le Vent êtant Venus au Nord lequel nous eumes Jus que le landemain, et depuis au Sud Sud Ouest avec de la pluie et de brouillards, apres avoir lavoye d'un bord â lautre l'espace de dix huit Jours sur les dits fonds pour pouvoir doubler le Cap de finisterre[6] â la fin nous eumes le vent nord nord Ouest faisant Cours sud vers l'isle de madere la quelle nous dêcouvrimes le 6 de mars elle nous restoit au sud un quart sud ouest et l'isle de Porto Santo[7] au sud sud est.

**Quelques úns ont Crús que Les Anciens** ont Connus Cette isle sous le noms de Junon et d'autolala[8]; Les portugais luy donnerent le nom de Madera qui en leur Langue Signifie bois ou foret; parce qu'ils la trouverent toute couverte d'arbres. il ÿ mirent le feu pour la rendre propre au labourage, et pendant le tems que dura cet ambrassement, ils se retirerent dans leurs vaisseaux, ou ils faillirent a mourir de soifs, faute d'eau douce, Cette isle à plusieurs petites montagnes, et de tres agreables Plaines qui sont egalement fertiles; les sources d'eau vive ÿ sont tres nombreúses. On â bâti sur huit grands ruisseaux des Moulins â scier du bois: et on ÿ travaille â des planches de bois d'if et de Cedre dont on fait grand trafic en Portugal.[9] elle est feconde en Cannes de sucre, en miel en Cire et en blé.[10] les vignes y produissent le meillieur Vin de la terre[11], les bêtes fauves sont en grand [3] nombre aussi bien que les pingeons, ramiers, les Cailles les paons sauvages et les serins.

---

**6** Cape Finisterre is a rocky headway, located in Galicia or northwestern Spain. It marks the westernmost point of the country.

**7** Porto Santo is an island in the Atlantic Ocean, located 43 kilometers northeast of Madeira.

**8** Juno was a Roman goddess. An island with this name – as well as another named Autolala – was commonly discussed in classical texts. The author here associates them with Madeira and Porto Santo. See William Smith (ed.), *Dictionary of Greek and Roman Geography, vol. 1* (London: James Walton, 1869), 346.

**9** Madeira was a key supplier of yew and cedar boards in the early Portuguese empire, as evident in its name. These woods were used in European furniture making, architecture and, in the case of hardwood yew, shipbuilding. See Thomas Bentley Duncan, *Atlantic Islands: Madeira, the Azores and the Cape Verdes in Seventeenth-Century Commerce and Navigation* (Chicago: University of Chicago Press, 1972), 10.

**10** As the Portuguese settled various Atlantic islands during the 1400s, they first focused on cultivating wheat as their principal export, for consumption in Europe. Madeira, which rarely had significant grain harvests, switched to growing sugarcane after midcentury. Felipe Fernández-Armesto, *Before Columbus: Exploration and Colonization from the Mediterranean to the Atlantic, 1229–1492* (Houndsmills: Macmillan Education, 1987), 195–200.

**11** See page 76, ft. 27.

La Ville de Funchal[12] qui est la Capitale est le sejour ordinaire d'un evêque suffragant de l'Archeveque de Lisbonne[13]; son port n'a point d'abbri assuré, quoÿ qu'il soit le meilleur d'isle, et l'on ne trouve de bon mouillage que dans les rades. l'isle de Porto Santo est au nord est de Madera. elle fut aussi decouverte par les Portugais en l'an 1420. elle est aussi abondante en blez en fruits et en bestiaux.[14]

Apres la decouverté de cette isle nous avons gouverné a l'ouest quart sud ouest Jusqu'a minuit et du depuis â L'ouest sud ouest Jus qu'a cinq heures du matin que nostre Commandant nous ordonna de faire route au sud ouest quart sud vers les Jsles de Canaries dont nous dêcouvrimes une d'elles nommeé Palma[15] environ les neuf heures du dit Jour au sud sud est vingt Lieuës de distance, nous gouvernames alors sud quart Ouest pour passer entre les isles du Cap Verd et le dit Cap; nous rencontrames icy les vents alisez qui ne nous quitterent que vers les trois degrez.

**Le 12 de mars 1723. noús Passames** le Celebre promontoire d'affrique nommé Cap Verd[16] dans la nigritie au midi de l'embouchure du Senega[17] et au Couchant de l'affrique. Cette Côtte est frequenteé par les europeens. les Jsles qui sont vers l'occident a cent cinquante lieuës de ce Cap, sont connuës sous le nom d'isles du Cap Verd, parce que ce cap est la partie de la terre ferme qui en approche le plus. elles sont rangees pres que [4] en forme de Croissant ou de demi Cercle dont la partie Convexe regarde la grande terre et les deux pointes la grande mer. les Portugais en sont les maîtres; elles ne sont pourtant pas tous habitéez, les principales sont saint Jaques,

---

12 Funchal, founded in 1424, was the principal settlement and port of Madeira. It was located on the island's southern coast. By the 1700s, the town linked trading networks in Europe, Africa and the Americas.

13 The Roman Catholic diocese of Funchal was elevated to the rank of Archdiocese from 1533 to 1551. Both before and after this period, and extending to the present day, it was under the Archdiocese of Lisbon. See Francis M. Rogers, *The Quest for Eastern Christians: Travels and Rumor in the Age of Discovery* (Minneapolis: University of Minnesota Press, 1962), 151–2.

14 The two preceding paragraphs were adjusted and copied from: Louis Moréri, *Le Grand Dictionaire Historique, vol. 3* (Amsterdam: Boom and Van Someren, 1694), 405.

15 San Miguel de La Palma is the northern- and western-most of the Canary Islands. The Spanish first landed on this island in 1405, but they did not successfully conquer it from the native Auaritas until 1493.

16 Cap-Vert is a rocky peninsula, located near Dakar, Senegal and along the country's Atlantic coast. It forms the westernmost point on the African continent.

17 Senegal is the westernmost country in Africa. It was a major focus of the Atlantic slave trade in the eighteenth century as well as a key market for the cottons Europeans shipped from the Indian Ocean. See James F. Searing, *West African Slavery and Atlantic Commerce: the Senegal River Valley, 1700–1860* (New York: Cambridge UP, 1993), 59–128; Pedro Machado, "Awash in a Sea of Cloth: Gujarat, Africa, and the Western Indian Ocean, 1300–1800", in: *The Spinning World: a Global History of Cotton Textiles, 1200–1850*, eds. Giorgio Riello and Prasannah Parthasarathi (New York: Oxford UP, 2009), 161–79.

saint nicolas[18], saint Lucie[19], saint Marie[20], l'isle de sal[21], l'isle de Mayo, Boa Vista[22], saint Anthoine[23], saint Vincent[24], isle de fuego[25], Brava[26] &[a]. elles ont environ cinq degré de longitude en largeur, et environ autant de latitude en Longeur, c'est â dire depuis pres de quatorze Jus qu'a 19 du nord.[27]

**Je ne sçaurais m'empecher a cette** occassion de vous faire part touchant l'isle de saint Iago â Cause que C'est la place ordinaire où nos Vaisseaux d'Ostende font leur relache pour prendre de l'eau et des refraichissemens, destinez pour les Jndes orientales. Cette isle â environ quarante cinq lieuës de longeur, dix de largeur et 95 ou cent de circuit, elle â une ville de même nom situeé au sud ouest de l'isle â quinze degré ou environ de latitude septentrionale, le gouverneur general et l'Eveque de tous les Isles du Cap verd ÿ font leur residence, les maisons de cette ville sont disperseés ça et lá sur les Cotez des deux montagnes entre les quelles il ÿ a une profunde valleé, qui a deux cent verges ou environ de largeur pres de la mer, et qui â ún quart de mile du rivage se retrecit Jusques â n'avoir pas plus de quarante verges de large. dans la valleé assez pres de la mer il ÿ a une ruë êcarteé avec des maisons d'un côte et d'autre et au bout un Couran d'eau qui se decharge dans une petite baye sabloneuse [5] ou la mer est ordinairement fort Calme; de sorte qu'on trouve ici de bonne eau, et qu'il est facile d'y âborder en tous tems; quoÿ qu'il y ait des rochers dans la rade et qu'elle soit dangereuse pour les vaisseaux tout aupres de l'endroit ou l'on aborde il ÿ a un petit fort, pres qu'â niveau dela mer, ou l'on tient toujours un Corps de guarde; sur le sommet dela montagne au dessus de la ville il y a un autre fort, et il semble par la muraille qu'on peut voir de la rade, qu'il est d'une assez grande êtenduë, il y â des pieces de canon en batterie; la ville peut consister en deux ou trois cens maisons toutes batties de pierre brute, il ÿ a d'aillieurs un couvent et un êglisse.

---

**18** São Nicolau is one of the windward Cape Verde islands. It is located about 30 kilometers southeast of Santa Luzia.

**19** Santa Luzia is the smallest of the windward Cape Verde islands. It is located eight kilometers east of São Vincente.

**20** The Ilhéu de Santa Maria is a small islet located just off the southern coast of Praia, Santiago in the Cape Verde islands.

**21** Sal is one of the windward Cape Verde islands. It is located 110 kilometers east and slightly north of São Nicolau.

**22** Boa Vista is one of the windward Cape Verde islands and the archipelago's easternmost. It is located 40 kilometers south of Sal.

**23** Santo Antão is the largest and westernmost of the windward Cape Verde islands.

**24** São Vicente is one of the windward Cape Verde islands. It is located about 15 kilometers southeast of Santo Antão. Given its lack of fresh water, it remained mostly uninhabited during the eighteenth century.

**25** Fogo is one of the leeward Cape Verde islands. It is located about 60 kilometers west of Santiago.

**26** Brava is one of the leeward Cape Verde islands. It is located about 20 kilometers west of Fogo.

**27** The preceding paragraph was adjusted and copied from: Louis Moréri, *Le Grand Dictionaire Historique, vol. 1* (Lyons: J. Gyrin and B. Rivière, 1683), 761.

**Tout le monde en gêneral ÿ est noir, ou** du moins basané[28], si vous en exceptes quelque peu de pesonnes des plus qualifieés, comme le gouverneur, l evêque quelques gentils hommes, et un petit nombre de prêtres dont quelques uns sont noirs; outre les vaisseaux des Autres nations qui abordent icÿ par hazard, il ÿ en arrive tous les ans un ou deux portugais qui touchent â Cette isle dans leur route au Bressil.[29] ces derniers y debittent quelque peu des marchandisses de l'europe, et ils prennent en êchange de la toille de coton raÿeé[30] qui est la principale manufacture du pais, et qu'ils transportent au bressil; on ÿ envoye aussi un autre Vaisseau du portugal pour ÿ Charger du sucre[31], et s'en retourner tout droit dans ce Roÿaume la du moins, on dit qu'il y a plusieurs petites sucreries dans Cette jsle, et que le portugal en tirre tous les ans pres de cent [6] tonneaux de sucre: il y croit d'aillieurs quantite de Coton, dont ces jnsulaires s'habillent eux mêmes, et dont ils envoÿent une bonne partie au bressil: ils ont aussy des vignes dont ils font quelque peu de vin: mais les vaisseaux europeens leur en fournissent de mëllieur, quoÿ qu'ils n'en boivent guêre d'aucune sorte. leurs principeaux fruits (outres les plantains qu'ils en ont en abondance) consistent en oranges, limons, citrons, milons d'eau, et musques, gauvas, grenades, Coins, pommes flan, paphas &ª.[32]

**A L'orient de Isle de S^t^. Jago il y** a un bon port nommé villa praÿa (lieu ordinaire ou nos vaisseaux font leur relache) le quel par sa comodite est rarement sans vaisseaux, car ç'â esté longtems le lieu ou les vaisseaux avoient accútumé de relacher, pour prendre de l'eau et des refraichissemens comme les Ostendois, Anglois, et françois destinez pour les Indes Orientales: plusieurs de ces Vaisseaux êtant charges pour la guineé[33] et les portugais pour le bressil, ce qui se fait ordinairement vers la fin de

28 The Cape Verde islands not only were colonized with the aid of African laborers and a frequent stop for transatlantic slave ships. Africans also regularly engaged in island markets as residents and visiting traders. For more on race and social status in the islands, see George E. Brooks, *Western Africa and Cabo Verde, 1790s–1830s: Symbiosis of Slave and Legitimate Trades* (Bloomington, IN: Authorhouse, 2010), 27–46.

29 Although sugarcane was present in Brazil since 1516, the Portuguese began building processing mills in Pernambuco and São Vicente, along its Atlantic Coast, during the 1550s. This rapidly expanded the regularity of Portugal's transatlantic commercial sailings. See Stuart B. Schwartz, *Sugar Plantations in the Formation of Brazilian Society: Bahia, 1550–1835* (New York: Cambridge UP, 1985).

30 This likely refers to a cheap, colored Indian cotton, often decorated with stripes or checks, known as guineas. They frequently were sold by European slave traders to residents of the western African coast.

31 Although the Portuguese tried to develop sugar monoculture on the Cape Verde islands, they never produced as much as other islands in the Atlantic Ocean. Schwartz, Sugar, 12–3.

32 The preceding four sentences were adjusted and copied from: *Voyage De Guillaume Dampier, Aux Terres Australes, A la Nouvelle Hollande &c. fait en 1699, vol. 1* (Amsterdam: Paul Marret, 1705), 27–9.

33 Guinea was a western African kingdom, located just south of modern Senegal and along the coast. It became a major hub of the transatlantic slave trade. Guinea and the Cape Verde islands were politically, economically and demographically very integrated in the 1700s. Brooks, Western, 27–46.

septembre: mais il y a peu des Vaisseaux qui passent par la en revenant en europe; quand ÿ â la des vaisseaux. les gens dela Campagne apportent leurs marchandisses pour les vendre aux matelots et passagers, ces marchandises sont de Jeunes taurreaux, des cochons, des chevres, dela volaille[34], des ëufs, des plantains, et des noix de cocos, qu'ils troquent pour des chemises, des haut=dechaussés ou autres nipes de [7] de toille, principalement de fil, car la laine n'y est pas beaucoup estimeé; ils ne soucient guêre de se dêfaire de leur betail â moins qu'on ne leur donne de l'argent, de la toille, ou quelque autre marchandise de prix. les voÿageurs doivent se donner de garde de ces gens la; car ils sont grands larrons et s'ils trouvent leur tems ils vous arrachent ce qu'ils peuvent attraper et s'en fuÿent. nous ne touchames cette isle pour cette fois la pour ne pas perdre du tems dans nostre voÿage.[35]

Le port de Praÿa est deffendus d'un fort bâti sur le sommet d'une montagne Commandant l'havre. il est tres fort dela nature, aÿant seulement un petit chemin fort êtroit pour l'approcher; ce fort est garde par un lieutenant gouveneur dêpendant â celuy d S.$^{t}$ jago, il â ordinairement sa demeure au côte gauche en entrent dans l'havre, les maisons de cette place sont disperseés ca et la fort pauvrement baties, il ÿ â d'ailleurs une Chapelle vis a vis le bois de Cocotiers.

**Laissant ces Isles a tribord et le vent** alisez soufflant assez gaillardement, nous en profitames le mieux qu'il nous fut possible, portant toutes les voiles que nous pouvions porter et arrivames â la faveur de ce vent vers le vingt et trois de mars â trois degré de lattitude meridionale; durant tout ce tems la nous ne rencontrames rien de remarquable, si ce n'est des poissons volans.[36] J'en consideraÿ un avec beaucoup d'exactitude qui avoit [8] environ douze pouces[37] de long: il ÿ en â peu de plus grands, et beaucoup d'un peu plus petits. le dos est d'un brun rousatre, marqueté de taches bleuves, tirand sur le verd, avec un peu de noir. le ventre nue de blanc et de bleu, et les Côtez couverts des petites escailles d'un roux obscur. les grandes ailes ou nagoires sont brunes, parsemeés de taches de ver de mer: les petites sont d'un gris Clair, et la queue aussi. l'ëuil est grand et êlevé, la prunelle large et bleue, et le rest blanc. Cé qui est pointille â la tête, est grisatre[38]; les naturalistes le nomment hirrondelle de mer[39],

34 The more arid Cape Verde islands, such as Santiago and Fogo, primarily were used to pasture cattle, horses, pigs and goats. These supplied local needs and provided fresh meat to anchored ships. Ibid., 27, 36.

35 The preceding paragraph was adjusted and copied from: Guillaume Dampier, *Nouveau Voyage autour du Monde, vol. 1* (Rouen: Jean-Baptiste Machuel, 1715), 99–100.

36 Ibid., 104.

37 This refers to the traditional English and French inch, which equates to 27.07 millimeters.

38 The preceding six sentences were adjusted and copied from: *Voyage et Avantures de François Leguat, & de ses Compagnons, vol. 1* (London: David Mortier, 1708), 10.

39 The flying fish, or "sea sparrow," typically was encountered in warm, tropical waters. It could glide above the water for up to one hundred yards, to avoid maritime – although not avian – predators.

et luÿ attribuent quantité de proprietez que Je laisse. il s'entrouve qui ont quatre ailes. Ceux que nous avons mangez ont assez le gout du harang.[40]

Ces pauvres petites bêtes, qu'on pourroit prendre pour le simbole d'une perpetuelle fraÿeur; sont aussy Continuellement en fuite et en s'êlevent, pour se sauver ils viennent assez souvent donner dans les voiles ils volent aussi longtems qu'il reste de l'humidité dans leurs ailes, qui des qu'elles sont seches, redeviennent aussitôt nageoires; force leur êtant de retomber dans l'eau. autrement, ils ont si grand peur, qu'ils s'en iroient au bout du monde.

Ces efforts qu'ils font de dêvenir plustôt habitans de l'air que de l'eau, sont pour eviter la persecution des dorades[41] et des bonites[42] qui leur font un guerre perpetuelle; mais les pauvres malheurex n'evitent un peril que pour se jetter Jncontinent dans un autre: des cruels oiseaux leurs ennemis irreconciliables [9] êtant toujours au guet, et en grosses bandes pour les englouttir des qu'ils entrent dans le nouvel êlement ou ils croiÿent trouver un asÿle. les marsouins font la même guerre aux dorades; et tout Cela nous est un image dela vie humaine, ou l'on est en de perpetuels dangers, et ou le foible est ordinairement la victime du fort.[43]

**Venant â la Latitude Septentrionale de** quatre degré 50 minutes le vent comenca âvarier et nous eumes en suitte de petits vents frais, avec quelques tourbillons. durant cet Jntervalle nous vimes quelques bonetas, et quelques requins:[44] et nous primes plusieurs de Ces derniers. pendant tous Ces Calmes, nous eumes l'occassion d'examiner le Courant que nous avions eu Jusqu'icÿ, et nous trouvames qu'il Couroit nord est quart â l'est 12 miles en vingt quatre heures; de sorte qu'il Courroit icy sur le pie d'un dêmy mile par heure; les pluies nous reprirent de tems en tems, Jus qu'a un degrez de latitude meridionale aveq des petits vents incertains des eclairs et de tonere venant par broullards, qui soufflоient presque tous du sud[45]; de sorte que nous ne gagnames le sud qu'avec beaucoup de lenteur. nous la rangeames le mieux qu'il nous fut possible, malgré tous ces obstacles, et d'abord qu'il venoit une bouffeé de vent d'est, nous continuames tout droit nostre route vers le sud, âfin d'arriver au plus vîte au lieu de nostre destination.

40 Herring, a shallow water fish native to the North Atlantic and North Pacific oceans, was a common catch among Dutch fishermen in the early eighteenth century. It then was salted or smoked for consumption.

41 The sea bream, or dorade, is a predatory fish, found in the Mediterranean Sea and northeastern Atlantic Ocean.

42 The bonita is a predatory fish, of the same family as tuna and mackerel. It is found in the Atlantic Ocean, Mediterranean Sea and Black Sea.

43 The preceding seven sentences were adjusted and copied from: Voyage et Avantures, vol. 1, 11–2.

44 See, for more on sharks and eighteenth-century seafaring, Marcus Rediker, "History from below the water line: Sharks and the Atlantic slave trade", in: *New Orleans in the Atlantic World: Between Land and Sea*, ed. William Boelhower (New York: Routledge, 2010), 131–43.

45 The preceding two sentences were adjusted and copied from: Voyage de Guillaume Dampier, vol. 4, 45.

**Nous passames la Ligne le premier** [10] d'avril et il me falloit assuÿer la ceremonie qu'on appelle du baptême[46] du moins ceux qui s'êtoient pas rencontré a pareille fête, ou qui ne vouloient pas se racheter pour de l'argent.

C'est une Coûtume ancienne qu'on auroit bien dela peine â abolir. cela se fait quelques fois aussi lorsqu'on passe sous le tropiques. voicy en peu de mots Comme Cette belle ceremonie se fit sur nostre vaisseau, un des matelots qui avoit dêja passé la ligne s'habilla d'haillons, se fit une Ceinture de Corde, des Cheveux et une barbe d'êtoupes, et se noirsit le visage de suye dé=trempée avec de l'huile dans Cet equipage tenant une Carte marine en une main, un sabre en l'autre et du noir a noircir, il se presenta sur le pont, accompagne de ses suffragans habillez aussi grotesquement que luÿ armez de grils, de poïles, de chaudrons &[a]. faisant aveq ces jnstrumens la musique qu'on peut s'imaginer.

Ils appellérent un â un ceux qui devoient estre Jnitiez, et apres les avoir fait asseoir sur le bord d'un cuveau plain d'eau, ils leur firent mettre la main sur la carta, et promettre qu'en pareille occassion ils feroient faire aux autres, la même Chose qu'on Exigeoit presentement d'eux. en suitte ils leur firent une marque au front avec le noir, leur mouillerent le vissage avec l'eau de mer et leur demanderent sils voulloient donner â l'equipage quelque chose pour boire, leur promettant que moÿennant cette liberalité ils les tiendroient quittes. ceux qui donnerent furent Jncontinent relachez, quelques uns mêmes êviterent ce desagreable prelude en donnant un peu grassement. il ne m'en couta que deux escu pour avoir [11] le previlege de Ces derniers. pour les autres, on leur fit faire la Cullebulte dans le Cuveau, où on les lava et les decrassa de tous les Côtez avec les balais du vaisseau, et Je pense bien que Cella dura un plus peu longtems qu'ils ne l'auroient voulu.

Comme la Chaloupe, n'avoit Jamais passe la ligne il falut qu'elle subisset la même loy. le Capitaine fut obligé de racheter l'eperon de sa Chaloupe les matelots disant qu'ils êtoient en droit de couper le nez a la chaloupe. l'argent que l'equipage ramassa fut destinez a se divertir en Commun â la premiere occassion. au reste Chaque nation pratique Cette redicule Ceremonie avecq quelque diversité.[47]

**Aÿant gagné Le sud dela Ligne, le** vent se tourna plus â l'est et alors nous fimes route sud ouest.[48] quart sud, et a mesure que nous avancames le sud le vent se rafraichit et se tourna â l'est. â deux degré et demÿ de latitude meridionale nous eumes le

---

46 For more on eighteenth-century equatorial baptisms, see Rediker, Between, 186–87; Simon J. Bronner, *Crossing the Line: Violence, Play, and Drama in Naval Equator Traditions* (Amsterdam: Amsterdam UP, 2007); Jaime Rodrigues, "A new world in the Atlantic: sailors and rites of passage crossing the Equator, from the 15th to the 20th century", in: *Revista Brasileira de História* 33.6 (2013), 233–75.

47 The preceding four paragraphs were adjusted and copied from: Voyage et Avantures, vol. 1, 25–7.

48 European ships could ride the Canary Current south until Cape Nao, Morocco, where it turned to the West. By sailing to about the Canary Islands, they then could catch a southeastern current that took their ships back along the western coast of Africa. Thornton, Cultural, 7–25.

vent sud est et a 16 Jus qu'a les 24. degré nous l'eumes est, et nord, nord est, petit vent et beau tems.[49]

Le 19 d'avril nostre Commandant nous fit signal de mettre en travers pour venir â nostre bord avec ses marchands pour prendre la soupe avec nous, en même tems nous deliberames sur le passé durant le trajet depuis la sortie d'ostende Jusqu'â Cette preditte hauteur.

Le 22 le vent sud est, et sud sud Est beau frais tems sombre avons Couru la bordeé de l'est nord est, Jus qu'a minuit que nous avons veu un navire au vent a nous environ un demi lieuë [12] nous avons en même tems viré de bord par ordre de nostre Commandant et Couru au sud sud Ouest, â midy par l'observation Je compris que nous êtions suivant mon hauteur êloigne dela ligne de 28 degré 32 minutes au sud, et de longitude occidentale de 7 degrez 54 Minutes du lezard en angleterre, nous trouvames la un degré vingt minutes de variation au nord est.

Estant le 27 d'avril â 23 degré 34 minutes de latitude nous eumes de gros vents estant presque toujours nord nord Ouest et Ouest avec beaucoup dela pluye, nous vimes une quantité prodigieuse de marsouvins. Ces annimaux ne sont pas eloigne dela figure du Cochon; ils ont la soye Courte mais plus rude que Celle des Chiens marins, et les piez qui leur servent aussi a nager, faits de même et de couleur noire.

Il ne se passa rien de remarquable depuis le 28 d'avril Jusques au 3 maÿ. mais nous vimes de tems en tems des herbages de mer apelé trompétte[50] et quelques petites balaines qui faisoient Jaillir l'eau, nous avions le vent nord qui nous servit a courir depuis le 34 degré 25 minutes de latitude meridionale Jus qu'a 36 degré 3 minutes, et nous eumes âlors 23 degrez 48 minutes de longitude Orientale dêpuis le Lezard, la variation augmentoit a present de plus en plus au nord Ouest. d'aillieurs nous eumes la visite d'un grand nombre d'oiseaux de mer, qui suivoient nostre vaisseau, il y en avoit de plusieurs especes, et ils differoient pour la grosseur la figure et le plumage. quelques uns estoient pres qu'aussi gros que des Oyes de couleur grisse aveq la poitrine [13] blanche, de même que le bec, les ailes et la queuë.[51] On y voyoit des pintados[52], ou oiseaux peints qui sont aussy gros que des canards et marquetez de blanc et de noir des friseurs d'eau des petrels, et quantité de plus gros oiseaux. nous en vimes des uns et des autres sur tout des pintados; Le pintado est un oiseau du pais

49 The preceding paragraph was adjusted and copied from: Dampier, *Nouveau, vol. 1*, 104.
50 The sea trumpet, or *Ecklonia buccinalis*, is a species of extremely large kelp, brown in color and native to the southern hemisphere. It especially is known to grow in the waters near Cape Town, thus providing clues as to the position of the ship.
51 This likely refers to one of the species of albatross – such as the shy, wandering or grey-headed albatross – that range in the southern hemisphere.
52 The pintado petrel, or Cape pigeon, is a seabird, which feeds on fish and squid in the southern hemisphere and makes its nest in rocky cliffside colonies. It has a dark-colored head and wings that are speckled black or brown and white, thus appearing to be painted and giving the bird a portion of its name.

meridional et de la partie tempereé de Cette Zone; du moins Je n'en ay Jamais guêre vu vers le nord du 30 degré de latitude meridionale. quoy qu'il soit aussi gros qu'un canard, il ne paroit en volant que de la grosseur d'un pigeon domestique, il â la queue courte et les ailes fort longues, comme les ont la plus part des oiseaux de mer, sur tout ceux qui s'êloignent beaucoup du rivage, et qui n'en aprochent presque pas; ils flottent sur l'eau pour se reposer; mais ils font leurs ëufs â terre, si je ne me trompe; il y a trois sortes de ces oiseaux, tous dela même forme et grosseur et qui ne different entreux que par le plumage. les uns sont noirs par tout, les autres ont le manteau gris, avec le Jabot et le ventre blanc, et les troisiemes, qui sont les vrais pintados sont admirablement bien mouchetez de blanc et de noir. Ceux cÿ ont la tête presque noire, de même que le bout des ailes et de la queuë: mais dans ce noir des aïles il y a des taches qui paroissent estre de la grandeur d'un dêmy êcu quand jls volent, c'est alors qu'on voit mieux leurs taches; leurs ailes sont aussi bordeés tout au tour d'un petit fil noir et l'on voit sur le milieu, qui est blanc une tache noire, qui s'eclairsit peu â peu, et aproche d'un gris obscur vers le dos de l'oiseau. le bord Jnterieur des ailes, et le dos même despuis la tête Jusques au bout de la queuë sont emaillez d'un nombre infini de [14] Jolie taches rondes, blanches et noires dela grandeur d'un sol marqué; le ventre les Cuisses les Cotez et le dessous des aïles sont d'un gris Clair. tous les pintados en general vont par troupes et ils balaÿent presque l'eau en volant.

**Le petrel ne differe pas beaucoup de** l'hirondelle mais il est plus petit, et il a la queuë plus courte; il est noir par tout, exepté sur le crupion, ou il a une tache blanche: il frise l'eau en volant de même que l'hirondelle. on n'en voit guêre quand il fait beau; c'est pour cela que nos matelots les appellent des oiseaux du mauvais tems, et lors qu'ils volent au tour des vaisseaux, on â sujet de craindre quelque orage; ils voltigent même sous la poupe, s'il a tempête, et â mesure qu'ils suivent la trace d'un vaisseau ils se mouillent les pieds â differentes reprises, de sorte qu'on diroit âles voir, qu'ils marchent plustôt qu'ils ne volent, et que par allusion â Saint Pierre qui marcha sur le lac de Gennesaret[53], nos matelots leur ont donné le nom de Pêtrels.[54]

**Le lendemain le 12 maÿ noús vimes** pazer pres de nous un oiseau noir[55], qui avoit le bec plat et blanchatre, nous observames avec autant plus de soin, que le pilote des Jndes Orientales parle de certains oiseaux, dela grosseur d'un corbeau, qui ont le bec plat et blanc, et le plumage noir, qui ne s'eloignent pas â plus de trente lieuës du Cap, et qui sont une marque qu'on en est pres. Selon nostre calcul, et eu [15] egard a

53 According to the Bible, Jesus Christ appeared to his disciples walking on Lake Gennesaret, or the Sea of Galilee, during a storm. Peter, one of his followers, asked to come to him and similarly walked atop the waves, as long as he had faith. The petrel, which appears to walk on water as it begins flight, derives a portion of its name from this story. Matthew 14:22–34, Mark 6:45–53, John 6:15–21.

54 The preceding two paragraphs were adjusted and copied from: Voyage de Guillaume Dampier, vol. 1, 78–80.

55 This might refer to the Crowned Cormorant, a seabird only found in the region around Cape Agulhas.

la longitude que les Cartes ordinaires donnent au Cap[56], nous ne devions estre pas loing du dit cap, â midi par l'estime nous Comprimes que nous êtions de la ligne de 36 degré 24 minutes et de longitude orientale du lezar suivant mon Compte de 25. degré 33 minutes, et nous trouvames par l'amplitude 13 degrez 15 minutes de variation occidentale, sur quoy nous sondâmes et trouve 95 brasses d'eau et la seconde 110 brasses fonds de sable fin, blanc, noir, et verdatre: cela nous fit voir que nous êtions â l'est du Cap de bonne esperance.

**Dans cette vuë nous fimes roûte Súd** est quart est tout voiles d'hors pour arriver plustôt â la nouvelle hollande[57], car quoy que Ce pais soit au nord est du Cap, tous les vaisseaux qui veulent au destroit de la sunde doivent courir quelque tems sous le même paralelle, ou dans une latitude entre les 35 et 40. degré du moins un peu au sud de l'est, afin de Continuer dans la route des vents variables; et ils ne doivent pas s'hazarder trop tôt a se mettre le Cap au nord, de peur de s'engager dans l'etenduë du vent alise, qui les detoúrneroit de leur route a l'est. le vent se rendit plus frais[58] avec de brouillards et de pluÿe.

**Le 14 dú même mois â la pointe dú joúr** nous vimes un navire devant nous un peu a tribord qui gouverna â l'est ¼ sud est il abora pavillon hollandais ce qui nous fit [16] croire que s'estoit un navire de la Compagnie, nostre Commandant et nous avons mis le nostre pareillement: poursuivant nostre route sans le parler. le vent Continuant au nord Ouest gros frais nous avons gouverne â l'est sud est, les huniers tout haut la grande voile cargué, le dit vent venant par brouillards avec dela pluÿe des esclairs et du tonnere.

**Le 20 de maÿ le vent nord et nord oûest** Jusqu'a l'ouest sud Ouest gros vent avec des brouillards et dela pluÿe des esclairs et du tonnere sur la minuit nous eumes une êclaircie pale et blanchatre aú nord ouest ce qui estoit signe d'un Orage, en effet le vent fraichit tout d'un Coup; la dessus nous serrames nos voiles de perroquet, nous serlames[59] nostre grande voile, et nous Courumes avec la seule voile de misaine, vers les 6 heures du matin la violence du vent redoubla, nous amenames la grande vergue sur le tilliac, et nous mimes le ciel au vent, qui se renforcoit toujours: le navire se manioit le mieux du monde et silloit â merveille. a sept heures du matin nous bais-

56 The preceding two sentences were adjusted and copied from: Voyage de Guillaume Dampier, vol. 4, 102.

57 Abel Tasman, a Dutch sailor, first applied the name "New Holland" to mainland Australia in 1644. It was used until the 1770s. The author here references the continent to note his ships' unique southerly course, in hopes of catching winds that might speed their sailing to the Straits of Sunda. The Ostend ships, in opposition to their EIC and VOC counterparts, often sailed this far southern course. Parmentier, Tea Time, 53–4.

58 The preceding three sentences were adjusted and copied from: Voyage de Guillaume Dampier, vol. 4, 113.

59 The original author, Guillaume Dampier, correctly wrote "ferlames." The author here, when copying this text, misspelled the word, by confusing the similar-looking "s" and "f".

sames nostre vergue de misaine de trois ou quatre pies et nous Courions fort vîte sur tout lors qu'un nuage noir nous envoyoit quelques Ondeés de pluÿe ou de grelle; parce que le vent souffloit avec la derniere Jmpetuosite. quoy que ces grains ne fussent pas de dureé, ils se suivoient de près les uns les autres. d'ailleurs la mer estoit fort grosse; mais nous aillons d'un Cours si rapide, vent en poupe, que les vagues ne nous [17] mouillerent presque point: il n'entra qu'un peu d'eau par les sabords du tilliac.

**Le vent ne dimínua de Sa violance** extraordinaire que Vers la nuit du dimanche 23 may, mais nous eumes un beau frais Jusques le 27, et un petit vent avec des Calmes Jusques au premier de Juin, dans Cett'espace nous avions courú au tour de quatre cent Lieuës, et le vent avoit presqûe toûjours soufflé de quelque point de l'ouest, c'est â dire depuis l'ouëst, Jusques au sud quart Ouëst. il souffloit avec plus de vehemence lors qu'il estoit â l'ouest ou entre le nord Ouest, mais lors qu'il tourna plus au sud le mauvais tems finit. J'aÿ plusieurs fois remarqué que dans ces mers aussitôt que le vent d'ouëst qui Causoit les tempêtes se rangoit au sud elles diminúent, et que si le vent se tournoit â l'est par le sud, nous avions de petits frais plus moderez, des calmes et un beau tems. pour ce qui est des vents d'Ouëst de ce côté du cap, leur Violance ne fait pas que nous les souhetions moins, parce qu'ils nous portent plus vite â l'est: aussi toutes les personnes qui vont â Cette partie des Jndes orientales qui est au sud de leur êquateur, comme Java, Sumatra, tous les vaisseaux destinez pour la Chine, et tous Ceux qui doivent passer le dêtroit de la Sunde ne soupirent qu'âpres ces vents la. d'abord qu'ils ont passe le Cap, ils rangent d'ordinaire le sud, enfin de trouver les vents d'Ouëst qui ne manquent presque Jamais de souffler en hÿver au sud du Cap: mais en esté, C'est âdire toujours â l'êgard de Ces [18] climats, il faut qu'ils aillent 40 degré au sud pour les rencontrer. nous n'avancames a plus de 37 degre 13 minutes de latitude, et souvent même nous fumes plus au nord, reduit a Changer nostre latitude toutes les fois que les vents et le tems le demandōit du moins dans ces voyages de long Cours, il vaut mieux accomoder sa route au vent qu'il fait, mais si en portant â l'est, nous estions obligez de Courir un peu au nord ou au sud il n'y auroit pas grand mal, puis qu'il ne faudroit que singler a 2 ou 3 points au dela du vent, lors qu'il est nord ou sud ce qu'il n'empeche pas seulement le vaisseau de faire trop d'effort; mais abrege plus le Chemin, que si l'on suivoit toujours le même rumb de vent comme font certains personnes.[60]

**Le 10. Juin noús êtions â 26 degré** 43 minutes de latitude meridionale et â 106 degré 9 minutes, de longitude du Lezard, et nous trouvames par l'amplitude 9. degré 30 minutes de variation occidentale; d'aillieurs il ne se presenta depuis le 20 de maÿ rien de fort remarquable, dans dans [sic] tout ce voÿage excepte que des oiseaux nous accompagnerent tout le long du Chemin depuis le Cap, sur tout des pintados; et que nous decoúvrions de tems en tems une baleine. mais â mesure que nous aprochions

---

**60** The preceding two paragraphs were adjusted and copied from: Voyage de Guillaume Dampier, vol. 1, 78–80.

de la Cote de la nouvelle hollande, nous en voÿions souvent trois ou quatre en semble. nous Commençames â voir des herbes marines; touttes de la mesme sorte[61], surquoÿ nous Jettames la sonde par un beau [19] tems, mais il n'y avoit pas Fond.

**Le 16 de Juin â 21 degré 4 minutes de latitude** meridionale et â 124 degre 6 minutes de longitude â l'est de teneriffe[62] le vent sud et sud est assé beau frais faisant route vers l'est, il faisoit tres beau ce Jour la, et la mer êtoit Couverte d'une espece de fort petite mousse[63] qui resembloit a des ëufs de poisson, il y avoit même quelque menu fretin qui l'accompagnoit.[64] â cinq heures du soir nous sondames, mais sans trouver fond et avons reste en pane depuis l'est quart sud est Jusqu'a l'est nord est, et avons reste ainsÿ Jusqu'a les 6 heures du matin que nous avons fait servir est nord est.

**Le 17 nous vimes quantité de petits globules** sur l'eau, qu'on auroit pris pour des perles[65], et dont quelques uns êtoient de la grosseur des pois secs, ils êtoient fort clairs et transperans: lors qu'on les escrasoit, il en sortoit une goute d'eau, et la pellicule qui la remfermoit estoit si delieé, qu'on avoit quelque peine a la discerner. il ÿ eut aussy des herbes marines qui passerent dans nostre voisinage; d'où nous conclumes que nous verions bientôt la terre.

**Le 18 nous en vimes flotter d'autres, tous les** oiseaux que nous avions vûs pendant le voÿage nous abandonnerent, et nous en vimes â present d'une toute autre espece qui estoient de la grosseur des vaneaux.[66] ils avoient le plumage gris [20] le tour des ÿeux noir, le bec rouge et pointu les ailes longues, et la queuë fourcheé Comme Celles des hirondelles, ils battoient les ailes en volant de même que les vaneaux. environ le soir nous rencontrames une espece de mareé ou de Courant qui venoit peut estre de quelque batture, mais nous l'avions dêja passeé avant que nous pussions Jetter le plomb. qu'oÿ qu'il ensoit, c'estoit un nouveau signe que nous approchions de terre[67]; nostre Commandant par Ces signes s'etant assuré d'estre assé â l'est des trials, se contenta sans voir la terre de la nouvelle hollande de faire route au nord vers l'isle de Java.

---

61 The preceding three sentences were adjusted and copied from: Ibid., 93.

62 Tenerife is the largest of the Canary Islands, located about 100 kilometers southeast of San Miguel de La Palma. It was conquered by the Spanish in 1494. Dutch cartographers used the island since the mid-1600s to mark the prime meridian and measure global locations to its east and west, a habit here adopted by the author.

63 This likely refers to the seaweed *Caulerpa lentillifera*, which has numerous small, green or bluish beads resembling grapes. It grows in the Indian and Pacific Oceans as well as along the east coast of Africa.

64 The preceding half-sentence was copied from: Voyage de Guillaume Dampier, vol. 4, 103.

65 This probably refers to another species of "sea grapes."

66 This refers to some sort of Australian sea- or shorebird, possibly the Antarctic, Caspian or Roseate terns. It also could indicate the Hooded Plover, but the St. Joseph would have had to be very close to the coast.

67 The preceding two paragraphs were adjusted and copied from: Voyage de Guillaume Dampier, vol. 4, 103.

**Il ne se passa rien de considerable, Jusqu'au** 24 a 8 heures du soir que nous avons veu un feu qui nous aparut trop grand pour estre le feu de quelque navire, en même tems nous avons fait signal â nostre Commandant en tirant un Coup de Canon l'ayant apercu il Carga ces basses voiles, et mit en pane sur les huniers pour nous attendre tellement que nous nous sommes parlés, et nous Commanda de rester en pane sur les deux huniers babord au vent Jus qu'au Jour au sud sud ouest qui ne veut dire que l'ouëst.

**Le 25 a cinq heures du matin noús avons** fait servir et presente au nord demÿ est Jus qu'a six heures que nous avons veu la terre de Java au nord nord est environs 13. lieuës de distance, terre haute et assé unie, nous l'avons un [21] peu aproche apres quoy nous avons gouverné au nord Ouest, â 8 heures la ditte pointe nous restoit au nord est quart est dix lieues de distance gouvernant au nord Ouest quart Ouëst Jus qu'a midi que J'aÿ eu hauter de 8 degré de latitude, et la terre la plus proche me restoit au nord est quart nord gouvernant a L'ouest nord Ouest avec un beau tems et la mer belle, a six heures du soir nous relevames un Cap qui nous restoit au nord ouest demy ouest distant de huit Lieuës. suivant mon observation ce cap est par sept degré 30 minutes de latitude meridionale. depuis ce dit Cap nous avons gouverne â l'ouëst Jus qu'a minuit et depuis ouest demÿ sud.

**Le 25. la terre qué noús Vimes, c'estoit** une terre de moyenne hauteur estant parsemeé de quelques mornes parmi les quels il y a de petites emminences qui resemblent fort a des dunes de sables, a 6 heures nous avons veu une isle au nord ouest quart nord, â 7 Lieuës de distance, elle nous parut d'assez belle hauteur, mais pas si haute que la grande terre Cette isle peut avoir une lieuë et demÿ de long. Comme elle n'avoit point de noms particulier dans nos Cartes nous nous servimes du previlege des gens de marine, et la nommerent l'isle de Sabina du Bois[68], â l'honneur de la femme[69] de nostre armateur monsieur Jaq.$^{s}$ Maelcamp.[70] On voit sur cette isle de beaux longs arbres au dessus, qui fait un fort beau aspect, â midÿ le millieu de Cette ditte isle me restoit au nord est demÿ nord distance de [22] sept Lieuës, J'estoit par sept degré 52 minutes de latitude observeé, et par 113 degré 8 minutes, de longitude â l'est du Lezard: et par 123 degré 44 minutes de longitude â l'est de tenerif, â soleil

**68** Place unknown.

**69** Sabine Maelcamp, née du Bois (ca. 1692–1765), married Jacques Maelcamp in Ghent in 1714. See Gustave Van Hoorebeke, *Le Nobiliaire de Gand* (Gand: A.I. Vander Schelden, 1850).

**70** Jacques-Fortunat Maelcamp (1683–1741) was a native of Ghent and the son of a city alderman. He became heavily invested, as a financier, in the Ostend trade. Together with his brother Charles and several Bruges associates, for example, he prepared the first Flemish ship to sail to the East Indies in 1715. The two brothers sent a ship to Malabar in 1717 and fitted out three vessels to trade in China in 1718. In 1721, the Maelcamps sought a 20-year monopoly of the China trade, which they did not receive. Jacques eventually became a director of the Ostend Company. See Jan Parmentier, "The Ostend Trade to Moka and India (1714–1735): the Merchants and Supercargos", in: *The Mariner's Mirror* 73.2 (1987), 129–30.

couchant nous vimes deux petits islets[71] proche la grande terre dont l'un est rond et l'autre plat, l'isle ronde me restoit au nord nord Ouëst dist:ᵉ de 2 Lieuës, et l'autre au nord de même distance, la grande terre est de belle hauteur couverte de longs arbres qui font plaisir â voir, pendant la nuit nous primes le large, et vers le Jour nous avons âproche de terre.

**Le 26. environs les neuf heures dú matin â** mesures que nous aprochions de terre nous en primes differentes vuës a plusieurs distances inegales, d'ou elle nous parut telle qu'on la voit icÿ representeé dans la table, dans la quelle J'ay adjute les terres les plus reconnoissables, vous pouvé observer aussy une fois pour toutes que les latitudes marqueés dans ces profils, ne sont pas la lattitude de la terre: mais du vaisseau lors qu'on prit Ces differentes vuës.[72]

**Le 27 â la pointe du Jour nous vimes de riere** nous deux navires avec pavillion hollandois, nous les repondimes avec le nostre faisants route Comme nous, Le vent Continuant â l'est sud est, beau frais faisant route le long de la terre â 6 heures du soir nous decouvrimes devant nous het boomkens Eylant ou bien l'isle aux arbres[73] au nord Ouest quart nord distan:ᵉ de 5 Lieuës [23] cette Jsle est tres remarcable par des grands et hauts arbres qu'elle a dessus autrement elle est basse et la pointe dela terre ferme nommée Wyncoopers hoeck[74] est une terre plus haute que la ditte Isle avec deux ou trois longs arbres venant en haussant devers le paÿs, Comme cette pointe n'est eloigneé du destroit de Sunde que de vingt cinq Lieuës â minuit nous avons sereé tous nos voilles et Cargué les basses voilles et mis en panne sur les huniers babord au vent, et reste de mesme Jusques â trois heures du matin que nous avons fait servir et gouverne au nord Ouest quart Ouest et Ouest nord Ouest sur les deux huniers Jusqu'au Jour que nous avons mis toutte voilles dehors, a 6 heures du matin nous vimes trauwers Eylant[75] au nord nord est quart est Jusqu'au nord est demy est distance de quatre lieuës, et Claps Eylant depuis le nord ouest quart nord Jusqu'au nord ouest demy ouest dist.ᵉ de 3 Lieuës. La pointe sud ouest de Java au nord nord ouest distance de 9 a 10 Lieuës; les dittes Jsles sont basses celle de Clappers est abondante en petits arbres, elles n'ont qu'environ quatre a cinc milles de circuit, la terre est Jeunatre et profunde, â midy la ditte pointe sud ouest de java nous restoit â l'est demy sud une lieuë de distance: pa la latitude observeé nous êtions par 6 degré 54 minutes et par 119 degré 43 minutes de longitude a l'est de tenerif.

---

71 These likely refer to modern-day Batu Nunggal and Batu Nusamanuk, located a short distance off the southern coast of Java.

72 The preceding two paragraphs were adjusted and copied from: Voyage de Guillaume Dampier, vol. 4, 106.

73 Place unknown.

74 Wynkoopers Hook, now Ujung Genteng, is a cape in southwest Java, located about 140 kilometers southeast of the entrance to the Straits of Sunda.

75 Trowers Island, now Pulau Tinjil, is located about 23 kilometers northeast of Clap's Island.

**Le vent venant de dessús la terre** avons Couru au plus pres du vent le long dela terre â midi et [24] demy avons entre dans le fameux Destroit de la Sunde par le behauden passage entre la grande terre de Java et l'isle du Prince, nous continuames de cottoïer la terre Jus qu'a neuf heures du soir que nous avons mouille l'ancre par les 19 brasses d'eau font de vaze dans le peperbay. le lendemain avec la pointe du Jour nous eumes la visite dela Chaloupe d'un vaisseau de la Compagnie d'hollande qui venoit de Suratte, comme aussy de plusieurs petites Canots ou pirogues de terre avec des pompelmissen de noix de coco et autres petits rafraichissemens, ces petits Pirogés sont tout d'une piece, et faits d'un tronc d'arbre Creuse, ils les manient fort bien et les font marcher en nageant avec leur petite rame d'une grande vitesse;

**Le 29 vers les 12 heúres le vent est venús** a l'ouëst en même tems avons levé l'ancre et gouverné au nord est le long de la terre, vers les neuf heures du soir nous passames les isles dwars inde Wegh[76], brabants hoetien[77], et toppers hoetien[78], en même tems nous avons parlé â nostre Commandant qui nous dit qu'il avoit escrit des lettres pour l'Europé et les avoit envoÿeés dans le navire le mary de londres[79], venant de batavia, allant â madras sur la Cotte de Coromandel[80] et de la en eúrope; le lendemain â quatre heures du matin toppers hoetien nous restoit au sud demÿ est 6 lieuës de distance, et la pointe de Bantam au sud sud est demÿ est â huit lieuës de nous, faisant route le long de la terre de Sumatra, â midy nous eumes les deux freres[81] â l'est, [25] Ces iles sont frequenteés Journellement par ceux de Bantam pour prendre des tortués[82], et en mesme tems faire la peche de poisons, qui est fort abondante, nous avons veu sortir de bantam â grand matin plus de Cent piroges qui alloient pour faire la pesche aux environs des dits isles.

76 This denotes the island Dwars-in-den-Wegh, now Pulau Sangiang.

77 This might refer to modern-day Pulau Rimaubalak, an island located about 10 kilometers northwest of Dwars-in-den-Wegh.

78 Toppers-hoetien, now Pulau Tempurung, is located northeast of Dwars-in-den-Wegh and in the Sunda Strait. It also may have been known as Button Island.

79 The Mary, of unknown rating, made several voyages for the EIC between 1708 and the 1730s. These primarily focused on the country trade with Madras and Bengal. McGilvary, Guardian, 4.

80 The Coromandel Coast is a region in southeastern India, extending southwards of the Bay of Bengal and including Madras. It initially had three Portuguese colonies but expanded to accommodate British, French and Ostend commercial claims in the 1700s. Seshan, Trade.

81 The Two Brothers, now Kepulauan Segama, are two wooded islands, located roughly 29 kilometers off the southeastern Sumatra coast. Ships sailing between the Sunda and Banca straits used them as navigational aides.

82 Sailors brought live turtles and tortoises onto transoceanic ships, to offer fresh meat supplies during long sailings. The latter, in particular, were reputed to be able to survive with no food or water for long periods of time. See Callum Roberts, *The Unnatural History of the Sea* (Washington, D.C.: Island Press, 2007), 74.

Ces isles sont fort abondantes en beaux et grands arbres, elles peuvent avoir environ deux milles de circuit Chacune, elles se resemblent si bien l'un â l'autre, qu'on les a donne pour tel raison le noms de deux freres.

**Le 30 â cinc heúres du matin noús** avons veu deux Jonques ou navires Chinois qui venoient de batavia faisant route Comme nous, depuis les six heures nous avons rangé plus a l'ouest pour nous aprocher de la terre de Sumatra, et a neuf heures nous decouvrimes de=vant nous au nord est l'isle de lucipara qui est devant le destroit de banca, en mesme tems veu un navire â l'ancre avec pavillion hollandois, â midy la ditte isle de Lucipara nous restoit au nord est trois lieues de distan:[e] elle nous parut comme cÿ desous.

**[Figure 1:** View of Lucepara Island]

a trois heúres apres midy nous entrames dans le dit destroit Côtoÿant de plus pres l'orient entre l'isle de Sumatra et celle de Banca, a Cause que l'entreé du destroit est fort peu profunde, ainsÿ il vaut mieux apres avoir eü lúcipara a l'est et est sud est [26] trois lieuës loing, gouverner au nord nord ouest et ranger la dite Cotte de Sumatre la sonde a la main ne venant pas a moindre eau que quatre brasses ou trois et demy pour le moins â Cause de deux bancs de Sabre et roches qui sont entre cette ditte Jsle et le milieu du destroit, qui son dangereux; quand on est dans le bon Canal on â la grande terre de banca nommeé de Lalarÿ[83] par la premiere pointe de sumatra l'un par l'autre, mais on la peut ranger d'une lieue ou une et demÿ et on trouvera pas moins de quatre brasses de fonds et si on range plus du Costé de sumatra l'eau amoindrit au lieu que quand on prend du Costé de lucipara elle augmente par ainsy on peut se tenir â un fonds â peu pres esgal selon qu'on trouve â propos.

**Le premier de Jullet noús continúames** de côtoÿer la terre de Sumatra distant d'une lieue et demy â midy la terre de manopin nous restoit au nord nord ouëst demi ouëst six lieuës de distance, et â six heures du soir elle nous restoit au nord est quart nord, en même tems nous avons veu un navire â l'ouest quart nord ouëst, et vers les huit heures la Chaloupe du dit navire, est venus a bord avec le Capitaine

**83** Lalary Point is a shoal on the southwestern coast of Banka. It is located opposite Sumatra's first point on the Banka Strait, when entered from the south.

nommé Pearsés[84], cet navire portoit pavillion anglois, il se dissoit estre de madras, entre tems qu'il estoit avec nous dans la grande Chambre nous nous fimes informer par nos officiers des matelots qui estoient venus avec la Chalupe sans pouvoir [27] sçavoir au Juste d'ou ils venoient et ou ils alloient les uns dissant d'une manière et les autres d'une autre ce qui nous fit presumer qu'il estoit forband, a dix heures du soir avons mouille l'ancre vis â vis la Riviere de Palimban[85]; ausitôt nous decouvrimes un prauwe ou petite barque hollandoisse, nostre Canot s'en fut â bord Chercher le maitre dela barque, il vint â nostre bord et il nous fit present de quelques poisons salez, il se dit estre hollandois, il ÿ avoit un mois qu'il croisoit devant la ditte Riviere de Palimban pour servir de Polotte aux vaisseaux dela compagnie hollandoisse qui devoient monter la ditte riviere ;

Les hollandois ont icy une loge ou factory[86] qu'ils entretiennent pour le Commerce du poivre le Roy[87] qu'ÿ demeure est assez puissant, dont la protection des hollandois qui ont une bonne forteresse le rend redoutable â ses voisins. Ils ont un traitte avecq ce Prince, qui leur livre tout le poivre de son paÿs, et qui en recoit la moitie du paÿement en toiles[88]; outre cette fortresse les hollandois ont encore trois ou quatre fortresses et comptoirs dans les estats du Roy d'Achem, et dans ceux de quelques autres petits princes[89]; entre autres Pedam[90] sur la coste sud ouëst et Jambi[91], ce qui

84 James Pearce (dates unknown) was an EIC captain and later associate of Thomas Hall, then captain of the Marquis de Prié, in the slave trade during the 1730s and 1740s. He additionally, as suggested here, may have been involved in regional smuggling. See James A. Rawley, *London, Metropolis of the Slave Trade* (Columbia: University of Missouri Press, 2003), 32.

85 The Musi River connected the city of Palembang, in southeastern Sumatra, with the Banka Strait.

86 The VOC first established a trading post in Palembang in 1619. Although it only lasted a few years, its merchants were able to reestablish this factory and secure a monopoly of the local pepper trade in 1642. See Iem Brown (ed.), *The Territories of Indonesia* (London: Routledge, 2009), 311.

87 The Aceh Sultanate was Sumatra's largest political entity from the sixteenth to eighteenth centuries, also extending at points to neighboring Banka. It vied in this timeframe with the Moloccas and Johor for control of the pepper trade. The kingdom's ruler, and twentieth sultan, in 1723 was Jamal ul-Alam Badr ul-Munir. He reigned from 1703 to 1726 and encouraged British traders from Madras to trade with his merchants. See Takeshi Ito (ed.), *Aceh Sultanate: State, Society, Religion and Trade, 2 vols.* (Leiden: Brill, 2015).

88 See especially Barbara Watson Andaya, "The Cloth Trade in Jambi and Palembang Society during the Seventeenth and Eighteenth Centuries", in: *Indonesia* 48 (1989), 27–46.

89 Additional early island kingdoms included Biar Lambry, Pedir, Piraada, Pase, Bata, Aru, Arcat, Rupat, Siak, Kampar, Tongkal, Indragiri, Capocam, Trimtall, Sekampung, Tulang Bawang, Andalas, Panchur, Baros, Singkel, Melabah, Daya, and Pirim. See *The Suma Oriental of Tome Pires: an Account of the East, from the Red Sea to China, written in Malacca and India in 1512–1515, vol. 1* (Delhi: Asian Educational Services, 2005), 135–6.

90 Padang was a largely Dutch-controlled settlement in mountainous central Sumatra. It competed commercially with Palembang and Jambi. See E.M. Jacobs, *Merchant of Asia: the Trade of the Dutch East India Company during the Eighteenth Century* (Leiden: CNWS Publications, 2006), 164.

91 Jambi was a Sumatran sultanate, located in central Sumatra near modern Mount Kerinci. Its capital was a key center of the pepper trade in the 1600s. See Elsbeth Locher-Scholten, *Sumatran Sultanate*

les rend en quelque sorte maîtres du negoce du poivre et de l'or de Cette isle; â l'êgard du fort Jambi la Compagnie ne l'entretient guêre que pour en tenir le Roÿ et ses sujets en respect, et empecher les projets des Anglois qui de tems en tems font des tentatives pour s'appropier le commerce du Poivre [28] dont l'isle produit une quantite incroyable, outre le poivre son principal Commerce Consiste en or, en argent en êtain, en Cuivre en fer, en diamans, et autres pierreries, en Cire[92], en miel, en Champre, en Casse[93], en Sandal, en bottou[94], en Souffre[95], en ris[96], en sucre, en gingembre[97], et en benjoin.[98]

L'or se trouve particulierement entre Ticou[99] et Manincabo[100] ou les habitans le receullënt au pied des montaignes dans des fosses qu'ils ÿ font, pour recevoir les eaux des torrens, qui dans le temps des pluÿes entrainnent beaucoup de ce metail avec elles; ces peuples n'ayant point encore l'art de travailler aux mines; ou bien leur paresse naturelle les empechant de s'exposer â un travail si dur.

Ceux qui font la recolte de l'or, sont des peuples a demy sauvages, qui n'ont aucun Commerce avec les estrangers et qui l'êchangent avec leurs voisins pour diverses mar-

---

*and Colonial State: Jambi and the Rise of Dutch Imperialism, 1830–1907* (Ithaca, NY: Southeast Asia Program Publications, 2003).

**92** Indonesian traders manufactured wax from the berries of several regional shrubs, including *Myrica querifolia* and *cordifolia*. This was used to make candles, claimed to last longer than their tallow alternatives. See John Splinter Stavorinus, *Voyages to the East-Indies, vol. 2* (London: G.G. and J. Robinson, 1798), 84.

**93** This refers to *Cinnamomum cassia*, a variety of evergreen tree indigenous to southeastern Asia. Its bark produced the spice popularly known – and much demanded in Europe – as cinnamon.

**94** The meaning of *bottou*, even among contemporaries, was not always clear. Some texts suggest it refers to "carret, ou écaille de tortue." See Jacques Savary des Brulons and Philemon-Louis Savary, *Dictionnaire universel de commerce, vol. 4* (Geneva: Cramer & Philibert, 1750), 915.

**95** Sulphur, or brimstone, was a chemical element, used in early modern medicine and in the making of gunpowder. It, as well as saltpeter, was mined in Indonesia, Burma, Siam and China.

**96** Rice was a regular food source and commodity in the country trade by the 1700s. While demanded by nearby VOC settlers, it did not play a major role in provisioning European ships. See R.D. Hill, *Rice in Malaya: a Study in Historical Geography* (Singapore: National University of Singapore Press, 2012), 30–40.

**97** Ginger is a flowering plant, indigenous to southeast Asia, whose root was used as both medicine and spice. By the late 1600s, some Europeans substituted it for pepper. Chaudhuri, Trading World, 322.

**98** Benzoin trees, native to Sumatra and Java, were tapped for their resin. This was popularly sold as a religious incense and medicine in the country trade, especially in India. See Leonard Y. Andaya, *Leaves of the Same Tree: Trade and Ethnicity in the Strait* (Honolulu: University of Hawaii Press, 2008), 146–72.

**99** Tiku is a coastal settlement in western Sumatra, located about 90 kilometers northwest of Padang. It became a stronghold of the island's Islamic community in the late 1500s, especially among merchants.

**100** The Minangkabau Highlands are a mountainous area in central Sumatra, located about 100 kilometers east of Tiku.

chandises; ceux de Manimcabo leur donnant des armes des outils de fer, ou de toilles de coton; et ceux de Priaman[101], du poivre, de l'acier, du sel, et de talis de Surate.[102]

Cet or n'est qu'a 30 ou 35 pour Cent melieur marche qu'en Europe le souffre se trouve a Pedir[103], ou il y en â une montaigne. C'est aussi proche de Cette ville, que Coule cette espêce de rasine, que l'on nomme Beaume de Sumatra.[104] les Diamans et les Pierreries y viennent de dehors particulierement de Borneo.[105] les autres drogues et marchandisses se trouvent et se Coultivent dans plusieurs endroits de l'jsle, sur tout dans le milieu des terres. outre les lieux [29] que Je vient de vous nommer on fait aussy du Commerce â Achem Pacam[106], Delÿ[107], Arau[108], Campo[109] &.[a110]

**Cette Isle est úne des trois grandes isles** de la Sunde, au midy et a l'occident de la presque isle de malaca[111]; elle est plus grande que l'Angleterre et l'escosse Jointes en semble. dans les terres, il y â des montaignes tres hautes: mais sur les Côtes et vers la mer il y a de belles Campagnes, et de bon paturages. un grand nombre de rivieres arrossent tout ce païs, et l'on y voit dans plusieurs endroits des beaux arbres, qui ne perdent Jamais leur verdure, l'equinoxial la Coupe presque par le milieu C'est

101 Pariaman is a coastal settlement in western Sumatra, located 45 kilometers northwest of Padang. The city officially was under Dutch control from 1663 to 1770.

102 The meaning of *talis de Surate*, even among contemporaries, was not always apparent. Savary des Brulons and Savary, Dictionnaire, vol. 4, 915.

103 Pedir was a Sumatran kingdom, which neighbored the Aceh Sultanate in northern Sumatra.

104 This refers a specific variety of benzoin, *Styrax enzoides craib.*

105 Borneo is an island, bordered by the Java and South China seas. It is located northeast of Batavia and east of Sumatra and the Malay Peninsula.

106 This might refer to a historical settlement near modern-day Lubuk Pakam, located in northeastern Sumatra and along the Melaka Strait.

107 The Sultanate of Deli was focused in northeast Sumatra, near modern-day Belawan. It was a rival of the Aceh sultanate, also located in northern Sumatra, after its founding in the 1600s. See Anthony Reid, *Southeast Asia in the Age of Commerce, 1450–1680* (New Haven: Yale UP, 1988).

108 Aru was a state in northeastern Sumatra, located along the Melaka Strait. See Anthony Miller, Edwards McKinnon and Tengku Luckman Sinar, "Aru and Kota Cina", in: *Indonesia* 26 (1978), 1–42; Suma Oriental, vol. 1, 147.

109 This likely refers to Kampar, a political entity in central Sumatra from the fourteenth to early sixteenth century. During the height of its power, it may have had coastal access on the Melaka Strait, but the kingdom shrunk to the island's interior and it became a client state of Melaka by 1700. There also was a small island known as Kampar off Sumatra's eastern coast, but this does not seem to be the author's reference. See Rebecca D. Catz (ed.), *The Travels of Mendes Pinto* (Chicago: University of Chicago Press, 1989), 34, 552, 558.

110 The preceding seven sentences were adjusted and copied from: Jacques Savary des Brulons and Philemon-Louis Savary, *Dictionnaire universel de commerce, vol. 1* (Amsterdam: Jansons, 1725), 1198.

111 Malacca, now Melaka, was not an island but a town on the western coast of the modern-day Malay Peninsula. It was located northeast of Sumatra. Because of its access to the nearby pepper trade, the city was repeatedly colonized – first by the Portuguese in 1511, then the Dutch in 1641. See Michael G. Vann, "When the World Came to Southeast Asia: Malacca and the Global Economy", in: *Education about Asia* 19.2 (2014), 21–5.

pour quoy les Chaleurs ÿ sont fort grandes. l'air est mal sain pour les êtrangers à Cause des lacs, les pluÿes sont fort grandes dans l'hiver pendant ce tems, les vents d'ouest ÿ exitent des tourbillons, et des orages; puis il survient des Calmes tout à Coup durant les quels le soleil attire des vapeurs puantes qui Causent de grands maladies. la terre de Cette isle est fertille et pourroit rapporter toutes sortes de grains, mais on n'ÿ seme que du ris, et du millet.[112] on y voit quantité des buffles, et beaucoup de poules, canards, et des sangliers n'y manquent pas. on rencontre dans les bois et au pied des montaignes quantité d'elephans sauvages, de tigres, de rinoceros, de porc êpis, de Civetes et de singes; quelques uns ont Cru que Sumatra estoit la traprobane des Anciens[113], et que C'estoit la ou les vaisseaux de Salomon alloit querir l'or et les autres Choses precieuses; dont parle l'escriture Sainte.[114] il ÿ en â qui disent que Cette isle â este detacheé dela [30] terre ferme par les Courans de la mer; mais Ce n'est qu'une Conjecture, et l'on pouroit autant dire du Pas de Calais[115], et de plusieurs autres places. L'isle de Sumatra est diviseé en plusieurs Roÿaumes, mais Comme nous ne fons voÿage que pour le negoce Je me suis Contente de dêcouvrir Ceux qui se font sur la Coste[116], laissant la relation de l'isle â Ceux qui ont fait un plus grand sejour que moÿ.

**Le 3 noús levames l'ancre poúr** Sortir du destroit faisant differentes routes à midy la pointe de manopin sur isle de Banca nous restoit au sud est quart sud distant de huit lieuës comme cy dessous.

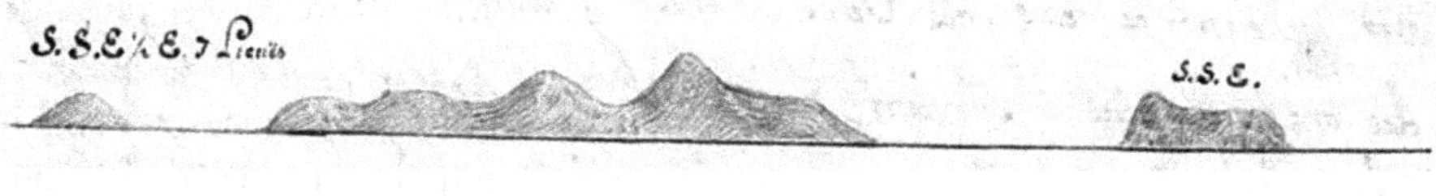


**[Figure 2:** View of Banka]

112 Millet was a variety of grain and, along with sorghum, one of the first cereals cultivated in Southeast Asia. It was introduced to the region from China likely at some point in the 1400s.

113 Taprobane was the name given by the ancient Greeks and Romans to Ceylon, now Sri Lanka. It is an island located about thirty kilometers off the southeast coast of India. See Stefan Faller, *Taprobane im Wandel der Zeit: das Śrî-Laṅkâ-Bild in griechischen und lateinischen Quellen zwischen Alexanderzug und Spätantike* (Freiburg i.B.: Franz Steiner Verlag, 2000).

114 According to the Bible, King Solomon amassed a large navy on the Red Sea, which he engaged in commerce. This trade especially focused on accessing foreign gold markets. I Kings 5:9, 9:26–28.

115 Calais is a port city in northern France, which was claimed by England from 1347 to 1558. The marshy plains around the town could be flooded with waters from nearby rivers as a defensive measure, transforming the city into an occasional island. Jean-Denis G.G. Lepage, *Vauban and the French Military under Louis XIV: an Illustrated History of Fortifications and Strategies* (Jefferson, NC: McFarland & Company, 2010), 151.

116 The preceding paragraph was adjusted and copied from: Louis Moréri, *Le Grand Dictionaire Historique, vol. 4* (Paris: Denys Mariette, 1707), 686–7.

Le vent Continuant au sud sud est assez Joly frais et beau tems nous decouvrimes Pulo Taÿa au nord ouest quart nord dist:e de 2 ou 3 lieuës

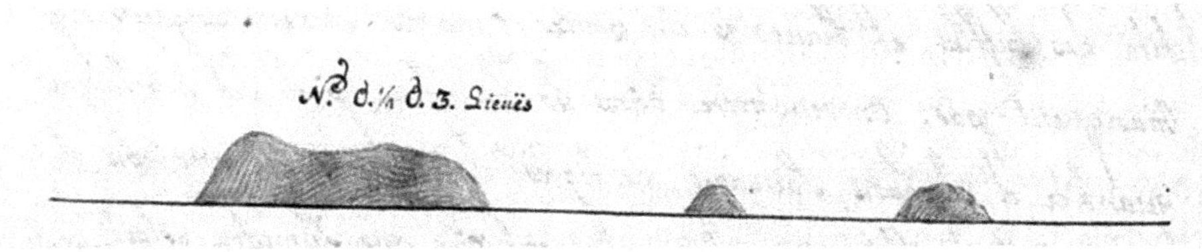

**[Figure 3:** View of Pulo Taÿa]

nous avons aussÿ veu deux ou trois petites isles qui nous restoient depuis l'ouëst nord ouëst Jus qu'au nord ouëst demÿ ouëst distance de quatre lieuës, et l'isle de Lingen[117] situe sous la ligne equinoctiale au nord Ouëst quart nord la veuë si loin qu'on puisse Voir du haut du mas, [31] faisant route au nord est quart nord, Le vent au sud sud ouest Jolÿ frais portant tout voille dehors.

**Entre Plusieúrs Isles qui se troúvent** au bout du destroit de malaca, nous passames â vingt Lieuës à l'est de la Riviere de Johore[118], Je ne me puis empecher en passant Cette riviere de vous donner part des honetetés que Ceux du vaisseau du Capitaine Solegar[119] passé huit à neúf ans receurent du Roy de Johore[120], le dit vaisseau appartenoit de livorno[121]; faisant voÿage pour la Chine avec pavillion Jmperial, ceux de Johore firent tout leur possible pour avoir Commerce avec nostre nation, mesme ils ont presente une petite isle qui est au milieu de la riviere, pour leur servir de loge, Je ne Scaÿ quelles raisons nos gens ont euës de ne pas continuer le negoce avec eux. les hollandois qui font un trafic tres considerable, ont fait tout leur devoir possible pour

**117** Lingen, now Lingga Island, is the largest island in the Lingga archipelago. It is located off the eastern coast of Sumatra and 10 kilometers northeast of Pulo Taya.

**118** The Johor River is located in the southern Malay Peninsula. It empties into the Johor Strait, which separates modern-day Johor from its southern neighbor, Singapore.

**119** Person unknown.

**120** The Johor-Riau Empire was an extensive regional power during the sixteenth and seventeenth centuries, based in the southern Malay Peninsula. It competed against the neighboring Aru and Acehenese kingdoms and, at the height of its reign, controlled territory across the peninsula and in modern-day Singapora, the Riau Islands, the Anamas, Sumatra and Borneo. See Peter Borschberg, "Batu Sawar Johor: a Regional Centre of Trade in the Early Seventeenth Century" (paper presented at the second Nicholas Tarling Conference on Southeast Asian Studies, Hanoi, Vietnam, 3–4 November 2011).

**121** Livorno was a port city, located on the western coast of Italy. It replaced Pisa, after the Arno River silted up in the fifteenth century, as Tuscany's main Mediterranean and transoceanic harbor, and several European firms began to regularly do business there, including those from England, Austria and the Southern Netherlands. See Francesca Trivellato, *The Familiarity of Strangers: the Sephardic Diaspora, Livorno and Cross-Cultural Trade in the Early Modern Period* (New Haven: Yale UP, 2009).

en avoir la predite isle, mais pas le sceu obtenir, a Cause qu'il n'avoit point long tems qu'ils avoient fait leur êffort pour porter le Roy à leur faire homage.

Ceux du mentionne Navire prirent icy une Cargaison de poivre et petittes Cannes pour Canton, la quelle ils vendirent avec 125 pour Cent de profit, ils menerent aussi de qualim[122], qui est marchandisse Courante en Chine, et abondante à Johore dont elle donne ordinairement 40 à 45 pour Cent d'avanse a Canton ; voÿe icy les pris des dits marchandisses au dit Johore.

Le poivre les 132 tt[123] pois d'angleterre à 6 ou 7 piastres.

Le qualim les 396 tt d° ........................ à _ 30 d.°

Les cannes fines[124] de la longeur de 32 pouses le 100,, 3 ½ d.°

[32] les cannes pour garnitures de Chieses sont de grand debit a Canton on les vend ordinairement avec 100, ou 125 pour cent de profit.

Outre les marchandises cÿ dessus mentionneés il y a abondance du bois de Sapan à 9 Schel:[125] les 100 tt donne à Canton 100 p. Cent d'avanse.

Le sago et l'or est aussy en abondance de la même qualité qu'en Chine.

En troque on enporte toutes sortes de grosses denrées de bengale les quels se Vendent avec un bon profit.

**La Ville qui donne Son Nom à ce** Roÿaume, est Situeé en la partie la plus meridionale de l'jnde pres de malaca, elle est bâtie sur des pilotis. pres la riviere du même nom qui se Jette dans la mer pres du promontoire de Sincapura[126] il y a un bon port, et on dit que la plus grande partie de la ville à nom Batusaber[127], et la plus petite Cottuabran.[128]

122 This might refer to kaolin, or China clay – a soft white clay indigenous to the Indonesian islands and China and especially used by the latter in the production of porcelain. It only was sent to Europe in ca. 1700.

123 This denotes *tonneau*, or barrels (as in a given number). The "pois d'angleterre" might refer to these barrels' specific sizing.

124 Rattan was a type of tropical palm, the stem of which provided thin reeds similar to bamboo but not hollow. These were woven into mats and used as packing materials by Europeans traders, who placed them between stacked boxes and chests to provide cushioning without the requirement of too much added space. Van Dyke, Merchants, 219, 272, 274, 281.

125 A schelling was a silver coin, commonly used in the Dutch Republic and the Southern Netherlands.

126 Singapore is an island, located off the southern coast of the Malay Penninsula. It primarily was governed by other empires in the eighteenth century – notably the Johor-Riau sultans in 1723.

127 Batu Sawar, near modern-day Kota Tinggi, was located on the Johor River, about about 30 kilometers from the Singapore Strait. It served as the capital of the Johor-Riau sultanate and its trading center during the 1600s.

128 Kota Seberang was a fort, located across the Johor River from Batu Sawar. It was constructed in ca. 1600. For its early modern description, see Peter Borschberg, *Hugo Grotius, the Portuguese, and Free Trade in the Early Indies* (Singapore: National University of Singapore Press, 2011), 207–8. The preceding two sentences were copied from: Moréri, Grand Dictionaire, vol. 3 (1698), 241.

Les habitans sont mahometans ils ont beaucoup de bravoure et un extreme passion pour le Commerce. ils se font un grand plaisir d'aller Sur mer; touttes les isles voisines êtant en quelque maniere des Colonies de Ce roÿaume et dependantes de Son gouvernament. ils trafiquent le long des Côtes dans leurs propres Vaisseaux, et vont en divers endroits de Sumatra malaca &.[a] leurs vaisseaux sont fort pointus aux deux bouts quoy qu'ils n'en fassent servir qu'un pour la prouë et au lieu d'un gouvernail ils ont à Chaque Cote dela poupe une espece de rame fort large, dont ils laissent tomber une dans l'eau à leur gré, selon qu'il faut aller d'un Cote ou d'autre, laissant toujour abatuë celle qui est au vent.[129]

Ils ont de barques, qu'ils appellent prauws extremement bien [33] travailleés et d'une grande propreté. elles s'elvent de Chaque bout au dessus de l'eau d'une telle manière qu'elles resemblent beaucoup a une demy lune qui a les Cornes en haut. ils en prennent un grand soin, elles vont bien à la voille et ils s'en servent beaucoup dans les guerres.[130]

**Nous estant enfin débarrassez de** toutes Ces isles, nostre Commandant mit son Canot à mer pour voir ou alloient les Courants, il a trouvé qu'il alloit au nord est faisant ⅓ de lieuë par heure qui fait huit lieuës par 24 heures.

Le 5 nous passames à dix lieuës de Celles de Pulo auro et Pulo timon. on touche souvent a Cette derniere place pour avoir du bois, de l'eau, et d'autres rafraichissemens; mais pour nous nous les doublames. entre plusieurs Choses que l'on trouve autour de ces Jsles, on ÿ voit une quantite de tortues verdatres, qui sont excellentes.[131]

**Le 9 le vent variable avecq de** brouillards et de la pluÿe aÿant gouverne au Nord est quart est à pres midi nous decouvrimes Pulo Condor[132] depuis le nord demy Ouest Jusqu'au nord est demÿ est. J'ay trouvent Suivant mon Compte que la ditte isle est à un degré 30 minutes à l'est de manopin; il a un demÿ ans que la Compagnie de france[133] avoit entrepris d'habiter Cette Isle par rapport de sa Situation qui est tres favorable pour aller et venir sur la route de la Chine [34] Japon, Manille[134], et de tous les lieux de

129 The preceding two sentences were copied from: M. Bruzen La Martiniere, *Le Grand Dictionnaire Geographique et Critique, vol. 4.2* (La Haye: C. van Lom and P. de Hondt, 1732), 83.

130 The preceding paragraph, except for the first two sentences, was copied from: Ibid.

131 The preceding paragraph was adjusted and copied from: Guillaume Dampier, *Suplement du Voyage autour du Monde* (Rouen: Jean-Baptiste Machuel, 1723), 6.

132 Pulo Condore, now Côn Sơn, is an island in the South China Sea, located 186 kilometers east of the southern tip of modern-day Vietnam. The EIC had a settlement there in 1702, but it was abandoned by 1705. See Danny Wong Tze-Ken, "The Destruction of the English East India Company Factory on Condore Island, 1702–1705", in: *Modern Asian Studies* 46.5 (2012), 1097–115.

133 The French *Compagnie des Indes Orientales* scouted Pulo Condore as the potential site for a commercial entrepôt from 1721 to 1723. Despite its central access, they ultimately decided not to establish there. See John Cady, *Southeast Asia: Its Historical Development* (New York: McGraw-Hill, 1964), 280.

134 Manila was a trading post, located about 1,150 kilometers southeast of Macao and in the modern-day Philippines. As the final destination of the Manila Galleons, or the ships that yearly sailed from the west coast of Spanish America loaded with New World silver, it attracted much business and

la Côte la plus orientale du Continent de l'Jnde soit qu on passe par le dêtroit de Sunde ou par Celuÿ de malaca, à Cause qu'on peut s'ÿ rafraichir et se pourvoir de tout de ce qu'on a bessoin, et outre le necessaire ordinaire on y trouve de mats, des vergues, de la poix et du godron[135] Mons.$^{r}$ du Brossaÿ Gardin[136] que J'aÿ trouve a Canton, et qui à este en qualité de Cap.$^{ne}$ sur Cette isle, me donna la relation, que J'ay Jointe icy à cause que Je scay qu'elle ne vous sera point desagreable.

**Plan de Jsle de Púlo Condore** oú jsle D'orleans[137]

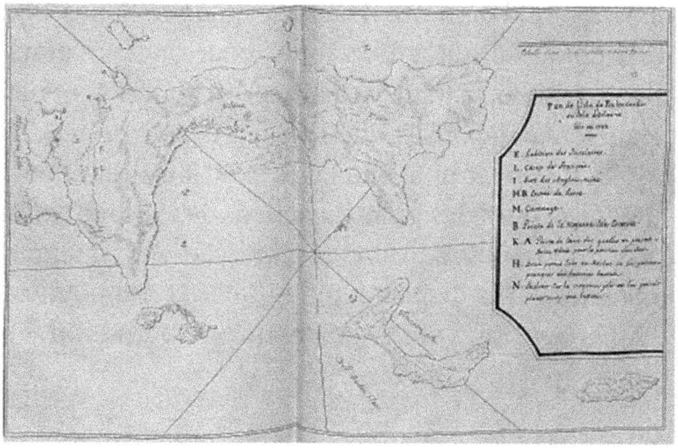

**[Figure 4:** "Plan de l'Isle de Poulo-Condor ou Isle d'Orleans fait en 1722"]

---

brought together an array of traders from the Americas, Europe, India and southeast Asia. See Dennis O. Flynn and A. Giráldez, "Silk for Silver: Manila-Macao Trade in the 17$^{th}$ Century", in: *Philippine Studies* 44.1 (1996), 52–68.

**135** This refers to the resin of the local damar tree, or *Dammara Orientalis*. Mariners in southeast Asia regularly used it to caulk their ships. The previous two sentences were adjusted and copied from: Guillaume Dampier, *Suite du Voyage autour du Monde, vol. 2* (Rouen: Jean-Baptiste Machuel, 1723), 84.

**136** Laurent Gardin du Brossay (b. 1685) was a native of Grenoble, France, who worked on VOC ships until the 1730s. He had been in Canton since May 13, 1721 and returned to France on July 24, 1724. As a prior student of medicine, he took notes of the curiosities he saw abroad and eventually published them in Europe between 1735 and 1748. See Xavier Beguin Billecocq, *Des voyageurs français au Cap de Bonne-Espérance* (Paris: Relations internationales et culture, 1996), 104 and Charles Le Gobien and Yves Mathurin de Querbeuf, *Lettres édifiantes et curieuses, écrites des missions étrangères: Mémoires de la Chine*, vol. 21 (Paris: J.G. Merigot, 1781), 445–6. A similar version of the following report on Pulo Condore, which Brossay had gotten from a certain Didier, is included in Gardin du Brossay's journal: *Voyage fait pendant les années 1720–1724 a la Chine, a Siam, a Malacca et autres pays de l'Inde, avec le testament de Kam hy Empereur de la Chine et un memoire des revolutions de cet empire*, in: Bayerische Staatsbibliothek München – Codex gallicus 624.

**137** The map appearing below is not part of the original text but, rather, taken from the aforementioned manuscript of Gardin du Brossay (ibid., inter p. 142–3). It is inserted here because the following abbreviations relating to Pulo Condor largely correspond with its abbreviations. This suggests that the map that originally was attached to the Ostend text must have been very similar to this example.

**Cette isle est à huit degré 38 minutes de** latitude Septentrionale, a 128 degré de longitude Suivant les vielles Cartes hollandoises[138] et à 15 lieuës de l'embouchure de la Riviere de Camboÿa[139], son havre est fort bon et tout a fait à l'abrÿ des vents ordinaires regles: on ÿ Sent pourtant quelque fois des bouffeés ou raffalles de Vent assez fortes et presque toujours oposeés à la direction du vent qui Souffle, ce qui provient de la hauteur et de la disposition des montagnes dont il est entouré qui donnent occassion au Vent de se reflechir diversement. Sa Situation est Sud est, Son entreé **H.B.** est au nord Ouest; ainsy l'entreé et la sortie en sont libres en toutte saison, et d'ailleurs elles sont faciles: on pourroit en Cas de besoin passer entre les ïles **C.D.** et entre l'isle **D.** et la pointe **Z.** car il y a de l'eau partout; au fond du havre il ne reste qu'un petit passage pour [35] les bateaux. Ce havre peut Contenir huit a dix vaisseaux de quelque grandeur qu'ils puissent estre, le mouillage est bon, le fond est de vaze, on pouroit Carener à l'endroit marque **M.** moÿenant quelques depenses que l'on feroit pour le rendre Commode; les mareés aux jours de la plaine et nouvelle Lune sont nord est et Sud ouest, C'est adire a trois heures, et dans le tems des grandes mareés des Equinoxes la mer monte et descend de neuf pieds. les Courans suivent les mareés, et sont quelque fois detourneés par les Vents, et ensuitte par la disposition des Côtes et des pointes, mais tous ces mouvemens Sont sy peu Sensibles si jrreguliers qu'on ne Sçauroit les determiner au juste.

**E.** habitation des Insulaires.

**L.** Camp des françois.

**C.B.-DZ.-CD.** Passes pour entrer dans lé havre.

**B.** P.te. dela moÿenne Isle escarpeé et Jmpraticable

**K.A.** Deux pointes de l'une des quelles on pouroit faire Choix pour la disposition d'un fort.

**H.** Deux petites Isles; ou Rochers ou l'on pouroit pratiquer des batteries basses.

**N.** endroit sur la moÿenne Isle ou lon pouvoit aussÿ placer une batterie.

**i.** Fort des Anglois ruiné

**HB.** Entreé du havre

**M.** Carenage.

Le terroir de ces Isles est pour la pluspart noiratres et asse profund. les montagnes seulement sont pierreuses. la partie Orientale dela plus grande jsle est Sabloneuse et à neamoins de diverses sortes d'arbres ils sont en general larges hauts et bons à tous usages. On en tire un Certain suc d'arbre dont on Compose de bon goudron en le lais-

138 The VOC initially attempted to keep navigational knowledge of, and thus economic competition within, its Southeast Asian entrepôts limited via cartographic secrecy. Ostend sailors, however, had little trouble accessing either Dutch or English maps during the early 1700s. Parmentier, Private, 85.

139 This refers to the Mekong River, which runs from the Tibetan highlands through the mainland of Southeast Asia. Its two primary branches empty into the South China Sea off the coast of modern-day Vietnam.

sant un peu boüillÿr, et si on le laisse trop bouillir il devient dur Comme de la poix. le terroir est assez bien arrossé Comme aussy des autres de petits ruisseaux d'eau douce, qui Coulent abondament dans la [36] mer durant dix mois de l'anneé, ils Commencent a tarir vers la fin des mars et au mois d'avril, alors il n'y a de l'eau que dans les fosses profondes, et quand el l'eau douce manque il y a des lieux ou l'on peut Creusser des puits;

Le pais est fort abondant en fruits Comme de Mangos dont le fruit n'en est pas plus gros qu'une petite peche; mais long et plus petit tirant vers le bout. il est Jaunatre quand il est mur ils sont d'un goût et odeur excellente.

Il y a aussy un certain arbre à grape dont le Corps est d'un pied ou plus de diametre, et fort droit, avec peu de branches. le fruit ou grapes Viennent par pelontons Comme à Celles de nos vignes tout autour du Corps de l'arbre, aussi elles ont un gout de vin fort agreable.

Il Croit dans les bois des Certains arbres qui produissent une espece de noix muscades sauvages[140], dont la noix est de la grosseur du noisetier, et beaucoup plus petite que la veritable le fruit Vient entre les branches Comme les noisettes. elle est enfermeé dans une gousse delieé, et dans une espece de fleur qui entoure la noix dans la gousse, mais elle n'en à ni l'odeur ni le gout.

Les animaux qu'on trouve, sont de cochons, des guanos[141], et de lezards, il ÿ a plusieurs Sortes d'oisseaux Comme pingeons, Perroquets Ramiers, et Perruches, il ÿ a un espe de Cocqs et de poules Sauvages qui resemblent au nostres, mais pas Si grand, et leur Chant est plus petit et plus aigre. C'est par ce Chant qu'on les trouve dans les [37] bois, leur Chair est fort delicate et blanche. on trouve aussi quantité de tortuës Vertes.

Les habitans de Cette Isle sont petits, assez bien formez ils ont le visage long, basanez, les Cheveux noirs et lisses les yeux petits et noirs, le nez d'une grasseur mediocre et assez êlevé, les levres minces, les dents blanches, et la bouche petite, ils sont fort polis mais extraordinairement pauvres, leur principial employ est de tirer le Jus des arbres dont on fait le goudron; ils font un grand trou horisontalement qui aille Jusq'au milieu du Corps de l'arbre et à environ un pie de terre, ils Coupent ensuite l'arbre au dessus; en descendant Jusques à ce qu'ils rencontrent la Cavité qu'on à fait en bas au milieu de l'arbre et travers. dans Ce tronc horisontal qui forme la figure d'un demi cercle, ils font un trou Comme un bassin qui Contient un ou deux pintes, alors le Suc tombe de la partie Superieure qu'on à Coupe à l'arbre, dans Cette Cavité, qu'ils vuident tous les Jours, a mesure qu'ils ramassent ils le gardent dans de baquets

---

**140** Nutmeg, the spice, is the seed of a small fruit that grows in southeast Asia. Europeans generally used it in small doses as a flavoring, meat preserver and medicine. Its wild variant has only a mild taste. Freedman, Out of the East.

**141** This probably refers to a large species of monitor lizard, the *Varanus indicus*, common on islands in Indonesia and the Pacific Ocean.

de bois, et quand ils ont leur Charge ils le transportent à la Conchinchine.[142] d'autres s'occupent a prendre des tortuës. ils en font bouillir le gras pour en tirer l'huile qu'ils transportent aussy a Cambodie ou Conchinchine[143]; ces peuples sont Jdolatres ils àdorent les Jmages de l'elephant et du cheval.[144]

Apres avoir veu Cette Isle de Pulo Condore nous avons Continue la routte du nord est un quart Est, et nord Est. le 14.$^{e}$ venant a l'hauteur de 15 degré 45 minutes de latitude Septentrionale et par 7 degré 35 minutes de distance meridionale a l'est de Pulo [38] Condore nous avons Veu les rochers dans le fond parsemees sur le sable surquoy nous avons Sonde et trouve 13. 14. et 15 brasses d'eau, un moment par apres pas eü fond avec une line de 50 brasses; nous avons trouve qu'il s'êtend est et Ouest, et aÿant pris le medium de plusieurs autres Vaisseaux qui ont Sonde sur le même banc, Sa longeur Seroit depuis l'est à l'ouest de 35 à 40 Lieuës, et depuis le nord au Sud de 15 a 20 Lieuës et trouve par differentes Sondes de puis les 40 brasses Jus ques les 10. Ce dernier est le moindre fond qu'on à trouve; Comme le dit banc n'est point marqué dans aucune Carte, J'aÿ Joint icy mons$^{r}$. la Sonde de differents vaisseaux pour Vous servir de plus grande explication.

Le Vaisseau la maison d'Autriche[145] sur la lattitude de 16 degré 14. minutes, et Sur celle de longitude 6 degré et 50 minutes à l'est de Pulo Condore à sonde 40. brasses fond de sable, et aÿant gouverné 30 Lieuës plus à l'est à trouve 26 brasses fond de Coral et depuis pas trouve de fond.

Le vaisseau l'essec[146] sur la lattitude de 15 degré 12 Minutes et du meridien à l'est de pulo Condore 4 degré 45 minutes 10 brasses fond de rochers.

---

**142** Cochinchina was a kingdom in Southeast Asia, concentrated in modern-day southern Vietnam. It was a key participant in the Chinese junk trade. See Li Tana, *Nguyen Cochinchina: Southern Vietnam in the Seventeenth and Eighteenth Century* (Ithaca, NY: Cornell UP, 1998); Olga Dror and K.W. Taylor (eds.), *Views of Seventeenth-Century Vietnam: Christoforo Borri on Cochinchina and Samuel Baron on Tonkin* (Ithaca, NY: Cornell UP, 2006), 23–67; Van Dyke, Merchants, 69.

**143** The preceding six paragraphs were adjusted and copied from: Dampier, Suite, vol. 2, 79–85.

**144** Southeast Asia was a religiously-diverse region, encompassing competing indigenous, Confucian, Buddhist and Islamic spiritualities. The elephant and horse mentioned here likely refer to Buddhist beliefs, where they represented mental-physical strength and energy respectively. See William G. Clarence-Smith, "Elephants, Horses, and the Coming of Islam to Northern Sumatra", in: *Indonesia and the Malay World* 32.93 (2004), 271–84; Tana, Nguyen Cochinchina, 102–11.

**145** The Maison d'Autriche, rated 400 tons, housed 80 crewmembers and 40 guns. She previously sailed twice to Canton from Ostend – the first time in 1719 captained by James Naish and the second in 1721 captained by Thomas Hall. Gill, Merchants, 17–23.

**146** The Essex, rating about 300 tons, housed between 60 and 64 crewmembers and 22 guns while active, from 1716 to 1727. She previously sailed for the EIC to India, under captains Charles Newton and John Pinnell.

Celuy nommé de Bonetta[147] Se trouvant Sur l'hauteur de 16 degré 33 minutes a l'est de l'isle du grand ladron 9 brasses fond de rochers.

Ayant passe le dit banc nous avons gouverné au nord nord ouëst et nord ouest quart nord Jus qu'au 16 à midy que nous avons Veu paroitre une grosse nuée qui estoit fort noire au pre de l'horison, dont elle estoit Vers la partie Superieure d'un Couleur rougeatre enforceé; plus haut encore, elle estoit plus brillante, et [39] ensuitte Jusques à Ses extremitez elle estoit pale et d'une Couleur blanchâtre qui êblouoït les ÿeux. Voÿant tous Ces signes d'un tÿphons[148] qui est une espece de violens tourbillons, qui regnent Sur les Côtes de la Chine aux mois de Juillet, et d'aoust et de septembre ordinairement lorsque la lune Change ou devient pleine; et apres avoir Veu Cette nueé affreuse qu'elle Commençoit a Se mouvoir avec rapidité et que le Vent Changoit d'un Moment à l'autre tout au tour du Compas, avons Serré tous nos voilles et laisse driver vent derriere, le Vent (un moment par apres) Commenca a Souffler avec Jmpetuosite du Nord Ouëst d'une maniere terrible, accompagné de terribles Coups de tonneres, avec de grosses pompes, dont il avoit une derriere nous tout proche Si grand qu'il faisoit peur de le Voir, il S'est êvallé Sans S'aprocher de nous d'avantage.

Ces Sortes de pompes est une meteore qui tire l'eau de la mer dans les nueés elle est faite Comme une Colonne qui se Communique avec les nueés, qui absorboient l'eau qui sembloit bouillir tout à l'entour de la dite Colonne; Si elle venoit à Crever sur un vaisseau elle l'abimeroit infalliblement, C'est de quoy nous avions peur, on la tache à Crever à Coup de Canon pour la dissiper, apres la dissipation du dit tourbillon nous eumes une pluÿe extraordinairement violente, qui dura environs d'une heure; le lendemain au matin le vent diminuant de Sa Caprice et Jmpetuosité avons en mesme tems largué les ris des basses Voilles et largue les hunniers tous les ris dedans et gouverné au nord Ouëst et nord nord ouest le Vent estant sud Ouëst.

**Le 19 Juillet le Vent Sud, l'air S'estant** [40] êclairci fimes route Vers le nord nord Ouest Jus qu'a les 10 heures du matin que nous avons Veu la terre de la Chine au nord distant de 6 a 7 lieuës, en mesme tems nous Vimes un batiment Chinois nostre Commandant envoÿa sa chaloupe a bord pour S'informer quelle terre est celle que nous avons veu mais il n'a pas eu aucun êclaircissement, a midy nous avons trouve par l'estime que nous estions au nord de la ligne de 21 degre 42 minutes, et 6 degré à l'est de pulo Condore, nous decouvrimes plusieurs autres isles droit devant nous au nord ouest et nord ouest quart nord elles nous parurent Comme vous pourris Conjecturer par le plan que J'ay mis icy dessous.

---

**147** The Bonita, an English country tradeship, sailed to India in 1716 with John Scattergood as chief supercargo and afterwards remaind in Asian waters. See the extant letters from Scattergood in: BL – Mss. Eur. C387/1–4.

**148** A typhoon is a tropical cyclone, which occurs in the region of the Pacific Ocean and especially in areas affected by seasonal monsoons. See Van Dyke, Merchants, 75–6; Paul D'Arcy, *People of the Sea: Environment, Identity and History in Oceania* (Honolulu: University of Hawaii Press, 2006).

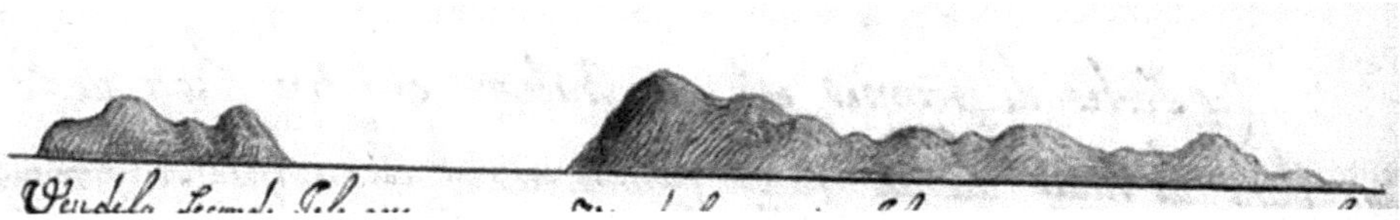

[**Figure 5:** Views of an unknown island, possibly modern-day Xiachuan Island, and of St. John's Island]

Veu dela seconde Isle[149] que nous Vimes de Vant nous un peu à tribord Nord nord Ouest demy ouest. Veu de la premiere Isle[150] que nous avons Veu à tribord de nous ou au nord quart Ouest 5 a 6 Lieues loin

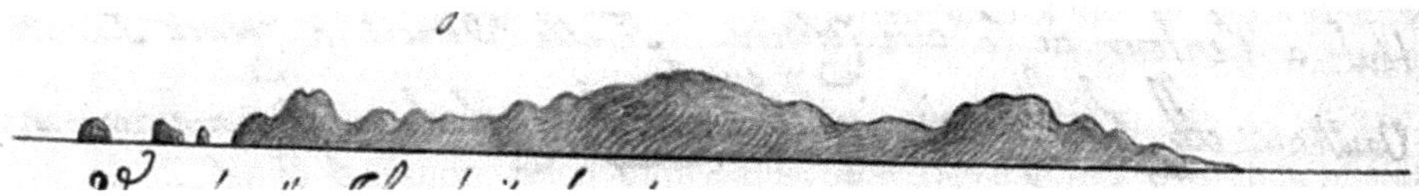

[**Figure 6:** View of St. John's Island]

Veue de Cette Jsle droit devant nous gouvernant au N.O. et N.O. ¼ N.

[**Figure 7:** View of St. John's Island]

Veu de Cette Isle a babord de nous un peu engouvernant au N.O. et N.O. ¼ N.

Estant venus proch de terre nostre Commandant à Demande à nostre Capitaine s'il en avoit Connoissance, aÿant repondu que non il gouverna d'abord à l'ouest Sud ouëst au plus pres du Vent le long de plusieurs Jsles, pour prendre Connoissance, à Cause que [41] l'un Se disoit à l'est et des autres a l'ouëst ainsy que tous les opinions des uns et des autres estoient differentes; pendant la nuit nous avons resté avec les basses Voilles cargueés sur les deux huniers amaré sur babord Courant au large, Vers les 3 heures apres minuit nous avons Vire le bord a terre et gouverné au nord quart nord Est et nord nord est Jus qu'a 6 heures du matin que nous avions reconnus que nous

**149** This likely refers to modern-day Xiachuan Island, located about 10 kilometers west of St. John's Island.
**150** This refers to St. John's Island, now Shangchuan Island.

estions à l'ouest de Macao par la Veuë d'une petite Jslet[151] qui deloin ressemble à un navire, elle nous restoit à l'ouëst quart nord Ouest distant de 4 a 5 Lieuēs.

**Les 21 le Vent Est** sud Est aÿant gouverné au nord est le long des Jsles Jusqu'a 4 heures apres midi que nous avons mouille l'ancre entre les dits isles par 7½ brasses d'eau fond de Sable Vazard a trois quart de lieü de terre vis a vis d'un passage par ou l'on peut aller à Macao Suivant que les Chinois d'un Champan ou barque qui Vint à bord (àpres que nous fumes muillés) ils nous dirent qu'il y avoit dans le dit Canal 8 brasses d'eau par tout, nous fimes aussi la sonde avec la Jole et trouve la moindre eau de 7 brasses 7 ½ et 8., en mesme tems Cap$^{n}$ Hall nostre Commandant nous fit visite à nostre bord; il ordonna à Ses gens de la Jole d'aller avec le second Pilote à terre pour voir s'il ne pourroit pas trouver un Pilote pour nous mener à macao, venant à terre il à trouvé un mandarin de qui il a esté fort bien receu, et traité à la maniere du pais, qui lüy a donne un homme pour nous Servir de pilote, le quel on à mené à nostre bord; nous Jnterrogames le dit Pilote pour Sçavoir Combien il vouloit avoir pour mener nos deux vaisseaux à Macao, ayant entendu Sa demande qui estoit de Cent theÿls[152] pris exhorbitant nous l'avons fait ramener à terre et repris l'homme qui nous avoit faleu laisser a terre à la place du [42] dit Pilote Chinois.

Vers les 4 heures du matin nous avons leve l'ancre et mis à la voile le vent estant nord Est Joly frais gouvernant au plus prés du Vent a l'est sud est à dix heures du matin nous decouvrimes les Jsles marquees dans la table **1** avec la lettre **A.** que nos gens prirent pour le Veritable passage de macao à Cause d'une tache blanche qui est Sur une des jsles à babord de nous qui se laisse Voir Comme la Veritable tache blanche qui est Sur l'jsle de Kosang[153] a l'Est du grand ladron.

**Le Vent Continuant** au nord Est gros frais avec des brouillards faisant route au plus pres du Vent pour entrer dans le Soubsonné passage de Macao, nous eumes le Malheur de rompre nostre mat d'hune du devant, en tombant il à rompu le grand mat de perroquet et dechiré la misene Comme aussy Celle de perroquet de devant avec la Voille, nous avons mis tout ce pratacage a bord le plus promptem.$^{t}$ qu'il nous fut possible apres quoÿ nous avons devergué la misene et envergue une autre, la pretendue isle du grand Ladron nous restoit au nord nord est 7 lieuës de distance.

**Le 22** à la pointe du jour avons veu un Jonque Sur la quelle nous fimes Voille pour tacher de prendre langue mais nous ne l'avons pas peu Joindre, nostre Commandant voyant qui ne la pouvoit àborder et que nous perdions beaucoup par le Courant qui nous drivoit à l'ouëst nous avons couru la bordeé du large et fait plusieurs bordeés

151 This likely refers to the Wizard Rocks, now the area around Xiaojin Dao. The small Wizard Rock, located northward of the largest island, had a white conical shape, which might explain the author's reference. Viados, or Coucok Island, also, however, had a rock off its southwestern coast which looks like a sailing ship.

152 This denotes the tael, the local Chinese currency.

153 Kosang, also known as Tyloo and now Gaolan Dao, had a point on its eastern coast that looked like a mizzenmast from the sea. It was located mid-way between St. John's Island and Macao.

Jusqu'a midy que nous decouvrimes la preditte islet ou Rocher qui resemble à un navire au sud Ouëst un quart Sud distant d'une lieue et demÿ.

Cette Roche est Connue dans les Cartes portugaisses sous le nom [43] de Carapucha de Mandarin[154], il y a au large de ce rocher bien une bon ne lieuë loin de rochers a fleur d'eau que nous voyons brisser la mer dessus de grand force, du Coté de la grand terre il y a un petit islet[155] qui nous restoit au sud ouëst distant d'un et trois quarts de Lieue, il y a aussy depuis le dit rocher Jus qu'a Cette petitte isle un banc de rochers de l'une a l'autre tout a fleur d'eau, l'isle ronde ou ovalle, dont J'ay parle cy devant, nous restoit à l'ouëst un peu nord, il y a aussi depuis Ce dit rocher qui est au large a moitie Chemin de l'une a l'autre un banc de rochers egalement Comme Celle des autres tout a fleur d'eau, nostre second Capitaine dans Son Voyage de l'anneé 1719 à trouve que la grande isle de ladrones est 76 minutes a l'est de ce dit rocher ce que nous avons trouve aussy Conforme, apres ces remarques faites nous avons Couru la bordeé de terre pour aller mouiller l'ancre Suivant le Signal de nostre Commandant, et a 5 heures nous avons mouille l'ancre par 5 ½ basses d'eau fond de Vaze, tandant que nous devions rester icÿ a l'ancre a Cause des vents Contraires nous avons mis le petit mas d'hunne, la vergue et petit hunie, en même tems avons garnÿ, les mats et les Vergues de perroquet et en Vergué le petit hunie;

Durant le sejour que nous ÿ fimes nous eumes le plaisir d'aller à terre dans le fonds de la Bay dans une des Isles nomeé isle de Jnhame[156] elle nous parrut d'une hauteur passable assez unie, et le terroir assez fertille. elle est Composeé en partie de Bois et en partie de paturages pour le betail. il y a quelques terres labourables qui produisent du ris. les bords de l'isle sont pleins de bois, et sur tout du Côte dela terre, Ce milieu est de paturages bons et herbeux, melez de quelque bois. les terres Cultiveés sont basses et humides, et produisent d'abondantes recoltes de ris[157], le seul grain que J'ay veu. les animeaux domestiques [44] qu'il y a dans Cette Isle sont de cochons, des Chevres, des buffles et quelques taureaux. les Oiseaux domestiques sont des Canards des Cocqs et des poules. Je n'ay vu que des petits oiseaux sauvages; voye icy monsieur le profil de la ditte Bay que vous peut servir de grande explication; Comme estant les isles les plus eloigneés à l'ouëst du grand ladrones, qui peut Servir de Marque aussureé qu'on est a l'ouëst de Macao.

---

**154** Island unknown.
**155** Island unknown.
**156** Island unknown.
**157** For more on rice cultivaton in eighteenth-century China, see Robert Marks, *Tigers, Rice, Silk and Silt: Environment and Economy in Late Imperial South China* (New York: Cambridge UP, 2004), 130–3, 163–94, 249–76.

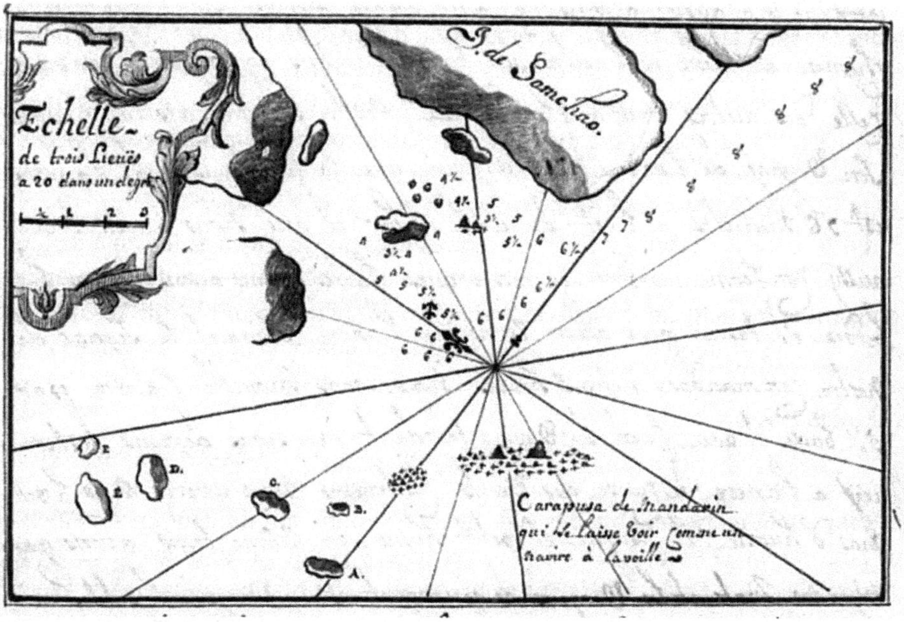


**[Figure 8:** Map showing St. John's Island and other islands west of Macao]

Prospectif des Isles Marqueés dans le Plan avec les lettres a.b.c.d.

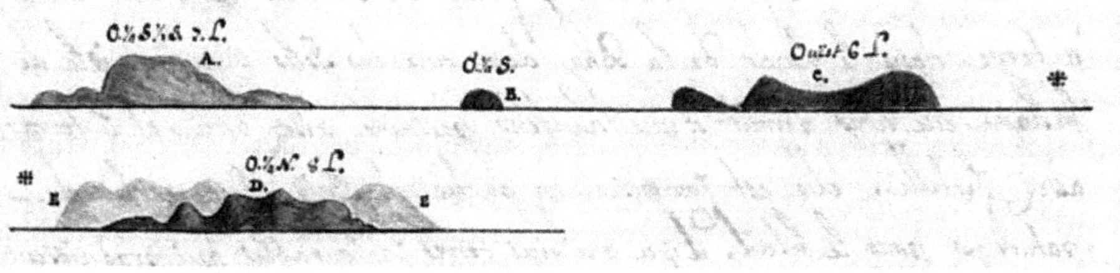

**[Figure 9:** Views of the islands in Figure 8]

apres avoir mis nostre Vaisseau en estat pendant que les gros Vents avoient duré, nous profitames du premier bon Vent qui Se presenta pour faire Voille du Côté de Macao. nous mimes à la Voille le 25 Juillet à trois heures apres midy avec une petite brise du sud, aÿant Couru [45] une petite bordeé au large, apresquoy nous avons Vire de bord, vers les 6 heures du Soir le Rocher blanc qui resemble a un navire nous restoit au Sud Ouest distance de trois Lieuës, pendant la nuit avons Couru au plus près du Vent le long des Isles, vers lessix heures du matin. le Vent est Venus au Sud ouest petit frais a mesure que nous àprochames de terre nous en primes differentes Vuës a plusieurs distances Jnegales, d'ou elles nous parurent telles qu'on les voit marqueés dans la table **1** sous la lettre **B.**

**A midÿ La place Blanche** sur l'isle de Viados[158] au Ouest sud Ouest distant 8 Lieuës le grand ladron au nord est quart nord distance de 14 Lieuës, il y a depuis la ditte place blanche Jusqu'a l'isle de Kosang (isle ou est le veritable artimon) de petites isles de distance en distance entre celles cy il ÿ a une nomeé l'isle de Viados qui est fort remarcable par une montagne qui vient en deux points Comme des oreilles d'âne au pres de la quelle il y a plusieurs places blanches qui peuvent Servir d'asse bonne remarque, Comme vous pourris Voir dans la Tab: **1.** Sous la lettre **C.**

**Le 26** nous decouvrimes Plusieurs autres Jsles que Je n'ay tiré, il y en à de toute Sorte de grandes, de moyennes de petites en quantité parsemeés parmis les grandes; a 6 heures apres midy nous Vimes la Veritable place blanche sur l'isle de kosangh qui resemble a un artimon de navire, a l'ouest distant quatre lieuës et la grande isle de Ladrones au Est demy nord [46] distant de huit lieuës marqueés dans la **Tab:**[e] **2.**[e] avec la lettre **E. F. & G.**

A neuf heures du soir nous mouillames au nord est de l'isle Montanha par 7 brasses d'eau font de Vaze. Voÿant les difficulteés qu'on a pour trouver le passage de Macao par rapport au grand nombre des isles qu'on rencontre qui forment un Archipel, et que Souvent on Se trompe par les marques qu'on ÿ prend qui Se trouvent aussi bien à l'est qu'a l'ouëst. J'ay adjute icy un petit extrait du Journal de Mons.[r] Lanszweert[159] à Cause que Je Sçay la Curieusité que vous avez pour les terrages et Comme nous n'avons point fait terrage du Coste de l'est, il vous Servira de plus grande esplication; il s'esplique de la maniere.

**Monsieur le 8 de Juillet 1725** à la pointe du Jour decouvrimes la terre a huit heures elle nous parut de la Manière Comme elle est Marqueé dans la table **2.** avec la lettre **A.** nostre Cap:[ne][160] Croÿant Connoistre la terre dit au Cap:[ne] Flanderin[161] que nous pourions estre Se Soir devant macao; mais il pouroit Se tromper, à 11 heures ces isles nous parurent Comme dans la ditte table **2**[e]. marqueés **B.** derierre Celles cÿ, vimes Jnfinité d'autres isles a perte de Vué. aÿant aproche des dits isles, decouvrimes, celles dans la d.[e] tab.[e] avec la lettre **C.** à un heure apres midy.

Un Jnfinité d'autres isles se faisoient voir derriere Celles cy, le Soir ne Vimes plus d'autres isles, et Commencions a Croire que nous estions fort à l'ouëst de la grande

---

**158** Viados, also known as Coucok and now likely Hebao Dao, was an island located between St. John's Island and Kosang.

**159** Andreas Lansweert (1698–ca. 1759) was a Flemish native and mariner, who sailed to China on the Ostend ship L'Impératrice from 1725 to 1726. The next two paragraphs are from his travels. See Jacques van Wijnendaele, *De familie Lanszweert en de stad Oostende* (Ostende: Oostendse Historische Publicaties, 2008), 21–46.

**160** Jan de Clerck (dates unkown) was captain of L'Impératrice during Lansweert's voyage. Ibid., 25.

**161** Andreas Jacobus Flanderin (1708–1763) was a Flemish native and Ostend Company supercargo. He additionally worked for the Swedish East India Company during the 1740s. See C. Koninckx, "Andreas Jacobus Flanderin. Een achttiende eeuwse middelgrote koopman", in: *Bijdragen tot de Geschiedenis* 56 (1973), 244.

ladrone, cepend:[t] [47] nostre Capitaine se crut à l'est Contre l'opinion de tout le monde, sur quoy on Vira de bord Vers l'ouest faisant tout la nuit tres peu de Voile;

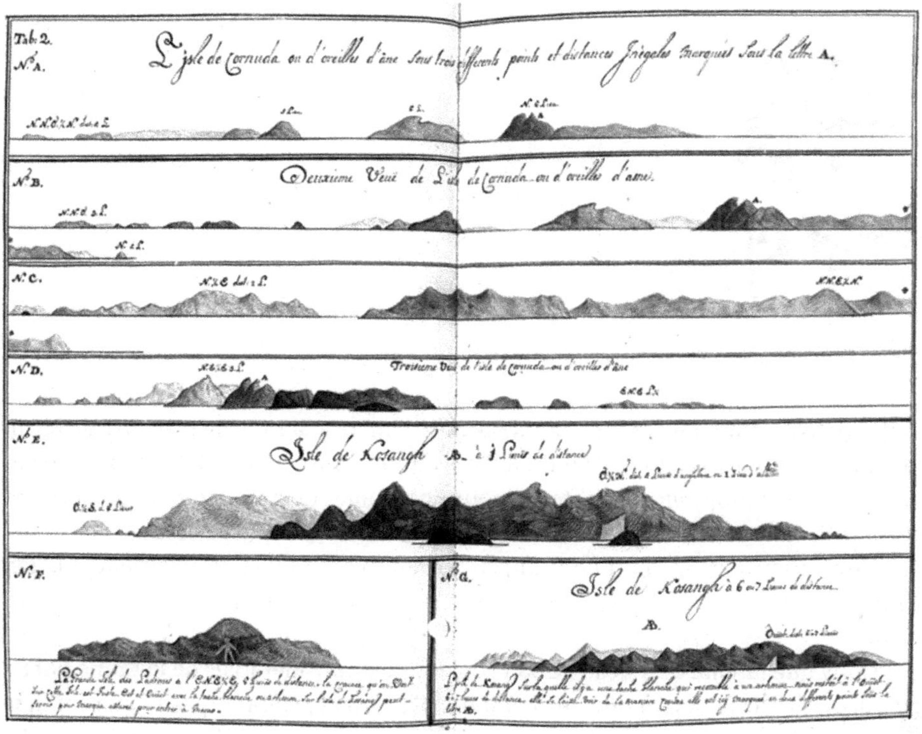

[**Figure 10:** Views of "L'jsle de Cornuda ou d'oreilles d'ane", the "Isle de Kosang" and "La Grand Isle des Ladrones."]

Le 9 nous Vimes ces Isles à la pointe du Iour tout Comme elles nous parurent hier au matin a 8 heures, nous les doublames et les aÿant au nord est 5 degré est, elles se faisoient voir Comme dans la table **2.** marqueés avec la lettre **D.** En mesme tems decouvrimes le Pic de la grande ladrone à l'ouest de nous Sans pourtant Sçavoir que C'estoit cette Isle mais a 10 heures Vimes l'isle de Kosang avec la tache blanche Comme un artimon, nous reconnumes à lors la grande ladrone, et l'avions au nord est de nous un quart de lieu: Mais Sans enagerer on peut dire qu'il ÿ a plus de deux Cent isles devant Macao; Ie suis &.[a]

**Voila** monsieur tout l'explication que Ie vous puise donner touchant les isles devant Macao, Ie ne Crois pas avoir rien oublie qui merite attention: Si Ie me resouviens de quelque Chause Considerable, Ie ne manqueraÿ pas de Vous en faire participant. apres avoir reste pendant tout la nuit à l'ancre, le lendemain Vers les cinc heures, nous mimes à la Voile et rengeames l'isle de Montanha, deux heures par apres nous entrames heureusement et nous mouillames dans la rade de Macao.

## Lettre Seconde Description de La Ville, du Port et des Fortifications de Macao. nommeé Par les chinois

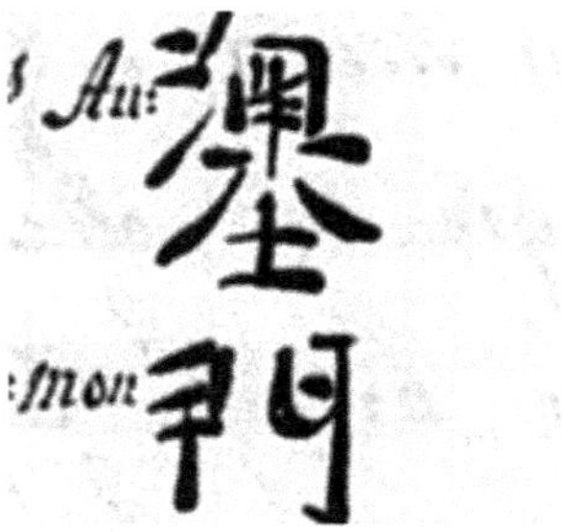


[**Figure 11:** Chinese letters, translated as "Macao"]

[48] **A peine, Monsieur avions noús moúillé** l'ancre a la rade de Macao avec Pavillion Imperial, que le gouvern:r nous envoÿa un Canot pour nous Saluer et prendre des nouvelles de l'Europe en mesme tems, nous Envoÿames Complimenter le gouverneur, et cependent nous le Saluames de neuf coups de canon chaque vaisseau;

Nous primes icy La mort de L'Empereur Kan̄ Kÿ[162] et que Son quatrieme fils Iōn̄ tchin̄[163] avoit Succede a tous ses estats et que les affaires de la Chine estoient assez bien;

Quoÿ que la Ville de Macao ne soit pas des plus considerables de la Chine par Sa grandeur, et par le nombre de Ses habitans, J'aÿ crû cependant qu'elle meritoit que Ie vous en fit mention en particulier non Seulement a Cause de la reputation qu'elle a toujours euë parmi Celles ou les Portugais Se Sont establis dans l'orient, et qu'ils ÿ possedént encore; mais aussi par ce qu'elle est la premiere par ou les Europeens se sont Ouverts le Commerce de ce grand Empire et qu'elle à este pendant pres [49] de deux Siecles la Seule ou il leur à esté permis de trafiquer.[164]

Cette Fameuse ville est situeé dans une presque Isle, sur l'jsle de Gaoram[165], sur la Coste de la province de Canton, cette Langue de terre ne tient même au reste de l'isle

---

162 This refers to the recent death of the K'ang-hsi Emperor.

163 Yinzhen, the Yung-cheng Emperor (1678–1735), was the fourth son of the K'ang-hsi Emperor and his successor. He mostly continued his father's policies of expansionism, although showed less favor to Christian missionaries in China. See Madeleine Zelin, "The Yung-cheng Reign", in: Cambridge History of China, vol. 9, 183–229.

164 The preceding paragraph was adjusted and copied from: Savary des Brulons and Savary, Dictionnaire, vol. 1, 1186.

165 Gaoram, now the Macao Penninsula, is the oldest portion of modern-day Macao. It connects to mainland China via a small isthmus of about 200 meters.

que par une gorge fort estroite ou l'on à basti une muraille de Separation[166]; au milieu de la quelle est une porte, ou se païent aux officiers de l'Empereur de la Chine les droits d'entreé et de Sortie pour toutes Marchandisses vivres et denrées qui Viennent à Macao ou qui en Sortent par terre; les portugais S'establirent au Commencement du Seizieme Siecle.[167]

Avant que les Chinois Se fussent apprivoisez avecq Ses nouveaux venus, qui Sous pretexte de Commerce, S'estoient déja emparez des plus fortes villes des Jndes[168], et dont les flottes avoient déja l'empire de toutes les mers d'orient, il estoit Seulement permis aux portugais de Venir tous les ans aporter leurs marchandisses dans l'isle deserte de Sanchan[169] et de les y étaler dans des Cabanes faites à la haste des branches d'arbres et de gazons, Sans pourtant y pouvoir bastir de maisons.

La Confiance augmentant, les portugais S'avancerént Jusqu'a Macao, a 10 Lieuës de Sanchan, ou se servant en suite des Conjonctures, ils eurent permission de bastir des maisons et des magacins, et d'entourer leur nouvelle ville d'une Simple muraille.

Les hollandois Jaloux du Commerce dela Chine ou ils ne pouvoient [50] estre reçûs tenterent d'en Chasser les portugais Cent ans apres que Ceux cy s'y estoient establis[170], mais ayant manqué leur Coup; leur entreprise ne Servit qu'a y mieux assurer l'establissement de leurs ennemis, qui prirent de la Occassion d'obtenir la liberté de faire de fortifications a leur ville les Chinois les aimant mieux pour voisins que les hollandois.[171]

Au Commencement elle fut gouverne par un Bourgemaître ou Consul que les marchands êtablirent pour leurs Chef en forme de republique[172], mais depuis que les hollandois ont fait plusieurs tentatives pour en Chasser les portugais ; ils ont demande

---

**166** The preceding sentence was adjusted and copied from: Jean Baptiste du Halde, *Description de l'empire de la Chine et de la Tartarie chinoise, vol. 1* (The Hague: Henri Scheurleer, 1736), 241.

**167** The preceding sentence was adjusted and copied from: Savary des Brulons and Savary, Dictionnaire, vol. 1, 1186–7.

**168** Two Yao communities, the She and Dan, inhabited Macao since the 200s BCE. They involved themselves in imperial Chinese politics since the Sung Dynasty (960–1279 CE). This included their conflicts with the Yüan Dynasty and the explorations of Admiral Zheng He. See Zhidong Hao, *Macau: History and Society* (Hong Kong: Hong Kong UP, 2011), 2–3, 12–6.

**169** This refers to St. John's Island.

**170** The first Dutch ships arrived in Macao in 1601, where they were surprised to find a Portuguese settlement and soon themselves were captured. After the successful seizing of the Santa Catarina, a Portuguese ship laden with Chinese cargo from Macao in 1603, the Dutch launched an unsuccessful offensive on the city that they repeated in 1607 and during later decades, notably in 1622. Ibid., 20.

**171** The preceding three paragraphs were adjusted and copied from: Savary des Brulons and Savary, Dictionnaire, vol. 1, 1186.

**172** This Senate, founded in 1583, was composed of six representatives elected by Macao's Portuguese population. It was the city's primary political and judicial governing body. Hao, Macau, 34–5, 129.

du viceroy de Goa[173] un gouverneur avecq trois Cent Soldats à leurs depenses pour deffendre leur Ville, ce qui leur fut accorde et envoÿe.

Le Gouverneur qui leur fut envoÿe l'an 1607. fut Don fran:co Mascarenhas[174], le quel ne fut pas trop bien reçue par Ceux de la Ville au lieu de luy donner la principale fortresse, ils luÿ donnerent une Simple maison pour Son logement; quand ce General leur commanda quelque chose par ordre du Roÿ Son maître, ils firent tout le Contraire en Se raillant de luÿ, avec un tel exces qu'il fut Contraint de Se Sauver dans le Couvent des Peres Augustins[175] ou il fut assiegé, et Canone par Ceux du fort S.t Paulo[176], dont trois balles percerent l'appartement du dit general; les quelles il fit dorer et Envoÿa une au Roÿ de portugal, un autre au Viceroÿ de Goa, et la troisieme il la Conserva en memoire du revolte.

[51] Comme il voÿoit qu'il ne pouvoit rien obtenir par force d'armes de ces gens il disimula quelque tems Ius qu'a ce qu'il trouva l'occassion de faire Semblant d'aller faire visite aux Revers: Peres Iesuites[177] pour Voir leur Cloistre et fortresse nommeé S:t Paúl, il Sçeút avecq un addresse et ordre fort grande S'en faire maitre de la fortresse devant que Ces bons Peres le peuvent decouvrir en faisant monter de tems en tems un homme, pendant qu'il entretenoit les dits Peres en un long discours et qu'ils ne Subsonoient rien de suprisse de ce General par les Sivilitées et parolles flatantes qui leur donnoit. le Soir S'approchant le R.P. Procurator dit au general de Se Vouloir retirer, a Cause qu'ils estoient oblige Selon Coûtume de Serer la porte à Soleil Couchant. le General leur repondit avec une mine fort froide mes Reverends P:s il ne Serat point necessaire que J'en Sorte, et que vous fermieés la porte, car J'aÿ fait estat de rester icy, et mes ordres sont desja donneés à mes gens pour la fermer, et ils n'ettendent qu'a vous Iusqu'a que Vous aurïes Sortis, Si non que Vous Voudrieés rester mes prisonniers, Car

173 Portugal's headquarters in the East Indies was established in Goa, located on India's western coast, in 1510. From here, a viceroy managed all Portuguese affairs in the Indian Ocean and Southeast Asia, including Macao. The viceroy from 1720 until his death in July 1723 was Francisco José de Sampaio e Castro. See R.P. Rao, *Portuguese Rule in Goa, 1510–1961* (Bombay: Asia Publishing House, 1963).

174 The first captain-general of Macao, appointed by the Viceroy of Goa, was Don Francisco de Mascarenhas (dates unknown). He held this post not in 1607 but from 1623 to 1626, and he was responsible for completing most of the city's wall. Mascarenhas' political assertiveness, evinced in the following story, made him unpopular. See Richard J. Garrett, *The Defenses of Macau: Forts, Ships and Weapons over 450 years* (Hong Kong: Hong Kong UP, 2010), 14; Charles Ralph Boxer, *Seventeenth-Century Macau in Contemporary Documents and Illustrations* (Hong Kong: Heinemann, 1984), 75–6.

175 This refers to Our Lady of Peñafrancia, an Augustinian hermitage located on Macao's Penha Hill. It shared this site with several early fortications, which were expanded after the 1622 VOC attack and eventually encompassed the religious structure. Garrett, Defenses, 36–7.

176 The Church of São Paulo, located on Macao's Monte Hill, was built by Jesuit missionaries beginning in 1582. It eventually housed a seminary and military fortress as well as served as a major center of city politics. Ibid., 8, 25.

177 For more on the Jesuits in early Macao, see Brockey, Journey; Hao, Macao, 119–35; Clive Willis, *China and Macau* (Burlington, VT: Ashgate, 2002), 65–74.

Cette place est deja Sous ma domination; ces paroles du general firent Comme enterer ces bons Peres de tel Sorte qu'ils ne prirent point la descente par la porte, mais par un Chemin Sousterain, lequel fut la mesme nuit bouché; ainsi le general mascarenhas par la Surprisse de Cette fortresse il Se fit maître de toutes les autres; par ce moÿen il eut aussy son tour de leur faire parler comme il Vouloit, dêpuis ce tems le Roÿ de Portugal a en proprieté cette place[178];

**Comme la Ville est Situeé sur une Colline** [52] et environnée de quelques montagnes[179] est Cause qu'il faut toujours monter et descendre par des degres de pierre ou taillez dans le roc. les maisons de Macao sont à l'europeené, mais un peu basses. les Chinois ÿ sont en plus grand nombre que les portugais, quoÿ que ceuci se disent les maitres de Cette place; ils ÿ ont mesme un gouverneur, mais les Chinois y ont aussy un Manderin[180], dont tout le paÿs depend;

Les fortifications de Macao Sont bonnes, la Situation en est avantageuse, les portugais ÿ ont presentement trois principales fortresses bâties Sur autant d'eminences, ou de petites Montagnes qui forment un triangle; la plus grande et la plus forte est nommeé S.[t] Paulo, construite à quatre bastions Sur une êminence haute de 185 degré, ce qui la rend Jmprenable, elle est munis de 40 pieces de Canon qui tirent 40 livres de balle; le Second est nommé nostra Señora de la penña de Francia Celle cÿ n'est pas Si haute ni Si forte munis de dix pieces de Canon, la troisieme qui est Situeé hors de la Ville Sur une haute montagne Se nomme N:[a] Señora de guia munis[181] de 6 pieces de Canon; celle cy Sert principallement pour Veiller Sur les Vaisseaux qui Viennent ou qui Vont au Sud ou Nord, et aussitot qu'ils S'appercoivent de quel qu'un ils font Signal a Ceux de la ville par le son d'une Cloche qui pend Sur le parapet, et S'il viend Sur la rade ils aborent pour lors un pavillion; outre ces fortresses la Ville est munis encorre de plusieurs autres forts et redoutes, Comme Celluÿ de la barra[182], nuestra Señora del bon Patto[183], S[t]. francisco[184], et S.[t] Juan[185], Celluÿ de barra est le plus grand de touts

178 See also Marco D'Avalo's description of Macao and of Mascarenhas' seizing of the Jesuit residence on Monte Hill, written in 1638. Boxer, Seventeenth-Century, 69–80.

179 Macao is surrounded by numerous peaks, including Jialin Shan, Baisha Mountain, Bijia Mountain and Nanshan Mountain.

180 Imperial officers were stationed in Macao by 1535. Hao, Macau, 17–22.

181 The Guia Fortress was constructed on the highest hill of Macao from 1622 to 1638. The fort shared its location with the hermitage of Our Lady of Guia, and it defended the city from the north. Garrett, Defenses, 48–52.

182 The fort of São Tiago da Barra, completed in 1629, was situated at the entrance to Macao's inner harbor. Its original expansion began in 1622. Ibid., 42–8.

183 Our Lady of Bom Parto, dating to 1622, was a small fort located on the Penha Hill that guarded the southern shoreline of Praia Grande. Ibid., 37–9.

184 The Fort of São Francisco was built in the 1720s, along the Praia Grande. It was Macao's first line of defense against attacks originating from the sea. Ibid., 67.

185 The fort of São João was located near Macao's Guia Hill. Ibid., 54.

les autres il Sert à la [53] ville de Cittadelle[186] c'est dans celuÿ ou le gouverneur general a Sa demeure, il defend l'entree du port à tous vaisseaux qui Voudroient entrer Sans permission; C'est une Ville de grand Commerce, à Cause de la Commodité de Son port qui est fort Sur et Vaste. il ÿ a un Evêque Suffragant de l'archeveque de Goa. on ÿ Compte cinc couvents quatre Eglises parochiales, Celle des Jesuittes Comme par tout aillieurs est la plus Magnifique on ÿ monte par 60 degré de pierre larges pour le moins de 50 pies, le frontespice de l'êglise est tres beau; la qu'elle est toute dorée par dedans;

Tout le Commerce des portugais estoit remfermé dans l'enceinte de macao, ou ils apportoient leurs marchandises et ou les Jonques de Canton, et des autres provinces Maritimes de la Chine[187], les venoient prendre en êchange de leurs soÿes de leurs êtoffes et des autres Manufactures, ou productions Chinoises; presentement ce commerce est presque reduit a rien, et ils ont peu Ioui des avantages du nouveau traité qu'ils avoient fait en 1680[188], avec la Cour de Pekin[189], par le qu'el, à l'exclusion de toute autre nation, ils avoient obtenu qu'ils feroient Seuls tout le negoce de la Chine: ce previlége n'aÿant duré qu'environ cincq ans; les ports de ce vaste empire aÿant esté Ouverts en 1685[190] a tous Ceux qui voudroient ÿ venir trafiquer, les Jndiens et les Européens Se Sont également empressez d'user de la liberté de ce nouveau commerce[191];

Aÿant pris un pilote Chinois à bord pour monter la Riviere [54] de Canton le 27 â 2 heures apres midÿ levames l'ancre avec un beau tems, apres avoir differentes fois mouille l'ancre à Cause du calme, le lendemain à huit heures du Soir nous mouillames dans le destroit de boca tigeris, en mesme tems quelques gens du hopoú ou

---

**186** This refers to a portion of the Jesuit estate on Macao's Monte Hill, initially commandeered by Don Francisco Mascarenhas in 1623. It served as the governor's residence until 1749. Ibid., 144.

**187** China's main maritime provinces in the early eighteenth century were Kwangtung, Fukien, Chexiang and Jiangsu. See pages 287, 312.

**188** Peking, now Beijing, was the imperial capital for much of the Ming and all of the Ch'ing dynasties. It is located in northeastern China, about 145 kilometers inland from the Bohai Sea.

**189** The Portuguese foothold at Macao was checked by the Chinese in the late 1600s, with the K'ang-hsi Emperor banning maritime trade several times because of civil unrest and with the seizure of thirteen country ships in 1663 and 1664. As a result, the Portuguese sent several ambassadors to the Peking court, notably Bento Pereira de Faria (dates unknown) in 1678. His goal was to show Portuguese support for the Emperor, to recommence overland commerce between Canton and Macao, and to exclude the VOC from this trade. See George Bryan Souza, *The Survival of Empire: Portuguese Trade and Society in China and the South China Sea, 1630–1754* (New York: Cambridge UP, 1986), 200–2.

**190** In 1684, and after settling several revolts, the K'ang-hsi Emperor declared his kingdom again unified and at peace. He then re-opened foreign commerce with all nations, so that the Chinese could "show the populous and affluent nature of our rule." This decree resulted in the creation of new customhouses and the formal permission to Europeans to begin trading with China in 1685. See Angela Schottenhammer, "Characteristics of Qing China's Maritime Trade Policies, *Shunzhi* through *Qianlong* Reigns", in: *Trading Networks in Early Modern East Asia*, ed. Angela Schottenhammer (Wiesbaden: Harrassowitz, 2010), 120–6; Souza, *Survival of Empire.*

**191** The two preceding sentences were adjusted and copied from: Savary des Brulons and Savary, Dictionnaire, vol. 1, 1187–8.

grand douanier Vinrent à nostre bord, ils nous demanderent les noms du Capitaine le nombre de l'equipage, la quantite des armes &.[a192] ils annotterent tout ce la, et demanderent quelque argent, on leur donna deux piastres[193], ils partirent apres nous avoir laisse trois hommes à bord: un moment apres Vint un autre Canot dont les gens firent la mesme Chose, on donna à Ceux cy qu'un piastre et ils partirent.

Nous levames l'ancre et mettions à la Voile pour passer la bouche du tigre qui est proprement l'entreé de la riviere de Canton; voicÿ comme elle Se fait Voir quand on a l'isle de lingting Sud Sud est, et les deux rochers[194] est ½ Sud.

**[Figure 12:** View of the Bocca Tigris]

Le lendemain à la pointe du jour nous passames le dêtroit de boca tigeris, que I'aÿ donne le nom de Dardanelles[195] Chateaux Sur les deux bords du dit destroit. à l'entreé de ce destroit on [55]

**[Figure 13:** View of ship entering the Bocca Tigris]

---

**192** Incoming ships to Canton cleared customs near the Bocca Tigris. Documentation then was checked at several different points, to ensure cargo was not unloaded and thus to inhibit smuggling. Van Dyke, Canton Trade, 1, 10, 19–34, 43.

**193** A piaster was a form of silver currency, introduced to the East Indies by the Spanish. The VOC equated one piaster to about .74 taels. Ibid., 156.

**194** Islands unknown.

**195** The Dardanelles is a narrow strait in northern Turkey, which connects the Aegean Sea and the Sea of Marmara. Here, the author invites a comparison to the slim width of the Pearl River at Bocca Tigris.

trouve deux Chateaux[196] vis a vis l'un de l'autre et le trajet est d'environ trois quarts de lieuë. celuÿ qui est placé sur une petite isle nomeé tigeris.[197] qui S'avance dans le dêtroit est de figure ovale flanque d'une bonne muraille, il ne Sont garnies de Canons braquez et Chargez, pour tirer Sur Ceux qui tenteroient le passage Sans permission: mais ces Canons ne Sont braquez que sur des gros morceaux de bois quarrez sans aucun affut: de Sorte que leurs premiers Coups êtant tirez il faut un tems Considerable pour les recharger et les rebraquer. et dans Cette Intervalle, une bordeé des Canons bien Chargez, tireé d'un Vaisseau qui Seroit devant pourroit facilement abattre une bonne partie de la muraille, et mettre ce Chateau en état d'estre pris d'embleé[198]; Le nouveau chateau de la terre ferme est placé su le penchant d'une Coline; il est d'une forme ronde. on ÿ voit environ Vingt Canons d'un mesme Calibre et d'une mesme porteé que Ceux du Chateau du tigre. lors qu'un Vaisseau marchand passe devant les dits Chateaux on Vous Vient [56] faire la visite pour avoir les droits du Passage.

Le vent estant O.S.O. petit frais de mareé motante poursuivimes nostre route Vers Wampou; venant devant la barre avons trouvé deux navires anglois[199] qui estoient mouilleés depuis hier n'aÿant par permission de monter plus haut Jus qu'a nouvelle ordre, a Cause de quelques difficulteés qui estoient Survenus touchant le vaisseau de Manilla qui avoit Charge plusieurs Marchandisses de Contrebande, dont l'armade Chinoise s'avoit saissi, la riviere estoit plaine de galeres, rangeés en forme de croisant, raison pourquoÿ nous mouillames l'ancre, en mesme tems nostre Commandant partit en Compagnie de nostre Capitaine avec la Chaloupe pour Canton, et tacher d'avoir la permission de Monter a Wampou, pour faire le Commerce comme cÿ devant, deux Iours par apres, nostre Commandant est retourne de canton avec la permission de monter la dite riviere, nous avons levé l'ancre et mis à la Voile et passé la barre, la riviere est encore tres large en Ces endroits, et bordeé des deux Cotez d'un tres beau paÿsage et de plusieurs petites Villes fort pres l'une a l'autre, il ÿ a aussÿ un asse grand fort[200] sur la montagne a l'ouëst en entrant, proche la premiere tour, dans la riviere qui ne paroissoit pas de grande Consequence;

Nous avions que peu de Vent, avant que d'arriver à [57] Wampou passames le fort que les hollandois avoient Commence pour S'establir en Chine; touchant ce paragraphe Ie vous diraÿ Monsieur que la compagnie d'hollande Se trouvant assez establie aux Indes, pour penser à ÿ Supplanter toutes les autres nations et plus encore

196 These castles may have been on modern-day Weiyuan, Dajiaotou or Hengdang islands, all of which were located at the entrance of the Bocca Tigris and were favored as sites for future Ch'ing Dynasty forts.

197 This refers to modern-day Dahushan Island, located in the Bocca Tigris.

198 The three preceding sentences were adjusted and copied from: Moréri, Grand Dictionaire, vol. 3 (1725), 573.

199 These were two of the EIC ships – the Montagu and the Duke of Cambridge.

200 This might refer to a tollhouse on the Pearl River, known as Huangpu Shuiguan and located near Whampoa. Van Dyke, Canton Trade, 22.

depuis 1641., qu'elle fut recuë dans le Iapon à l'exclusion de tous autres européens[201], elle tourna toute Son attençion à S'emparer aussÿ du Commerce de la Chine, la ditte Comp:e fit d'abord quelque commerce à macao; mais les portugais ÿ aÿant un trop puissant êtablissement Ceux la formant de nouveau desseins, Surprirent l'isle de Samptpou nommeé autrement Piscadores[202], et y battirent un fort. les Chinois, qui ne les Voulurent pas Souffrir Si pres de leurs Côtes; permirent pourtant qu'ils prissent poste dans l'isle de formosa[203], plus grande, plus fertile, et plus peupleé: mais plus êloigneé d'eux de 12 ou 15 lieuës. C'est dela que, pendant de vingt anneés la Comp:e hollandoise fit un grand Commerce avecq la Chine; dont les marchandisses Iointes aux peaux de Cerf que cette compagnie tiroit en abondance de l'isle même êtoient tres utiles pour Soutenir leur Commerce du Iapon qui n'en est environ qu'a deux Cens quarante cincq lieuës; l'êtat florissant de la Colonie de formosa dura Jus qu'en 1661, que Coxinga[204] Roÿ dela Chine, qui s'estoit retiré dans les isles voisines, apres l'invasion des tartares[205] de la Chine qui ÿ regnent presentement se trouva obligé par la situation de ses affaires, d'en Chasser les hollandois dont il prit les forts dela providence et de

**201** Beginning in 1641, only Dutch and Chinese ships were allowed to enter Japan and only at the harbor of Nagasaki on its southwestern coast. The VOC initially tried to insert itself into the China trade as middlemen, shipping much demanded Chinese deerskins to Japan via Taiwan. These were used in garments, furniture and leather goods. In the 1640s, they obtained a monopoly on a portion of this export trade, which excluded native Chinese merchants. See Thomas O. Hollman, "Formosa and the Trade in Venison and Deer Skins", in: *Emporia, Commodities and Entrepreneurs in Asian Maritime Trade, c. 1400–1750*, ed. Roderich Ptak (Stuttgart: Franz Steiner, 1991), 261–90; Cheng Wei-chung, *War, Trade and Piracy in the China Seas, 1622–1683* (Leiden: Brill, 2013).

**202** The VOC established themselves in the Penghu Islands, or Pescadores, after their failed assault on Macao in 1622. These are an archipelago of 64 islands, including main island Penghu, and are located about 45 kilometers off the western coast of Taiwan. See John E. Wills, Jr., "Relations with maritime Europeans, 1514–1662", in: Cambridge History of China, vol. 8, 368–9.

**203** Taiwan, historically known as Formosa, is an island in the East China and Philippine seas, located about 180 kilometers east of mainland China. It was an area of contest between rival Chinese, Portuguese and Dutch powers in the late 1600s. See ibid., 369–72; Tonio Andrade, *How Taiwan became Chinese: Dutch, Spanish and Han Colonization in the Seventeenth Century* (New York: Columbia UP, 2008).

**204** Cheng Ch'eng-kung, or Koxinga (1624–1662), was a Japanese native and Chinese military leader. A Ming loyalist, he led several successful efforts against the Ch'ing Dynasty and their Dutch allies along the Fukien coast and in Taiwan before his early death. See K'o-ch'eng Chen, "Cheng Ch'eng-kung's maritime expansion and early Ch'ing coastal prohibition", in: *Development and decline in Fukien Province in the 17th and 18th Centuries*, ed. E.B. Vermeer (Leiden: E.J. Brill, 1990), 222–41.

**205** The Tartars were a series of ethnic kingdoms, based north of China and originally on the Mongolian Plateau. The term at various points referred to the Mongols and to Turkish-speaking Islamic communities. But the author here denotes the imperial conquests of the northern Manchu in 1644, which commenced the Chinese Ch'ing Dynasty. The Manchu were a distinct group from the Han, which remains the dominent ethnic group in China. See Pierre Joseph d'Orléans and Nicholaas Witsen, *History of the Two Tartar Conquerors of China*, ed. Richard Henry Major (Cambridge: Cambridge UP, 2010); Gertraude Roth Li, "State Building before 1644", in: Cambridge History of China, vol. 9, 9–72.

Zeelande[206], apres un Siege assez long, et assez meurtrier. la Compagnie priveé de la Commodité d'un poste si avantageux [58] pour le commerce de la Chine, qu'elle auroit pu mesme Soutenir, Sans la mesintelligence du conseil de batavia, et du gouverneur de formosa, sembloit ÿ avoir renoncé, Sur tout par ce que les anglois et les portugais faisoient tout celuÿ de macao, ou les Hollandois n'osoient aller qu'en cachette: mais l'empereur de la Chine (comme I'aÿ remarqueé ci devant) aÿant ouvert les ports de Son empire à tous les nations en 1685. ils firent partir une nombreuse ambasade, avec plus d'esperance du Succes, que celle qu'ils ÿ avoient envoÿeé en 1659 ou ils furent fort traversez par le credit que les Iesuites ont en Cette cour[207];

Apres avoir passe le plus beau paÿsage qui puisse S'offrir nous mouillames l'ancre a Wampou, plase ordinaire ou tous les Vaisseaux d'europe s'arretent, nous ÿ trouvames un Vaisseau anglois nommeé le Walpoel cap:$^{n}$ Bantem qui nous dit que 30 Iours passez la mareé avoit monté pendant 36 heures Sans Continué d'ou tout le paÿs avoit este jnondé et qu'il ÿ a eu même à la Ville de Canton plus de dix mille maisons qui ont esté emportees par ce dilûge.

## Lettre 3.$^{e}$ Description dú Port et dela Ville de Canton, du Paÿs d'alentour, et dela Chine en General.

[59] **C'est Monsieur le premier d'aoúst** 1723 que nous mouillames a Wampou dans la Riviere Ta[208] à trois lieuës de Canton. d'abord que nous eumes Ietté nos ancres Ie m'en allay à terre avec les deux Capitaines et nous arrivames a Canton vers le midÿ: a moitie Chemin de la Ville de Canton et Wampou, il ÿ a une petite ville ou il ÿ a un fort[209], aux extremitez des faubourgs du dit canton, qui sont d'une êtendue extraordinaire, nous rencontrames une machine ou flaut qui montoit la riviere[210], construit d'une infinité de gros et menu bois lié en Semble avec des bamboes, il ÿ avoit plusieurs cabanes et une Infinité de monde dessus, ce qui nous fit croire que ce gens apparement n'avoient pas assez de terrain pour demeurer a terre puis qu'ils habitoient la riviere.

---

206 Fort Zeelandia was the principal VOC fortress in Taiwan, established between 1624 and 1634. It was surrendered to Chen Ch'eng-kung in 1662, after a nine-month siege. This ended Dutch rule on the island. Wills, Relations, 371–5.

207 The preceding paragraph, except for the first sentence, was adjusted and copied from: Savary des Brulons and Savary, Dictionnaire, vol. 1, 980–1.

208 This refers to the Pearl River, now *Zhū Jiāng*, which was the main sea-route to Canton. The river expands near the city with the addition of three tributaries – the *Běijie*, *Xijiāng* and *Dongjiāng*. See page 341.

209 This might denote the military post known as Dongpaotai, or "French Folly," located just south of Canton and along the Pearl River. Van Dyke, Canton Trade, 22–3.

210 A portion of Canton's population lived on the water, in sampans that provided housing, shelter for animals, markets and warehouses. These could be tied together to form floating neighborhoods. Ibid., 59–60.

Au Commencement des faubourgs nous passames l'isle Sodomique[211] noms que nous avons donne par rapport que Sont [60] tous les ladres, lepreux, veneriens &.[a] qui demeurent, au milieu de la ditte isle il ÿ a un arbre d'une grandeur enorme sous l'ombre du quel tous ces malades estoient Couchez.

En Suitte nous passames au travers de milliers de Champans qui Sont au rivage du faubourg de Canton, nous arrivames enfin à la maison de nostre Correspondent Sinqua[212] que nous occupames en attendent que Celle que nous avions loueé fut en estat.

Quelques Iours ensuitte nous primes possession de nostre factorie, c'est une maison grande et belle situeé a bord de la riviere aÿant la porte de devant dans les rues du faubourg, et celle de derriere Sur le fleuve, par la quelle on Charge les marchandises;

Comme nostre factorie donnoit Sur la riviere I'ay vu plusieurs fois la nuit une Vingtaine de Iampans qui paressoient tout de feu, et de tems en tems on Jettoit des papiers dorez brulants dans l'eau au bruit de leur musique et Charivarÿ de plusieurs Jnstruments: une nuit entre autres Ie vis driver plus de trois Cents feux Sur la riviere Sans Voir aucun bateau, Ie crois que C'estoit quelque Composition brulante qu'on avoit mis dans des escuelles de bois, en mesme tems nous Vimes paroitre un grand feu d'artifice ou ils presenterent de Caracteres et de figures d'une maniere qui nous souprenoit. Ces apparences durerent l'espace d'un quart d'heure, la matiere S'etant Consume elles disparurent faisant les traces de fumeé dans tous les endroits ou la figure avoit paru. la depense de Ces Sortes de feu n'est [61] pas Considerable, car un Iour pour nous divertir pour deux Theyls nous eumes un feu de trois ou quatre représentations.

Le lendemin nous eumes le plaisir de Voir la fête dela nouvelle Lune[213], fêtes que les Chinois ont dans chaque saison de l'anneé. Comme les Villes sont diviseés par quartiers, chaque quartier a son jour fixe pour faire cette fête: les Bonses[214] en habit de sacrificateurs portants des morceaux d'yvoire courbez en arc, vont chercher leurs Ydoles dans la Pagode[215], ou Temple de faux Dieux, et les transportent dans des certaines maisons orneés de differentes figures tres petites et en grand Nombre,

**211** Place unknown.

**212** This likely refer to Tan Suqua, who – along with Cudgin – primarily supplied the Ostend Company in the early 1720s. It also could refer to the former's bookeeper, Chinqua.

**213** The Autumn Moon Festival is a popular Chinese harvest celebration, traditionally observed on the first full moon of late summer or early autumn. See Liming Wei, *Chinese Festivals* (New York: Cambridge UP, 2011), 48–50; Yang Lemei, "China's Mid-Autumn Day", in: *Journal of Folklore Research* 43.3 (2006), 263–70.

**214** This specifically refers to Buddhist monks. For more on Buddhism, generally, see pages 290–2.

**215** Architecturally, the term *pagoda* denotes a tall tower, typical in southeast Asia, whose levels are distinguished by eaves. The French term *pagode*, however, here distinguishes only a space of non-Christian worship.

representants des anciens Manderins a cheval qui se battent contre les Tartares, des Bonses, des Pagodes, des Palaÿs, l'Empereur et sa Cour, et mille autres drogues de cette Nature: au milieu il y a une place pour les Ydoles, et une table pour ÿ mettre l'offrande, qui consiste en plusieurs Sortes de Viandes, et une espece de vin de ris qu'ils appellent Samsou:[216] devant cette table on voit un grand bassin rempli des cendres des papiers dorez et argantez qu'on ÿ brulle; il ÿ a aussi une bande de Musiciens qui jouent pendant tout le tems que l'Ydole est dans Cette maison: aprez que le Sacrifice des Viandes a esté offert avec toutes Ses ceremonies, ceux dela maison les mangent, en suitte on transporte les jdoles dans d'autres Maisons, ou on fait la meme Chose, le Soir il ÿ à des illuminations d'en milliers de lanternes devant les portes de chaque Maison, et comme les rues Sont fort droites et êtroites donne le plus beau coup d'oeil du monde: en même tems on donne la Comedie[217] au peuple en plusieurs endroits dans la rue, et cela dure tout la nuit.

Il n'y a rien de Si Commun Monsieur que ces Comedies, il ne leur faut pas de grands Sujets pour cela, par Exemple quand [62] une Ionque est arriveé de Batavia, Manille, Tonquin[218], Iapon &a les Interessés portent leurs Ydoles en procession à bord dela jonque, au Son de leurs trompettes et plusieurs autres jnstruments bisares, Je ne Scaurois dire quelle ceremonie ils ÿ font, mais aprez bien du tintamare qu'ils font Sur des bassins d'arrain, ils rapportent leurs Ydoles dans leur Pagode ou Temple et les jnvitent pour Venir assister à la Commedie qui Se donne pendant toute la nuit pour remercier leurs Dieux de ce que leur Vaisseau a fait un heureux Voÿage. un Iour il se donna une Commedie au peuple le teatre êtoit bâti sur l'eau tout contre notre factorie vis a vis une petite rue ou debarquoient ordinairement les passagers, le Sujet pourquoÿ se donnoit cette comedie estoit pour remercier l'Ydole de ce qu'il n'estoit arrivé aucun malheur dans le debarquement pendant Cette anneé, on avoit posé une petite loge vis a vis du theatre ou on place une demi dousaine d'Ydoles a demi roties, et tout a fait noires dela fumeé des Sacrifices qu'on leur avoit offert, la Comedie Commenca par des prosternations de tous les acteurs devant ces Ydoles, au son de toute leur Musique extravagante composeé de grands bassins d'airains qu'ils frappent avec des battons, d'autres bassins d'airains qu'ils frappent avec des battons, d'autres bassins faits comme des plats à barbe, qu'il frappent l'un Contre l'autre avec grand bruit, des tambours, des longues trompettes faisants le bruit d'une corne de Vache, un espece de flute traversiere des jnstruments d'airain aÿants a peu pres la forme

**216** Samsou refers to any type of fermented rice wine, popular among the Chinese. It was cheap and easy to produce.

**217** For more on early Chinese theatre, see Chung-wen Shih, *Golden Age of Chinese Drama* (Princeton, NJ: Princeton UP, 1976); Fu Jin, *Chinese Theatre* (New York: Cambridge UP, 2010); Marvin Carlson, *Theatre: a Very Short Introduction* (New York: Oxford UP, 2014), 9–13, 34–5.

**218** Tonkin was a kingdom in Southeast Asia, located north of Cochinchina and in modern-day northern Vietnam. The EIC and VOC established factories there during the 1600s, and its residents regularly did business with China via the country trade. Dror and Taylor, Views, 15–22, 74–84.

d'un hautbois[219], un Carillon d'une dousaine de Sonnetes faites en forme de bassin, pendues perpendiculairement en quatre rangs[220], et quelques jnstruments a Corde qu'ils pincent Comme le luth[221], tout cela entremélé fait un discord admirable, cependant ils observent une Mesure tres exacte, [63] qui Se donne avec deux morceaux de bois, que l'on manie comme on feroit chez nous d'une paire de Castaignettes[222], vers le Soir le Soleil estant fort bas dardoit ses Rayons divertement Sur ces Ydoles, les acteurs recommencerent leurs prosternations devant ces Ydoles, et on les rapporta a leur Pagode, nous demandames a quelques Chinois pourquoÿ ils n'attendoient pas la fin dela Commedie pour remporter leurs Ydoles qu'ils nomment Poussas, ils nous repondirent. ne voÿez vous pas que le Soleil les jncomode, et outre cela ils sont las de voir la Commedie: Cette reponse fait voir l'extreme aveuglement de Cette Nation qui d'allieurs est Si fine et si ruseé.

Le Premier de Septembre 1723 nous fumes jnvitez en ville par le Vice Roy ou Fou ÿuen, il nous envoia un de ses premiers Manderins pour nous Conduire en ville en habit Europiens dont nous fumes portes en palanquins ouverts[223], le Manderin marchand devant, car Sans cela on auroit des affronts a essuyer dela populace, la quelle comme par tout allieurs ÿ est jnsolente, d'abord qu'ils appercoivent un Europien, ils Se mettent a Crier fan quei fanquei, qui veut dire diable blanc.[224]

lors que nous fumes arrivez a la porte dela Ville Tartare[225], Je remarquay en pasant que cette porte êtoit d'une épaisseur prodigeuse, garnie de Cloux ou plustot

---

**219** This might refer to the suona, a traditional, double-reeded Chinese instrument. It is constructed of wood, fashioned in a conical shape, and makes a high-pitched sound. See Yuan-Yuan Lee and Sin-yan Shen, *Chinese Musical Instruments* (Chicago: Chinese Musical Society of North America, 1999), 76–9.

**220** The Chinese had been playing bells as chimes since at least the 400s BCE. The most famous are the sets of large *bianzhong*, which were played with a mallet. The carillon referenced here was a medieval European term for a series of bells, similarly arranged so that they could be struck melodically. Ibid., 24–31.

**221** A lute is a plucked string instrument, typically with a long neck and rounded back. The Chinese had several traditional instruments that fit this description, including the liuquin, pipa, ruan, sanxian and yueqin.

**222** Castanets are Mediterranean percussion instruments, composed of two small, wooden shells. They can be clicked together to keep and maintain rhythm within a group or used to add musical accents.

**223** A palanquin, or *jiao*, was a wheelless form of human transport, which consisted of a wooden carriage or chair and two poles and which was carried by at least two porters. They typically suggested social standing.

**224** For more on xenophobia in early China, see Louis Dermigny, *La Chine et l'Occident: le Commerce à Canton au XVIIIe siècle, 1719–1833, vol. 2* (Paris: SEVPEN, 1964).

**225** Ethnic divisions also featured prominently among the Chinese. During the Ch'ing Dynasty, the political and military elite Manchus spatially settled in the northern Old City of Canton, also known as the "Tartar Quarter." See Valery M. Garrett, *Heaven is High, the Emperor Far Away: Merchants and Mandarins in Old Canton* (New York: Oxford UP, 2002), 13–20.

de grosses Chevilles de fer, munie par derriere, et pour Surcroit de Sureté d'une barre aussi de fer qui est proportionneé au reste.[226] apres avoir passé la porte nous trouvames environs Cent Soldats Tartares de tres bonne mine, un second Manderin du Fou: ÿuen [64] nous recut a cette porte, qui nous Conduisit par des rues tres manifiques ou il n'y a que de boutiques des Choses les plus belles, apres avoir passé ces ruës, nous entrames dans la principale, ou nous rencontrions d'abord une rangeé d'arc de Triomphe[227] de pierre de taille a trois etages au milieu on ÿ voit eslevé un grand portail en voute, accompagne de Côté et d'autre d'une porte d'une moindre hauteur: et au haut dela voute est representé en Caracteres Chinoises les tropheés de Ceux qui l'avoient merité, ce qui fait un fort bel aspect au travers des dites voutes, et que les ruës Sont Si droites que la Veuë est libre d'un bout a l'autre,

Aprez avoir fait une bonne lieue de Chemin nous arrivames au palais de Fou: ÿuen, l'entreé en estoit de peu d'apparence a Cause qu'on entre par une Simple porte cochere, mais aussitot que nous fumes entreés dans la bassecour ou esplenade nous Vimes une belle porte gardeé de Cent fantasins et 50 Cavaliers, nous entrames par cette porte dans une place tres Spacieuse, ou il ÿ avoit des rochers de marbre Construits artificiellement, plains d'arbres et belles fleurs, au milieu il y avoit une Salle tres spacieuse Soutenue par plusieurs piliers ouverte de tout cotez, hormis dans le fond, enfin nous montames dans le principal appartement ou nous trouvames le Fou: yuen ou Viceroÿ assis sur une estrade Couverte d'un manifique tapis, nous arrivames a son estrade et aprés l'avoir Salué, il nous fit dire par Son jnterprete de nous asseoir.

Jl nous commenca par nous faire quelques questions generales sur le pais d'ou nous Venions, et Sur nostre [65] voyage; a quoy ayant Satisfait, il nous assura desa protection: ensuite il nous fit présenter le theé, et des Confitures du pais. il estoit fort affable, et avoit l'air fort dous. il estoit dans une grande Veneration par tout le pais, apres avoir tenu plusieurs discours, nous primes Conge avec toute la Satisfaction possible, il ordonna a Son premier Manderin de nous laisser voir les principales places dela ville.

Il faut avouer qu'on ne peut rien voir de plus beau en son genre, que les ruës de Canton, elles sont propres et nettes, paveés de pierre et Si droites, que la veuë est libre d'une porte à l'autre, nous trouvames les murs dela ville, dont elle est entoureé a l'antique dont le parapet est percé par quantité de Creneaux, qu'ils defendent ordinairement a Coup des fleches et d'artillerie, qu'ils disent ÿ etre en usage parmi eux d'un tems jmmemorial[228];

---

**226** The preceding sentence was adjusted and copied from: Roque, Voyage, 41.

**227** For a midcentury representation of such triumphal arches, see "Plate 45. A Trimphal Arch at Canton," in *A New General Collection of Voyages and Travels, vol. 4* (London: T. Astley, 1747).

**228** The preceding half-sentence was copied from: Allain Manesson-Mallet, *Description de l'univers, vol. 1* (Paris: Denys Thierry, 1683), 50.

Jl y a Sept portes dont celles qui regardent le nord sont sans fossé, garanties de plusieurs tours ou pateés Situeés Sur des eminences, les batteries que nous Vimes estoient de Canon de fonte, dont quelques uns Sont de Soixante livres de balle, ils ne Sont braquez que Sur des gros morceaux de bois quarrez sans aucun affut, de Sorte que les premiers coups etant tirez, il faut un tems considerable pour les recharger et les rebraquer. ces batteries sont gardeés par des Soldats tartares, qui font la patrouille pendant la nuit, et qui durant le jour se tiennent aux portes pour empecher les desordres et les friponneries, car en ce pais les tartares Sont fort Jaloux de leur Domination, et dela tranquilité publique; ils amenent les Coupables devant le Manderin de justice, qui sur le rapport [66] de l'offier qui Commande ses gardes les fait punir Severement.

Nous montames sur une Colline entre les deux Portes du nord ou est la Pagode[229] construit a l'honneur de la famille Taiming elle est la seule qui est batie a cinc étages, dela nous allames a Celle de Confusius[230] qui est au milieu dela Ville Tartare, un peu plus au Nord on trouve une tour[231] qui ne se distinge pas seulement du reste, mais qui efface les plus rares ouvrages dela Ville par sa propreté, et par la beauté de sa Construction, elle a neuf êtages qui ont Chacun leur voute, et Chacun une galderie en déhors dont les appuis ou garde foux sont disposeés avec tant de Simetrie et d'art que nos plus fameux architectes en admireroient le travail, et la Construction, le Corps du Batiment Compris entre Chaque galerie est uni et plombe par de hors, l'on diroit à voir ce superbe edifice que cette Tour n'est qu'un miroir pour l'eclat des pierres vernisés de verd et rouge dont l'email est le plus êclatant et brillant que l'on puisse voir, toutes les pierres ÿ sont si bien assambleés l'une à cote de l'autre, qu'il est difficile d'en discerner la liaison[232];

Au Sud dela ditte Tour, nous en rencontrames une autre de figure ronde Sans aucun ornement[233], les Chinois nous dirent que Cette tour avoit este batie par les Tartares, qui en ce tems la avoient envahÿ et pillé la Chine: d'ou vient que les Tartares de

229 The Zhenhai Tower, also known as the Five Story Pagoda, originally was constructed in 1380 during the Ming Dynasty. It was located on the northern edge of the eighteenth-century city, along the city wall.

230 Confucius (ca. 551–479 BCE) was an early Chinese politician, teacher and philosopher. His teachings – including a focus on family bonds, moral self-edification and reciprocity – aimed at improving secular relations, although many of his followers practiced them religiously. They gained popularity in the Han and T'ang dynasties. See Annping Chin, *Confucius: a Life of Thought and Politics* (New Haven: Yale UP, 2008); Michael Schuman, *Confucius and the World He Created* (New York: Basic Books, 2015).

231 The Hua Ta, or Flower Pagoda, forms part of the Buddhist Liurong Temple and was located in central Canton. Initially constructed in 537, it appears to have nine levels on its exterior but really has seventeen.

232 The preceding sentence was adjusted and copied from: Manesson-Mallet, Description, vol. 1, 38.

233 This round, unadorned tower forms the minaret of the Huaisheng Mosque. It was constructed in 627, making it part of one of the world's oldest Muslim mosques. See Nancy Steinhard Shatzman, "China's Earliest Mosques", in: *Journal of the Society of Architectural Historians* 67.3 (2008), 330–361.

ce tems cÿ la Conservent comme un Chef d'euvre que leurs ancetres ont fait batir, et Comme un tropheé de leurs victoires.

Ayant passe au côte de l'ouest nous entrames dans la [67] maison dela Propaganda fide[234], qui est batie a l'Italiene, mais un peu negligeé, nous fumes d'abord Saluer le Reverend Pere Peroni[235] providiteur dela ditte Congregation, Cette Maison est batie par le Cardinal de Tournon[236], qui fut envoye en qualité de Legat du Saint Siege[237] par le Pape Clement Onze[238], pour aller dans l'Empire dela Chine, ou il arriva au mois d'avril 1705. il estoit muni d'un decret du Pape[239], qui n'estoit point encore publié en Europe, Contre le Culte superstitieu des Chinois que quelques Missionaires permettoient aux nouveaux Chretiens. en Vertu du Decret, le Legat defendit par un Mandement publié a Nanquin[240] le 7 fevrier 1705 de mettre dans les Eglises un tableau

---

**234** The Holy Congregation for the Propagation of Faith was a Roman Catholic institution founded in 1622, which aimed to encourage and manage missionary activity overseas. It increasingly came into conflict with the Jesuits – who had been present in China since 1579 – during the late 1600s. This was at the same moment that new missionaries, especially the Dominicans and Franciscans, began to evangelize in China and complain about their predecessor's perceived lax conversion styles. Brockey, Journey, 12, 185.

**235** Domenico Perroni (ca. 1674–1729) was an Italian Jesuit and procurator of the Holy Congregation for the Propagation of Faith in Canton from 1721 to 1729. See Ludwig Koch (ed.), *Jesuiten-Lexikon, vol. 2* (Löwen-Heverlee: Verlag der Bibliothek SJ, 1962), 1383–4.

**236** Carlo Tomasso Maillard de Tournon (1668–1710) was a cardinal and papal legate to the East Indies. In 1703, Pope Clement XI sent him to India and Southeast Asia, to ensure Catholic missions there were observing church orthodoxy. He eventually was imprisoned in Macao for conjoined spiritual-political reasons by the emperor and died while under house arrest in 1710. Brockey, Journey, 186–204.

**237** A papal legate is an individual personally selected to represent the pope and official Roman Catholic theological teachings to overseas congregations or foreign nations. Typically, this role is filled by a cardinal.

**238** Pope Clement XI (1649–1721) was the spiritual and diplomatic head of the Catholic church from 1700 until his death. During his reign, he fought against church heresies and for religious uniformity in the East. J.N.D. Kelly and M.J. Walsh (ed.), *The Oxford Dictionary of Popes* (New York: Oxford UP, 2010), 294–6.

**239** The K'ang-hsi Emperor officially allowed Christianity in China with his 1692 Edict of Toleration, which permitted all religions present before 1691 to worship so long as they did not conflict with state-sponsored Confucianism. To draw converts, some missionaries began to incorporate the secular habits of eastern belief-systems – such as adopting Buddhist habits of dress, participating in seasonal Confucian activities and allowing for ancestor worship (together known as the Chinese Rites) – into Roman Catholic religious life. The practice was banned by Pope Clement XI in his 1704 brief *Cum Deus optimus*, which Cardinal de Tournon was to communicate to the emperor. In response, the K'ang-hsi Emperor banned all Christian missionaries in 1706 who did not have an imperial *piao*, or license. To obtain such permission, ministers had to swear an oath to accept the Chinese Rites. Many Jesuits accepted the *piao*. Brockey, Journey, 167; 186–204.

**240** Nanking, now Nanjing, is a city in eastern China, located on the Yangtze River Delta. It served as an imperial capital for several Chinese dynasties.

avec cette jnscription King tien[241], c'est à dire, adorez le Ciel, ni de pratiquer les Cultes que les Chinois rendent aux Esprits, aux Ancetres, a Confusius, et aux Planetes. le Cardinal etant arrivé a Pekin[242], fut d'abord bien recu de l'Empereur dela Chine; il ÿ fit venir Monseig.r l'Eveque de Conon Vicaire Apostolique[243], le quel aÿant declaré par ecrit et de vive voix à l'Empereur, que la Doctrine et les cultes des Chinois ne s'accordoient pas avec la religion Chretienne, fut arreté et ensuitte banni. le Cardinal de Tournon avoit eté renvoyé quelque tems auparavant, le 28 aoust 1706 il fut conduit a Maccao, apres avoir donné un mandement le 25 Ianvier 1707[244]. pour servir de reglement a la Conduite que doivent garder les Missionaires, quand ils sont jnterrogés sur les Cultes des Chinois. etant a Macao il y a toujours ête retenú en prison dan la maison des Peres Iesuites par l'ordre du dit Empereur dela Chine, et ÿ est mort en reputation de Sainteté au mois de Iuin 1710 sans que les mauvais traitemens qu'il ÿ a Souffert aÿent [68] pu le faire Changer de sentiment, ni êbranler Sa fermeté. le Pape a honore sa memoire par un Exellent èloge que Sa Sainteté a recité en plein Consistoire le 14 octobre 1711.[245]

Apres avoir pris une tasse de theé et avoir parle touchant l'êtat present dela Religion Chretienne a la Chine, nous primes Congé du dit Père Peroni. nous revinmes dans la grande rue qui va à la Porte meridionale, apres avoir traverse plusieurs Arcs de triomphe, nous passames par la porte nommeé parmi eux Chia non men[246], qui veut dire, Porte Meridionale de la Ville Chinoise, par ce qu'elle regarde la ditte Ville, dont elle est separeé de Celle des Tartares par une muraille de pierre de taille qui sert aux derniers de Citadelle, qui tiennent devant un Corps de garde de Cent hommes, Situeé entre les deux portes, et un autre en dedans avec un pareil nombre. I'aÿ remarquaÿ en passant que Cette Porte est la plus forte de toutes Celles dela ville, à cause

241 This likely was a play on the Confusion-inspired phrase "Jing Tiam," or "Revere Heaven." The latter was used by the Jesuits in their churches, to make their rituals more adaptive to Chinese customs. It was often written in the emperor's calligraphy, thus indicating his approval. Brockey, Journey, 187.

242 Cardinal de Tournon had two audiences with the K'ang-hsi Emperor at his palace in Peking in December 1705 and June 1706. While the first was friendly, the Catholic legate and his associates were ordered away and back to Macao from the second, after it became clear they would not approve any integration of the Chinese Rites into church rituals. Ibid., 186–7.

243 Charles Maigrot (1652–1730) was apostolic vicariate of China from roughly 1700 to 1708. Although once held in the Emperor's favor, and seemingly supportive of the Chinese Rituals, Maigrot was sent to Macao with Cardinal de Tournon after the latter's second and failed imperial audience in June 1706. Ibid., 181–8.

244 Cardinal de Tournon officially published the papal mandates banning the Chinese Rituals in January 1707 in Nanking. Violators thereafter risked official excommunication. Ibid., 188–9.

245 The preceding paragraph, except for the first sentence, was adjusted and copied from: Louis Moréri, *Supplément aux anciennes éditions du Grand Dictionaire Historique, vol. 2* (Amsterdam: Pierre Brunel, 1716), 588.

246 The Great South Gate, or *Tae nan mun*, was the principle southern entrance to Canton's Old City from its New City. Garrett, Heaven, 13, 16, 29.

d'un petit ruisseau qui court le long de la muraille, et qu elle est garantie par deux Portes d'une êpaisseur prodigieuse, garnie des Cloux ou plustot de grosses Chevilles de fer, et pour Surcroit de Sureté, d'une Sarasine[247], qui est un assemblage de grosses pieces de bois, mises en treilles, qui est Suspendue au dessus des Portes à une corde qu'on lache pour Se garantir des Surprises.

Nous entrames par cette Porte dans la Ville Chinoise, elle ne nous parut pas si considerable que celle des Tartares nous ne trouvames aucune Chose qui merita attention, hormis les boutiques qui sont remplis des plus belles marchandisses du monde ce qu[i] Contribue a la beauté des rues à cause que chaque maison est garnié a deux coteés de tablettes qui sont aussi hautes que les [69] portes, sur les quelles on escrit en caracteres d'or sur un fond rouge, verd ou bleu, tout se qu'on vend de denreés dans la ditte Maison.

Nous avons trouvé aux environs de Canton beaucoup de Pagodes ou Cloiters Chinois remplis de Bonzes ou Pretres Chinois: vis a vis de notre factorie a l'autre bord de la Riviere il y avoit une Pagode[248] d'une Vaste etendue, ou nous allions quelque fois, lorsque les affaires nous donnoient quelque relache. on entre premierement dans une grande bassecour, et là traversant sous des alleés d'arbres, nous montames par quelques degrez dans un grand portique et le traversant, nous trouvames à chaque Côté une Ydole haute pour le moins de trente pieds, nous descendimes encore une fois pour traverser une autre cour et pour monter dans la Pagode, qui est un Corps de logis grande de quatre Cent pieds de diametre en son quarez, on ÿ entre de touts côtez, car a la facade seule il ÿ a plus de douze portes, nous vimes trois Deeses[249] assises hautes environ de vingt cinc pieds doreés entierrement d'une grandeur et fisionemie êgale, et plusieurs autres figures a droit et a gauche, comme nous êtions a examiner toutes ces ydoles, nous vimes sortir une Soisantaine de Bonzes marchands tous sur une ligne l'un apres l'autre avec grande modestie, ils entroient dans l'Eglise, et si mirent debout sur trois rangs, un d'eux en tonna quelque hymne, et un autre donnoit la mesure sur un jnstrument fait [70] comme une noix de coco ouverte par le milieu, un autre frappoit d'une main sur quelques petites Sonnettes et de l'autre Sur un tambour grand comme quatre des nôtres aprez bien des genuflexions de celuÿ qui officioit devant chacune de ces trois Deeses et aprez qu'il eut bien battu la terre de Sa tête (maniere d'adorer chez eux) il prit une petite tasse remplie de quelque liqueur: et

---

**247** A sarrasine, or portcullis, is a heavy grate of wooden or iron bars, which can be lowered to block a doorway, should it require added protection.

**248** The Haizhuang Temple is located on the north shore of the Pearl River, directionally south of Canton and its factories. It was built as a site of Buddhist worship during the tenth-century Southern Ming Dynasty.

**249** The Grand Hall of the Haizhuang Temple historically featured three gold-colored buddha statues. They signified the Buddhas of the Three Worlds, or *Trailokya*, being the realms of desire, form and formless. Garrett, Heaven, 114; Damien Keown, *Buddhism: a Very Short Introduction* (New York: Oxford UP, 2013), 39.

un autre ou il ÿ avoit quelques grains de ris, et aprez l'avoir offert aux Ydoles avec bien de grimaces il vint devant la porte du milieu, et il repandit la tasse de liqueur sur un tripied en trois diverses parties, et il fit la même Chose avec le Ris.

Ensuitte ils Commencerent une procession faisant trois fois le tour de la Pagode ou Temple, et chantants toujoúrs ces Paroles: O. mi. to. Foe[250], qui signifie Grand Dieu Foe, Sauvez moi, ils portent aussi des rosaires sur les quels ils recitent incessament ces quatre parolles.

Aprez la procession ils allerent prendre leur Souper qui ne consiste que dans de legumes, car ils ne peuvent pas manger de ce qui a receu vie: Cependent ils le font en cachette, ces Bonzes ne portent point de queue, ou tresse de cheveux comme les autres Chinois, et son habillez autrement aussi, portants encore leurs anciens habits Chinois, ces Bonses sont gens de la lie du peuple, ignorans jusques au fondements de leur Regilion la plus part, e[t] capables des plus grands Crimes. le Reverend Pere Appiani[251] nous conta un jour, que dans la Pagode ou il [71] êtoit prisonnier ils avoient tué leur Superieur par ce qu'il avoit environ Cent theÿls en argent.

Derriere cette Pagode il ÿ avoit une cour aboutissante à une Seconde Pagode, ensuitte une Troisieme[252], l'enceinte de ces trois Pagodes etoit composeé de grand nombre d'appartemens parmi les quels nous decouvrimes plusieurs autres petites Pagodes, comme Chapelles qui contenoient differentes Ydoles.

Ces Pagodes ou Bonseries, sont comme chez nous les Couvents, mais il ÿ a plusieurs autres Pagodes publiques, ou Chacun vient Sacrifier, voicÿ la description d'une, que J'aÿ eu occasion de bien examiner.

Devant la porte il ÿ avoit plusieurs astrologues[253], et diseurs de bonne avanture, car les Chinois sont fort adoné a l'astrologie judiciaire: quoÿ qu'ils Soyent fort ignorans dans cette Science: mais ils sont fort Superstitieux a l'egard des jours heureux, qu'ils pretendent que ces Astrologues ignorans savent predire.

---

**250** The mantra "A Mi Tuo Fo," loosely translates as the "boundless Buddha." It refers to the name of the celestial Buddha, Amitābha, who was especially popular in eastern Asia.

**251** Luigi Antonio Appiani (1663–1733) was an Italian native and Lazarist missionary to China between 1699 and 1726. He also served as Cardinal Tournon's interpretor during his travels in 1705 and 1706 and was similarly imprisioned by the emperor thereafter. Nicolas Standaert (ed.), *Handbook of Christianity in China, vol. 1* (Leiden: Brill, 2001), 349.

**252** It was common for Buddhist temples to have several separate pagodas. This might refer to the Hall of the Heavenly Kings and the Hall of the Sixth Patriarch, which also were located at the Haizhuang Temple.

**253** Astrology relates to the predicting of earthly events, based on celestial observations. This tradition flourished in ancient China and eventually integrated into imperial spiritual-systems, especially Daoism. See Xiaochun Sun and Jacob Kistemaker, *The Chinese Sky during the Han: Constellating Stars and Society* (Leiden: Brill, 1997).

Dans le vestibule dela Pagode, il ÿ avoit une boutique ou on vendoit du papier doré, Argenté[254], pour bruler devant les jdoles, et une composition de bois odoriferant[255], dont ils font des petits batons qu'ils allument devant les Ydoles, aiant avance cinc à six pas, je trouvai une machine de cuivre haute de cinc pieds, qui servoit de foyer pour bruler les papiers dorez, a trois pas dela, il y avoit un autre foyer, ou on bruloit des bois Odoriferants, au fond dela pagode, il ÿ avoit la principale Ydole[256] representante un homme assis gravement dans un fauteuil, aÿant la barbe fort longe [72] et par articles, a sa droite etoient quatres Ydoles, dont la Premiere representoit une femme aiant la phisionemie fort modeste[257], les trois autres etoient de figures d'hommes[258] hautes d'huit pieds, armez de differentes Sortes d'armes jnconnus parmi nous, et aiants la vue horrible, ala gauche dela principale Ydole etoient quatre figures d'hommes[259] comme les precedentes, hormis le dernier qui avoit la tête et les griffes d'un aigle.

Je ni voiois point de Bonse dans cette Pagode, et J'observay que chacun sacrifioit pour soi meme, de sorte qu'un domestique portoit les viandes destineés pour le sacrifice dans une ou deux Banastres, il ÿ avoit des poules bouillies, du Porc, des Crabes, quelques fruits &.[a] de chaque viande differente il coupe un morceau le quel morceau il met tout entier dans une coupe de porselaine, et la presente au maitre, qui la mit sur une grande table devant la principale jdole: ensuitte il prend trois petites tasses de porselaine qu'il remplit de Samsou (vin Chinois) et les mit aussi dessus la table, il se mit a genoux et bat la terre de la tête trois fois, en marmottant toujours quelques paroles entre les dents, il se leva et offroit la viande et le vin a l'jdole, et aprez bien de genuflexions et ceremonies, il repand le vin dans une machine ou reservoir de fer

---

**254** Chinese Daoists and some Buddhists burn joss paper – a bamboo material covered in gold or silver foil and fashioned to look like money – as a symbol of family wealth in their religious ceremonies. It especially is used in rituals of ancestor worship. See Gary Seaman, "Spirit Money: an Interpretation", in: *Journal of Chinese Religions* 10.1 (1982), 80–91. For more on Daoism, generally, see pages 289–90.

**255** Incense long played a role in Chinese Daoist rituals, symbolizing the rising of personal or communal prayers to the gods. Buddhism's arrival increased this habit as well as introduced new fragrances. See John Kieschnick, *The Impact of Buddhism on Chinese Material Culture* (Princeton, NJ: Princeton UP, 2003), 277–8.

**256** This likely refers to the Buddhist bodhisattva known as the *Maitreya*, or Future Buddha. According to tradition, he is the earthly successor of the current Buddha, Siddhattha Gotama. He is often depicted seating on a throne and is attended by the Four Heavenly Kings. Denise Patry Leidy and Donna Strahan, *Wisdom Embodied: Chinese Buddhist and Daoist Sculpture in the Metropolitan Museum of Art* (New Haven: Yale UP, 2010), 10, 198–205.

**257** Guanyin typically is depicted as a female bodhisattva, revered by both Daoists and Buddhists as a giver of mercy, compassion and the relief of suffering. Leidy and Strahan, Wisdom, 14, 75, 86, 104.

**258** Figures unknown.

**259** These probably represent the Four Heavenly Kings – mythological Buddhist figures who represent the four cardinal directions and symbolically protect the temple from harm.

sous la table, le quel coule par un trou sur la terre, aprez il se remet a prier devant l'Ydole battant la terre de Sa tête de tem[s] en tems.

Ayant finis sa priere il prend de dessus la table un êtui [73] haut d'un pied, Contenant environ cincquante petits batons de bamboux[260], et il le Secoue, Jusqu'a ce qu'il en tombe par terre, il le ramasse avec pricipitation, pour voir ce qui etoit ecrit dessus, ce qu'ayant lu, il prend deux morceaux de bois, ayant la forme d'un roignon, de porc Coupé en deux, les jette en lair, et observe Soigneusement leur Situation, lors qu'ils êtoient tombé par terre, apparement qu'il en etoit content, car il fit bien des Compliments a mons.[r] l'Ydole, il reitere ce jeu Iusques à trois fois, et paroissoit plus ou moins content, selon que le dit Ydole, lui avoit accordé ou refusé sa demande, par ces petits batons et morceaux de bois, aprez avoir bien fatigué la terre de sa tête, il se leve, et prend une poigneé de ces petits batons de bois Odoriferant, que l'on achete a la porte de la Pagode, et les allume a un des foÿers, et il en met deux a trois devant chacun des huit Ydoles, qui etoient a gauche et a droite de l'Ydole Principale; I'observai qu'il ne fit qu'une simple jnclination de tête pour ces Ydoles, apparement que ces Messieurs etoient d'un rang inferieur a l'autre, ensuitte il prend quelques morceaux de papier doré, et les brule dans le foÿer destine pour cela, et Sorte aprez avoir fait la reverence en Inclinant la tête profondement, aÿant les mains Iointes, qui est leur maniere de saluer, l'un l'autre, en disan tsin:tsin[261], plusieurs autres Chinois Venoient ensuitte, et Sacrifioient a peu pres de la meme maniere, ils donnent la Viande, qui a este offerte a l'Ydole, aux domestiques, parce qu'ils croÿent que le dit Ydole en à Succé la melieure Substance.

## 4.[e] Lettre Qatrieme de la Religion Chr:[e] et. Des sectes Differentes qui sont dans L'Empire dela Chine.

[74] Monsieur il est difficile de decider qu'elle à esté la Religion Ancienne des Chinois et combien du tems, la Connoissance du Vraÿ Dieu que les Enfans de Noé[262] donnerent a leurs descendens s'est conserveé dans cette partie du Monde. On ne peut

260 This refers to the augury practice of Kau Cim, which originated in China in about the third century. According to tradition, a worshipper at a Daoist or Buddhist temple drops one of one hundred bamboo slivers from a cup while simultaneously asking a question. This refers them to an oracle, which answers their query. See Michel Strickmann, *Chinese Poetry and Prophecy: the Written Oracle in East Asia* (Stanford, CA: Stanford UP, 2005), 151–2, ft. 10.

261 This refers to the Confucian principle of graded love, wherein many spiritual adherents believed they should retain more affection for their family than for others. See Home H. Dubs, "The Development of Altruism in Confucianism", in: *Philosophy East and West* 1.1 (1951), 51–5.

262 Noah (dates unknown) is a figure from the Old Testament, selected by the Christian God to survive a devastating flood. He and his sons, as a result, were perceived as the ancestors of all humanity. Genesis 6–10.

gueres faire de fond sur ce que raporte l'histoire dela Chine de leurs premiers Empereurs: elle à tout à fait l'air d'une histoire fabuleuse. quoÿ qu'il en soit les Missionaires dela Chine conviennent que ce Peuple êtoit enseveli dans les tenebres de l'Ydolatrie environ huit cent ans avans la naissance de Iesus Christ.[263]

Quelques uns Croyent que Saint Thomas porta la foÿ Chretienne dans la Chine[264], et que certains peuples de cet Empire en ont encore quelque reste, a cause de ce qu'on Voit dans leurs Pagodes, comme une Ydole a trois têtes[265], qui se regardent, des Peintures de douze personnes Vénérables[266], et des tableaux d'une fille, qui porte un enfant entre ses bras[267], assurant qu'elle fut Vierge apres l'enfantement. toutes ces Choses s'appliquent par les speculatifs, au mÿstere dela Trinite, aux douze Apôtres, et à la Sainte Vierge.[268]

Ce qu'il ÿ a devraÿ, c'est que le Christianisme commenca a être prêché a la Chine par des Prestres qui y êtoient allez de Syrie[269], l'an 636. de Iesus Christ, par rapport

---

263 The preceding paragraph was adjusted and copied from: Noël Alexandre, *Apologie des dominicains missionnaires de la Chine*, 2nd ed. (Cologne: Corneille d'Egmond, 1700), 7. Jesus Christ (ca. 6 BCE–30 CE) was a native of modern-day Palestine and Jewish teacher, whose life and preachings eventually founded Christianity. See Linda Woodhead, *Christianity: a Very Short Introduction* (New York: Oxford UP, 2014).

264 Some Christians believed Thomas, one of the early disciplines of Jesus Christ, evangelized in India, China and Japan during the first century. See, for example, Juan González de Mendoza, *The History of the Great and Mighty Kingdom of China* (1586).

265 This might refer to the Asura – lesser Buddhist deities or demons that had three heads and six arms. See Sampa Biswas, *Indian Influence on the Art of Japan* (New Delhi: Northern Book Centre, 2010), 72–5.

266 This likely relates to the twelve deities of the Chinese zodiac, which correspond to the twelve lunar months and which are depicted both as animals and as men. See Stephen Little and Shawn Eichman, *Taoism and the Arts of China* (Chicago: The Art Institute of Chicago), 29, 141.

267 This might refer to the Daoist deity Bixia Yuanjun, the goddess of dawn and childbirth. She was especially popular during the Ming (1368–1644) and Ch'ing (1644–1912) dynasties, and she sometimes was displayed with a child in her arms. It also may refer to Songzi Niangniang, a Daoist fertility goddess. Ibid., 278–80.

268 The preceding paragraph was adjusted and copied from: Moréri, Grand dictionaire, vol. 1 (1683), 882.

269 The first form of Christianity to arrive in China was Nestorianism, a spirituality centered in modern-day Syria and Palestine. It was known as *Jingjiao* in Asia. Nestorianism broke with the western church in 431, after its founder Nestorius continued to argue that the divine and human persons of Jesus Christ were separated. Its accommodative nature made it popular in seventh and eighth century China, as it adapted to include Chinese rhetoric and Buddhist teachings. The faith's initial tenure in China ended in 845, when Emperor Wuzong banned both it and Buddhism. See Huaiyu Chen, "The Encounter of Nestorian Christianity with Tantric Buddhism in Medieval China", in: *Hidden Treasures and Intercultural Encounters: Studies on East Syriac Christianity in China and Central Asia*, ed. Dietmar W. Winkler and Li Tang (Vienna: Lit, 2009), 195–214.

de ce monument[270] [75] Chinois que l'on a trouvé l'an 1625 dans le Roÿaume de Chen si[271] qui merite bien que Ie vous en donne icy un petit detail. c'est une grande pierre graveé en caracteres chinoises et Syriaques, qui a neuf palmes et demÿ de longeur et dix de largeur, Son epaiseur est d'un palme, on quatre pouces. elle fut trouveé l'an 1625 en creusant les fondamens d'une Maison, dans un Village proche la ville de Singanfou[272] qui est la Capitale dela Province de Chen si, un Spectacle Si curieux attira un nombre infini de toute Sorte de Personnes pour voir cette espece d'epithaphe. le Gouverneur meme Y accoúrut, et fit porter ce monument de l'antiquité dans le temple ou Pagode des Bonses pour le faire examiner par les Scavans, et en decouvrir l'explication, il ordonna en meme tems, qu'on taillat une pierre dela même grandeur et que l'on gravat fidelement toutes les lettres et toutes les figures de ce monument. il ÿ a deux jnscriptions qui marquent l'anneé que cette pierre fut graveé, l'une Chinoise, et l'autre Syriaque et qui Semblent ne Se pas accorder: car l'jnscription Chinoise porte que ce fut Sous le Regne du Grand Tam[273], le Second anneé de King: tsong ou kim çum[274], c'est à dire l'an de Iesu Christ 782, et l'jnscription Syriaque marque l'an 1092, Selon les Grecs. pour concilier ces deux dates, les Sçavans observent qu'il y avoit en ce tems la deux Sortes de Supputations d'anneés, la premiere etoit Ecclesiastique[275], et servoit aux Chretiens dela Chine, dont l'epoque Commencoit ala naissance de Iesu Christ. la seconde etoit politique et ètoit commune aux Arabes, aux Caldeens[276], aux [76] Syriens, et aux Egiptiens et presque a tout l'orient ou l'on Comptait les anneés depuis l'Ere appelleé des Seleúsides[277], qui Commencoit douze ans apres la Mort

---

**270** For more on this monument, see Michael Keevak, *The Story of a Stele: China's Nestorian Monument and its Reception in the West, 1625–1916* (Hong Kong: Hong Kong UP, 2008).

**271** Shensi, now Shaanxi, Province was the administrative center of the T'ang Dynasty, which ruled China between 618 and 907. It was located in north central China and along the Great Wall.

**272** This refers to the city of Chang'an, located in Shensi. It was the capital of the T'ang Dynasty as well as its largest city. The Nestorian Stele was found near its Congren Temple. Keevak, Story, 1.

**273** The first complete reign period of Te-tsung was named Chien-chung, and extended from 780 to 783.

**274** Te-tsung (742–805) was the oldest son of Tai-tsung and the tenth emperor in the T'ang Dynasty. See C.A. Peterson, "Court and province in mid- and late T'ang", in: Cambridge History of China, vol. 3, 497–513.

**275** The Christian Church marks the start of their chronology, or 1 CE, with the proposed date of the birth of Jesus Christ. See Denis Feeney, *Caesar's Calendar: Ancient Time and the Beginnings of History* (Berkeley: University of California Press, 2007).

**276** Chaldea was a small kingdom that emerged in the Middle East, specifically on the west coast of the Persian Gulf, between the tenth and sixth centuries BCE. It eventually integrated into Babylonia, although the term was used again in the Middle Ages to refer to Roman Catholics from the region. See John Joseph, *The Modern Assyrians of the Middle East: Encounters with Western Christian Missions, Archaeologists, and Colonial Powers* (Cologne: Brill, 2000), 3–9.

**277** The Seleucids ruled much of the territory previously conquered by Alexander the Great from 312–63 BCE, with a focus on modern-day Syria and Palestine. The Seleucid calendar starts its chrod'Alexandre le Grand[278], l'an 310 devant Iesu Christ. cette reflexion fait connaitre, que l'an 1092, des Grecs, ètoit l'an 782 depuis la naissance du Sauveur, car ajoutant 310 a 782. cela fait 1092.

Le premier qui travailla a decouvrir les Secrets de cette pierre fut Leon Manderin[279], le quel êtant nouvellement converti, mit un livre aujour pour en donner l'explication. ensuite le Pere Alvares Semedo[280] Iesuite portugais, qui fut un des premiers Peres a qui l'on permit de batir une maison et une Eglise a Singan fou, l'an 1628. s'appliqua avec un soin particulier a chercher l'jntelligence des mots et des figures qui paroissent sur le monument, mais le Pere Kircher[281] ÿ a le mieux reussi, Ie Vous donneraÿ ici un petit precis de ce qu'il explique fort au long.

Aú haut dela pierre on voit un Croix Ciseleé sur des nuages dont les bras Sont recourbez par le bout a peu pres en facon de fleurs de lÿs: au dessous de cette Croix il y a neufs mots Chinois en trois petites lignes. l'ecriture contient soixante et deux lignes en caracteres Chinois, que l'on distinge en vingt neuf colomnes qui se lisent de haut en bas. a côte de cette êcriture, principalement au cote gauche et au bas, il ÿ a plusieurs mots Syriaques et quelques uns Chinois. les mots qui sont à coté de la premiere colomne, s'expliquent ainsi, la Pierre digne d'une Eternelle louange, et le prologue de la tres jllustre Loi promulgué dans la Chine [77] fait par Kim cym[282], prêtre de l'Eglice de Ta cyn[283] (cest à dire) de Iudeé. les discours des vingt neuf colomnes contient les articles de Foi, et les ceremonies dela Religion. il est parlé du mistere de la tres Sainte

nology with Emperor Seleucus I's re-conquest of Babylon in 312 BCE, and it remained popular among residents of the Middle East until the sixth century. Feeney, Caesar's Calendar, 139.

**278** Alexander III (356–323 BCE) was a Macedonian king, who spread Hellenistic culture through his vast military conquests from Greece to Persia, Syria, Egypt, Babylon and India. Ibid., 40, 48, 63, 142.

**279** Leon Li Zhizao (1565–1630) was a Chinese official and early elite convert to Christianity. He aided European missionaries in their evangelization efforts, especially by translating texts to his native tongue. He also made the Jesuits aware of the Nestorian Stele, once informed himself by friend and scholar Zhang Gengyu. Li Zhizao published the first commentary on the stele in 1625. Keevak, Story, 10–2, 65.

**280** Alvarez Semedo (1586–1658) was a Portuguese Jesuit, who worked as a missionary in China since 1610. He was the first European to visit the Nestorian Stele as well as the first person to identify its Syriac text. His account of the discovery was included in *History of the Great and Renown Monarchy of China*, published in the 1640s. Ibid., 13–5, 31–5, 90.

**281** Athanasius Kircher (1602–1680) was a German Jesuit who specialized in the study of linguistics and foreign cultures, especially those of Egypt and China. While he never traveled to the East, he first published the inscription on the Nestorian Stele in his *China Illustrata* (1667). Ibid., 29–60.

**282** Jingjing, or Adam in Syriac (dates unknown), was an eighth-century Nestorian Christian living in China, who composed the text engraved on the Nestorian Stele. Ibid., 148.

**283** Ta-Ch'in, or Daquin, was the early Chinese name for the nearby Roman Empire. It specifically referred to the Byzantine and Arabic provinces of Syria and Palestine. Biblically, this region was known as Judea. The name applied after 745 to all Christian monasteries in China that followed the Nestorian tradition. Ian Gillman and Hans-Joachim Klimkeit, *Christians in Asia before 1500* (London: Routledge, 1999), 270.

Trinité, de lá Creation du monde, de l'jncarnation du fils de Dieu[284], de Sa Vie, de Sa Mort, et de sa resurrection. puis dela discipline ecclesiatique, du purgatoire[285], de la messe, et des Roÿs Chretiens de ce pais.

La date Chinoise de l'erection de cette pierre est l'an 782. les mots Syriaques qui Sont en marge, marquent les noms des Docteurs et des hommes Apostoliques qui florissoient dans la Chine, lors que cette pierre fut graveé, et errigeé pour Servir a la posterité d'un monument eternel de la Religion de ce Roÿaume, avec la date de l'an 1092 Selon les grecs, qui revient a l'an 782 de Iesus Christ.

Sous le Regne de Tai tsong ven hoam[286], en viron l'an 636 Olo puen[287] pasa dela Iudeé dans la Chine pour y preher l'evangile, et ÿ fut fort bien receu. le fils et successeur de l'Eempereur, qui Se nommoït Cao cum[288], etablit Olo puen Eveque de la grande loÿ de l'evangile. le quel êtoit receu dans tout cet Empire. pendant le regne de Xim lie[289], il s'eleva en 699, une persecution contre les fideles, exiteé par les Bonses qui vouloient retablir leur Pagodes, mais l'Empereur Hiven çum chi tao[290] la fit cesser

284 The Incarnation refers to the Christian belief that God became fully human – while also remaining fully divine – through the person of Jesus Christ, conceived of Mary. An early text that aimed to teach this doctrine in China was: Giulio Aleni, *Illustrated Explanation of the Incarnation of the Lord of Heaven* (1637). See *Catechism of the Catholic Church* (Vatican: Libreria Editrice Vaticana, 1993), 456–63; Brockey, Journey, 305, 395–6.

285 Purgatory, according to the Roman Catholic Church, is a space of purification, experienced by souls on their way to heaven. *Catechism*, 1030–2.

286 T'ai-tsung (598–649) was the second emperor in the Chinese T'ang Dynasty. His liberal policies and military conquests expanded both Buddhism and Nestorian Christianity. He issued formal protections for the latter faith in 638 and, according to the Nestorian Stele, arranged for the translation of several Christian works. See Howard Wechsler, "T'ai-tsung (reign 626–49) the consolidator", in: Cambridge History of China, vol. 3, 118–241.

287 Alopen (dates unknown) was the first known Christian missionary in China, having arrived in the imperial capital of Chang'an, now Xi'an, from the Persian or Syrian empires in 635. His details only are known via the Nestorian Stele. See Daniel H. Bays, *A New History of Christianity in China* (Malden, MA: Wiley-Blackwell, 2012), 7–11.

288 Kao-tsung (628–683) was ninth son of T'ai-tsung and the third emperor in the T'ang Dynasty. He extended his father's accomodation towards Christianity, by establishing Alopen as "Great Lord of the Law, Guardian of the Realm" and by building Christian worship sites in each of his provinces. See Denis Twitchett and Howard J. Wechsler, "Kao-sung (reign 649–83) and the empress Wu: the inheritor and usurper", in: Cambridge History of China, vol. 3, 242–89.

289 Wu Chao (624–705) was the second wife of Kao-tsung and effectively took over his reign following a stroke. She was empress in her own right from 690–705, during the brief Chou Dynasty. A devout Buddhist, Wu declared it the state religion in 691 and allowed the informal persecution of Christians and the destruction of their institutions during her reign. See ibid., 251–72; Richard W.L. Guisso, "The reigns of the empress Wu, Chung-tsung and Jui tsung (684–712)", in: Cambridge History of China, vol. 3, 290–320.

290 Hsüan-tsung (685–762) was the grandson of Wu Zetian and the seventh emperor in the T'ang Dynasty. During his 43 year reign, the Christian church in China began its recovery from persecution. See Denis Twitchett, "Hsüan-tsung (reign 712–56)", in: Cambridge History of China, vol. 3, 333–408.

en 719, par le moyen de Iean Eveque des Chretiens[291], So:çum:nen:men[292] fut encore plus Zelé pour la foy Chrestienne, et recut avec Ioÿe un Pretre de la Iudeé nomme Kié hò[293], qui vint en la Chine [78] l'an 757 et ÿ fit refleurir le Christianisme. son successe[u]r Taiçum-ven-vū[294] Emploÿa toute son autorité pour maintenir les fideles dans la paix: et enfin Kïem-çum Surpassa tous Ses predecesseurs en Zele en pieté et fit eviger en 782 ce fameux Monument Chinois (dont j'ay parle ci devant) en caracteres chinois et Sÿriaques.[295]

Voila Monsieur en Substance l'histoire de l'etablissement du Christianisme à la Chine. on n'en avoit pas fait mention dans les histoires dela Chine; le Père Coúplet[296] Iesuite, avoit tire de l'jnscription meme, ce qu'il en a dit dans son abregé chronologique. ne Seroit ce pas que les histoires Chinoises auroient èté fabriqueés dans un tems ou on ne Scavoit plus qu'il ÿ avoit eu des Chretiens a la Chine. Depuis Saint francois Xavier[297] forma le dessin d'y aller prècher; mais il mourut en ÿ abordant; les Missionaires Apostoliques qui l'ont Suivi ont ete plus heureux ils ont êté reçus dans l'Empire[298] l'an 1583[299] Sous le Regne de l'Empereur Van lie.[300]

**291** Person unknown.

**292** Su-tsung (711–762) was the son of Hsüan-tsung and the eighth emperor in the T'ang Dynasty. He fought in the An Shi Rebellion in 756 to gain his father's throne. Twitchett, "Hsüan-sung," 380, 423–5, 460–1.

**293** Bishop George, or Chi-ho (dates unknown), traveled from Syria to China in 744, in the company of an abott and several other monks. There, he obtained permission to hold mass at a palace owned by the imperial family. See Yoshirō Saeki, *The Nestorian Documents and Relics in China* (Tokyo: Academy of Oriental Culture, 1951), 95.

**294** Tai-tsung (727–779) was the oldest son of Su-tsung and the ninth emperor in the T'ang Dynasty. See Michael T. Dalby, "Court politics in late T'ang times", in: Cambridge History of China, vol. 3.1, 567.

**295** The preceding five paragraphs were adjusted and copied from: Moréri, Grand dictionaire, vol. 3, 335.

**296** Philippe Couplet (1623–1693) was a native of the Southern Netherlands and Jesuit missionary in China, since 1656. He published several works on the early Chinese church. Keevak, Story, 49, 154.

**297** Francis Xavier (1506–1552) was a Spanish missionary to Asia and, as a companion of Ignatius of Loyola, one of the initial monks to join the Jesuit order. His ministry had much success in India during the 1540s, and he additionally evangelized in Japan, Borneo, Portuguese Malacca and off the Chinese coast. He died in 1552 on St. John's Island, never having made it to mainland China. Brockey, Journey, 28–9.

**298** The preceding paragraph was adjusted and copied from: Moréri, Grand dictionaire (1731), 127.

**299** Matteo Ricci and Michele Ruggieri obtained the first Jesuit foothold in China in 1583, after being invited to stay in Zhaoqing. Although expelled in 1589, Ricci was able to keep their presence permanent by then relocating—with permission—to Shaozhou. Brockey, Journey, 33–41.

**300** Chu I-chün, or the Wan-li Emperor (1563–1620), was the thirteenth emperor in the Chinese Ming Dynasty. He ruled for 48 years and invited Matteo Ricci to join the imperial court as an advisor in 1601. Ray Huang, "The Lung-ch'ing and Wan-li reigns, 1567–1620", in: Cambridge History of China, vol. 7, 514–584; Brockey, Journey, 41–9.

Une nouvelle persecution contre les fideles s'eleva dans la Province de Fokien[301], le Tsong tou[302] non content d'avoir proscrit la Religion Chretienne dans la Province de Son Gouvernement, il S'addressa en Cour par requete, et apres avoir rendu Compte dela conduite des Missionaires dans les termes les plus forts, et le danger qu'il ÿ avoit de permettre cette Loi êtrangere que prechoient les Europeéns, il Supplioit Sa Maj.[té] par Zele qu'elle avoit pour le bien du peuple et le repos de l'Empire, de faire Sortir tous les Europeéns des Provinces et d'ordonner, ou qu'ils [79] Soient Conduits a la Cour, ou qu'ils Soÿent envoyez a Maccao, et que leurs temples Soÿent employez a d'autres usages.

L'Empereur envoya aussitôt cette requête au tribunal des Rits[303], et sa decision fut, que les Europeéns qui Sont a la Cour, Y Sont utiles pour le Calendrier[304], et d'autres Services qu'ils rendent, mais que ceux qui Sont dans les Provinces, ne Sont de nulle utilité, qu'au contraire ils elevent des Eglises et attirent a leur Loi le peuple, les hommes et les femmes &.[a] que Conformement à ce que le Tsong tou de Fokien propose, il faut laisser a la Cour ceux qui Sont utiles, et faire conduire les autres a Maccao. l'Empereur recút cette deliberation du tribunal le 10 Ianvier 1723[305], et des le lendemain il ecrivit avec le pinceau rouge, la sentence suivante.

Qu'il soit fait ainsi qu'il a este determiné par le tribunal des Rits: les Europeens Sont des etrangers, il ÿ a bien des anneés qu'ils demeurent dans les Provinces de l'Empire, maintenant il faut s'entenir a ce que propose le Tsong tou de Fokin. mais comme il est à craindre que le peuple ne leur fasse quelque jnsulte; j'ordonne au Tsong tou et aux vicerois des Provinces de leur accorder un demi anneé, ou quelques

**301** Fukien, now Fujian, is a mountainous province, located about 650 kilometers northeast of Canton and along the southeastern Chinese coast. It was a key site of missionary work by both Jesuits and Dominicians. An official effort to stop Christianity was launched in Fukien during the 1720s, as indicated below. This included the faith's outright ban locally, the confiscation of church property and the dissolution of several female religious orders. Brockey, Journey, 199–200.

**302** This refers to the *zongdu* or *tsongtu* – the provincial Viceroy. The *zongdu* of Fukien and Chexiang Province in the 1723 was Gioro Mamboo (1673–1725). See page 201, ft. 54.

**303** The Board of Rites, or *libu*, was an imperial ministery, founded during the T'ang Dyanasty (618–907) and lasting until 1911. It managed imperial ceremonies, upkept shrines and temples, and monitored the behavior of spiritual adherents residing in China as well as dealt with foreign diplomats. See Donald F. Lach and Edwing J. Van Kley, *Asia in the Making of Europe, vol. 3.4* (Chicago: University of Chicago Press, 1993), 1582–3.

**304** Jesuits at the imperial court in the fifteenth and sixteenth centuries – notably Johann Adam Schall (1591–1666) – used their astronomical training to suggest reforms to the Chinese calendar. See William Peterson, "Calendar Reform Prior to the Arrival of the Missionaries at the Ming Court", in: *Ming Studies* 1 (1986), 45–61.

**305** Soon after ascending the throne, the Yung-cheng Emperor accepted *zongdu* Mamboo's view of Christianity as one of China's "perverse sects and sinister doctrines." Criticism included the faith's ban on ancestral worship and support of sexual chastity, which left no posterity and was seen as filial disobedience. The emperor endorsed the prohibition of Christianity in 1723, allowing missionaries not at court six months to remove to Macao. Brockey, Journey, 198–9; Marinescu, Defending, 286, 297–8.

mois, et pour les conduire ou a la Cour, ou a Maccao, de leur donner un Manderin qui les accompagne dans les Provinces, qui prenne soin d'eux, et qui les garantisse de toute jnsulte. qu'on observe cet ordre avec respect.

Les Missionaires qui êtoient a la Cour se donnerent tous les mouvemens posibles, soit aupres des amis qu'ils avoient au tribunal des Rits, soit aupres des Princes qui les protegeoient et qui avoient le plus de credit sur l'esprit de l'Empereur, pour detourner un coup Si fatal a la Religion: tout l'adoucissement qu'ils purent [80] obtenir, c'est que le lieu d'Exil fut changé, et qu'au lieu deles Conduire a Maccao on leur permit de demeurer a Canton, encore ne leur accordat on cette grace, qu'a Condition qu'ils ne donneroient aucun sujet de plainte.

La Sentence que l'Empereur Yong tching venoit de porter contre la loi Chretienne fut bientot annonceé par les gazettes publiques, plusieurs Manderins se haterent de l'executer quoy qu'elle n'ait ête envoÿeé dans les Provinces que le 17 fevrier 1723.

Tous les Missionaires sans distinction furent Chassez de leurs Eglises et conduits a Peking ou a Canton; encore l'Empereur declarat il dans un livre[306] qu'il avoit compose pour l'jnstruction de Ses Sujets, qu'il n'en toleroit quelques uns ala Cour qu'à cause de l'utilité que l'Empire recoit de leur habilité dans les Arts et les Sciences.

Plus de trois cent Eglises furent ou detruites, ou converties en usages profanes, ou devinrent des temples du Demon, les Ydoles ayant èté Substitueés a la place du Vraÿ Dieu. Plus de trois cent mille Chrestiens Se Virent destituez de Pasteurs, et livrez a la rage des Jnfideles. enfin les traveaux et les Sueurs de tant d'hommes Apostoliques Se trouverent presque aneantis, Sans qu'on vit aucune lueur d'esperance, qui presentat le moindre adoucissement a tant de maux.

Tel est le triste etat d'une mission, qui etoit auparavant Si florissante. on a pris des mesures, pour ne laisser pas [81] tout a fait Sans Secours Spirituel, une Chretiente Si nombreuse, quelques Prêtres Chinois[307], à qui il est plus aisé de Se cacher, parcourent les Chretientez des Provinces, et S'emploient avec Zele au Salut de leurs Compatriotes. mais comme le nombre d'ouvriers Evangeliques est fort petit dans un Empire si vaste, et pour suppleér a ce defaut on envoÿe chaque anneé dans les Provinces des Catechistes habiles et bien Choisis, qui Se repandent dans les diverses Chretientez qui ÿ raniment la foi des Neophites, qui leur fournissent des Calendriers, des livres, et des jmages de pieté, qui examinent les catechistes particuliers remplisent leurs obligations et qui Se presentent même aux Manderins, et leur offrent des presens, pour gagner leur amitié et leur protection. C'est tout ce qu'on peut faire pour maintenir

306 Text unknown.
307 The Jesuits did not ordain their first Chinese priests until 1688. These individuals, with a few additions, were responsible for ministering to imperial Christians after their European counterparts were expelled in 1723. Standaert, Handbook, vol. 1, 380–403; Brockey, Journey, 143, 201, 280.

la foi dans l'ame de tant de nouveaux fideles, Jus qu'à ce qu'il plaise au Seigneur de Changer le Coeur d'un Prince qui paroit aliené des ministres du Vray Dieu.[308]

Les Religions dominantes dans la Chine Se reduissent a deux la Premiere est celle des Idolatres, la Seconde est celle des gens de lettres et des Savans.[309] celle des Idolatres est diviseé en deux Sectes. Le Philosope Li-chao-kiun[310] donna commencement a la premiere. il est un peu plus ancien que Confusius. Ses Sectateurs que les Chinois appellent Tao-Sseë[311], font Croire a ce peuple que Sa naissance fut miraculeuse, que Sa Mere [82] le porta quatre vingts et un an dans Ses flancs, d'ou il Sortit enfin par le Côté gauche, qu'il S'ouvrit lui même un moment avant la mort de celle qui lui donna la vie.

Il ecrivit, dit on, plusieurs livres ou il traita dela vertu, de la fuite des honneurs, du mepris des richeses, et de cette heureuse solitude dont l'ame peut jouir en S'elevant au dessus de toutes les Choses de la terre, et rentrant en elle même;

La Maxime fondamentale de sa philosophie, que Ses disciples ont toujours dans la bouche, est que la loi ou la raison a produit deux, deux on produit trois, et trois ont produit toutes Choses[312]; il enseigna que le Dieu Souverain êtoit Corporel, et qu'il gouvernoit les autres Divinités, comme un Roÿ gouverne ses sujets.

Ses Disciples s'adonnerent à la magie, et firent croire qu'ils avoient trouvé le Secret de rendre les hommes jmmortels, les ministres de cette Secte furent appellez Tien-Sseë[313], c'est a dire Docteurs Celestes. ils eleverent des Temples a Li-chao-kiun leur maitre, et persuaderent au peuple de l'honnorer d'un Culte Divin.

---

308 The preceding six paragraphs were adjusted and copied from: Jean Baptiste du Halde, Description, vol. 3, 153–4.

309 The author identifies "idolaters" as Daoists and Buddhists and "savants" as Confucianists. For his discussion of each respective faith, see pages 289–90, 290–2, and 293–5, 306–11.

310 Laozi (ca. sixth century BCE), to whom the following story relates, was an ancient Chinese poet and philosopher. He either was a contemporary of or slightly predated Confucius. He often is credited with writing the *Daodejing*, one of the foundational Daoist texts, and, in some communities, he is revered as a Daoist deity. See Livia Kohn, *Introducing Daoism* (London: Routledge, 2009), 22, 31–4.

311 Daoism is a philosophical and religious tradition, indigenous to ancient China in the sixth and fifth centuries BCE. Some adherents maintain a Taoist pantheon. The belief-system, however, has no standard gods but promotes living habits informed by natural rhythms, balance, understanding and acceptance. Kohn, Introducing.

312 This quote is from a foundational Daoism text, *Daodejing* (sixth century BCE). It refers to the creation of the universe and the initial balance of the forces of Yin and Yang. Religiously, it relates to three forms of celestial energy, also called the Three Pure Ones. Kohn, Introducing, 93–4.

313 The title of Celestial Master, or *Tianshi*, refers to a Daoist religious leader. It first appeared in the second century, when a series of disasters caused minister Chang Tao-ling (34–156) to espouse a spiritual version of the philosophy. *Tianshi* encourage rituals of repentance and cosmic renewal. Ibid., 86–7.

Cette secte a multiplie les Idoles, mettant au nombre des Dieux plusieurs anciens Empereurs dela Chine et faisant honnorer differens esprits sous le nom de Chang ti ou le souverain Empereur[314] qui gouvenoient chacun leur element.

La Seconde Secte des Idoles de la Chine, est celle des Ho.chan[315] [83] ou des Bonses, qui adorent un Idole nommeé Fo ou Foë[316] elle est passeé des Indes dans la Chine[317]; quelques Chinois rapportent que Confusius leur Philosophe assuroit qu'il ÿ avoit dans le Pais d'occident un Saint homme, a cause qu'on luy entendoit repéter souvent ces paroles: Si:fang yeou chin gin.[318] on jgnore de qui il vouloit parler. mais ce qu'il y a de certain, ç'est que 65 ans apres la naissance de Iesus Christ, Ming-ti quinzieme[319] Empereur dela famille des Han, êgalement frappé des paroles de ce Philosophe, et de l'jmage d'un homme qui se presenta a lui durant le sommeil venant d'occident, envoÿa de ce Côté la deux Grands de l'Empire nommez Tsai tsing[320], et

**314** Chang-ti, or the Sovereign Emperor, is the supreme deity in religious Daoism. Also known as the Jade Emperor, he was the patron god worshipped by the imperial family since the ninth century. Ibid., 164, 198.

**315** *Heshang*, or *hochan*, was the title given to Buddhist monks in China. It translated as "revered."

**316** Siddhattha Gotama, or the Buddha (ca. 566–486 BCE), was a native of northeastern India and a spiritual leader. His teachings form the basic tenents of Buddhism – here named Fo or Foë – and, in some sects, he also is revered as an eternal being. Buddhism, although divided into different branches, generally promotes worldly asceticism, non-harmful and ethical conduct, and a striving towards spiritual enlightenment. Keown, Buddhism.

**317** This sentence and the preceding five paragraphs were adjusted and copied from: Noël Alexandre: *Apologie des Dominicains missionaires de la Chine, vol. 1* (Cologne: Corneille d'Egmond, 1699), 153–4.

**318** This phrase, ascribed to Confucius, translates as: "that in the West the Most Holy was to be found." Tomoko Masuzawa, *The Invention of World Religions: or, How European Universalism was Preserved in the Language of Pluralism* (Chicago: University of Chicago Press, 2005), 124.

**319** Liu Yang, or the Ming-ti Emperor (28–75), was the second ruler in the Eastern Han Dynasty. It was during his reign that Buddhism advanced into China, possibly with the support of his half-brother. See Erik Zürcher, *The Buddhist Conquest of China: the Spread and Adaptation of Buddhism in Early Medieval China* (Leiden: Brill, 2007), 22.

**320** Ts'ai Yin, or Caiyin (dates unknown), was a minister in the court of the Ming-ti Emperor. According to the legend recounted here, he was sent with seventeen other officials to India in 65, to further explore Buddhism. They returned in 68, bringing with them spiritual texts as well as two Buddhist monks. Historians generally dispute this story's accuracy, instead contending Buddhism arrived in China via trading-routes. See Adamek Wendi, *The Teachings of Master Wuzhu: Zen and the Religion of No-Return* (New York: Columbia UP, 2011), 69–73; Jason Neelis, *Early Buddhist Transmission and Trade Networks: Mobility and Exchange within and beyond the Northwest Borderlands of South Asia* (Leiden: Brill, 2011), 289–310.

Tsin king[321], avec ordre de ne point revenir qu'ils n'eussent trouvé le Saint que le ciel lui avoit fait connoitre, et qu'ils n'eussent appris la loi qu'il enseignoit.[322]

mais etant arrivez dans un Canton des Indes ils s'arreterent a Considerer une fameuse Idole, nommeé Fo ou Foë representant un Philosophe qui avoit vêcu dans les Indes cinc cens ans avant Confusius. ils emporterent cette Idole dans la Chine, avec des Instructions sur le culte qu'on lui rendoit. heureux, si au lieu de cette abonible doctrine, ils eussent raporté quelques lumieres dela Religion Chrestienne, que S.t Thomas Apotre prechoit en ce tems là dans les Jndes[323]

La Superstition que ces ambassadeurs Jntroduissirent dit qu'il qu'il [sic] sortit du coté droit de Sa mere[324], qui mourut dans les douleurs de l'enfantement. qu'aussitot qu'il fut né, il se tint debout, et qu'il fit sept ou huit pas, montrant le ciel [84] d'une main, et la terre de l'autre: qu'il parla même disant, Ie suis le seul qui doit etre honoré, dans le Ciel et sur la terre. a l'age de dix sept ans, il se maria, et il eut un fils nommé par les Chinois Mo heu lo.[325]

A l'age de dixneuf ans, il Se retira dans une Solitude avec quatre philosophes Indiens qu'il êcouta comme ces maitres. a l'age de trente ans regardant l'etoile qui annonce le lever du Soleil, il fut (disent ils) tout d'un Coup penetré de la divinité, il devint Dieu, et il S'attira la Veneration des peuples.[326] il eut un nombre jnfini de Sectateurs, qui se repandirent par tout l'orient, les Chinois les appellent Ho-chan, les tartares Lamas, les Europeens Bonses.

Cet Imposteur mourut en sa soixante et dixneufvieme anneé declarant a ses disciples qu'il avoit caché Jusqu'a Cette heure la Verité au monde, que tous Ses discours avoient este envelopez de paraboles et que toutes Ses expresions avoient ète figures: mais qu'etant prest de quitter la terre, il vouloit leur reveler le Secret de Sa doctrine. jl ne faut point, (leur dit il) chercher hors du neant et du vuide le principe de toutes Choses. c'est du neant que tout doit retomber. voila là fin de toutes nos esperances.

C'est ainsi qu'a sa mort il jnspira l'atheisme, apres avoir etabli l'jdolatrie pendant Sa Vie. Sur Ses principes les Ho-chan ou les Bonses enseignent un double loi qu'ils

---

**321** Ch'in Ching, or Qin Jing (dates unkown), was an academician in the court of the Ming-ti Emperor, who supposedly accompanied Ts'ai Yin on his exploratory voyage to India. Ibid.

**322** The preceding paragraph, except for the first sentence, was copied from: Halde, Description, vol. 2, 387.

**323** The preceding paragraph was copied from: Moréri, Grand dictionaire, vol. 2 (ca. 1700), 236.

**324** The Buddha, according to tradition, was conceived of his mother immaculately, when she dreamed of a white elephant. Following her death, he was brought up by her younger sister. Keown, Buddhism, 20–1.

**325** Rāhula (b. ca. 534 BCE) was the only son of Buddha and his wife-cousin, Yaśodharā. He and his mother both later became disciples of his father. Ibid., 20.

**326** The Buddha, again according to tradition, spent 49 days in meditation before finally achieving enlightenment, a stage of awakening that offered peace of mind free from the sufferings of the world. This allowed him to end his own cycle of death and rebirth and start a heavenly existence upon death. Ibid., 23–47.

[85] appellent la loi exterieure, et la loi interieure. l'une, Selon eux doit preparer l'esprit a recevoir l'autre: Semblable aux cintres qui Sont necessaires pour Soutenir la Voute qu'on veut faire, et que l'on ôte quand elle est achevee.[327]

Leur Doctrine exterieure fait le discernement du bien et du mal, elle enseigne que les bons seront recompensez et les mechans punis en des lieux destinez pour cela: que la beatitude S'obtient par trente deux figures, et par quatre vingts qualitez:[328] que Fo ou Foë est un Dieu et le Sauveur des hommes, dont il expie les crimes, et qu'il fait renaitre dans l'autre monde.

Ils deffendent d'oter la vie à aucun être vivant, tel qu'il puisse etre: ils ordonnent de S'abstenir du larcin de l'jmpureté, du vin, et du mensonge. ils recomandent les œuvres de misericorde particulierement envers les ministres du Dieu Fo.

Leur Doctrine Secrete est un atheisme tout pur, le Vuide[329] qu'ils reconnoissent pour principe de toutes choses, est, disent ils, Souverainement parfait et tranquille, Sans commencement, et sans fin, sans mouvement, sans connoissance, sans desirs. C'est pourqoui ceux qui veulent être heureux, doivent faire tous leurs efforts pour se rendre semblables a ce principe, en domtant et Supprimant toutes leurs passions; de Sorte qu'ils Soient jnsensibles a tout et qu'abimez dans la plus haute contemplation, Sans aucune reflexion, sans aucun usage de leur raison, ils jouissent de ce divin repos qui fait tout le bonheur de l'homme.

Lors qu'ils ÿ Sont arrivez ils peuvent enseigner aux autres la doctrine et la maniere commune de vivre, et la pratiquer a l'exterieur, ne s'appliquant jnterieurement qu'a jouir de [86] cette tranquilité secrete qui est le caractere d'une Vie Celeste.

C'est la le mistere de cette Secte qui ne fait dans le fond aucune difference du bien et du mal, qui fait consister la vertu a ne point penser n'ÿ travailler a estre Vertueux qui ne reconnoit point de recompense ni de peines apres la mort, qui ne croit point de providence, ni l'jmmortalité de l'ame, qui reduit toute choses a un Vuide confus et a un Simple neant, comme a leur principe et a leur fin, et qui met la perfection dans une parfaite jndifference, une apathie et une quietude Souveraine.

---

**327** The preceding three paragraphs were adapted from the following publication: Louis le Comte, *Memoirs and Observations Topographical, Physical, Mathematical, Mechanical, Natural, Civil and Ecclesiastical Made in a Late Journey through the Empire of China, and Published in Several Letters* (London: Benjamin Tooke, 1697), 323–5.

**328** Adherents believed there were 32 main physical characteristics, *lakkhana*, and 80 sub-features, *anubyanjana*, that distinguish all enlightened Buddhas. They include level feet, slender fingers, full shoulders, even teeth, a deep voice, a stately gait, and unwrinkled skin, among other traits. See Yuvraj Krishan, *The Buddha Image: its Origin and Development* (New Delhi: Munshiram Manoharlal Publishers, 1996).

**329** *Śūnyatā*, or emptiness, is a central concept in Buddhism, which refers to a particularly desirable state of meditation. Its attainment is believed to reveal the interrelatability of all worldly things. Keown, *Buddhism*, 73–4.

**Dela Secte des Lettrez.**

La Secte des Savans ou Lettrez est devenuë la plus celebre quoi qu'elle ne Soit pas plus commune dans la Chine; Elle commença l'an mil soixante et dix, Sous les Empereurs de la race de Song[330], qui aimoient les lettres, mais elle fit peu de progés J'usqu'a l'an mil quatre cens, que l'Empereur Yonglo[331] Choisit quarante quarante deux Docteurs des plus habiles aux quels jl ordonna de faire un corps de Doctrine tireé des livres classiques des anciens[332] particulierement des Philosophes, Confusius, et Mencius.[333]

Les Lettrez ou Savans dela chine parlent dela nature comme d'une Divinité.[334] ils disent que c'est un principe tres pur, tres parfait, qui n'a ni commencement ni fin, que c'est la Source de toutes choses, l'essence de chaque estre, et ce qui en fait la veritable difference.

mais quelques pompeúses que Soient ces expressions, elles ne [87] prouvent pas que la Secte des lettrez reconnoisse et adore le vrai Dieu. ils n'entendent par ces beaux termes qu'une ame jnsensible du Monde, qu'ils croient repanduë dans la matiere ou elle produit tous les Changemens: et on ne voit dans leurs Ouvrages qu'un Atheisme rafiné, et un eloignement de tout Culte religieux.

Ils font ala verité proffession d'adorer le Ciel, qu'ils appellent Tien[335] en chinois, et le Souverain Empereur, qu'ils appellent Chang ti:[336] mais ils donnent a ces paroles un sens jmpie, qui detruit la Divinite, et qui etoufe tout Sentiment de Religion.

---

**330** Emperor Wu-ti declared Confucianism the imperial ideology in 136 BCE, but it experienced an official revival during the Sung Dynasty (960–1279 CE). A prominent proponent of this faith was Wang An-shih (1021–1086), who promoted political reform based on its moral ideas. He was a favored councilor of the Sung Dynasty's sixth emperor, Shen-tsung (1048–1085). Schuman, Confucius, 50–2.

**331** Chu Ti, the Yung-lo Emperor (1360–1424) was the third emperor in the Chinese Ming Dynasty. See Hok-lam Chan, "The Chien-wen, Yung-lo, Hung-hsi, and Hsüan-te reigns, 1399–1435", in: Cambridge History of China, vol. 7, 205–75.

**332** The Yung-lo Encyclopedia was an extensive inventory of textual knowledge, commissioned by the emperor and completed between 1403 and 1408. Its 22,937 manuscript rolls contained the titles of all writings on Confucianism as well as a range of other subjects then-known in China. See Sarah Foot and Chase F. Robinson (eds.), *The Oxford History of Historical Writing, vol. 2* (New York: Oxford UP, 2012), 42.

**333** Mencius (ca. 370–289 BCE) was a Confucian philosopher, who argued in favor of innate human goodness, the role of the environment in developing moral character and virtuous political rulership. See David Shepherd Nivison, "The Classical Philosophical Writings", in: *The Cambridge History of Ancient China: from the Origins of Civilization to 221 B.C.*, eds. Michael Loewe and Edward L. Shaughnessy (New York: Cambridge UP, 1999), 770–778.

**334** Nature is a particularly strong entity in Daoism. Adherents believe the Dao, or "way," manifests itself organically through the rhythms of the natural world. Kohn, Introducing, 24–5.

**335** *Tian* translates to the Daoist and Confucian concept of heaven. Confucius, in particular, promoted the idea of a heavenly will guiding and sometimes protecting individuals on earth. Schuman, Confucius, xviii, 47.

**336** *Shangdi* is the ancient Chinese name for the Supreme Deity.

Ils n'entendent parla que le Ciel materiel a qui ils en offrent des Sacrifices, comme ils font aussi aux esprits des fleuves, et des montagnes, c'est adire aux fleuves et aux montagnes même. car ils n'entendent pas par le nom d'esprits des Substances Spirituelles, et jmmortelles, la pluspart n'en reconnoissent point de veritables, semblables aux Sadduceéns[337] qui ne crojoient ni resurection, ni Anges, ni esprits.

Le Roÿ d'en haut ou le souverain Empereur n'est don autre chose, selon le Sens des lettrez dela Chine, que la vertu active du Ciel materiel, ou les jnfluenses par les quelles ils crojent qui se produissent les diverses Choses du monde, l'esprit dela terre, n'est autre chose que la terre materielle et Corporelle, ou la Vertu naturelle qu'elle à, de produire Ses effets, l'esprit de l homme est la partie la plus subtile en la qu'elle il se resout quand il meurt: car il devient cadavre quand la partie aërienne se separe dela partie grossiere, la premiere s'elevant [88] en haut, et l'autre retournant en bas.

Pour ce qui regarde les expressions des livres Classiques, et les manieres populaires de parler, le Perre Appiani me dit qu'ils admettent deux Sortes d'esprits, ceux des generations et des corruptions, qu'on peut appeller des esprits Phisiques et naturels, et ceux des Sacrifices, qu'on peut nommer des esprits civils et politiques.

Les premiers sont les causes naturelles des generations et des corruptions qui arrivent dans l'univers, et ils entendent par les esprits la Substance même des choses qui agissent, ou leurs qualitez ou la formalité pour ainsi dire de leur vertu active.

Les seconds ont eté jntroduits dans l'etat a fin de tenir le peuple dans le devoir, luÿ faisant conserver ces esprits du ciel, et de la terre, des montagnes, des fleuves, des villes, des defunts Comme capables de faire du bien et du mal aux hommes: ce que les anciens Paÿens de l'Europe crojoient aussi de Iupiter, de Mars, de Saturne, de Neptune, et de toutes leurs fausses divinitez.[338]

Dans cette Secte il y a deux Sortes de Doctrines, une Secrete pour les gens d'esprit, l'autre publique et apparente pour les Simples. ils crojent que la premiere est la Seule veritable et que la derniere est absolument fausse.

Ainsi pour decouvrir leurs Vrais Sentimens, on ne doit point S'arrester a quelques textes dans les quels ils ont parlé expres d'une maniere qui a pu faire jmaginer au [89] peuple qu'il ÿ avoit des esprits et des Divinitez Vivantes qu'il devoient reverer et craindre.

C'est la fin des Sacrifices qu'ils offrent au Ciel, et aux esprits des Montagnes des Rivieres, des Villes, et des defunts. ainsi la Doctrine des lettrez est un Mêlange d'Atheisme et d'Jdolatrie.

---

**337** The Sadducees were a Jewish sect, active in the Middle East from ca. 150 BCE to 70 CE. They were conservative followers of Mosiac law, believing only in the written Torah. Matthew 22: 23–40; Acts 23:8.

**338** These are an assortment of Greco-Roman deities, each associated with a different, mostly natural phenomenon. Jupiter was god of the sky, Mars was god of war, Saturn was god of agriculture, and Neptune was god of water. See Edith Hamilton, *Mythology* (New York: Little, Brown and Company, 1942), 49–52.

Ils sont ÿdolatres Selon leur Doctrine apparente, et populaire: ils Sont atheés Selon leur doctrine Secrete. ils disent dans leur Cœur: il n'y a point de Dieu. ils rapportent tout à la nature et ils disent en public, il faut adorer le Ciel, il faut offrir des Sacrifices au Souverain Empereur et aux esprits.[339]

Je ne dis rien icÿ de la Secte des Mahometans[340], qui est tolereé a la Chine par ce qu'ils Sont en petit nombre. Je ne dis rien aussi d'une nouvelle Secte qui prit naissance a Hing-hoa-fou[341] dans la Province de Fokien vers l'an 1540, et qui eut pour auteur un lettré nommé Lin.[342] On l'appelle San-kiao-tung[343], c'est à dire, la Communication et l'union des trois autres Sectes, de Confusius, De Foë, et de Lao-kun. Ie n'ay eu dessin de traiter a fond Monsieur que des Sectes principales et Dominantes de ce grand Empire.[344]

Avant que de finir ma lettre des Sectes Chinoises, il me manque à vous dire Monsieur Comment quelques Missionaires de la chine ont volou faire Croire en Europe que l'empereur de la Chine Kan-hy avoit embrassé la Religion Chretienne [90] par le present qui leur fit, de l'honneur de son estime, et qu'il traita avec beaucoup de distinction d'une tablette ou ces deux mots Chinois êtoient écrits de sa propre main King-Tien, c'est à dire adorez le Ciel, les uns les eleverent dans la cour, les autres Sur le frontespice de l'Eglise, et quelques uns les placerent Sur l'Autel même.

**339** The veneration of ancestors was a key component in Confucianism and the Confucian state, which lauded filial piety. Such acts were believed to result in spiritual aid. They also were understood as moral goods, in that they caused believers to invest in a non-interal world. See William Lakos, *Chinese Ancestor Worship; a Practice and Ritual Oriented Approach to Understanding Chinese Culture* (Newcastle upon Tyne: Cambridge Scholars Publishing, 2010).

**340** Islam arrived in China primarily through traders and administrators for the Mongols, beginning in the seventh century. A distinct Chinese form of the faith especially developed between the sixteenth and eighteenth centuries. See Zvi Ben-Dor Benite, *The Dao of Muhammad: a Cultural History of Muslims in Late Imperial China* (Cambridge, MA: Harvard UP, 2005); James D. Frankel, *Rectifying God's Name: Liu Zhi's Confucian Translation of Monotheism and Islamic Law* (Honolulu: University of Hawaii Press, 2011).

**341** Putian is a coastal city in eastern Fukien province. The Putian Chinese – who were of the Han cultural group – also were known as *Xinghua*. Lin Zhao'en, mentioned in the next footnote, originated here.

**342** Lin Zhao'en (1517–1598) was a spiritual reformer and teacher, who proposed in the 1540s and 1550s a form of Confucianism, which also merged elements of Buddhism and Daoism. He was revered as a deity after his death. See Kenneth Dean, *Lord of the Three in One: the Spread of a Cult in Southeast China* (Princeton, NJ: Princeton UP, 1998), 3–29; Judith Berling, *The Syncretic Religion of Lin Chao-en* (New York: Columbia UP, 1980).

**343** *San-chiao hui-pen*, or the Joint Chronicle of the Three Teachings, was the syncretic sect proposed by Lin Zhao'en in the mid-sixteenth century. This included combining Buddhist rituals of meditation and Daoist incantations with Confucian views on secular moral development. See ibid.; Lin Guoping, "On the Rise, Decline and Evolution the Three-in-One Teaching", in: *Popular Religion and Shamanism*, eds. Ma Xisha and Meng Huiying (Leiden: Brill, 2011), 123–66.

**344** The preceding twenty-three paragraphs were adjusted and copied from: Jean Jovet, *L'histoire des religions de tous les royaumes du monde* (Paris: Montalant, 1724), 437–45.

Plusieurs autres les rejetterent, persuadez que le dessin de l'Empereur n'etoit pas de recommander la Religion Chretiene par ces deux mots: mais la Chinoise, don la Secte des Lettrez fait profession, et dont la Majeste Imperiale est le Chef. ces paroles n'êtoient qu'une exhortation à adorer le Ciel materiel, dont ils regardent le culte comme les premiers de leurs devoirs.[345]

I'aÿ trouve bon de vous donner icÿ le dernier discours que le dit Empereur fit, devant avoir rendu sa pauvre ame a la merci de son Createur, le quel j aÿ donné au public Sous le nom de Testament de l'Empereur Kan-hy monarque du grand Empire de la Chne [sic] &.[a], pour qu'on voiroit que le dit Empereur durant Sa vie a exercé l'atheisme qu'il etablit dans les livres de Philosophie qu'il a Composez et qu'il a donné au public; jl offroit tous les ans des Sacrifices au Ciel materiel et a la terre Selon la Coutume de Ses predecesseurs, et il fit lui même les fonctions de Sacrificateur. Il est le Chefs de la Secte des lettrez et de la Religion Chinoise il n'est don pas vraisemblable qu'il ordonne autre Chose par ces paroles King-Tien, adorez le Ciel, que le [91] culte du Ciel materiel, ni qu'il exhorte d'adorer le Dieu des Chrestiens, don il ne croit pas la religion veritable. vous voire icÿ comment il S'explique.[346]

Testament de l'Empereur

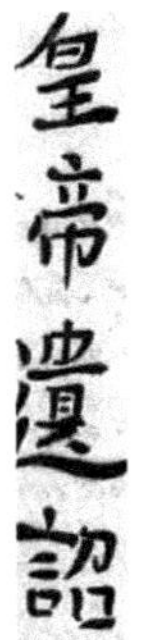

Hoâṅ

tý

ŷ

tcháo

**Testament de l'Empereur.**

Kāṅ-hÿ Monarque du grand Empre de la Chine, et des deux Tartaries Orientale et Septentrionale mort le 20 decembre 1722 agé de 69 ans Sept mois 25 Iours et de son Regne la 61.[e] anneé 10 mois 13 Iours, Son 4.[e] fils agé de 40 et tant d'anneés a Succede a tous ses etats il est Surnommé yōn-tchi'n

**[Figure 14:** Chinese letters, beginning the K'ang-hsi Emperor's Testament]

345 The preceding two paragraphs were adjusted and copied from: Alexandre, *Apologie* (1700), 73–4.
346 Contemporary European newspapers published other versions of K'ang-hsi's testament. See, for example, *The Historical Register* 10 (1725), no. 37, 1–8. For the historical significance of this document and its reputed varieties, see Zelin, Yung-cheng, 183–9.

[**Figure 15:** Chinese letters, translated as "J'aÿ Receu du Ciel ma destineé a L'Empire / L Empereur Mande et dit"]

Depuis le commencement jus qu'a present de tous les Empereurs qui ont gouverné l'Empire on n'en a pas encore veu qui n'ait pas reveré le ciel et jmité Ses ancetres, comme etant la principale chose à la quelle ils doivent S'apliquer de toutes leurs forces.

La Veritable reverence envers le ciel, et la Veritable jmitation [92] envers les ancetres, Consiste a traiter benignement les êtrangers des paÿs eloignés, et Scavoir bien gouverner Ses propres Sujets, tenir le peuple dans l'abondance, et dans la paix, luÿ et Son Empire, faire un usage reciproque des richeses Contenues dans les quatres mers avec les autres nations, conformer ses jnclinations a celles de tout L'Empire, preserver le paÿs de tout danger.

L'exellence du bon gouvernement consiste à faire en Sorte qu'il n'y ait point de troubles, matin et Soir Sans discontinuer, Soit qu'on veille, Soit qu'on dorme, il ne faut pas oublier les moÿens necessaires pour gouverner long tems le Roÿaume en paix. observant toutes ces regles on approche de la Veritable reverence envers le Ciel, et de la veritable jmitation envers les Ancetres. mon age est de Septante ans. I'aÿ occupé le throne Soixante et un ans.

Veritablement je reçeus ces grands biens faits par le Secours jmpenetrable du Ciel, de la Terre[347], de mes ancêtres, et du Dieu qui preçede a toutes les generations, ce n'est nullement par ma foible vertu que j'aÿ vecu et regné si longtems: ayant lû attentivement les Chronologies des Empereurs, depuis le Siecle de l'Empereur Hoân-tÿ[348] jusqu'aujourdhuÿ il ÿ a quatre mille trois cents cinquante tant d'anneés, en tout trois cent un Empereur. Il n'y en à pas un Seul qui ait regné tant que moÿ. quand j'arrivaÿ a la vingtieme anneé de mon regne, je n'osois pas me flater d'arriver à la trentieme, à la

347 This note appears in the left margin: "Esprit de la Terre."

348 Huang Di, or the Yellow Emperor (r. 2697–2597 BCE), was a legendary ruler in ancient China. He is accredited with advancing Chinese culture, particularly medicine, politics and writing. See Kwang-chih Chang, "China on the Eve of the Historical Period", in: Cambridge History of Ancient China, 70.

tentieme, je n'osois pas me flater d'arriver à la quarantieme: aujourdhuÿ[349] me voicy à la Soixante unieme de mon Regne,

Le livre Classique Chán-chū-kīn[350] au chapitre Hôṅ-fán[351] marquant [93] Ce qui fait la felicité de l'homme, dit 1.° la longe vie, 2.° les richesses, 3.° la Santé la tranquillité et la joye, 4.° aimer toujours les Choses vertueuses, 5° etant parvenu a une grande Vieillesse, faire une belle mort. de ces cinc chefs de felicitez, la bonne mort dans la Vieillesse est marqueé le cinquiéme ou le dernier, parce qu'il est veritablement difficile de trouver des gens qui ajent cela. Presentement me voicy parvenu a Septante ans, dans mon opulence je possede tout ce qui est Contenu dans les quatre mers[352], mes enfans et petits Sont au nombre de cent cinquante, et tant de personnes[353], L'Empire jouit d'une heureuse paix, mon bonheur est fort grand. c'est a dire que S'il me faloit murir, mon cœur est fort tranquille, pensant a tout ce qui c'est passé depuis le commancement de mon regne jus qu'a present, quoy que je n'ose pas dire de moi même que je suis capable de faire changer les mauvaises Coutumes en bonnes

J'ay la Consolation de voir que mes peuples ont de quoÿ, Sont dans l'abondance et font Suffisament leur devoir. J'aÿ imité les Empereurs[354] des trois anciennes dinasties qui Sont estimez Saints.[355] j'ai voulu porter la paix dans lès quatre parties de l'Empire et jus qu'a la mer; Sous mon regne chacun à exercé Son art en paix et avec joÿe continuellement et Sans jnterruption, j'ay èté Vigilent et attentif, matin et Soir on ne m'a pas veu jndolent, je n'ay jamais cessé d'avoir Soin de l'Empire, pendant plusieurs dixaines d'anneés jusqu'apresent j aÿ travaillé pour le bien de mon peuple de tout mon Cœur et de toutes mes forces, comme Si ce n'eust eté qu'un jour, ce qu'on appelle travail, peine, et fatige n'aproche pas de ce que j'ay Souffert [94] pour bien

349 This note appears in the left margin: "61 ans mois 15 jours."

350 The *Shu jing*, or *Classic of History*, is an ancient Chinese text, which collects philosophical and political rhetoric and histories purportedly extending from the eleventh to the fourth or third centuries BCE. It has ties to Confucianism and historically served as a guide for state leaders. See Walter Gorn Old, trans., *The Shu King* (London: Theosophical Publishing Society, 1904); Michael Nylan, *The Five "Confucian" Classics* (New Haven: Yale UP, 2001), 120–167.

351 This refers to chapter 11 of the *Shu jing*, entitled *Hóng fàn* or "The Great Plan." Old, Shu, 160–71.

352 This note appears in the right margin: "Mers qui environment la Chine." It alludes to the believed borders of ancient China, which were the northern Lake Baikal, eastern East China Sea, southern South China Sea and western Qinghai Lake.

353 This note appears in the right margin: "En comptant les fils et les filles les petits fils et les petites filles."

354 This note appears in the right margin: "Les Empereurs Yu-tchān-oûen et son fils Où." The former name corresponds to the Chinese phrase *Tiānhuáng*, meaning "heavenly sovereign." Its specific reference is unknown.

355 The three *Huang*, or August Ones, were legendary rulers in ancient China, extending from ca. 2852 to 2070 BCE. Also revered as demigods, these individuals shared their knowledge with their subjects in an effort to improve their lives, including fire and farming. Their identities vary across ancient Chinese texts. See David Leeming, *A Dictionary of Asian Mythology* (New York: Oxford UP, 2001), 36–38.

gouverner l'Empire, les Empereurs des presedentes dinasties, n'ont pas regné long tems, les historiographes de l'Empire disent que l'jvrognerie et l'jmpureté ont abregé leurs Iours, tous ces escrivains se plaisent a critiquer les actions des Empereurs, quoÿ qu'un Empereur Soit tres bon et tres parfait.

Certenainement ils trouveront quelque chose a repondre en luy aujourdhuÿ moÿ pour l'amour de ces Empereurs des precedentes dinasties je distinge clairement et dis: parce que les affaires de l'Empire Sont sans nombre ne pouvant pas Supporter le pesant fardeau de ces affaires ils en ont êtez accablez, et c'est ce qui à abregé leurs jours. Le grand Tchū-kĕ-[356] leán[357] disoit j'epuise mes forces, etant mort j'auraÿ finis glorieusement ma course.

Que les Ministres de l'empire considerent Seulement Tchū-kĕ-leán et tachent de Se rendre capable de l'jmiter, Si un Prince prend Sur Ses èpaules le tres pesant fardeau de l'empire, il ne luÿ est pas permis de S'en decharger Sur un autre, les peines et les traveaux de Ses ministres ne peuvent pas egaler les Siennes, les ministres peuvent prendre une charge et la quitter, S'ils veulent cesser d'exerser leur emploÿ ils cessent d'abord, etant devenus vieux ils Se demetent pour toujours de leur Charge, et s'en retournent dans leur famille, ou ils ont la consolation de tenir entre les bras leurs enfans encore petits, et badinent avec leurs petits fils ils ont tout a Souhait, vivent tranquilles et Contens d'eux même

Quandt a l'Empereur toute Sa vie est un tissu de peine d'jnquietude et de travail, il n'a pas un Seul jour de repos, tel fut l'empereur Chún[358] quoy que le monde dit qu'il ne faisoit [95] rien pour bien gouverner l'empire, cependant ala fin de ses jours accablé de travail et de fatige, il mourut dans le terroir de Tsāñ-vóu[359] fort eloigne de sa famille.

L'Empereur ÿù[360] voyaga long tems en differentes manieres arpentant lui même la terre accablé de travail et de fatige mourut a la Ville hóey-k'ÿ-hién[361] trés èloigne de la famille, c'est ainsi que ces deux Empereurs ont Souffert, pour les affaires de

356 This note appears in the left margin: "Ministre d'un Empereur de la Famile Han."
357 Person unknown.
358 Shun (ca. 2294–2184 BCE) was a legendary emperor of ancient China. Leeming, Dictionary, 38.
359 This note appears in the right margin: "Pays de la Province de Quān-Sÿ, C'est luÿ qui secha la Chine auparavant jnnondeé." This refers to Cangwu, the site in the Jiuyi Mountains and Kwangsi Province where Emperor Shun died and was buried. See Wendy Swartz, Robert Ford Campany, Yan Lu and Jessey J.C. Choo (eds.), *Early Medieval China: a Sourcebook* (New York: Columbia UP, 2014) 264, ft. 5.
360 Yu (ca. 2200–2100 BCE) was a legendary emperor of ancient China as well as the founder of the Xia Dynasty. He was known for his hydrographical improvements, as well as his moral character. See Chang, China, 71–3; Donald Harper, "Warring States Natural Philosophy and Occult Thought", in: Cambridge History of Ancient China, 872–73.
361 This note appears in the right margin: "Ville du troisieme ordre sous la Cité Chao-hin-fou Province de Tche-kiān." Emperor Yu, according to legend, died after a 45-year reign on Mount Kuaiji, near Shaoxing in Fukien Province. It is located near modern-day Hangzhou Bay and the eastern Chinese coast.

l'empire, ils alloient eux même Sur les lieux examiner toutes les affaires, et n'ont pas Ozé prendre un Seul lieu de repos, peut on dire qu'il n'avoit rien a faire et qu'il etoit oisif etant Empereur.

Dans le livre classique Yĕ-kīn[362] a la figure Tün-koûa et a la petite figure Loŭ-yâo[363] il n'est rien dit contre la conduite des Empereurs, il est aisé de voir que ces empereurs n'ont eu un seul lieu de repos, ou ils aÿent peu pour un tems abandonner les reines de l'Empire, vivre toujours jnquiet epuiser nos forces, Voila ce qu'on peut appeller le partage d'un Empereur, depuis l'antiquité la plus reculeé de tous les Empereurs qui ont occupé le throne avec equité, il n y en à pas un Seul dont le regne Soit comparable aû mien, mon aÿeul[364] et mon Pere[365] au commencement ne pensoit pas à prendre l'Empire. leur armeé etant arriveé à Peking tous les ministres dirent qu'il devoit prendre l'empire. L'Empereur mon Pere dit. la famille jmperialle Mîn[366] avec mon Royaume n'ont jamais èté bien en paix, presentement je puis me Saisir fort aisement de Son Empire Seulement je pensois c'est le Veritable Seigneur dela Chine il ne convient pas dela luy enlever après le fameux [96] brigand Lÿ-tsen-tchiñ[367] batit et renversa les murailles de Peking, L'Empereur Tsôn-tchin[368] se pendit luÿ même, les manderins et le peuple vinrent à l'envÿ jnviter mon Pere a entrer dans la Chine, pour exterminer le fameux brigand Lÿ-tséu tchîn, il entra et receut l'Empire, il examina les rites et les ceremonies, et pour les enterrements des Empereurs, et enterra honorablement L'Empereur Tstôn-tchin conformement a ces rites, autrefois Hán-kāo-tsòủ[369]

---

362 The *Yijing*, or *Book of Changes*, is an ancient Chinese divination manual and its oldest text, dating as a composed work to about the ninth century BCE. It was absorbed into imperial cosmology in the second century BCE. See Richard John Lynn (trans.), *The Classic of Changes: a New Translation of the* I Ching *as Interpreted by Bi Wang* (New York: Columbia UP, 1994).

363 This likely refers to two of the sixty-four hexagrams, or *gua*, found in the *Yijing*.

364 Hung Taiji, or Abahai (1592–1643), was an early Ch'ing Dynasty ruler, who laid the groundwork for the Ming conquest and expanded China. He died in the midst of his military campagain, without designating an heir. Roth Li, State.

365 Fu-lin, or the Shun-chih Emperor (1638–1661) was the third emperor in the Ch'ing Dynasty and the first to rule over China. See Jerry Dennerline, "The Shun-chih Reign", in: Cambridge History of China, vol. 9, 73–119.

366 This note appears in the right margin: "C'est la derniere famille des Empereu[rs] qui regnoit avant q[ue] le Roÿ de la tartarie [...] enta le Pere de cet E[m]pereur entra dans l[a] chine et envahit la Chine."

367 Li Tzu-ch'eng (1606–1645) was a military leader from central China, who led a revolt against the Ming Dynasty from 1642 to 1644. He ultimately deposed the last emperor and established himself as first ruler of a new dynasty in 1644. See Huang, Lung-ch'ing, 563–74; William Atwell, "The T'ai-ch'ang, T'ien-ch'i and Ch'ung-chen reigns, 1620–1644", in: Cambridge History of China, vol. 7, 635–56.

368 Chu Yu-chien, the Ch'ung-chen Emperor (1611–1644), was the sixteenth and final emperor in the Chinese Ming Dynasty. He faced numerous rural revolts and a Manchu invasion during his reign. He ultimately hung himself as rebel armies, led by Li Zicheng, approached his court in Peking. Atwell, Tai-ch'ang, 611–37.

369 Liu Pang, or the Kao-ti Emperor (ca. 256–195 BCE), was the first ruler in the Chinese Han Dynasty. See Michael Loewe, "The Former Han dynasty", in: Cambridge History of China, vol. 1, 110–127.

fondateur de la famille jmperialle Hán, n'etoit qu'un simple commissaire du quartier Séu-tchàn.[370]

Miñ-táÿ-tsòu[371] le fondateur de la famille Imperialle Mîn etoit Bonse, de la Bonserie Hoân-kio-seû, Le general Hân-yù[372] leva des armeés[373], et disputa de l'empire, cependant l'empire resta a la famille Hân, à la fin du Regne yûen, Le general tchîn-yèou-lean[374], et autres capitaines mirent des armeés jnnombrables Sur pied[375], cependant l'Empire resta a la famille Mîn.

Ma famille qui possede a present l'Empire dela Chine vient des Roÿs de la tartarie orientale obeisant au Ciel, et ce conformant a la volonté des peuples, elle a obtenu l'Empire, c'est ainsÿ que quand on a veu les manderins et le peuple dans le desordre et dans le brigandage, celuÿ qui a eteint ces desordres, et ces brigandages, en faisant mourir ou chassant ces brigands, est devenu le Veritable maitre. tout Empereur à certainement l'ordre du Ciel, devant regner long tems, les hommes ne peuvent pas faire qu'il ne regne longtems. devant regner en paix, les hommes ne peuvent pas faire [97] qu'il ne regné en Paix.

De ma Ieunesse j'aÿ etudié la Doctrine des Anciens et des nouveaux, je Scaÿ un peu des uns et des autres. etant jeunes et dans le fort de ma Vigeur je pouvois bander un arc de 150 livres, et tirer une fleche de 13 poigneés de long. conduire des armeés donner des batailles, ce Sont Choses, ou je Suis fort habile, qouy que je Sois grand guerrier: de ma vie je n'aÿ fait mourir un Seul homme injustement, I'aÿ fait mourir les

370 This note appears in the left margin: "d'une Ville de la Province de Nanquin." This refers to modern-day Pei County, located in Jiangsu Province in eastern China. It was the birthplace of the Kao-ti Emperor, who worked there as a patrolman before joining the rebellion that ultimately brought him to power.

371 Chu Yüan-chang, also known as T'ai-tsu or the Hung-wu Emperor (1328–1398), was the first ruler in the Chinese Ming Dynasty. He was born into a poor family and spent much of his youth training as a Buddhist monk. He raised an army, after his monastery was destroyed in a 1352 revolt against Mongol rule, and successfully lead these rebels to victory across China by 1381. Frederick W. Mote, "The rise of the Ming dynasty, 1330–1367", in: Cambridge History of China, vol. 7, 11–57; Edward L. Dreyer, "Military origins of Ming China", in: ibid. 58–106; John D. Langlois, Jr., "The Hung-wu reign, 1368–1398", in: ibid., 107–81.

372 Lan Yü (d. 1393) was a Chinese Muslim and general at the founding of the Ming Dynasty. He was heavily rewarded by the Hung-wu Emperor for his military skill and earned the title General-in-Chief in 1388. Ultimately perceived as an imperial threat, he was accused of plotting a revolt and executed in 1393. Langlois, Hung-wu, 125, 129, 144–6, 158–61, 170–2.

373 This note appears in the left margin: "contre la famille Hañ."

374 Ch'en Yu-liang (1320–1363) was a political and military rebel against the Mongol Yüan as well as the Ming Dynasty. He declared himself the new Han emperor in 1358. Dreyer, Military Origins, 65–89.

375 This note appears in the left margin: "tartares occidenteaux."

trois Roÿs[376] nettoyé l'Empire de la famille mŏpĕ[377], l'aÿ fait tout cela par mes seules lumieres, et par ma bonne fortune quand au thresor Imperial, je ne m'en Suis Servi que pour entretenir les armeés en tems de guerre et nourir le peuple en tems de famine, je n'aÿ pas ozé m'en Servir pour aucunne depence jnutille: parce que tous ces thresors Sont la Sueur et le Sang de tout le peuple. Tous les Palais qui Sont pour me loger dans mes vojages, Sont peu ornez et meublez, la depence pour chacun de ces palais, ne passe pas dix ou vingt mille Taëls[378], pour les digues et fleuves on depense tous les ans trois millions et tant de dix milles Taëls, ainsi pour mes palais on ne depence pas la Centiesme de ce qu'on depence pour les digues des rivieres.

Autre fois l'Empereur Leân-ou-tÿ[379] obtint l'Empire par ces actions heroiques, ensuite agé de 80 ans son ministre nommé Heóu-kīn[380] le detruisit, en l'enferment entre quatre murailles ou il mourut de fain.

[98] L'Empereur Soûiy-oûen-tÿ́[381] obtint aussi l'empire par hazar et ne peut pas prevoir la mechancetté de Son fils Yân-tÿl[382] pour le quel il fut mis miserablement a mort, l'un et l'autre ne Se mirent pas en garde de bonne heure contre la malice de ces mechans hommes; = mes fils et petits fils sont au nombre de cent et tant, mon age est de 70 ans, tous les Roys, les Grands, Ministres, les Manderins, les Soldats, et le peuple, jusqu'au Môn-kòu[383] et autres, il ni en à pas un qui ne m'aime, et qui n'ait de l'affection pour moÿ Vieillard. presentement quoi que je Sois dans un grand age, Ie

---

**376** This note appears in the right margin: "de Iunan quānton et Foûkien." It refers to Wu San-kuei, king of Yunnan (1612–1678), Shang K'o-hsi, king of Kwangtung (1604–1676), and Keng Ching-chung, king of Fukien (d. 1671). All three men were vassal rulers of the K'ang-hsi Emperor in southern China and initially welcomed by the Manchus.

**377** The Revolt of the Three Feudatories began in 1673, when three vassal kings of the Ch'ing Dynasty in southern China rose against perceived aggressions to their rule. The emperor, in particular, tried to force Wu Sang-kuie – the general behind his prior military successes – to dismantle his army so as to consolidate power. The K'ang-hsi Emperor did not completely suppress the rebellion until 1681, and each king died during the course of the war. Spence, K'ang-hsi, 136–44.

**378** This note appears in the right margin: "Tartarres occidenteaux."

**379** Hsiao Yen, the Wu-ti Emperor (464–549), was the first ruler in the Liang Dynasty, based in southern China. His reign was mostly peaceful, but ended with rebellion and his death while under house arrest. See Albert Dien, *Six Dynasties Civilization* (New Haven: Yale UP, 2007), 43, 72.

**380** Hou Ching (d. 552) was a Chinese general, who usurped control of the Liang Dynasty from roughly 549 to 552. He briefly declared himself emperor during this period. Ibid., 10, 43–5.

**381** K'ai-huang, or the Wen-ti Emperor (541–604), was the first Emperor in the short-lived Chinese Sui Dynasty. See Arthur F. Wright, "The Sui Dynasty", in: Cambridge History of China, vol. 3, 48–149.

**382** Ta-yeh, or the Yang-ti Emperor (569–617) was the second emperor in the Chinese Sui Dynasty. He was an unpopular ruler, rumored to have murdered his father. His building and military campaigns left his kingdom bankrupt and unsettled. He was strangled by a rebellious general and the Sui Dynasty disintegrated soon thereafter. Ibid.

**383** Person unknown.

Suis fort contant, vojant que même les fils et petits fils des deux Roys Lȳtsīn-van et Iâo-yû-vân[384] mes oncles Sont encore tous vivants et en paix.

Apres ma mort vous autres mes Parens Si vous pouvez vivre et vous Conserver tous dans une grande union, Je meurs avec plaisir.

Yōn-tsiṅ-vân mon quatrieme fils Surnomme Y'n-tchīn, est un homme d'une grande capacite, il me resemble beaucoup. Certainement il pourra bien gouverner tout l'Empire, Ie luy ordonne apres ma mort de prendre possession de mon throne conformement aux ceremonies de l'Empire; qu'on garde le deüil Vingt Sept Iours. apres ce tems qu'on cesse le deüil, qu'on en fasse la publication a la Cour et dans les Provinces. que tout l'Empire le sçache

Du Regne de l'Empereur Kāṅ-hÿ la
61.e anneé le 13e de la 11.me Lune le 20 decembre
1722. Edit Imperial

### Lettre 5.e Sur les Enterremens des Chinois et des honneurs qu'ils rendent a leurs Ancetres

[99] Monsieur les Enterremens des Chinois se font avec de grandes Ceremonies.[385] lors qu'un malade est a l'article de la mort, tous les Parens, et les amis s'assemblent autour deluÿ, et luy demandent bonnement, ou il veut aller, et pour quoy il les quitte: questions fort èdifiantes et fort a propos! ils luy disent qu'il n'a qu'a faire Savoir ce qui luÿ manque et l'assurent fort obligeament qu'on le luÿ donnera tout jncontinent. quand il a rendu Sa pauvre ame ala merci de Son Createur, on met le Corps dans un lit de parade le plus riche, ou le plus beau qu'il est possible d'avoir, et quelque tems apres il est porté en terre dans ce même lit sur les epaules de plusieurs hommes, de telle maniere que tout le monde le Voit a decouvert. une grande foule de peuple marche Confusement devant et apres le Corps qui est jmmediatement Suivi par des Prêtres ou Bonzes et par des pleureuses de profession, qui Sont habillieés de blanc. Ces pleureuses se tourmentent beaucoup et demandent toujours au mort pourquoÿ il a ainsi abandonné [100] le monde? de quoÿ il manquoit, et pour quoÿ il ne le veut pas dire? puis qu'assurement il obtiendroit ce qu'il Voudroit sur le Champ. C'est ainsi que le Corps est porté dans le lieu destiné a Sa Sepulture, qui est aux environs de Canton. On enterre quelques pieces d'argent avec luÿ, et on porte tous les jours de la Viande,

---

384 These probably refer to T'ung Kuo-kang (d. 1690) and T'ung Kuo-wei (d. 1719), the two brothers of K'ang-hsi's mother. Both men served official roles at court, and the latter's daughter became an imperial consort and, in 1689, the Empress. Standaert, Interweaving, 278, ft. 75.

385 For more on Chinese burial rituals, see Mu-chou Poo, "Ideas Concerning Death and Burial in Pre-Han and Han China", in: *Asia Major* 3.2 (1990), 25–62; Dieter Kuhn, *Burial in Song China* (Heidelberg: Edition Forum 1994); James L. Watson and Evelyn S. Rawski (eds.), *Death Ritual in Late Imperial and Modern China* (Berkeley: University of California Press, 1988), Standaert, *The Interweaving of Rituals*.

et des présens Sur le tombeau pendant un an Comme dans le dessein de faire du bien et de l'honneur au defunt.[386]

Les Parens font la Ceremonie Solemnelle a l'honneur des Ancetres defunts dans les temples qui leur Sont dediez; le 14.ᵉ et le troisiéme et de la Septieme Lune de l'anneé Chinoise.[387] tous ceux qui doivent ÿ assister, Se trouvent de grand matin a la porte et chacun Se place en son rang. le plus Considerable par Sa qualité qui doit faire la fonction de Prêtre est appellé Chuchi[388] en langage du paÿs, C'est à dire le Seigneur qui Sacrifie. jl est accompagné de deux ministres qui font comme l'office de Diacre et de Sousdiacre qui S'appellent Fúchÿ'[389], C'est adire Ceux qui aident le Sacrificateur. jl ÿ en a d'autres qui font comme l'office d'acolythes qui S'appellent Ché cú.[390] ils doivent jeusner trois jours avant ces fonctions ; ils doivent aussi [101] S'abstiner des devoirs du Mariage et du Bain, ne manger de Viande, ne point boire de Vin, ne point aller dans les maisons ou il y a ds [sic] malades, eviter les spectacles, et les Concerts. ils nettoient et ornent les temples, ils ÿ expossent les jmages de leurs Ancetres, et les rangent chacune à leur place. On prepare tout ce qui est necessaire pour la Ceremonie, des tables, des sieges, des plats, des êcuelles, un Vase pour offrir le vin, de l'eau, un linge pour essujer les mains, des Chairs de Porc, des poules, des testes de Chevres, des Poissons, des fruits, du vin, des parfums et des Cierges. On prepare aussi un homme de paille, qu'ils appellent Maò-xà[391], qui represente le corps du defunt, et ils mettent cette figure Sous une table.

Tout etant ainsi disposé celuÿ qui fait la fonction de Prêtre Se lave les mains puis accompagné de Ses Ministres il S'approche avec beaucoup de gravité et de respect du lieu ou Sont remfermez les tableaux ou tablettes des Ancestres dans un Tabernacle fort propre Couvert d'un rideau de Soÿe. ces tablettes ou tableaux (Comme S'jmaginent et comme Crojent les Chinois) Sont le Siege et le throne des Ames ou des Esprits des morts.

---

**386** The preceding paragraph was adjusted and copied from: Voyage et Avantures, vol. 2, 119–21.

**387** Typically, the fifteenth day of the third and seventh Chinese moons were set aside to worship ancestors. *Qingming* is celebrated after the third moon and usually involves tidying family tombs and leaving gifts. The Ghost Festival, meanwhile, is celebrated in the seventh month and encourages gifting and ritual storytelling that provide for the dead in the afterlife and remember their lives on earth. See Stephen Teiser, *The Ghost Festival in Medieval China* (Princeton, NJ: Princeton UP, 1988); Francis L.K. Hsu, *Under the Ancestors' Shadow: Kinship, Personality and Social Mobility in China* (Stanford, CA: Stanford UP, 1971), 195.

**388** This probably refers to a *daoshi*, or formally ordained Daoist priest. It also could reference the higher position of *zhuchi*, or senior Daoist abbot.

**389** *Fashi* were lay practioners of Daoism, or a sort of secondary sacrifier, who performed many of the same ritual roles as *daoshi*. They typically lived in the communities they served.

**390** Reference unknown.

**391** Effigies were commonplace in Chinese burial ceremonies. See Stuart E. Thompson, "Death, Food and Fertility", in: *Death Ritual in Late Imperial and Modern China*, eds. James L. Watson and Evelyn S. Rawski (Berkeley: University of California Press, 1988), 85–6.

[102] Le Prêtre tire ces tableaux ou ces tablettes avec respect et tous les assistans S'etant mis a genoux il les encense et leur offre des parfums et lors le Maitre des Ceremonies qu'ils appellent Lÿ"Señg[392], dit a haute voix: nous qui sommes les enfans obeisans, de nos Ancestres, nous vous servons et nous vous honorons aujourd'huÿ; et nous prions ces tableaux de venir au milieu de nous sur cette table, afin que nous leur faissions nos offrandes. Ensuitte le Maitre de Ceremonies dit a haute voix. ɔaÿ[393], C'est adire, qu'on se mette a genoux et tout le monde S'ÿ met aussitot. un peu apres il dit du même ton, Hing[394], c'est adire, levez vous, et tout le monde se leve. cela Se fait jus qu'a trois fois avec beaucoup de gravité et de Solemnité. ensuite le Maitre de Ceremonie dit. que le Sacrificateur vienne a Sa place, qu'il fasse des reverences aux esprits. les Esprits sont dêja descendus, qu'on leur offre les Viandes. Apres cela un des ministres prend le vin et le presente au prêtre qui le repend Sur l'homme de paille, ausitot ces assistans flechissent les genous, et se levent, ce qu'ils font quatre fois de Suite, Selon l'ordre du Maitre des Ceremonies. ensuite le Sacrificateur et les Ministres prennent le Chevre et les [103] autres viandes et les offrent devant les tableaux. Le Maitre de Ceremonies dit, Chý chý eū[395], Sacrifie le vin, et le Prêtre êleve le vin dans une vase, comme les Prêtres du vraÿ Dieu êlevent le Calice à la messe. le Maitre des Ceremonies dit: Iufō chieū[396], beuvez le vin qui est le gage de tous biens et de toute Sorte de prosperité, et le Prestre le boit. Pendant toutes ces fonctions, il fait bruler plusieurs fois des parfums devant les tablettes des Ancestres. ensuite le Prêtre dit à haute voix: nos Ancestres vous avez commandé au Maitre des Ceremonies de nous promettre de nous promettre [sic] de votre part beaucoup des faveurs, et des biens Sans fin. vous avez aussi procuré a vos enfans et a vos descendans des dons magnifiques du Ciel, des anneés fertiles et abondantes et une longe vie et ces bien faits sont perpetuels. apres cela tout la monde Se met a genoux et Se leve par trois fois par ordre du Maitre des Ceremonies. Cela fini, le sacrificateur et le ministres prennent les tablettes des Ancestres[397], et les remettent avec respect dans le tabernacle ou dans l'ormoire d'ou il les ont tirez, et ils la Couvrent d'un rideau de Soÿe. on distribue les viandes du Sacrifice a tous les assistans. Enfin le Maitre des Ceremonies dit a haute voix : tenez

---

**392** *Lǐshēng*, or ritual masters, were Confucian spiritual leaders, who guided the celebration of nuptials, funerals and other spiritual rites. See Yonghua Liu, *Confucian Rituals and Chinese Villagers: Ritual Change and Social Transformation in a Southeastern Chinese Community, 1368–1949* (Leiden, Brill: 2013), 47–70. For more on the format of *lǐshēng* rituals, as well as a translation of commonly used rites, see ibid., 72–6, 88–9, 279–84; Standaert, *Interweaving of Rituals*, 10–20.

**393** This might correspond to the Chinese phrase *guì*, meaning "to kneel or genuflect."

**394** This might correspond to the Chinese phrase *tǐng lì*, meaning "to stand erect."

**395** Phrase unknown.

**396** Phrase unknown.

**397** Many Confucian households had family altars. After a death, relatives prepared an ancestral tablet, or soul seat, for the deceased, which was placed on this altar and mourned. Standaert, *Interweaving of Rituals*, 11–4; Thompson, "Death, Food and Fertility," 43–5.

vous pour assurez qu'en recompense de ce sacrificé vous recevrez toute sortes [104] de faveurs, et de bonheur, des richesses, un grand nombre d'enfans, des honneurs, une longe vie, le repos et la paix. Celuy qui a fait la fontion de prêtre, repete la même chose. on met le feu a un monceau de papiers preparez au de hors du Temple ou Pagode, qui Sont argenteés et doreés les Chinois crojent qu'ils se Changent en argent pour l'usage des morts.[398] Voila Monsieur les Ceremonies sur les quels on a disputé Si longtems entre les Peres Iesuites et autres Missionaires, Si elles Sont Superstitieuses ou non, et Si on pouvoit laisser avoir part aux noúveaux Chretiens dans les dits Ceremonies.[399] pour moÿ Monsieur comme je trouve la matiere dèlicate, et que je scaÿ qûe vous est assez jnstruit de l'affaire, je me Contenteraÿ de vous dire avec Saint Paul. si quis non habet Spiritum Christi hic non est ejus. Que si quelqu'un n'a point l'esprit de Iesu Christ il n'est point a luÿ.[400] Rom: 8.V9.

## Lettre Sixieme Des honneurs que les Chinois rendent a Confucius

[105] Ie ne me puis pas empecher Monsieur, de Vous donner Sur votre demande le recit des honneurs que les Chinois rendent a Confucius. qu'ils reconnoissent pour leur maitre et leur Legislateur, jl nâquit l'an 550 avant la Venue de Iesu Christ dans le Roÿaume de Lū[401], qui est maintenant la Province de Chan tong. quelques autheurs Chrestiens n'on pas ète honteux de Soutenir qu'il à conu et adoré le vraÿ Dieu. et qu'il a este un modèle de Vertu et de Sainteté, par les exemples qu'il donna d'une moderation, d'une fidelité, d'une equité, et d'une douceur Sans ègale. jl meprisa les honneurs et les richesses, S'appliquant uniquement a repandre Sa doctrine dans le monde. l'humilité que les Philosophes de l'Europe ont regardeés comme une bassesse d'ame, etoit sa Chere vertu. jl parloit toujours de Soÿ même, et de tout ce qui avoit quelque rapport a Sa personne avec beaucoup de modestie, jl faisoit un aveu publicq de Ses defauts et une profession Sincere de n'etre pas l'auteur dela Doctrine qu'il enseignoit, mais d'en etre redevable [106] aux anciens, et principalement des Roÿs Yao[402] et Xun[403] qui l'avoient precedé de plus de quinze cent ans. il fit profes-

398 The preceding three paragraphs were adjusted and copied from: Alexandre, Apologie, 27–31.

399 For more on this debate, see pages 276–7.

400 This also translates as: "whoever does not have the Spirit of Christ does not belong to him."

401 Lu was a vassal state during the Chou Dynasty, founded in the eleventh century and lasting until the mid-third century BCE. It was located in eastern China and covered a portion of Shantung Province.

402 Yao (ca. 2356–2255 BCE) was a legendary emperor of ancient China. He is considered one of the Five August Emperors. See Lihui Yang and Deming An, *Handbook of Chinese Mythology* (New York: Oxford UP, 2005), 227–9.

403 Shun (ca. 2294–2184 BCE) was a legendary emperor of ancient China. He inherited his rule from Yao, although unrelated, because of his moral reputation. Ibid., 203–4.

sion publique d'enseigner la Philosophie morale: et sa reputation luy attira plus de trois mille Disciples. dont il assembla soixante et douze, comme a fait Iesu Christ, qui surpasserent les autres en Science et en vertu, et pour qui les Chinois ont encore à present une veneration particuliere, jl choisit dix ou douze de ce nombre qui estoient la fleur de son école, pour en faire comme Ses Apostres.[404] peu s'en faut qu'on ne le fasse passer pour un Prophete, Comme j'aÿ leu dans un certain Autheur qui parle de Confucius en ce termes. Son humilité et sa modestie, donnerent lieu de juger que ce n'a pas eté un pur Philosophe formé par la raison, mais un homme jnspiré de Dieu pour la reforme de ce nouveau monde.[405]

Confucius divisa Sa Doctrine en quatre parties, et Ses disciples en un pareil nombre de Classes. le premier ordre êtoit de ceux S'etudioient à aquerir les Vertus. le Second rang êtoit de Ceux qui apprenoient l'art de raisonner et l'eloquence. dans la troisieme classe on traitoit du gouvernement de l'etat et du [107] devoir des Magistrats. la quatrieme classe s'occupoit à discourir noblement sur tout ce qui regarde la Science des meurs. quelques Chinois rapportent qu'il assuroit qu'il ÿ avoit un Saint homme en occident qui enseignoit une loix Sainte, nommé Sifain-ren-ximgun[406]; ou Sisam-ren chimgim; dont on ne dit rien davantage, et on ne scay disent ils, de qui il parloit, ni par quel esprit. il est Certain que l'Empereur Mimti envoÿa des Ambassadeurs en Occident soixante et six ans apres la naissance de Jesu Christ pour chercher ce Saint homme dont on disoit que Confucius avoit parlé, et que estant abordez a une isle assez proche dela Mer Rouge[407], ils n'oserent passer outre, et rapporterent l'Idole Fo (dont jaÿ parle cÿ devant) et l'execrable doctrine de sa secte, dans la Chine. Cela justifie bien la prophetie de Confucius, voicy Mons^r ce qui prouve son humilité pretendue, cet admirable Philosophe prevojant la fin de ses jours, et Considerant le desordre dela Cour du Roÿ de Lû[408], chanta ce vers entremêlez de soupirs, Montagne jmmense ou est tu tombé? la grande machine est renverseé: les hommes sages et les Vertueux ont manqué: les Roÿs, ajoutat-il ne suivent pas mes maximes je ne Suis plus utile au monde, ainsi il est tems que j'en Sorte. jl tomba dans [108] une lethargie qui dura Sept jours et murut a fin agé de 73 ans. jl fut enterré dans le royaume de Lu, ou il est

---

**404** According to tradition, Confucius returned to Lu from a self-imposed exile at age 68. There, he began a school and instructed roughly 70 students in his moral and political beliefs. Schuman, Confucius, 13–4.

**405** The preceding paragraph was adjusted and copied from: Alexandre, Apologie, 16–7.

**406** This note appears in the right margin: "escrit par un Missionaire Portugais, qui prononcent le Kimgim comme les franc[ais] chimgim."

**407** The Red Sea is an inlet of the Indian Ocean, which separates the Asian and African continents.

**408** Lu was a dukedom during Confucius' lifetime, although constantly threatened by three competing aristocratic families. The ruler at the time of his death in 479 BCE was Jiang, or Duke Ai. Chin, Confucius, 65–6, 128–9.

retourné avec Ses disciples, proche de la Ville de Kio-fu[409], Sur le bord dela Riviere Sú. Son tombeau est dans l'accadamie même ou il faisoit Ses leçons la quelle est fermeé de murailles comme un Bourg.

Depuis plus de deux mille ans, ce philosophe a toujours esté en grande Veneration dans la Chine, et personne n'est êlevé a la qualité de Manderin et aux charges de la robe, qu'apres avoir êté reçu Docteur[410] dans la Science de Confucius. en toutes les Villes, il ÿ a des Palais qui luÿ sont Consacrez, et lorsque quelqu'un des officiers de Robe passe devant, il descend de Son palanquin, et fait quelques pas a pié, pour rendre honneur a Sa memoire. Sur le frontispice des Palais qui luÿ Sont Consacrez, on voit ses êloges en grandes lettres d'or, avec de semblables titres: au grand Maitre: a l'jllustre: au Sage Roÿ des lettres. il restoit encore en 1646. un de ses descendans qui tenoit un rang Considerable dans l'Etat : et Chun:tchi[411] Roÿ Tartare qui conquit la Chine le reçut avec beaucoup d'honneur. Ceux [109] de cette famille Sont Manderins nez, etont un previlége qui ne leur est Commun qu'avec les Princes du Sang, de ne payer aucun tribut[412] a l'Empereur. Outre cela, tous ceux qui recoivent le titre de Docteur doivent faire un present au Manderin dela race de Confusius. on peut juger parla que les Missionaires, qui vont precher l'Evangile dans la Chine Sont obligez de Scavoir la Doctrine de ce Philosophe, et de Se Servir de Son autorité, pour Se mettre en Credit parmi les Chinois[413], et pour disposer les esprits a recevoir les lumieres dela foi.

---

**409** Qufu is a city located along the Si River in Lu. It was Confucius' hometown and also where he was buried. It quickly became a pilgrimage site after his death.

**410** In order to qualify for political office and the title of mandarin in imperial China, men had to pass an intense civil service exam, which included thorough knowledge of Confucianism. Even then, the number of students who could pass the exam in each province was limited. See Charles O. Hucker, "Governmental Organization in The Ming Dynasty", in: *Harvard Journal of Asiatic Studies* 21 (1958), 13–14; Benjamin A. Elman, *Civil Examinations and Meritocracy in Late Imperial China* (Cambridge, MA: Harvard UP, 2013); Adam Yuen-chung Lui, "Syllabus of the provincial examination (*hsiang-shih*) under the early Ch'ing (1644–1795)", in: *Modern Asian Studies* 8.3 (1974), 391–6.

**411** This note appears in the left margin: "par les Portugais Xunchi." This refers to Fulin, or the Shun-Chih Emperor.

**412** China maintained tributary relationships with many neighboring states since the Han Dynasty. Most often, these took the form of formalized gifts to and prostrations before the emperor to procure trading rights. While the Chinese emperor had the option of arbitrating disputes between tributaries, the kingdoms in this system mostly managed their own domestic and foreign affairs. See John E. Willis, Jr., *Past and Present in China's Foreign Policy: From "Tribute System" to "Peaceful Rise"* (Honolulu: University of Hawaii Press, 2011).

**413** Some Jesuits, in particular, used their scientific training to permeate the imperial court, hoping their knowledge would impress and convert Confucian elites and then trickle down to lower social orders. Their willingness to engage and sometimes adopt Chinese religious and non-religious customs (notably dress) earned them much criticism in Europe. Brockey, Journey, 25–56.

car la Doctrine de cet homme, qu'ils ont en Veneration, est tres Conforme à la raison: et les Savans du paÿs n'ecouteront jamais des gens qui mepriseront Confusius.[414]

Les honneurs extraordinaires et Divins que les Chinois rendent a Confucius se font deux fois l'anneé, Scavoir au printems et dans l'automne[415], le Manderin ou Gouverneur de chaque ville doit offrir le Sacrifice à Confusius, et les Lettrez ÿ doivent assister. il ÿ en à entre eux qui ÿ font des fonctions qui ont quelque ressemblance a celles de Diacre, de Sousdiacre, et de Maitre des Ceremonies dans le Ministeré de nos autels. [110] Le Sacrificateur Se prepare ala Ceremonie par le Jeune et par la Continence. ils disposent des la veille le ris et les autres Semences et fruits de la terre qui Se doivent offrir, et les pieces d'etoffe de Soÿe qui Se doivent bruler a l'honneur de Confucius, et ils les rangent Sur des tables. le tableau ou la Cartouche ou le nom de Confusius est êcrit, est placé sur un autel paré de beaux ornemens de Soÿe. Celuÿ qui fait l'office de Prêtre met sur un autre table dans la Cour qui est devant la Chapelle, des Cierges, des brasieres, et des parfums. il eprouve ensuite les Pourceaux et les autres animaux qu'on doit Sacrifier, en leur mettant du vin chaud dans les Oreilles. S'ils Secouent la tête on les choisit comme propres au Sacrifice, S'ils ne Se donnent point ce mouvement, on les rejette. avant qu'on tue le pourceau, le Prêtre fait une reverence et un jnclination profonde et ensuite on le tue en Sa presence. apres qu'on l'a ègorgé, il fait une autre jnclination. on enrase ensuite les poils, on en prend les jntestins et on en garde le Sang pour le jour Suivant. Le lendemain des le Chant du coq, on donne le Signal. le Sacrificateur et les officiers estant venus, chacun d'eaux êcrit sur un beau papier rouge[416] [111] d'une figure ronde des caracteres chinoises pour jnviter l'esprit de Confucius a venir recevoir les offrandes qu'on luÿ va faire. le Sacrificateur lave Ses mains, on allume les Cierges et on jette les parfums Sur les brasiers. le Maitre des Ceremonies fait chanter les musiciens et le Prêtre êtant devant le tableau de Confusius, le maitre des Ceremonies dit: qu'on offre le Sang et les poils des betes mortes. alors le Prêtre leve des deux mains le bassin ou Sont ces poils et ce Sang. le Maitre des Ceremonies dit ensuitte: qu'on enterre ces poils et ce Sang. et ausitot tous les assistans Se levent, et le Prêtre aÿant le bassin entre les mains Sort en procession avec les ministres, et on les enterre dans la Cour qui est devant la Chapelle. on decouvre ensuite les Chairs des victimes, et le Maitre des Ceremonies dit: que l'esprit de Confucius descende. ausitot le Sacrificateur leve en haut un vase plein de vin, qu'il repend Sur un home de palle. apres cela il prend le tableau de Confucius,

**414** The preceding two paragraphs were adjusted and copied from: Moréri, Grand Dictionaire (1689), vol. 3, 381–2.

**415** The *shih-tien*, or Twice Yearly Confucian Ceremony, is held in the spring and fall, and is heavily associated with the state. It includes three offerings to Confucius and other spiritual worthies in a Confucian temple and is exclusively led by the mandarin elite. See Rodney L. Taylor, *The Way of Heaven: an Introduction to the Confucian Religious Life* (Leiden: Brill, 1986), 14–26.

**416** This likely refers to red xuan – or rice – paper, the durability yet fine texture of which makes it popular for Chinese calligraphy.

et le met sur l'autel en disant cette oraison: grandes, admirables et exelentes Sont vos Vertus, ô Confusius; Si les Roÿs gouvernent leurs Sujets, ils vous en Sont obligez; c'est par le Secours de votre Doctrine. tout ce que nous offrons est pur. que votre esprit Si êclairé vienne donc vers nous [112] et qu'il nous honore de Sa Sainte presence. cela etant fait, le Maitre des Ceremonies dit. Cĭvi, mettons nous a genoux: et tout le monde S'agenouille. quelques moments après il dit: Kÿ[417], levez vous et tout le monde se leve. le Sacrificateur lave Ses mains. un des Ministres luÿ presente une piece d'etofe de soÿe dans un bassin, et un autre du Vin dans un Vase. le maitre des Ceremonies dit a haute Voix: que le Sacrificateur S'approche du thrône de Confucius. ausitôt le Prêtre S'agenouille, et pendant que la musique Chante, il prend l'etoffe de Soÿe, il la leve de deux mains, et il loffre a Confucius. jl prend aussi le Vase de Vin, et l'êleve. le Maitre des Ceremonies dit Comme auparavant : qu'on s'agenouille, et ensuitte qu'on se leve. on brule ensuitte la piece d'êtoffe de Soÿe, avec le papier rouge dont on a parle, dans un brasier prepare pour cela, et le Sacrifiant fait cette priere. Depuis le tems que les hommes ont Commencé à naitre jusqu'a ce jour, qui d'eux a pû ou peut surpasser les Vertus magnifiques et surabondantes de Confuciús? le Seul esprit ou l'ame de ce Roÿ Surpasse tous les Saints du tems passé ces offrandes et cette êtoffe de Soÿe sont prepareés pour la Ceremonie que nous faisons en votre presence et a votre honneur tout ce que nous vous offrons est peu de Chose. la Saveur et l'odeur n'en Sont pas fort agréables: mais nous vous [113] les offrons Seulement enfin que Votre esprit nous êcoute. apres plusieurs jnclinations, le Sacrifiant prend le Vase de Vin, et adresse encore deux Oraisons à Confucius, ou apres avoir dit qu'il luÿ offre avec un grand Zele d'exelent Vin, et sans mêlange, et des Chairs de Pourceaux, de Chevres de lievres, de Poules, &.[a] il le prie de recevoir ces offrandes, Supposant que Son esprit est present a la Ceremonie. le Maitre des Ceremonies dit ensuite au Sacrificateur: mettez vous a genoux, tirez la table d'Yvoire de Votre Sain, approche vous du thrône de Confucius, et beuvez le vin de la felicité. aussitot le Sacrifiant le boit. apres quoÿ un des ministres luÿ met entre les mains la Chair qu'il eleve en haut, pendant que le maitre des Ceremonies dit: prenez la chair du sacrifice. le Prêtre dit ensuite une Oraison qui finit en ces termes: nous vous avons fait ces offrandes avec beaucoup de Joÿe, et nous sommes certains qu'en vous offrant toutes ces Choses, nous recevons toute Sorte de bonheur d'honneurs, de faveurs et de biens. Les Viandes qui ont esté offertes se distribuent aux assistans, et ceux qui en mangent Croyent que Confucius leur faira du bien et les preservera du mal.

La derniere fonction du Sacrifice consiste a reconduire [114] l'esprit de Confucius au lieu d'ou il est descendu, en luÿ adressant cette Oraison: nous Vous avons fait ces offrandes avec un profund respect: nous Vous avons Servi avec beaucoup de joÿe, Vous jnvitant de venir à nous pour recevoir agreablement les Choses que nous Vous avons offertes. Apres cela nous reconduisons et nous accompagnons votre Esprit,

417 This might correspond to the Chinese word *qilai*, meaning "to stand up."

et nous le prions de retourner au lieu d'ou il est descendu: et ces offrandes estant Consommeés, nous nous tenons assurez de toute sorte de prosperitez et des biens Comme si nous les avions déjà receus.[418] apres cette oraison faite Chacun retourne a Sa maison.

## Lettre Septieme Ideé Generale de l'Empire de la Chine

[115] Ie reprend Monsieur le Sujet de notre voyage, qui êtoit l'achat, le transport et les Cargaisons de Porselaine, thé et Soyeries que nous devions porter en Europe, pour cela il est bon avant toutes Choses de vous faire Connoitre le paÿs qui produit une plante Si cherÿ et que l'on vient Chercher de Si loin

Comme on est extremement Curieux de tout ce qui regarde ce grand Empire, c'est pourquoÿ je vous donne icÿ un petit Memoire que I'aÿ eu du tres R.ᵉ P.ᵉ Ioseph Labbe[419] Iesuite de la Mission françoise a canton, et Sur les observations faites par plusieurs Peres qui on demeure longtems ala Cour de l'Empereur.

Les Tartarres Occidentaux nommés Mongols l'appellent Cataÿ, et par les Tartarres Mantcheoux[420], Nican courou, et par les Chinois Tchong koué (qui veut dire Roÿaume du milieu) Sans qu'on puisse dire au vrai ce qui à donne occassion en Europe au nom de Chine[421], quoÿ qu'il en soit du nom il est Certain que la Chine est le plus grand [116] et le plus beau Roÿaume de l'univers, et un paÿs qui abonde plus qu'aucun autre en toutes les Choses qui peuvent Contribuer a rendre la Vie Commode et même deli-

**418** The preceding three paragraphs were adjusted and copied from: Alexandre, Apologie, 19–24.

**419** Joseph Labbe (1697–1745) was a French Jesuit and Chinese missionary, See Louis Pfister, *Notices biographiques et bibliographiques sur les jésuites de l'ancienne mission de Chine, 1552–1773, vol. 2* (Nendeln: Kraus Reprint, 1971), 633–5.

**420** The Mongols, Cathay and Manchu Tartars were different, but overlapping, ethnic groups indigenous to northern China, although the author uses their names synonymously in the text. The Khitan, or Cathay, were a nomadic community that ruled much of northern China from 907 to 1125. The Mongols, meanwhile, dominated the Mongolian Plateau by the 1100s and defeated China's Sung Dynasty in 1279 – controlling all of China under their new Yüan Dynasty. Their reign ended in 1368, and conflict with the Jurchens of modern-day Manchuria led to the tribe's disintegration during the 1600s. The Manchus were the descendants of these Jurchen people, who once were tributaries of the Cathay, Mongol and Han Chinese states. They rose against the Ming Dynasty in the late 1600s and conquered China, establishing the Ch'ing Dynasty. The first use of the ethnic name Manchu was in 1635. Franke and Twitchett, Cambridge History of China, vol. 6; Mark C. Elliott, *The Manchu Way: the Eight Banners and Ethnic Identity in Late Imperial China* (Standord, CA: Stanford UP, 2001).

**421** *Zhōngguó* was a Chinese word meaning "Middle Kingdom," used to denote China and conquered territories. The name Cathay, too, sometimes was as a synonym for China in medieval and early modern Europe and in the Middle East. See Joseph W. Esherick, "How the Qing Became China", in: *Empire to Nation: Historical Perspectives on the Making of the Modern World*, eds. Joseph W. Esherick, Hasan Kayah and Eric Van Yong (New York: Rowman & Littlefield Publishers, 2006), 232–3; Denis Twitchett and Klaus-Peter Tietze, "The Liao", in: Cambridge History of China, vol. 6, 43.

cieuse c'est la partie du Monde la plus abondante, si on ne voit pas Certains fruits et autres Chauses semblables qui sont Communes en Europe il ÿ en à une jnfinité d'autres que l'Europe n'a jamais produit et qu'elle ne sauroit produire.

Ce grand Empire est Composé de quinze Provinces. Celles de Pekin ou Petchili, de Chansi[422], et de Chensi, s'etendent le long de la fameuse muraille[423] qui la divise au septentrion de la tartarie, celles de Chantong[424], de Fokien, de Kiangnan[425], de Tche kiang[426] sont sur la Mer Orientale, Celles de Quang tong[427], de Quansi[428], de Yunnan[429], de Setchuen[430], sont les bornes du midÿ et de l'occident, celles de Honan[431], de Hou quang[432], de Koei tcheou[433], et de Kiangsi[434], occupent le milieu.

Leautung[435] depend aussi de la Chine. Cette Province n'est separeé en partie du Roÿaume de Coreé[436] par un bras de Mer elle est au dela de la grande muraille. les Tartarres S'etant rendus maitres de Cette Province, establirent [117] leur Cour dans la Ville Capitale[437], et Se mêlerent parmi les Chinois, qu'ils distinguent fort depuis ce tems la des habitans des autres Provinces: car les Chinois de Leautung passent à

**422** Shansi, now Shanxi, was a province in north central China and along the Great Wall.

**423** The Great Wall of China is a series of conjoined defensive structures along China's northern border, built between the seventh century BCE and fourteenth century CE to keep out frontier raiders. See Arthur Waldron, *The Great Wall of China: from History to Myth* (New York: Cambridge UP, 1992).

**424** Shantung, now Shandong, was a province in northeastern China, located along the Bohai and Yellow seas.

**425** Jiangsu, is a coastal province in eastern China. It formed part of seventeenth-century South Chihli province, along with modern-day Anhui.

**426** Chexiang, now Zhejiang, was a coastal province in eastern China.

**427** Kwangtung, now Guangdong, was a costal province in southern China, which housed the Pearl River delta. It was the center of Europe's Chinese trade during the early 1700s.

**428** Kwangsi, now Guangxi, was a province in southern China, along the Gulf of Tonkin.

**429** Yunnan is a province in southwest China.

**430** Szechwan, now Sichuan, was a province in west central China.

**431** Honan, now Henan, was a province in central China.

**432** Hukwang, now Huguang, was a province in central China during the Yüan and Ming dynasties. It now is composed of Hubei and Hunan provinces.

**433** Kweichow, now Guizhou, was a province in southern China.

**434** Kiangsi, now Jiangxi, was a province in southeastern China.

**435** Liaodong was a peninsular province, located in northeast China and bordering the Bohai Sea and Korea Bay. The name still is used for the peninsula proper, but historically it corresponded to all of modern-day Liaoning Province.

**436** Korea was a historical kingdom, located on a peninsula northeast of China and bordering Liaoning Province. It was a Ch'ing tributary but reasserted an autonomous political, economic and cultural identity by 1700. See Susan Naquin and Evelyn S. Rawski, *Chinese Society in the Eighteenth Century* (New Haven: Yale UP, 1987), 28.

**437** The Manchus established numerous capital cities in Liaodong, including Xingjing (1616–1621), Dongjing (1621–1625) and Shengjing (1625–1644). They moved their capital to Peking after the Ch'ing conquest in 1644.

la Chine pour Tartares, et jouissent de tous le Previleges de cette nation. ainsi qu'on enfait une Seixieme Province.

Il y a dans Chaque Province un grand nombre de Villes du premier, du Second et du troisiemé ordre, la pluspart sont baties sur les Rivieres navigables. les Capitales sont tres grandes et ont de chaque Coté (comme toutes les autres Villes) de fort grands fauxbourgs. outre ces villes, il ÿ a quantité de bourgs et de Villages sur tout les premiers qu'on appelle tching[438], qui peuvent aller de pair avec les villes pour leur grandeur, le nombre des habitans, et le grand Commerce qui s'y fait, Fochan[439] Bourg qui depend de Canton dont il n'est qu'a quatre lieues est devenu Celebre par la grande quantité de manufactures qu'on a etabli, ne doit ceder à rien pour ses richeses ni pour la multitude de ses habitans, a la plus grande ville.

Chaque Province est Subdiviseé en Certain nombre de Iuridictions, qu'on nomme Fou, d'ou dependent [118] d'autres beaucoup moins etendües, nommeés Tcheou et Hien[440], de la meme maniere comme nos Magistrats subalternes sont subordonneés aux Presidiaux: les Presidens de celles la sont nommés Tchi-fou, et les Administrateurs de celles ci, s'appellent Tchi:tcheou, et Tchi:hien.[441] dela vient qu'on trouve toujours dans l'enceinte d'une seule ville appelleé Fou, un Manderin nommé Tchi:fou, et au moins un autre qui est Tchi:hien: car dans les plus grandes Villes, outre le Tchi:fou, sont encore deux Manderins jnferieurs avec le titre de Tchi:hien, on partage le territoire en deux Districts a cause de leur trop d'etendu, dont chacun resortit en premiere jnstance au tribunal de son Tchi:hien, l'un et l'autre Tribunal ~~de son Tchi : hien, l'un et l'autre Tribunal~~, releve jmmediatement de celuÿ du Tchi:fou, par Exemple outre les six grandes Cours Souveraines[442] qui sont a Pekin Capitale de l'Empire, il ÿ a encorre le tribunal propre de cette ville, qui est nommeé Chun:tien[443], sous ce Tribunal il ÿ a encorre deux Subalternes de deux Hien ou villes du troisieme ordre, dont l'une s'ap-

**438** This might refer to a *xiāng*, meaning an administrative township.

**439** Foshan is a city in Kwangtung Province, located about 20 kilometers southwest of Canton. It was a key economic center on the Pearl River in the 1700s and reknown for its warehouses of regional produce.

**440** *Fu* was the Chinese term for "office." It was used during the Ming and ensuing dynasties to describe an administrative prefecture or a provincial capital city. A *chou* was a sub-prefecture, and *hsien* comparable to modern-day counties. For more on local government in imperial China, see Thoma G. Nimick, *Local Administration in Ming China* (Minneapolis, MN: Society for Ming Studies, 2008); Hucker, Governmental; Tung-Tsu Ch'un, *Local Government in China under the Ch'ing* (Stanford, CA: Stanford UP, 1962).

**441** A *chih-fu* was a Chinese prefect, or the chief governing official of a *fu*. Similarly, *chih-chou* and *chih-hsien* were subprefects and magistrates, which managed affairs at the level of *chou* and *hsien* respectively. See Charles O. Hucker, "Ming government", in: Cambridge History of China, vol. 8, 88–90.

**442** The main administrative tasks of the Ming and Ch'ing dynasties were centralized and monitored by six ministries, based in Peking. These were the Ministry of Personnel, Ministry of Revenue, Ministry of Rites, Ministry of Defense, Ministry of Justice and Ministry of Works. Hucker, Governmental, 31–6.

**443** The prefecture at Peking had the specific title of *Shun-t'ien fu*. Hucker, Ming government, 89.

pelle Tai:hing[444] et l'autre Venping[445], le nom de ces deux villes tai:hing et venping, s'entend aussi de plusieur[s] autres villes a proportion de l'etenduë des terres que [119] les habitans possedent, il ÿ a des autres Villes dans les Provinces, qui ont des Tribuneaux qui s'appellent Ouei[446], dont les Manderins qui sont des officiers de guerre ont le titre de Ouei:cheou:pei[447], leur Jurisdiction ne s'etend pas d'ordinaire hors des murs tous ces Tribuneaux de Tchi:fou, Tchi:hien, Ouei:cheou:pei, dependent du Viceroÿ et des quatre autres officiers Generaux qui Sont Ses assesseurs, Suivant la nature des affaires; S'il S'agit des Finances et des matieres Civiles, l'affaire est porteé au Tresorier General ou Poútchingse[448]; Si c'est une Cause Criminelle, elle est renvoÿeé au Lieutenant Criminel, Ngan-tcha-se.[449] S'il S'agit des affaires qui regardent les Postes, le Sel, &.[a] on a recours a l'yen tao.[450] Si c'est des Vivres qu'on leve en tribut, on S'addresse au Leang tao[451]; outre ces affaires attacheés a leur tribunal, le Peuple peut encorre s'addresser a eux pour differentes affaires, a Cause que tous les tribuneaux Subalternes dela Province dependent d'eux, les Conseillers ou Manderins qui Composent ces tribunaux Subalternes, Sont obligez plusieurs fois chaque mois de Se rendre au tribunal de ce Grand Mandarin ou Viceroÿ pour deliberer, Sur ce qui Se passe de plus jmportant dans la Province; Les officiers des Troupes dependent aussi en quelque Sorte du Viceroÿ, et ils sont obligez sous de grandes peines, de l'jnformer des moindres Choses; qui Surviennent dans l'etendue de leurs departemens, ainsÿ [120] que toutes les affaires soit Civiles, soit Crimineles, soit Militaires, reviennent anfin au tribúnal de son Gouvernement, il est si respectable, que les Cours Souveraines de Pekin, ne decident ordinairement que Sur les jnformations et qu'elles ratifient presque toujours la Sentence qu'il a porteé Contre les Manderins, qu'il a droit de Casser, en leur ôtant même le Sceau par avance. non obstant son grand pouvoir, le Tresorier General et le Lieutenant Criminel peuvent accuser le viceroÿ, mais Comme ils Craignent d'avoir le dessous, et qu'ils se perdent mutuellement par cette dissension, que les loix Condamnent Comme nuisible au bien public, raison pourquoÿ qu'ils ferment les ÿeux sur la Conduite l'un de l'autre, L'Empereur Yong-tching a present regnant, ÿ a apporté des remedes efficaces en fournissant liberalement aux fraix que

**444** Ta-hsing Hsien, now Daxing, was a historical county that included part of eastern Peking. The city was split between counties, so as to divide its potential political power. See Susan Naquin, *Peking: Temples and City Life, 1400–1900* (Berkeley: University of California Press, 2000), 172–3.

**445** Wan-p'ing hsien, now Wanping, was a historical county that included part of Peking. Ibid.

**446** *Wei* was the title given to the Chinese guard. Hucker, Governmental, 59–60.

**447** The title *tsung-ping kuan* was given to the commander of Chinese troops within a particular *fu*. Ibid., 62.

**448** Provinces often had two *pu-cheng shih*, who managed civic administration, such as gathering census data, assessing taxes, construction and water control. Ibid., 43.

**449** This might refer to the provincial judge, *t'i-hsing an-ch'a shih*, who supervised regional justice and post-related services. Ch'un, *Local Government*, 6.

**450** The *i-yen tao* was the postal and salt intendant. Hucker, Governmental, 47, 54.

**451** The *tu-liang tao* was the provincial tax intendant circuit. Hucker, Ming government, 88–9.

ses envoÿes sont obligez de faire dans les Voÿages qu'ils font par Son ordre dans les Provinces pour les affaires et le bien du peuple, et en punissant rigoureusement ceux qui Se Sont laisse Corrompre par des presents et ceux qui les ont donne.

Les Censeurs Publics de l'Empire nommez Cantao:ÿu-se[452] qui resident a Pekin n'ont pas seulement l'jnspection [121] sur tout l'Empire, mais encorre chacun d'eux sur une Province, ils sont les plus redoutez de tous les Grands Manderins , ils sont aussi tres vigilants, et ils ont leurs espions par tout, ainsi ils nepeuvent gueres jgnorer ce qui Se passe, et il est de leur jnterets que le bon ordre ÿ regne, si quelque Manderin manque a Son devoir et que le Viceroÿ n'en avertisse pas au plustot, ils Sont obligez d'en jnformer les Cours Souveraines et l'Empereur et S'ils Sont les premiers parqui l'Empereur apprenne le desordre, cela leur fait beaucoup d'honneur, S'ils ÿ manquent ils risquent de perdre leur Charge. On ne demande d'eux aucunne preuve, jl suffit que leur denontiation ait une apparence de Verité qui puisse donner lieu aux jnformations qu'en suite on à Coutume de faire, Ces Catao-ÿu-se ou Censeur public, sont regarde de toute la nation Comme les Peres dela Patrie, la Crainte qu'on à d'eux, est peut estre ce qui Contribue le plus à maintenir l'ordre et les Coutumes anciennes, et a prevenir les desordres que la nouveauté pouroient causer; dont le Peuple n'est que trop Susceptible, au reste, quoÿ que le Gouverneur de la Province ait sous luÿ les quatre grands officiers, dont j'aÿ parle cÿ devant, et que les Manderins de justice subalternes aÿent toujours un et quelque fois deux assesseurs, les affaires toutes fois ne Sont point ordinairement jugeés àla [122] pluralité des Voix, Chaque Magistrat grand ou Petit, à son tribunal ou Yamen[453], et des qu'il S'est fait jnstruire par les parties, apres quelques procedures en petit nombre dresseés par quelques gens de pratique, il prononce tel arrêt qu'il luÿ plait. quelque fois apres avoir Iugé les deux Parties, il fait encorre donner la bastonade[454] a celuÿ qui a perdu son proces, pour l'avoir jntente mal a propos, ou soutenu contre toutte apparence de bon droit.[455]

Apres avoir donne cette jdeé generale des Magistrats et des Jurisdictions, il est bon de vous faire connoitre, que la Chine compte cent soixante treize tribunaux ou jurisdictions jmmediatement soumises aux officiers Generaux et Gouverneurs de chaque Province, nommez en Chinois Fou. il ÿ a mil quatre Cent huit tribunaux jnferieurs ou jurisdictions Subalternes, qui dependent jmmèdiatement des Tchi:fou, dont onze

---

**452** *Ch'ien tu yü-shih* were assistant censors-in-chief, delegated to each province but resident in Peking. These men monitored the behaviors of the court and imperial nobles as well as military officers. They additionally had punitive powers. Hucker, Governmental, 48–51.

**453** A *yaman* was the administrative office of a local mandarin.

**454** This note appears in the bottom margin: "La bastonade, qui consiste a frapper le Criminel sur les fesses avec de grosses Cannes de telle sorte que souvent il en meurt, et on le donne suvent presque sans aucune forme de justice." Physical retribution for wrongdoing did not extend to mandarins. For more on corporal punishment in imperial China, see Terance Miethe and Hong Lu, *Punishment: a Comparative Historical Perspective* (New York: Cambridge UP, 2005), 124–8.

**455** The preceding two paragraphs were adjusted and copied from: Du Halde, Déscription, vol. 2, 2–5.

cent soixante treize on le titre de Hien, et deúx Cent trente cinq ont celui de Tcheou. Ceux cÿ cependent different un peu entre eux. la plûpart n'ont nulle autorité sur les Hiens, et quelques uns ont une jurisdiction sur un, d'eux, et quelque fois sur quatre Hien, presqu'egale a celles de Tchi:fou. il ÿ en a meme plusieurs qui ne dependent point du Tchi:fou, et qui relevent jmmediatement du viceroÿ.[456]

[123] L'Histoire des Roÿs dela Chine est fort obscure, Cette Confusion se peut attribuer a la Vaste êtenduë de ce Roÿaume qui a veu naistre des historiens en differentes Provinces sous des Roÿs ou des Tirans Cantonnez en même tems, en divers endroits: de Sorte que Chaque escrivain a reconnu Son Prince particulier pour le Veritable possesseur dela Monarchie, et a Supprimé la mémoire du Concurrent.

Quelques uns de leurs historiens disent que le premier de leurs Roys appellé Paoneus[457] fut tiré du Caos, lorsque la masse premiere fut developeé par l'autheur de la nature. d'autres donnent le nom de Viteÿ[458] au fondateur dela Monarchie, et disent qu'il jnventa l'art de faire des habits et des bâtimens, il batit un Temple nommé de la Paix, qui dedia à Chang:ti, c'est-à-dire au Souverain Monarque du Monde, qu'il divisa les terres en Provinces, et distribua les diverses habitations des hommes en Villes. Bourgades, Villages, et Chateaux. il orna Sa tête d'un Diadême, et choisit la Couleur Iaune, qu'il dêfendit à tous Ses Sujets, ils le reconnoissent aussi pour leur Legislateur, et disent qu'il êtoit d'une taille Si excessive, qu elle rêpondoit àpres de cinc aunes[459] de nos mesures. ils ajoutent qu'il Commanca a Regner l'an 1417, environ deux cent trente neuf ans avant le Deluge[460] et qu'il a vecu Cent anneés et qu'il à eu Vingtcinc enfans de quatre femmes: ils disent qu'il ÿ a eu pendant l'espace de 2257 anneés [124] le nombre de Cent Seize Roys de sa ligneé qui finit ala Personne de Tuintzon[461], qui fut êgorgé avec tous les Princes de son sang.[462]

---

**456** The preceding paragraph was adjusted and copied from: Ibid., 8.

**457** According to Chinese mythology, Pangu was the first being to emerge from primordial chaos. He created and eventually, after his death, also became part of the earth. Leeming, Oxford, 73–4; 307.

**458** King Vitey is a Chinese mythological figure, believed by some to be the first king of China. Mendoza, History, 69–72.

**459** An aune, or ell, was a unit of length, especially used to measure textiles. It equaled about 1.2 meters.

**460** For contemporary European attempts to date this flood, see David E. Mungello, *Curious Land: Jesuit Accommodation and the Origins of Sinology* (Honolulu: University of Hawaii Press, 1989), 126–7.

**461** Ch'in Shih-huang-ti (259–210 BCE) became China's first emperor by conquering the competing kingdoms of Hann, Chao, Wei, Ch'u, Yen and Ch'i between 230 and 221 BCE. Unsuccessful in his campaigns to the north, he unified several smaller walls into a larger defensive structure, which became the Great Wall of China. See Derek Bodde, "The state and empire of Ch'in", in: Cambridge History of China, vol. 1, 40–5.

**462** The preceding paragraph was adjusted and copied from: Manesson-Mallet, Description, vol. 2, 40.

Les plus habiles historiens Chinois Conviennent que c'est Fohi[463] qui a jetté les premiers fondemens de leur Monarchie, et que si quelques auteurs ont taché de pousser plus loin l'origine, tout ce qu'ils ont avancé est compté pour fabuleux[464], il fut nommé Tient:tse[465], c'est à dire, fils du Ciel. et qu il civilisa les peuples, êtablit des loix, fit un livre d'astrologie, jnventa la musique, et choisit un dragon[466] pour Symbole de la nation Chinoise, que les Empereurs prirent en suite pour leur Armes.[467]

Les historiens Chinois Conviennent encore des Successeurs qu'a eu Fo:hi et qui sont au nombre de six Iusques a l'Empereur Yao, savoir Chinnong[468], Hoang:ti, Chao:hao[469], Tchuen:hio[470], Tico[471], et Tchi.[472] mais en quell tems a paru Fohi? quelle a esté la dureé du Regne de ces six Empereurs jusqu'a Yao? C'est ce qui selon eux est tres jncertain, et dont on n'a point de Connoissance asse sure pour ranger ce tems la Sous une exacte et Vraÿe Chronologie.[473]

Pour renger en quelque façon au Vraÿ ils Commencent leur Chronologie depuis Yao, qui Commenca a Regner 2357.[as] a[vant] Iesu Christ dans le tems que le Deluge couvrit la terre elle se trôuve tres bien conduite: le nom des Empereurs, la dureé de leur [125] Regne, les Divisions, les revolutions, les Interregnes tout est marqué dans un grand detail. cette Chronologie est tellement etablie par tous les Scavans historiens dela Chine, que Si quelqu'un s'avisoit de rapprocher d'avantage de nos tems l'origine de leur Empire, ils Seroit regardé Comme l'Inventeur d'une Doctrine Orronneé, et exposé à des grandes peines.[474]

**463** Fuxi is a Chinese mythological figure, credited with creating, alongside sister-wife Nü Wa, the first humans and with teaching them the skills of agriculture, cooking, hunting and writing. Leeming, Oxford, 73, 140.

**464** The preceding sentence was adjusted and copied from: Du Halde, Déscription, vol. 1, 260.

**465** This corresponds to the Chinese phrase *T'ien-tze*, meaning "son of heaven."

**466** The dragon was believed to be one of the most powerful mythical creatures – able to control the rain, clouds, rivers and sea. Legends suggest Fuxi encountered the first dragon in 2962 BCE. Yan and An, Handbook, 100–10.

**467** The preceding half-sentence was adjusted and copied from: Moréri, Grand Dictionaire, vol. 2 (1694), 156.

**468** Shen Nong was a mythological emperor of ancient China, credited with the development of Chinese agriculture and pharmacoloy. Chang, China, 43.

**469** Shaohao (ca. 2600 BCE) was a legendary emperor of ancient China and believed to be the son of Huang Di, the Yellow Emperor. He is considered one of the Five August Emperors. Yang and An, Handbook, 187–9.

**470** Zhuan Xu was a mythological emperor of ancient China, associated with the separation of Heaven and Earth and the creation of the calendar. He was the grandson of Huang Di and nephew of Shaohao. He is considered one of the Five August Emperors. Chang, China, 70–1.

**471** Ku, or Gaoxin, was a mythological emperor of ancient China, associated with the advancement of music. He is considered one of the Five August Emperors. Yang and An, Handbook, 98–100.

**472** Zhi was a mythological emperor of ancient China and the son of Ku. Ibid., 99.

**473** The preceding paragraph was adjusted and copied from: Du Halde, Déscription, vol. 1, 260.

**474** The preceding sentence was adjusted and copied from: Ibid.

Il est jmpossible d'accorder leur Supputation avec celle dela Vulgate[475], a la quelle nous nous attachons, amoins que de Supposer que les Chinois ont eu des Empereurs, plusieurs Siecles avant le Deluge: ce qui est jncroiable. si on Voudroit exposer ce qui contient leurs monuments, ils ne paroitront gueres plus surs en Chronologie, que le calcul dont les Chaldeéns et les Egiptiens se servoient autrefois, pour prouver l'ancienneté fabuleuse de leurs Empires.[476]

Vous pouvez Conjecturer Monsieur par ce peu de lignes, comment ces genealogies Sont Suspectes, et en quel aveuglement le Peuple Chinois est enseveli, qu'ils ne Connoissent rien de ce qui est de la Creation de notre Premier Pere Adam[477], car si on les devroit croire ler premier Pere seroit mil ans plus vieux qu'Adam. Ils comptent Vigt deux Dÿnasties ou familles Imperiales qui ont occupé Successivement le trône dont ils Ignorent la dureé des sept premiers Empereurs, et pour vous donner une jdeé breve de leur Chronologie, [126] Ie joint icÿ l'ordre et suite de leurs Empereurs qui ont occupé successivement le trône Iusques a Yong tching maintenant regnant.

**Noms des Empereurs qui ont Gouverne**
**L'Empire de la Chine**[478]
**Fohi, Chin:nong, Hoang:ti, Chao:hao, Tchuen:hio, Tico, Tchi.**

C'est une chose certaine parmi les Chinois que ces Empereurs ont êté les fondateurs de leur Empire: mais ils jgnorent quelle a esté la dureé de leur Regne. il n'est pas de même des Suivans, dont ils ont une Chronologie êxacte et suivie.

**Yao.**

a regné seul 72 ans, et 28 avec **Chún**, qu'il associa à l'Empire

**Chun.**

à regne seul 50 ans

**Ordre et suite des XXII. Dÿnasties ou Familles Imperiales, qui ont occupé successivement le Trône.**

**1.e Dynastie**

475 The Vulgate was a Latin translation of the Bible, largely completed by Christian scholar Jerome, which was the Roman Catholic Church's official version after the sixteenth-century Council of Trent.

476 The preceding paragraph was adjusted and copied from: Moréri, *Grand Dictionaire*, vol. 2 (1718), 330.

477 According to tradition, Adam was the first human being created by the Christian God. All human life followed from him and his partner, Eve. Genesis 1–5.

478 This entire catalogue, including the heading and the introductory paragraph, was copied from: Du Halde, Description, vol. 1, 266. The author does not account for those periods when there were several competing Chinese kingdoms. Rather, he follows a straight evolution, typically favoring dynasties that had their capital in Peking or were located in southeast China. For a modern rendering of these dynasties, see Brunhild Staiger, Stefan Friedrich and Hans-Wilm Schütte (eds.), *Das große China-Lexikon* (Darmstadt: Primus, 2008), xi.

Nommeé **Hia**[479], elle Compte 17 Empereúrs dans l'espace de 458 ans.
**2.ᵉ Dÿnastie**
Nommeé **Chang** ou **Yng**[480], elle Compte 28 Empereurs dans l'espace de 644 ans
**3ᵉ** Dÿnastie
Nommeé **Tcheoú:**[481] elle Compte 35 Empereurs dans l'espace de 873 ans
**4ᵉ** Dÿnastie
Nommeé **Tsin.**[482] elle Compte 4 Empereurs dans l'espace de 43. ans
**5.ᵉ** Dÿnastie
Nommee **Han.**[483] Elle Compte 25 Empereurs dans l'espace de 426 ans
[127] **6.ᵉ** Dÿnastie
Nommeé **Heou:han.**[484] elle Compte 2 Empereurs dans l'espace de 44 ans
**7ᵉ** Dÿnastie
Nommeé **Tsin.**[485] elle Compte 15 Empereurs dans l'espace de 155. ans
**8.ᵉ** Dÿnastie
Nommeé **Song.**[486] elle Compte 8 Empereurs dans l'espace de 59. ans
**9.ᵉ** Dÿnastie
Nommeé **Tsi.**[487] elle Compte 5 Empereurs dans l'espace de 23. ans
**10.ᵉ** Dÿnastie

---

**479** The Xia Dynasty, founded by Emperor Yü, extended from ca. 2070 to ca. 1600 BCE. It was the first dynasty in recorded Chinese history and rumored to have received its rule from the Five August Emperors. Chang, China, 71–3.

**480** The Shang Dynasty extended from ca. 1556 to 1046 BCE. See David N. Keightley, "The Shang: China's First Historical Dynasty", in: Cambridge History of Ancient China, 232–91.

**481** The Chou Dynasty extended from ca. 1025 to 256 BCE. It politically and military dominated China only until 771 BCE, in a period known as the Western Chou. See Edward L. Shaughnessy, "Western Zhou History", in: Cambridge History of Ancient China, 292–351.

**482** The Ch'in Dynasty extended from 221 to 207 BCE. Its was the first imperial dynasty, after founder Ch'in Shuh-huang-ti conquered six competing kingdoms. Bodde, State, 20–102.

**483** The Han Dynasty extended from 210 BCE to 6 CE and then again from 9 to 220. Its long reign created relative peace and encouraged economic and cultural development, including the Silk Road. See Loewe, Former Han, 103–222; Hans Bielenstein, "Wang Mang, the restoration of the Han dynasty, and Later Han", in: Cambridge History of China, vol. 1, 223–90.

**484** The Three Kingdoms lasted from 220 to 228, when China was divided between three states. The author here follows the western Shu, which extended from 221–263. Its founder descended from the Han clan and thus proclaimed himself to be its legitimate successor. See Dorothy Perkins, *Encyclopedia of China: the Essential Reference to China, its History and Culture* (New York: Routledge, 1999), 56, 203.

**485** The Chin Dynasty extended from 265 to 420. Ibid., 246.

**486** The Sixteen Kingdoms lasted from 304 to 439, following the fracturing of northern China and the Chin Dynasty. The state that followed the Chin in southern China was the Sung Dynasty, which extended from 420 to 479 and governed from Nanking. Denis Twitchett, "Introduction", in: Cambridge History of China, vol. 3, 5.

**487** The Southern Ch'i Dynasty extended from 479 to 502. It governed southern China from Nanking. Ibid.

Nommeé **Leang.**[488] elle Compte 4 Empereurs dans l'espace de 55. ans
**11.**ᵉ Dÿnastie.
Nommeé **Tchin.**[489] elle Compte 5 Empereurs dans l'espace de 33. ans
**12.**ᵉ Dÿnastie
Nommeé **Souÿ**. elle Compte 3 Empereurs dans l'espace de 29. ans
**13**ᵉ Dÿnastie
Nommeé **Tang.**[490] elle Compte 20 Empereurs dans l'espace de 289. ans
**14.**ᵉ Dÿnastie
Nommeé **Heoú:leang.**[491] elle Compte 2 Empereurs dans l'espace de 16. ans
**15.**ᵉ Dÿnastie
Nommeé **Heoú:tang.**[492] elle Compte 4 Empereurs dans l'espace de 13. ans
**16.**ᵉ Dÿnastie
Nommeé **Heoú:tsin.**[493] elle Compte 2 Empereurs dans l'espace de 11. ans
**17 Dÿnastie**
Nommeé **Heou:han.**[494] elle Compte 2 Empereurs dans l'espace de 4. ans.
[128] **18.ᵉ Dynastie**
Nommeé **Heoú:tcheoú.**[495] elle Compte 3 Empereurs dans l'espace de 9. ans
**19.**ᵉ Dÿnastie
Nommeé **Song.**[496] elle Compte 18 Empereurs dans l'espace de 319 ans
**20.**ᵉ Dÿnastie
Nommeé **Yúen.**[497] elle Compte 9 Empereurs dans l'espace de 89. ans
**21.**ᵉ Dÿnastie
Nommeé **Ming.** elle Compte 16 Empereurs dans l'espace de 236. ans

---

**488** The Liang Dynasty extended from 502 to 557. It governed southern China from Nanking. Ibid, 5–6.
**489** The Ch'en Dyasty extended from 557 to 589. It governed southern China from Nanking. Ibid.
**490** The T'ang Dynasty extended from 618 to 907, with a short interruption from 690 to 705. Imperial power became increasingly centralized in this period and also was felt in neighboring kingdoms, such as Korea and Cochinchina. Ibid.
**491** The Five Dynasties and Ten Kingdoms period lasted from 907 to 979, following the fall of the T'ang Dynasty to a military coup. The state to emerge from this rebellion was the later Liang Dynasty, which extended from 907 to 923. See Paul Jakov Smith, "Introduction: the Sung Dynasty and its Precursors, 907–1279", in: Cambridge History of China, vol. 5, 1–11.
**492** The Later T'ang Dynasty extended from 923 to 936. Ibid.
**493** The Later Chin Dynasty extended from 936 to 946. Ibid.
**494** The Later Han Dynasty extended from 947 to 950. Ibid.
**495** The Later Chou Dynasty extended from 951 to 960. It was the last of the Five Dynasties and again ended in a military coup. Ibid.
**496** The Sung Dynasty extended from 960 to 1279. Twitchett and Fairbank, Cambridge History of China, vol. 5.
**497** The Yüan Dynasty extended from 1271–1368. Established by Kublai Khan, its imperial family was from the Mongol ethnic group. See Morris Rossabi, "The reign of Khubilai kan", in: Cambridge History of China, vol. 6, 414–89.

**22.e** Dÿnastie
Nommeé **Tsing** Maintenant regnante elle Compte Iusqu'a ce jour 1724 trois Empereurs.

Pour donner plus d'jntelligence a cette Chronologie, il me reste a vous dire que vous devez observer, pour ne pas tomber en erreur, que l'anneé de la mort de chaque Empereur en quelque mois qu'elle arrive, est compteé toute entierre par mi celles de Son Regne, et quoÿ que Son Successeur Soit deja reconnu, on fait l'honneur au defunt Prince d'expedier toutes les affaires Sous Son nom. le nouvel Empereur ne donne presque jamais le Sien qu'a l'anneé suivante, amoins que la Couronne ne passe dans une autre famille, car alors l'anneé de Son regne, commence le même jour qu'il a monte sur le trône.[498]

L'Empereur Tsin.chi:hoang[499] pour Se garantier des Invasions Continueles que les Tartares faisoient dans la Chine, fit Construire cette fameuse muraille qui n'a gueres moins de 500. lieuës, Si lon Compte tous les detours. elle est fortifieé [129] de tours d'espace en espace, a peupres comme les murailles des Villes de guerre et dans les endroits les plus aisez a forcer, on ÿ a êlevé tout de Suite deux ou trois remparts qui se defendent les uns les autres. elle Serpente tout le long des plus hautes Colines, tantot plus haute, et tantot plus basse Selon la disposition du lieu et l'jrregularité du terrain et non pas tireé par tout au niveau comme quelques uns l'ont Crû. D'elle-même elle n'egale pas les murailles ordinaires de leurs Villes, et Sa largeur n'est que de quatre ou cinq pieds tout au plus. Presque tout l'ouvrage est de brique, et si bien batie qu'il est encore presque tout entier, quoi que faite l'an 221 avant Iesu Christ. Cette Celebre Barriere n'a pas empeche les Tartares d'entrer dans ce Vaste Empire, et de le ravager Souvent, Sur tout au 17.e Siecle[500] que les Tartares Orienteaux jnvahirent tout l'Empire, cette revolution fut d'un exemple funeste, car elle a este Suivie dela ruine entiere dela Dynastie nommeé Ming qui finit par Hoai tsong ou tsong tching[501], pour faire place a celle des Tartares qui gouvernent encore maintenant ce Vaste Empire aveq un autorité absolué Sous le nom de Tsing.

Pour vous donner Mons.r une Ideé d'un evenement Si remarquable, Ie Vous joint icÿ un petit detail, qui vous jnstruira Comment les Tartares ont pû Conquerir et conserver un Empire Si Considerable comme la Chine avec un armeé de 80 mille hommes; il arriva que vers l'an [130] 1644. un des petits Roÿs dela Tartarie Orientale, s'etant plaint de quelque jnjustice faite a Ses Sujets par les marchands Chinois[502], sans en avoir eu

498 The preceding sentence was adjusted and copied from: Du Halde, Déscription, vol. 1, 265.
499 This refers to Emperor Ch'in Shih-huang-ti.
500 The preceding paragraph was adjusted and copied from: Moréri, Grand Dictionaire, vol. 2 (1718), 326.
501 This refers to the Ch'ung-chen Emperor, the last ruler in the Ming Dynasty.
502 The Manchu initally were a Ming tributary population and depended on annual diplomatic visits to Peking to trade. The Ch'ung-chen Emperor began to curb the number of tributaries – or as the Man-

Satisfaction; entra pour se Venger, dans le Leanton avec une nombreuse armeé: ainsi la guerre S'alluma, durant laquelle un nomme Le Chinois[503] fit revolter les Provinces les plus êloigneés et marcha droit a Pekin, dont il sçavoit que les meilleures troupes êtoient sorties, pour aller sur la frontiere s'opposer aux Tartares. l'Empereur[504] ÿ avoit pourtant encore 70 mille hommes; mais presque tous gagnez par les emissaires des revoltez qui leur ouvrirent les portes, et leur Chef mit tout a feu et a Sang. ce pauvre Prince se voÿant ainsi trahi, proposa de Sortir de Son palais, a la tete de 600. gardes qui lui restoient, pour mourir glorieusement les armes a la main; mais pas un d'eux ne voulut le Suivre. De quoÿ dêsesperé, il Se retira dans un Iardin avec sa fille[505], ou, apres avoir êcrit de Son propre Sang ces paroles sur le bord de Sa veste: Les miens m'ont abandonné: fais de moi tout ce qu'il te plaira, mais êpargne mon peuple; il fit tomber a Ses pieds d'un Seul coup de Sabre, cette jeune Princesse, et Se pendit lui même a un arbre. Apres Sa mort tout plia Sous la puissance de l'usurpateur, exepte le Commandant[506] des troupes Chinoises et Tartares, qui ne voulant point Se Soumettre, fut assiegé dans Le Leanton, mais jnutilement; quo[ique] le Tÿran pour le reduire, lui fit voir son pere charge de fers, protestant qu'il l'êgorgeroit a ses ÿeux s'il differoit [131] a Se rendre. ce grand homme prefera Son devoir a toute la tendresse naturelle, et le Sang qu'il vit répandre ne Servit qu'a l'animer davantage a la Vengeance. Ainsi setant reconcilié avec le Tartare, ils Ioignirent leurs troupes ensemble et marcherent droit a l'ennemi[507], qui n'ayant osé les attendre regagna Pekin; et apres ÿ avoir brûlé le Palais, et tout ce qui avoit echape a Sa premiere fureur, il s'enfuit dans la Province de Chensi, chargé des depouilles de l'Empire et dela malediction des peuples. on le poursuivit, mais il Se cacha avec tant de Soin, qu'on ne put jamais le decouvrir, ni

chu used them, merchants – allowed on these trips in the early 1600s, a decision which correlated with a period of economic hardship in the north. This certainly contributed to the Manchu decision to invade the south. More directly, however, the Manchu conflict resulted from Seven Grievances they issued in 1618, which accused Ming emperors of murder and of encouraging political rebellion. Fredrick W. Mote, *Imperial China, 900–1800* (Cambridge, MA: Harvard UP, 2003), 784–810.

**503** This might refer to the nickname *Chuang Wang*, or "Dashing King," given first to Gao Yingxiang, leader of the Chinese peasant revolt, and then passed on to his successor, Li Tzu-ch'eng. See Roger V. Des Forges, *Cultural Centrality and Political Change in Chinese History: Northeast Henan in the Fall of the Ming* (Stanford, CA: Stanford UP, 2003), 182, 193.

**504** This again denotes the Ch'ung-chen Emperor.

**505** Princess Kunya (1630–1644) was the daughter of the Ch'ung-chen Emperor and Empress Zhou. She supposedly was murdered by her father, when he faced incoming enemy troops. For more on her death, see Frederic E. Wakeman, Jr., *Telling Chinese History* (Berkeley: University of California Press, 2009), 67.

**506** Wu San-kuei (1612–1678) was a brigade general in the Ming Dynasty and one of their last military hold-outs. He offered his loyalty to the Ch'ing Dynasty after the emperor's death but eventually led a rebellion against Emperor K'ang-hsi from 1674 until his own death in 1678. Dennerline, Shun-chih, 80–2; Spence, K'ang-Hsi, 138–43.

**507** This again denotes Li Tzu-ch'eng.

même Savoir ce qu'il etoit devenu. Cepedendant les Tartares entrerent dans Pekin, et tournèrent tellement les esprits en leur faveur, qu'on les pria même de prendre Soin de l'empire, dont ils se rendirent bientot les maitres absolus. Le Roÿ Tartare nomme Tsong:té[508], n'eut pas le tems de jouir de Sa nouvelle Conquête. il mourút en ÿ entrant et laissa à Amavan[509] Son frere, le gouvernement de l'etat, et de l'education de Son fils, qui n'avoit encore que Six ans.

Amavan acheva de Soumettre toutes les Provinces. Prince veritablement grand par Son Courage, par Sa Sagesse, par Ses Succés; mais plus recommandable par Sa fidelité et Son desjnteressement: car pouvant retenir l'Empire pour lui, il le remit entre les mains de Son neveu Chun:tchi des que ce jeune Monarque eut atteint l'age de gouverner.[510]

Ou san gueÿ General Chinois reconnut trop tard la faute ~~la faute~~ qu'il avoit faite, d'avoir eu recours aux Tartares [132] pour se delivrer du Tyran, et il disoit quelque fois qu'il avoit fait venir des Lions pour chasser les Chiens. cependant il receut des mains de Chun tchi la dignité de Roÿ et le titre de Ping si[511], qui Signifie pacificateur d'occident. on luÿ assigna pour le lieu de Sa residence la ville de Si:nganfou Capitale de la Province de Chensi, la quelle avoit été ravageé par le fer et par le feu.

Chun:tchi se voyant maitre des Provinces Septentrionales tourna ses armes vers les Meredionales[512], les quelles il soumit en peu de tems a Son obeisance, apres avoir pris le petit fils de l'Empereur Hong:quang.[513] qu'il fit conduire a Pekin ou il fut étranglé. il prit aussi un autre petit fils[514] de Chin:tsong treizieme Empereur dela derniere dynastie qu'il fit decapiter. il assiega la ville de Tche:kiang[515], Capitale de la Province

---

**508** This refers to Hung Taiji.

**509** Prince Dorgon, also known as Ama Van to the Jesuits (1612–1650), was a Manchu general and regent for nephew Fulin, or the Shun-Chih Emperor, from 1643–1650. Ibid., 73–104; Dennerline, Shun-chih, 70–2.

**510** The preceding two paragraphs were adjusted and copied from: Moréri, Grand Dictionaire, vol. 2 (1718), 336.

**511** Emperor Shun-Chih rewarded Wu San-kuei with the title of *Pingxi Wang*, or "Prince Pacifier of the West" and sent him to Yunnan Provinces in the early 1670s. It was from here he began his rebellion in 1674.

**512** The Southern Ming was a loyalist movement that emerged around Nanking and in the southwest after the Ming Dynasty collapsed in 1644. It extended until 1683, when its final supporters were captured by Ch'ing armies. See Lynn A. Struve, "The Southern Ming, 1644–1662", in: Cambridge History of China, vol. 7, 641–725.

**513** Chu Yu-sung, also known as Hóngguāng and the Prince of Fu (1607–1646), was a grandson of Emperor Wanli and the first ruler in the Southern Ming Dynasty. He was captured in Nanking in 1646, after ruling only one year. Ibid., 642.

**514** This likely refers to Chu Yu-lang, the Yongli Emperor (1623–1662), who was the fourth and final ruler in the Southern Ming Dynasty. He and his son were captured in Burma in 1662 and executed, likely by strangulation and not decapitation. Ibid., 678–725; Spence, K'ang-hsi, 136–7.

**515** This refers to modern-day Hangzhou, a city in northern Chexiang Province that became the latter's capital in 1132.

du dit nom ou Lo:vang[516] en etoit Roÿ et qui refusa le titre d'Empereur, monta sur les murailles, et a genoux il Supplia les Tartares d'epargner Son peuple, et que S'il leur falloit une Victime, il S offroit volontiers pour Sauver la vie a Ses Sujets. en même tems il Sort de la ville, et S'abandonne a la discretion du vainquer.[517]

Il ÿ avoit deja treize Provinces[518] reduites Sous la puissance de l'Empereur Tartare, quand A:ma:van, oncle et touteur de l'Empereur vint a mourir. il fut autant regretté apres Sa mort, qu'il S'etoit fait estimer des chinois [133] c'est proprement luÿ qui a affermi Sur le trône la famille regnante des Tartares.

Son frere[519] pretendit lui Succeder dans la tutelle du Ieune Empereur: mais tous les Grands S'y opposerent, sur ce que l'Empereur aÿant quatorze ans, il etoit capable de gouverner l'Empire par lui même. il fut donc reglé que ce Prince prendroit en main les rênes du gouvernement. il le fit d'une manière qui lui gagna d'abord le Ceur des peuples, au lieu que les Empereurs Chinois avoient Coutume de se tenir renfermez dans leur Palais, Chun:tchi plus populaire commenca par Se montrer en public, et donner un acces facile aupres de Sa personne.

Il ne Changea rien, ni dans les Loix, ni dans le Gouvernem.t de la Chine. il conserva les six Tribuneaux Souverains:[520] mais ~~mais~~ il voulut qu'ils ne fussent qu'a Peking. et il regla qu'outre le President Chinois, il ÿ en auroit aussi un autre Tartare[521]

L'Empereur aÿant Epouse[522] la veuve d'un Seigneur Tartare le quel il avoit envoÿe à l'autre monde pour marier sa veuve, la fit declarer Reine, il en eut un fils qui fut fort Cheri de l'Empereur, il vecut que trois mois et Sa Mere le Suivit de pres au tombeau. l'Empereur fut jnconsolable de cette perte. il laissa aller Si loin les exes de tristesse, qu'en peu de jours ce Malheureu Prince fuit reduit a l'extremité et l'on desespera de Sa vie. il fit approcher quatre Seigneurs de Sa Cour[523] et les declara tuteurs de Son

**516** Place unknown.

**517** The preceding paragraph was adjusted and copied from: Du Halde, Description, vol. 1, 467.

**518** Before his death in 1650, Dorgon conquered all but Kweichow and Yunnan provinces. Dennerline, Shun-Chih, 116–7.

**519** Ajige (1605–1651) was a Manchu general, who lead a failed military coup after his brother Dorgon's death. Ibid., 74–102.

**520** This refers to the six ministries at the center of the Ming and Ch'ing administrations. See page 313, ft. 442.

**521** The preceding three paragraphs were adjusted and copied from: Du Halde, Description, vol. 1, 470.

**522** Hsiao-hsien (1639–1660) was a favorite consort of Emperor Shun-chih, who died while grieving the recent death of her son. See "Empress Xiao Xiao of the Dongoo clan", in: *Biographical Dictionary of Chinese Women*, eds. Lily Xiao Hong Lee, Clara Lau and A.D. Stefanowska, vol. 1 (New York: Routledge, 1998), 344–5.

**523** Emperor Shun-chih appointed four ministers to oversee his young son's reign in 1661. These were Soni (1601–1667), Suksaha (d. 1667), Ebilun (d. 1674) and Oboi (ca. 1610–1669). They governed China in the latter's stead until 1669. Spence, K'ang-hsi, 126–9.

plus Ieune fils nommé Cang:hi[524] qui n'avoit encore que huit ans. puis il fit apporter [134] le Manteau Imperial, il s'en revetit, et en se ramassant sur son lit en une espece de peloton: voila que je vous quitte, leur dit il, et au même moment il expira vers le milieu dela nuit a l'age de vingt quatre ans. Le lendemain Cang:hi monta sur le Trône, ou il recut les hommages de tous les Grands de l'Empire.

Tout fut assez tranquille sous le gouvernement des quatre tuteurs. les premieres marques d'autorité qu'ils donnerent, fut de faire trancher la téte au Chef des eunuques[525], qui avoit êté l'auteur et la source de tant de malheurs arriveés durant le regne du defunt Empereur, qui regreta fort, avant mourir, son affection pour les Eunuques,

Il parut ensuite un Edit[526] par le quel il étoit ordonné sous peine de la vie, a tous Ceux qui habitoient les cotes de la mer, de quiter leurs habitations, et d'aller S'etablir a trois lieux plus loin dans l'jnterieur des terres. on rasa aussi toutes les Villes, Forteresses, et Bourgades maritimes, et le commerce de la Mer fut absolument interdit: pour affoiblir par la la puissance du fameux Pirate Tching:tching:cong[527], qui s'etoit rendu maitre de la Mer.[528]

Lors qu'il n'etoit encore âgé que de 15 a 16 ans il commenca de tenir les resnes de Son Empire, il S'applica avec tant de Soin a le gouverner, qu'il a toujours. voulu prendre connoissance de toutes les affaires, et les regler par lui même après avoir entendu le Sentiment de ses Ministres et de Son conseil.

[135] L'application jnfatigable de ce grand Prince a toutes les affaires de Son Etat, fit que la Chine jouissoit d'une profonde Paix. toút occupé qu'etoit ce Prince du Gouvernement de Son Empire, il trouva encore le loisir de S'appliquer aux Sciences pour les quelles il avoit un gout et un genie particulier, c'est ce qui l'engage a Souffrir les Missionaires, pour S'jnstruire des arts et les Sciences des Europeéns, et il permit dans tout l'Empire la Religion Chrêtienne.

Il s'est acquis une plus grande gloire en arrestant toutes les dangereuses revoltes et maintenant l'Empire de la Chine tout entier Sous Son obeisance contre tant de Si

---

**524** This refers to the K'ang-hsi Emperor.

**525** Eunuchs were castrated men, often assigned as bureaucrats and guards in the imperial household. Wu Liang-fu (d. 1661) was the favorite eunuch of Emperor Shun-chih and joined in several of his military and political campagins. He was executed soon after the latter's death, in an effort to recentralize power in the imperial court. Dennerline, Shun-chih, 112–3; Spence, K'ang-hsi, 161, 166–7.

**526** In 1661, the four regents issued an imperial edict, ordering all coastal residents in modern-day Guangdong, Fukien, Zhejian, Jiangsu and Shantung provinces to relocate their residences about 45 kilometers inland. Ostensibly, this effort was a military maneuver, but it really intended to crack down on illegal trading, which officials believed was removing Chinese specie during a period of economic hardship. See Ramon H. Myers and Yeh-Chien Wang, "Economic Developments, 1644–1800", in: Cambridge History of China, vol. 9, 565.

**527** This refers to Cheng Ch'eng-kung, a Ming loyalist.

**528** The preceding three paragraphs were adjusted and copied from: Du Halde, Description, vol. 1, 472–4.

grands ennemis qu'il a fallu Conquerir, que ne S'en est acquis ce fameux A:ma:van Son oncle tuteur de Son Pere, dont jaÿ parle ci devant. en effet il ne couta presque rien aux Tartares, les Chinois Se detruissant eux mêmes les uns les autres, et les plus braves d'entre eux Combattant pour les Tartares contre leur propre nation.

Apres avoir eteint toutes ces Revoltes, et donné la paix à ce Vaste Empire et avoir establi le bon ordre, et avoir reformé les abus qui S'y êtoient glisez durant la licence dela guerre, et a faire regner la vigeur des loix la Sureté et abondance. dans toutes les Provinces, il eut soin de mettre de bons officiers habiles et jntelligens et d'une probité reconnue dans les Charges les plus Considerables de la Cour et des Provinces c'est aussi a en faire un bon Choix, et a maintenir dans [136] le devoir ceux qu'il établit, qu'il s'etudia principalement.

En éffet, le gouvernement de la Chine est parfaitement Monarchique; tout s ÿ rapporte à un Seul. les officiers inferieurs dependent entierement des Superieurs, dans une ville c'est le Gouverneur, qui Seul a le pouvoir de decider de toutes les affaires de cette Ville, dans une Province c'est le viceroÿ ou le Gouverneur de la Province: et cette forme de Gouvernement qui de Soy est tres parfaite, demande que les Gouverneurs des Villes et des Pronvinces entre les mains des quels reside toute l'aútorité du Prince, Soient des gens d'une grande probité et d'une jntegrité a l'épreuve, pour ne se pas laisser Corrompre, et pour ne vendre la Justice.[529] ainsi qu'on ne doit pas acuser les Tartares d'avoir troublé le bon ordre, au contraire l'Empereur kāṅ:hȳ ou Cang:hÿ a fait revivre le bon ordre et la plus belle Police telle comme Je vous l'aÿ escrit aú commencement de Cette lettre.

L'Empereur ayant donne une Paix Solide a L'Empire il Songa pour laisser apres Sa mort un Successeur qui put Supporter l'jmportante Charge de Gouverner eficacement l'Empire, il desherita Son Second fils Hoang:tai:tçe[530] (c'est a dire, Prince heritier) par ce qu'il l'avoit eu de la Princesse[531] qui à le titre d'Imperatrice dont les enfans Succedent à l'Empire preferablement aux enfans des autres femmes, etant encore tout Ieune fut ètabli Successeur de l'Empire, [137] L'Empereur l'aimoit extremement, il ne Se pouvoit pas Se Separer de luÿ. Venant a l'age de 30 ans l'esprit lui tourna et vint Comme fou, L Empereur prevoÿant qu'il Seroit difficile, qu'il put Supporter l'jmportante Charge de Sacrifier aú Ciel, a la terre, et aux Ancestres, non obstant toutes les

529 The preceding three paragraphs were adjusted and copied from: Joachim Bouvet, *Histoire de l'empereur de la Chine* (The Hague: Meyndert Uytwerf, 1699), 43–5.

530 Yin-jêng (1674–1725) was K'ang-hsi's second surviving son and his favored *Huang Taiz*, or crown prince, during two different periods, 1676–1708 and 1709–1712. A frequent target of court politics, he was accused of plotting against the emperor, alongside his uncle Songgotu (1636–1703) and stripped of his title in 1708. K'ang-hsi restored Yin-jêng in 1709 but again deprived him of his title in 1712, possibly after evidence of mental illness. Spence, K'ang-hsi, 123, 155–61.

531 Hsiao-ch'êng (1654–1674) was K'ang-hsi's first wife and first empress. She died after giving birth to their second surviving son, Yin-jêng. See Jonathan D. Spence, *Emperor of China: Self-Portrait of K'ang-hsi* (New York: Vintage Books, 1988), 115–7.

diligences possibles que le Pere Moron[532] Iesuite fit pour le maintenir dans la Succession, il n'a pas pu S'empecher de le desheriter une Seconde fois, apres avoir attendu dix a douze anneés Ses grandes jnfirmitez Continuerent comme auparavant, L'Empereur au jour de Sa mort declara pour Successeur en sa place, Son quatrieme fils de la Reÿne Té[533] Surnommé Jōn:tchin ou Iong:tching.[534]

L'Empereur Kân:hÿ ou Cang:hÿ mourut le 20 decembre 1722 agé de 69 ans sept mois 25 jours, apres avoir regne 61 ans 10 mois 13 Iours. Le lendemain Le Nouvel Empereur âgé d'environ quarante cinq ans, S'assit Sur le trône à cinq heures du matin et prit le nom de Iong:tching, qui Signifie paix ferme, Concorde jndissoluble. il fut reconnu de tous les Princes, de tous les Grands, et des Mandarins qui Composent les tribuneaux.

Des Son avenement a la Couronne ce Prince donna des marques du mècontentement qu'il avoit de quelques uns de Ses freres, et Sur tout du Second nommé Hóang:-tai:tse qu'il envoya en Exil en Tartarie avec le Père Moron. Il rapella ensuite à Pekin son quatorzieme frere[535] qui Commandoit l'armeé Chinoise; son huitieme[536], neuvieme[537], et dixieme frere[538] tomberent de même dans sa disgrace. jl n'y a que le 13me.[539] [138] auquel il donna toute Sa Confiance, et qu'il fit entrer dans toutes les affaires du Gouvernement, en même tems il fit de Capiter plusieurs des Principaux Manderins de la Cour, qui estoient pour son frere Hoang:tai:tse, il rapella aussi plusieurs Gouverneurs des Provinces qu'il Subsonoit, dont quelques uns firent mis a mort, et les autres envoÿé en exil. ausitot il fit publier le Manifeste qui suit.

---

**532** João Mourão (1681–1726) was a Portuguese Jesuit, who allied himself with Yin-t'ang during his conflicts with the K-ang-hsi Emperor. He was exiled to northwestern China alongside with the prince in the 1720s and eventually strangled by Yung-cheng's supporters. Wills, Jr., China, 169.

**533** Hsiao-kung (1660–1723) was one of K'ang-hsi's favorite consorts and the mother of his successor. She thus earned in 1723 the title Empress Dowager. See "Empress Xiao Gongren of the Uya clan", in: Biographical Dictionary, 349–50.

**534** This refers to the Yung-cheng Emperor.

**535** Yin-t'i (1688–1756) was K'ang-hsi's fourteenth surviving son and one of Yung-cheng's chief competitors for the Ch'ing succession. He led patrols of China's northwest frontier between 1718 and 1722, a privileged military position, although he later was placed under house arrest by his brother. Some of his supporters claimed K'ang-hsi's final will was a forgery and Yin-t'i the rightful imperial heir. Zelin, Yung-cheng, 185–7.

**536** Yin-ssu (1681–1726) was K'ang-hsi's eighth surviving son and another of Yung-cheng's chief competitors for the Ch'ing succession. The court supported him to replace Yin-t'i, but he later endorsed the faction behind Yin-t'i. He ultimately died while imprisoned during Yung-cheng's reign. Ibid., 186–7.

**537** Yin-t'ang (1683–1726) was K'ang-hsi's ninth surviving son and Yin-ssu's chief political ally. He was removed to northwest China and later arrested duing Yung-cheng's reign. Ibid., 187.

**538** Yin'e (1683–1741) was K'ang-hsi's tenth surviving son and another supporter of Yin-ssu. Ibid.

**539** Yin-hsiang (1686–1730) was K'ang-hsi's thirteenth surviving son and Yung-cheng's chief political ally and primary advisor during his early reign. Ibid., 196, 204.

**Nouvelle Promulgation Faite à la Premiere anneé du Regne de l Empereur Yoñg:tchiñg par la quelle Sa Majesté a la bonté d'ordonner qu'on pardonne aux criminels.**

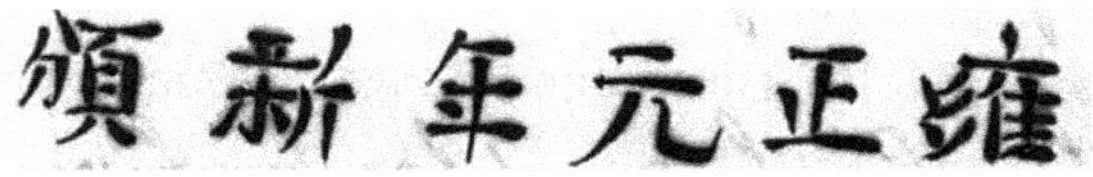


on lit ces Mots chinois par la droite oú nous finissons la ligne

pān : sīn : niên : yuên_ tching_ Yong

[**Figure 16:** Chinese letters, translated as "L Empereur Yong:tching mande et dit"]

qui veut dire L Empereur Yong:tching mande et dit.

Hoân

ngēn

tcháo

ché

[**Figure 17:** Chinese letters, translated as "J'ay Receu du Ciel ma destine a L'Empire"]

C'est a dire J'ay Receu du Ciel ma destiné a L'Empire

Ma Famille Roÿalle à este assisteé du Ciel a Commencer [139] depuis mes saints et divins ancetres Jusqu'apresent l'Empereur mon aÿeul surnomme l'jllústre par sa force a fonde notre Monarchie a la Chine, le Deffunt Empereur mon Pere à gouverne cet Empire soixante et un ans, Sa vertu à fleuri, son merite à esté eminent, il a este admirable dans la Science de la robbe et de l'epeé[540], il a tenus la terre et la mer en paix. Son Regne à esté de longe dureé. Lorsque nous ÿ pensions le moins il a quitté les Manderins et le peuple, ausitot il est monté au Ciel porté Sur un Char traisné par le dragon. apres m'avoir luÿ meme remis Son divin pouvoir pour gouverner l'Empire.

540 This note appears in the right margin: "il a este l'etoille fixe des Manderins de robbe, et la planette des Manderin[s] d'armes." The Ch'ing Dynasty divided its administration into separate civil and military offices, which in turn were subdivided into nine different rankings. See Beverly Jackson and David Hugus, *Ladder to the Clouds: Intrigue and Tradition in Chinese Rank* (Berkeley, CA: Ten Speed Press, 1999), 129–38.

Ie Suis le fils de sa Dame Té Reÿne du feu l'Empereur mon Pere, cÿ devant le second fils de l'Empereur étant encore tout jeune fut ètabli Successeur de l'empire, l'Empereur l'aimoit il ne pouvoit pas Se Separer de luÿ, apres avoir eu la bonté de le declarer Son Successeur, il l'aima encore plus qu'au paravant, tout cela n'a pas eu une bonne Suite car a l'age de[541], virilité l'esprit lui tourna, ses jnfirmites l'ont rendus comme fou, feu l'Empereur mon Pere pensant qu'il Seroit difficile que ce second fils put Supporter l'jmportante Charge de Sacrifier au Ciel, à la terre, et aux Ancêtres, il n'a pas pû S'empecher de le desheriter une Seconde fois apres avoir attendu dix et tant d'anneés, Ses grandes infirmites Continuerent comme auparavant, et n'a jamais peu Se retablir, c'est pour cela que l'Empereur mon Pere au jour de Sa mort, m'ordonna de continuer la Monarchie de nos Ancêtres, me Chargant de l'empire, mes freres aines, Cadets, et neveus, Sont en tres grand nombre, mon dessin est Seulement que nous ne Soions qu'un, que nous Sojons tres unis, et qu'il n'y ait nul deffaut dans notre union, [140] que le bonheur de la Paix nous soit Commun et que notre gouvernement Soit toujours fondé Sur la pierre ferme. Confucius dit pendant trois ans il ne faut rien Changer a la methode de son Pere.

Feu l'Empereur mon Pere depuis le Commencement de Son Regne jusqu'apresent, ses beaux reglemens et ses admirables actions, peuvent Servir de modelle a tous les Siecles à venir, Ie Suis obligé de me conformer toujours a Sa maniere de gouverner; Ie n'oserai pas ÿ faire le moindre Changement, pour quoi Se contenter de ne rien changer à la methode de Son Pere seulement pendant trois ans. qùand au feu mon Pere il connoissoit Veritablement les gens, et Scavoit de quoi chacun etoit capable, il êtoit tres clair voÿant et tres ferme, pour moi apresent je Souhaite ardement que vous tous grands Mandarins dela Cour tant ceux du dedans du Palais que ceux du de hors m'assisties, afin que nous nous protegions toujours mutuellement, vous deves travailler pour moi de tout Votre Coeur de tous vos forces et en toute verité, vous m'honnorez par Votre moderation et par votre temperence, et vous feres en sorte que I'augmenterai mes bienfaits envers vous Anciens officiers dela Couronne, et que je remplirai le devoir d'honnorer mon Pere, que si vous ne gardés pas les obligations des Manderins vous violeres vous-même les loix de l'empire, par la vous mepriseres les bienfaits de l'Empereur mon Pere qui vous avoit Choisi et elevé chacun dans votre charge, vous mepriseres aússi le jouste Amour que j'aÿ pour vous grands Ministres, les officiers des Parlements et autres cours Souveraines tous les Mandarins de Pekin de Nanking et de chaque Province doivent aussi agir veritablement, [141] etre purs et equitables ne pas renvoÿer les affaires aux Mandarins Superieurs negligent eux mêmes leurs devoirs.

O! vous tous peuples de l'Empire vous avez receux pendant long tems les biensfaits de mon Pere vous n'avez pas eu dequoi payer le tribut, il vous l'a remis dans le tems de famine, il vous à nouris et cela pendant longtems, il vous à exhorté a la Vertu, et vous à empeches de tomber dans le Vice, recompensent le bien et punisant le mal,

541 This note appears in the right margin: "30 ans."

Si par hazard quelqu'un du peuple à violé la loix, quand on à montré leur proces à feu l'Empereur mon Pere, il les a Certainement tous examinés quoi qu'ils fussent en tres grand nombre, il les à regardés tous les uns apres les autres et quand il ÿ a eu le moindre jour à leur sauver la Vie, il les à delivres, leur faisant misericorde, quiconque est de mon peuple doit honnorer ses Parens, porter respect a Ses Superieurs, qu'on craigne et le Chatiment par la Vous et moi jmiterons le feu Empereur mon Pere qui comme le Ciel vouloit la vie et non la mort des hommes.

Presentement parce que les Roÿs, les Marquis, les Comtes, les Grands officiers de la Couronne et autres tant de Robbe que d'epeé disent tous qu'il ne m'est pas permis de laisser longtems le thrône de l'Empire vuide, qu'il faloit certainement êtablir au plûtôt un Sacificateur des temples des Ancetres du Ciel et de la Terre, étant venus par trois fois reiterer leurs jnstances et leurs prieres, Ie suis forcé d'y Consentir, Si bien que je Suis contraint d'etouffer d'abord dans mon Coeur ma grande douleur, et d'arréter mes gemissemens Sur la mort de mon Pere.

Le 20.me Iour de l'onzieme lune.[542] Je Signifiay respectueusement [142] au Ciel, à la terre, à mes Ancetres, au Dieu tutelaire du terroir[543] qui preside à tous les generations, et au Dieu des grains[544] que j'allois prendre ausitôt possession du Trône Imperial par la cette anneé appelleé Koùci mào[545] est la premiere anneé de mon Regne, mon unique but est de Suivre les jntentions de mon predecesseur pour remplir mon devoir, disant ardement d'affermir longtems l'Empire, maintenant Je manifeste mes nouvelles loix qui doivent Servir d'exemple pour porter mes peuples au bien, mon dessin est de Surpasser en bienfaits le Regne presedent, je vais marquer cÿ dessous tout ce qui est du devoir d'un Empereur.

**Denombrement**

1.e Ie Recompense tous ceux de ma Cour depuis les Roÿs jusqu'aux Mandarins du neuvieme ordre.

2.e Ie recompense ceux qui Sont hors de la Cour depuis les Roÿs Iusqu'aux Ducs.

3.e Ie recompense les Filles, et les petites filles de l'Empereur tant celles dela Cour que celles du d'hors.

4.e Quand aux Mandarins Soit Tartares, Soit Chinois, tant ceux dela Cour que ceux du d'hors, pour ceux du premier ordre je recompense leurs Parens deffunts, a remon-

542 This note appears in the right margin: "le 22.me de xbrê 1722."

543 Tutelary gods, known as *chenghuang*, were deities that presided over specific Chinese cities or geographical spaces.

544 This probably refers to Shen Nong, a mythical emperor also worshipped as the God of Five Grains. See page 317, ft. 468.

545 *Guĭ-măo* was the name for the fortieth year in the sixty-year Chinese lunar cycle. It correlated with 1723, or the first complete year of Yung-cheng's reign.

ter jusqu'a la deuxieme generation, pour les Mandarins du 4.e, 5.e 6e, et 7.e ordre[546], Ie recompense de même leur Pere et Mere, Ceux du 8.e et 9.e ordre[547] Ie recompense leur Personne par des lettres honnoraires.

5.e Exceptes les Tartares des cinq bannieres[548] du Palais, et ceux qui leur appartienent, que je ne recompense pas.

Ie recompense tout ceux des huit bannieres hors du Palais, tous les fusiliers[549], Canoniers, tous les gens de pied et de Cheval [143] tant Tartares Orientaux, Occidentaux que Chinois, leur accordant gratis a Chacun la paÿe d'un mois.

6.e Quand a Ceux qui ont èté à la derniere Guerre Contres les jndustans[550], soit des huit bannieres, tant Tartares Orienteaux, tant soldats Chinois que Tartares occidentaux, qui pour avoir du merite, ont èté d'eux mêmes a cette guerre, ajant Compasion d'eux, je leur remets le fond et l'usure de l'argent qu'ils ont empruntez au thresor Roÿal.

7.e Quand aux Soldats des huit bannieres et a leur Mandarins, qui autrefois ont èté à l'armeé et qui faute seulement d'un degré de merite, ne peuvent pas obtenir le Mandarinat. etant tous gens qui ont merité en expossant leur vie, on doit en avoir Compassion, je les remets au Parlement des Armes, pour qu'il examine ceux qui ne manque qu'un degré de merite pour obtenir le Mandarinat, et qu'on m'en avertisse de

---

**546** Fourth-rank mandarins "of the robe" included directors of the imperial household, circuit intendants and prefects. Fifth included sub-prefects and assistant instructors and librarians. Sixth included tutors in the imperial academy and Buddhist and Daoist priests. Seventh included district magistrates and certain secretaries. Fourth-rank mandarins "of the sword" included lieutenant colonels and captains. Fifth included police captains and first lieutenants. Sixth included bodyguards. Seventh was made up of ensigns and first class sergeants. Jackson and Hugus, Ladder, 134–5.

**547** Eighth-rank mandarins "of the robe" included assistant district magistrates and salt examiners. Ninth included jail wardens, tax collectors and police commissioners. Eighth-rank mandarins "of the sword" was made up of ensigns and first-class sergeants. Ninth was made up of lower sergeants, corporals and privates. Ibid.

**548** The Ch'ing administration was divided into Eight Banners, essentially military units. The highest three banners were held by the emperor himself, whereas the remaining five "inferior" banners went to members of the imperial household, such as siblings and children. Every Manchu belonged to one banner, as did those Mongols and Han Chinese who aided their conquest. The superior banners were bordered yellow, plain yellow and plain white. The remaining were bordered white and variations of red and blue. Elliott, Manchu.

**549** A fusilier, as used in the European context familiar to the author, was an ordinary infantry soldier.

**550** Hindustan was a Mughal kingdom, located on the Gangetic Plain of modern-day Pakistan, northern India and Bangladesh during the 1600s and 1700s. This may reference the K'ang-hsi Emperor's conflicts with the Oöled Mongol tribes north of this region, which mostly ended in 1697. Peter C. Perdue, *China Marches West. The Qing Conquest of Central Eurasia* (Cambridge, MA: The Belknap Press of Harvard UP, 2010), 148–89.

même pour les Soldats et Mandarins de Six bannieres Chinoises[551] qui Sont dans le même cas des presedents, qu'on en fasse l'examen et qu'on m'en avertisse.

8.ᵉ Pour tous Ceux qui ont èté à l'armeé et qui ont Combattu pour dissiper l'Industan, j'ordonne qu'on marque distinctement leurs belles actions et qu'on m'en avertisse.

9.ᵉ Quand a Ceux qui ont èté anciennement a la guerre qui ètant devenus Vieux ne font plus la fonction de Soldats n'ayant plus la paÿe ne peuvent pas se nourrir, on doit avoir Compassion d'eux, si leur fils ou petit fils ont une paÿe de soldats, qu'on ne fasse aucun examen la dessus. Si au contraire leurs fils et petit fils n'ont pas cette paÿe, comment faire pour les nourrir, qu'on examine Clairement par qu'el endroit on pourra leur donner une paÿe, et qu'on m'en donne avis.

[144] 10.ᵉ Pour les Criminels soit grands petits Mandarins, soit soldats, peuple et autres, exepte le crime de revolté, des petits fils qui ont tués leurs ayeuls, des fils qui ont tués leur Pere et Mere, l'jnceste des femmes et des Concubines qui ont tué encaisé leurs maris, des esclaves[552] qui ont tué leurs maitres, ceux qui ont comis le Crime d'avoir tué une famille, de trois personnes ceux qui eventrent les femmes enceintes pour avoir leur fruit et en faire des Sortileges, les meurtriers par fraude, par haine, lorsque la mort S'ensuit, le poison lent, les malefices, le poison Violent qui tue d'abord, les brigandages, les exciteurs de revoltes, ce dix Sortes de mechancetez et autres semblables ce sont de crimes qui meritent Veritablement la mort et que je ne pardonne pas, je ne pardonne pas non plus aux traitres qui donnent des avis aux ennemis contre le bien dela patrie, pour les autres moindres Crimes comis depuis le Commencement du regne de mon Pere qui a duré Soixante et un an Ius qu'au matin 20.ᵉ jour de la 11.ᵉ lune[553] que je pris possession de l'Empire, soit connus, soit cachez, soit qu'on en ait porte Sentence ou non, je les pardonne tous, s'il Se trouve quelqu'un qui accuse un autre pour les crimes qu'on Vient de pardonner, l'accusateur subira la peine de l'accusé.

11.ᵉ Quand aux Sacrifices des cinq principales montagnes[554], des quatre principaux fleuves[555] et autres pour les quels on doit envoÿer des Mandarins pour presider aux dits Sacrifices, qu'on garde les anciennes Coutumes.

---

**551** The Ch'ing emperors eventually expanded their banner-system to incorporate the Han Chinese. Two *Hànjūn*, or infantry, banners were integrated in 1637, two more in 1639, and the final four in 1642. There were a total of eight Chinese banners, not six. Elliott, Manchu, 74–8.

**552** For more on unfree labor in imperial China, see Hsieh Bao Hua, *Concubinage and Servitude in Late Imperial China* (New York: Lexington Books, 2014).

**553** This correlates to 27 December 1722, when the Yung-cheng Emperor began his reign.

**554** The Five Sacred Peaks were sites of imperial pilgrimage as well as Daoist and Buddhism ritual, popularized in the third century BCE. They were Tài Shāni in Shantung Province, Huà Shān and Héng Shān in Shansi Province, Héng Shān in Hukwang Province, and Sōng Shān in Honan Province. Wang Gungwu, "Ming Foreign Relations: Southeast Asia", in: Cambridge History of China, vol. 8, 305.

**555** These four rivers were the modern-day Yellow, Yang-tze, Huai and Tsi waterways.

12.e Pour les Mandarins de Robbe qui Sont ala Cour depuis le quatrieme rang Jusqu'au premier ceux qui Sont hors de la cour depuis le troisieme rang[556] Iusqu'au premier, pour les Mandarins d'armes du premier et du second rang[557], tant ceux dela Cour que ceux du d'hòrs, que chacun d'eux envoÿe ún de [145] ses fils au College Imperial[558] pour y etudier.

13.e Les soldats Tartares Orientaux qui a Cause des blessures receues dans le combat ne peuvent plus faire la fonction de Soldats les viellards qui ne peuvent plus rien faire recevront tous recompense.

14.e Quand au nombre déja fixé des Licenties qui doivent recevoir le Doctorat, que le parlement des lettres attende le tems de l'examen[559] qu'alors il vienne demander mes ordres pour en augmenter le nombre, pour l'Examen[560] des Bacheliers a la Licence qui se fait hors la Cour que dans les grandes Provinces, on augmente le nombre des nouveaux Licenties jusqu'a trente, dans les moÿennes Provinces, jusqu'a vingt, dans les petites jus qu'a dix.

15.e Pour les Bacheliers de deux Cours et de chaque Province n'jmporte qu'il soit dé l'école des Villes du premier, du second, du troisieme ordre ou des Villes des Exilés[561] à chaque école au lieu d'un Kon:sen[562] on en fera deux.

16.e Dans chaque Province au nombre fixé des Lettrez qui deviennent Bacheliers qu'on en adjute aux grandes ècoles jusqu'a sept, aux ècoles moÿennes jus qu'a cinq, et aux petites jus qu'a trois, ce bienfait est accordé une fois Seulement a la premiere anneé de Yōng:tching, apres quoÿ il n'y aura plus cette Coutume, et on Suivra l'ancien usage.

17.e Tous Mandarins de Robbe ou d'Epeé qui avoit des proces contre les quels on n'avoit pas encore porté Sentence Sur la qualité de leur faute et de leur Chatiment soit ceux qu'on avoit privé de leurs appointements en peine de leurs fautes, Ie leur par-

**556** Third-rank mandarins "of the robe" included provincial judges, Assistant Vice Presidents in the Censorate, and salt controllers. Jackson and Hugus, Ladder, 134.

**557** First- and second-rank mandarins "of the sword" included field marshalls, lieutenant generals, major generals, colonels and commanders of the imperial bodyguard. Ibid., 135.

**558** Much Chinese learning focused on the imperial exams. Some students worked with tutors, but private schools and academies, or *shūyuàn*, also offered preparation. Select students moved on to the *Kuotzuchien*, or Imperial College, the empire's highest educational body. See Adan Yuen-chung Lui, "The imperial college (*Kuo-tzu-chien*) in the early Ch'ing (1644–1795)", in: *Papers on Far Eastern History* 10 (1974), 147–66.

**559** This note appears in the right margin: "L'examen se fait à la Cour pour tous les Licenties de la Chine." There were three levels of exams during the Ming and Ch'ing dynasties, which were offered every two to three years. These were the *shengyuan* (prefectural), *chü-jen* (provincial) and *chin-shih* (national). Contemporary Europeans often described these exams in terms of bachelor's, master's and doctoral degrees. Elman, Civil Examinations, 13–45, 95. See also page 308, ft. 410.

**560** This note appears in the right margin: "cet Examen se fait dans chaque Capitale ou Metropole."

**561** Place unknown.

**562** This note appears in the right margin: "Titre des Lettres entre les Bacheliers et les Licenties."

donne à tous, pour les Mandarins dela Cour qui ont èté demis de leur Charge a Cause de leurs maladies ou de leur grand age, on leur permet de prendre leur Charge.

18.ᵉ que dans chaque Ville du premier, du second du troisieme ordre et du lieu des Exilés que dans chaque lieu on fasse Connoitre les gens de bien pour leur donner le Bonnet et l'habit de Mandarin du Sixieme Ordre, afin d'honnorer leur personne en attendent [146] qu'il y ait des ordres pour Se Servir d'eux qu'on S'applique de toutes ses forces à Choisir de Veritables Sujets, Ie ne veux pas qu'on fasse ce choix a l'etourdie;

19.ᵉ Le labourage est le principal soutien de l'Empire que dans chaque ville de tous ces ordres et dans les lieux des exilez ÿ ajent veritablement des laboureurs qui travaillent de toutes leurs forces, que les Manderins des lieux les recompensent en tout tems pour exiter les autres a travailler Comme eux.

20.ᵉ Pour les Provinces ou le peuple n'a pas achevé de paÿer le tribut j'ordonne au Parlement qui a Soin du thresor Royal d'examiner clairement cette affaire pour m'en donner avis, ceux qui doivent depuis longtems et a qui il faut pardonner qu'on attende mes ordres pour accorder ce pardon.

21ᵉ. Ceux qui Sont en faute jmpersonnelle et qui pour chatiment eux et ceux de leur famille ont èté faits esclaves de Kÿ-Hia[563] j'ordonne qu'on en fasse l'examen qu'on m'en donne avis pour pardonner a ceux de la famille du Criminel.

22ᵉ. Ces derniers anneés les Soldats et les exilez qui ont porté les depèches publicques ont beaucoup Souffert, j'ordonne aux Tson:tou et aux Viceroÿs des Provinces d'en avoir bien Soin.

23ᵉ. Pour les Viellards de tout tems on a eu de grands ègards pour eux Soit Tartares Soit Chinois depuis 80 ans au dessus exeptez les esclaves, que les parlemens examinent clairement qu'el titre de Mandarin on doit leur donner et qu'on m'en donne avis.

24ᵉ. Quand aux Mandarins des Six bannieres parmi lesquels il y en a qui n'ont pas de quoi S'entretenir on doit en avoir compassion, j'ordonne que les Parlèmens mandent aux Madarins des lieux aux Tson:toù et aux Viceroÿs d'examiner clairement s'ils Sont veritablement Mandarins de merite et qu'ils n'ajent pas de quoÿ S'entretenir, qu'on voye Comment on pourra leur [147] faire du bien et que les parlemens m'en donnent avis.

25.ᵉ Pour les Mandarins des peuples non Chinois et soumis à l'empire ils ont toujours merité et ils n'ont pas encore receu de l'Empereur aucun Mandarinat que chaque

563 This note appears in the left margin: "Les Kÿ-hia sont [l]es chinois qui sont [s]oumis aux Tartares [e]t qui sont esclaves de l'Empereur." This likely refers to the Yung-cheng Emperor's 1723 efforts to improve the inherited status of *yue* households in his kingdom. See Matthew H. Sommer, *Sex, Law and Society in Late Imperial China* (Stanford, CA: Stanford UP, 2000), 260–304; Anders Hansson, *Chinese Outcasts: Discrimination & Emancipation in Late Imperial China* (Leiden: Brill, 1996).

Tson:tou et Viceroÿ examine ceux qui Sont Mandarins de ces peuples Soumis qui ont du merite qu'ils m'en donnent avis pour les recompenser Selon leur merite.

26.e Il y a dis Peuples sur les Montagnes et dans la Mer qui habitent des lieux forts d'assietes qui ne Sont pas Soumis à nostre gouvernement S'ils veulent venir tous ensemble Se Soumettre je leur pardonne tout le passé aÿant èprouvé leurs merites, je les èleverai aux dignites, ou je leurs donneraÿ d'autres recompenses Selon l'ancien usage.

27.e Pour les Voleurs de chaque lieu particulier S'ils Sont devenus voleurs ou a Cause de la famine n'ajant pas de quoi manger à cause du froid n'ayant pas des habits pour Se vetir ce qui les met hors d'état de Subsister, ou S'ils ÿ ont èté contraints ils Sont dignes de Compassion, s'ils veulent changer et venir d'eux mêmes Se Soumettre, je promets de leur pardonner.

28.e Pour tout on doit rechercher ceux qui retiennent les biens d'autrui injustement, qu'on examine les biens qu'ils ont S'ils les ont tous dissipez et n'ont pas le pouvoir de restituer je leur pardonne à tous il ne faut pas rechercher leurs parens ou ceux de leurs familles la dessus.

29.e Si les Mandarins des deux Cours et des Provinces portant le tribut aux thresors ont èté volez en chemin ou dans les hostelleries et que pour cella on les recherche et les tourmente encore Ie leur pardonne et remets le tout.

[148] 30.e Pour les soldats et les gens du peuple ages de 70 ans au dessus on leur permet d'avoir un homme pour avoir Soin d'eux, et cet homme Sera dispensé des traveaux publics, les Mandarins ne pourront pas les envoÿer autrepart ny le prendre a leur Service, ceux de 80 ans et au dessus qu'on leur donne une piece de Saÿa Saÿa[564], une livre de Cotton, un Pic de ris, dix livres de Cochon, a ceux de 90 et tant d'anneés qu'on leur donne le double.

Ah! quand je Considere les beaux faits de feu mon Pere, je ne scaurois les oublier jour et nuit, je pense a marcher sur ces traces, Ses exelentes vertus Sont en tres grand nombre et Sont repandus depuis longtems dans tous l'Empire, vous tous mes Parens, Gens de bien, Mandarins de Robbe, Mandarins d'armes de mon Roÿaume montrez vous gens de Probité, que chacun de vous me fasse Connoitre qu'il est homme de Coeur, afin que je me Serve de luÿ, pour Continuer Sans fin, les beaux faits de mes Ancétres, et comuniquer à jamais, le bonheur de la Paix, qu'on publie cecÿ dans tous l'Empire, pour que tout le monde le Sçache.

Soit que ce Prince n'ait pas pour les Sciences le même gout qu'avoit Son Pere, du reste il est tres applique aux affaires de l'Etat, dont il S'occupe tout entier; il est ferme et decisif, toujours pret a recevoir des memoiriaux, et a ÿ repondre, et gouverne

564 A *saya* is a monochromatic and twilled silk, first exported from China during the Ming Dynasty.

entierrement par luÿ même: de Sorte qu'il n'est pas possible de voir un Maitre plus absolu et plus reduté.[565]

L'Empereur fut si vivement prévénu contre les Missionaire[s] par diversses requestes que luy presenterent les Lettrez, et qui furent fortement appuyeés par le Tsong:tou de Fo:kien[566], qu'il [149] Proscrit la Religion Chrestienne il fit confisquer les Eglises, chassa les Missionaires de toutes les Provinces, exceptez de la ville de Peking et de Canton et ordonna de faire Apostazier les Chrêtiens, ce Malheureux Edit Monsieur a èté executé a notre depart de la Chine le premier de decembre 1724. tous les Missionaires sont Chassez de leurs Eglises, et la pluspart ont èté Conduits dans la Ville de Canton, plusieurs Chretiens dans les Provinces du Nord ont beaucoup Souffert; quatre Princes de la famille Imperialle ont èté Chargez de chaines et envoÿez en exil pour la foy.[567] La Province de Canton à moins Soufferte que les autres à cause que les Missionaires Sont assez amis du Viceroÿ; la Persecution est grande dans le Tonquin et plusieurs Missionaires ont perdu la vie.[568]

La Cour de Rome allarmeé d'un èvenement Si fatal pour la Religion Chrêtienne, envoÿa a la Cour de Peking les R.$^{s}$ P.$^{s}$ Godard[569] et Idelphonse[570] Carmes chargez de lettres et de Presens pour l'Empereur, pour le feliciter sur son avenement Sur le trône, et pour luÿ demander la liberté des Missionaires Prisoniers qui depuis l'an 1705 (du tems que le Cardinal de Tournon fut envoyé en qualité de Legat du S.$^{t}$ Siege par le Pape Clement Onze), avoient ete emprisonnez, Il ècrivit en reponce au Pape Regnant les deux lettres Suivantes.

---

**565** The preceding paragraph was adjusted and copied from: Du Halde, Description, vol. 1, 483.

**566** See pages 287–9.

**567** This likely refers to several sons of Sunu (ca. 1648–1725), a cousin of the Yung-cheng Emperor and imperial official. His son, Suerjin, introduced Catholic texts to the family in 1712, encouraging their conversion. Sunu himself may or may not have become Christian, but he was exiled by the emperor because of his sons' beliefs in July 1724. Brockey, Journey, 195–9; Standaert, Handbook, vol. 1, 445–6.

**568** The church in Tonquin frequently was the target of general social unrest between the 1730s and 1760s. For more on regional Christianity, see Adriano di St. Thecla, *Opusculum de Sectis apud Sinenses et Tunkinenses*, trans. Olga Dror (Ithaca, NY: Cornell UP, 2002).

**569** Emeric Plaskowitz, or Gotthard a Santa Maria (1700–1757), was a discalced Carmelite priest, who arrived in China in 1725 as a member of the third papal legate. He was sent with gifts for the Yongheng Emperor, so as to win his favor towards Christianity. See Standaert, Handbook, vol. 1, 362; Giovanni Stary, "The Rediscovery of Yongzheng's Letter of 1725 to Pope Benedict XIII", in: *Manuscripta Orientalia* 4.4 (1998), 28.

**570** Ildefonso a Nativitate (1699–1742) was a discalced Carmelite priest, who also arrived in China in 1725 as a member of the third papal legate. Ibid.

**Au Grand Pontife:**
Par ordre du Ciel, l'Empereur d'aujourdhuÿ envoÿe cette lettre à Kiac-vam[571], Roi d'Italie, et Grand Pontife.

I'aÿ connu la Sincerité de votre Cœur, ô Roi! par la lettre que vous m'avez ècrite, et les Presens[572] que vous m'avez envoÿez en même tems [150] Ie vous assure que tous les Mandarins et tout le Peuple, non Seulement de mon Empire, mais encore tous les ètrangers, ont montré par leurs larmes une grande consternation dans la mort du defunt Empereur mon Pere: il avoit toûjours eu grand soin de conserver avec toutes les nations les plus èloigneés, la Paix et l'amitie; ce qui fait qu'a mon Avenement au Trône, I'aÿ apporté tous mes Soins à Continuer ce que mon Pere avoit si bien Commencé. ainsi, Ie me rejouis que le Grand Pontife Se Souvienne des bienfaits de mon Pere, en me souhaitant par sa tres honnête lettre, toutes les prosperitez et felicitez de mon Empire.

Ceux que tu as eu la bonté de m'envoÿer, Ie les aÿ recûs et traitez avec tous les honnetetez par rapport aux autres Europeéns qui demeurent en mon Empire.

Moÿ, Empereur, qui regarde les Choses de l'univers avec une substance, je leur ai ordonné de se Contenir en Paix et tranquilité, et S'ils observent mes loix toute leur vie, ils Seront dignes de ma misericorde: Certainement, je les aimerai et protegerai.

Or, par Vos envoyez, qui à present retournent dans votre Roÿaume, Ie vous envoye cent Pieces de Soirie brodeé:[573] acceptez les ô Roÿ! et connoissez par la la bien veillance que I'aÿ pour vous

Signé Yoñg: tching
A Peking le 25 de la 35.e Lune et le 21 novembre 1725 de l'Ere Chretien.

**Seconde Lettre de L'Empereur au Grand Pontife.**
Par Ordre du Ciel, L'Empereur d'aujourdhuÿ envoÿé cette lettre a Kiac:Vam, Roÿ d'Italie et Grand Pontife.

---

571 *Kiaó Vam̃* was derived from the Manchu *jiao wang*, which was used to signify "pope" but translated as "King of the Religion." The current pope in 1725 was Benedict XIII (1649–1730), an Italian-born Dominican. Immediately after assuming the pontificate in 1724, he sent delegates to China in hopes of ending Christian persecutions and reopening the kingdom to evangelization. Stary, Rediscovery, 29, 33.

572 Among the gifts Pope Benedict XIII sent the Yung-cheng Emperer in 1725 were "eleven ivory embedded snuffboxes; a pair of snuff canisters and leisure items such as snuff bottles" as well as snuff tobacco. See Carole Benedict, *Golden-Silk Smoke: a History of Tobacco in China, 1550–2010* (Berkeley: University of California Press, 2011), 113–4.

573 A brocade is any textile with a raised, woven supplementary pattern. It often looks like embroidery and is very costly. Yung-cheng's gifts were much more extensive than listed here, including not only brocades but a variety of colored silks as well as 300 ounces of silver. Stary, Rediscovery, 30.

Vous m'avez prie par votre deuxieme lettre de donner la liberté aux deux europeéns prisonniers a Canton nommez Petien Sing[574] [151] et Ky-Jen-Sang:[575] Je l'ai donné a un troisieme, nommé Te-like.[576]

Mon Pere le defunt Empereur, sachant que Te-li-ke etoit etranger, eut de la Clemence pour lui, ordonnant Seulement de le mettre en Prison. il avoit rapporté à l'Empereur des choses qui n'etoient pas vraÿes: mais apres que j'ai receû la dignité Imperiale, pour montrer a tout le monde ma clemence, et pour que les Coupables reconnoissent leurs fautes; I'ai fait publier une ordonnance generale de Pardon.[577] Te-li-ke etant un des Coupables, il a eu sa grace; et si les Mandarins de Canton m'avoient averti de ces deux Prisonniers, ils Seroient Sortis comme les autres: mais a present que j'ai reçû votre lettre, ô Roÿ! I'ordonne aux Mandarins de Canton de leur donner la liberté, pour montrer au peuple et aux Etrangers, le desir de regner avec Clemence et bonté.

Apresent que vos envoÿez Ta-ta-tu[578], et Ie-sang[579] retournent dans Votre Roÿaume, Ie les charge dela Racine de Ien-sing[580] et de quinze differentes choses de mon Empire: acceptez les, ô Roÿ! et connoissez par la la bienveillance que I'ai pour vous.

signe Yoñg tchiñg
A Peking le 7.^e Jour de la 43.^me Lune et le 4.^me Mars 1726 de l'Erre Chretien.

Tout aliené que ce Prince paroisse dela Religion, a laquelle il n'a pû cependant refuser Son estime, on ne Scauroit s'empecher de louer Son application jnfatigable dans le travail: il a fait plusieurs beaux Reglements soit pour etablir la forme d'un Sage

574 This note appears in the left margin: "Appianÿ." It refers to Luigi Antonio Appiani, or *Pi T'ien-hsiang*, an Italian priest imprisoned in China since 1706. See page 279, ft. 251.
575 This note appears in the right margin: "Guiguel de la mai[son] de Sorbonne de Paris." Antoine Guignes, or *Chi Yu-kang* (d. 1741), was a French priest, member of the Paris Foreign Missions Society and missionary to China since 1706. He was imprisoned in China since 1717. See Lo-shu Fu, *A documentary chronicle of Sino-Western relations, 1644–1820* (Tucson: University of Arizona Press, 1966), 506–7, 649.
576 This note appears in the right margin: "Pedrini." Teodorico Pedrini, or *To-li-ko* (1671–1746), was an Italian native and Lazarist missionary in China since 1710. Pedrini was held under house arrest in Peking from 1721 to 1723, after Cardinal Tournon's unsuccessful legate. See Joseph Van den Brandt, *Les Lazaristes en Chine, 1697–1935: Notes biographiques* (Beijing: Imprimerie des Lazarists Pei-T'ang, 1936), 2.
577 See page 332.
578 This note appears in the right margin: "Godard." Gotthard a Santa Maria also was known as *Ka-ta-tu*.
579 This note appears in the right margin: "Idelphonse." Ildefonso a Nativitate also was known as *I-te-feng*.
580 Ginseng is a plant, indigenous to North America and the cooler climates of Asia. Its root was prized as an aphrodisiac and preventative medicine in early modern China.

Gouvernement et procurer le bonheur de Ses Sujets, Soit pour honnorer le merite et recompenser la Vertu, soit [152] pour mettre de l'emulation parmi les Labureurs, ou pour Secourir les peuples dans les anneés Steriles.

Le treizieme frere de l'Empereur qui avoit l'Intendance de tout l'Empire, et qui protegoit les Missionaires, mourut le 9 Iuin 1730, l'Empereur fut jnconsolable de cette perte, c'etoit un Prince qui possedoit tous les qualitez qu'on pouvoit dessirer de lui, il partagoit avec l'Empereur tout le poids des affaires, il S'etoit Consumé par l'excés du travail auquel il Se livroit jour et nuit, Sa Mort fut fatalle pour les Missionaires qui avoient été Chasses des Provinces de l'empire, et Relegez à Canton, car aÿant perdu celui qui les protegoit, ils furent chassez de Canton même, et renvoyez a Macao le 20 aoust 1732.[581]

L'Empereur apres avoir gouverné ses vastes Etats avec une autorité absolue, Mourut a Peking le 8.$^{e}$ octobre 1735 a l'age de 54 ans, et dans la 14.$^{me}$ de son Regne.

Voila Monsieur tout ce que Ie peu dire en peu de mots de plus Iuste et de plus precis, touchant le Present Gouvernement de Ce vaste Empire depuis la Conquêté par les Tartares, et comme Je n'ay en vue que de vous donner une Ideé de Son Commerce, Se Seroit vous ennujer par un recit de repetition de ce qu'on vous à dêja donné par plusieurs relations, Ie me borneraÿ a vous donner, par ma lettre Suivante, une Connoissance entierre de la Province de quang:tong, que nous nommons Canton, par la quelle I'espere que vous aurez une plus ample Information [153] de Son Commerce qui Se fait avec les Europeéns, ce que tant d'autres ont neglige de vous donner, Ie me flatte qu'elle satisfaira parfaitement Votre Curieusité.

## Lettre húitieme

Monsieur comme la Province de Quang:tong nommeé par les Europeéns Canton est la principale ou nos vaisseaux Europeens traffiquent, me donne occassion de Vous la faire connoitre en particulier; elle est la plus Considerable des Provinces Meridionales de la Chine, elle à pour Ses limites au couchant le Roÿaume de Tong:king[582], et au nord ouest la Province de Quang:si, au Septentrion celle de Kiang:si dont elle n'est separé que par des Montagnes[583]; Fo:kien au nord est, elle est borneé au midi par la mer ou l'on trouve quantité de Ports Commodes. elle est diviseé en dix contreés, qui Contiennent dix Villes du premier ordre, et quatre vingt quatre Villes tant du second

581 In August 1732, the Yung-cheng Emperor issued his third edict allowing Christian persecutions in China – this time expelling all foreign missionaries to Macao. See Lars Peter Laamann, *Christian Heretics in Late Imperial China: Christian inculturation and state control, 1720–1850* (New York; Routledge, 2006), 60–1.

582 For these provinces' modern-day equivalents, see pages 287, 312.

583 The Yün-k'ai-ta mountains separate the provinces of Kwangtung and Kwangsi.

que du troisieme ordre, Sans ÿ comprendre plusieurs forts ou places de guerre[584], sa capitale nommeé Quang:tc̈heu:Fou ou Canton et Macao Sont devenues cèlebres en Europe.

De toutes les Provinces dela Chine, il n'y en à point de plus abondante ni de plus riche que Celle cÿ, le Paÿs est partie plat, partie Montagneux; les terres Sont si fertilles, qu'elles produisent du grain deux fois chaque anneé. tout ce qui peut Contribuer aux delices de la vie, s'y trouve en abondance. Elle fournit de l'or, salpetre[585], fer, acier, Etain, vifargent, sucre, soÿes, du cuivre, de l'ebene[586], du bois d'Aigle[587] et [154] plusieurs sortes de bois de Senteur. aussi elle est la plus fertille en bled, Ris, et toutes Sortes de fruits, comme des grenades, des raisins des poires des prunes, ces trois Sortes des fruits ont de la peine à meurir, en revenge elle produit d'autres qui sont excellens; tels sont les Bananes, les Ananas, les Litchi[588], les Orangers, et les Citrons de toutes les Sortes.[589] elle abonde ausi en tous Sortes de Paturages, Elle est aussi la plus saine et la plus Riche en negoce, qui Se fait dans Sa Capitale, avec toutes les nations du Monde, les Vaisseaux d'Europe seulement trafiquent Chaque anneé pour plusieurs millions de florins[590], sans ÿ Compter les vaisseaux de Manilla, Madras, de la Côte, et autres vaisseaux mores qui viennent annuellement, je vous donneray en particulier le recit de Son Commerce.

On voit une Chose extraordinaire dans cette Province, c'est la prodigieuse quantité de Canards domestiques, que ces peuples nourisent avec jndustrie: jls font èclore leurs oeufs dans un foúr où dans du fumier: ils les mettent sur de petits bateaux, et en menent de grandes bandes, pour paitre sur les bords de la Mer ou des Rivieres, nonobstant la grande quantité des bateaux, qui vont ensemble et que les Canards se trouvent melez sur le Rivage. des qu'on frappe sur un bassin chaque bande retourne sur son bateau.

Ce qu'il ÿ a encorre de rare dans cette Province c'est le bois de fer[591], qui est Si dur et Si pesent qu'il Sert aux Vaisseaux, pour faire les Ancres des Vaisseaux, on voit

---

**584** The preceding sentence was copied from: Duhalde, Description, vol. 1, 221.

**585** Saltpeter, or potassium nitrate, is a naturally-occuring compound in India and Southeast Asia. It was a primary ingredient in Chinese gunpowder. See David Cressy, *Saltpeter: the Mother of Gunpowder* (New York: Oxford UP, 2013).

**586** Ebony is a dark and heavy hardwood, especially found along the Coromandel Coast.

**587** Calambac, or eaglewood, is a highly-prized resinous hardwood, found in southeast Asia. It especially was valued as a perfume and disinfectant.

**588** A litchi is a small, red tropical fruit indigneous to Kwangtung and Fukien provinces.

**589** The preceding four sentences were adjusted and copied from: Duhalde, Description, vol. 1, 221.

**590** Although the original florin referred to a gold coin from Florence, this denotes the Dutch gilder, or *gulden*, which borrowed the name. The guilder was a silver coin, and one tael was worth 4.4 guilders.

**591** Ironwood was the name give to several varieties of trees known for their hardness. This might refer to the lumber of the *Metrosideros vera* or the *Mesua ferrea*.

aussi un autre Sorte de bois qu'on nomme bois de Rose[592] à Cause de Son odeur, dont les Chinois se Servent pour faire des meubles, ils est d'un noir tirant Sur le rouge, marqué de Veines et peint naturellement: [155] jl croit encore une Sorte d'ozier qui est tres souple, et qui ne se rompt pas aisement, dont les Chinois S'enservent pour faire des Cables et des Cordages de navire: on les Separe en de filets, dont on fait des Corbeilles, des panniers, des sieges et de nattes fort propres.[593]

Le principal fleuve qui arrose la Province est nommé Ta, il est tres vaste son cours en general est du midi au nord, il à sa source dans la province de Quang:si, il est nommé devant Canton Ta:ho par ce que elle recoit les Vaisseaux qui viennent de la Mer, il se va decharger par le dêtroit de la Porte du Tigre nommé par les Chinois Hou:men[594], et le long des isles de Macao dans la Mer: elle est fort riche en poisons de tout Sortes, elle nourit en abondance tout le pais à fort bon marché.

Comme cette Province est la plus eloigneé de la Cour et frequanteé par toutes sortes de nations etrangeres, Son Gouvernement est aussi un des plus Considerables de l'Empire. celuÿ qui en est Tsong:tou, l'est aussi dela Province de Quang:si; et c'est pour cette raison qu'il reside à Tchao:king[595], qui en est plus voisine, afin d'etre plus a porteé d'y donner Ses ordres.[596]

Ie suis obligé Monsieur Sur les plaintes que vous me fites de ce que la description ambulante que Ie vous aÿ donné de la Ville de Canton, ne Seroit pas assez detailleé pour ètré jnstruit de sa veritable Situation et des meurs de ses habitans, pour Satisfaire a votre Curieusité je vous la donne icÿ, telle, comme vous la dessiré.

La Capitale de la Province de Quang:tong que Ceux du paÿs nomment Quang:tcheou:fou, et les Europeéns Canton [156] est situeé sous le 23.[e] deg.[e] 10 min.[s] 58 sec.[s], et de 130 deg.[s] 43 min.[s] 15 sec.[s] de longitude de l'isle de fer[597]; Elle est la premiere que l'on trouve dans la Chine en ÿ entrent par Macao, la Riviere Ta:ho qui lui Sert d'un fort bon Port, lui attire un nombre prodigieux de Marchands, par la grande quantité d'argent que les vaissaux Europeens et des Indes ÿ apportent, de sorte qu'on trouve dans cette Ville tout ce qu'il ÿ a de Curieux et de rare dans tout l'empire. Les habitans sont fort laborieux, tres adroits et extremement habiles a imiter tous les Ouvrages qu'on leur montre, Comme les Ouvriers de cette grande Ville ne Sont pas

---

592 Rosewood is a fragrant and richly-hued wood, found throughout Asia and the Americas. Furniture made of the timber polishes well, which made it an apt substitute for mahogany in the eighteenth century.

593 The preceding two paragraphs were copied from: Duhalde, Description, vol. 1, 230–1.

594 The *Porte du Tigre* and *Hŭmén zhèn* both refer to Bocca Tigris.

595 Zhaoqing was a city in Kwangtung Province, located about 80 kilometers west of Canton and along the Pearl River.

596 The preceding paragraph was adjusted and copied from: Du Halde, Description, vol. 1, 231.

597 El Hierro, also known as *l'île de Fer*, was the smallest and southernmost of the Canary Islands. Since 1634, it had been used as the prime meridian for measuring longitude on continental European maps.

à un assez grand nombre pour fournir au grand Commerce qui Se fait, on est obligé d'avoir recours au fameux Bourg de Fo:chan qui n'est qu'a quatre lieux de Canton sur un des bras de la Riviere[598], par le quel on va a Macao par des petits Bataux; cette Bourgade qui à au moins trois lieues de Circuit, ne doit ceder en rien a Canton, ni pour les richesses, ni pour la multitude de Ses habitans, et pour le trafic des Soÿeries qui Se fait; neamoins les ètoffes de Soÿe qu'on fabrique à Canton qu'on nomme Cha[599], sont les plus estimeés de tout la Chine, sur tout celles qui sont Semeés de fleurs, perceés au jour comme des dentelles, dont l'usage est fort commun pendant l'êté, elles Sont à bon marche et d'une proprete acheveé.

Cette Ville est de figure quareé comme vous pourez Conjecturer par Son plan que j'ay icÿ Ioint, les Tartares en Si placant obligerent les Chinois de Se loger hors des murailles, ou ils batirent en peu de tems une nouvelle Cité, qui etant plus longue que large, fait avec la Ville une figure jrreguliere. de maniere que [157] Canton est Composeé de deux villes, l'une se nomme la Ville des Tartares parce qu'il n'y à qu'eux qui S'y puissent ètablir, on appelle l'autre, la ville des Chinois[600], moitie aussi grande, mais beaucoup plus peupleé que la premiere, toutes deux ensemble font un Circuit[601] de trois grandes lieues d'allemagne[602], et peupleé par une grande multitude d'habitans.

Elle est revetue de bonnes murailles à l'antique, les rues sont etroites, et paveés de grandes pierres plattes et fort dures, elles sont si droites que la vuë est libre d'un bout à l'autre. les maisons[603] sont tres basses Sans aucunes fenêtres Sur la rúe, et presque toutes en boutiques qui Sont remplis des plus belles marchandisses du Monde, dont les ruës font un fort bel aspect à cause que Chaque maison est garnié a deux côteés de tablettes ou planches qui Sont aussi hautes que les portes, Sur les quelles on ècrit en Caracteres d'or sur un fond rouge, verd ou bleu, tout ce qu'on vend de denreés dans la ditte maison, ces especes de pilastres rangez de deux Côtez des rues et presque dans une egale distance, font une Collonade qui a quelque rapport a nos theatres.

---

**598** This refers to the Dongping Waterway.

**599** Canton cambric, or *cha-pou*, was a lightweight textile. Here, the author suggests it was a silk but, by the nineteenth century, the term referred to a linen appropriate for summer weather. See *The London Journal of Arts, Sciences, and Manufactures, and Repertory of Patent Inventions, vol. 24* (London: W. Newton, 1846), 53.

**600** The Han Chinese predominated in the southern New City of Canton. Garrett, Heaven, 37–48.

**601** The preceding paragraph was adjusted and copied from: *Atlas historique, ou nouvelle introduction a l'histoire, a la chronologie,* & à *la geographie ancienne & moderne* (Amsterdam: L'Honoré & Chatelain, 1719), 155.

**602** The German and Dutch league equated to 6.4 kilometers, when measured on land.

**603** For more on imperial architecture, see Sun Dazhang, "The Qing Dynasty", in: *Chinese Architecture*, ed. Nancy S. Steinhardt (New Haven: Yale UP, 2002), 261–344; Klaas Ruitenbeek, *Carpentry & Building in Late Imperial China: a Study of the Fifteenth-Century Carpenter's Manual* Lu Ban Jing (Leiden: Brill, 1996).

Les plus beaux quartiers resemblent assez aux ruës de la foire Saint Germain à Paris[604]; et il ÿ a presque autant de peuple qu'a cette foire, aux heures qu'elle est bien frequenteé. on voit peu de femmes sur les ruës, mais au Contraire les hommes Y fourmillent, presque tous sont chargez de quelque fardeau, n'ÿ aiant point d'autre Commodité pour voiturer ce qui se Vend et ce qui s'achette, que les êpaules des hommes. Ces portefaix vont ordinairement la tête et les pieds nuds, quelques fois pourtant, ils se Couvrent d'une [158] espece de Chapeau de paille de figûre bizare[605], pour se dêfendre de la pluje ou du soleil.[606]

On trouve dans Canton d'assez belles places et des arcs de triomphe mangnifiques à la maniere du pais, dont j'aÿ parlé ci devant, ils sont dresses à l'honneur des Vaillans hommes, des Docteurs Cêlebres, et de ceux qui ont rendu quelque service Considerable a leur patrie.

Il ÿ a des portes au bout de toutes les ruës, pour les fermer pendant la nuit[607], les quelles Sont gardeés par un chef de la rue qui doit veiller à tout ce qui Se passe dans la Cloture de Sa rue, et avertir le Mandarin des querelles, des nouveautez, des êtrangers qui ÿ arrivent ou qui en sortent. les maisons Voisines se doivent garder mutuellement, et Sont obligeés de se prêter main forte en cas d'allarme; de Sorte qu'elles sont responsables, par exemple, des vols nocturnes qui s'y commetent. enfin en chacue famille les Peres repondent de desordres de leurs enfans, et de leurs domestiques.

On voit sur la Riviere une espece de Ville flotante[608], les barques Se touchent et forment des ruës; chaque barque loge toute une famille, et à des Compatimens pour tous les usages du menage selon que leur famille est grosse, le petit peuple qui habite ces maisons flotantes decampe tous les matins pour aller pecher ou travailler au ris qu'on receuille trois fois l'anneé[609], ce Sont ordinairement les femmes qui nagent avec l'aviron, et la plûpart ayant sur le dos un enfant qui tete encore; il ÿ a deux petites îles[610] dans la Riviere sur chacun des quels il ÿ a un fort dont celui du côté d'ouest est de figure ovalle, et l'autre est quaré assez bien entretenus.

Les Yamen ou Palais des Mandarins ont quelque Chose qui surprend, et l'on arrive au lieu ou ils donnent audience, qu'aprés [159] avoir traversé un grand nombre

604 The Faubourg Saint-Germain is a Parisian neighborhood, located on the left bank of the Seine River. After the building of the Luxembourg Palace in the 1600s, it became a fashionable space for the French nobility.

605 This refers to the *dǒulì*, a conical straw or bamboo hat.

606 The preceding two paragraphs, except for the first half-sentence, were adjusted and copied from: *Memoires pour l'Histoire des Sciences & des beaux Arts* (Paris: Jean Boudot, 1703), 234–5.

607 The preceding two sentences were adjusted and copied from: Moréri, Supplément, vol. 1 (1716), 394.

608 See page 270, ft. 210.

609 The preceding two sentences were adjusted and copied from: Moréri, Supplément, vol. 1 (1716), 394.

610 These probably refer to the islands which housed Dongpaotai, or the slightly downriver "French Folly," and the "Dutch Folly," nearer the Canton factories.

de Cours: quand ils Sortent leur train est nombreux Selon leur rang, quelsques uns ajant Ius qu'a cent hommes à leur Suite, au milieu des qu'els paroit le Mandarin êlevé sur une Chaise bien garnie, que six ou huit hommes portent sur leurs êpaules.[611]

Les Temples d'jdoles environnez de cellules de Bonzes, ont quelque chause de singulier, la Sale de Confucius, aussi bien que l'Acadamie[612] ou les Lettrez s'assemblent pour faire leurs Compositions, Sont de Morceaux Curieux en leur genre.[613]

Cette ville à beaucoup Souffert dans la derniere guerre contre les Tartares[614], c'est aussi l'unique qui resta fidele a Son Empereur Yong:lié, les Tartares furent obligeés pour soumettre cette Ville d'envoÿer trois fortes armeés, Celles de Nan king et de Kiang si, qui êtoient allieés avec celle de Canton, aÿant entendus la marche de ces trois nombreuses armeés, furent tellement effraÿez, quelles abandonnerent celle de Canton, et Se Soumirent Volontairement aux Tartares[615], quoi que cette Ville Se trouva tout Seule, elle resitat vigureusement un an tout entier contre les forces des Tartares, et les assiegeés leur firent Souffrir de fort grandes pertes les aÿant repousez vigureusement dans trois assauts, enfin apres une deffense vigoureuse et opiniatre, elle fut forceé et prise d'assaut le 4 novembre de l'anneé 1650, le masacre ÿ fut terrible, car plus de cent mille hommes ÿ perirent par le fer du Vainqueur. Les autres Villes dela Province voiant leur Capitale prise envojerent des Deputez aux Tartares pour jmplorer leur clemence, ce qui leur fût accordé Sans peine.

C'est dans Cette Ville que réside le Fou:ÿuen ou Viceroÿ le ressort de cette Capitale Comprend dix sept villes, dont une est du Second ordre, et les seize autres du troisieme.[616]

Les Environs de Canton Sont d'une Veuë fort agreable, il faut [160] avouer qu'on ne peut rien voir de plus beau en Son genre que les Pagodes, Tombeaux, Maisons de Campagne entremelleés d'haÿes d'arbres toujours Verds, et les petites Villes ou Bourgs qui Sont fort pres l'un de l'autre. le terroir est compose en partie de Montagnes et en partie de valons; le Sud de la grande Riviere, qui est coupé par plusieurs Caneaux qui forment autant d'isles, est d'une hauteur passable, assez unie et d'une fertilité jncroiable, Car tout ce qu'on ÿ Seme ÿ vient en fort peu de tems en maturité.

---

**611** The preceding paragraph was adjusted and copied from: Moréri, Supplément, vol. 1 (1716), 394

**612** See page 333, ft. 558.

**613** The preceding paragraph was adjusted and copied from: Martinière, *Grand dictionnaire*, vol. 8, 4.

**614** The Ch'ing Dynasty conquered Canton, a Ming loyalist bastion, in January 1647. The city soon rebelled and came under the control of the Yongli Emperor of the Southern Ming Dynasty. After a siege of eight and a half months, however, it again fell to Ch'ing armies in 1650. See R. Kent Guy, *The Qing Governors and their Provinces: the Evolution of Territorial Administration in China, 1644–1796* (Seattle: University of Washington Press, 2010), 310; Struve, Southern Ming, 678–714.

**615** Nanking surrendered without further resistance in June 1645, after the Yangzhou massacre. The final Ming bastion in Kiangsi was besieged in May 1646. Struve, Southern Ming, 674.

**616** The preceding paragraph was adjusted and copied from: Du Halde, Description, vol. 1, 232.

Les bords des dits Caneaux ou petites rivieres Sont pleins de petits chateaux de plaisance, et Sur tout du Côté dela grande Riviere, Ce milieu est de paturages bons et herbeux, melez de quelque bois. les terres qui produisent le ris sont basses et humides et produissent d'abondantes rêcoltes, et celles qui donnent le froment, Sont d'une hauteur raisonable.

Le terroir qu'ils prennent pour Semer le ris, quand la terre est labureé resemble a une masse de bouë. ils labourent avec une petite Charuë tireé par une bufle, un homme tenant la Charruë et faisant aller la bête, quand le ris est mûr et Cueilli, ils le foulent avec des boufles dans une grande place ronde sur un pavé dur, et fait expres pour cela. ils attachent trois u quatre bufles a la queuë des uns des autres, et les font marcher en rond comme un Cheval de moulin, en sorte que ces bêtes foulent tout.[617]

Les Chinois qui rendent leurs terres si fertilles à force de les arroser, n'ont point trouvé de meilleur moyen de distribuer l'eau egalement, qu'en mettant touttes les terres de niveau, Sans quoÿ les plus hautes demeureroient dans la Secheresse, tandis que les fonds seroient noÿ[és.] c'est ainsi qu'ils en usent, même dans la Culture des Colines, car ils les Coupent par ètages, et par degré depuis le pied Iusqu'au [161] Sommet, afin que les pluÿes se repandent ainsi egalement par tout, et n'entrainent pas avec elles les Semences et les terres.[618]

La Plante de thé appelleé autrement Tcha[619] qui croit aux environs de Canton, n'est pas Si bone en qualité, que celle qui croit dans le district de kun:ning:fou[620], Ville de la Province de Fokien

L'arbre de thé ou arbrisseau, se plait dans les Valeés et au pied des montagnes, les terroirs pierreux lui convenant le mieu, ensuite les terres legeres, et apres les terres Iaunes, et qu'on la prepare tout de même Comme nos paisans le font pour Semer l'houblon[621], On Seme ordinarement la graine dans des terres exposeés au midÿ, et ils portent trois ans aprez avoir été Semez. leur racines ressemblent a celles du pêcher. leurs feuilles sont d'un Verd obscur, allongeés par la pointe, et assez etroites d'un pouce ou d'un pouce ou demi de long, denteleés tout au tour. leurs fleurs Sont assez faites comme les roses blanches Sauvages. leur fruit de differente figure, tantot rond, tantot long, quelque fois triangulaire, est de la groseur d'une fêve, et renferme

---

617 The preceding paragraph was adjusted and copied from: Dampier, Suite, vol. 2, 86–7.

618 The preceding paragraph was adjusted and copied from: M. Bruzen de la Martinière, *Introduction à l'histoire de l'Asie, de l'Afrique, et de l'Amérique, vol. 1* (Amsterdam: Zacharie Chatelain, 1735), 177.

619 The Chinese word for tea is *chá*.

620 This likely refers to a settlement either in the northern Wuyi Mountains or in southern Anxi County, both key tea production regions in Fukien Province.

621 The hops plant, or *Humulus lupulus*, produces a flower, which is used as a stabilizer and flavor in fermenting beer.

deux ou trois pois d'un gris de Souris[622] au dessus, et qui ont un amande blanche au dedans. ce Sont ces pois qui Servent de Semence pur les multiplier.

Ces arbres S'elevent en hauteur depuis deux pieds, jus qu'a Vint, et l'on en trouve que deux hommes auroient dela peine a embrasser, tandis qu'il ÿ en a qui n'ont que quelques foibles tiges, et qui rampent presque comme les moindres plantes.

Le tems le plus propre pour faire la récolte des feuilles de thé est Vers le printems, lors qu'elles Sont encore petites, tendres, et pleines de Suc. quand elles ont été Cueilleés, on les passe sur des plaques de fer qu'on fait Chauffer[623] pour les [162] amoitir, et ensuite on les laisse refroider Sur des nates fines, apres ils le mettent une Seconde fois Chauffer à petit feu sur les dits plaques ou terrines de fer, qu'ils scavent par une addresse de main les faire rouler de la maniere qu'on les apporté en europe, on les cêche de la maniere Jus qu'a deux ou trois fois, alors on les Conserve dans des Canastres garnis de plomb.

Touchant le the bou ou vou ÿtcha dont je parle, nait dans la Province de Fokien, et tire Son nom dela fameuse montagne Vou:ÿ:chan[624], dont la terre est legere blanchatre et Sablonneuse. on lui donne trois differens noms, celui dela premiere recolte qui Se fait dans le mois d'avril, Se nomme Peko, la deuxieme qui se fait dans le mois de Mey, Congo, et la troisieme qui Se fait dans tout le mois de juin vou ÿ tcha[625], pou etre bon il faut qu'il ait l'odeur de Violette ou de Rose, aussi ces trois sortes de vou:y:t-cha sont les plus recherches pour l'usage dans l'empire.

Le thé Singlo ou Son-glo-tcha que nous appellons the verd est tout un autre espece, la Culture des arbrisseaux est la même, que celle des arbrisseaux vou-ÿ-tcha. La Seule difference qu'il y ait c'est que les feuilles Sont plus longes et plus pointues, il le faut Choisir odoriferant le plus entier qu'il Se peut, et Sur tout prendre garde qu'il ne Soit point êvente.[626]

On croit que l'usage de cette boisson preserve les Chinois de la pierre et de la goutte, dont ils ne Sont jamais jncommodez. il est certain quelle nettoÿe les reins, qu'elle purge le Cerveau, qu'elle empêche les cruditez et les jndigestions, et en prennent un peu aprés le repas, et qu'elle Chasse la [163] melancolie et le Sommeil: ce qui est commode a ceux qui êtudient beaucoup, et on peut dire qu'elle Surpasse

---

**622** The *Camellia sinensis* plant produces small spherical seeds, which are not edible themselves but used to produce cooking oil.

**623** The preceding three paragraphs were adjusted and copied from: Jaques Savary des Brûlons, *Dictionnaire universel du commerce, vol. 2* (Paris: Jacques Estienne, 1723), 1723–4.

**624** The *Yù Shān*, or Jade, Mountain is the highest peak in modern-day Taiwan.

**625** This likely refers to a variety of oolong, which is a semi-fermented black tea. Liu, Dutch, 68.

**626** The preceding half-sentence was adjusted and copied from: Savary des Brûlons, Dictionnaire, vol. 2, 1724.

en bonté le Café[627] des Turcs, et le Chocolat[628] des Americains, car le Café excite ordinairement la bile, et le Chocolat êchauffe trop en été: mais le the a une qualité fort tempereé, et ne nuit point, quoique l'on en prenne plusieurs fois par jour.[629]

Les Orangers que I'aÿ vû aux environs et dans les Iardins de la ville de canton, sont en tres grands nombre, les arbres qui produissent les oranges sont aussi grands que nos Pommiers, ses feuilles Sont larges, grosses, lisseés, odoriferantes, et pointues par le bout, Sa fleur, est blanche avec plusieurs petits dards garnis d'une êtamine jaunatre. il Conserve Sa feuille, (comme tous les autres arbres) toute l'anneé; on Croit que les Portugais (apres la decouverte dela chine) en aporterent les premiers les plantes en Europe[630], depuis ce tems la on trouve ces Sortes d'arbres êgalement en Espagne, Italie &.ª aussi bien qu'a la Chine, mais il faut Convenir, que ceux de la Chine sont d'un autre gout, melieur et plus dou, ils ont aussi de plusieurs Sortes que nous n'avons pas en Europe.

Nous avons trouve a Canton un exellent fruit qu'ils nomment Li-tchi qui est dela grosseur d'une datte; Son noyau est êgalement long et dur: il est Couvert d'une chair molle, pleine d'eau, et d'un gout exquis: il ne Conserve ce goût qu'en partie, lors qu'il se Seche, et il devient noir et vide comme nos prunes ordinaires: la Chair est renfermeé dans un ècorce, qui au dehors ressemble a du Chagrin, mais qui est unie au dedans, et d'une figure pres qu'ovale.[631]

Les animaux Domestiques, qu'on ÿ trouve Sont de cochons [164] des Chevres, des bufles des Vaches, Taureuax, Mouttons &ª Les cochons sont tous noirs, ont la tête petite, le Cou court et epaix, le ventre gros, et touchant ordinairement a terre, et les jambes courtes. ils mangent peu, et sont neamoins fort gras pour la plûpart, apparement parce qu'ils dorment beaucoup.

---

**627** Coffee reached Europe, through the Middle East, during the sixteenth century. See Brian Cowan, *The Social Life of Coffee: the Emergence of the British Coffeehouse* (New Haven: Yale UP, 2005).

**628** The Spanish encountered chocolate, or *cacao*, early in the sixteenth century. The tools for making chocolate beverages arrived in Europe around midcentury. See Marcy Norton, *Sacred Gifts, Profane Pleasures: a History of Tobacco and Chocolate in the Atlantic World* (Ithaca, NY: Cornell UP, 2008).

**629** The preceding paragraph was adjusted and copied from: Moréri, Grand Dictionaire, vol. 4 (1702), 445.

**630** For more on the import of non-indigenous plants to early modern Europe, see Vinita Damodaran, Anna Winterbottom and Alan Lester (eds.), *The East India Company and the Natural World* (Houndsmills, UK: Palgrave Macmillan, 2015); Paula Findlen, *Possessing Nature: Museums, Collecting and Scientific Culture in Early Modern Italy* (Berkeley: University of California Press, 1996); Daniela Bleichmar, *Visible Empire: Botanical Expeditions and Visual Culture in the Hispanic Enlightenment* (Chicago: University of Chicago Press, 2012).

**631** This paragraph, except for the first sentence, was adjusted and copied from: Du Halde, Description, vol. 1, 19–20.

Les Oiseaux Domestiques Sont de Canards, des Coqs, des Poules[632], des Pauvons[633], des faisans &.[a] on trouve tout Sorte de gibier en quantite et fort bon marche, c'est enfin un Païs fort agreable et delicieu. on feroit un livre entier de tout ce qu'il ÿ a de particulier à dire des fruits, des Arbres fruitiers, du arbre qu'on tire de l'huile, de celui qui porte le Suif[634], et de l'arbre ou l'on prend la Cire, du Bamboux, et celuy du vernis et des tout autres qu'on trouve dans cette Province.

Monsieur les Chinois en general Sont grands, droits et peu chargez de graisse. ils ont le Visage long et le front haut, mais les jeux petits. leur nez est assez large, et êlevé dans le milieu, leur bouche n'est ni grande ni petite; et leurs levres Sont assez delieés. ils Sont d'un teint Couleur de cendre[635], et ont les cheveux noirs. ils ont peu de barbe, mais celle qu'ils ont est longe; car ils S'arrachent le poil, et n'en laissent venir au manton que quelques uns fort longs, êparpillez parci parla, dont ils se font grand honneur. jls les peignent souvent, ils ont aussi a chaque côté de le levre Superieure de longs poils qui resemblent a des Moustaches. les Anciens Chinois êtimoient fort leurs Cheveux qu'ils laissoient venir fort longs, et les jettoient (comme eux meme m'on dit) Soigneusement derriere avec la main: en Suitte ils les entortilloient au tour d'un poinçon, et les jettoient derriere la tête, ce qui Se pratiquoit par l'un [165] et par l'autre Sexe. mais apres que les Tartares eurent conquis la Chine, ils oterent aux Chinois de vive force cette Coûtume[636] dont dont [sic] ils etoient si entetez. aussi cette jnjure leur fut plus sensible que leur Servitude, et fut cause qu'ils se rebellerent, mais ayant encore êté vaincus, ils furent forcez d'obeir, et ils suivent encore aujourd'huÿ la mode des Tartares leurs vainqueurs, se rasent la tête et ne laissent qu'un toupet que les uns nouent et que les autres laissent prendre aussi long et aussi Court qui leur plait.

Le Commun peuple n'a ni chapeau ni bonnets ni turbans, mais quand ils Sortent ils ont ala main un petit parasol qu'ils tiennent sur la tête pour se garantir du Soleil ou de la pluje. S'ils ne vont pas loin ils se Contentent de prendre un grand evantail de

632 This sentence and the preceding paragraph were adjusted and copied from: Dampier, Suite, vol. 2, 82.

633 This likely refers to peafowl, a type of pheasant of which several species are native to India, Indonesia and Southeast Asia. The male bird—the peacock—was used as a symbol of the Ming Dynasty.

634 The Chinese tallow tree, or *Triadica sebifera*, was indigenous to eastern China and Japan. It produced seeds with waxy coatings, which were used to make candles and soaps for regional use.

635 For more on racial categorization in eighteenth-century Europe, see David Bindman, *Ape to Apollo: Aesthetics and the Idea of Race in the 18th Century* (Ithaca, NY: Cornell UP, 2002); Michael Keevak, *Becoming Yellow: a Short History of Racial Thinking* (Princeton, NJ: Princeton UP, 2011).

636 The queue was a traditional Manchu hairstyle, wherein men shaved the front portion of their heads and wore their remaining hair gathered in a braid behind. In July 1645, Dorgon ordered all conquered Han Chinese to adopt the custom or face execution within ten days. It remained the standard hairstyle during the Ch'ing Dynasty. Han styles favored long hair, often worn by men in a bun atop their heads. Struve, Southern Ming, 662; Dennerline, Shun-chih, 87; Elliott, Manchu, 400, ft. 104.

papier ou de Soÿe, fait comme ceux de nos Dames, chacun à Son evantail, dont il se couvre la tête, S'il n'a pas de parasol, quand ce ne seroit que pour traverser la ruë.[637]

L'habit ordinaire[638] des hommes est une tunique et un haut de chausse, les bas qu ils portent sont de Coton ou de Soÿe, leurs souliers ou pantoufles sont faits differemment, les Chinois de qualitez portent de longes robes de Soÿe et fort legerés et communement blanches et un haut bruin, olive, ou violet, et un autre qui leur sert de Casaque, est noir. leurs Calecons sont amples qui descendent jus qu'aux talons, et au lieu de Souliers ils portent de boutines de Soÿe.

Les Chinois Sont fort attachez aux civilitez et aux compliments. ils affectent un air modeste, et un Contenance Serieúse [166] jls marchent toujours avec un évantail ala main, sont bien vetus, et ne se decouvrent point la tête quand ils saluent, mais font une jnclination du Corps, et joignent leurs mains[639] ensemble en forme de Cercle.

Les femmes n'y passent point pour belles, si elles n'ont de petits pieds, c'est pourquoi[640] on leur lie les pieds de leur enfance aussi fort qu'elles le peuvent souffrir, et des qu'elles peuvent marcher jusques a ce qu'elles soient en âge de ne plus Croitre, on les bande tous les Soirs.[641] en use ainsi pour les empecher de grossir parce qu'ils regardent la petitese du pied comme une grande beauté. mais cette ridicule Coûtume les prive en quelque maniere de l'usage des pieds et au lieu de marcher, elles vont en chancelant autour de leurs maisons, et retombent incontient, reduites qu'elles Sont par maniere de dire a demeurer assises tout le tems de leur vie.

Elles Sortent rarement, et l'on croiroit Volontiers comme quelques uns ont fait, que l'entetement des chinois par une Coûtume Si raisonable à été une ruse des maris pour empêcher leurs femmes de Courir et de se rejouir ensemble, et pour les retenir au logis. elles Sont toujours cloueés a leur ouvrage, et habiles a l'aigille, dont elles font plusieurs curieuses broderies et même leurs Souliers.

Les pauvres femmes vont dans les ruës avec beaucoup de peine sans bas ou sans souliers, celles ci n'ont pas besoin d'avoir de petits pieds, etant comme elles le Sont obligeés de gagner leur vie.[642]

---

**637** The preceding two paragraphs were adjusted and copied from: Dampier, Suite, 83–4.

**638** For more on contemporary dress, see Valery Garrett, *Chinese Dress: from the Qing Dynasty to the Present* (Tokyo: Tuttle Publishing, 2007), 8–26, 64–87, 158–171; Antonia Finnane, *Changing Clothes in China: Fashion, History and Nation* (New York: Columbia UP, 2008), 43–51; Timothy Brook, *The Confusions of Pleasure: Commerce and Culture in Ming China* (Berkeley: University of California Press, 1998), 218–37.

**639** The preceding three sentences were copied from: Moréri, Grand Dictionaire, vol. 2 (1707), 155.

**640** The preceding sentence was copied from: Ibid., vol. 2 (1702), 155.

**641** Female foot binding popularized in China during the Sung Dynasty and, although associated with elites, eventually spread to encompass wider social ranks. The K'ang-hsi Emperor tried to ban the habit in 1644 – seeing it as a form of non-Manchu ethnic expression – but failed. See Dorothy Ko, *Cinderella's Sisters: a Revisionist History of Footbinding* (Berkeley: University of California Press, 2005).

**642** The preceding three paragraphs, except for the first sentence, were copied from: Dampier, Suite, 100–1.

Les hommes Sont obligez d'assigner la dot des filles qu'ils veulent êpouser[643], et la nouvelle marieé la remet a son Pere, pour la peine qu'il a eü de l'êlever.[644] quand un riche Chinois se [167] fiance a Canton, apres que le Contract est signé, il va le soir voir sa maitresse et se fait porter dans une Chaise magnifique porteé par deux ou quatre hommes selon sa qualité presedeé par plusieurs domestiques qui portent chacun un fallot ou Lanterne. la Chaise est jmmediatement Suivie d'un grand nombre d'jnstruments de musique a leur maniere, qui à l'egard dela nôtre est un Veritable charivari. les Pretres ou Bonzes viennent apres avec de longues robes violettes et des bonnets noirs quarrez: le galant va voir sa maitresse en cet equipage, et s'en retourne de même.[645]

On fait les même façons quand ils vont s'epouser avec cette difference seulement que la femme à une Chaise Couverte de telle maniere qu'elle peut voir tout le monde sans être vûe. quand la céremonie du mariage est acheveé, les hommes disnent tous ensemble en public, et les femmes sont dans un autre chambre ou les hommes n'entrent point. les tables dans les deux Chambres, sont disposeés de telle maniere que le mari et la marieé se trouvent ce jour la justement dos a dos, la muraille entre deux. le soir l'epoux fait l'honneur a son Epouse dela recevoir a Sa table, faveur qui ne lui est jamais plus accordeé: car les hommes ont une telle Sorte de mepris pour les femmes, que les maris mêmes ne regardent et ne traitent les leurs que comme des Veritables esclaves, de meme que tous les autres Orientaux, ils Sont extremement Ialoux[646], volupteux, non obstant qu ils ont plusieurs femmes, ils Se donnent fort àla Sodomie.[647]

Il n'est pas permis aux Chinois de repudier leur femme, si ce n'est en cas d'adultere, et en quelques autres occasions qui sont tres rares. pour lors ils les vendent a qui il leur plaît[648], et en achetent une autre. parmis les gens de qualité, cela n'arrive guere, mais le peuple en use ordinairement ainsi. que si un homme êtoit assez hardi que [168] de vendre sa femme sans raison, celui qui l'acheteroit et celui qui la vendroit secretement, sont Severement punis Sans pourtant obliger le premier Mari à la reprandre.

---

643 For more on this nuptial process, see Richard J. Smith, *The Qing Dynasty and Traditional Chinese Culture* (New York: Rowman & Littlefield, 2015), 354–356.

644 The preceding sentence was copied from: Moréri, Grand Dictionaire, vol. 2 (1707), 211.

645 The preceding three sentences were adjusted and copied from: Voyage et aventures, 116–7.

646 The preceding paragraph was adjusted and copied from: Ibid., 117.

647 For more on homoeroticism in imperial China, see Bret Hinsch, *Passions of the Cut Sleeve: The Male Homosexual Tradition in China* (Berkeley: University of California Press, 1990).

648 Marriage was a marker of social adulthood in Ming and Ch'ing China. As a result, divorce was greatly frowned upon. For more on licit and illict wife-selling, or *mai xiu*, see ibid.; Matthew H. Sommer, *Polyandry and Wife-Selling in Qing Dynasty China: Survival Strategies and Judicial Interventions* (Berkeley: University of California Press, 2015).

Quoiqu'en chaque famille il n'y puisse avoir qu'une femme legitime il est neamoins permis de prendre autant de Concubines[649] qu'on en Veut tous leurs enfans ont egalement droit à la Succession[650], parce qu'ils sont censez appartenir a la veritable femme, ils l'appellent tous leur Mere, et elle est en effet l'unique maitresse de la maison, les concubines la Servent, l'honnorent, et n'ont d'autorité qu'autant qu'elle Veut bien leur en Communiquer.[651]

Les Chinois font grand Chère de tous Sortes de ragous[652], mais le principal est la viande de pourceau qui est un mets tres delicieux chez eux. ils mangent tres proprement quoi que Sans nape ni Serviete. ils ne prennent point la Viande avec les doits, et Comme on la sert toute découpeé ils la portent à la bouche en la serrant entre deux petîts bâtons[653], longs de six a sept pouces, qui Sont Vernis proprement.[654]

Leur boisson ordinaire est le thé et le vin de Ris qu'ils font par destillation. il à la Couleur d'ambre et à un gout assé agreable, selon que je l'ay gouté il Approche à la boison que nous appellons hidromel.[655] les chinois le nomment vin de Mandarin.

On dit que les Chinois n'aiment point a monter les degrez d'un escalier, ce que j'aÿ trouvé contraire, car les maisons des Mandarins que nous avons frequenteés nous les avons trouveés avec des appartemens haut aussi bien que bas, il est vrai qu'ils occupent preferablement le bas de la maison, [169] c'est une Coutume que nous observons aussi bien qu'eux.

Ils partagent leurs maisons qui sont fort espacieuses en Sales et en chambres, sans aucunes fenetres sur la ruë ils nous dirent, qu'il n'est pas honnête de s'en servir. Le dedans de leurs maisons est manifique[656] et proprement meubleés.

L'appartement le plus retiré est pour les femmes, qui ÿ Sont êtroitement gardeés, Sans voir les hommes et sans avoir aucunne familiarité avec eux. ils mettent devant la porte un Idole domestique nommeé Choang Loyé[657] qui est un Mandarin assis dans

**649** Chinese men sometimes had additional recognized sexual partners, known as *qie* or concubines. These women were subservient to his wife. Hua, Concubinage, 41–94.

**650** A Chinese wife had control over all of her husband's household, including the upbringing, marriages and property of his children with concubines. All sons in this extended household, in turn, were entitled to equal shares of their paternal inheritance. Ibid., 51.

**651** The preceding two paragraphs were adjusted and copied from: Louis Le Comte, *Nouveaux Mémoires Sur L'Etat Present De La Chine, vol. 2* (Paris: Jean Anissson, 1701), 85.

**652** For more on Chinese foodways, see Thomas O. Hollmann, *The Land of Five Flavors: a Cultural History of Chinese Cuisine* (New York: Columbia UP, 2010).

**653** This refers to chopsticks, or *kuai-tzi*.

**654** The preceding paragraph, except the first half-sentence, was adjusted and copied from: *Voyage et avantures*, vol. 2, 114.

**655** Mead is a yellow alcoholic beverage, made by fermenting honey and water.

**656** The preceding paragraph was adjusted and copied from: Moréri, Grand Dictionaire, vol. 3 (1725), 141.

**657** This might refer to Zhang Lang, or Zao Jun, a popular Daoist deity believed to guard the hearth and family.

un fauteuil, aÿant un homme[658] derriere lui d'une phisionomie hideuse qui lui souffle dans l'oreille: C'est un Mandarin Tartare, comme les Missionaires m'on dit, qui a gouverné les peuples fort Sagement, et qui à rendu de grands services à l'Empereur Chinois, c'est pourqoui il a este Deifie par le peuple, et en tel reveren, qu'il n'y a point de maison, meme la moindre petite barque qui n'aÿe la dite jdole.

Comme les Chinois croÿent la metempsÿchose[659] ils se persuadent qu'il leur est avantageux quand leurs enfans viennent à mourir que leurs ames passent en d'autres Corps, et qu'ils viennent des enfans d'un homme plus riche. Ce desir d'avoir du bien fait encore qu'ils ne Souffrent point d'oisifs, et le Soupçon leur inspire une grande aversion pour les êtrangers. jls ont divers jeux semblables a Ceux que nous avons, et sur tout pour les Cartes et les êchecs, qui Sont peu differens des notres.

Ils ont un grand Soin de toutes les Choses publiques; ils ont aussi des inventions particulieres pour le Soulagement des ouvriers, presque en toute sorte de profession[660], cela provient, que la [170] loÿ du Paÿs oblige chaque Chinois a Suivre la profession de son Pere[661], et jl n'oseroit Changer que par la permission des Mandarins: d'ou il S'ensuit que les arts Sont florisans, il leur est rigureusement defendu de sortir du Paÿs, et de vojager sans un ordre expres dela Cour.

Depuis le Philosophe Confucius (dont j'aÿ parlé) la morale à esté en si grande reputation, que des trois Sortes de Sectes de Philosophie qu'on ÿ permet, la Sienne nommeé de Lettrez à Si fort l'avantage que tous les grands du Royaume en font profesion; et meme il n'y a que les Mandarins Lettrez, formez dans Son êcole qui aÿent part au gouvernement[662], ainsi que toute la noblesse vient des scienses, sans avoir êgard à la naissance, hormis dans les familes Royales, plus un homme est docte, plus il est avancé aux honneurs et aux dignitez.[663]

L'Empereur Choisit ceux qui sont les plus Doctes d'entre les Lettrez pour deservir la Charge de Quong:fou nommé par les Europeens Mandarin[664] et comme dans le Mandarinat il y a plusieurs Ordres, et en chaque ordre deux degrez; l'Empereur êleve

658 Reference unknown.

659 Metempsychosis, or reincarnation, argues for the persistence of an individual's consciousness or soul through more than one bodily lifespans. The idea especially developed in China after the arrival of Buddhism, although several Confucian emperors claimed to be the reincarnations of earlier rulers. See Joanna Waley-Cohen, *The Culture of War in China: Empire and the Military under the Qing Dynasty* (London: I.B. Tauris, 2006), 103.

660 This sentence and the preceding paragraph were adjusted and copied from: Moréri, Grand Dictionaire, vol. 1 (1683), 881.

661 This tradition was noted by Marco Polo during his travels in Yüan China. Manuel Komroff, *The Travels of Marco Polo* (London: The Modern Library, 1926), 197–8.

662 The preceding paragraph was adjusted and copied from: Moréri, Grand Dictionaire, vol. 1 (1683), 881.

663 The preceding paragraph was adjusted and copied from: Ibid, vol. 2, 155.

664 This note appears in the left margin: "nom que les Portugais leur donnerent, à Mandado, les appelants jndifferement os Mandarinos, ne pouvant prononcer le mot Quong:fou." The Chinese word

ses officiers à ces ordres et a ces degrez à proportion de leur merite et de leur Services: mais quand il n'est pas content de leur conduite, il les abbaisse d'un degré ou d'un ordre et ces officiers ainsi abbaissez Sont obligez de le marquer dans leurs qualitez, ce qui les humilie beaucoup et les oblige pour ôter cette tache, a servir le Prince avec plus de fidelité et de Zele. car par exemple celuÿ du troisieme ordre venant dans la presence [171] de celuÿ du deuxieme ordre, doit Se prosterner devant luy, comme celuÿ cÿ doit faire devant celuÿ du premier Ordre, et le Mandarin du Premier Ordre devant l'Empereur.

La Marque de Cette dignité est un petit Chapeau[665] pointu d'une nate tres fine, double avec un brocard d'or, auquel est attache un boutton d'ambre de six rais: dela pointe de ce Chapeau sort une ombelle de Soÿe cramoisi, descendent jus qu'au bord du Chapeau. quand ils Sortent leur train est nombreux, de cinquante ou Cent hommes, qui portent des êtandarts, des grands Sabres et autres tropheés Selon le rang du Mandarin, au milieu des quels paroit le Mandarin êleve sur une Chaise bien garnie, que Six ou huit hommes portent Sur leurs epaules.

Apres que l'Empereur a fait Mandarin ces Lettrez il leur donne d'ordinaire le gouvernement de quelque Province de son Etat, hors du paÿs de leur naissance; ou ils ont un fort beau palais. dans la principale Salle de Ce Palais, et dans un lieu fort êlevé est l'effige de l'Empereur, devant la quelle le Manderin se met à genoux en faisant une profunde reverence avant que de s'asseoir sur le siege de justice, et de Commencer aucune affaire de consequence. tout le peuple leur porte un tel respêt et honneur qu il ne leur parlent jamais qu'a genoux ou par requétes, et lorsque quelques uns de ces Mandarins passe par les ruës tout le monde se tire a l'êcart a fin de lui faire place.[666]

Les Chinois se servent ordinairement de palaquins ou litieres porteés par des hommes, la pluspart d'eux, ont peú de Coeur et [172] n'aiment pas les fatiges de la guerre comme les Tartares: cest pourquoi ils ont plus de Mandarins de Robbe, que des Mandarins d'êpeé.[667]

---

for "mandarin" was *guān*. This phrase might also refer to the word *gōngfū*, which signified a skill mastered through much effort.

**665** For more on mandarin dress, see Garrett, Chinese Dress, 70–5.

**666** The preceding paragraph was adjusted and copied from: Manesson-Mallet, Déscription, vol. 2, 44.

**667** The preceding paragraph was adjusted and copied from: Moréri, Grand Dictionaire, vol. 2 (1724), 155.

Leur maniere d'êcrire differe fort dela notre[668], jls emploÿent le pinceau qui leur Sert de plume, leur encre n'est pas liquide comme la notre: c'est une matiere êpaise[669], dont la Couleur est noire ou rouge[670] si connú en Europe, ils le broÿent sur une pierre qui leur Sert d'ecritoire, sur la quelle ils trempent le pinceau: leur papier est plus fin, et plus uni que le nôtre, mais il n'est pas Si blanc, ni aussi fort, cela est Cause qu'ils n'y êcrivent que d'un Côté. Leur maniere d'êcrire, est de Conduire les lignes de haut en bas par Colomnes, commencent par le Côté droit, retournant à la gauche, ils commencent leurs livres ou nous les finissons.[671]

Quelques autheurs croÿent que l'art d'jmprimerie[672], ÿ est plus ancien que dans l'europe, et Selon que j'aÿ apris d'eux même, il ÿ auroit bien cinq Cent ans qu'ils s'en servent, leur jmprimerie est aussi fort differente de la notre. Comme nous avons peu de Caracteres, nous les assemblons aisement, et nous en formons des planches qui Servent à Imprimer; Mais ala Chine, comme ils ont plus de quatrevingt mille Caracteres, la dépence des Caracteres seroit jnfinie, et l'assemblage presque jmposible. ainsi ils ont pris le parti de graver leurs lettres sur des planches de bois, dont ils se servent de la meme maniere que nous nous servons icÿ des planches de Cuivre pour Jmprimer en taille douce.[673]

Leur maniere de chiffrer est aussi differente de la nòtre, nous [173] employons pour cela nos lettres de Chiffre: mais quoi qu'ils en ajent aussi a leur maniere, ils ne Scavent les assembler comme nous; ils ont une planche de deux ou trois pieds de long et un et demi de large dans le quels il ÿ a six ou sept petits battons qui Sont paralelles la longeur de la boite, sur les quels on broche plusieurs petites globes l'une

---

668 Calligraphy, or *shūfǎ*, is a form of stylized writing, in which brush-drawn characters represent both words and phrases. It was employed for all imperial records since the T'ang Dynasty. See Lothar Ledderose, "Chinese Calligraphy: Its Aesthetic Dimension and Social Function", in: *Orientations* 17.10 (1986), 35–50; Kwo Da-Wei, *Chinese Brushwork in Calligraphy and Painting: its History, Aesthetics and Techniques* (Mineola, NY: Dover Publications, 1981); Chen Tingyou, *Chinese Calligraphy* (New York: Cambridge UP, 2010).

669 Chinese ink was composed of lampblack, or a finely powdered soot, bonded with an animal adhesive. Calligraphers grinded and mixed inksticks with water on a clay or natural inkstone to obtain their desired consistency. Savary des Brulons and Savary, Dictionnaire, vol. 1, 131; Da-Wei, Chinese, 125–32.

670 The preceding two sentences were adjusted and copied from: Moréri, Grand Dictionaire, vol. 5 (1725), 25.

671 The preceding paragraph was adjusted and copied from: Ibid.

672 The earliest printing originated in third-century China. Bi Sheng, a Chinese native, then developed moveable type between 1041 and 1048, or several hundred years before Johannes Gutenberg. See Joseph Needham, *Science and Civilisation in China, vol. 5.1* (New York: Cambridge UP, 1993).

673 The preceding paragraph, except for the first sentence, was copied from: Charles le Gobien, *Histoire de l'édit de l'empereur de la Chine en faveur de la Religion Chrestienne* (Paris: Jean Anisson, 1698), 57.

plus grande que l'autre, les quelles ils font glisser le long des dits battons, de même qu'en Europe on fait avec les jettons.[674]

Les Chinois n'ont point des lettres disposeés en Alphabeth, ils ont autant des figures que de mots qui sont tous d'une Silabe. il faut Scavoir meme que leurs declinaisons et conjugaisons Sont contenuës dans ces figures, dont le nombre êgale celui de leurs penseés: qu'en S'exprimant ou en êcrivant avec des figures qui signifient quelque fois deux ou trois mots, et souvent meme des periades entières ils marquent ces diferentes Significations par des Caracteres diferentes.

Par Exemple, Cĩu, si on le prononce simplement ne signifie rien. si on le on le [sic] prononce Ciúúúú en allongeant la pronontiation de l'u[675], et en êclaircissant toujours la voix il signifie Monsieur. si on le prononce Ciú en allongeant l'u[676], et lui Conservant toujours le meme son, il signifie pourceaú. Ciu prononcé avec beaucoup de vitesse[677], est la cuisine; et prononcé d'une voix forte et afoiblie sur la fin[678], signifie les pieds d'une escabelle.

Par la, il est bien aisé de Consevoir que toute la force de Cette langue consiste dans la diversité des accens, des jnflexions des tons, des aspirations et des autres Changemens dela Voix [174] qui sont dificiles et en tres grand nombre. mais outre les cinq figures que l'on employe pour les cinq diferentes Significations de ciu, si l'on a dessin d'ecrire bon jour Monsieur, on ne se sert ni du Caractére qui signifie bon, ni de celui qui Signifie jour, ni de celui qui Signifie Monsieur, mais d'un Caractere tout diferente de ceux la, qui expliquera Seul, les trois mots bon jour Monsieur: et Si l'on veut êcrire oui Monsieur, il faudra de même laisser la figure qui Signifie oui, et celle qui Signifie Mons.[r], et se servir d'une autre qui Signifie Seule, oui Monsieur.

Ces caracteres etant jnfinis, il est hors de doute que pour en faire le juste discernement, la Vie d'un homme ne peut pas Sufire: nul parmi les Chinois, n'est crû Savant, S'il n'en connoit pour le moins quatrevingt mille, quoi que l'on n'en ait besoin que de dix mille pour posseder parfaitement cette langue. avec tout cela, elle est si pauvre, qu'elle ne Contient que trois cent trente mots. ce qu'il ÿ a de fâcheux est qu'un Seul mot Signifie bien Souvent quinze ou vingt choses toutes differentes, par la maniere dont on le prononce, et elle est tres difficile par rapport aux equivoques.[679] I'aÿ remarqué quand ils parlent qu'ils emploÿent cinq tons de musique, et parlent pour ainsi dire en Chantant. Il leur est jmposible de prononcer le R., mais lors qu'ils veulent S'efforcer de le faire, ils ne prononcent qu'une suite de L.L.L.

---

**674** This likely refers to the *suànpán*, or Chinese abacus. Dating at least to the second century, it was used both for decimal and hexadecimal computation.

**675** This might refer to the Chinese word *jūn*, meaning "sovereign or master."

**676** This refers to the Chinese word *zhü*, meaning "hog" or "swine."

**677** This refers to the Chinese word *chuï*, meaning "to cook."

**678** Word unknown.

**679** The preceding three paragraphs were adjusted and copied from: Urbain Chevreau, *Histoire du monde, vol. 7* (Paris: Hilaire Foucault, 1717), 375–7.

La langue Vulgaire de Canton[680] n'est pas entendue des Mandarins et differe aussi de Celle des Provinces voisinnes, et je crois que [175] chaque Province à une langue Vulgaire différente l'une a l'autre: mais celle des Mandarins est universelle dans toute l'Empire.

Ie vous aÿ dit aillieurs Monsieur que l'jnvention de l'jmprimerie leur etoit duë, comme aussi l'jnvention dela poudre à Canon, et il ÿ a pres de seize cent ans, qu'ils en ont l'usage. leurs feux d'artifices sont même d'autant plus beaux et au dessus des nôtres, qu'ils Savent donner à la flamme, la couleur et la figure qu'il leur plait de donner, et ils representent en l'air[681] differentes Sortes de figures, comme des Caracteres, dragons &.[a]

A l'egard dela Geographie et l'Astrologie, les Savans n'en Sçavent que ce que les Peres Missionaires leur en ont appris, car autrefois ils croÿoient que la Superficie de la terre êtoit plane[682], mais on leur à fait voir facilement qu'elle est ronde,

Le peuple n'est pas encore defait dela fole croÿance d'un dragon d'une enorme grandeur qui a Sa residence dans la vaste etendue des airs, et s'approche quelques fois du Soleil ou de la Lune pour le devorer: et suivant eux, c'est la Cause de l'êclipse: il m'est arrivé qu'un marchand Chinois Gikoang[683] êtoit assez Sot pour me demander si nous avions aussi une Lune en Europe, et aÿant rêpondu qu'ouÿ, il demanda Si c'êtoit la meme qu'on voÿoit ala Chine: Le peuple font pour lors un tintamare diabolique avec leurs bassins de Cuivre, pour effrayer le dit Dragon, âfin qu'il n'avale pas le Soleil ou la Lune: cependant les Mandarins et les gens Lettrez ont été desabusez de Cette folle jdeé par les Missionaires qui leur ont donné l'explication.

[176] Cependent les Chinois n'ont pû porter l'art dela navigation au point de perfection qu'elle est parmi nos Europeéns: car ils ne Savent pas se servir d'hauteur, d'azimuth, et du Cours des Astres, comme nos Pilotes: aussi toute leur navigation n'est proprement qu'un Cabotage, Ils navigent sur la Connoissance des terres ou Côtes et par l'aide d'un Compas qui n'a que huit rumbs de vent.

Les cotes principales ou ils navigent Sont le Iapon, Conchinchine, Tonquin, Manille, Malacca, Batavia, Achin et Surate, mais ils n'oseroient naviger au large du grand Occean, quand ils navigent dans les paÿs susdits, c'est dans la Saison des Moussons favorables lors qu'ils n'ont point de tempêtes ou tÿphons à Craindre, autrement ils n'oseroient S'y risquer:

**680** Yue, or Cantonese, is the regional dialect of Chinese, which includes differences in vocabulary, pronunciation and tone. Mandarin, or *guānhuà*, was the official language of the Ch'ing Dynasty. See Don Snow, *Cantonese as Written Language: the Growth of a Written Chinese Vernacular* (Hong Kong: Hong Kong UP, 2004), 67–100.

**681** The preceding paragraph was adjusted and copied from: Chevreau, Histoire, vol. 7, 378–9.

**682** The Ancient Chinese believed the earth was flat, with a dome-like struture above encompassing the heavens. The belief persisted at least to the arrival of Jesuit Matteo Ricci in the late sixteenth century. William Peterson, Learning, 805–6.

**683** Person unknown.

Ils ont aussi des navires de guerre faites en forme de Galeres[684] et qui vont fort bien a la rame, mais qui ne sont propres que dans les Rivieres, ils n'ont point de Canon: mais quelques pieriers qu'ils gouvernent avec la main: les ancres de leur Vaisseaux sont de bois et n'ont qu'une pâte, leurs Cables d'une espece de Pitre.

Leurs Ionques ou Vaisseaux de mer Sont tout autrement construits que les notres, leurs gabaret n'est pas si beau[685], ils sont tous a plate Varange. La pruë en est coupeé et sans esperon, la poupe Ouverte par le milieu afin que le gouvernail, qu'on ÿ enferme, soit defendu par les cotez des coups de mer, il est aussi plus large que les notres[686], ils ont sur le tillac de petites Chaumures ou toits Couverts de feuilles de Palmite et hautes d'environ 5 a 6 pieds, ou les matelots Se logent. ils ont une grande Cabane avec un grand autel sur le quels jls p[la]cent leur Idole, devant du quel ils ont une lampe ardente.

Le fond de Calle est divisé en plusieurs Separations, toutes Si [177] propres et si bien jointes, que S'il entre de l'eau dans quelqu'une, elle ne peut aller plus loin, par ce moÿen ne fait du dommage qu'aux marchandisses qui sont au fond de la Chambre. Il ÿ a dans chaque Chambre un ou deux marchands ou plus, chacun y Serre ses marchandisses, et S'y loge dans le voÿage.[687]

Ces Vaisseaux ont trois mâts comme les notres, mais tout autrement mâtes, leur mât de misene est tout sur l'avant, et le gros mast n'est pas loin du lieu ou nous plaçons notre mast de misene, un Cordage qui se transporte du basbord à stribord selon que le vent change leur sert d'estraÿ et d'aubans. le beaupré et l'artimon qui sont tres foibles, sont à basbord êloignez considerablement du milieu, ou nous avons Coutume dele placer.

Leurs masts de hune sont fort courts, mais le grand mast des gros Vaisseaux me parut aussi gros que les masts de nos Vaisseaux de guerre du troisieme rang, Cependent ils ne sont pas de deux pieces comme les nôtres, je n'aÿ jamais vu de Si gros mâts d'une seule piece si longs, et diminuents Si proprement en haussant. Leurs basses Voiles sont de nattes fort êpaisses. garnies de deux en deux pieds dans toute leur largeur de lattes d'un bois tres leger, ces voiles Sont êtroites comme celles de nos barques, elles sont composeés de differens pans qui tombent en se doublant les uns sur les autres, comme Ceux d'un paravant, elles Sont attacheés au mât par le moÿen de plusieurs chapelets; quand le tems est beau, on met une voile de perroquet, mais quand le tems vient mauvais on dêcend Sur le tillac et la voile et la verge Sans ÿ monter pour la ferler. quand le vent est arriere ou fort largue, ces vaisseaux font

**684** Covered swoopers, or *Meng chong*, could be used as maritime battering rams.

**685** Europeans who traveled to the East Indies often ridiculed Chinese ships, which they perceived as unwieldy and bulky. See Jobst Broelmann, "Der chinesische Weg im Schiffbau", in: China, eine Wiege der Weltkultur, ed. Arne Eggebrecht (Mainz: von Zabern, 1994), 139.

**686** The preceding sentence was adjusted and copied from: Le Comte, Nouveaux Mémoires, vol., 348–9.

**687** The preceding paragraph was adjusted and copied from: Dampier, Suite, vol. 2, 106.

beaucoup de Chemin, et Sont aussi bon voiliers que les notres, mais de bouline, ils ne font que deriver.

[178] On Se Sert point de godron pour les Calfas, mais ils emploient une Composition de Chaux, et d'huile avec la filasse de bambou rapé, ce sorte de Calfas est Si bon que les Vaisseaux ne font presque point d'eau, aussi n'usent ils jamais de pompe, un ou deux puits suffisent pour mettre le fond de cale à sec.[688]

Dans les gros Vaisseaux les Ancres Sont de fer, dans les moindres ils sont d'un bois dur et pesant garnis de fer, pour vous donner une jdeé entierre de ces Sortes de Batimens, J'ay joint icy le dessin[689] que I'aÿ tire apres une de leurs Ionques qui voguoît avec nous, en entrant devant Macao.

Si les Chinois sont mauvais Marins, ils remplacent cela par leur grande addresse à naviger Sur les Rivieres: ils ÿ ont des grands bateaux[690] de 150 a 170 pieds de longs, les quels ils font marcher et gouvernent avec Six a Sept rames aussi grandes que celles de nos galeres, avec les quels ils nagent par derriere, et Se tirent fort bien d'affaire malgre les Courans, et les Roches cacheés Sous l'eau.

Je passe sous silance Monsieur plusieurs autres Choses qui Consernent les Chinois. je crois ne devoir pas entrer dans un plus long detail. aÿez la bonté de Vous Souvenir que ce n'est qu'une lettre que je vous êcris et non pas une histoire. avant que de finir je vous[691] entretiendrai encore un moment de nos affaires particulieres.

Apres avoir demeure deux mois[692] sans pouvoir contracter avec aucun Chinois pour la Cargaison du thé pour nos deux Vaisseaux, par rapport des grandes pertes que les Chinois avoient Souffert l'anneé precedente, par la grande abondance des dits marchandisses, et le peu des Vaisseaux qui etoient venus cette anneé la pour trafiquer, ils furent obligois d'envoÿer leur thé a Batavia[693] [179] pour tacher de le vendre par cette voÿe sans perte, mais le transport fut si grand que le thé se trouva a plus bon marché a Batavia qu'a Canton, dont plusieurs d'eux se trouverent ruinez dans ce Commerce, ainsi qu'il ne resta que fort peu de thé a Canton, comme effectivement nous l'avons trouvé.

---

**688** The preceding three sentences were adjusted and copied from: Le Comte, Nouveaux, vol. 1, 389.
**689** There is no attached picture.
**690** For more on China's naval development, see Lo Jung-pang, *China as a Sea Power, 1127–1368: a Preliminary Survey of the Maritime Expansion and Naval Exploits of the Chinese People during the Southern Song and Yuan Periods*, ed. Bruce A. Elleman (Hong Kong: Hong Kong UP, 2011); Timothy Brook, "Communications and commerce", in: Cambridge History of China, vol. 8, 604–5.
**691** The preceding paragraph was adjusted and copied from: Étienne de Barbinais le Gentil, *Nouveau voyage autour du monde, vol. 1* (Amsterdam: Pierre Mortier, 1728), 303.
**692** Ostend ships stayed in Canton for shorter periods than their European counterparts, averaging 120 days and generally leaving in late November rather than early January. Parmentier, Private, 87.
**693** The K'ang-hsi Emperor prohibited overseas Chinese navigation in 1719, which necessitated that the ongoing trade with Batavia now be conducted through (more costly) Portuguese intermediaries. This sometimes resulted in market shortages in Canton. Van Dyke, Merchants, 458.

Nous nous trouvames forcé pour faire l'achat de thé, a cause que la saison avancoit pour notre depart, nous fimes semblants aupres des petits marchands qui se trouvoient avec de thé, d'avoir dêya fait notre emplette de thé pour nos deux Vaisseaux avec une personne qui etoit en état pour nous fournir toute la Cargaison, chacun d'eux S'jmagina que s'êtoit avec Chiuqua[694] notre Correspondent, et comme ces petits marchands êtoient jnformez dela force de cet homme dans le negoce ils Commencerent àlors à presenter leur thé a vendre, au Comencement nous rejettames leurs presentations. Comme si nous aussions dêja eu nôtre thé pour nôtre Charge ce qui les obliga a venir nous presenter leur thé, l'un le vouloit donner pour un tel pris, et un autre pour un moindre, àla fin nous fimes accord pour Cent Caisses avec un marchand nomme Chin qua[695], temoignant que c'etoit pour lui faire plaisir que nous prenions ces cent Caisses; pendant que nous recevions ce thé, tous les autres marchands s'jmaginerent pour lors que nous leur avions dit la Verité. ceçi alarma un peu ces petits marchands qui auroient été obligez de garder leur thé encor cette anneé Sans pouvoir le vendre, ce qui fit qu'ils [180] baisserent le pris, et nous fimes Contract avec eux a l'jncuë de l'un et de l'autre.

notre achat êtant à peu pres fait, alors ils connurent qu'ils avoient été trompeés à Cause qu'ils voÿoient que nous ne recevions aucun thé de notre dit Correspondent, et que nous paquettions dans l'un et autre maison des petits Marchands. Ils Commencerent àlors a Se plaindre de nous, mais pour les âdoucir, nous en achetames une plus grande partie d'eux, et primes un tiers de leur vieux thé; En cas que nous n'ussions pas fait dela sorte, il auroit fallu acheter le thé d'un tiers plus Cher, par ce moÿen nous avons eu la Charge des deux Vaisseaux pour les 15 a 22 theÿls le Piquel.

Il faut agir avec les Chinois fort politiquement, et ne pas donner aussitôt a Conôitre les marchandises qu'on doit acheter au Contraire il leur faut faire croire le Contraire, car autrement ils font entre eux des monopoles qui font quelque fois, que les Europeéns doivent acheter les marchandisses a un fort haut pris, comme il est arrivé aux Marchands des Vaisseaux Anglois, que par leur grande demande qu'ils firent tous à la fois de l'or, il leur a fallu payer 20 pour cent plus que les autres anneés.

Les achats que nous faissons actuellement du thé, n[e] donna aucunne alteration dans ce negoce, au Contraire le pris êtoit ala fin plus bas qu'au Commencement, Cela provient [181] de notre bon menagement et jntelligence dans ce Commerce. A mesure que nous avions paquetté nos Caisses de porselaine, soÿeries, thé &.[a] nous les avons envoye a nos vaisseaux, pour ne point perdre de tems, a Cause que la saison avancoit pour nôtre depart, à la fin, apres que nous eumes receu nos soÿries et le reste du thé

694 *Hong* merchants typically went by several trade names. This makes their specific identification in the historical record difficult. According to data collected by Paul A. Van Dyke, the Ostenders primarily traded with Tan Suqua, Tan Hunqua, Cudgin and Pinky in 1723. Van Dyke, Merchants, 293, 316, 399, 419.
695 Ibid.

avec le restant de notre Cargaison nous les fimes embarquer avec les provisions de bouche.

## Lettre 9.me

Monsieur Comme ma principale jntention est de vous faire Connoitre en detail le negoce dela Chine, ainsi il faut que je vous fasse Connoitre premierement ses Richesses, sa politique, et la grande science de ses habitans dans le Commerce, et Comment notre nation flamande s'est avisé de faire en droiture le Commerce dans cette Vaste partie de la terre, la plus Orientale de l'Asie, et la plus Celebre par sa fertilité qui lui fournit avec abondance tout ce qui peut entretenir un grand Commerce.

Ce qui rend la Chine plus propre au Commerce qu'aucun autre Etat de l'Orient, est le génie de ses habitans qui plus qu'aucun peuple du monde, savent employer en toutes sortes de Manufactures, et d'ouvrages, les Riches productions de toutes [182] especes, qui croissent et qui se trouvent dans les quinze Provinces de ce Vaste Empire, qui sont traverseés au dedans d'une grande quantité de Rivieres et de Caneaux qui facilitent le transport des marchandisses d'une Province dans l'autre.

La Politique des Chinois qui Craignoient d'être Corrompus dans leurs Loix par la frequantation des Etrangers dans leurs Ports qui se trouvent dans Six de ses Provinces, qui sont baigneés de L'ocean Oriental et la Crainte qu ils eurent que les êtrangers n'entreprissent sur leur liberté sous le pretexte du Commerce, les avoit obligé pendant plusieurs milliers d'anneés de fermer l'entreé de leur Empire à toutes sortes de nations, et de se Contenter du negoce jnterieur qu'ils faisoient eux mêmes, mais enfin L'Empereur defunt Kăñg Hy, ayant oúvert les trois Port de Canton ou Quang tong, Fo:kien, et Ning:po:foú[696] que les Anglois ont appelle Liampo, a toút le monde en l'an 1685 a l'exclusion des Hollandois, dont je vous ay parle cy devant, les Indiens, et les Europeéns Se sont êgalement empressez d'user de la liberté de ce nouveau Commerce; et l'on â vu même dans la Flandre Austrichene des Riches Marchands et d'autres personnes d'un grand Credit S'associer, et y former une Compagnie de Commerce[697] Octroÿeé par Sa Maj.te Imperiale et Catholique Charles VI.[698] dans l'an

---

**696** Ningo, known to Europeans as Liampó, was a seaport city, located on the southern coast of Hangzhou Bay and in Chexiang Province. The Portuguese had a settlement here from roughly the 1520s to 1545.

**697** The preceding two paragraphs were adjusted and copied from: Savary des Brûlons, Dictionnaire, vol. 1, 1174.

**698** Charles VI (1685–1740) governed as the Holy Roman Emperor from 1711 to 1740. See Max Braubach, "Karl VI., Kaiser", in: *Neue Deutsche Biographie, vol. 11* (Berlin: Duncker & Humblot, 1977), 211–8.

1723 sous le nom et titre de Compagnie Imperiale et Royale Sous la protection de S.t Charles[699], et la faculté de naviger et negocier aux Indes Orientales et occidentales.

Le Commerce des Etrangers dans la Chine n'a pas seulement [183] êté Ouvert du Côté dela Mer, leurs Caravanes ont êté pareillement recues du Côté dela Terre: et outre les Tartares Orientaux qui ÿ ont toujours envoÿé les leurs particulierement depuis les Empereurs de leur nation qui gouvernent cet Empire, On Voit tous les ans arriver a Peking une nombreuse Caravane de Moscovites[700] qui part de Moscou[701] et de Petersbourg[702], cette nouvelle et Celebre ville situeé au fond de la Mer Baltique[703], qui doit son nom et sa fondation au Czar Pierre Alexiovits[704], Prince qui de nos jours a rendu ses sujets egalement habiles dans la guerre, dans les sciences, et dans le Commerce de terre et de Mer.

Il n'y a point de nation plus propre au Commerce et qui l'entende mieux, que la Chinoise; aussi ne refuse t'elle aucun gain qui se fasse par le negoce, Trafiquant de tout et profitant sur tout avec une grande habilité, mais non pas avec cette fidelité qui aillieurs est regardeé comme l'ame du Commerce.

En un mot, les Chinois sont en Asie comme les Iuif[705] dans L Europe, repandus par tout ou il à quelque chose à gagner, trompeurs, usúriers, sans parole, pleins de souplesse et de subtilité pour menager une bonne occassion, et tout cela sous une apparence de simplicité et de bonne fois, Capables de Surprendre les plus attentifs

**699** This refers to Charlemagne (ca. 742–814), the first Holy Roman Emperor. He was canonized by one of the competing popes, Paschal III, during the twelfth century. Because Saint Charles was considered patron of his office, the giving of his name to the Ostend Company signified their current emperor's protection and support.

**700** The kingdom of Muscovy emerged around the city of Moscow during the fourteenth century, after a period of Mongol political dominance. It became the basis of the Tsardom of Russia in 1547. For more on its early relations with China, see Donald Ostrowski, *Muscovy and the Mongols: Cross-Cultural Influences on the Steppe Frontier, 1304–1589* (New York: Cambridge UP, 1998); Perdue, China, 74–88.

**701** Moscow was a Russian imperial city, located along the western Moskva River.

**702** Saint Petersburg was a Russian imperial city, located along the Neva River and near the Baltic Sea. The city was founded by Tsar Peter I in 1703 and served as Russia's capital from 1712. It is located roughly 650 kilometers northwest of Moscow.

**703** The Baltic Sea is a large inlet of the northern Atlantic Ocean, bordered by modern-day Scandinavia, Finland, the Baltic States, Poland and Germany. Russia also has access to the waterway, via the Gulf of Finland.

**704** Peter Alexeyevich, also known as Peter I or "Peter the Great" (1672–1725), was tsar, then emperor of Russia from 1682 until his death. See Paul Bushkovitch, *Peter the Great: the Struggle for Power, 1671–1725* (New York: Cambridge UP, 2001).

**705** For more on Sephardic activity in early modern trade, see Trivellato, Familiarity; Jonathan I. Israel, *Empires and Entrepots: the Dutch, the Spanish Monarchy and the Jews, 1585–1713* (London: The Hambledon Press, 1990); Richard L. Kagan and Philip D. Morgan (eds.), *Atlantic Diasporas: Jews, Conversos, and Crypto-Jews in the Age of Mercantilism, 1500–1800* (Baltimore: The Johns Hopkins UP, 2009).

et les plus defians.[706] Ils ne sont point honteux lors qu'on decouvre leur friponerie, et qu'on la leur reproche, mais ils vous diront en riant: vous êtes un homme d'esprit vous avez beaucoup de lumiere, vous avez de bons yeux &.[a]

Comme une des maximes du gouvernement Chinois à toujours [184] êté de donner un grand cours au commerce dans tout l'Empire, l'on peut dire que tout le monde s'en mêle, n'y aÿant guêre de Chinois, même des Mandarins qui ne le fasse, au moins en societé en donnant leur argent a des Marchands, pour le faire valoir dans le negoce.

Un des principaux Commerce dela Chine tant au dedans qu'au dehors, Consiste dans les soyes, et dans les êtoffes ou únis, ou mêleés d'or et d'Argent[707], qui s'y fabriquent, y en aÿant en si grande quantité que la plûpart du Peuple sont habillez de Satin[708] ou de Damas.

On nourrit des vers a Soye dans presque toutes les Provinces de l'Empire; mais Nang kin et Che kiang particulierement cette derniere, sont celles ou il S'en recueille davantage, et ou il ÿ a le plus de manufactures d'etoffes de Soye; n'y ayant point d'anneé qu'elles n'envoyent a Peking pres de quatre cent barques chargeés de draps d'or, de Damas, de Satins, de Velours[709]; outre celles qui se fabriquent expres pour l'Empereur, qui en fait des presens à ses femmes aux Princes et a toute la Cour.

Toutes les autres Provinces payent aussi une partie de leurs tributs en soÿe, et en êtoffes de soÿe, qui pour l'ordinaire se revendent pour le Compte de l'Empereur, mais qui n'aprochent pas toutes ensemble à la moitie de ce qu'en fournit Che kiang toute Seule.

On Croit Communement qu'il ÿ auroit 150 a 200 pour Cent [185] à gagner sur les Soyes crues dela Chine, Si nous les pouvions tirer de Nanking en droiture et qu'elles ne passassent pas par les mains de Ceux de Canton[710], Les Messieurs francois[711] qui hivernerent a Canton m'assurerent d'avoir gagn[és] en les faisant venir de droiture de Nanquing 60 p. Cent en les revendant à Canton.

C'est dans la Province de Nanking que se fabriquent les plus belles etoffes; et c'est ou presque les meilleurs ouvriers Viennent etablir leur manufactures. Les Etrangers cependent n'enlevent guere de Celles ci, et presque toutes les êtoffes que nous

**706** The preceding three paragraphs were adjusted and copied from: Savary des Brûlons, Dictionnaire, vol. 1, 1175.
**707** For more on luxury silks in early China, see James C.Y. Watt and Anne E. Wardwel, *When Silk was Gold: Central Asian and Chinese Textiles* (New York: The Metropolitan Museum of Art, 1997), 127–64.
**708** Satin refers to any smooth, shiny cloth made from silk fibers with a satin weave. It originated in China and commonly was used for court dress and domestic furnishings in eighteenth-century Europe.
**709** Velvet, or velour, is a plush textile, typically made of silk and featuring a densely piled surface.
**710** The preceding five paragraphs were adjusted and copied from: Savary des Brûlons, Dictionnaire, vol. 1, 1175–6.
**711** Persons unknown. As Europeans generally were not allowed to stay in Canton year round, this remark seems strange. The only Frenchmen who might have remained there was the priest Antoine Guignes. See page 338, ft. 575.

Chargons et que nous apportons en Europe, aussi bien que les Soyes êcruës, se font a Canton et a Fochan fameux Bourg a quatre Lieux du dit Canton Capitale dela Province.

On fait a la Chine de toutes les étoffes de soye pure ou meleés d'Or et d'Argent, qu'on fabrique à Anvers, entre autres des brocards à fleurs, sans Or, et avec Or, des Velours, des Pannes[712], des sattins, des Damas, des Crepons[713], des taffetas, et plusieurs autres, qu'on ne Connoit pas en Europe. il ÿ a même dont l'or et l'argent ne sont que de papier doré[714], tels que vous avez vû par le Chantillon que je Vous aÿ apporté pour la Curieusité.

Les teintures[715] de ces manufactures Sont jnfiniment meilleures que les notres, et leurs Couleurs primitives Sont a l'epreuve de l'eau, et si on les veut faire travailler dans notre gout, ils ne seront pas jnferieurs à nos ouvriers.[716]

Pour vous donner l'explication de toutes ces êtoffes tant celles dont on a raporté le noms Chinois que les autres, I'ay mis icÿ [186] la facture d'achat des Marchandisses que nous fimes a Canton pour nos deux Vaisseaux tel comme nous les avons trouvees dans l'anneé 1723 et 1724.

---

**712** Panne is a highly-sheened cloth, typically made by further compressing satin or velvet.

**713** Crêpe is a lightweight fabric, here of silk or cotton, which features a finely crinkled surface.

**714** The preceding two paragraphs were adjusted and copied from: Savary des Brûlons, Dictionnaire, vol. 1, 1176.

**715** For more on contemporary textile dying, see Beverly Lemire and Giorgio Riello, "East & West: Textiles and Fashion in Early Modern Europe", in: *Journal of Social History* 41.4 (2008), 887–916; Harriet T. Zurndorfer, "The Resistant Fiber: Cotton Textiles in Imperial China", in: Spinning World, ed. Riello and Parthasarathi, 43–62.

**716** The preceding paragraph was adjusted and copied from: Barbinais le Gentil, Nouveau voyage, vol. 2, 20.

## Facture des Marchandisses Chargeés dans le Vâisseaú Le Marquïs de Prié pour le Comte de la societé a Sçavoir

| | | Theyl. | M. | Cat. | C.’[717] |
|---|---|---|---|---|---|
| | 167„ Caisses de Porselaine et 1950 Roulaux qui ont Coute | 8703 | 5 | – | |
| Sago qui sert a paquetter les petits assortimens de Porselaine dans les Caisses | 4 Piquel et 38 catti a 3.$^{th:}$ 5$^{m}$ le piquel qu’on a repandus dans les caisses entre la Porselaine | 15 | 3 | 3 | |
| | 300 Pots dans des petits tobes du vif Argent pesent Netto 149$^{Piq:}$ 50 $^{Cat:}$ a 40 th: par piquel | 5980 | – | – | |
| | 3 caisses de Cambogium[718] pes.$^{t}$ net 9$^{Pic:}$ 24$^{Cat:}$ a 20 th: par Piquel | 184 | 8 | – | |
| Marchandisses qui servent a remplir le vuide entre les Caisses dans le fond de Cale du Vaisseau pour ne pas perdre de la place | Galing[719] 69 piq: 65 Catt: a 1 th: 7 mas le piquel | 118 | 4 | – | |
| | Radix China[720] Ou Esquine 178 piq: et 65 catt:$^{s}$ a 1 th: 5 m: 6 C: p.$^{r}$ piq. | 345 | 8 | 6 | 4 |
| | 20 Caisses de thé. Peko qui pesent 39 piq: et 52 catt:$^{s}$ a 25 th: le piquel | 988 | – | – | |

717 These columns denote taels, mace, catties and candareens. For their interrelated values, see pages 43, ft. 101; 203, ft. 60; 217, ft. 82.
718 Gamboge refers to several products, produced from the resin of the *Garcinia cambogia* and *Garcinia indica* trees of Southeast Asia. These include a saffron- or brownish-colored textile dye and a medical purgative.
719 Galangal, or galinga, is a plant in the ginger family and traditionally used by residents of Southeast Asia in cooking and as an herbal medicine.
720 This refers to China root. See page 60, ft. 91.

**Thé Bou[721] 951 Caisses acheté** en divers tems de differents marchands pour menager

| The boú | Les prix | Piq: | Catt: | thei: | theÿl. | M. | C. | C. |
|---|---|---|---|---|---|---|---|---|
| 200 | Caisses achetees de Congo qui pesent | 417 | 67¼ | a 21 le piq:l | 8771 | 1 | 7 | 5 |
| 64. | ditto de Tinqua[722] | 135 | 88 | a 16 ditto | 2174 | _ | 3 | _ |
| 134. | ditto de Cowlo[723] | 292 | 34 | a 21 d° | 6139 | 1 | 4 | _ |
| 136. | ditto de Tinqua | 283 | 64 | a 21 d° | 5956 | 4 | 4 | _ |
| 66. | ditto de Cowlo | 105 | 21 | a 21 d:° | 2209 | 4 | 1 | _ |
| 100. | ditto de Ionqua[724] | 208 | 51 ¼ | a 17,,6 d:° | 3669 | 8 | 6 | 4 |
| 50. | ditto de Tonsoÿ[725] | 96 | 49 | a 20 d° | 1929 | 8 | _ | _ |
| 17. | d° de Cowlo | 24 | 11 | a 21 d° | 506 | 3 | 1 | _ |
| 60. | d° de ditto | 119 | 30 | a 19 d° | 2266 | 7 | _ | _ |
| 42. | d° de Tinqua | 87 | 1 | a 21 d° | 1827 | 2 | 1 | _ |
| 40. | d° de Jong Congo[726] | 81 | 35 | a 17 d° | 1382 | 9 | 5 | _ |
| 41 | d° Pinké[727] | 84 | 82 | a 11 d° | 933 | _ | 2 | _ |
| 1. | d.° de Tonsoÿ | 2 | 71 | a 22 d° | 59 | 6 | 2 | _ |
| 951 Caisses qui Pesent Netto .... 1939,,05. Porte la Somme de .... 37825,,7,,1,,9 | | | | | | | | |

**721** This refers to Bohea tea.
**722** This likely refers to a Tinqua (dates unknown) from Amoy, who was active in the Canton trade in the early 1700s. Cheong, Hong Merchants, 38–9.
**723** Cowlo (dates unknown) was a native of Fukien, who traded in Canton in the early decades of the eighteenth century. He partnered in business with Old Quiqua, before retiring in the 1730s. Cheong, Hong Merchants, 34, 38, 45, 49.
**724** Ton Tonqua (dates unknown) was a business partner of Tan Suqua during the 1720s and one of the wealthiest traders in Canton. Ibid., 34, 42–3, 45, 68, 135.
**725** Merchant unknown.
**726** Merchant unknown.
**727** Zhang Zuguan, alias Pinky (dates unknown), regularly supplied Ostend Company ships during the 1720s and early 1730s. He especially was known to supply porcelain. Van Dyke, Merchants, 199–202.

### Thé Bing 252 Caisses a scavoir

| Caisses de the Bing | Pic: | Cat. | th: | m: | |
|---|---|---|---|---|---|
| 61. Caisses acheteés de Cowlo qui pes.$^{t}$ | 35 | 73 | a 29 | 5 p. Pic. | 768,,1,,9,,5 |
| 131. d° de Chinqua | 77 | 29 | a 19 | d° | 1468,,5,,2,,_ |
| 60. d° de Hudson[728] | 36 | 0 | a 20 | d° | 720,,_,,_ |
| 252. caisses qui Pesent Netto .... 149,,02 qui Portent la Somme de .... 2956,,7,,_,,5 | | | | | |

### Heÿsan Thé 20 Caisses a scavoir

20 Caisses acheteé. de Quicong[729] qui P.$^{t}$ 12$^{Pic.}$ 20$^{Cat.}$ a 20$^{th:.m}$ p.p. 244,,_,,_

Transport a l'autre Coté 57362,,3,,2,,5

### [187] Thé Congo 87 Caisses a scavoir

| Caisses | Pic: | Cat: | th: | th: | m | c | c |
|---|---|---|---|---|---|---|---|
| 32 Achettees de Cudgin[730] qui pesent | 72 | 82 | a 26 p. pic: | 1966 | 1 | 4 | _ |
| 35 ,, de Tinqua ,, | 42 | 31 | a 31 d° | 1311 | 6 | 1 | _ |
| 20 ,, de Hunqua[731] ,, | 38 | 87 | a 32 d° | 1243 | 8 | 4 | _ |
| 87 Caisses qui Pesent Netto .... 154,, .... qui Montent ensemble 4521,,5,,9,,_ | | | | | | | |

### Thé Singlo ou thé Verd 252 Caisses

| | Caisses | Pic. | Cat: | th | th: | m | c | c |
|---|---|---|---|---|---|---|---|---|
| de petites Caises | 203 Acheteés d'Honqua qui pesent | 119 | 27 | a 13. p. P.$^{c}$ | 1557 | _ | 1 | _ |
| | 96 ,, de Tinqua ,, | 27 | 60 | a 10 d° | 276 | _ | _ | _ |
| de grandes | 100 ,, de Chiúqua[732] ,, | 116 | _ | a 15. d° | 1740 | _ | _ | _ |
| | 20 ,, de ditto ,, | 24 | _ | a 12. d° | 288 | _ | _ | _ |
| Petites - | 310 ,, de ditto ,, | 182 | 90 | a 15. d° | 2734 | 5 | _ | _ |
| Balottusen[733] | 252 Caisses qui Pesent Netto .... 470,,27 qui montent en semble 8604,,5,,1,,_ | | | | | | | |

728 Merchant unknown.
729 Merchant unknown.
730 See page 217, ft. 83.
731 Chen Fangguan, alias Tan Hunqua (d. 1760), was a prominent hong merchant in Canton. He was active in the country trade with Macao and Batavia by 1713 and traded with the GIC several times in the 1720s. He accused his competitor, Tan Suqua, of commercial mispropriety in 1730 and was himself arrested several times during the ensuing proceedings. Van Dyke, Merchants, 99–116.
732 Chen Kuiguan, alias Mandarin Quiqua (d. 1742), was a native of Amoy, who regularly supplied Ostend and later VOC ships during the 1720s and early 1730s. Van Dyke, Merchants, 169–80, 393.
733 This might refer to a ballotine, or small rolled article.

## Etoffes de Soÿe

| | | | Prÿs | | | | | | |
|---|---|---|---|---|---|---|---|---|---|
| Noms des Marchands de qui on a fait les achats | | Cubits de Long.r | Th: | m. | c | Theÿls | m | c | c |
| Chinqua | 3850 Pieces de taffetas Long | 38 a | 3 | 9 | la P.e | 15015 | _ | _ | _ |
| | 1690. ditto Gorgorans | 45 a | 5 | 9 | ,, | 9971 | _ | _ | _ |
| | 1430. d.o Gosies[734] ou Damas | 45 a | 5 | 6 | ,, | 8008 | _ | _ | _ |
| | 330. d.o Chagrins[735] | 45 a | 4 | 6 | ,, | 1518 | _ | _ | _ |
| | 250. d.o Gosies ou Damast | 38 a | 4 | 7 | ,, | 1175 | _ | _ | _ |
| | 143. d.o ditto unies | 38 a | 4 | 5 | ,, | 643 | 5 | _ | _ |
| | 120. d.o Chagrins | 38 a | 3 | 9 | ,, | 468 | _ | _ | _ |
| | 120. d.o Posies ou Satins unies | 38 a | 5 | 4 | ,, | 648 | _ | _ | _ |
| | 100. d.o ditto | 45 a | 6 | 4 | ,, | 640 | _ | _ | _ |
| | 300. d.o Gorgorans | 45 a | 6 | 4 | ,, | 1920 | _ | _ | _ |
| | 1000. d.o Posies ou Damast | 45 a | 6 | 6 | ,, | 6600 | _ | _ | _ |
| | 200. d.o Sattins Rayeés | 45 a | 6 | 4 | ,, | 1280 | _ | _ | _ |
| | 390. d.o Taffetas | 38 a | 4 | _ | ,, | 1560 | _ | _ | _ |
| | 360. d.o Posies ou Damast | 38 a | 5 | 6 | ,, | 2016 | _ | _ | _ |
| | 90 di.o ditto Brosteés[736] | 45 a | 7 | _ | ,, | 630 | _ | _ | _ |
| Chinqua | 219. d.o Gorgorans | 45 a | 5 | _ | ,, | 1095 | _ | _ | _ |
| | 200. d.o Taffetas | 38 a | 4 | _ | ,, | 800 | _ | _ | _ |
| | 178 d.o Gorgorans | 45 a | 5 | 6 | 5 ,, | 1005 | 7 | _ | _ |
| | 120. d.o Chagrins | 45 a | 4 | 4 | ,, | 528 | _ | _ | _ |
| Hinqúa | 200. d.o Posies ou Damast | 45 a | 6 | 3 | 5 ,, | 1270 | _ | _ | _ |
| | 110. d.o Gosies ditto | 45 a | 5 | 3 | 5 ,, | 588 | 5 | _ | _ |
| Caulo | 300. d.o Dimitis[737] | 45 a | 5 | 6 | ,, | 1680 | _ | _ | _ |
| | 200. d.o Posies ou Damast | 45 a | 6 | 4 | ,, | 1280 | _ | _ | _ |

734 A goshee probably was a silk-cotton textile. It was retailed under a different name in Europe. Lee-Whitman, Silk Trade, 28–30.

735 A chagrin is a silk cloth, constructed with a pebbled face to imitate leather.

736 This probably is a derivation of brosser, meaning "brushed." Brushed silks have a softer surface.

737 A dimity is a lightweight, usually white cotton textile.

| | | | | | | | | | | |
|---|---|---|---|---|---|---|---|---|---|---|
| Tinqua | 500. d.° Taffetas | | 38 a | 3 | 7 | ,, | 1850 | _ | _ | _ |
| | 500. d.° Gorgorans | | 45 a | 6 | 5 | ,, | 3250 | _ | _ | _ |
| | 500 d.° Posies ou Damast | | 45 a | 6 | 3 | 5 ,, | 3175 | _ | _ | _ |
| | 500 d.° ditto | | 38 a | 5 | 3 | 5 ,, | 2675 | _ | _ | _ |
| | 46 d.° Pelongs | qui pesent | 986th a | 1 | 6 la piece | | 91 | 2 | _ | _ |
| | 11 d.° ditto | | | | | | | | | |
| 13957 Pieces de Soÿeries assorties qui Montent a la Somme .... 71380,,9,,_,,_ | | | | | | | | | | |

Transporté cÿ derrieré 141869,,3,,2,,5

[188] **Soÿes Crues**[738]

| Caisses | Picq.[l] | Catt: | th: | th: | m. | c | [Theÿls m c. c.] |
|---|---|---|---|---|---|---|---|
| 9 ,, acheteés de Kung qua[739] qui Pes.t Netto | 19 | 45 | à 130 le P.t | 2525 | 9 | _ | |
| 14,, ditto de Tinqua | 25 | 14 | a 133 d° | 3343 | 6 | 2 | 5869,,5,,2,,_ |
| 23 caisses qui Pesent Netto 44 ,,59 | | | | | | | |

**Gensing** deux petits paquets qui Pesent ensemble 1½ Catti a 100 theyls le Catti 150,,_,,_,,_

**Somme totale d'Achat en Th.s** 147888,,8,,4,,5

A nôtre Retour a Ostende, la facture cÿ dessus mentionneé, apres vente et tous fraix fait, elle a rendue de profit a la Societé 124 poúr Cent de profit.

---

738 Europeans developed a domestic silk manufacturing industry long before establishing comparable sites for cotton textiles. Chaudhuri, Trading World, 343–58.

739 This might refer to Koonqua (dates unknown), a nephew of Tan Hunqua. Van Dyke, Merchants, 104.

**Prix des Marchandisses a La Chine**

A.° 1723 & 1724.

| | Theyls | m | c | c |
|---|---|---|---|---|
| Le Picol d'Argent vif ou Mercure | 40 | _ | _ | _ |
| Le Picol de sucre Candÿ | 4 | 5 | _ | _ |
| Le Picol de toutenage | 6 | _ | _ | _ |
| Le Picol de nacre de Perle[740] | 6 | _ | _ | _ |
| Le Picol de the Bouÿ depuis les 11 th: a | 22 | _ | _ | _ |
| Le Picol de thé Congo depuis les 27 th: a | 32 | _ | _ | _ |
| Le Picol de the Pekau depuis les 26 th: a | 29 | _ | _ | _ |
| Le Picol de the Bing ou Imperial depuis les 19 th: a | 21 | _ | _ | _ |
| Le Picol du Heÿsan thé depuis les 17 th: a | 20 | _ | _ | _ |
| Le Picol de thé Singlo ou thé Verd depuis 12 th: a | 15 | _ | _ | _ |
| Le Picol de Soyes Crües depuis 130 th: a | 133 | _ | _ | _ |
| Le Picol de Rubarbe[741] depuis 15 th: a | 20 | _ | _ | _ |
| Le Picol d'esquine ou Radix China | 1 | 5 | 6 | _ |
| Le Picol de galanga | 1 | 7 | _ | _ |
| Le Picol de Sago | 3 | 5 | _ | _ |
| Le Picol de Curcuma[742] | 2 | _ | _ | _ |
| Le Picol de Mirrhe[743] | 12 | 9 | 6 | _ |
| Le Picol de GommeLack[744] en bâton | 6 | 4 | 4 | _ |

740 Nacre, or mother of pearl, is an iridescent material product by some molluscs. See Molly A. Warsh, *Adorning Empire: a History of the Early Modern Pearl Trade, 1492–1688* (PhD diss., The Johns Hopkins University, 2009).

741 The roots of the rhubarb plant were used medicinally in China as a laxative and purgative.

742 Tumeric – notably the variety *Curcuma longa* – was a popular Chinese condiment and also cultivated in order to produce a yellow dye. The plant was indigenous to India and Southeast Asia.

743 Myrrh is an aromatic resin, derived from trees in the *Commpihora* genus. It was used in medical treatments as well as a personal and religious incense.

744 Shellac is a resin, produced on certain insect-inhabited trees in India and Southeast Asia. It was used as a lacquer, or finishing, on eighteenth- and early-nineteenth-century European furniture.

[189]

| | | quantites des Fillets | Longeur en Cobits | a Paisant en theil | Prix | | |
|---|---|---|---|---|---|---|---|
| | | | | | Theil | mas | can |
| Etoffes de Soÿe | Les Pequins a fleur dit brostes | 6 | 38 | 26 | 3 | 9 | _ |
| | Les Pequins de | 6 | 45 | 30 | 4 | 2 | _ |
| | Les Pequins de | 5 | 45 | 28 | 4 | _ | _ |
| | Les Pequins de | 4 | 38 | 24 | 3 | 7 | _ |
| | Les Chagrins de | 4 | 38 | 25 | 3 | 9 | _ |
| | Les Gourgourans de | 8 | 38 | 38 | 6 | _ | _ |
| | Les Gourgourans de | 6 | 45 | 42 | 6 | 4 | _ |
| | Les Damas dit Poesies de | 8 | 38 | 38 | 5 | 6 | _ |
| | Les dits de | 8 | 45 | 46 | 6 | 6 | _ |
| | Les Damas a Meuble | 10 | 38 | 46 | 7 | 6 | _ |
| | Les Damas dit Poesies de | 6 | 38 | 30 | 4 | 7 | _ |
| | Les dits de | 6 | 45 | 35 | 5 | 6 | _ |
| | Les Satins de | 8 | 38 | 35 | 5 | 4 | _ |
| | Les dits de | 8 | 45 | 40 | 6 | 4 | _ |
| | Les Gelons crepés | _ | 46 | _ | 3 | _ | _ |
| | Les Paches unis et a fleur | _ | 55 | _ | 2 | 8 | _ |
| | Les Pelongs | _ | 20 | _ | 1 | 6 | _ |
| | Les Lampes ou Parteres | _ | 38 | _ | 8 | _ | _ |
| | Les Lampes de | _ | 52 | _ | 11 | _ | _ |
| | La pair de bas de Soÿe a homme | _ | _ | _ | 1 | 2 | _ |
| | La pair de ditto a femme | _ | _ | _ | _ | 6 | _ |

Pour un lit brodde d'un beau dessin coute ordinairement 130 th:

Pour tout les autres quinquailleries on les achette au prix qu'on peut, aÿant point de prix fixe

L'on fabrique encore ala Chine quatre Sortes d'Etoffes de soÿe [190] qui sont peu Connuës en Europé, l'une qu'on nomme Toua[n]se[745] qui approche de ce qu'on

745 A touanse is a flat satin, which was either monocolored or decorated with colorful blossoms and figures.

appelle en flandre Furies[746], ou Satins faconnez, l'autre qu'on nomme Cha[747] plus legere, et qui Sert l'eté, est une sorte de taffetas ordinairement a fleurs perceés au joûr comme des dentelles[748] de Brusseles, la troisieme est aussi un taffetas tres seré, qu'on nomme Pelongs, mais Si maniable, qu'il ne Conserve jamais son pli. il ÿ a le Kiem tchou[749] ou Panches fait avec la soÿe de Vers sauvages: elle n'engraisse jamais et on la lave Comme dela toille.

Il y a quantité de Laine dans plusieurs Provinces de la Chine, mais ils n'en scavent point faire de draps a la mode d'Europé, ils s'en servent pour faire des serges[750] de plusieurs sortes qui leur servent en hÿver de Couvertures.[751]

Les Draps d'Engleterre ÿ sont tres estimez non obstant les Chinois n'en achetent que fort peu, coutant jncomparablement plus que les plus belles étoffes de soÿe, c'est pour tel raison qu'ils S'en Servent de diverses fourures, des hermines, des Martres, et telles que sont le petit gris[752], pour doublures de leurs habits, ils en fourrent aussi leurs leurs [sic] bonnets d'hiver, et les selles de leurs Chevaux. toutes ces fourures leur Viennent de la moscovie par les Caravanes qu'on voit tous les ans arriver à Peking et de Tartarie; il ÿ en à de Si cheres qu'une doublure d'habit revient Souvent a cinq cent theÿls.

Les autres Marchandisses qu'on tire dela Chine outre les soÿes et les êtoffes[753], des cuivres Iaunes[754] en plaque et en Saumons du Tutenague mêtail blanc qui approche du Cuivre, du thé, du Camfre, du musc[755] du Lin, du sucre, du sel, du Gengembre [191] confit, du Vifargent du Vermillon, du Lapis[756], du Vitriol[757], de l'ambre gris[758],

---

**746** This refers to an Asian silk, whose irregular decoration makes it appear as if designed by a madman or fury.

**747** Cha was a lightweight, plain-weave Chinese silk, often printed with floral patterns and used for summer dress.

**748** Dentelles here referred to a type of lightweight, handmade and presumably silk lace.

**749** Fabric unknown.

**750** Serge is a durable twill textile, constructed from wool or worsted and especially used for linings and warm outer garments.

**751** The preceding two paragraphs were adjusted and copied from: Savary des Brûlons, Dictionnaire, vol. 1, 1176–7.

**752** The Chinese nobility established a regular fur trade with Siberian merchants by the 1600s. Perdue, *China Marches West*, 27–8, 84–91, 164–5.

**753** The preceding sentence was copied from: Savary des Brûlons, Dictionnaire, vol. 1, 1177.

**754** Yellow copper was a mineral, mined in China and regularly used for local currency and in the country trade.

**755** Musk is a secretion, gathered from a gland of the male mule deer indigenous to central Asia and China. It gives off a strong odor and thus was used both as a perfume and in traditional medicine.

**756** Lapis lazuli refers to a deep blue-colored, semiprecious stone, sometimes found in China but especially imported from neighboring kingdoms. It was used to make a costly dye and paint in early modern Europe.

**757** Vitriol refers to a range of chemical sulfates. Some were used in cloth dyeing.

**758** Ambergris is a digestive secretion, produced by spermwhales. It had been imported to China from Africa since 1000 BCE and was used in making perfume.

dela Rubarbe, du Galanga de l'equine ou Radix China, de l'ancre dela Chine[759], de la Porcelaine, des ovurages delaque et de vernis[760], de l'or tres fin, de l'etain, du fer, de l'açier, du quinquina[761] et de l'ambre[762] jaune et rougeatre.

A l'egard des marchandisses étrangeres qui Sont propre pour le Commerce dela Chine, l'argent en est comme la basse, soit qu'il soit en piastres, soit qu'il Soit en barres, ou en monoÿe: les Chinnois qui n'en ont point l'estiment beaucoup, et l'echangent Volontiers contre leur Or, et leur meillieures marchandisses.

Les êpiceries et le Poivre ÿ sont encore d'un bon debit particulierement ce dernier dont les Anglois de Madras font une partie de leur Cargaison. on ÿ porte aussi des toilles de plusieurs Sortes, des draps, des serges, des êtamines de diverses especes et Coúleurs, dont les rouges, les blancs et les noires sont les plus rechercheés, du Bois de Sandal, des dents d'Elephant[763], de l'ambre, et du corail rouge[764], mais pâle.[765]

Ie vous aÿ parlé des richeses dela Chine et de son negoce et ce qu'on doit apporter pour trafiquer avec eux, à present il me manque a vous dire Comment on se doit gouverner en arrivant avec le Vaisseau audit Empire. quand on arrive devant devant [sic] la ville de Macao, on s'informe comment les affaires vont a Canton, et S'il n'ÿ a point de troubles dans l'Empire, soit des revoltes ou autrement. sachant que tout est en paix et le Commerce libre, on prend un Pilote dans cette Ville pour [192] monter la Riviere, venant a l'embouchure de Boca tigris nommé par les Chinois Hou:men, le Mandarin du fort vous vient voir, pour prendre note du nombre de l'equipage et de la quantité d'armes &.[a] cecÿ fait on luÿ paye pour droit du passage deux Piastres, et il vous laisse deux hommes de Sa garde pour veillerd sur le Vaisseau ou il va et si n'y fraude pas les droits de l'Empereur.

Apres avoir passe ces deux forts, on entre dans la Riviere de Canton, et on reste avec Son Vaisseau devant la premiere barre, jusqu'a ce que le Contrat avec L'Hoú poú

759 This again refers to Chinese ink.

760 Europeans often referred to this styling of ceramics as "japanning." See page 203, ft. 62.

761 The genus *Cinchona* refers to a group of evergreen plants, native to South America but introduced by Europeans to the East Indies. Their bark was used as an antimalarial. See Jeyamalar Kathirithamby-Wells, "Unlikely Partners: Malay-Indonesian Medicine and European Plant Science", in: East India Company, eds. Damodaran and Winterbottom, 193–218.

762 Amber is fossilized tree resin. It was used as a fragrance and for domestic decor in imperial China.

763 Chinese elephants were extinct by 100 BCE, but ivory sculptures for domestic use – mostly made from the tusks of African and Asian elephants –were especially popular during the 1700s.

764 Mediterranean red coral, *Corallium rubrum*, was much demanded in imperial China, for use in jewelry and as markers of status. See Pippa Lacey, "The Coral Network: the Trade of Red Coral to the Qing Imperial Court in the Eighteenth Century", in: *The Global Lives of Things: the Material Culture of Connections in the Early Modern World*, eds. Anne Gerritsen and Giorgio Riello (New York: Routledge, 2015), 81–102.

765 The preceding two paragraphs were adjusted and copied from: Savary des Brûlons, Dictionnaire, vol. 1, 1177–8.

ou grand Douanier soit arreté: sitôt le premier Marchand doit aller a Canton pour contracter avec le dit Hoú poú touchant les droits qu'on doit payer d'entreé et sortie.

**Contract de Commerce que nous arrêtames avec le Fou:yuen ou Viceroy et L'Houpoü a Canton l'anneé 1723**

1

Que le Capitaine et supercargos allant en Chaloupe avec leur Pavillion; seront examté des visites des Iampans du Houpou sans etre moleste, ou poursuit.

2.

Que l'on ne payera aucuns droits pour le necessaire des Vaisseaux ni pour biere, vin, et toutte autre amonition de bouche pour la factorie, et de la factorie aux Vaisseaux.

3.

Que l'on jmposera aucun droits sur les Jampans que l'on envoyera avec des lettres aux vaisseaux.

4.

Que nous pouvons engager nos Jnterpretes, Comprador, et autres [193] serviteurs, de même que l'on ne paÿera aucun droits pour la factorie ou Gan[766] qui est loueé.

5.

Que l'on aura un Chap Permettant le negoce avec un Chacun soit Gan oú Bouticquiers[767] sans que l'on sera obligez de payer aucunne chose extraordinaire.

6.

Que L'on ne sera pas responsable dela mauvaise Conduite des matelots, se devant Contenter du Saisissement de leurs effects.

7.

Que l'on poura sans exception quelquonques, envoÿer touttes sortes de soyeries et Couleurs sans paÿer aucunne nouvelle jmposition ni par nous ou par les Vendeurs, de même que de les molester, que l'on ne paÿera aucun droits pour l'argent, mais seulement pour les marchandisses que nous ferons embarquer

8.

Que les officiers du Hoú poú seront toujours prest quand on les aura besoin, que notre grand Chap pour notre depart ne poura pas etre suspendu; que nous serons traitté sur le pied et Privileges accordes aux Vaisseaux Europeéns par le Defunt Empereur Kang hÿ, et pour encourager le negoce nous aurons la refaction sur les droits, accordé par le dit defunt Empereur, que l'on nous donnera un chap de tous ces Articles qui sera affiche devant la factorie ou Gan.

Apres la Conclusion du dit Contract le Capitaine fait monter son vaisseau a Wampou place ordinaire dans la Riviere ou les Vaisseaux Europeéns restent a L'ancre; un jour

**766** This likely is a misspelling of the word *hong*.

**767** This likely refers to non-*hong* merchants.

ou deux par apres L'Hoú poú vient faire le messurage du Vaisseau avec une nombreuse suitte, entre les quels il ÿ à plusieurs [194] qui viennent pour attraper quelque presents, pour ce tems la, il faut que chacun prenne garde de ses petites raretez qu'il porte d'Europe, car tout ce qu'on Vend à ces gens, c'est pour un chinchin[768], qui est une sorte d'argent qui s'evanouit dans un Compliment.

Quand on voit venir L'houpou les Capitaines vont ordinairement a sa rencontre avec leurs leurs [sic] Chaloupes pour le recevoir, en même tems on le salue de quelques coups de Canon, étant monté abord avec La Suite de ses principaux officiers, il S'assit dans un fauteil tout contre le mat d'Artimon, et on mesure avec une corde la distance du mât de misaine au mât d'artimon et suivant que cette distance est grande on paÿe les droits de l'Empereur. on lui presente quelques petites raretez, ensuite il parte avec le même Cortege Comme il est venus, et on le salue de quelques Coups de Canon.

Le Mesurage etant finis on tache alors de faire son negoce les plus avantageusement qu'on peut, il ne faut pas divulger ou donner à Connoitre (comme je vous aÿ deja dit) dans le moment son jntention, le Tarif des droits d'entreé et de Sortie, comme aussi ceux des especes, dont on se sert au negoce a Canton Amoy &.[a] sont comme vous pourez conjecturer par le Plan que vous trouverez cÿ aprez, avant de finir cet article il faut que je vous dise auparavant de ne pas donner a Connoitre combien d'argent on ÿ porte par rapport que les marchands avec qui vous fait vos ampletes sont souvent taxé des Mandarins [195] a payer de recognoissances selon les deniers qu'on lui a paÿe pour l'achat, c'est pour Cette raison qu'on tache d'amener tant d'argent qu'on peut du Vaisseau, sans Connoissance des douanes, a la factorie, non obstant qu'on le peut faire sans paÿer aucun droit.

On ne trouve dans la Chine qu'une seule monnoÿe, frapeé au coin du Prince.[769] elle est de Cuivre, avec un trou au milieu, pour la commodite du Commerce, s'en filant ordinairement plusieurs ensemble, dont on Compose des Cordons, qui valent plus ou moins, suivant qui sont plus ou moins longs. Cette monnoÿe S'appelle casché[770]

**768** This likely refers to the attempts of Chinese officials to get the latest rarities from European ships for the Emperor during measuring ceremonies, without paying large sums for them. See, for an example, pages 218–9.

**769** The earliest Chinese currency emerged as a copper coin, with a square hole in its center during the Ch'in Dynasty. This model persisted until the twentieth century, with some regional variations. Silver circulated throughout the empire by the 1723, but it was not officially minted into coins until the late nineteenth century. For more on Ming and Ch'ing efforts to issue and regulate coinage, see Richard von Glahn, "Chinese Coin and Changes in Monetary Preferences in Maritime East Asia in the Fifteenth-Seventeenth Centuries", in: *Journal of the Economic and Social History of the Orient* 57.5 (2014), 629–68; Bruce Rusk, "Silver, Liquid and Solid: The Matter of Money in the Ming-Qing Marketplace" (paper presented at the Conference on Coin of the Realm: Money and Meaning in Late Imperial China, Cambridge, MA, 18 April 2014).

**770** A cash was a Chinese denomination of weight. It also was the name given to the primary official currency circulating in China from the second century BCE until the twentieth century CE –a copper coin.

et ne vaut guêre plus qu'un deniers[771] de flandre, les dix casches ne faisant que trois liards[772] de flandre, leur grandeur et figure est comme icÿ a margé.

On Compte neamoins encore au nombre des monnoyes les Canderins, le mas, et le theÿl: dix câches font un Canderin, dix Canderins, un mas; et dix mas un theÿl.

Ie vous aÿ dêja dit cÿ devant, que l'Or et l'argent sont marchandisses à la Chine, et non pas monnoÿe, cependant quoi que ces meteaux ne sojent point marquez, ils ont cours comme les especes qui en sont fabriqueés comme on le voit dans les autres Etats, mais seulement au poids, chaque morceau d'une Certaine pesanteur valant un certain prix.

La raison que l'on apporte pour quoÿ il n'y a point de moñoÿe dans la Chine, est que les Chinois; qui sont egalement âdroits et de mauvaise foÿ ne manqueroient pas d'en fabriquer de fausse, sur tout pour l'argent ayant le secret de fixer le mercure, [196] et le rendre maleable en sorte qu'il n'y a que l'épreúve dú feú qui en puisse faire reconnoitre la friponerie.

L'or se vend en masse que nous appellons pains[773], ou bateau: il ÿ en a de differens poids, depuis les cinq theÿls jus qu'à Cent. on le detaille même quelque fois comme l'argent, et ainsi l'on pourroit dire en ce sens que comme les chinois ont leur êcu, et ses diminutions ils ont aussi des pistoles[774], des demies et des quarts, dependant de Chaque marchand de donner l'or dans le negoce, a si petits poids qu il le veut.

L'on doit remarquer a propos du negoce d'or et d'argent qui se fait ala Chine, que l'argent n'ÿ êtant par rapport a l'or, que comme un a dix, et etant Communement en europe, comme un a quinze, le profit est dans cet êchange selon que la demande est grande ou moindre.[775]

L'argent qui se trouve dans la Chine ÿ est presque tout apporté du dehors: L'Or s'y receuille dans les sables et les bouës que les torrens entrainent des montagnes, et cet or qu'on ramasse en tres grande quantité, est d'un titre tres haut. ce n'est pas qu'il n'y ait dans plusieurs Provinces du Royaume, des mines tres riches de ces deux meteaux, mais les Princes qui ont gouverne jus qu'a present, aiment mieux n'y point faire travailler et les laisser jnutiles, que d'exposser dans un travail si penible et Si hazardeux, la Vie de leurs Sujets.

---

**771** A denier was a small medieval coin, otherwise referred to as a silver penny. Three deniers equated to one liard.

**772** The liard was a small copper coin and one of the main currencies of the Austrian Netherlands.

**773** This again refers to sampans.

**774** A pistole was the French name given to a sixteenth-century Spanish gold coin, or other later gold coins of equal value. It typically equated to ten livres or three écus.

**775** The preceding six paragraphs were adjusted and copied from: Savary des Brûlons, Dictionnaire, vol. 1, 1176–7.

Le Titre de l'or se divise en Cent parties, qu'on nomme des toques[776], et se recoit dans le commere depuis 80 Jus qu'a [197] Cent, au dessous on le rejette.[777] nous l'avons acheté a Canton 97 theÿl d'argent du titre 94, pour les 10 theyls d'or de Conchinchine aloi de 93. Pour vous donner une Ideé parfaite de ce Commerce, je vous donne icÿ le Tarif qui vous jnstruira du profit que vous pourois faire en achetant de l'or en Chine pour le revendre en Europe.

## Tarif pour l'achat de l'Or

| Finnesse de l'or selon l'es-tandart d Angleterre | N1 | Finnesse de l'or selon la Touche Chinoise N2 | La valeur d'un Once de 4 £ Stl. selon le standart N3 | Gain quand on Achette a 5 par dessus Touche N4. | Gain quand on Achette au pair de la Touche N.5. | Gain quand on Achette a 5 par dessous la touche N6. | Gain a 10 sous la touche N7. |
|---|---|---|---|---|---|---|---|
| Meillieur que Standarad | Carad $q^{r}$. | | £ per C.$^{t}$ | £ per C.$^{t}$ | £ per C.$^{t}$ | £ per C.$^{t}$ | £ per C.$^{t}$ |
| | 1,,3 | 100,,4,,_ | 4,,5,,10 | 62,,87,,_ | 70,,97,,_ | 79,,94,,_ | 89,,90,,_ |
| | 1,,2 | 99,,3,,_ | 4,,5,,_ | 62,,92,,_ | 71,,12,,_ | 80,,19,,_ | 90,,28,,_ |
| | 1,,1 | 98,,2,,_ | 4,,4,,2 | 62,,93,,_ | 71,,27,,_ | 80,,45,,_ | 90,,67,,_ |
| | 1,,_ | 97,,2,,_ | 4,,3,,4 | 63,,3,,_ | 71,,42,,_ | 80,,71,,_ | 91,,7,,_ |
| | _,,3 | 96,,1,,_ | 4,,2,,6 | 63,,9,,_ | 71,,57,,_ | 80,,98,,_ | 91,,48,,_ |
| | _,,2 | 95,,1,,_ | 4,,1,,8 | 63,,14,,_ | 71,,73,,_ | 81,,25_ | 91,,90,,_ |
| | _,,1 | 94,,_,,_ | 4,,_,,10 | 63,20,,_ | 71,,88,,_ | 81,,53,,_ | 92,,33,,_ |
| | _,,_ | 93,,_,,_ | 4,,_,,_ | 63,,26,,_ | 72,,4,,_ | 81,,81,,_ | 92,,77,,_ |
| Standard | _,,1 | 92,,0,,- | 3,,19,,1 | 63,,15,,_ | 72,,2,,_ | 81,,90,,_ | 93,2,,_ |
| | _,,2 | 90,,9,,_ | 3,,18,,2 | 63,,4,,_ | 72,,1,,_ | 82,,2,,_ | 93,,27,,_ |
| | _,,3 | 89,,8,,_ | 3,,17,,3 | 62,,92,,_ | 71,,99,,_ | 82,,12,,_ | 93,,53,,_ |
| | 1,,_ | 88,,8,,_ | 3,,16,,4 | 62,,80,,_ | 71,,97,,_ | 82,,23,,_ | 93,,80,,_ |
| | 1,,1 | 87,,7,,_ | 3,,15,,5 | 62,,68,,_ | 71,,95,,_ | 82,,34,,_ | 94,,8,,_ |
| | 1,,2 | 86,,7,,_ | 3,,14,,6 | 62,,56,,_ | 71,,93,,_ | 82,,46,,_ | 94,,36,,_ |
| | 1,,3 | 85,,6,,_ | 3,,13,,7 | 62,,43,,_ | 71,,91,,_ | 82,,58,,_ | 94,,65,,_ |

776 A toque, or touch, was the rating of either gold or silver, as related to their alloy content. By the late 1700s, 100 touch equated to 24 carats.

777 The preceding four sentences were adjusted and copied from: Savary des Brûlons, Dictionnaire, vol. 1, 1179.

| Finnesse de l'or selon l'estandart d Angleterre | N1 | Finnesse de l'or selon la Touche Chinoise N2 | La valeur d'un Once de 4 £ Stl. selon le standart N3 | Gain quand on Achette a 5 par dessus Touche N4. | Gain quand on Achette au pair de la Touche N.5. | Gain quand on Achette a 5 par dessous la touche N6. | Gain a 10 sous la touche N7. |
|---|---|---|---|---|---|---|---|
| Moins que Standard | 2,,_ | 84,,5,,_ | 3,,12,,8 | 62,,30,,_ | 71,,90,,_ | 82,,70,,_ | 94,,95,,_ |
| | 2,,1 | 83,,5,,_ | 3,,11,,9 | 62,,17,,_ | 71,,88,,_ | 82,,83,,_ | 95,,27,,_ |
| | 2,,2 | 82,,4,,_ | 3,,10,,10 | 62,,3,,_ | 71,,86,,_ | 82,,96,,_ | 95,,60,,_ |
| | 2,,3 | 81,,4,,_ | 3,,9,,11 | 61,,89,,_ | 71,,83,,_ | 83,,9,,_ | 95,,92,,_ |
| | 3,,_ | 80,,3,,_ | 3,,9,,_ | 61,,74,,_ | 71,,81,,_ | 83,,22,,_ | 95,,25,,_ |

La Troisieme Colonne Contient les Prix En Angleterre d'une Once d'Or de la finesse. Dans les premiers et 2.e colonnes, Le standard des Roupies d'or ètant a 4 £ Stl. par Once, en diminuant 4 den.s pour les fraix du rafinage de chaque Carat[778], selon qu'il est moindre en qualitez que le standard, les 4e dernieres Colonnes montrent Combien on gagne pour Cent, en Achetant de l'or a la Chine, et le Vendant en Angleterre, en supposant le standard a 4 £ Sterl. l'once, eú l'argent avec le quel vous Achettez l'or a 5 schillins l'Once. NB Les Anglois usent du Troÿ weÿghts[779] pour peser l'or et l'argent, qui est plus fort que le poids de marc[780], comme vous le trouverez dans la reduction de ces deux poids cÿ apres

[198] Avant que Ie vous donne les Tarifs des Especes, et celuÿ des Droits d'entré et de Sortie, il est necessaire que vous Sachez que les Chinois n'ont autre poids pour peser leur Or et Argent, et tout ce qu ils Vendent Jus qu'a du Bois, que de theÿls, mas, canderins et cassies; dont les dix Cassies, font un Canderin, les dix Canderins, un mas, et les dix mas un theÿl, et le theÿl en poids de marc d'Europe un Once, un gros, 57 grains[781] et 6/10 de grain. Ils ont aussi un Piquel que nous nommons quintal[782] qui fait 122 ll poids de marc et d'Ostende 125 ll, et du pays 100 Cattÿ et le Cattÿ 16 theÿls &.[a]

La balance qui sert a peser l'or et l'argent, et que Chaque marchand porte toujours dans sa poche, ou a sa ceinture, est une espece de petite romaine[783], etant Composeé d'un petit plat, d'un bras ou branche et d'un poids courant, le bras est d'yvoire ordinairement de la longeur et grosseur d'une plume à ecrire, divisé en de tres petites

**778** A carat is a unit of mass, often used for evaluating the density and related quality of gemstones. One carat equates to 200 milligrams, and 24 carats of gold equated to roughly 373 VOC guilders. Liu, Dutch, xvii.

**779** Troy weight is a system used for calculating mass, typically of gold, silver and gemstones. A troy pound equates to 5,760 grains.

**780** This refers specifically to the Dutch troy weight system, which was based on the medieval mark. A Dutch troy pound equated to 3,798 grains.

**781** Ounces, gros, and grains all were Europeans units of weight. A grain, as used in England and France, equated to the weight of a single grain of barley or wheat, or roughly 65 milligrams. About 437.5 grains equated to eight gros and to one ounce.

**782** The *quintal* was the French hundredweight, a unit of weight equating to about 48.95 kilograms.

**783** The preceding sentence was adjusted and copied from: Savary des Brûlons, Dictionnaire, vol. 1, 1179.

parties sur trois faces differentes, et suspendu par des fils de soÿe à l'un des bouts, en trois differentes points, afin de pouvoir peser avec plus de facilité toutes sortes de pois, si petits qu'il soÿent. quand cette balance a une longeur un peu Considerable, elle est d'une precision si grande, que le moindre poids fait pencher sensiblement le bassin. pour la rendre plus portative, on la renferme ordinairement dans un ètuÿ de bois vernissé fort leger et tres propre.[784] les Europeens ne se Servent guêre de celles cÿ, que dans des petits achats, nous nous servimes de la balance ordinaire a deux bassins pour peser notre [199] Argent, et pour peser le thé et les autres marchandisses de grand poids, nous nous servimes d'une Romaine de leur façon calculeé à 1600 theÿl le Piquel, marqueé avec notre marque pour ne pas ètré friponné des Chinois.

L'aune est une mesure qu'ils nomment Cove ou Cubitus avec la quelle ils messurent tout sortes de Choses, comme leurs êtoffes, arbres, vaisseaux, Terres, Rivages &.[a] car ils n'usent point d'autre mesure pour mesurer, ils ne Connoisent ce qui est de Toises, pieds, bonnier, Joúrnal, verge[785] &.[a] Elle Consiste en dix ponto[786], et chaque ponto, de dix Canderins, elle à la longeur de douze poúses juste, ainsi que trois Cúbitus, deúx ponto, et six Canderins font un aune de Paris de quarante quatre pouses, dont dix Cubitús font 3 1/15 aunes de Paris, et 11 ¼ Cubitus font cinc aunes d'Ostende.

Voicÿ a Coté la moitie du Cubitus de la Chine par le quel vous pourois facillement Iuger de leur messúre, et quelle difference il ÿ a entre celle cÿ et celle de Paris ou de Flandre.

[200] **Tarif de ce qúe Le Marc d'Argent produit à la** Chine, un Marc paise et produit, 6 theÿls 5 mas, 3 Canderins, 6 parties de Caisse, comme on le peut voir par le tarif.

| un Marc | Pese et produit | Theÿls | Mas | Cânder | Chassies | 1/10 Cass. |
|---|---|---|---|---|---|---|
| 1 | | 6 | 5 | 3 | - | 6 |
| 2 | | 13 | - | 6 | 1 | 2 |
| 3 | | 19 | 5 | 9 | 1 | 8 |
| 4 | | 26 | 1 | 2 | 2 | 4 |
| 5 | | 32 | 6 | 5 | 3 | - |
| 6 | | 39 | 1 | 8 | 3 | 6 |
| 7 | | 45 | 7 | 1 | 4 | 2 |
| 8 | | 52 | 2 | 4 | 4 | 8 |

**784** The preceding two sentences were adjusted and copied from: Ibid., 216.

**785** Fathoms, feet, bonniers, journal and vergée all were units of length or surface measurement (as related to land). A fathom equated to six feet or about 3.8 square meters. One bonnier, a Flemish standard, equated to four journal. A vergée, or French yard, equated to between 1,630 and 1,800 meters squared or a little over 0.4 acres.

**786** A *ponto*, or point, was the smallest measurement of length, equating to about 0.188 millimeters.

| un Marc | Pese et produit | Theÿls | Mas | Cânder | Chassies | 1/10 Cass. |
|---|---|---|---|---|---|---|
| 9 | | 58 | 7 | 7 | 5 | 4 |
| 10 | | 65 | 3 | - | 6 | - |
| 11 | | 71 | 8 | 3 | 6 | 6 |
| 12 | | 78 | 3 | 6 | 7 | 2 |
| 13 | | 84 | 8 | 9 | 7 | 8 |
| 14 | | 91 | 4 | 2 | 8 | 4 |
| 15 | | 97 | 9 | 5 | 9 | - |
| 16 | | 104 | 4 | 8 | 9 | 6 |
| 17 | | 111 | - | 2 | - | 2 |
| 18 | | 117 | 5 | 5 | - | 8 |
| 19 | | 124 | - | 8 | 1 | 4 |
| 20 | | 130 | 6 | 1 | 2 | - |
| 30 | | 195 | 9 | 1 | 8 | - |
| 40 | | 261 | 2 | 2 | 4 | - |
| 50 | | 326 | 5 | 3 | - | - |
| 60 | | 391 | 8 | 3 | 6 | - |
| 70 | | 457 | 1 | 4 | 2 | - |
| 80 | | 522 | 4 | 4 | 8 | - |
| 90 | | 587 | 7 | 5 | 4 | - |
| 100 | | 653 | - | 6 | - | - |
| 200 | | 1306 | 1 | 2 | - | - |
| 300 | | 1959 | 1 | 8 | - | - |
| 400 | | 2612 | 2 | 4 | - | - |
| 500 | | 3265 | 3 | - | - | - |
| 600 | | 3918 | 3 | 6 | - | - |
| 700 | | 4571 | 4 | 2 | - | - |
| 800 | | 5224 | 4 | 8 | - | - |
| 900 | | 5877 | 5 | 4 | - | - |
| 1000 | | 6530 | 6 | - | - | - |
| 2000 | | 13 061 | 2 | - | - | - |
| 3000 | | 19 591 | 8 | - | - | - |
| 4000 | | 26 122 | 4 | - | - | - |
| 5000 | | 32 653 | - | - | - | - |
| 6000 | | 39 183 | 6 | - | - | - |
| 7000 | | 45 714 | 2 | - | - | - |
| 8000 | | 52 244 | 8 | - | - | - |
| 9000 | | 58 775 | 4 | - | - | - |
| 10 000 | | 65 306 | - | - | - | - |

### [201] **Tarif de ce qúe les Onces produissent en arg.$^{t}$ de la Chine**

| Once | Pese et Prod. | Theils | Mas | Când | Cass.$^{s}$ | 1/10 Cas | 1/10 | 1/10 | 1/10 |
|---|---|---|---|---|---|---|---|---|---|
| 1 | | - | 8 | 1 | 6 | 3 | 2 | 5 | - |
| 2 | | 1 | 6 | 3 | 2 | 6 | 5 | - | - |
| 3 | | 2 | 4 | 4 | 8 | 9 | 7 | 5 | - |
| 4 | | 3 | 2 | 6 | 5 | 3 | - | - | - |
| 5 | | 4 | - | 8 | 1 | 6 | 2 | 5 | - |
| 6 | | 4 | 8 | 9 | 7 | 9 | 5 | - | - |
| 7 | | 5 | 7 | 1 | 4 | 2 | 7 | 5 | - |
| 8 | | 6 | 5 | 3 | - | 6 | - | - | - |

### **Tarif de ce que Les gros produissent a La Chine**

| Gros | Pesent et Prod: | Theils | Mas | Cander | Cassies | 1/10. Cass. | 1/10 p.$^{s}$ | 1/10 p.$^{s}$ | 1/10 p.$^{s}$ | 1/10 p.$^{s}$ | 1/10 p.$^{s}$ |
|---|---|---|---|---|---|---|---|---|---|---|---|
| 1 | | _ | 1 | _ | 2 | _ | 4 | _ | 6 | 2 | 5 |
| 2 | | _ | 2 | _ | 4 | _ | 8 | 1 | 2 | 5 | _ |
| 3 | | _ | 3 | _ | 6 | 1 | 2 | 1 | 8 | 7 | 5 |
| 4 | | _ | 4 | _ | 8 | 1 | 6 | 2 | 5 | _ | _ |
| 5 | | _ | 5 | 1 | _ | 2 | _ | 3 | 1 | 2 | 5 |
| 6 | | _ | 6 | 1 | 2 | 2 | 4 | 3 | 7 | 5 | _ |
| 7 | | _ | 7 | 1 | 4 | 2 | 8 | 4 | 3 | 7 | 5 |
| 8 | | _ | 8 | 1 | 6 | 3 | 2 | 5 | _ | _ | _ |

### **Tarif de ce que les Grains produissent en theils**

| Grains | Pesent et Pro.$^{d}$ | Theils | Mas | Cand.$^{s}$ | Cassies | 1/10 Cas. | 1/10 p.$^{s}$ | 1/10 p.$^{s}$ | 1/10 p.$^{s}$ | 1/10 p.$^{s}$ | 1/10 p.$^{s}$ |
|---|---|---|---|---|---|---|---|---|---|---|---|
| 1 | | - | - | - | 1 | 4 | 1 | 7 | 2 | 3 | 1 |
| 2 | | - | - | - | 2 | 8 | 3 | 4 | 4 | 6 | 2 |
| 3 | | - | - | - | 4 | 2 | 5 | 1 | 6 | 9 | 3 |
| 4 | | - | - | - | 5 | 6 | 6 | 8 | 9 | 2 | 4 |
| 5 | | - | - | - | 7 | - | 8 | 6 | 1 | 5 | 5 |
| 6 | | - | - | - | 8 | 5 | - | 3 | 3 | 8 | 6 |
| 7 | | - | - | - | 9 | 9 | 2 | - | 6 | 1 | 7 |
| 8 | | - | - | 1 | 1 | 3 | 3 | 7 | 8 | 4 | 8 |
| 9 | | - | - | 1 | 2 | 7 | 5 | 5 | - | 7 | 9 |

| Grains | Pesent et Pro.d | Theils | Mas | Cand.s | Cassies | 1/10 Cas. | 1/10 p.s | 1/10 p.s | 1/10 p.s | 1/10 p.s | 1/10 p.s |
|---|---|---|---|---|---|---|---|---|---|---|---|
| 10 | | - | - | 1 | 4 | 1 | 7 | 2 | 3 | 1 | - |
| 11 | | - | - | 1 | 5 | 5 | 8 | 9 | 5 | 4 | 1 |
| 12 | | - | - | 1 | 7 | - | - | 6 | 7 | 7 | 2 |
| 13 | | - | - | 1 | 8 | 4 | 2 | 4 | - | - | 3 |
| 14 | | - | - | 1 | 9 | 8 | 4 | 1 | 2 | 3 | 4 |
| 15 | | - | - | 2 | 1 | 2 | 5 | 8 | 4 | 6 | 5 |
| 16 | | - | - | 2 | 2 | 6 | 7 | 5 | 6 | 9 | 6 |
| 17 | | - | - | 2 | 4 | - | 9 | 2 | 9 | 2 | 7 |
| 18 | | - | - | 2 | 5 | 5 | 1 | - | 1 | 5 | 8 |
| 36 | | - | - | 5 | 1 | - | 2 | - | 3 | 1 | 6 |
| 72 | | - | 1 | - | 2 | - | 4 | - | 6 | 3 | 2 |

[202] **Tarif de Ce que Les Monnoÿes de la Chine Pesent en Marcs, Onces, Gros et Grains**

| Theil | Pese et Produit | Marc. | Once | Gros | Grains | P. | P. | P. |
|---|---|---|---|---|---|---|---|---|
| 1 | | - | 1 | 1 | 57 | 6 | - | 2 |
| 2 | | - | 2 | 3 | 43 | 2 | - | 6 |
| 3 | | - | 3 | 5 | 58 | 8 | - | 6 |
| 4 | | - | 4 | 7 | 14 | 4 | - | 8 |
| 5 | | - | 6 | 1 | - | - | 1 | - |
| 6 | | - | 7 | 2 | 57 | 6 | 1 | 2 |
| 7 | | 1 | - | 4 | 43 | 2 | 1 | 4 |
| 8 | | 1 | 1 | 6 | 28 | 8 | 1 | 6 |
| 9 | | 1 | 3 | - | 14 | 4 | 1 | 8 |
| 10 | | 1 | 4 | 2 | - | - | 2 | - |
| 11 | | 1 | 5 | 3 | 57 | 6 | 2 | 2 |
| 12 | | 1 | 6 | 5 | 43 | 2 | 2 | 4 |
| 13 | | 1 | 7 | 7 | 28 | 8 | 2 | 6 |
| 14 | | 2 | 1 | 1 | 14 | 4 | 2 | 8 |
| 15 | | 2 | 2 | 3 | - | - | 3 | - |
| 16 | | 2 | 3 | 4 | 57 | 6 | 3 | 2 |
| 17 | | 2 | 4 | 6 | 43 | 2 | 3 | 4 |
| 18 | | 2 | 6 | - | 28 | 8 | 3 | 6 |
| 19 | | 2 | 7 | 2 | 14 | 4 | 3 | 8 |
| 20 | | 3 | - | 4 | - | - | 4 | - |

| | | | | | | | | |
|---|---|---|---|---|---|---|---|---|
| 30 | | 4 | 4 | 6 | - | - | 6 | - |
| 40 | | 6 | 1 | - | - | - | 8 | - |
| 50 | | 7 | 5 | 2 | - | 1 | - | - |
| 60 | | 9 | 1 | 4 | - | 1 | 2 | - |
| 70 | | 10 | 5 | 6 | - | 1 | 4 | - |
| 80 | | 12 | 2 | - | - | 1 | 6 | - |
| 90 | | 13 | 6 | 2 | - | 1 | 8 | - |
| 100 | | 15 | 2 | 4 | - | 2 | - | - |
| 200 | | 30 | 5 | - | - | 4 | - | - |
| 300 | | 45 | 7 | 4 | - | 6 | - | - |
| 400 | | 61 | 2 | - | - | 8 | - | - |
| 500 | | 76 | 4 | 4 | 1 | - | - | - |
| 600 | | 91 | 7 | - | 1 | 2 | - | - |
| 700 | | 107 | 1 | 4 | 1 | 4 | - | - |
| 800 | | 122 | 4 | - | 1 | 6 | - | - |
| 900 | | 137 | 6 | 4 | 1 | 8 | - | - |
| 1000 | | 153 | 1 | - | 2 | - | - | - |
| 2000 | | 306 | 2 | - | 4 | - | - | - |
| 3000 | | 459 | 3 | - | 6 | - | - | - |
| 4000 | | 612 | 4 | - | 8 | - | - | - |
| 5000 | | 765 | 5 | - | 10 | - | - | - |
| 10 000 | | 1531 | 2 | - | 2 | - | - | - |

[203] **Tarif de ce que les Mas produissent en Marc, onces &.**[a]

| Mas | Pese et Produit | Marc | Once | Gros | Grains | P | P. | P. | P. | P | P |
|---|---|---|---|---|---|---|---|---|---|---|---|
| 1 | | - | - | - | 70 | 5 | 6 | - | 2 | - | |
| 2 | | - | - | 1 | 69 | 1 | 2 | - | 4 | - | |
| 3 | | - | - | 3[787] | 67 | 6 | 8 | - | 6 | - | |
| 4 | | - | - | 3 | 66 | 2 | 4 | - | 8 | - | |
| 5 | | - | - | 4 | 64 | 8 | - | 1 | - | - | |
| 6 | | - | - | 5 | 63 | 3 | 6 | 1 | - | - | |
| 7 | | - | - | 6 | 61 | 9 | 2 | 1 | 4 | - | |
| 8 | | - | - | 7 | 60 | 4 | 8 | 1 | 6 | - | |
| 9 | | - | 1 | - | 59 | - | 4 | 1 | 8 | - | |
| 10 | | - | 1 | 1 | 57 | 6 | - | 2 | - | - | |

**787** This should be a “2”. The mistake is in the original.

**Ce qûe Les Canderins produissent**

| Canderins | Pese et Produit | Marc | Once | Gros | Grains | P. | P. | P. | P | P | P. |
|---|---|---|---|---|---|---|---|---|---|---|---|
| 1 | | - | - | - | 7 | - | 5 | 6 | - | 2 | |
| 2 | | - | - | - | 14 | 1 | 1 | 2 | - | 4 | |
| 3 | | - | - | - | 21 | 1 | 6 | 8 | - | 6 | |
| 4 | | - | - | - | 28 | 2 | 2 | 4 | - | 8 | |
| 5 | | - | - | - | 35 | 2 | 8 | - | 1 | - | |
| 6 | | - | - | - | 42 | 3 | 3 | 6 | 1 | 2 | |
| 7 | | - | - | - | 49 | 3 | 9 | 2 | 1 | 4 | |
| 8 | | - | - | - | 56 | 4 | 4 | 8 | 1 | 6 | |
| 9 | | - | - | - | 63 | 5 | - | 4 | 1 | 8 | |
| 10 | | - | - | - | 70 | 5 | 6 | - | 2 | - | |

**Ce qûe Les Cassies produissent.**

| Cassies | Pese et Produit | Marc | Once | Gros | Grains | P. | P. | P. | P. | P. | P |
|---|---|---|---|---|---|---|---|---|---|---|---|
| 1 | | - | - | - | - | 7 | - | 5 | 6 | - | 2 |
| 2 | | - | - | - | 1 | 4 | 1 | 1 | 2 | - | 4 |
| 3 | | - | - | - | 2 | 1 | 1 | 6 | 8 | - | 6 |
| 4 | | - | - | - | 2 | 8 | 2 | 2 | 4 | - | 8 |
| 5 | | - | - | - | 3 | 5 | 2 | 8 | - | 1 | - |
| 6 | | - | - | - | 4 | 2 | 3 | 3 | 6 | 1 | 2 |
| 7 | | - | - | - | 4 | 9 | 3 | 9 | 2 | 1 | 4 |
| 8 | | - | - | - | 5 | 6 | 4 | 4 | 8 | 1 | 6 |
| 9 | | - | - | - | 6 | 3 | 5 | - | 4 | 1 | 8 |
| 10 | | - | - | - | 7 | - | 5 | 6 | - | 2 | - |

[204] **Tarif de ce que Le Marc, et Onces produit en Onces** Pennÿ weights et grains du Troÿ Weights ou poids de Troy des Anglois

| Onces du poids de Marc | Produit | Onces du poids de Troÿ | Penny weights[788] | Grains | Explication du Troÿ Weights |
|---|---|---|---|---|---|
| 1 | | - | 19 | 18½ | 32 Grains ou Weat<br>24. Grains<br>20. Pennÿ Weights<br>12. Onces<br>} fait {<br>24 Grains artificiels<br>1 Penny Weights<br>1. Once<br>1 Livre Troÿ |
| 2 | | 1 | 19 | 13 | |
| 3 | | 2 | 19 | 7½ | |
| 4 | | 3 | 19 | 2 | |
| 5 | | 4 | 18 | 20½ | |
| 6 | | 5 | 18 | 15 | |
| 7 | | 6 | 18 | 9½ | |
| un Marc } | Produit Onces du Poids de Troÿ des Anglois | | | | Advertence |
| 1 | | 7 | 18 | 5 | Comme les Anglois se servent ala Chine pour Peser l'or et l'argent dú Poids de Troÿ, au lieú que nous nous servons du poids de Marc, il est venu (par la longeur du tems) en usance parmis tous les Marchands chinois, et comme jl pouvoit arriver que vous n'auriois poins amene ave vous une balance avec le poids de Marc, jl est necessaire que vous soÿez Instruit de ce poids, c'est pourquoÿ que je Vous donne icÿ Ce Tarif pour vous demontrer la difference qu'il a du Poids de Troÿ a celluy du poids de Marc, par Cette petite explication et les Tarifs qui suivent, vous serez assez jnstruit pour faire votre negoce |
| 2 | | 15 | 16 | 10 | |
| 3 | | 23 | 14 | 15 | |
| 4 | | 31 | 12 | 20 | |
| 5 | | 29 | 11 | 1 | |
| 6 | | 47 | 9 | 6 | |
| 7 | | 55 | 7 | 11 | |
| 8 | | 63 | 5 | 16 | |
| 9 | | 71 | 3 | 21 | |
| 10 | | 79 | 2 | 2 | |
| 20 | | 158 | 4 | 4 | |
| 30 | | 237 | 6 | 6 | |
| 40 | | 316 | 8 | 8 | |
| 50 | | 395 | 10 | 10 | |
| 60 | | 474 | 12 | 12 | |
| 70 | | 553 | 14 | 14 | |
| 80 | | 632 | 16 | 16 | |
| 90 | | 711 | 18 | 18 | |
| 100 | | 791 | - | 20 | |
| 200 | | 1582 | 1 | 16 | |
| 300 | | 2373 | 2 | 12 | |

**788** A pennyweight is a unit of mass in the troy weight system. One pennyweight equates to 24 grains, and 240 pennyweights equate to one troy pound.

| | | | | | |
|---|---|---|---|---|---|
| 400 | | 3164 | 3 | 8 | |
| 500 | | 3955 | 4 | 4 | |
| 600 | | 4746 | 5 | - | |
| 700 | | 5537 | 5 | 20 | |
| 800 | | 6328 | 6 | 16 | |
| 900 | | 7119 | 7 | 12 | |
| 1000 | | 7910 | 8 | 8 | |
| 2000 | | 15 820 | 16 | 16 | |
| 3000 | | 23 731 | 5 | - | |
| 4000 | | 31 641 | 13 | 8 | |
| 5000 | | 39 552 | 1 | 16 | |
| 6000 | | 47 462 | 10 | - | |
| 7000 | | 55 372 | 18 | 18 | |
| 8000 | | 63 283 | 6 | 16 | |
| 9000 | | 71 193 | 15 | - | |
| 10 000 | | 79 104 | 3 | 8. | |

[205] **Tarif de ce que L'once d'Argent poids d'Angleterre** produit a la Chine, Un Once Pese et produit 8 mas, 2 Canderins, 6 cassies et 1/10 partie de Cassie.

Ce Tarif est environ ún par mil plus petit que Celuÿ des Chinois, que je vous donne icy apres, et au Contraire un par mil plus grand, que Celuÿ dela Compagnie Angloise ainsi que ce Tarif est le medium des deux Tarifs des Anglois et des Chinois Marchands.

| Once Angloise | Pese et Produit en | Theÿls | mas | Cand: | Cassies | 1/10 p.e de C. |
|---|---|---|---|---|---|---|
| 1 | | - | 8 | 2 | 6 | 5 |
| 2 | | 1 | 6 | 5 | 3 | - |
| 3 | | 2 | 4 | 7 | 9 | 5 |
| 4 | | 3 | 3 | - | 6 | - |
| 5 | | 4 | 1 | 3 | 2 | 5 |
| 6 | | 4 | 9 | 5 | 9 | - |
| 7 | | 5 | 7 | 8 | 5 | 5 |
| 8 | | 6 | 6 | 1 | 2 | - |
| 9 | | 7 | 4 | 3 | 8 | 5 |
| 10 | | 8 | 2 | 6 | 5 | - |
| 20 | | 16 | 5 | 3 | - | - |
| 30 | | 24 | 7 | 9 | 5 | - |
| 40 | | 33 | - | 6 | - | - |
| 50 | | 41 | 3 | 2 | 5 | - |

| Once Angloise | Pese et Produit en | Theÿls | mas | Cand: | Cassies | 1/10 p.e de C. |
|---|---|---|---|---|---|---|
| 60 | | 49 | 5 | 9 | - | - |
| 70 | | 57 | 8 | 5 | 5 | - |
| 80 | | 66 | 1 | 2 | - | - |
| 90 | | 74 | 3 | 8 | 5 | - |
| 100 | | 82 | 6 | 5 | - | - |
| 200 | | 165 | 3 | - | - | - |
| 300 | | 247 | 9 | 5 | - | - |
| 400 | | 330 | 6 | - | - | - |
| 500 | | 413 | 2 | 5 | - | - |
| 600 | | 495 | 9 | - | - | - |
| 700 | | 578 | 5 | 5 | - | - |
| 800 | | 661 | 2 | - | - | - |
| 900 | | 743 | 8 | 5 | - | - |
| 1000 | | 826 | 5 | - | - | - |
| 2000 | | 1653 | - | - | - | - |
| 3000 | | 2479 | 5 | - | - | - |
| 4000 | | 3306 | - | - | - | - |
| 5000 | | 4132 | 5 | - | - | - |
| 6000 | | 4959 | - | - | - | - |
| 7000 | | 5785 | 5 | - | - | - |
| 8000 | | 6612 | - | - | - | - |
| 9000 | | 7438 | 5 | - | - | - |
| 10 000 | | 8265 | - | - | - | - |

## [206] **Ce que Les Pennÿ Weights rendent**

| Pennÿ Weights | Rendent et Pesent en | Theyls | mas | Cand. | Cassies | 1/10 p de C. |
|---|---|---|---|---|---|---|
| 1 | | - | - | 4 | 1 | 3 |
| 2 | | - | - | 8 | 2 | 6 |
| 3 | | - | 1 | 2 | 3 | 9 |
| 4 | | - | 1 | 6 | 5 | 3 |
| 5 | | - | 2 | - | 6 | 6 |
| 6 | | - | 2 | 4 | 7 | 9 |
| 7 | | - | 2 | 8 | 9 | 2 |
| 8 | | - | 3 | 3 | - | 6 |
| 9 | | - | 3 | 7 | 1 | 9 |
| 10 | | - | 4 | 1 | 3 | 2 |

**Ce que Les Grains rendent.**

| Grains | Pesent et Rendent | Theÿls | mas | Cande-rins | Cassies | 1/10 p: de C | 1/10 p: C. |
|---|---|---|---|---|---|---|---|
| 1 | | - | - | - | 1 | 7 | 2 |
| 2 | | - | - | - | 3 | 4 | 4 |
| 3 | | - | - | - | 5 | 1 | 6 |
| 4 | | - | - | - | 6 | 8 | 8 |
| 5 | | - | - | - | 8 | 6 | - |
| 6 | | - | - | 1 | - | 3 | 2 |
| 7 | | - | - | 1 | 2 | - | 4 |
| 8 | | - | - | 1 | 3 | 7 | 6 |
| 9 | | - | - | 1 | 5 | 4 | 8 |
| 10 | | - | - | 1 | 7 | 2 | - |
| 11 | | - | - | 1 | 8 | 9 | 2 |
| 12 | | - | - | 2 | - | 6 | 4 |
| 13 | | - | - | 2 | 2 | 3 | 6 |
| 14 | | - | - | 2 | 4 | - | 8 |
| 15 | | - | - | 2 | 5 | 8 | - |
| 16 | | - | - | 2 | 7 | 5 | 2 |
| 17 | | - | - | 2 | 9 | 2 | 4 |
| 18 | | - | - | 3 | - | 9 | 6 |
| 19 | | - | - | 3 | 2 | 6 | 8 |
| 20 | | - | - | 3 | 4 | 4 | - |
| 21 | | - | - | 3 | 6 | 1 | 2 |
| 22 | | - | - | 3 | 7 | 8 | 4 |
| 23 | | - | - | 3 | 9 | 5 | 6 |

[207] **Tarif que Ceux de la Compagnie Angloise se servent** pour Peser leur Argent en Chine, dont l'once du Troÿ Weights (dont je vous aÿ donne cÿ devant le tarif) pese et produit 8 mas, 2 Canderins 5 Cassies 1/10 p. de Cassie et 1/10 d'un 1/10., Ce tarif est un per mil plus petit que le Tarif de Londre

| Onces de la Comp.e Ange | Pesent et Rendent | Theyls | mas | Cand: | Cassies | 1/10 C. | 1/10 de C |
|---|---|---|---|---|---|---|---|
| 1 | | - | 8 | 2 | 5 | 7 | 6 |
| 2 | | 1 | 6 | 5 | 1 | 5 | 2 |
| 3 | | 2 | 4 | 7 | 7 | 2 | 8 |
| 4 | | 3 | 3 | - | 3 | - | 4 |
| 5 | | 4 | 1 | 2 | 8 | 8 | - |
| 6 | | 4 | 9 | 5 | 4 | 5 | 6 |
| 7 | | 5 | 7 | 8 | - | 3 | 2 |
| 8 | | 6 | 6 | - | 6 | - | 8 |
| 9 | | 7 | 4 | 3 | 1 | 8 | 4 |
| 10 | | 8 | 2 | 5 | 7 | 6 | - |
| 20 | | 16 | 5 | 1 | 5 | 2 | - |
| 30 | | 24 | 7 | 7 | 2 | 8 | - |
| 40 | | 33 | - | 3 | - | 4 | - |
| 50 | | 41 | 2 | 8 | 8 | - | - |
| 60 | | 49 | 5 | 4 | 5 | 6 | - |
| 70 | | 57 | 8 | - | 3 | 2 | - |
| 80 | | 66 | - | 6 | - | 8 | - |
| 90 | | 74 | 3 | 1 | 8 | 4 | - |
| 100 | | 82 | 5 | 7 | 6 | - | - |
| 200 | | 165 | 1 | 5 | 2 | - | - |
| 300 | | 247 | 7 | 2 | 8 | - | - |
| 400 | | 330 | 3 | - | 4 | - | - |
| 500 | | 412 | 8 | 8 | - | - | - |
| 600 | | 495 | 4 | 5 | 6 | - | - |
| 700 | | 578 | - | 3 | 2 | - | - |
| 800 | | 660 | 6 | - | 8 | - | - |
| 900 | | 743 | 1 | 8 | 4 | - | - |
| 1000 | | 825 | 7 | 6 | - | - | - |
| 2000 | | 1651 | 5 | 2 | - | - | - |
| 3000 | | 2477 | 2 | 8 | - | - | - |
| 4000 | | 3303 | - | 4 | - | - | - |
| 5000 | | 4128 | 8 | - | - | - | - |

| Onces de la Comp.e Ange | Pesent et Rendent | Theyls | mas | Cand: | Cassies | 1/10 C. | 1/10 de C |
|---|---|---|---|---|---|---|---|
| 6000 | | 4954 | 5 | 6 | - | - | - |
| 7000 | | 5780 | 3 | 2 | - | - | - |
| 8000 | | 6606 | - | 8 | - | - | - |
| 9000 | | 7431 | 8 | 4 | - | - | - |
| 10 000 | | 8257 | 6 | - | - | - | - |

[208] **Ce qûe Les Pennÿ Weights rendent.**

| Penny Weights | Pesent et pro-duisent | Theyls | mas | Cand: | Cassies | 1/10 p: | 1/10 p.e |
|---|---|---|---|---|---|---|---|
| 1 | | - | - | 4 | 1 | 2 | 8 |
| 2 | | - | - | 8 | 2 | 5 | 6 |
| 3 | | - | 1 | 2 | 3 | 8 | 4 |
| 4 | | - | 1 | 6 | 5 | 1 | 2 |
| 5 | | - | 2 | - | 6 | 4 | - |
| 6 | | - | 2 | 4 | 7 | 6 | 8 |
| 7 | | - | 2 | 8 | 8 | 9 | 6 |
| 8 | | - | 3 | 3 | - | 2 | 4 |
| 9 | | - | 3 | 7 | 1 | 5 | 2 |
| 10 | | - | 4 | 1 | 2 | 8 | - |
| 11 | | - | 4 | 5 | 4 | - | 8 |
| 12 | | - | 4 | 9 | 5 | 3 | 6 |
| 13 | | - | 5 | 3 | 6 | 6 | 4 |
| 14 | | - | 5 | 7 | 7 | 9 | 2 |
| 15 | | - | 6 | 1 | 9 | 2 | - |
| 16 | | - | 6 | 6 | - | 4 | 8 |
| 17 | | - | 7 | - | 1 | 7 | 6 |
| 18 | | - | 7 | 4 | 3 | - | 4 |
| 19 | | - | 7 | 8 | 4 | 3 | 2 |

**Ce que Les Grains rendent.**

| Grains | Pesent et rendent | Theÿls | mas | Cand: | Cassies | 1/10 Cassie | 1/10 p: C |
|---|---|---|---|---|---|---|---|
| 1 | | - | - | - | 1 | 7 | 2 |
| 2 | | - | - | - | 3 | 4 | 4 |
| 3 | | - | - | - | 5 | 1 | 6 |
| 4 | | - | - | - | 6 | 8 | 8 |
| 5 | | - | - | - | 8 | 6 | - |
| 6 | | - | - | 1 | - | 3 | 2 |
| 7 | | - | - | 1 | 2 | - | 4 |
| 8 | | - | - | 1 | 3 | 7 | 6 |
| 9 | | - | - | 1 | 5 | 4 | 8 |
| 10 | | - | - | 1 | 7 | 2 | - |
| 11 | | - | - | 1 | 8 | 9 | 2 |
| 12 | | - | - | 2 | - | 6 | 4 |
| 13 | | - | - | 2 | 2 | 3 | 6 |
| 14 | | - | - | 2 | 4 | - | 8 |
| 15 | | - | - | 2 | 5 | 8 | - |
| 16 | | - | - | 2 | 7 | 5 | 2 |
| 17 | | - | - | 2 | 9 | 2 | 4 |
| 18 | | - | - | 3 | - | 9 | 6 |
| 19 | | - | - | 3 | 2 | 6 | 8 |
| 20 | | - | - | 3 | 4 | 4 | - |
| 21 | | - | - | 3 | 6 | 1 | - |
| 22 | | - | - | 3 | 7 | 8 | 4 |
| 23 | | - | - | 3 | 9 | 5 | 6 |

[209] **Tarif du Poids de Troÿe qúe les Marchands Chinois** úsent pour Peser l'argent qu'on leur paÿe, le quel est un par mil plus fort que celuÿ que ceux dela Compagnie Anglois usent pour peser leur argent à Canton dans les payements qu'ils font aux Marchands Chinois

| Onces du Troy weight | qui Pese et Produit | Theÿls | mas | Cand. | Cassies | 1/10 Cassie | 1/10 p. C |
|---|---|---|---|---|---|---|---|
| 1 | | - | 8 | 2 | 7 | 4 | 4 |
| 2 | | 1 | 6 | 5 | 4 | 8 | 8 |
| 3 | | 2 | 4 | 8 | 2 | 3 | 2 |
| 4 | | 3 | 3 | - | 9 | 7 | 6 |

| Onces du Troy weight | qui Pese et Produit | Theÿls | mas | Cand. | Cassies | 1/10 Cassie | 1/10 p. C |
|---|---|---|---|---|---|---|---|
| 5 | | 4 | 1 | 3 | 7 | 2 | - |
| 6 | | 4 | 9 | 6 | 4 | 6 | 4 |
| 7 | | 5 | 7 | 9 | 2 | - | 8 |
| 8 | | 6 | 6 | 1 | 9 | 5 | 2 |
| 9 | | 7 | 4 | 4 | 6 | 9 | 6 |
| 10 | | 8 | 2 | 7 | 4 | 4 | - |
| 11 | | 9 | 1 | - | 1 | 8 | 4 |
| 12 | | 9 | 9 | 2 | 9 | 2 | 8 |
| 13 | | 10 | 7 | 5 | 6 | 7 | 2 |
| 14 | | 11 | 5 | 8 | 4 | 1 | 6 |
| 15 | | 12 | 4 | 1 | 1 | 6 | - |
| 16 | | 13 | 2 | 3 | 9 | - | 4 |
| 17 | | 14 | - | 6 | 6 | 4 | 8 |
| 18 | | 14 | 8 | 9 | 3 | 9 | 2 |
| 19 | | 15 | 7 | 2 | 1 | 3 | 6 |
| 20 | | 16 | 5 | 4 | 8 | 8 | - |
| 30 | | 24 | 8 | 2 | 3 | 2 | - |
| 40 | | 33 | - | 9 | 7 | 6 | - |
| 50 | | 41 | 3 | 7 | 2 | - | - |
| 60 | | 49 | 6 | 4 | 6 | 4 | - |
| 70 | | 57 | 9 | 2 | - | 8 | - |
| 80 | | 66 | 1 | 9 | 5 | 2 | - |
| 90 | | 74 | 4 | 6 | 9 | 6 | - |
| 100 | | 82 | 7 | 4 | 4 | - | - |
| 200 | | 165 | 4 | 8 | 8 | - | - |
| 300 | | 248 | 2 | 3 | 2 | - | - |
| 400 | | 330 | 9 | 7 | 6 | - | - |
| 500 | | 413 | 7 | 2 | - | - | - |
| 600 | | 496 | 4 | 6 | 4 | - | - |
| 700 | | 579 | 2 | - | 8 | - | - |
| 800 | | 661 | 9 | 5 | 2 | - | - |
| 900 | | 744 | 6 | 9 | 6 | - | - |
| 1000 | | 822 | 4 | 4 | - | - | - |
| 2000 | | 1654 | 8 | 8 | - | - | - |
| 3000 | | 2482 | 3 | 2 | - | - | - |
| 4000 | | 3309 | 7 | 6 | - | - | - |

| Onces du Troy weight | qui Pese et Produit | Theÿls | mas | Cand. | Cassies | 1/10 Cassie | 1/10 p. C |
|---|---|---|---|---|---|---|---|
| 5000 | | 4137 | 2 | - | - | - | - |
| 6000 | | 4964 | 6 | 4 | - | - | - |
| 7000 | | 5792 | - | 8 | - | - | - |
| 8000 | | 6619 | 5 | 2 | - | - | - |
| 9000 | | 7446 | 9 | 6 | - | - | - |
| 10 000 | | 8274 | 4 | - | - | - | - |

[210] **Ce que Les Penny Weights Produissent.**

| Pennÿ Weights | Pesent et produissent | Theyls | mas | Cand: | Cassies | 1/10 Cassie | 1/10 p.d.C | 1/10 p: de C |
|---|---|---|---|---|---|---|---|---|
| 1 | | - | - | 4 | 1 | 3 | 7 | 2 |
| 2 | | - | - | 8 | 2 | 7 | 4 | 4 |
| 3 | | - | 1 | 2 | 4 | 1 | 1 | 6 |
| 4 | | - | 1 | 6 | 5 | 4 | 8 | 8 |
| 5 | | - | 2 | - | 6 | 8 | 6 | - |
| 6 | | - | 2 | 4 | 8 | 2 | 3 | 2 |
| 7 | | - | 2 | 8 | 9 | 6 | - | 4 |
| 8 | | - | 3 | 3 | - | 9 | 7 | 6 |
| 9 | | - | 3 | 7 | 2 | 3 | 4 | 8 |
| 10 | | - | 4 | 1 | 3 | 7 | 2 | - |
| 11 | | - | 4 | 5 | 5 | - | 9 | 2 |
| 12 | | - | 4 | 9 | 6 | 4 | 6 | 4 |
| 13 | | - | 5 | 3 | 7 | 8 | 3 | 6 |
| 14 | | - | 5 | 7 | 9 | 2 | - | 8 |
| 15 | | - | 6 | 2 | - | 5 | 8 | - |
| 16 | | - | 6 | 6 | 1 | 9 | 5 | 2 |
| 17 | | - | 7 | - | 3 | 3 | 2 | 4 |
| 18 | | - | 7 | 4 | 4 | 6 | 9 | 6 |
| 19 | | - | 7 | 8 | 6 | - | 6 | 8 |

## Ce que Les Grains Produissent

| Grains | Pesent et pro-duissent | Theÿls | mas | Cand: | Cassies | 1/10 Cas. | 1/10 p. C. | 1/10 p C |
|---|---|---|---|---|---|---|---|---|
| 1 | | - | - | - | 1 | 7 | 2 | 4 |
| 2 | | - | - | - | 3 | 4 | 4 | 8 |
| 3 | | - | - | - | 5 | 1 | 7 | 2 |
| 4 | | - | - | - | 6 | 8 | 9 | 6 |
| 5 | | - | - | - | 8 | 6 | 2 | - |
| 6 | | - | - | 1 | - | 3 | 4 | 4 |
| 7 | | - | - | 1 | 2 | - | 6 | 8 |
| 8 | | - | - | 1 | 3 | 7 | 9 | 6 |
| 9 | | - | - | 1 | 5 | 5 | 1 | 6 |
| 10 | | - | - | 1 | 7 | 2 | 4 | - |
| 11 | | - | - | 1 | 8 | 9 | 6 | 4 |
| 12 | | - | - | 2 | - | 6 | 8 | 8 |
| 13 | | - | - | 2 | 2 | 4 | 1 | 2 |
| 14 | | - | - | 2 | 4 | 1 | 3 | 6 |
| 15 | | - | - | 2 | 5 | 8 | 6 | - |
| 16 | | - | - | 2 | 7 | 5 | 8 | 4 |
| 17 | | - | - | 2 | 9 | 3 | - | 8 |
| 18 | | - | - | 3 | 1 | - | 3 | 2 |
| 19 | | - | - | 3 | 2 | 7 | 5 | 6 |
| 20 | | - | - | 3 | 4 | 4 | 8 | - |
| 21 | | - | - | 3 | 6 | 2 | - | 4 |
| 22 | | - | - | 3 | 7 | 9 | 2 | 8 |
| 23 | | - | - | 3 | 9 | 6 | 5 | 2 |

# Abbreviations

## General Abbreviations

| | |
|---|---|
| BL | British Library |
| C | candareen (fr. candarins) or catty |
| Cand. | candareen |
| Cat. | catty |
| d.° | ditto |
| EIC | United English East India Company |
| ft. | footnote |
| GIC | *Generale Keijserlijcke Compagnie* |
| IOR | India Office Records |
| ll | livres |
| M. | mace |
| p. | per |
| Piq | picul |
| Th. | tael |
| tt | barrels (fr. tonneaux) |
| UP | University Press |
| VOC | *Verenigde Oostindische Compagnie* |

## Nautical Abbreviations

| | |
|---|---|
| A | all |
| Amp | amplitude |
| Azim | azimuth |
| B | by or both |
| Bro | broaching to |
| d | degree |
| D | double |
| dis | distance |
| E | east |
| F | fore |
| fa | fathoms |
| H | hoisted |
| I | in |
| lat | latitude |
| lea | league |
| long | longitude |
| m | minutes |
| M | main |
| N | north |
| O | out |
| R | reefed |
| S | south or sail |
| T | top |
| $Tk^t$ | tacked |
| W | west |

# Glossary of Nautical Terms

**aft** Towards the stern of a ship.

**amplitude** The angular distance of a celestial body (i.e. sun, moon, planets, stars) east and west of the horizon at a specific locale. By 1600, navigators brought amplitude charts with them on their sailings. By comparing their compass readings to these printed aides, they could determine any necessary accounting for magnetic variation.

**azimuth** Azimuth, as calculated by eighteenth-century mariners with the aid of azimuth compasses, was the angular distance between the rising or setting sun and true north. It, too, was used to account for magnetic variation.

**backstay** A piece of rigging that connects from the top of the mast to the ship's stern.

**ballast** Any material or cargo that provides weight, and thus stability, to a ship.

**bearing away** To steer a ship away from the wind. The tactic often was done so as to make repair work easier.

**benting** To attach new square sails to a ship's lowest yards. Sailors typically did this before leaving port, unless their sails were damaged in route or they expected heavy weather and wanted better canvas.

**berthing** To moor a vessel, either in a harbor, attached to a buoy or in a fixed spot with an anchor.

**boatswain** A senior crewmember, charged with monitoring the deck and his fellow sailors.

**boom** A spar, or rod, that runs along the bottom of a sail and controls its shape.

**boot-tops** Markings on a ship's external bow, which note its differing draughts when loaded and unloaded. These indicate the part of the vessel most exposed to the elements and thus most likely to decay and need repairs.

**bow** The frontmost portion of a ship.

**bower** Anchors stowed at a ship's bow. The starboard anchor is the "best bower", while its portside counterpart is the "small bower". Both are of equal size.

**bowsprit** A ship extension, attached to the bow and to which the masts are secured.

**breadroom** A compartment used to store a ship's dry provisions. It was located in in the aftmost part of the hold and well-lined with boards and sometimes tin plates, to prevent water seepage.

**brig** A two-masted sailing vessel, with square-rigged sails. Brigs moved quickly, which made them popular for military and commercial use in the early 1700s.

**broaching to** To turn a ship sideways in a heavy sea or to turn it into the waves, so as to combat any diminished steering capacity brought on by rear waves and wind.

**bulkhead** A partition wall within a ship's hull. Bulkheads were especially common on Chinese junks, where they prevented cargos from shifting as well as increased the vessel's water tightness, even when damaged.

**cap truss** A truss is a thick cable, which attaches the center of a ship's yard to its mast and thereby maintains the shape of its sails. The cap is a block of wood, which supports the topmast.

**cabotage** Maritime navigation, within sight of land. The term derives from the French word *caboter*, meaning "to travel by the coast".

**caulking** To make a vessel watertight, by packing its seams with materials like pitch, tar and tallow.

**cross jackyard** The lowest yard on a ship's mizzenmast.

| | |
|---|---|
| **dhow** | A one- or more-masted sailing vessel with triangular sails, commonly used in the Indian Ocean. |
| **draught** | The amount of a ship that sits underwater, as measured from the waterline to the bottom of its hull. |
| **fathom** | A unit used to calculate water depth. One fathom equals 1.82 meters. |
| **fore** | Towards the bow of a ship. |
| **foremast** | Typically the first, or foremost, mast on a ship. |
| **frigate** | A three-masted, square-rigged military ship, which carried – according to the English Admiralty's use of the term – at least 28 guns on one or more decks. |
| **furl** | To roll up or stow a sail. This typically is done to prevent damage in bad weather. |
| **gammon** | The chains, ropes or iron bands that attach a vessel's bowsprit to its bow. |
| **gun carriage** | The frame and mount that supported a ship's artillery (guns and cannon). Gun carriages were made of wood and had two or four wheels, to allow for recoil. |
| **gun deck** | A level on a ship, often located just below its main deck, where the cannons are mounted. |
| **hawsehole** | A hole is the bow of a vessel, through which its anchor rope passes. |
| **hawser** | A thick rope used for towing or securing ships. A bridle arrangement takes the load of a central hawser and divides it among several different points on a ship, to ease strain. |
| **hoisted** | To haul up a ship's sail or sails so as to decrease the pressure or slow down. |
| **hold** | The lower, interior portions of a ship, used for storing cargo. The forehold is nearest the bow. The afterhold is between the mainmast and stern. |
| **hoy** | A small, European sailing vessel, used for coastal navigation and for carrying heavy loads into shallow waters. |
| **hull** | The hollow, lowermost portion of a ship, which is located below the main deck and partially submerged. |
| **jolly** | A small boat, carried on a larger ship. The term, as used in these sources, is synonymous with "yawl". |
| **junk** | A term used to describe a variety of traditional Chinese sailing vessels, all of which have full batten – or rigid, horizontally-supported – sails. |
| **kedge anchor** | A ship's smallest anchor, mostly employed in calm water. It especially was used to pull moored ships free of sandbars and to change a vessel's direction when lacking wind. |
| **ketch** | A two-masted, square-rigged sailing vessel, similar to a yawl. |
| **knot** | A unit for measuring a ship's speed. One knot equates to about 1.85 kilometers per hour. |
| **larboard** | The left side of a ship, when viewed from aboard and facing the bow. |
| **latitude** | The angular distance of a particular site north or south of the Equator. Latitude was calculated visually in the early 1700s, by sighting the altitude of the noon sun or other specific celestial bodies. This was done with the aid of quadrants and back-staffs. |
| **lazaretto** | A small storage space, located between the decks of ships and near the stern. Mariners typically used it to store drinking water and provisions. |
| **league** | A unit of length. At sea, one league equated to three nautical miles or about 5.5 kilometers. |
| **lighter** | A flat-bottomed, oar- and current-powered barge, used to lighten the loads of heavier ships that needed to anchor in deep waters. |

**longboat** The longest and heaviest vessel carried aboard early modern ships. Longboats often had a removable mast and sails, given that they doubled as lifeboats. They usually, however, were powered by manual oaring and used for smaller tasks, such as locating channels, fishing, and transferring passengers to shore.

**longitude** The angular distance of a specific site east or west of another location, or a standard meridian. It was difficult to calculate longitude precisely in the early 1700s. Ship captains primarily relied on calculated guesses, or estimations of the distance and speed their vessels sailed east or west from prior navigational markers. There was no agreed upon prime meridian in 1723, although some ships tried to use the Lizard in England or El Hierro in the Cape Verde islands as a standard zero (or prime) meridian. Greenwich, England only came to be used as a popular prime meridian marker in the late nineteenth century.

**magnetic variation** The difference between true north and magnetic north, as indicated on a compass. It varied due to location and the amount of metals on a ship.

**mainmast** The tallest mast on a ship, typically located near its center.

**meridian distance** This refers to a new attempt to calculate longitude, as measured east or west of a standard meridian, in the early eighteenth century. It involved recording the location of the noon sun and then mathematically relating this observation to the standard with the help of print guides.

**midshipman** An experienced naval officer, charged with keeping watch, completing deck side repairs, and recording some navigational measurements.

**mizzenmast** The third mast on a three- or more-masted ship, located behind the mainmast.

**moor** To secure a ship in a fixed position, whether by tying it to a dock or securing its anchors in open water. A mooring is the location to which a vessel is or can be secured.

**mooring swivel** An extra anchor, to prevent an anchored ship from swaying with the wind or tides.

**pinnace** A small boat, powered by oars or sails. It was stored on ocean-going ships and used to transport mail, goods and passengers between anchored ships and to the shore.

**port** The left side of a ship, when viewed from aboard and facing the bow.

**proa** A multi-, usually two-hulled sailing vessel, popular near the Indonesian islands and South China Sea in the 1700s. Their light weight made them very quick.

**quartermaster** A naval officer, responsible for aiding with the watch and manning the helm.

**reefing** To reduce the part of a sail exposed to the wind, typically by folding or rolling up one edge. This tactic improves a ship's performance and stability in high winds. It is possible to insert several reefs into one sail, thereby reducing the amount of cloth exposed to the wind.

**rigging** The ropes and cables, used to support and control the masts, yards and sails of a sailing vessel.

**river pay** The amount of money due a ship's crew for work done before formally setting sail. River pay typically was given in-full and sometimes accompanied by two months' forward wages. This gave mariners spending money for their travels.

**rhumb lines** Diagonal lines drawn onto a map, made across all longitudinal meridians at the same angle and extending from pole to pole. They were used as navigational tools. Ships that travelled along rhumb lines, especially near the Equator, travelled in a straight line and the shortest distance between two points, as they accounted for the earth's curvature. To employ this aid, mariners only needed to know their latitude.

| | |
|---|---|
| **sampan** | A largely flat-bottomed, wooden boat, common in eighteenth-century China. It was propelled by oars. |
| **schooner** | A two- or more-masted sailing vessel. Smaller than ocean-going ships, such as frigates, they could travel easily and quickly into shallow waters, which made them ideal for coastal traders as well as pirates and smugglers. |
| **service** | A marked amount of anchor rope that can be released from a moored vessel. This is crucial, because it indicates portions of the cable that are reinforced and can sustain the continued pressure of the hawsehole. A long, or leeward, service is the marked section located almost at the end of the anchor rope. |
| **shoring** | To prop a ship upright, with the aide of wooden beams and wedges. |
| **shrouds** | Standard pieces of rigging that secure and hold up a ship's mast. They bind the top of each mast to the hull in parallel ways on both port and starboard sides. |
| **sloop** | A one-masted sailing vessel, commonly used for fishing and coastal trade. |
| **sounding** | The process by which the water-depth under a ship is determined. In the early 1700s, this was calculated by dropping a weighted cable with marked-off measurements overboard. Soundings also were used to determine if a ship was nearing land, indicated by diminished depths or any collected seabed materials. |
| **starboard** | The right side of a ship, when viewed from aboard and facing the bow. |
| **stern** | The backmost portion of a ship. |
| **steward** | A naval officer, charged with guarding food supplies and dispensing rations to the crew. He sometimes also acquired additional provisions, when anchored. |
| **stream anchor** | A small anchor, used primarily in rivers and in harbors with weak tides. |
| **tacking** | A sailing tactic, whereby a vessel turns its bow to change the direction that the wind blows into its sails. It is often used to move into the direction of the wind. |
| **tailor** | A crewmember charged with accommodating mariners' clothing needs. This included new garments fit for naval activities and adjusting existing garments for fluctuating body shapes. |
| **topgallant mast** | The section of the mast above the topmast. |
| **topmast** | The second lowest of four sections on each mast. The topmast adjoins the lower mast, which then connects each mast to the vessel. It, like all masts, is used to support the sails. |
| **warping** | A method of moving a ship, usually against the wind. It involves throwing out a kedge anchor in the intended route of movement and then – by hauling this anchor in – pulling the vessel in that direction. |
| **wearing** | To turn a ship in such a manner that its mainsail is pulled across the deck and catches the wind on its opposite side. This switches the windward side of the vessel and thus its sailing direction. The tactic also is referred to as "jibing." |
| **whipstaff** | A piece of vertical timber in eighteenth-century sailing vessels that controlled the direction of the rudder, thus steering the ship. It was located at the stern. |
| **yard** | A horizontal spar on a vessel's masts, to which its sails are connected. |
| **yawl** | A two-masted sailing vessel. Yawls initially were used for fishing but here are used for navigational tasks, like locating channels and moving kedge anchors. |

For more on early modern ship constructions and naval activities, see Jean Sutton, *Lords of the East: the East India Company and its Ships* (New York: Conway Maritime Press, 2000); Peter Kemp, ed., *The Oxford Companion to Ships and the Sea* (New York: Oxford UP, 1976); Rediker, Between; Horst Nowacki and Matteo Valleriani (eds.), *Shipbuilding practice and ship design methods from the Renaissance to the 18th century* (Berlin: Max Planck Institut für Wissenschaftsgeschichte, 2003).

# Bibliography

## Archival Material

Bayerische Staatsbibliothek – Codices gallici 624, 674
British Library – IOR/E/3/101, IOR/B/51–185, IOR/G/12/32, IOR/L/MAR/A/CXLIV, IOR/L/MAR/B/656-I(2), IOR/L/MAR/B/700D(2), Mss. Eur. C387/1–4
Landesarchiv Aurich – Rep. 4, B IVe, Nr. 179.
Staatsarchiv Hamburg – 111-1, Cl VII, Lit. Ka 165, vol. 4a.

## Online Material

Bibliography on the History of the Ostend Company: http://www.oostende.be/product.aspx?id=5974 [12.11.2015].
Sound Toll Registers Online: http://dietrich.soundtoll.nl/public/stats.php?stat=py [23.10.2015].

## Printed Sources

*A chart of the China Sea from the island of Sanciam to Pedra Branca with the course of the river Tigris from Canton to Macao, corrected from the surveys made by Captn. Jph. Huddart and Captn. J.P. Larkins* (London: Laurie and Whittle, 1794).
*A New General Collection of Voyages and Travels, vol. 4* (London: T. Astley, 1747).
*A New Nautical Directory of the East-India and China Navigation* (London: S. Couchman, 1804).
*A Register of Ships, Employed in the Service of the Hon. The United East India Company* (London: Charles Hardy, 1800).
Giulio Aleni, *Illustrated Explanation of the Incarnation of the Lord of Heaven* (1637).
Noël Alexandre, *Apologie des dominicains missionnaires de la Chine, vol. 1* (Cologne: Corneille d'Egmond, 1699, [2]1700).
*Atlas historique, ou nouvelle introduction a l'histoire, a la chronologie, & à la geographie ancienne & moderne* (Amsterdam: L'Honoré & Chatelain, 1719).
Peter Auber, *An Analysis of the Constitution of 'The East India Company'* (London: Kingsbury, Parbury, & Allen, 1826).
Étienne de Barbinais le Gentil, *Nouveau voyage autour du monde, 2 vol.* (Amsterdam: Pierre Mortier, 1728).
Joachim Bouvet, *Histoire de l'empereur de la Chine* (The Hague: Meyndert Uytwerf, 1699).
*Calendar of Treasury Books and Papers, 1729–1730, vol. 1*, ed. William A. Shaw (London: Her Majesty's Stationery Office, 1897).
*Catalogue des Livres imprimé et manuscrits composant la bibliothèque de Feu M. le Comte Daru* [...] (Paris: J.S. Merlin, 1830).
Rebecca D. Catz (ed.), *The Travels of Mendes Pinto* (Chicago: University of Chicago Press, 1989).
Urbain Chevreau, *Histoire du monde, vol. 7* (Paris: Hilaire Foucault, 1717).
Louis le Comte, *Memoirs and Observations Topographical, Physical, Mathematical, Mechanical, Natural, Civil and Ecclesiastical Made in a Late Journey through the Empire of China, and Published in Several Letters* (London: Benjamin Tooke, 1697).
Ibid., *Nouveaux Mémoires Sur L'Etat Present De La Chine, 2 vol.* (Different places: different publishers, 1697–1701).

Pieter van Dam, *Beschryvinge van de Oostindische Compagnie*, eds. F.W. Stapel and C.W. Th. van Boetzelaer (The Hague: Nijhoff, 1977).
*Catechism of the Catholic Church* (Vatican: Libreria Editrice Vaticana, 1993).
Guillaume Dampier, *Nouveau Voyage autour du Monde, vol. 1* (Rouen: Jean-Baptiste Machuel, 1715).
Ibid., *Suite du Voyage autour du Monde, vol. 2* (Rouen: Jean-Baptiste Machuel, 1723).
Ibid., *Suplement du Voyage autour du Monde* (Rouen: Jean-Baptiste Machuel, 1723).
*The Gentleman's Magazine: or, Monthly Intelligencer* (London: F. Jefferies, 1731).
Charles le Gobien, *Histoire de l'édit de l'empereur de la Chine en faveur de la Religion Chrestienne* (Paris: Jean Anisson, 1698).
Ibid. and Yves Mathurin de Querbeuf, *Lettres édifiantes et curieuses, écrites des missions étrangères: Mémoires de la Chine, vol. 21* (Paris: J.G. Merigot, 1781).
Francis J. Grund, *The Merchant's Assistant* (Boston: Hilliard, Gray & Company, 1834).
Jean Baptiste du Halde, *Description de l'empire de la Chine et de la Tartarie chinoise, 3 vol.* (The Hague: Henri Scheurleer, 1736–1737).
Charles Hill, *List of Europeans and others in the English Factories of Bengal at the time of the Siege of Calcutta in the year 1756* (Calcutta: Office of the Superintendent of Government Printing, 1902).
*The Historical Register, Containing An Impartial Relation of all Transactions, Foreign and Domestick* 10–13 (1725–1728).
James Horsburgh, *India Directory, or Directions for Sailing* (London: W.H. Allen & Co., 1836).
Jean Jovet, *L'histoire des religions de tous les royaumes du monde* (Paris: Montalant, 1724).
*The London Journal of Arts, Sciences, and Manufactures, and Repertory of Patent Inventions, vol. 24* (London: W. Newton, 1846).
*The London Magazine: or, Gentleman's Monthly Intelligencer* (January 1735).
Richard John Lynn (trans.), *The Classic of Changes: a New Translation of the* I Ching *as Interpreted by Bi Wang* (New York: Columbia UP, 1994).
Allain Manesson-Mallet, *Description de l'univers, 2 vol.* (Paris: Denys Thierry, 1683).
M. Bruzen La Martiniere, *Le Grand Dictionnaire Geographique et Critique, vol. 4.2, 8* (Different places: different publishers, 1732, 1737).
Ibid., *Introduction à l'histoire de l'Asie, de l'Afrique, et de l'Amérique, vol. 1* (Amsterdam: Zacharie Chatelain, 1735).
*Memoires pour l'Histoire des Sciences & des beaux Arts* (Paris: Jean Boudot, 1703).
Juan González de Mendoza, *The History of the Great and Mighty Kingdom of China* (1586).
Louis Moréri, *Le Grand Dictionaire Historique, 5 vol.* (Different places: different publishers, 1683–1725).
Ibid., *Supplément aux anciennes éditions du Grand Dictionaire Historique, 2 vol.* (Amsterdam: Pierre Brunel, 1716).
J.W. Norie, *Sailing directions for the river Thames, from London, to the Nore and Sheerness* (London: J.W. Norie and Co., 1817).
Walter Gorn Old (trans.), *The Shu King* (London: Theosophical Publishing Society, 1904).
Pierre Joseph d'Orléans and Nicholaas Witsen, *History of the Two Tartar Conquerors of China*, ed. Richard Henry Major (Cambridge: Cambridge UP, 2010).
John Pinkerton, *A General Collection of the Best and Most Interesting Voyages and Travels in Various Parts of Asia, vol. 2* (London: Longman, Hurst, Rees, Orme & Brown, 1819).
*The Present State of Europe: or, the Historical and Political Monthly Mercury* (May 1723).
Floris Prims, *De oorlog van Mijnheer Cobbé; geschiedenis van de reis van Cobbé, van zijn onderhandelingen met den Nabab en van zijn Oorlog tegen de Mooren 1722–1724* (Antwerpen: Leeslust, 1927).

Charles C. Prinsep, *Record of Services of the Honourable East India Company's Civil Servants ... as well as lists of the directors of the East India Company; Chairmen and Deputy Chairmen of the Direction* (London: Trübner & Company, 1885).
John Purdy, *The Oriental Navigatory: or, Directions for Sailing to, from, and upon the coasts of, the East-Indies, China, Australia, &c.* (London: James Whittle and Richard Holmes Laurie, 1816).
*Isaac Pyke: Twice Governor of St. Helena* (London: Taylor and Francis, 1937).
*Records of Fort St. George: Diary and Consultation Book of 1722, 1723* (Madras: Government Press, 1930).
*Remarks on Trade in a Dialogue between a Committee-man and an Interloper* (London, 1683).
Jean de La Roque, *Voyage de l'Arabie Heureuse* (Paris: André Cailleau, 1716).
J. Rotsaert, *De reis van het keyserlyck compagnieschip genaempt De Keyzerinne, gemonteerd met 30 stukken canon en 108 zielen. Equipatie gecommandeert per Capteyn Joan de Clerck, gedestineerd naar Canton in China, uyt gevaren van Oostende op den 20 January 1725* (Sint-Andries: Heemkundige Kring "Maurits Van Coppenolle", 1963).
*Sailing Directions for the Oriental, or East-India Pilot* (London: Robert Sayer and John Bennett, 1778).
Adriano di St. Thecla, *Opusculum de Sectis apud Sinenses et Tunkinenses*, trans. Olga Dror (Ithaca, NY: Cornell UP, 2002).
Jaques Savary des Brûlons, *Dictionnaire universel du commerce, vol. 2* (Paris: Jacques Estienne, 1723).
Ibid. and Philemon-Louis Savary, *Dictionnaire universel de commerce, 4 vol.* (Different places: different publishers, 1725–1750).
William Smith (ed.), *Dictionary of Greek and Roman Geography, vol. 1* (London: James Walton, 1869).
John Splinter Stavorinus, *Voyages to the East-Indies, vol. 2* (London: G.G. and J. Robinson, 1798).
*The Suma Oriental of Tome Pires: an Account of the East, from the Red Sea to China, written in Malacca and India in 1512–1515, vol. 1* (Delhi: Asian Educational Services, 2005).
Jacob Swart, *Verhandelingen en Berigten betrekkelijk het Zeewezen, de Zeevaartkunde en de Daarmede in Verband Staande Wetenschappen* (Amsterdam: G. Hulst Van Keulen, 1857).
Wendy Swartz, Robert Ford Campany, Yan Lu and Jessey J.C. Choo (eds.), *Early Medieval China: a Sourcebook* (New York: Columbia UP, 2014).
George Walter Thornbury, *Old and New London: a Narrative of its History, its People and its Places* (London: Petter & Galphin, 1878).
Paul A. Van Dyke and Cynthia Viallé (eds.), *The Canton-Macao Dagregisters, 3 vol., 1762–1764* (Macau: Instituto Cultural, 2006–2009).
Gustave Van Hoorebeke, *Le Nobiliaire de Gand* (Gand: A.I. Vander Schelden, 1850).
*Voyage De Guillaume Dampier, Aux Terres Australes, A la Nouvelle Hollande &c. fait en 1699, 4 vol.* (Amsterdam: Paul Marret, 1705–1723).
*Voyage et Avantures de François Leguat, & de ses Compagnons, 2 vol.* (London: David Mortier, 1708).

## Books, Articles, Chapters

Michel Aghassian and Kéram Kévonian, "The Armenian Merchant Network: Overall Autonomy and Local Integration", in: Merchants, eds. Chaudhury and Morineau, 74–94.
David Denis Aldridge, *Admiral Sir John Norris and the British Naval Expeditions to the Baltic Sea 1715–1727* (Lund: Nordic Academic Press, 2009).
Edward A. Alpers, *The Indian Ocean in World History* (Oxford: Oxford UP, 2014).
Leonard Y. Andaya, *Leaves of the Same Tree: Trade and Ethnicity in the Strait* (Honolulu: University of Hawaii Press, 2008).

Tonio Andrade, *How Taiwan became Chinese: Dutch, Spanish and Han Colonization in the Seventeenth Century* (New York: Columbia UP, 2008).

Kenneth R. Andrews, *Trade, Plunder and Settlement: Maritime Enterprise and the Genesis of the British Empire, 1480–1630* (New York: Cambridge UP, 1985).

Robert J. Antony, *Elusive Pirates: Pervasive Smugglers: Violence and Clandestine Trade in the Greater China Seas* (Hong Kong: Hong Kong UP, 2010).

David Armitage, *The Ideological Origins of the British Empire* (New York: Cambridge UP, 2000).

Sebouh Aslanian, *From the Indian Ocean to the Mediterranean: the Global Trade Networks of Armenian Merchants from New Julfa* (Berkeley: University of California Press, 2011).

Martin Åberg, "The Swedish East India Company 1731–66. Business Strategy and Foreign Influence in a Perspective of Change", in: *Scandinavian Journal of History* 15 (1990), 97–108.

William Atwell, "The T'ai-ch'ang, T'ien-ch'i and Ch'ung-chen reigns, 1620–1644", in: Cambridge History of China, vol. 7, 585–640.

Ernst Baasch, "Hamburg und die Compagnie von Ostende", in: *Zeitschrift für Social- und Wirthschaftsgeschichte* 5 (1897), 309–19.

R. Baetens, "Investering en rendement bij de Generale Indishe Compagnie: de handel op Bengalen vergeleken met de Chinahandel", in: *Album aangeboden aan Charles Verlinden ter gelegenheid van zijn dertig jaar professoraat* (Ghent: Universa, 1975), 17–42.

Vahé Baladouni and Margaret Makepeace, *Armenian Merchants of the Seventeenth and Early Eighteenth Centuries: English East India Company Sources* (Philadelphia: American Philosophical Society, 1998).

Iídio Cabral Baleno, "Pressões externas. Reacções ao corso e à pirataria", in: *História geral de Cabo Verde, vol. 2*, ed. Maria Emília Madeira Santos (Lisboa: Instituto de Investigação Científica Tropical, 1995), 125–88.

R. N. Banerji, *Economic Progress of the East India Company on the Coromandel Coast (1702–1746)* (Nagpur: Nagpur University, 1974).

Daniel H. Bays, *A New History of Christianity in China* (Malden, MA: Wiley-Blackwell, 2012).

James Bender, *Dutch Warships in the Age of Sail, 1600–1714: Design, Construction, Careers and Fates* (Yorkshire: Seaforth Publishing, 2014).

Zvi Ben-Dor Benite, *The Dao of Muhammad: a Cultural History of Muslims in Late Imperial China* (Cambridge, MA: Harvard UP, 2005).

Carole Benedict, *Golden-Silk Smoke: a History of Tobacco in China, 1550–2010* (Berkeley: University of California Press, 2011).

Ric Berman, *Schism: the Battle that Forged Freemasonry* (Brighton: Sussex Academic Press, 2013).

Arne Bialuschewski, "Pirates, Slavers, and the Indigenous Population in Madagascar, c. 1690–1715", in: *The International Journal of African Historical Studies* 38.3 (2005), 401–25.

Hans Bielenstein, "Wang Mang, the restoration of the Han dynasty, and Later Han", in: Cambridge History of China, vol. 1, 223–90.

Xavier Beguin Billecocq, *Des voyageurs français au Cap de Bonne-Espérance* (Paris: Relations internationales et culture, 1996).

David Bindman, *Ape to Apollo: Aesthetics and the Idea of Race in the 18th Century* (Ithaca, NY: Cornell UP, 2002).

Daniela Bleichmar, *Visible Empire: Botanical Expeditions and Visual Culture in the Hispanic Enlightenment* (Chicago: University of Chicago Press, 2012).

Judith Berling, *The Syncretic Religion of Lin Chao-en* (New York: Columbia UP, 1980).

Sampa Biswas, *Indian Influence on the Art of Japan* (New Delhi: Northern Book Centre, 2010).

Jeremy Black, *Trade, Empire and British Foreign Policy, 1689–1815* (London: Routledge, 2007).

Leonard Blussé, "John Chinaman Abroad: Chinese Sailors in the Service of the VOC", in: *Promises and Predicaments: Trade and Entrepreneurship in Colonial and Independent Indonesia in the*

*19th and 20th Centuries*, eds. Alicia Schrikker and Jeroen Touwen (Singapore: National University of Singapore, 2015), 101–12.

Derek Bodde, "The state and empire of Ch'in", in: Cambridge History of China, vol. 1, 20–102.

Peter Borschberg, "Batu Sawar Johor: a Regional Centre of Trade in the Early Seventeenth Century" (paper presented at the second Nicholas Tarling Conference on Southeast Asian Studies, Hanoi, Vietnam, 3–4 November 2011).

Ibid., *Hugo Grotius, the Portuguese, and Free Trade in the Early Indies* (Singapore: National University of Singapore Press, 2011).

M. Boucher, "The Cape and Foreign Shipping, 1714–1723", in: *South African Historical Journal*, 6.1 (1974), 3–29.

Pierre Boulle, "French Mercantilism, Commercial Companies and Colonial Profitability", in: *Companies and Trade: Essays on Overseas Trading Companies during the Ancien Régime*, eds. Leonard Blussé and Femme Gaastra (The Hague: Leiden UP, 1981), 97–117.

H.V. Bowen, *The Business of Empire: the East India Company and Imperial Britain, 1756–1833* (Cambridge: Cambridge UP, 2006).

Ibid., Margarette Lincoln and Nigel Rigby (eds.), *The Worlds of the East India Company* (Woodbridge: The Boydell Press, 2004).

Charles Ralph Boxer, *Seventeenth-Century Macau in Contemporary Documents and Illustrations* (Hong Kong: Heinemann, 1984).

Joseph Van den Brandt, *Les Lazaristes en Chine, 1697–1935: Notes biographiques* (Beijing: Imprimerie des Lazarists Pei-T'ang, 1936).

Liam Matthew Brockey, *Journey to the East: The Jesuit Mission to China, 1579–1724* (Cambridge, MA: The Belknap Press of Harvard UP, 2007).

Jobst Broelmann, "Der chinesische Weg im Schiffbau", in: China, eine Wiege der Weltkultur, ed. Arne Eggebrecht (Mainz: von Zabern, 1994), 139–45.

Timothy Brook, "Communications and commerce", in: Cambridge History of China, vol. 8, 579–707.

George E. Brooks, *Western Africa and Cabo Verde, 1790s–1830s: Symbiosis of Slave and Legitimate Trades* (Bloomington, IN: Authorhouse, 2010).

Simon J. Bronner, *Crossing the Line: Violence, Play, and Drama in Naval Equator Traditions* (Amsterdam: Amsterdam UP, 2007).

Timothy Brook, *The Confusions of Pleasure: Commerce and Culture in Ming China* (Berkeley: University of California Press, 1998).

Iem Brown (ed.), *The Territories of Indonesia* (London: Routledge, 2009).

Kevin Brown, *Poxed and Scurvied: the Story of Sickness and Health at Sea* (Barnsley: Seaforth Publishing, 2011).

Jaap R. Bruijn, "Between Batavia and the Cape: Shipping Patterns of the Dutch East India Company", in: *Journal of Southeast Asian Studies* 11.2 (1980), 251–65.

Ibid., *Commanders of Dutch East India Ships in the Eighteenth Century* (Woodbridge: The Boydell Press, 2011).

Ibid. and Femme S. Gaastra (eds.), *Ships, sailors and spices. East India Companies and their shipping in the 16th, 17th and 18th centuries* (Amsterdam: NEHA, 1993).

Paul Bushkovitch, *Peter the Great: the Struggle for Power, 1671–1725* (New York: Cambridge UP, 2001).

John Cady, *Southeast Asia: Its Historical Development* (New York: McGraw-Hill, 1964).

*The Cambridge History of Ancient China: from the Origins of Civilization to 221 B.C.*, eds. Michael Loewe and Edward L. Shaughnessy (New York: Cambridge UP, 1999).

*The Cambridge History of China, 15 vol.*, general ed. Denis Crispin Twitchett (Cambridge: Cambridge UP, 1986–).

Marvin Carlson, *Theatre: a Very Short Introduction* (New York: Oxford UP, 2014).

Hok-lam Chan, "The Chien-wen, Yung-lo, Hung-hsi, and Hsüan-te reigns, 1399–1435", in: Cambridge History of China, vol. 7, 205–75.
Kwang-chih Chang, "China on the Eve of the Historical Period", in: Cambridge History of Ancient China, 37–73.
K.N. Chaudhuri, *The Trading World of Asia and the English East India Company 1660–1760* (Cambridge: Cambridge UP, 1978).
Ibid., *The English East India Company: the Study of an Early Joint-Stock Company* (London: Routledge, 1965).
Ibid., *Trade and Civilization in the Indian Ocean: an Economic History from the Rise of Islam to 1750* (New York: Cambridge UP, 1985).
Ibid., "The English East India Company's Shipping (c. 1660–1760)", in: Ships, ed. Bruijn and Gaastra, 49–80.
Sushil Chaudhury and Michel Morineau (eds.), *Merchants, Companies and Trade: Europe and Asia in the Early Modern Era* (New York: Cambridge UP, 1999).
Huaiyu Chen, "The Encounter of Nestorian Christianity with Tantric Buddhism in Medieval China", in: *Hidden Treasures and Intercultural Encounters: Studies on East Syriac Christianity in China and Central Asia*, ed. Dietmar W. Winkler and Li Tang (Vienna: Lit, 2009), 195–214.
K'o-ch'eng Chen, "Cheng Ch'eng-kung's maritime expansion and early Ch'ing coastal prohibition", in: *Development and decline in Fukien Province in the 17th and 18th Centuries*, ed. E.B. Vermeer (Leiden: E.J. Brill, 1990), 222–41.
Weng Eang Cheong, *The Hong Merchants of Canton: Chinese Merchants in Sino-Western Trade* (Richmond: Curzon, 1997).
Ibid., "The Age of Suqua, 1720–1759: the Early Hong Merchants", in: *Asian Trade Routes: Continental and Maritime*, ed. Karl Reinhold Haellquist (London: Curzon Press, 1991), 217–30.
Annping Chin, *Confucius: a Life of Thought and Politics* (New Haven: Yale UP, 2008).
May-Bo Ching, 'Chopsticks or Cutlery? How Canton Hong Merchants Entertained Foreign Guests in the Eighteenth and Nineteenth Centuries", in: Narratives, ed. Johnson, 99–116.
Ng Chin-keong, *Trade and Society: the Amoy Network on the China Coast, 1683–1735* (Singapore: Singapore UP, 1983).
Tung-Tsu Ch'un, *Local Government in China under the Ch'ing* (Stanford, CA: Stanford UP, 1962).
William G. Clarence-Smith, "Elephants, Horses, and the Coming of Islam to Northern Sumatra", in: *Indonesia and the Malay World* 32.93 (2004), 271–84.
J.J. Colledge and Ben Warlow, *Ships of the Royal Navy; the Complete Record of All Fighting Ships of the Royal Navy* (London: Greenhill, 2003).
Andrew S. Cook, "Establishing the Sea Routes to India and China. Stages in the Development of Hydrographical Knowledge", in: *Worlds*, eds. Bowen, Lincoln and Rigby, 119–36.
Douglas Coombs, *The Conduct of the Dutch: British Opinion and the Dutch Alliance during the War of the Spanish Succession* (The Hague: Martinus Nijhoff, 1958).
Brian Cowan, *The Social Life of Coffee: the Emergence of the British Coffeehouse* (New Haven: Yale UP, 2005).
David Cressy, *Saltpeter: the Mother of Gunpowder* (New York: Oxford UP, 2013).
Barry Crosbie, *Irish Imperial Networks: Migration, Social Communication and Exchange in Nineteenth-Century India* (New York: Cambridge UP, 2011).
Gregory Cushman, *Guano and the Opening of the Pacific World: a Global Ecological History* (New York: Cambridge UP, 2013).
Michael T. Dalby, "Court politics in late T'ang times", in: Cambridge History of China, vol. 3.1, 561–681.
Richard Dale, *The First Crash: Lessons from the South Sea Bubble* (Princeton, NJ: Princeton UP, 2005).

Vinita Damodaran, Anna Winterbottom and Alan Lester (eds.), *The East India Company and the Natural World* (Houndsmills, UK: Palgrave Macmillan, 2015).

Paul D'Arcy, *People of the Sea: Environment, Identity and History in Oceania* (Honolulu: University of Hawaii Press, 2006).

Ashin Das Gupta, *Malabar in Asian Trade: 1740–1800* (New York: Cambridge UP, 1967).

Henry Davidson Love, *Vestiges of Old Madras, vol. 2* (London: J. Murray, 1913).

Kwo Da-Wei, *Chinese Brushwork in Calligraphy and Painting: its History, Aesthetics and Techniques* (Mineola, NY: Dover Publications, 1981).

Sun Dazhang, "The Qing Dynasty", in: *Chinese Architecture*, ed. Nancy S. Steinhardt (New Haven: Yale UP, 2002), 261–344.

Kenneth Dean, *Lord of the Three in One: the Spread of a Cult in Southeast China* (Princeton, NJ: Princeton UP, 1998).

Jerry Dennerline, "The Shun-chih Reign", in: Cambridge History of China, vol. 9, 73–119.

Gang Deong, *Maritime Sector, Institutions, and Sea Power of Premodern China* (Westport, CT: Greenwood Press, 1999).

Louis Dermigny, *La Chine et l'Occident: le Commerce* à Canton au XVIIIe siècle, 1719*–1833, vol. 2* (Paris: SEVPEN, 1964).

Albert Dien, *Six Dynasties Civilization* (New Haven: Yale UP, 2007).

Stephan Diller, *Die Dänen in Indien, Südostasien und China (1620–1845)* (Wiesbaden: Harrassowitz, 1999).

Edward L. Dreyer, "Military origins of Ming China", in: Cambridge History of China, vol. 7, 58–106.

Olga Dror and K.W. Taylor (eds.), *Views of Seventeenth-Century Vietnam: Christoforo Borri on Cochinchina and Samuel Baron on Tonkin* (Ithaca, NY: Cornell UP, 2006).

Home H. Dubs, "The Development of Altruism in Confucianism", in: *Philosophy East and West* 1.1 (1951), 48–55.

Heinz Duchhardt, *Das Zeitalter des Absolutismus* (München: R. Oldenbourg Verlag, 1998).

Thomas Bentley Duncan, *Atlantic Islands: Madeira, the Azores and the Cape Verdes in Seventeenth-Century Commerce and Navigation* (Chicago: University of Chicago Press, 1972).

Mark C. Elliott, *The Manchu Way: the Eight Banners and Ethnic Identity in Late Imperial China* (Standord, CA: Stanford UP, 2001).

Benjamin A. Elman, *Civil Examinations and Meritocracy in Late Imperial China* (Cambridge, MA: Harvard UP, 2013).

Victor Enthoven, "Dan maar oorlog! De reactive van de Republiek op de Oostendse Compagnie", in: Noord-Zuid, ed. Parmentier, 131–48.

Emily Erikson, *Between Monopoly and Free Trade: the English East India Company* (Princeton: Princeton UP, 2014).

Joseph W. Esherick, "How the Qing Became China", in: *Empire to Nation: Historical Perspectives on the Making of the Modern World*, eds. Joseph W. Esherick, Hasan Kayah and Eric Van Yong (New York: Rowman & Littlefield Publishers, 2006), 232–47.

Chris Evans, Owen Jackson and Göran Ryden, "Baltic Iron and the British Iron Industry in the Eighteenth Century", in: *Economic History Review* 55.4 (2002), 642–65.

Stefan Faller, *Taprobane im Wandel der Zeit: das Śrî-Laṅkâ-Bild in griechischen und lateinischen Quellen zwischen Alexanderzug und Spätantike* (Freiburg i.B.: Franz Steiner Verlag, 2000).

Jonathan Farris, "Dwelling Factors: Western Merchants in Canton", in: *Investing in the Early Modern Built Environment: Europeans, Asians, Settlers and Indigenous Societies*, ed. Carole Shammas (Boston: Brill, 2012), 163–90.

Denis Feeney, *Caesar's Calendar: Ancient Time and the Beginnings of History* (Berkeley: University of California Press, 2007).

Felipe Fernández-Armesto, *The Canary Islands after the Conquest: the Making of a Colonial Society in the Early Sixteenth Century* (New York: Oxford UP, 1982).
Ibid., *Before Columbus: Exploration and Colonization from the Mediterranean to the Atlantic, 1229–1492* (Houndsmills: Macmillan Education, 1987).
Paula Findlen, *Possessing Nature: Museums, Collecting and Scientific Culture in Early Modern Italy* (Berkeley: University of California Press, 1996).
Antonia Finnane, *Changing Clothes in China: Fashion, History and Nation* (New York: Columbia UP, 2008).
Dennis O. Flynn and A. Giráldez, "Silk for Silver: Manila-Macao Trade in the 17th Century", in: *Philippine Studies* 44.1 (1996), 52–68.
Sarah Foot and Chase F. Robinson (eds.), *The Oxford History of Historical Writing, vol. 2* (New York: Oxford UP, 2012).
Roger V. Des Forges, *Cultural Centrality and Political Change in Chinese History: Northeast Henan in the Fall of the Ming* (Stanford, CA: Stanford UP, 2003).
Andre Gunder Frank, *ReOrient: Global Economy in the Asian Age* (Berkeley: University of California Press, 1998).
Caroline Frank, *Objectifying China, Imagining America: Chinese Commodities in Early America* (Chicago: University of Chicago Press, 2011).
James D. Frankel, *Rectifying God's Name: Liu Zhi's Confucian Translation of Monotheism and Islamic Law* (Honolulu: University of Hawaii Press, 2011).
Jeremy Franks, "Eighteenth-Century Chinese Vessels at Canton. The Paintings at Skärva, Sweden", in: *The Mariner's Mirror* 83.1 (1997), 21–40.
Paul Freedman, *Out of the East: Spices and the Medieval Imagination* (New Haven, CT: Yale UP, 2008).
Marc Frey, "Eurasian Interactions: Siam and the Dutch East India Company during the Seventeenth Century", in: *Southeast Asian Historiography: Unravelling the Myths*, ed. Volker Grabowsky (Bangkok: River Books, 2011), 162–75.
Robert I. Frost, *The Northern Wars. War, State and Society in Northeastern Europe, 1558–1721* (London: Routledge, 2000).
Lo-shu Fu, *A documentary chronicle of Sino-Western relations, 1644–1820* (Tucson: University of Arizona Press, 1966).
Holden Furber, *Rival Empires of Trade in the Orient, 1660–1800* (Minneapolis: University of Minnesota Press, 1976).
Ibid., "Asia and the West as Partners before 'Empire' and After", in: *The Journal of Asian Studies* 28.4 (1969), 711–21.
Femme S. Gaastra, "War, Competition and Collaboration: Relations between the English and Dutch East India Company in the Seventeenth and Eighteenth Centuries", in: Worlds, eds. Bowen, Lincoln and Rigby, 49–68.
Ibid., "Private Money for Company Trade. The Role of the Bills of Exchange in Financing the Return Cargoes of the VOC", in: *Itinerario* 18 (1994), 65–76.
Alison Games, *The Web of Empire: English Cosmopolitans in an Age of Expansion, 1560–1660* (New York: Oxford UP, 2008).
Richard J. Garrett, *The Defenses of Macau: Forts, Ships and Weapons over 450 years* (Hong Kong: Hong Kong UP, 2010).
Valery M. Garrett, *Heaven is High, the Emperor Far Away: Merchants and Mandarins in Old Canton* (New York: Oxford UP, 2002).
Ibid., *Chinese Dress: from the Qing Dynasty to the Present* (Tokyo: Tuttle Publishing, 2007).
James Geiss, "The Chia-ching reign, 1522–1566", in: Cambridge History of China, vol. 7, 440–510.

G.C. Gibbs, "Britain and the Alliance of Hanover, April 1725–February 1726", in: *The English Historical Review* 73 (1958), 404–30.
Conrad Gill, *Merchants and Mariners of the 18th Century* (London: Edward Arnold, 1961).
Ian Gillman and Hans-Joachim Klimkeit, *Christians in Asia before 1500* (London: Routledge, 1999).
Richard von Glahn, "Chinese Coin and Changes in Monetary Preferences in Maritime East Asia in the Fifteenth-Seventeenth Centuries", in: *Journal of the Economic and Social History of the Orient* 57.5 (2014), 629–68.
Kristof Glamann, *Dutch-Asiatic Trade 1620–1740* ('S-Gravenhage: Martinus Nijhoff, 1981).
Erik Gøbel, "Danish Companies Shipping to Asia, 1616–1807", in: Ships, eds. Brujin and Gaastra, 99–120.
Richard W.L. Guisso, "The reigns of the empress Wu, Chung-tsung and Jui tsung (684–712)", in: Cambridge History of China, vol. 3, 290–332.
Wang Gungwu, "Ming Foreign Relations: Southeast Asia", in: Cambridge History of China, vol. 8, 301–32.
Lin Guoping, "On the Rise, Decline and Evolution the Three-in-One Teaching", in: *Popular Religion and Shamanism*, eds. Ma Xisha and Meng Huiying (Leiden: Brill, 2011), 123–66.
R. Kent Guy, *The Qing Governors and their Provinces: the Evolution of Territorial Administration in China, 1644–1796* (Seattle: University of Washington Press, 2010).
Alastair Hamilton, Alexander H. de Groot, and Maurits H. van den Boogert (eds.), *Friends and Rivals in the East: Studies in Anglo-Dutch Relations in the Levant from the Seventeenth to the Early Nineteenth Century* (Boston: Brill, 2000).
Edith Hamilton, *Mythology* (New York: Little, Brown and Company, 1942).
David Hanock, *Oceans of Wine: Madeira and the Emergence of American Trade and Taste* (New Haven: Yale UP, 2009).
Valerie Hansen, *The Silk Road: a New History* (New York: Oxford UP, 2012).
Anders Hansson, *Chinese Outcasts: Discrimination & Emancipation in Late Imperial China* (Leiden: Brill, 1996).
Zhidong Hao, *Macau: History and Society* (Hong Kong: Hong Kong UP, 2011).
Donald Harper, "Warring States Natural Philosophy and Occult Thought", in: Cambridge History of Ancient China, 813–84.
Mark Harrison, *Medicine in an Age of Commerce and Empire: Britain and its Tropical Colonies, 1660–1830* (New York: Oxford UP, 2010).
Gerald B. Hertz, "England and the Ostend Company", in: *English Historical Review* 22 (1907), 255–79.
R.D. Hill, *Rice in Malaya: a Study in Historical Geography* (Singapore: National University of Singapore Press, 2012).
G. Hinchcliffe, "An Ostend East Indiaman, 1718–1720", in: *The Mariner's Mirror* 59.3 (1973), 291–7.
Bret Hinsch, *Passions of the Cut Sleeve: The Male Homosexual Tradition in China* (Berkeley: University of California Press, 1990).
Thomas O. Hollman, "Formosa and the Trade in Venison and Deer Skins", in: *Emporia, Commodities and Entrepreneurs in Asian Maritime Trade, c. 1400–1750*, ed. Roderich Ptak (Stuttgart: Franz Steiner, 1991), 261–90.
Ibid., *The Land of Five Flavors: a Cultural History of Chinese Cuisine* (New York: Columbia UP, 2010).
Helma Houtman-de Smedt, "The ambitions of the Austrian Empire with reference to East India during the last quarter of the eighteenth century", in: Merchants, eds. Chaudhury and Morineau, 227–39.
Francis L.K. Hsu, *Under the Ancestors' Shadow: Kinship, Personality and Social Mobility in China* (Stanford, CA: Stanford UP, 1971).

Hsieh Bao Hua, *Concubinage and Servitude in Late Imperial China* (New York: Lexington Books, 2014).
Ray Huang, "The Lung-ch'ing and Wan-li reigns, 1567–1620", in: Cambridge History of China, vol. 7, 514–84.
Charles O. Hucker, "Governmental Organization in the Ming Dynasty", in: *Harvard Journal of Asiatic Studies* 21 (1958), 1–66.
Ibid., "Ming government", in: Cambridge History of China, vol. 8, 9–105.
Michel Huisman, *La Belgique commercial sous l'empereur Charles VI. La Compagnie d'Ostende.* Étude historique de politique commerciale et colonial (Bruxelles: Lamertin 1902).
Douglas A. Irwin, "Strategic Trade Policy and Mercantilist Trade Rivalries", in: *The American Economic Review* 82.2 (1992), 134–9.
Jonathan I. Israel, *Empires and Entrepots: the Dutch, the Spanish Monarchy and the Jews, 1585–1713* (London: The Hambledon Press, 1990).
Takeshi Ito (ed.), *Aceh Sultanate: State, Society, Religion and Trade, 2 vols.* (Leiden: Brill, 2015).
Beverly Jackson and David Hugus, *Ladder to the Clouds: Intrigue and Tradition in Chinese Rank* (Berkeley, CA: Ten Speed Press, 1999).
E.M. Jacobs, *Merchant of Asia: the Trade of the Dutch East India Company during the Eighteenth Century* (Leiden: CNWS Publications, 2006).
Fu Jin, *Chinese Theatre* (New York: Cambridge UP, 2010).
Christine R. Johnson, *The German Discovery of the World: Renaissance Encounters with the Strange and Marvelous* (Charlottesville: University of Virginia Press, 2009).
C.J.A. Jörg, *Porcelain and the Dutch China Trade* (The Hague: M. Nijhoff, 1982).
Kendall Johnson (ed.), *Narratives of Free Trade: the Commercial Cultures of Early US-China Relations* (Hong Kong: Hong Kong UP, 2012).
John Joseph, *The Modern Assyrians of the Middle East: Encounters with Western Christian Missions, Archaeologists, and Colonial Powers* (Cologne: Brill, 2000).
Lo Jung-pang, *China as a Sea Power, 1127–1368: a Preliminary Survey of the Maritime Expansion and Naval Exploits of the Chinese People during the Southern Song and Yuan Periods*, ed. Bruce A. Elleman (Hong Kong: Hong Kong UP, 2011).
Richard L. Kagan and Philip D. Morgan (eds.), *Atlantic Diasporas: Jews, Conversos, and Crypto-Jews in the Age of Mercantilism, 1500–1800* (Baltimore: The Johns Hopkins UP, 2009).
Henry Kamen, "The Destruction of the Spanish Silver Fleet at Vigo in 1702", in: *Bulletin of the Institute of Historical Research* 39 (1966), 165–73.
Jeyamalar Kathirithamby-Wells, "Unlikely Partners: Malay-Indonesian Medicine and European Plant Science", in: East India Company, eds. Damodaran and Winterbottom, 193–218.
John Keay, *The Honourable Company. A History of the English East India Company* (London: HarperCollins, 1991).
Michael Keevak, *The Story of a Stele: China's Nestorian Monument and its Reception in the West, 1625–1916* (Hong Kong: Hong Kong UP, 2008).
Ibid., *Becoming Yellow: a Short History of Racial Thinking* (Princeton, NJ: Princeton UP, 2011).
David N. Keightley, "The Shang: China's First Historical Dynasty", in: Cambridge History of Ancient China, 232–91.
J.N.D. Kelly and M.J. Walsh (ed.), *The Oxford Dictionary of Popes* (New York: Oxford UP, 2010).
Peter Kemp (ed.), *The Oxford Companion to Ships and the Sea* (New York: Oxford UP, 1976).
Damien Keown, *Buddhism: a Very Short Introduction* (New York: Oxford UP, 2013).
Eric Kerridge, *Textile Manufactures in Early Modern England* (Manchester: Manchester UP, 1985).
John Kieschnick, *The Impact of Buddhism on Chinese Material Culture* (Princeton, NJ: Princeton UP, 2003).

Dorothy Ko, *Cinderella's Sisters: a Revisionist History of Footbinding* (Berkeley: University of California Press, 2005).
Ludwig Koch (ed.), *Jesuiten-Lexikon, vol. 2* (Löwen-Heverlee: Verlag der Bibliothek SJ, 1962).
Livia Kohn, *Introducing Daoism* (London: Routledge, 2009).
Manuel Komroff, *The Travels of Marco Polo* (London: The Modern Library, 1926).
C. Koninckx, "Andreas Jacobus Flanderin. Een achttiende eeuwse middelgrote koopman", in: *Bijdragen tot de Geschiedenis* 56 (1973), 243–90.
Yuvraj Krishan, *The Buddha Image: its Origin and Development* (New Delhi: Munshiram Manoharlal Publishers, 1996).
Dieter Kuhn, *Burial in Song China* (Heidelberg: Edition Forum 1994).
Lars Peter Laamann, *Christian Heretics in Late Imperial China: Christian inculturation and state control, 1720–1850* (New York; Routledge, 2006).
Donald F. Lach and Edwing J. Van Kley, *Asia in the Making of Europe, vol. 3.4* (Chicago: University of Chicago Press, 1993).
Pippa Lacey, "The Coral Network: the Trade of Red Coral to the Qing Imperial Court in the Eighteenth Century", in: *The Global Lives of Things: the Mateiral Culture of Connections in the Early Modern World*, eds. Anne Gerritsen and Giorgio Riello (New York: Routledge, 2015), ■.
William Lakos, *Chinese Ancestor Worship; a Practice and Ritual Oriented Approach to Understanding Chinese Culture* (Newcastle upon Tyne: Cambridge Scholars Publishing, 2010)
John D. Langlois, Jr., "The Hung-wu reign, 1368–1398", in: Cambridge History of China, vol. 7, 107–81.
Philip Lawson, *The East India Company: A History* (London: Longman, 1993).
Lothar Ledderose, "Chinese Calligraphy: Its Aesthetic Dimension and Social Function", in: *Orientations* 17.10 (1986), 35–50.
Lily Xiao Hong Lee, Clara Lau and A.D. Stefanowska (eds.), *Biographical Dictionary of Chinese Women, vol. 1* (New York: Routledge, 1998).
Yuan-Yuan Lee and Sin-yan Shen, *Chinese Musical Instruments* (Chicago: Chinese Musical Society of North America, 1999).
Leanna Lee-Whitman, "The Silk Trade: Chinese Silks and the British East India Company", in: *Winterthur Portfolio* 17.1 (1982), 21-41.
David Leeming, *A Dictionary of Asian Mythology* (New York: Oxford UP, 2001).
Denise Patry Leidy and Donna Strahan, *Wisdom Embodied: Chinese Buddhist and Daoist Sculpture in the Metropolitan Museum of Art* (New Haven: Yale UP, 2010).
Yang Lemei, "China's Mid-Autumn Day", in: *Journal of Folklore Research* 43.3 (2006), 263–70.
Beverly Lemire, "Transforming Consumer Custom: Linen, Cotton and the English Market, 1660–1800", in: *The European Linen Industry in Historical Perspective*, eds. Brenda Collins and Philip Ollerenshaw (New York: Oxford UP, 2003), 187–208.
Ibid. and Giorgio Riello, "East & West: Textiles and Fashion in Early Modern Europe", in: *Journal of Social History* 41.4 (2008), 887–916.
Mary Lindemann, *The Merchant Republics: Amsterdam, Antwerp and Hamburg, 1648–1790* (New York: Cambridge UP, 2014).
Stephen Little and Shawn Eichman, *Taoism and the Arts of China* (Chicago: The Art Institute of Chicago).
Yong Liu, *The Dutch East India Company's Tea Trade with China, 1757–1781* (Boston: Brill, 2007).
Yonghua Liu, *Confucian Rituals and Chinese Villagers: Ritual Change and Social Transformation in a Southeastern Chinese Community, 1368–1949* (Leiden, Brill: 2013).
Elsbeth Locher-Scholten, *Sumatran Sultanate and Colonial State: Jambi and the Rise of Dutch Imperialism, 1830–1907* (Ithaca, NY: Southeast Asia Program Publications, 2003).
Michael Loewe, "The Former Han dynasty", in: Cambridge History of China, vol. 1, 103–222.

Adan Yuen-chung Lui, "The imperial college (*Kuo-tzu-chien*) in the early Ch'ing (1644–1795)", in: *Papers on Far Eastern History* 10 (1974), 147–66.
Pedro Machado, "Awash in a Sea of Cloth: Gujarat, Africa, and the Western Indian Ocean, 1300–1800", in: Spinning World, eds. Riello and Parthasarathi, 161–79.
Carlos Daniel Malamud Rikles, *Cádiz y Saint Malo en el Comercio Colonial Peruano (1698–1725)* (Cádiz: Diputación de Cádiz, 1986).
Catherine Manning, *Fortunes à Faire: The French in Asian Trade, 1719–1748* (Surrey: Ashgate Publishing, 1996).
Paul W. Mapp, *The Elusive West and the Contest for Empire, 1713–1763* (Chapel Hill: University of North Carolina Press for the Omohundro Institute of Early American History and Culture, 2011).
Robert Marks, *Tigers, Rice, Silk and Silt: Environment and Economy in Late Imperial South China* (New York: Cambridge UP, 2004).
Tomoko Masuzawa, *The Invention of World Religions: or, How European Universalism was Preserved in the Language of Pluralism* (Chicago: University of Chicago Press, 2005).
Sucheta Mazumdar, *Sugar and Society in China: Peasants, Technology, and the World Market* (Cambridge, MA: Harvard UP, 1998).
Anne E.C. McCants, "Poor consumers as global consumers: the diffusion of tea and coffee drinking in the eighteenth century", in: *The Economic History Review* 61 (2008), 172–200.
George K. McGilvary, *Guardian of the East India Company: the Life of Laurence Sulivan* (New York: Tauris Academic Studies, 2006).
Ibid., *East India Patronage and the British State: the Scottish Elite and Politics in the Eighteenth Century* (New York: Tauris Academic Studies, 2008).
Annerose Menninger, *Genuss im kulturellen Wandel. Tabak, Kaffee, Tee und Schokolade in Europa (16.–19. Jahrhundert)* (Stuttgart: Franz Steiner, 2008).
Søren Mentz, *The English Gentleman Merchant at Work: Madras and the City of London, 1660–1740* (Copenhagen: University of Copenhagen Press, 2005).
L. Michielsen, "Het einde van de Oostendsche Kompagnie", in: *Bijdragen tot de geschiedenis* 28 (1937), 128–43.
Terance Miethe and Hong Lu, *Punishment: a Comparative Historical Perspective* (New York: Cambridge UP, 2005).
Anthony Miller, Edwards McKinnon and Tengku Luckman Sinar, "Aru and Kota Cina", in: *Indonesia* 26 (1978), 1–42.
M.I. Moire, *A General Guide to the India Office Records* (London: The British Library, 1988).
Derek Morris, "Stepney and Trinity House", in: *East London Record* 13 (1990), 33–8.
H.B. Morse, *The Chronicles of the East India Company trading to China, 1635–1834, vol. 1* (Oxford: Clarendon Press, 1926).
Frederick W. Mote, "The rise of the Ming dynasty, 1330–1367", in: Cambridge History of China, vol. 7, 11–57.
Ibid., *Imperial China, 900–1800* (Cambridge, MA: Harvard UP, 2003).
David E. Mungello, *Curious Land: Jesuit Accommodation and the Origins of Sinology* (Honolulu: University of Hawaii Press, 1989).
Ramon H. Myers and Yeh-Chien Wang, "Economic Developments, 1644–1800", in: Cambridge History of China, vol. 9, 563–646.
Jürgen G. Nagel, *Abenteuer Fernhandel. Die Ostindienkompagnien* (Darmstadt: WBG, 2007).
Susan Naquin, *Peking: Temples and City Life, 1400–1900* (Berkeley: University of California Press, 2000).
Ibid. and Evelyn S. Rawski, *Chinese Society in the Eighteenth Century* (New Haven: Yale UP, 1987).
Joseph Needham, *Science and Civilisation in China, vol. 5.1* (New York: Cambridge UP, 1993).

Jason Neelis, *Early Buddhist Transmission and Trade Networks: Mobility and Exchange within and beyond the Northwest Borderlands of South Asia* (Leiden: Brill, 2011).
*Neue Deutsche Biographie, vol. 11* (Berlin: Duncker & Humblot, 1977).
Chris Nierstraz, "The Popularization of Tea: East India Companies, Private Traders, Smugglers and the Consumption of Tea in Western Europe, 1700–1760", in: *Goods from the East, 1600–1800: Trading Eurasia*, ed. Maxine Berg (New York: Palgrave Macmillan, 2015), 263–276.
Thoma G. Nimick, *Local Administration in Ming China* (Minneapolis, MN: Society for Ming Studies, 2008).
Marcy Norton, *Sacred Gifts, Profane Pleasures: a History of Tobacco and Chocolate in the Atlantic World* (Ithaca, NY: Cornell UP, 2008).
Horst Nowacki and Matteo Valleriani (eds.), *Shipbuilding practice and ship design methods from the Renaissance to the 18th century* (Berlin: Max Planck Institut für Wissenschaftsgeschichte, 2003).
Michael Nylan, *The Five "Confucian" Classics* (New Haven: Yale UP, 2001).
Jürgen Osterhammel, *Die Entzauberung Asiens. Europa und die asiatischen Reiche im 18. Jahrhundert* (München: C.H. Beck, [2]2010).
Donald Ostrowski, *Muscovy and the Mongols: Cross-Cultural Influences on the Steppe Frontier, 1304–1589* (New York: Cambridge UP, 1998).
James Parker, *The Directors of the East India Company* (PhD diss., University of Edinburgh, 1977).
Jan Parmentier, *Oostende & Co. Het verhaal van de Zuid-Nederlandse Oost-Indiëvaart 1715–1735* (Gent: Ludion Press, 2002).
Ibid., *Tea Time in Flanders. The Maritime Trade between the Southern Netherlands and China in the 18th Century* (Gent: Ludion Press, 1996).
Ibid., "The Private East India Ventures from Ostend: The Maritime and Commercial Aspects, 1715–1722", in: *International Journal of Maritime History* 5.2 (1993), 75–102.
Ibid., *De holle compagnie. Smokkel en legale handel onder Zuidnederlandse vlag in Bengalen, ca. 1720–1744* (Hilversum: Verloren, 1992).
Ibid., "The Ostend Trade to Moka and India (1714–1735): the Merchants and Supercargos", in: *The Mariner's Mirror* 73.2 (1987), 123–38.
Ibid., "In the Eye of the Storm: the Influence of Maritime and Trade Networks on the Development of Ostend and Vice Versa during the Eighteenth Century", in: *Trade, Migration and Urban Networks in Port Cities, c. 1640–1940*, eds. Robert Lee and Adrian Jarvis (Liverpool: Liverpool UP, 2008), 67–80.
Ibid., "Vriend en vijand: de Zuid-Nederlanders en de VOC tijdens de achttiende eeuw", in: Noord-Zuid, ed. ibid., 149–66.
Ibid. (ed.), *Noord-Zuid in Oost-Indisch perspectief* (Zutphen: Walburg pers., 2005).
Ibid. and Karel Degryse, "Maritime Aspects of the Ostend Trade to Mocha, India and China (1715–1732)", in: Ships, ed. Bruijn and Gaastra, 139–75.
David Patrick and Francis Hindes Groome (eds.), *Chambers Biographical Dictionary* (London: W&R Chambers, 1902).
Helen Julia Paul, *The South Sea Bubble: an Economic History of its Origins and Consequences* (London: Routledge, 2010).
M.N. Pearson, *Merchants and Rulers in Gujarat: the Response to the Portuguese in the Sixteenth Century* (Berkeley: University of California Press, 1976).
Amelia Peck (ed.), *Interwoven Globe: the Worldwide Textile Trade, 1500–1800* (New Haven: Yale UP, 2013).
C.R. Pennell, *Piracy and Diplomacy in Seventeenth Century North Africa: the Journals of Thomas Baker, English Consul in Tripoli, 1677–1685* (London: Associated UP, 1989).

Norman Penney, "The Quaker Family of Eccleston", in: *The East Anglian: or, Notes and queries on subjects connected with the counties of Suffolk, Cambridge, Essex and Norfolk* 13 (1910), 25–6.
Peter C. Perdue, *China Marches West. The Qing Conquest of Central Eurasia* (Cambridge, MA: The Belknap Press of Harvard UP, 2010).
Dorothy Perkins, *Encyclopedia of China: the Essential Reference to China, its History and Culture* (New York: Routledge, 1999).
C.A. Peterson, "Court and province in mid- and late T'ang", in: Cambridge History of China, vol. 3, 497–513.
Willard Peterson, "Learning from Heaven: the introduction of Christianity and other Western ideas into late Ming China", in: Cambridge History of China, vol. 8, 789–839.
Ibid., "Calendar Reform Prior to the Arrival of the Missionaries at the Ming Court", in: *Ming Studies* 1 (1986), 45–61.
Louis Pfister, *Notices biographiques et bibliographiques sur les jésuites de l'ancienne mission de Chine, 1552–1773, vol. 2* (Nendeln: Kraus Reprint, 1971).
C.H. Philips, "The Secret Committee of the East India Company", in: *Bulletin of the School of Oriental and African Studies* 10.2 (1940), 299–315.
Mu-chou Poo, "Ideas Concerning Death and Burial in Pre-Han and Han China", in: *Asia Major* 3.2 (1990), 25–62.
Om Prakash, *On the Economic Encounter Between Asia and Europe, 1500–1800* (Surrey: Ashgate Publishing, 2014).
Earl H. Pritchard, "Private Trade between England and China in the Eighteenth Century", in: *Journal of the Economic and Social History of the Orient* 1.2 (1958), 221–56.
Rogério Miguel Puga, *The British Presence in Macau, 1635–1793* (Hong Kong: Hong Kong UP, 2013).
Jeroen Puttevils, *Merchants and Trading in the Sixteenth Century: the Golden Age of Antwerp* (London: Pickering & Chatto, 2015).
R.P. Rao, *Portuguese Rule in Goa, 1510–1961* (Bombay: Asia Publishing House, 1963).
James A. Rawley, *London, Metropolis of the Slave Trade* (Columbia: University of Missouri Press, 2003).
Marcus Rediker, *Between the Devil and the Deep Blue Sea: Merchant Seamen, Pirates, and the Anglo-American Maritime World, 1700–1750* (New York: Cambridge UP, 1987).
Ibid., "History from below the water line: Sharks and the Atlantic slave trade", in: *New Orleans in the Atlantic World: Between Land and Sea*, ed. William Boelhower (New York: Routledge, 2010), 131–43.
Anthony Reid, *Southeast Asia in the Age of Commerce, 1450–1680* (New Haven: Yale UP, 1988).
Giorgio Riello, *Cotton: The Fabric that Made the Modern World* (New York: Oxford UP, 2015).
Ibid. and Prasannan Parthasarathi (eds.), *The Spinning World: a Global History of Cotton Textiles, 1200–1850* (New York: Oxford UP, 2009).
Lindsay Ride and May Ride, *An East India Company Cemetery: Protestant Burials in Macao* (Hong Kong: Hong Kong UP, 1996).
Victor Ring, *Asiatische Handlungscompagnien Friedrich des Großen. Ein Beitrag zur Geschichte des preußischen Seehandels und Aktienwesens* (Berlin: Carl Heymanns Verlag, 1890).
Callum Roberts, *The Unnatural History of the Sea* (Washington, D.C.: Island Press, 2007).
Jaime Rodrigues, "A new world in the Atlantic: sailors and rites of passage crossing the Equator, from the 15th to the 20th century", in: *Revista Brasileira de História* 33.6 (2013), 233–75.
Francis M. Rogers, *The Quest for Eastern Christians: Travels and Rumor in the Age of Discovery* (Minneapolis: University of Minnesota Press, 1962).
Morris Rossabi, "The reign of Khubilai kan", in: Cambridge History of China, vol. 6, 414–489.
Gertraude Roth Li, "State Building before 1644", in: Cambridge History of China, vol. 9, 9–72.

Stephen Royle, *The Company's Island: St. Helena, Company Colonies and the Colonial Endeavour* (New York: Palgrave, 2007).

Klaas Ruitenbeek, *Carpentry & Building in Late Imperial China: a Study of the Fifteenth-Century Carpenter's Manual* Lu Ban Jing (Leiden: Brill, 1996).

Bruce Rusk, "Silver, Liquid and Solid: The Matter of Money in the Ming-Qing Marketplace" (paper presented at the Conference on Coin of the Realm: Money and Meaning in Late Imperial China, Cambridge, MA, 18 April 2014).

Yoshirō Saeki, *The Nestorian Documents and Relics in China* (Tokyo: Academy of Oriental Culture, 1951).

Allison Sandman, "Controlling Knowledge: Navigation, Cartography, and Secrecy in the Early Modern Spanish Atlantic", in: *Science and Empire in the Atlantic World, 1500–1800*, eds. Nicholas Dew and James Delbourgo (New York: Routledge, 2007), 31–52.

Matthias Schnettger, *Der spanische Erbfolgekrieg* (München: C.H. Beck, 2014).

Angela Schottenhammer, "Characteristics of Qing China's Maritime Trade Policies, *Shunzhi* through *Qianlong* Reigns", in: *Trading Networks in Early Modern East Asia*, ed. Angela Schottenhammer (Wiesbaden: Harrassowitz, 2010), 101–54.

Ernst Schütz, *Die Gesandtschaft Großbritanniens am immerwährenden Reichstag zu Regensburg und am Kur(Pfalz-)Bayerischen Hof zu München 1683–1806* (München: C.H. Beck, 2007).

Michael Schuman, *Confucius and the World He Created* (New York: Basic Books, 2015).

Stuart B. Schwartz, *Sugar Plantations in the Formation of Brazilian Society: Bahia, 1550–1835* (New York: Cambridge UP, 1985).

Gary Seaman, "Spirit Money: an Interpretation", in: *Journal of Chinese Religions* 10.1 (1982), 80–91.

James F. Searing, *West African Slavery and Atlantic Commerce: the Senegal River Valley, 1700–1860* (New York: Cambridge UP, 1993).

Romney Sedgwick (ed.), *The House of Commons, 1715–1754: the History of Parliament* (New York: Oxford UP, 1970).

Michael W. Serruys, "The Port and City of Ostend and the Process of State Consolidation in the Southern Netherlands in the Seventeenth and Eighteenth Centuries: a Geopolitical Approach", in: *International Journal of Maritime History* 19.2 (2007), 319–47.

Radhika Seshan, *Trade and Politics on the Coromandel Coast: Seventeenth and Early Eighteenth Centuries* (Delhi: Primus Books, 2012).

Edward L. Shaughnessy, "Western Zhou History", in: Cambridge History of Ancient China, 292–351.

David Shepherd Nivison, "The Classical Philosophical Writings", in: Cambridge History of Ancient China, 745–813.

Chung-wen Shih, *Golden Age of Chinese Drama* (Princeton, NJ: Princeton UP, 1976).

Carl T. Smith and Paul A. Van Dyke, "Muslims in the Pearl River Delta, 1700 to 1930", in: *Review of Culture* 10 (2004), 6–15.

Paul Jakov Smith, "Introduction: the Sung Dynasty and its Precursors, 907–1279", in: Cambridge History of China, vol. 5, 1–11.

Richard J. Smith, *The Qing Dynasty and Traditional Chinese Culture* (New York: Rowman & Littlefield, 2015).

Don Snow, *Cantonese as Written Language: the Growth of a Written Chinese Vernacular* (Hong Kong: Hong Kong UP, 2004).

Dava Sobel, *Longitude: the True Story of a Lone Genius who Solved the Greatest Scientific Problem of His Time* (New York: Walker, 1995).

Matthew H. Sommer, *Sex, Law and Society in Late Imperial China* (Stanford, CA: Stanford UP, 2000).

Ibid., *Polyandry and Wife-Selling in Qing Dynasty China: Survival Strategies and Judicial Interventions* (Berkeley: University of California Press, 2015).

George Bryan Souza, *The Survival of Empire: Portuguese Trade and Society in China and the South China Sea, 1630–1754* (New York: Cambridge UP, 1986).
Ibid., "Country Trade and Chinese Alum: Raw Material Supply in Asia's Textile Production in the Seventeenth and Eighteenth Centuries", in: *Revista da Cultura* 11 (2004), 136–53.
Jonathan Spence, "The K'ang-hsi Reign", in: Cambridge History of China, vol. 9.1, 120–82.
Ibid., *Emperor of China: Self-Portrait of K'ang-hsi* (New York: Vintage Books, 1988).
Brunhild Staiger, Stefan Friedrich and Hans-Wilm Schütte (eds.), *Das große China-Lexikon* (Darmstadt: Primus, 2008).
Nicolas Standaert (ed.), *Handbook of Christianity in China, vol. 1* (Leiden: Brill, 2001).
Ibid., *The Interweaving of Rituals: Funerals in the Cultural Exchange between China and Europe* (Seattle: University of Washington Press, 2008).
Giovanni Stary, "The Rediscovery of Yongzheng's Letter of 1725 to Pope Benedict XIII", in: *Manuscripta Orientalia* 4.4 (1998), 27–34.
Niels Steensgaard, "The growth and composition of the long-distance trade of England and the Dutch Republic before 1750", in: *The Rise of Merchant Empires. Long-Distance Trade in the Early Modern World, 1350–1750*, ed. James D. Tracy (Cambridge: Cambridge UP, 1994), 102–52.
Tristan Stein, "Passes and Protection in the Making of a British Mediterranean", in: *Journal of British Studies* 54.3 (2015), 602–31.
Nancy Steinhard Shatzman, "China's Earliest Mosques", in: *Journal of the Society of Architectural Historians* 67.3 (2008), 330–361.
Philip J. Stern, *The Company-State: Corporate Sovereignty and the Early Modern Foundations of the British Empire in India* (New York: Oxford UP, 2011).
Ibid., "Politics and Ideology in the Early East India Company-State: the Case of St. Helena, 1673–1709", in: *The Journal of Imperial and Commonwealth History* 35.1 (2007), 1–23.
David James Stewart, *The Sea Their Graves: an Archaeology of Death and Remembrance in Maritime Culture* (Gainesville: UP of Florida, 2011).
Michel Strickmann, *Chinese Poetry and Prophecy: the Written Oracle in East Asia* (Stanford, CA: Stanford UP, 2005).
Lynn A. Struve, "The Southern Ming, 1644–1662", in: Cambridge History of China, vol. 7, 641–725.
Xiaochun Sun and Jacob Kistemaker, *The Chinese Sky during the Han: Constellating Stars and Society* (Leiden: Brill, 1997).
Jean Sutton, *Lords of the East: the East India Company and its Ships* (New York: Conway Maritime Press, 2000).
Ibid., *The East India Company's Maritime Service, 1746–1834: Masters of the Eastern Seas* (Woodbridge: The Boydell Press, 2010).
John Styles, "Product Innovation in Early Modern London", in: *Past & Present* 168 (2000), 124–69.
Eric Tagliacozzo and Wen-Chin Chang (eds.), *Chinese Circulations: Capital, Commodities, and Networks in Southeast Asia* (Durham, NC: Duke UP, 2011).
Li Tana, *Nguyen Cochinchina: Southern Vietnam in the Seventeenth and Eighteenth Century* (Ithaca, NY: Cornell UP, 1998).
Rodney L. Taylor, *The Way of Heaven: an Introduction to the Confucian Religious Life* (Leiden: Brill, 1986).
Stephen Teiser, *The Ghost Festival in Medieval China* (Princeton, NJ: Princeton UP, 1988).
M.A. Thompson, "Louis XIV and the Origins of the War of the Spanish Succession", in: *Transactions of the Royal Historical Society* 4 (1954), 111–34.
Stuart E. Thompson, "Death, Food and Fertility", in: *Death Ritual in Late Imperial and Modern China*, eds. James L. Watson and Evelyn S. Rawski (Berkeley: University of California Press, 1988), 71–108.
John Thornton, *A Cultural History of the Atlantic World, 1250–1820*, (New York: Cambridge UP, 2012).

Chen Tingyou, *Chinese Calligraphy* (New York: Cambridge UP, 2010).
Adrian Tinniswood, *Pirates of Barbary: Corsairs, Conquests, and Captivity in the Seventeenth-Century Mediterranean* (New York: Riverhead Books, 2010).
Francesca Trivellato, *The Familiarity of Strangers: the Sephardic Diaspora, Livorno and Cross-Cultural Trade in the Early Modern Period* (New Haven: Yale UP, 2009).
Denis Twitchett, “Hsüan-tsung (reign 712–56)”, in: Cambridge History of China, vol. 3, 333–463.
Ibid., “Introduction”, in: Cambridge History of China, vol. 3, 1–47.
Ibid. and Howard J. Wechsler, “Kao-sung (reign 649–83) and the empress Wu: the inheritor and usurper”, in: Cambridge History of China, vol. 3, 242–89.
Ibid. and Klaus-Peter Tietze, “The Liao”, in: Cambridge History of China, vol. 6, 43–153.
Danny Wong Tze-Ken, “The Destruction of the English East India Company Factory on Condore Island, 1702–1705”, in: *Modern Asian Studies* 46.5 (2012), 1097–115.
Shelagh Vainker, *Chinese Silk: a Cultural History* (London: The British Museum Press, 2004).
Paul Arthur Van Dyke, *Merchants of Canton and Macao: Politics and Strategies in Eighteenth-Century Chinese Trade* (Hong Kong: Hong Kong UP, 2011).
Ibid., “The Ye Merchants of Canton, 1720–1804”, in: *Review of Culture* 13 (2005), 6–47.
Ibid., “Bookkeeping as a Window into Efficiencies of Early Modern Trade: Europeans, Americans and Others in China Compared, 1700–1842”, in: Narratives, ed. Johnson, 17–32.
Ibid., *The Canton Trade: Life and Enterprise on the China Coast, 1700–1845* (Hong Kong: Hong Kong UP, 2007).
Michael G. Vann, “When the World Came to Southeast Asia: Malacca and the Global Economy”, in: *Education about Asia* 19.2 (2014), 21–5.
Tijl Vanneste, *Global Trade and Commercial Networks: Eighteenth-Century Diamond Merchants* (London: Pickering & Chatto, 2011).
Jacques van Wijnendaele, *De familie Lanszweert en de stad Oostende* (Ostende: Oostendse Historische Publicaties, 2008).
François R. Velde, “Was John Law’s System a bubble? The Mississippi Bubble revisited”, in: *The Origins and Development of Financial Markets and Institutions: from the Seventeenth Century to the Present*, eds. Jeremy Atack and Larry Neal (New York: Cambridge UP, 2009), 99–120.
Cynthia Viallé, “Daily Life of the Dutch in Canton and Nagasaki: a Comparison Based on the VOC *Dagregisters* and Other Sources”, in: *Itinerario* 37.3 (2013), 153–71.
Mary Doreen Wainwright and Noel Matthews, *A Guide to Western Manuscripts and Documents in the British Isles relating to South and South East Asia* (New York: Oxford UP, 1965).
Frederic E. Wakeman, Jr., *Telling Chinese History* (Berkeley: University of California Press, 2009).
Arthur Waldron, *The Great Wall of China: from History to Myth* (New York: Cambridge UP, 1992).
Joanna Waley-Cohen, *The Culture of War in China: Empire and the Military under the Qing Dynasty* (London: I.B. Tauris, 2006).
Michal Wanner, “The Establishment of the General Company in Ostend in the Context of the Habsburg Maritime Plans, 1714–1723”, in: *Prague Papers on the History of International Relations* (2007), 32–61.
Ibid., “Bankibazar – Ostend and Imperial Factory in Bengal, 1722–1744”, in: *Prague Papers on the History of International Relations* (2009), 107–18.
Kerry Ward, *Networks of Empire: Forced Migration in the Dutch East India Company* (New York: Cambridge UP, 2009).
Molly A. Warsh, *Adorning Empire: a History of the Early Modern Pearl Trade, 1492–1688* (PhD diss., The Johns Hopkins University, 2009).
Barbara Watson Andaya, “The Cloth Trade in Jambi and Palembang Society during the Seventeenth and Eighteenth Centuries”, in: *Indonesia* 48 (1989), 27–46.

James L. Watson and Evelyn S. Rawski (eds.), *Death Ritual in Late Imperial and Modern China* (Berkeley: University of California Press, 1988).
James C.Y. Watt and Anne E. Wardwel, *When Silk was Gold: Central Asian and Chinese Textiles* (New York: The Metropolitan Museum of Art, 1997).
Howard Wechsler, "T'ai-tsung (reign 626–49) the consolidator", in: Cambridge History of China, vol. 3, 118–241.
Liming Wei, *Chinese Festivals* (New York: Cambridge UP, 2011).
Cheng Wei-chung, *War, Trade and Piracy in the China Seas, 1622–1683* (Leiden: Brill, 2013).
Adamek Wendi, *The Teachings of Master Wuzhu: Zen and the Religion of No-Return* (New York: Columbia UP, 2011).
Eyer Wilbur, *The East India Company, and the British Empire in the Far East* (New York: Oxford UP, 1945).
Basil Williams, "The Foreign Policy of England under Walpole", in: *The English Historical Review* 15 (1900), 665–98.
Clive Willis, *China and Macau* (Burlington, VT: Ashgate, 2002).
John E. Wills, Jr., "Relations with maritime Europeans, 1514–1662", in: Cambridge History of China, vol. 8, 333–75.
Ibid., *Past and Present in China's Foreign Policy: From "Tribute System" to "Peaceful Rise"* (Honolulu: University of Hawaii Press, 2011).
Ibid., *China and Maritime Europe, 1500–1800. Trade, Settlement, Diplomacy, and Missions* (New York: Cambridge UP, 2011).
Linda Woodhead, *Christianity: a Very Short Introduction* (New York: Oxford UP, $^2$2014).
Arthur F. Wright, "The Sui Dynasty", in: Cambridge History of China, vol. 3, 48–149.
Lihui Yang and Deming An, *Handbook of Chinese Mythology* (New York: Oxford UP, 2005).
Adam Yuen-chung Lui, "Syllabus of the provincial examination (*hsiang-shih*) under the early Ch'ing (1644–1795)", in: *Modern Asian Studies* 8.3 (1974), 391–6.
Madeleine Zelin, "The Yung-cheng Reign", in: Cambridge History of China, vol. 9, 183–229.
Erik Zürcher, *The Buddhist Conquest of China: the Spread and Adaptation of Buddhism in Early Medieval China* (Leiden: Brill, 2007).
Harriet T. Zurndorfer, "The Resistant Fiber: Cotton Textiles in Imperial China", in: Spinning World, eds. Riello and Parthasarathi, 43–62.

# Index

Numbers in italics refer to the additional material online:
http://www.degruyter.com/view/product/456197?format=B&rskey=5ZojLY&result=3